Essex

Manchester University Press

Essex

The cultural impact of an Elizabethan courtier

edited by Annaliese Connolly and Lisa Hopkins

Manchester University Press

Published by Manchester University Press
Altrincham Street, Manchester M1 7JA, UK
www.manchesteruniversitypress.co.uk

British Library Cataloguing-in-Publication Data is available

Library of Congress Cataloging-in-Publication Data is available

ISBN 978 1 7849 9354 2 *paperback*

First published by Manchester University Press in hardback 2013

This edition first published 2016

Printed by Lightning Source

Contents

List of illustrations *page* vii
Acknowledgements viii
Notes on contributors ix

Introduction
Annaliese Connolly and Lisa Hopkins 1

Part I Essex: patron and patronage

1 'Cleverly playing the stoic': the Earl of Essex, Sir Philip Sidney and surviving Elizabeth's court 25
Richard Wood

2 Essexianism and the work of Gervase Markham 47
Matthew Steggle

3 Robert Devereux, 2nd Earl of Essex, and the practice of theatre 63
Grace Ioppolo

4 Essex's international agenda in 1595 and his device of the Indian Prince 81
Linda Shenk

Part II Self-fashioning

5 'Achilles alter': the heroic lives and afterlives of Robert Devereux, 2nd Earl of Essex 101
Andrew Hiscock

6 'Bringing rebellion broached on his sword': Essex and Ireland 133
Chris Butler and Willy Maley

7 Essex's last campaign: the fall of the Earl of Essex and manuscript circulation 153
Andrew Gordon

8 'Idle papers': *An Apology of the Earl of Essex* 179
Hugh Gazzard

9 'Toucht with bolt of Treason': the Earl of Essex and Lady Penelope Rich 201
Chris Laoutaris

10 The Earl of Essex and 'politic history' 237
Alexandra Gajda

Part III Afterlives

11 Prodigality and the Earl of Essex 263
Mary Partridge

12 The Earl of Essex and the Duke of Windsor: Elizabeth and Essex on film 279
Lisa Hopkins

Select bibliography 295
Index 321

List of illustrations

1 'Young Man among the roses'. Miniature by Nicholas Hilliard, c. 1588. Victoria and Albert Museum, London. 170

2 'Interview between Queen Elizabeth and the Earl of Essex'. Line engraving by Thomas Milton, after Robert Smirke, published 1806. © National Portrait Gallery, London. 171

3 'Sir Henry Unton'. Portrait by unknown artist, c. 1596. © National Portrait Gallery, London. 172

4 'Robert Devereux, 2nd Earl of Essex'. Portrait by Marcus Gheeraerts the Younger, 1596–97. Reproduced by kind permission of his Grace the Duke of Bedford and the Trustees of the Bedford Estates. 173

5 Letter from Essex to Elizabeth, August 1599. MS 601 f.98v. Richard Mynshall Lute book. Reproduced by kind permission of the Royal Academy of Music, Robert Spencer Collection. 174

6 Verse in Richard Mynshall's hand. MS. 601 f.98r. Richard Mynshall Lute book. Reproduced by kind permission of the Royal Academy of Music, Robert Spencer Collection. 175

7 Scribal copy of the letter from Essex to Egerton with Antony Grenlinge's annotations. BL Harley MS. 3787, f. 178v. Reproduced by kind permission of the British Library. 176

8 'Lady Penelope Rich?' c. 1589. Miniature portrait by Nicholas Hilliard. Supplied by Royal Collection Trust. © HM Queen Elizabeth II 2012. 177

9 Essex meets Elizabeth for the last time. Bette Davis and Errol Flynn in Michael Curtiz's *The Private Lives of Elizabeth and Essex*, Warner Brothers, 1939. Courtesy of the Wisconsin Center for Film and Theater Research, University of Wisconsin-Madison. 178

Acknowledgements

We would like to thank all the contributors for their exemplary promptness and attention to detail and for their patience while we prepared the final draft. Thanks also to the anonymous reader for their careful reading of the volume and to the City campus library staff at Sheffield Hallam University.

Notes on contributors

CHRIS BUTLER is currently an Associate Lecturer at Sheffield Hallam University; his PhD (completed at Sheffield Hallam University, 2012) explored relations between religion, cognition and author-function in works by Sir Edward Dyer, Saint Robert Southwell, Thomas Lodge and Shakespeare. Chris Butler's published scholarly works include an article on connections between *As You Like It* and the second Earl of Essex's Irish campaign of 1599 (forthcoming in *Celtic Shakespeare*, eds Rory Vincent Loughnane and Willy Maley); an article on the religious meaning of Dyer's lyric poem 'Hee That His Mirth Hath Loste', in *New Perspectives on Tudor Cultures*, eds Mike Pincombe and Zsolt Almási (2012); the entry on *As You Like It* for the *Facts on File Companion to Shakespeare* (2012) and a short note on pricking in *The Faerie Queene* (*Notes and Queries*, 2008).

ANNALIESE CONNOLLY is Senior Lecturer in English at Sheffield Hallam University. Recent publications include 'Guy of Warwick, Godfrey of Bouillon, and Elizabethan Repertory' in *Early Modern England and Islamic Worlds*, eds Linda McJannet and Bernadette Andrea (2011), the entry for George Peele in *The Encyclopedia of English Renaissance Literature* (2011) and a chapter on the performance history of Middleton's *Women Beware Women* in *Middleton: Women Beware Women* (2011). Her current project is a monograph on George Peele.

ALEXANDRA GAJDA is John Walsh Fellow and Tutor at Jesus College, Oxford University. Her monograph, *The Earl of Essex and Late Elizabethan Political Culture* was published in 2012. Other publications include: 'The State of Christendom: History, Political Thought and the Essex Circle', *Historical Research* 81 (August 2008); 'Debating War and Peace in Late Elizabethan England', *Historical Journal* 52 (2009), pp. 851–878; 'Tacitus and Political Thought in Early Modern Europe, c.1530–c.1640', in *The Cambridge Companion to Tacitus*, ed. A. J. Woodman (2009); 'Education as a Courtier', in *The Oxford Handbook to John Donne*, eds J. Shami, T. Hester and D. Flynn (2009).

HUGH GAZZARD has held several posts at Oxford, and currently lectures in English at St Hugh's College. His doctoral thesis was about the networks of patronage (literary, cultural, political, religious, military) around the Earl of

Essex. He now pursues broad research interests within early modern literature, especially poetry and drama.

ANDREW GORDON lectures in Literature at the University of Aberdeen where he is also Co-Director of the Centre for Early Modern Studies. He is the author of *Writing Early Modern London: Memory, Text and Community* (2013) and has edited several collections including *Literature, Mapping and the Politics of Space in Early Modern Britain,* with Bernhard Klein (2001), and *The Arts of Remembrance in Early Modern England* with Thomas Rist (2013). His work on the manuscript culture of early modern England has included studies of the letters of the Earl of Essex, Francis Bacon, John Donne and the culture of libels and has been published in *ELR, Journal of Medieval and Early Modern Studies,* and in various collections. He is currently involved in a collaborative project with James Daybell under the rubric *Cultures of Correspondence in Early Modern Britain.*

ANDREW HISCOCK is Professor of English at Bangor University, AHRC Research Fellow 2011–12 and a Fellow of the English Association. He has published widely on early modern literature and his most recent monograph is *Reading Memory in Early Modern Literature* (2011). Other publications include *The Uses of this World: Thinking Space in Shakespeare, Marlowe, Cary and Jonson* (2004) and an edited critical collection entitled *Middleton: Women Beware Women* (2011). He edited the double issue of the MHRA's *2008 Yearbook of English Studies* devoted to Tudor literature, and is co-editor with Lisa Hopkins of the Continuum Renaissance Drama Series. He is English Editor for *MLR.*

LISA HOPKINS is Professor of English at Sheffield Hallam University and co-editor of *Shakespeare,* the journal of the British Shakespeare Association. Her recent publications include *Shakespeare's The Tempest: The Relationship Between Text and Film* (2008) and *Goddesses and Queens: The Iconography of Elizabeth I,* co-edited with Annaliese Connolly (2007).

GRACE IOPPOLO is Professor of Shakespearean and Early Modern Drama in the Department of English Literature at the University of Reading. She is the Founder and Director of the Henslowe-Alleyn Digitisation Project (www.henslowe-alleyn.org.uk) and an elected Fellow of the Society of Antiquaries of London. She is the author of *Revising Shakespeare* (1991) and *Dramatists and their Manuscripts in the Age of Shakespeare, Jonson, Middleton and Heywood: Authorship, Authority and the Playhouse* (2006), as well as numerous scholarly articles on early modern manuscripts, including the letters of Robert Devereux, 2nd Earl of Essex, and his sister Penelope Rich. With Peter Beal she is the co-editor of *Elizabeth I and the Culture of Writing* (2007). She edited *King Lear* and *Measure for Measure* for the Norton Critical Series and *Hengist, King of Kent* and *The Honest Man's Fortune* for the Malone Society. She is the General Editor of the 10-volume *The Collected Works of Thomas Heywood* (forthcoming).

CHRIS LAOUTARIS was awarded a prestigious Birmingham Fellowship at the Shakespeare Institute in 2013. Before that he lectured at University College London, where he was Renaissance Literature Course Convener. He is author of *Shakespearean Maternities: Crises of Conception in Early Modern England* (2008) and *Shakespeare and the Countess: The Battle that Gave Birth to the Globe* (2014), which was awarded a British Academy Post-Doctoral Fellowship and short-listed for the Tony Lothian Prize (sponsored by the Duke and Duchess of Buccleuch). He is contributor to *Performing Maternity in Early Modern England* (2007) and *Performing Pedagogy: Gender and Instruction in Early Modern England* (2011), edited by Kathryn M. Moncrief and Kathryn R. McPherson. He has also published a survey of activist female translators and historical writers in *History of British Women's Writing: 1500–1610* (2010), edited by Caroline Bicks and Jennifer Summit. Laoutaris is currently working on two articles which reveal the mysterious female subjects of well-known Renaissance portraits for the *British Art Journal*; a study of early modern Robotics and Artificial Life; and a project for the Shakespeare Institute called *Team Shakespeare: The First Folio and the Men who Created the Shakespeare Legacy* (forthcoming).

WILLY MALEY is Professor of Renaissance Studies at the University of Glasgow. He is the author of *A Spenser Chronology* (1994); *Salvaging Spenser: Colonialism, Culture and Identity* (1997); and *Nation, State and Empire in English Renaissance Literature: Shakespeare to Milton* (2003). He is editor, with Andrew Hadfield, of *A View of the Present State of Ireland: From the First Published Edition* (1997). He has also edited eight collections of essays: with Brendan Bradshaw and Andrew Hadfield, *Representing Ireland: Literature and the Origins of Conflict, 1534–1660* (1993); with Bart Moore-Gilbert and Gareth Stanton, *Postcolonial Criticism* (1997); with David J. Baker, *British Identities and English Renaissance Literature* (2002); with Andrew Murphy, *Shakespeare and Scotland* (2004); with Alex Benchimol, *Spheres of Influence: Intellectual and Cultural Publics from Shakespeare to Habermas* (2006); with Philip Schwyzer, *Shakespeare and Wales: From the Marches to the Assembly* (2010); with Michael Gardiner, *The Edinburgh Companion to Muriel Spark* (2010); and with Margaret Tudeau-Clayton, *This England, That Shakespeare: New Angles on Englishness and the Bard* (2010).

MARY PARTRIDGE received her doctorate from the University of Birmingham in 2008. She was awarded the Royal Historical Society's Alexander Prize for 2007. Publications include 'Thomas Hoby's Translation of Castiglione's Book of the Courtier', *Historical Journal* 50 (2007), p. 769; 'Lord Burghley and il Cortegiano: Models of Courtliness in Elizabethan England', *Transactions of the Royal Historical Society*, 6th series 19 (December 2009), pp. 95–116; and 'A "surprising shock" in the Cathedral: getting Year 7 to Vocalise Responses to the Murder of Thomas Becket', *Teaching History* 143 (June 2011), pp. 22–31. She is currently working as a teacher of history at Solihull School.

LINDA SHENK is Associate Professor at Iowa State University. Her publications include *Learned Queen: The Image of Elizabeth I in Politics and Poetry* (2010) as well as articles on Elizabeth I, the Earl of Essex, John Lyly, and Elizabethan university drama. She is currently working on a monograph examining the intersection of drama and diplomatic culture in late sixteenth-century England.

MATTHEW STEGGLE is Professor of English at Sheffield Hallam University. His publications include *Richard Brome: Place and Politics on the Caroline Stage* (2004); *Laughing and Weeping in Early Modern Theatres* (2007); and *Volpone: A Critical Guide* (2011). He is a Contributing Editor to *Richard Brome Online* (2010) and to *The Cambridge Works of Ben Jonson* (2012). His current project is a monograph on Gervase Markham.

RICHARD J. WOOD is an Associate Lecturer in the English Department at Sheffield Hallam University, where he recently completed his doctorate on Sir Philip Sidney's *Arcadia*. He is the author of journal articles on Sidney's *Arcadia* in the *Sidney Journal* and *Early Modern Literary Studies,* and has contributed an essay on Sidney to a forthcoming collection on maternity in early modern romance, edited by Naomi Miller and Karen Bamford. He is also the author of the chapters on Shakespeare's *Venus and Adonis* and *The Rape of Lucrece* in *The Facts on File Companion to Shakespeare* (2012), the entry on Shakespeare's poetry in *The Year's Work in English Studies,* and the biographical essay on Mary Sidney (the Countess of Pembroke) in *The Literary Encyclopedia* (2012).

Introduction

Annaliese Connolly and Lisa Hopkins

The life of Robert Devereux, the second Earl of Essex, has often been refracted through the biographical lens of two other figures from the period: Queen Elizabeth I and William Shakespeare. In many ways Essex's career has served as an adjunct to the dominant narratives created for these two iconic figures and as a consequence our understanding of the earl and his life is overshadowed and constrained by these rather imposing parameters. As one of Elizabeth's favourites, Essex's relationship with the queen has been used to explore pervasive questions about the queen's sexuality and her unmarried state. Their tumultuous relationship as detailed in popular accounts of Elizabethan history is frequently summarised by three key events: Elizabeth boxing Essex's ears; his hasty return from Ireland; and his bursting in upon the queen while she was in dishabille.[1] Finally his imprisonment and execution and its effect upon the queen is often framed by the apocryphal story of the ring given by Elizabeth to Essex which he is to return to her in time of need to secure her assistance.[2] Essex's career has also functioned as a conduit between the queen and Shakespeare at two significant junctures.[3] The first is the possible allusion to Essex in Shakespeare's *Henry V* and his imagined return from Ireland as a victorious warrior, where Shakespeare provides the only direct reference in his plays to contemporary events; the second is the contemporary record of a payment for a performance of a play about Richard II for members of Essex's circle before his abortive uprising in 1600 and subsequent speculation about whether this was in fact Shakespeare's *Richard II* or another play on that subject, and in each case critics have used these plays to try and work out what they might reveal about Shakespeare's attitude towards the earl and the queen and the relationship between the theatre and the state.

The aim of this collection of essays about the earl is to break away from such paradigms by resituating his life and career within the richly diverse contours of his cultural and political milieu and to identify the ways in which his biography has been variously interpreted both during his own lifetime and since his death in 1601. This critical shift in historiography is a consequence of the development in critical theory and practice since the early 1980s. The influence of the work of new historicist, cultural materialist and feminist scholars as well as those working in the field of theatre history has resulted in a rethinking of older historicising approaches to text and context, to biography and to the theatre as both a commercial enterprise and part of a patronage network. One significant development has been to consider history as a cultural construct, composed of circulating and competing texts which exist within a discourse of power.[4] This collection approaches the rich and diverse figure of the earl by looking at a wealth of diverse visual and textual manifestations of Essex produced during the sixteenth century and up to the present day. Included in the discussion are not just those texts of which Essex is the subject, such as poems, portraits or films, but also those texts produced by Essex himself, including private letters, prose tracts, poems and entertainments. One important area of discussion is the transmission and circulation of texts by the earl as an important means of disseminating his political views. The collection also provides a corrective to the biographical-historicist approach which has tended to view the career of Essex as a teleological narrative, culminating in his execution in 1601. One of the ways in which this is achieved is by the adoption of a range of different critical perspectives, some of which utilise the life and works of less well-known contemporaries as an opportunity to expand our understanding of the earl and his circle, as well as the ways in which his identity was shaped and refashioned during and after his life. In addition to essays which offer single author studies as a means of prising open long-held assumptions about the earl's life, others provide a diachronic approach to the earl's career, identifying crucial events such as the Irish campaign and the uprising in order to re-evaluate their significance and critical reception.

The earl was a figure who loomed very large indeed in late Elizabethan culture, and one whose memory was by no means forgotten later. Essex is memorialised in the sonnet below, printed in *A Poetical Rhapsody*, a poetry miscellany, in 1602, a year after the earl's execution in February 1601.

> Worthily famous lord, whose virtues rare,
> Set in the gold of never-stain'd nobility,
> And noble mind shining in true humility,
> Make you admir'd of all that virtues are:
> If, as your sword with envy imitates
> Great Caesar's sword in all his deeds victorious;
> So your learn'd pen would strive to be glorious
> And write your acts perform'd in foreign States;
> Or if some one with deep wit inspired
> Of matchless Tacitus would them historify
> Then Caesar's works so much we should not glorify,

And Tacitus would be much less desired.
But till yourself, or some such out them forth,
Accept of these as pictures of your worth.[5]

The author of the sonnet and compiler of the collection was Francis Davison, a poet who operated on the fringes of the Essex circle.[6] The poem's prefatory material suggests that perhaps it was presented to the earl as a gift before his death, but in any case the miscellany went through three editions, with the second printed in 1608 and the third in 1611. While the lyric may not be an example of great sonneteering, it is significant for the snapshot it provides of early responses to the earl's career and his death. The poem's classical sphere of reference situates the earl firmly within the intellectual milieu of his own circle, members of which were intimately acquainted with the writing of the Roman historian Tacitus, with Sir Henry Savile producing a translation of his *Histories* and *Agricola* in 1591. Just as Tacitus used Roman history to offer a series of exemplars of political power which were utilised by the earl and his circle as a lens through which to interpret the current Elizabethan polity, so Davison seems to suggest that Essex's own career can be used in a similar way by his contemporaries. If, and when, the history of Essex is written it would eclipse the writings of both Tacitus and Caesar for future generations.

In view of Davison's links to the earl it is not surprising that the poem works to recuperate Essex's reputation and to distance him from the charges of treason and ambition for which he was put to death. Instead the emphasis is placed upon Essex as a Protestant hero, a soldier defending England and her allies from the threat of imperial Spain whose military exploits are to be recorded and emulated. Essex's virtues, although implied rather than itemised here in the sonnet, suggest a complete code of behaviour, an alternative perspective from which to view the world.

Davison's sonnet is just one example of the many texts and dedications written for and about Essex; it has been noted that the earl received more book dedications during the 1590s than anyone else in early modern England, even than the queen.[7] The reason for the contemporary interest expressed in Essex was that he appeared to many not simply as a patron but as warrior, poet, favourite of the queen, aspiring arbiter of the succession to the throne, champion of Protestantism, depressive and valetudinarian, would-be spymaster, exemplar of chivalry, tournament star, a new Achilles, patron of poets, painters, musicians and Tacitean historians, and ultimately failed conspirator. As even the briefest outline of the earl's career makes clear, he was many things to many men.

Born on 10 November 1565, he was the elder son of Walter Devereux, 1st Earl of Essex, and his wife Lettice Knollys, a cousin of Queen Elizabeth I on the Boleyn side. As well as Robert, there was another son, Walter, who would die at the siege of Rouen in 1591, and two older daughters, Dorothy and Penelope, the latter of whom enjoyed great influence over her brother the earl and was the 'Stella' of Sir Philip Sidney's sonnet sequence *Astrophel and*

Stella. Neither sister fared well in marriage: Dorothy first eloped with the relatively impecunious Sir Thomas Perrot and after his death made an unhappy second marriage with Henry Percy, 9th Earl of Northumberland, sometimes known as 'the wizard earl', while Penelope was effectively forced to marry Sir Robert Rich, a union whose only obvious benefit was the scope it afforded poets to play with her new surname. Although she apparently rejected the advances of Sir Philip Sidney she did succumb to those of Charles Blount, a close friend of her brother the earl, and was soon more or less openly living with him and bearing him children.

The first earl died in 1576, aged only thirty-seven, while serving in Ireland, and within a very short time his widow Lettice had secretly married the queen's favourite, Robert Dudley, Earl of Leicester, who was already the young earl's godfather and was sometimes rumoured to be also his father, since there had been longstanding gossip about him and Lettice. When the marriage eventually became public knowledge Queen Elizabeth was outraged, but she eventually forgave Leicester, and his handsome stepson the new Earl of Essex shared in her favour, especially after Leicester died in 1588. Although the young earl spent his early years principally at his family seats of Chartley in Staffordshire and Lamphey in Pembrokeshire, with his guardian Lord Burghley or his grandfather Sir Francis Knollys, or between 1577 and 1581 at Trinity College Cambridge, Leicester was a consistent and important presence in his life during this period, and it was under his aegis that the young Essex made his first appearance at court in September 1585.

Court, however, was not where Essex most wanted to be. Barely three months later he was accompanying Leicester again, this time on his way to the war against the Spanish in the Netherlands, where he was given the largely nominal role of colonel-general of the cavalry. Nine months after that, in September 1586, he took part in the fight at Zutphen at which Leicester's nephew Sir Philip Sidney was mortally wounded; the dying Sidney bequeathed to Essex his second-best sword, and at some stage subsequent to his return to England the month after Zutphen, Essex cemented his connection with Sidney's memory by secretly marrying Sidney's widow Frances, daughter of Elizabeth's spymaster Sir Francis Walsingham, though the marriage did not become public knowledge until late 1590 when it became apparent that Frances was pregnant. That Essex was more interested in Frances's status as Sidney's widow than in Frances herself is suggested by the number of his affairs after the marriage, some of which also had uncomfortably visible consequences in the shape of pregnancies. A further consequence of the death of Sidney was that it left his uncle Leicester, whose own son had already died, without his planned heir, with the result that his support for his stepson Essex became if anything even more determined and wholehearted, especially because he saw Essex as a useful counterweight to the influence of his enemy Sir Walter Ralegh.

Partly as a result of his stepfather's backing but also partly because of the queen's growing fondness for him personally, Essex was appointed master of the horse in June 1587, and other favours and appointments soon followed. He was made a knight of the garter in April 1588 and after Leicester's death in 1588 Essex was awarded the late earl's extremely valuable monopoly on sweet wines in January 1589, something which was particularly welcome because throughout his life he was chronically impecunious. In due course there were other honours: membership of the privy council in 1593, the mastership of the ordnance in 1596, the office of earl marshal in 1597, and the chancellorship of the University of Cambridge in 1598, which was especially welcome since he had failed to be awarded that of Oxford in 1592. Leicester's death also left other gaps to fill, and from this period Essex came to see himself as the political and military heir of his late stepfather as well as of his own father and of Sir Philip Sidney. In due course he would also come to see himself as the heir of his father-in-law, Sir Francis Walsingham, and in the second half of his career the earl worked hard to establish an intelligence network of his own, in a calculated attempt to rival Elizabeth's chief minister Lord Burghley and his son Sir Robert Cecil.[8] In the earl's mind, this dabbling in espionage, which is touched on here in Chapter 5 by Andrew Hiscock and Chapter 9 by Chris Laoutaris, was also part of his self-appointed role of militant champion of Protestantism and destined reviver of the military glory which had once been England's.

It was to this end that, despite the fact that Elizabeth was unimpressed by military endeavours in general and by the cost of them in particular, Essex very soon embarked on a series of hugely ambitious military and naval ventures designed to advance the cause of Protestantism and to make England into a major player on the pan-European stage. The first of these came in April 1589 when against Elizabeth's express orders he joined Sir Francis Drake and Sir John Norris on an unsuccessful attempt to capture Lisbon, in Spanish hands since Philip II's effective annexation of Portugal after the death of the childless King Henry. This failure was followed by others. In August 1591 Essex led a force to Normandy to the aid of Henri IV, but within weeks his beloved brother Walter had been killed at the siege of Rouen and by the time he returned to London in January 1592 it was clear that nothing had been achieved by the campaign. Undeterred, the earl tried again to win glory in June 1596, this time by leading a raid on the Spanish port of Cadiz; in fact this was reasonably successful, but Essex was nevertheless disappointed because he had hoped not just to storm the city but actually to capture and garrison it, restoring to England the foothold on the Continent which she had lacked ever since the recapture of Calais by the French in the reign of Mary I. In the summer of 1597 the earl was charged with weakening Spanish forces with an attack on the Spanish port of Ferrol, but storms wrecked the initial expedition and instead Essex was forced to rethink his mission and decided to head for the Azores and attempt to capture the Spanish silver fleet as it sailed past on its return from South America. The English fleet failed to intercept it and returned to Falmouth to the embarrassing discovery that in his absence the port had narrowly avoided suffering a Spanish counter-raid.

Far worse was to come though when in April 1599, after a serious quarrel with the queen during which he put his hand to his sword in her presence and that of his fellow privy councillors, he took up his father's command in Ireland as part of the ongoing English attempt to bring this rebel 'colony' to heel. The earl's expedition to the country where his father had died was a disaster from the outset and would in due course come to appear as a classic instance of one of the chief dangers Tacitus had warned against, which was how easy it was for political opponents to 'banish with offices of imployment'.[9] Willy Maley and Chris Butler in Chapter 6 trace the critical assessment of the earl's decision to undertake a campaign in Ireland and consider the suggestion that his political enemies considered it politically expedient to have the earl personally embroiled in a foreign war.[10] Bad roads, difficult terrain, lack of local knowledge and the difficulty of communicating with London meant that the earl, like others before him, struggled. After Elizabeth objected to his having met the rebel leader, the Earl of Tyrone, to discuss possible terms, Essex returned to London without orders in September 1599 to explain himself. Popular accounts of Essex's return have it that, arriving early in the morning, he surprised the queen without her wig and make-up. This account was popularised by a number of eighteenth- and nineteenth-century paintings and engravings, including Thomas Milton's line engraving entitled 'Interview between Queen Elizabeth and the Earl of Essex', published in 1806 (Figure 2). Michael Dobson and Nicola J. Watson note that during the nineteenth century in particular there was a shift in the way that this incident was depicted, with an emphasis upon Elizabeth as a visibly aged tyrant who responds vindictively to the intrusion rather than as a woman who is forced to choose between love and duty.[11] Grace Ioppolo in Chapter 3, however, qualifies the traditional account by pointing to the circumstances and transmission of this story which were to be found in contemporary letters and argues that as a consequence the details were liable to exaggeration depending on the audience for whom the account was written. Whatever the exact nature of the encounter, the queen was furious at his return and deprived him of the monopoly on the sale of sweet wines, his major source of income. Driven into effective exile from the court (the meeting at Nonsuch would be the last time he ever saw the queen), threatened with political impotence, and desperate to vindicate both his own reputation and the essentially warrior culture which he saw himself as embodying, Essex, encouraged by his sister Penelope Rich and his close friend the Earl of Southampton, decided to lead an armed uprising against the government.

The spark was lit on Saturday 7 February 1601, when the earl received a summons to attend the Council. He feared that this was a pretext to arrest him, and it may indeed have been a provocative measure masterminded by

Essex's principal enemy, Sir Robert Cecil, in an attempt to force him to show his hand. As often in the past, the earl excused himself on the grounds of illness. To prime Londoners for the forthcoming *coup*, he also sent one of his followers, Sir Gelly Meyrick, to persuade the Lord Chamberlain's Men (the leading troupe of actors in London, whose principal dramatist was Shakespeare) to perform a play about Richard II. (As many essays here note, there is debate about whether this was Shakespeare's play or another on the same subject.)[12] Reminding an audience of the deposition of one monarch seemed like a good way of encouraging them to think of doing the same to another, and it further helped the earl's cause that Henry IV, who deposed Richard II, was his own ancestor.

Despite the performance, however, the rebellion which the earl launched the next day, Sunday 8 February, was an abject failure. The government had taken precautions (which may well be evidence that Cecil had been in control of the situation from the outset): they doubled the guards at the palace at Whitehall, making it impossible for Essex and his followers to attempt to seize control of the court as they had originally planned; they sent messengers through the streets of London to tell the citizens to lock their doors and remain inside; and they sent four lords of the Council including Essex's uncle, Sir William Knollys, and the Lord Chief Justice, Sir John Popham (great-uncle of the Caroline dramatist John Ford, on whose work the Essex story has been seen as an influence),[13] to Essex House to assure the earl of a fair hearing if he would come with them peacefully. Instead, a panicking Essex locked the four lords in a room, with his sister Penelope loudly calling for Popham's head, and decided to appeal to the citizens. He and his followers marched through Ludgate and along the Strand to St Paul's, a popular gathering place where books were sold in the churchyard and where the earl had planned to make a speech. However, the citizens, obeying the Council's orders, stayed resolutely indoors, and there was no one to make speeches to. Essex walked on through the City, shouting out as he went that he was the victim of a plot, that there were plans to murder him, and that Sir Robert Cecil was determined to betray England by ensuring that the queen's successor would be the Spanish Infanta, daughter of England's hated enemy Philip II of Spain, who had sent the Armada against England in 1588. Even this had no effect. Eventually, the earl turned back and made for Essex House again. He had to fight his way through Ludgate, where the Bishop of London had posted soldiers, but he eventually won through. Safely back at Essex House, he burned as many of his papers as he could and toyed with the idea of a desperate last stand, but when the Lord Admiral, Charles Howard, Earl of Nottingham, appeared outside with guns, it was clear that the situation was hopeless, and Essex, reluctant to risk the safety of his sister and of the other women in the house, gave himself up without a fight. The Essex Rebellion was over, and Essex knew he was doomed; Elizabethan treason trials had only one possible outcome, a verdict of guilty, and when the trial of Essex and his friend Southampton, whom Essex himself had knighted in the field on the Azores expedition and who had followed him loyally, was held on 19 February 1601 it was no exception. A particular betrayal was that Sir Francis Bacon, to whom Essex had always been a friend and patron, was one of the prosecuting counsel. A little under a week later, on 25 February, the earl was executed. Southampton, however, was spared the death penalty and ultimately pardoned, and so was Penelope Rich, despite the fact that she had been deeply and visibly implicated in her brother's activities.

The earl was by no means forgotten after his death and when James VI and I, whose succession Essex was widely believed to have supported, finally came to the throne, 'The Venetian ambassador reported that James I "has received the twelve-year-old son of the Earl of Essex and taken him in his arms and kissed him, openly and loudly declaring him the son of the most noble knight that the English had ever begotten"'.[14] (James's kindness was not reciprocated: that twelve-year-old boy grew up to become a parliamentary general fighting against, and ultimately helping depose, King Charles I.) Davison's eulogy in sonnet form earlier in the chapter suggests one interpretative approach to Essex's career after his death, but during James's reign other contemporary responses suggest a less positive reading of the earl's life as exemplar, reading it instead in terms of the *de casibus* pattern of pride and ambition leading to a fall. Plays such as Samuel Daniel's *Philotas* and Jonson's *Sejanus* make use of classical history to reflect on the earl's demise and offer a pointed warning to other political overreachers.[15]

During the late seventeenth and early eighteenth centuries the earl's career was formulated less in terms of his political, Tacitean persona and more in terms of his role as one of Elizabeth's favourites, with a tendency to explore the parameters of that relationship in terms of their respective personalities and of Elizabeth's status as an unmarried queen. This popular impulse can be traced from early prose writing such as *The Secret History of the most renown'd Q. Elizabeth and the E. of Essex by a person of quality* (1680) and John Banks's play *The Unhappy Favourite* (1682).[16] Here Essex is used as a character in courtly intrigue with Elizabeth and the Cecils and to populate apocryphal stories. In these instances his primary function is to allow authors to explore the personality of the queen as a woman torn between private affections and public duty.

This biographical and historiographical trend continued into the twentieth century, perpetuated by studies of Elizabeth and Essex which sought to apply recent developments in literary criticism and psychology to their relationship, while approaching the queen and Essex as though they were characters in a play. The best examples of this kind of work on Essex are Lytton Strachey's *Elizabeth and Essex: A Tragic History*, published in 1928, and Robert Lacey's *Robert, Earl of Essex: An Elizabethan Icarus*, published in 1971.[17] In Strachey's psychobiography the role of Essex as a favourite is used to explicate the queen's sexuality and her unmarried state. Whereas earlier Victorian writers had sought to distance the queen from Essex and neutralise any sense of an inappropriate relationship between them, Strachey develops Essex's prominence in the queen's reign in order to suggest that Elizabeth's refusal to marry comes from trauma in her childhood linked to the execution of her mother Anne Boleyn and her stepmother's husband Thomas Seymour. As Michael Dobson and Nicola J. Watson remark,

> To Strachey, it is the Essex imbroglio which makes retrospective sense of Elizabeth's 'mysterious organism', illuminating much of her past career (both public and private) even as it brings that career to a culminating crisis. It is not political expediency but depth psychology which explains Elizabeth's conduct throughout, and Essex's death is dictated by a passion of outraged vanity and a sense of agonised betrayal which stirs up the darkest recesses of her childhood self.[18]

The motivation for Essex's execution is prompted by the personal rather the political, whereby the queen can exact retribution on men in general and on her father in particular:

> She felt her father's spirit within her; and an extraordinary passion moved the obscure profundities of her being, as she condemned her lover to her mother's death ... but in a still remoter depth there were still stranger stirrings ... was this, perhaps, not a repetition but a revenge? ... Manhood – the fascinating, detestable entity, which had first come upon her concealed in yellow magnificence in her father's lap – manhood was overthrown at last, and in the person of that traitor it should be rooted out.[19]

Robert Lacey's biography is influenced in part by a strand of literary criticism used to discuss the life and works of Christopher Marlowe. Harry Levin's study *The Overreacher: A Study of Christopher Marlowe*, published in 1952, uses the life of the dramatist as the key to reading the works, with aspects of Marlowe's personality and events from his career being mapped onto the plots and characters in the plays. Marlowe's tragedies are defined by the figure of Icarus, an ambitious overreacher who is doomed to fall. Lacey applies this teleologically over-determined narrative to Essex's career, beginning in the preface with the lines from Francis Bacon who applied the emblem of Icarus to the earl in a letter of 1600: 'I was ever sorry your Lordship should fly with waxen wings, doubting Icarus' fortune'. Lacey suggests that Essex's downfall is partly predetermined, casting him in the role of tragic hero and that any power he was able to exercise was fragile since it was derived from his ability to flatter and please the queen:

> When Francis Bacon compared him to Icarus, his soaring flight destroyed by the sun, he captured not only the spirit of the man but the essence of the historical tragedy in which he was trapped. His political power was based on the personal attraction he exercised over Queen Elizabeth I, but when he presumed to pursue that attraction he was struck down.[20]

The influence of literary criticism is clearly felt in the description of Essex's personality which is described in terms of qualities exhibited by Shakespeare's tragic heroes:

> He could be as mercurial and inspiring as Henry V, as amorous and captivating as Anthony, but then too he could be haughty and domineering as Coriolanus, uncertain and moody as Hamlet, ambitious as Macbeth and obtuse as Othello.[21]

The persistence of the narrative of Essex's career in terms of his role as Elizabeth's favourite has also influenced the discussion of the portraiture of the earl. Roy Strong in his seminal text on Elizabethan portraiture and culture *The Cult of Elizabeth: Elizabethan Portraiture and Pageantry* described the significance of the miniature *The Young Man Among Roses*, thought to be an early image of Essex, in the following terms:

> Above all, it has to be seen as one of the supreme artistic expressions of one of the greatest and most passionate romances of the age, that between a lonely ageing female ruler in her middle fifties and a dashing aristocratic youth of twenty.[22]

Strong considers the frustrations of the male lover of this image largely in terms of his concern that the queen may choose to shift her affections to another male courtier. More recent scholarship influenced by new historicist criticism has sought to query the power relations between Elizabeth and her subjects, particularly in portraiture and courtly entertainments. Rather than these texts simply reinforcing the power of the monarch and confirming the subordinate role of courtiers to their monarch, critics have argued that many of these texts provide the locus for a struggle for power and demonstrate the limitations of the queen and her government to exercise control over these allegorised texts.[23] The influence of this strand of scholarship can be seen in Chris Laoutaris's consideration of *The Young Man Among Roses* in Chapter 9. Laoutaris situates his discussion of the soubriquet the 'weary knight' given to the earl by his sister, Penelope Devereux, in her coded correspondence in the wider iconographical context of the portraits and courtly entertainments associated with Essex, including the early Hilliard miniature. By juxtaposing these two images of the earl Laoutaris suggests that Penelope Devereux is re-appropriating Essex's earlier persona of the passive, forlorn lover to make a more pointed protest about the ways in which the queen has frustrated the political and military ambitions of the earl and his circle.

The influence of twentieth-century literary criticism and earlier biography can also be seen in the depiction of the earl on the celluloid screen and in television dramatisations. Michael Curtiz's 1939 *The Private Lives of Elizabeth and Essex* is discussed below; more recently two television series about Elizabeth I have featured the Earl of Essex, including the two-part drama series *Elizabeth I* screened on Channel Four in 2005. This starred Helen Mirren as Elizabeth and concentrated on her relationships with the Earl of Leicester, played by

Jeremy Irons, in episode one and with Hugh Dancy as the Earl of Essex in episode two.[24] The second drama series, for the BBC and called *The Virgin Queen*, starred Anne Marie Duff as the queen and Hans Matheson as Essex. The four episodes traced Elizabeth's life, starting with her imprisonment in the Tower, up to the 1590s and her relationship with Essex.[25] In each case however, despite the inclusion of some details about Essex's life, his purpose was in a supporting role to the queen, which eliminated the potential for a more nuanced portrait of the earl.

The BBC television series *Elizabeth R*, transmitted in 1971, is particularly notable because it offers a snapshot of the ways in which Essex's biography demonstrates the triangulated relationship between Essex, Elizabeth and Shakespeare, as well as providing an interesting intervention in one of the ongoing and critically charged debates about the circumstances of the Essex Rising in 1601. The final episode of the series, entitled 'Sweet England's Pride', traces the relationship between Elizabeth, played by Glenda Jackson, and Essex, played by Robin Ellis, against the backdrop of his campaign in Ireland, his abortive rising and his execution. The episode demonstrates an awareness of Elizabethan drama and the theatrical trends of the late 1580s and 1590s, as Essex declares in a moment of bravura to the Earl of Southampton 'We do not crawl. We command. We are Tamburlaine'.[26] This reference to Marlowe's influential play of the same name is used as a shorthand method of sketching Essex's character in the mould of a Marlovian character. The queen also articulates the performative nature of Essex's life and the rebellion when she considers the punishment of the Earl of Southampton, Essex's close friend and Shakespeare's patron. Elizabeth remarks 'He has a fondness for the theatre, but he has no place in this (Pause) dramatic spectacle' (p. 526). The episode reinforces the popular but erroneous belief that Essex was in attendance at a performance of a play about Richard II before the uprising as it depicts the earl and his associates watching a performance of Shakespeare's *Richard II*, specifically the deposition scene in Act IV, scene 1, up to Richard's response to Bolingbroke's question 'Are you contented to resign the crown?' As Richard hands over the crown and sceptre Essex begins to applaud and remarks 'We have much to do. She has cut me off from her exchequer. All she sends me are conditions. Conditions, my friends. Her conditions are as crooked as her carcase. Come, my friends, we have much to do' (p. 524). For Essex, in this television series at least, Shakespeare's play seems to provide the motivation for the uprising.

The historical source for this fictional vignette is an account provided by Augustine Phillips, a member of the Lord Chamberlain's Men, who recounted how a group of Essex's associates asked the company

> to have the play of the deposyng and kyllyng of Kyng Richard the second to be played the Saturday next promysyng them xls. [forty shillings] more than their ordynary to play yt. Wher thys Examinate and hys fellowes were determyned to have played some other play, holdyng that play of Kyng Richard to be so

> old & so long out of use as that they shold have small or no company at yt. But at their request this Examinate and his fellowes were Content to play yt the Saterday and had their xls. More then their ordynary for yt and so played yt accordyngly.[27]

This testimony by Phillips is often discussed alongside a conversation which took place between William Lambarde and the queen, in which Elizabeth identifies herself with Richard II, while Lambarde alludes to Essex's own appropriation of that history for his own ends.[28] The Lambarde family manuscript records the following:

> her majestie fell upon the reign of King Richard II. Saying, 'I am Richard II. know ye not that?'
> W[illiam L[ambarde]. 'Such a wicked imagination was determined and attempted by a most unkind Gent[leman] the most adorned creature that ever your Majestie made.'
> Her Majestie. 'He that will forget God, will also forget his benefactors; this tragedy was played 40[tie] times in open streets and houses.'[29]

Historians and critics have long been exercised by questions relating to these two incidents. Does Phillips' allusion to a play about Richard II refer to Shakespeare's own play, and if so what might this tell us about Shakespeare's own political views? Is he a supporter of Essex and of subversive politics? Is the queen alluding to Shakespeare's *Richard II* in her conversation with Lambarde? Two camps quickly emerged during the twentieth century as critics attempted to answer these questions: those who argued that the play performed on the eve of the Essex rebellion was Shakespeare's *Richard II* and those who argued for another potential candidate, a play based on the recently published history of Henry IV by Sir John Hayward. Those who have argued that it was not Shakespeare's play have tended to present the dramatist as moderate or even neutral in his politics, pointing to the fact that Shakespeare, unlike many of his contemporaries, managed to avoid any trouble with the law.

Ian Rodger, the author of the final episode of *Elizabeth R*, was certainly aware of these arguments and of the two competing texts, Shakespeare's play and Hayward's history. Earlier in the episode Robert Cecil and Francis Bacon discuss the publication of Hayward's book and in the following scene Elizabeth reads aloud to Bacon Hayward's dedication of the book to Essex and indicates that it contains a detailed account of the deposition of Richard II. Elizabeth makes it clear that an analogy between Richard and herself is intended: 'Of all the history in England, they choose this one incident. The idea behind it is treason' (p. 497). The scene concludes with Elizabeth demanding the suppression of the book. Later when Elizabeth considers how to punish Essex for his conduct in Ireland and his hasty return, Cecil warns Elizabeth that if she revokes his monopolies she may provoke him into rebellion, to which she retorts: 'For his sake, Sir Robert, I pray God it will not. I play no Richard the Second to his Bolingbroke' (p. 521).

The debate about the relationship between Elizabeth, Essex and Richard II was played out in the late 1920s and early 1930s in the work of Evelyn May Albright and Ray Heffner.[30] Albright in her article of 1927 made the case for the association between Elizabeth I and Richard II and indicated the political resonances of a play like Shakespeare's *Richard II* for the queen in the 1590s. Albright suggested that the play performed before Essex's associates was Shakespeare's play, but she argued for a direct link between Shakespeare's *Richard II* and Hayward's history, suggesting that Hayward's account of the reign of Richard II served as a source for Shakespeare's play. Heffner responded directly to these suggestions arguing that Elizabeth in her comments to Lambarde was referring not to Shakespeare's play but a dramatisation of Hayward's book. Heffner concluded emphatically 'There is no evidence to connect Shakespeare's *Richard II* with either Hayward or Essex'.[31] The dispute was reactivated in the 1980s when Shakespeare's play and the attendant contemporary details outlined above were utilised by New Historicist and Cultural Materialist critics to confirm their theory of the political relationship between the theatre and the state and that theatrical performance was by its very nature subversive of royal power. Stephen Greenblatt in his landmark essay of 1982 compared his own reading of Shakespeare's *Richard II* and Elizabeth's comments to Lambarde with that of J. Dover Wilson. Whereas Greenblatt attends to the subversive potential of the play, Wilson reads *Richard II* in the context of the providential nature of the two tetralogies, with the deposition of Richard leading ultimately to the accession of the Tudors.[32] Jonathan Dollimore also brings together Elizabeth and Shakespeare's play to make a similar point which emphasises the role of the theatre and Shakespeare's work in providing a space for popular dissent. He remarks that

> A famous attempt to use the theatre to subvert authority was of course the staging of a play called Richard II (probably Shakespeare's) just before the Essex rising in 1601; Queen Elizabeth afterwards anxiously acknowledged the implied identification between her and Richard II, complaining also that 'this tragedy was played 40 times in open streets and houses'.[33]

Leonard Tennenhouse concurs with the position adopted by Greenblatt and Dollimore in his discussion of Shakespeare's history plays as he notes that

> He [Essex] obviously had Bullingbroke's method of challenging Richard II in mind, for he requested Shakespeare's company to revive *Richard II* the night before the rebellion.[34]

In an important response to the practices adopted by proponents of New Historicism and cultural materialism Leeds Barroll used the example of Shakespeare's *Richard II* and its relationship with Elizabeth and Essex to point out some of the potential blind spots in the arguments which emphasised the seditious nature of the theatre and its dramatists. He argued that the desire to link Shakespeare to Essex via Richard II came from 'a narrative promoted by a nineteenth-century aristocratic ideology that constantly sought to raise Shakespeare to the status of confidant with the peerage'.[35] Barroll was alert to the totalising effect of focusing simply on a selection of contemporary narratives about the play and he assured his readers that 'It is methodologically important to break this traditional story of the *Richard II* performance out of its amber'.[36] The way in which Barroll attempts to achieve this is to broaden out the debate and consider a wider range of contemporary documents as a context for the Essex rebellion, namely the publication of Hayward's book in 1599. The article traces the consequences of its publication and argues that printed books were considered more troublesome to the authorities than individual theatrical performances:

> If one looks beyond the locus that has been used to demonstrate the subversive value of Shakespeare's play, one finds other loci that add new readings of history. One could argue, in fact, that the Elizabethan authorities perceived in connection with the Essex plot a threat much more serious than acted plays: i.e. the printed book.[37]

More recently Blair Worden has revivified Ray Heffner's claim that the play performed on 7 February 1601 was not in fact Shakespeare's play at all but a version of Hayward's history for the stage. The ensuing discussion between Worden and Frank Kermode can be traced in the *London Review of Books.*[38] Other critics are prepared to accept that it was Shakespeare's play, but use a number of sources to explicate how Shakespeare's play works in conjunction with a number of other texts to provide a fuller context for the uprising. Paul Hammer, for example, argues that critical misunderstanding of the nature of the Essex rebellion has itself skewed the ways in which the performance of *Richard II* has been read. Events which precipitated Essex's entrance into the City of London happened so rapidly that the performance of the play on Saturday 7 February did not have any direct bearing on the events of the following day. The accepted narrative of the uprising cites a direct correlation between the commissioning of a play and the subsequent rebellion but in fact the play had been organised in conjunction not with the uprising that actually happened but with a more ordered intervention planned for at least a week later by the earl and his followers.[39]

The opening two chapters by Richard Wood and Matthew Steggle offer important insights into the composition and ethos of the Essex circle. Wood begins by revisiting the biographical commonplace that Essex identified himself with the chivalric code valued by Sir Philip Sidney and actively fashioned an identity for himself as Sidney's heir. Wood suggests that the relationship between Essex and Sidney is triangulated by the influential figure of Mary Sidney and argues that this complicates traditional narratives about the earl's personality, the political attitudes of his associates and the factionalism which has characterised the 1590s. Wood argues that if the revised *Arcadia* is read through the lens supplied by the interpretation of Sidney's sister the

Countess of Pembroke rather than through the Tacitean one of his friend Fulke Greville it can in fact be seen as pragmatic and as advocating conciliation rather than as a gospel for doomed idealists. This chapter invites the reassessment of the privileging of the influence of Tacitus on Essex and his circle and suggests that the consideration of Mary Sidney's pragmatic stoicism illustrates a range of competing viewpoints within the Essex circle.

Steggle's chapter also contributes to the discussion surrounding the identity and ethos of the Essex circle initiated by Wood, by arguing that texts by Sidney and Spenser offer ways of understanding Essexianism: the mindset which characterised this grouping. Steggle brings to our attention Gervase Markham, a prolific author in his own right but significant here as one of the earliest biographers of Essex; Markham, Steggle argues, sought to translate Essex's chivalric philosophy into a lived reality. In Chapter 3, Grace Ioppolo provides an important intervention in the debate about the relationship between Essex and the theatre and Essex and Shakespeare, considering his role not as the subject of plays like *Henry V*, for example, but as a patron of a company of players. Between 1575 and 1594 Essex supported a touring company, the Earl of Essex's men. This fresh perspective situates the earl within the tradition of theatre patronage established by both his father Walter Devereux and his stepfather the Earl of Leicester. The chapter also highlights the role of Lettice Knollys as the patron of her husband's company of players and underlines the importance of a number of powerful women who were linked to the earl.

Linda Shenk in Chapter 4 turns her attention to Essex's use of nonprofessional theatrical entertainments at court in 1595 to promote an agenda he had shared with Sidney by campaigning for an increased level of English involvement in international affairs. The chapter deals with a frequently neglected entertainment called the device of the Indian Prince, referred to here as *Seeing Love* as it dramatises the story of the blind Indian prince whose sight is restored by the queen and whose identity is revealed to be that of Cupid, the god of love. As an entertainment focused on a prince of the West Indies this has a specific political context, namely Spanish expansionism in the Americas and Caribbean, so that Essex is able to promote his own political agenda for English intervention not just in the West but in France more particularly. This entertainment is significant in that it demonstrates that Essex was capable of exercising subtlety and careful negotiation in his efforts to persuade the queen of his position on foreign policy. This provides another corrective to the dominant depiction of Essex in his dealings with Elizabeth, in which he is either a petulant child or a vengeful, competitive bully.[40] The chapter also makes important contributions to our understanding of the recording of entertainments and the portraiture of the earl. Whereas many of the entertainments provided to celebrate occasions such as the queen's Accession Day are recorded either in first-hand accounts or in poems, Shenk argues that there is a visual record of Essex's device captured in the Henry

Unton memorial portrait. What Shenk's essay makes clear is that Essex and his associates were skilled not only in utilising a range of media to promote their own agenda but also in deploying a range of personae for the earl in order to achieve this.

Andrew Hiscock in Chapter 5 provides a comprehensive survey of the classical and biblical figures deployed by and for the earl. It situates the earl in his intellectual milieu as a man of considerable classical learning in his own right. While a great deal of work has been done on the iconography of Elizabeth, this chapter charts the ways in which the earl was engaged in similar practices of representation. The process of self-fashioning was necessarily a two-way process in that the deployment of allegorical representations of the earl meant that its meaning could be appropriated and redefined by a range of recipients. The recurrent figuring of Essex as Achilles discussed by Hiscock demonstrates the unstable nature of the earl's image. The chapter also provides a sense of the trajectory of the earl's biography in the mid-seventeenth century and beyond whereby Essex's career is reduced to a narrative about his status as a favourite of the queen.

In their jointly authored Chapter 6 Chris Butler and Willy Maley re-examine the circumstances under which the earl undertook the commission to subdue Ireland in order to problematise assumptions about Essex's attitude to foreign policy and his career as a military figure. They argue that Shakespeare and Spenser in particular mediate the earl's career in texts such as *A View of the Present State of Ireland, The Faerie Queene* and *Henry V.* Adopting Juliet Dusinberre's dating of the first performance of *As You Like It* as 14 February 1599, the chapter also goes on to suggest that Shakespeare uses the play as a means of engaging with the earl's political agenda. Maley and Butler read the courtly invasion of the Forest of Arden against the earl's proposed mission to secure the Ard peninsula in Ireland as part of a wider colonisation project.

Some of the most important textual traces of the earl can be found in his extant letters, poems and prose tracts. Andrew Gordon in Chapter 7 focuses upon Essex's absence from court at times when he was on campaign, during his not infrequent periods of pique, illness or depression, and finally during his effective exile. Gordon traces how this exclusion from court in 1598 produced the personal and political manifesto known as Essex's *Apology* and other written texts to compensate for the earl's loss of a personal voice. In particular the chapter details two specific instances of the ways in which letters and other writing by the earl circulated in manuscript form and were appropriated by others. Gordon notes that 'The sustained appeal of these texts cannot be confined to a desire for model letters or a general historical interest, they also provide a touchstone for political reflection in debates over tyranny and royal authority, supplied the grounds for comparative analysis of topical issues ... as well as registering within the conceptualisation of an oppositional politics more generally'. The first example is a letter from

Essex to the queen in August 1599 which was found in a contemporary manuscript lute book, compiled by Richard Mynshall. The musical context for this letter provides important insights into Essex's role as a musical patron and of the lutenists within his circle. Essex's letter is considered alongside a poem by Mynshall which responds to Essex's position in his letters to the queen and offers a sympathetic view of a soldier's lot. The second example of letters by Essex which were reproduced and circulated is provided by his correspondence with Sir Thomas Egerton. Gordon discusses a copy of one of these letters which has been annotated by Anthony Grenlinge, the brother-in-law of William Sancroft, the Archbishop of Canterbury (1617–93), an important collector of Essex manuscripts and materials. As with the Mynshall material, Grenlinge's annotation of Essex's letter is a way of demonstrating his sympathies for the earl and provides some useful insights into the ways in which the earl's views were utilised by subsequent generations.

Hugh Gazzard's chapter is a case study of the earl's *Apology* which casts new light on the circumstances behind both the composition and the printing of this document and also on its reception. Gazzard reminds us that this tract was printed alongside a letter written by the earl's sister Penelope Devereux, to the queen, begging for the queen's mercy in her dealings with Essex. The chapter is accompanied by an appendix which offers a census of the manuscript copies of the *Apology*, which will prove invaluable to scholars who wish to pursue work in the field.

In Chapter 9 Chris Laoutaris also considers Penelope's letter as part of his general examination of the relationship between Essex and his sister and the part she played in the rebellion. What emerges from Laoutaris' chapter is a woman of extraordinary talents, accomplishments and attractions without whom Essex's story might well not have unfolded as it did. The chapter makes use of extensive manuscript resources to trace Penelope's involvement in the covert correspondence between the earl's circle and James VI of Scotland. Laoutaris demonstrates the ways in which the ciphers deployed by Penelope in her letters provide examples of the ways in which royal iconography was re-appropriated in order to critique the queen.

Lastly in this group Alexandra Gajda offers a detailed examination in Chapter 10 of Essex's relationship with another dangerously public discourse, 'politic history', by tracing the influence of a range of competing texts, including Hayward's *The first part of the life and raigne of King Henrie the IIII*, Antonio Perez's *Pedacos de Historia o Relaciones* (1594), *A Conference about the Next Succession to the Crown of England* (1594/5) and *The State of Christendom.* The chapter considers the extent to which the study of Tacitean history was seen by the earl and his circle as constituting a blueprint for political action, this being a mode of writing which D. R. Woolf sees as distinguished by 'its vivid character depiction, its pointed Tacitean style and its Machiavellian analysis of political events'; 'it transcended the confines of the annal and ... sought the causes of the events it depicted in human nature rather than providence, fate, or fortune',[41] and so extensive was the influence of Tacitus on writing associated with Essex's circle that when John Hayward, apparently without permission, controversially dedicated to the earl his history of Henry IV, who was not only Essex's own ancestor but also a successful usurper, Francis Bacon quipped to the queen that he thought the book's real crime was not treason but felony, since so many of its passages had been stolen from Tacitus.[42] The chapter examines the various ways in which the events of the uprising might be read against the historical analogies offered in these texts.

Finally, the last two chapters both consider different manifestations of the earl's posthumous reputation. Mary Partridge discusses the play performed at court in 1602 entitled *A Pleasant Comedie, Shewing the Contention Betweene Liberalitie and Prodigalitie: As it was Playd Before her Maiestie* and situates it within the context of other plays performed by the children's companies which alluded to the career of the Earl of Essex, such as *Cynthia's Revels, Philotas* and *Sejanus.* The essay provides a study of a critically neglected play whose 1602 performance and prodigal son narrative mediates another set of contemporary responses to the earl's life and career. Lisa Hopkins focuses on the representation of the earl in the 1939 Michael Curtiz film *The Private Lives of Elizabeth and Essex*, which was influenced by Strachey's dual biography as well as by the contemporary politics of the 1930s. Hopkins argues that the paradigm of the abdication of Edward VIII offers a useful way of reading the depiction of Essex in Curtiz's film, whose values are dismissed as outmoded and impractical but in which the earl himself remains, as he has done for so long, a source of fascination and a potent image of doomed glamour and of a lost alternative to the established order.

Notes

1 There are numerous biographies of Elizabeth and a smaller number for Essex but the following provide a brief overview of the field: Lytton Strachey, *Elizabeth and Essex* (London: Chatto and Windus, 1928); J. E. Neale, *Queen Elizabeth* (New York: Harcourt, Brace and Company, 1934); G. B. Harrison, *The Life and Death of Robert Devereux, Earl of Essex* (London: Cassell and Co., 1937); Robert Lacey, *Robert, Earl of Essex: an Elizabethan Icarus* (London: Weidenfeld and Nicolson, 1970); and Alison Weir, *Elizabeth the Queen* (London: Jonathan Cape, 1998).

2 See Strachey, *Elizabeth and Essex*, pp. 259–260; and Michael Dobson and Nicola J. Watson, *England's Elizabeth: An Afterlife in Fame and Fantasy* (Oxford: Oxford University Press, 2002), pp. 89–94.

3 For discussion of the actual and imagined relationship between Elizabeth and Shakespeare for example, see Helen Hackett, *Shakespeare and Elizabeth: The Meeting of Two Myths* (Princeton, NJ: Princeton University Press, 2009).

4 For a brief overview of some of these critical developments relevant to this collection see for example, Louis A. Montrose, 'Professing the Renaissance: The Poetics and Politics of Culture', in *The New Historicism*, ed. H. Aram Veeser (London: Routledge,

1989), pp. 15–36; Stephen Greenblatt, *Renaissance Self-Fashioning: From More to Shakespeare,* 2nd edn (Chicago: University of Chicago Press, 2005); and Stephen Greenblatt, 'Invisible Bullets: Renaissance Authority and its Subversion', in *Political Shakespeare: Essays in Cultural Materialism,* eds Jonathan Dollimore and Alan Sinfield (Manchester: Manchester University Press, 1985), pp. 18–47.

5 Francis Davison, *A Poetical Rapsody containing, diuerse sonnets, odes, elegies, madrigalls, and other poesies, both in rime, and measured verse. Neuer yet published. The bee and spider by a diuerse power, sucke hony' & poyson from the selfe same flower* (London: John Baily, 1602), sig. E9^{v}. All further quotations will be taken from this edition and reference will be given in the text.

6 John Considine, 'Davison, Francis (1573/4–1613x19)', in *Oxford Dictionary of National Biography,* ed. H. C. G. Matthew and Brian Harrison (Oxford: Oxford University Press, 2004), hereafter *ODNB*; online edn, ed. Lawrence Goldman, January 2008, hereafter *ODNB online,* www.oxforddnb.com/view/article/7300, accessed 17 March 2013. See also R. C. McCoy, 'Lord of Liberty: Francis Davison and the Cult of Elizabeth', in *The Reign of Elizabeth I: Court and Culture in the Last Decade,* ed. J. Guy (Cambridge: Cambridge University Press, 1995), pp. 212–228 and Paul E. J. Hammer, *The Polarisation of Elizabethan Politics: The Political Career of Robert Devereux, Second Earl of Essex, 1585–1597* (Cambridge: Cambridge University Press, 1999), pp. 183 and 372.

7 See Paul E. J. Hammer 'Devereux, Robert, Second Earl of Essex (1565–1601)', in *ODNB*; and Franklin B. Williams, Jr, *Index of Dedications and Commendatory Verses in English Books before 1641* (London: The Bibliographical Society, 1962).

8 See for instance Charles Nicholl, *The Reckoning: The Murder of Christopher Marlowe* (London: Vintage, 1992), pp. 222–223; and Paul E. J. Hammer, 'A Reckoning Reframed: the "Murder" of Christopher Marlowe Reconsidered', *English Literary Renaissance* 26 (1996), pp. 225–242, and Hammer, *The Polarisation of Elizabethan Politics,* pp. 152–198.

9 BL, Harleian MS 1327, fol. 58^{v}.

10 Hammer, *The Polarisation of Elizabethan Politics,* p. 133; Rudolf B. Gottfried, 'Spenser's *View* and Essex', *PMLA* 52:3 (1937), pp. 645–651, p. 646; and L. W. Henry, 'The Earl of Essex as Strategist and Military Organizer (1596–7)', *English Historical Review* 68 (1953), p. 388.

11 See Dobson and Watson, *England's Elizabeth,* pp. 159–168.

12 This question was first debated in a series of articles in *Publications of the Modern Language Association of America*: E. M. Albright, 'Shakespeare's *Richard II* and the Essex Conspiracy', *PMLA* 42 (1927), pp. 686–720; Ray Heffner, 'Shakespeare, Hayward and Essex', *PMLA* 43 (1930), pp. 754–780; E. M. Albright, 'Shakespeare's *Richard II,* Hayward's History of Henry IV, and the Essex Conspiracy', *PMLA* 46 (1931), pp. 695–719; Ray Heffner, 'Shakespeare, Hayward and Essex again', *PMLA* 47 (1932), pp. 898–899; and E. M. Albright, 'Reply to Ray Heffner's "Shakespeare, Hayward and Essex again"', *PMLA* 47 (1932), pp. 899–901. More recently, Blair Worden in 'Which Play Was Performed at the Globe Theatre on 7 February 1601?', *London Review of Books* 25: 13 (10 July 2003), pp. 22–24 has argued that it was not Shakespeare's, and Paul E. J. Hammer, in 'Shakespeare's *Richard II,* the Play of 7 February 1601, and the Essex Rising', *Shakespeare Quarterly* 59: 1 (2008), pp. 1–35, has replied to argue that it was. Chris Fitter also takes the play in question to be Shakespeare's in his essay 'Historicising Shakespeare's *Richard II*: Current Events, Dating, and the Sabotage of Essex', *Early Modern Literary Studies* 11: 2 (September 2005), http://extra.shu.ac.uk/emls/11-2/fittric2.htm, accessed 5 March 2013.

13 See Lesel Dawson, 'Dangerous Misogyny: John Ford's *The Queen* and the Earl of Essex's 1601 Uprising', *Explorations in Renaissance Culture* 33: 1 (2007), pp. 64–82.

14 Lesel Dawson, 'The Earl of Essex and the Trials of History: Gervase Markham's *The Dumbe Knight*', *The Review of English Studies* 53 (August 2002), pp. 344–364, p. 356.

15 See Hugh Gazzard, '"Those Graue presentments of Antiquitie": Samuel Daniel's *Philotas* and the Earl of Essex', *The Review of English Studies* 51 (2000), pp. 423–450; and Peter Lake, 'From *Leicester his Commonwealth* to *Sejanus his Fall*: Ben Jonson and the politics of Roman (Catholic) Virtue', in *Catholics and the 'Protestant Nation': Religious Politics and Identity in Early Modern Britain*, ed. Ethan H. Shagen (Manchester: Manchester University Press, 2005), pp. 128–161.

16 See Winifred Smith, 'The Earl of Essex on the Stage', *PMLA* 39: 1 (March 1924), pp. 147–148. Smith also other discusses French and Italian plays featuring Essex.

17 Strachey, *Elizabeth and Essex*; and Lacey, *Robert, Earl of Essex*.

18 Dobson and Watson, *England's Elizabeth*, p. 223.

19 Strachey, *Elizabeth and Essex*, p. 258.

20 Lacey, *Robert, Earl of Essex*, p. xi.

21 Lacey, *Robert, Earl of Essex*, p. 26.

22 Roy Strong, *The Cult of Elizabeth: Elizabethan Portraiture and Pageantry* (London: Thames and Hudson, 1977), p.57. For further discussion of the portraiture of Essex see also Roy Strong, 'Queen Elizabeth, the Earl of Essex and Nicholas Hilliard', *Burlington Magazine* 101 (1959), pp. 145–149 and D. Piper, 'The Lumley Inventory: Hilliard, Segar and the Earl of Essex' (in two parts), *Burlington Magazine* 99 (1957), pp. 231, 299–302.

23 For texts which consider the entertainments and portraiture of Essex in this context see Paul Hammer, 'Upstaging the Queen: The Earl of Essex, Francis Bacon and the Accession Day Celebrations of 1595', in *The Politics of the Stuart Court Masque*, eds David Bevington and Peter Holbrook (Cambridge: Cambridge: 1998), pp. 41–66; and R. C. McCoy, '"A dangerous image": the Earl of Essex and Elizabethan Chivalry', *Journal of Medieval and Renaissance Studies* 18 (1983), pp. 316–323. For more general discussion of the Elizabethan royal image see John N. King, *Tudor Royal Iconography: Literature and Art in an Age of Religious Crisis* (Princeton, NJ: Princeton University Press, 1989); Susan Frye, *Elizabeth I: The Competition for Representation* (Oxford: Oxford University Press, 1993); Louis Adrian Montrose, '"Shaping Fantasies": Figurations of Gender and Power in Elizabethan Culture', *Representations* 2 (1983), pp. 61–94 and Louis Montrose, *The Subject of Elizabeth: Authority, Gender, and Representation* (Chicago: University of Chicago Press, 2006).

24 For details of the series including interviews with Helen Mirren and the script writer Nigel Williams see the HBO website, www.hbo.com/movies/elizabeth-i/index.html#/movies/elizabeth-i/inside/interviews/interview/helen-mirren.html.

25 For details of the series and an opportunity to watch clips from the series see the BBC website, www.bbc.co.uk/drama/virginqueen/.

26 Ian Rodger, 'Sweet England's Pride', in *Plays of the Year Special: Elizabeth R*, ed. J. C. Trewin (London: Paul Elek, 1972), p. 477. All subsequent quotations will be taken from this edition and reference will be given in the text.

27 Quoted in Hackett, *Shakespeare and Elizabeth*, p. 125. On the anecdote and what we can learn from it see Leeds Barroll, 'A New History for Shakespeare and His Time', *Shakespeare Quarterly* 39: 4 (Winter 1988), pp. 441–464; and Cyndia Susan Clegg, 'Archival Poetics and the Politics of Literature: Essex and Hayward Revisited', *Studies in the Literary Imagination* 32: 1 (Spring 1999), pp. 115–466.

28 For a detailed discussion of the contemporary comparisons made between Elizabeth and Richard II see E. K. Chambers, *William Shakespeare: A Study of Facts and Problems*, 2 vols (Oxford: The Clarendon Press, 1930); William Shakespeare, *King Richard II*, ed. Charles R. Forker (London: Thomson Learning, 2002), pp. 5–16; and Jonathan Bate, *Soul of the Age: The Life, Mind and World of William Shakespeare* (London: Viking, 2008), p. 278.

29 Chambers, *William Shakespeare*, vol. 2, pp. 326–327.

30 Dobson and Watson, *England's Elizabeth*, pp. 159–168.

31 Heffner, 'Shakespeare, Hayward and Essex', p. 780.

32 Stephen Greenblatt, 'Introduction' to 'The Forms of Power and The Power of Forms In the Renaissance', *Genre*, 15 (1982), pp. 3–6.

33 Jonathan Dollimore, 'Introduction: Shakespeare, cultural materialism and new historicism', in *Political Shakespeare*, eds Dollimore and Sinfield, pp. 18–47.

34 Leonard Tennenhouse, *Power on Display: The Politics of Shakespeare's Genres* (London: Methuen, 1986), p. 88.

35 Barroll, 'A New History for Shakespeare and his Time', p. 443.

36 Barroll, 'A New History for Shakespeare and his Time', p. 444.

37 Barroll, 'A New History for Shakespeare and his Time', p. 452.

38 Worden, 'Which Play Was Performed at the Globe Theatre on 7 February 1601?'

39 Hammer, 'Shakespeare's *Richard II*, the Play of 7 February 1601, and the Essex Rising'.

40 See Hammer, 'Upstaging the Queen', pp. 41–66; and McCoy, '"A dangerous image".

41 D. R. Woolf, 'Genre into Artifact: the Decline of the English Chronicle in the Sixteenth Century', *Sixteenth Century Journal* 19: 3 (1988), pp. 350 and 322.

42 F. J. Levy, 'Hayward, Daniel, and the Beginnings of Politic History in England', *Huntington Library Quarterly* 50: 1 (Winter 1987), p. 19.

PART I

Essex: patron and patronage

1

'Cleverly playing the stoic': the Earl of Essex, Sir Philip Sidney and surviving Elizabeth's court

Richard Wood

As the title of Paul E. J. Hammer's landmark book indicates, the political career of Robert Devereux, second Earl of Essex is associated with the polarisation of Elizabethan politics towards the end of the sixteenth century.[1] And, although, as Hammer notes, the traditional image of Essex, as 'the ill-fated favourite of Elizabeth', who 'lost his head, both metaphorically and literally', and whose career historians have employed as 'an easy explanation for the political problems of the 1590s', is a 'caricature', there is a persistent sense that the earl's personal qualities, often characterised as exclusively negative, were the most significant factors in determining the events of the period. That several scholars (including Hammer) have repeatedly countered this impression over a long period of time has not completely debased its currency.[2] In the entry on Essex published in the *Dictionary of National Biography* in 1888, Sidney Lee observes that

> Essex's character is a simple one. He was devoid of nearly every quality of which statesmen are made. Frank, passionate, and impulsive as a schoolboy, he had no control whatever over his feelings; and at a court like Elizabeth's, split into warring factions, whose members strove to supplant one another by intricate diplomacy, his attempt to make a great political position by force of his personal character was doomed to failure.[3]

This nineteenth-century example of a caricature of Essex's career contains the essential elements of many others: he is painted as an over-ambitious, arrogant courtier, who lacked the self-control and diplomatic ability to survive in the already overheated atmosphere of the late Elizabethan court. In Hammer's entry in the 2004 edition of the *Oxford Dictionary of National Biography*, he outlines a 'more complex', 'modern historiographical image of Essex' in which research demonstrates that

> Essex developed a coherent military strategy for the war against Spain and examined the broader cultural context which helped to shape his career. More

> recent works have illuminated his role in intelligence gathering and his patronage of university scholars, whose research helped to serve his political needs.[4]

This latter view of Essex echoes that presented by Mervyn James, in his influential book, *Society, Politics and Culture: Studies in Early Modern England.* In a chapter entitled 'At a crossroads of the political culture: the Essex revolt, 1601', James acknowledges that time was running out for figures in Essex's mould, but, even so, prefers to emphasise the earl's political and cultural sophistication. Indeed, he asserts that 'the most interesting feature of the Essex revolt is not so much the fact of its failure, as that it was the last of its kind'. For James, 'the revolt was motivated by, and arose out of, a specific aspect of the political culture of Elizabethan England: the cult of honour and its code'; 'it was the last honour revolt'; Essex himself, a product of his 'aristocratic lineage, his military career, and the tradition he inherited', was 'a paradigm of honour'.[5] Moreover, a dominant feature of Essex's make-up, according to James, was a new chivalric romanticism, 'a synthesis of honour, humanism and religion', inherited from Sir Philip Sidney and epitomised by his prose romance, the *Arcadia.*[6]

And so, building on the work of historians like James and Hammer, and in order to further the ongoing reappraisal of the political and cultural career of the Earl of Essex, this chapter will examine the relationship between the earl and the 'specific aspect of the political culture of Elizabethan England' (that 'synthesis') that is 'Sidneian chivalric romanticism'.[7] More specifically, it will read the *Arcadia,* Sidney's prose romance and the chief source for what James terms 'Sidneian romanticism', with reference to the issues of counsel and court factionalism, which have particular relevance for Essex's career and the 1590s in general. Employing the work of historians of the late Elizabethan polity, this chapter will argue that the revised *Arcadia* in particular, written in the 1580s, ought to be read in accordance with a distinctly feminine discourse of pragmatic stoicism and principled anti-factionalism. This reading privileges the philosophy of Mary Sidney Herbert, the Countess of Pembroke, Sidney's sister and supervisor of the publication of the 1593 edition of the *Arcadia,* over that of Fulke Greville, Sidney's friend, biographer and editor of the 1590 edition.

The first version of the *Arcadia,* completed by 1581, has come to be known as the *Old Arcadia.*[8] Sidney's reworking of his romance 'might have begun', according to Victor Skretkowicz, 'as early as 1582 and continued into 1584'.[9] This revised version, though incomplete at the time of Sidney's death in 1586, is known as the *New Arcadia.* In 1590, Sidney's closest friend, Fulke Greville, supervised the publication of an edition based on Sidney's incomplete revision of the *Arcadia.* Three years after the publication of what has come to be seen as Greville's edition, Sidney's sister, Mary Sidney Herbert, the Countess of Pembroke, supervised the publication of another *Arcadia,* combining the revised work with the third, fourth and fifth books of the *Old Arcadia*; this is often referred to as 'the composite *Arcadia*'. The *Old Arcadia* circulated in manuscript in the 1580s, but was not available to a modern readership until after Bertram Dobell's discovery of three copies in the years 1906–07. The first printed *Arcadias*, Greville's of 1590 and those supervised by the countess (of 1593, and the slightly emended version of the same text of 1598) were much more widely available.[10] Indeed, it is from the printed text of 1593 that Gervase Markham took the inspiration to write the two volumes of his prose completion: *The English Arcadia, Alluding his Beginning from Sir Philip Sidney's Ending* (1607) and *The Second and Last Part of the First Book of the English Arcadia* (1613).[11] During the 1590s, Markham's works were, as Matthew Steggle notes, 'strongly identified with the faction of the earl of Essex'.[12] From its first appearances in contrasting print versions, the ethos of the *Arcadia* has been contested, and that contest has always involved a subordinate struggle over which version of the text has priority. In the very act of supervising its publication, Greville backed the incomplete revised version, unencumbered by any older additions; likewise, the Countess of Pembroke blessed the composite text published in 1593.

The basic plot of the *Arcadia* is recognisably similar in both the *Old* and *New* versions: two princes, Pyrocles and Musidorus, of Macedon and Thessalia respectively, disguise themselves (the former as an Amazon warrior, the latter as a shepherd) to gain access to their beloved Arcadian princesses, Philoclea and Pamela, who have been secreted in a remote pastoral location; the princesses' father, King Basilius, has sought to preserve his daughters' safety after consulting the oracle at Delphi; both Basilius and his wife, Gynecia, fall in love with Pyrocles (disguised as an Amazon), which, understandably, complicates the prince's courtship of Philoclea; the eventual resolution of this narrative, with the marriage of the two young couples, brings the *Old Arcadia* to a happy ending. Indeed, the *Old Arcadia* might fairly be described as 'a relatively light-hearted chivalric pastoral-romance'.[13]

The incomplete revision that is the *New Arcadia*, however, does not benefit from such a felicitous conclusion. Indeed, compared to the five books (or acts) of the original, the revised text ends mid-sentence, before the conclusion of the third book. Nevertheless, so substantial are Sidney's additions to his romance that the revised version is still significantly longer than the original. In what amounts to a change in genre, away from the comedic and towards the epic, Sidney introduces considerably more involutions to the narrative, including a wholly new episode in which the princesses and Pyrocles (still disguised as an Amazon) are kidnapped by Basilius's sister-in-law, Cecropia, who wishes to remove Basilius from his throne in favour of her own son, Amphialus. What becomes, in effect, Amphialus's rebellion against his uncle's rule institutes a significantly greater number of martial exploits, which, in keeping with the epic tone, multiply Sidney's allusions to the *Iliad*, the *Odyssey* and the *Aeneid*. Nevertheless, it is those passages dealing with the princesses' captivity that are of most interest here.

As both Greville's and Sidney Herbert's editions contain the three books of the revised romance, the key to understanding their differing philosophies lies in their contrasting editorial practices rather than any fundamental differences between the captivity episodes in the two texts. In order to fulfil his (and what he believed to be Sidney's) vision for the *Arcadia*, Greville omitted certain eclogues, divided the text into chapters, to which he added didactic chapter summaries, and left the romance without an ending. As Joel Davis persuasively argues, Greville's editorial decisions 'impose a Stoic interpretive frame-work [on the *Arcadia*], allowing Greville to highlight [what Greville believed to be] philosophical similarities between himself and Sidney'. Greville, according to Davis, wished to align himself and the *Arcadia* with the factionalism and the pessimistic Taciteanism of the circle of the Earl of Essex. This is evident in the chapter summaries for the captivity episode in the 1590 text, where Greville highlights 'the reactions of Pamela and Philoclea to their captivity and torture' as 'direct examples of ... passive female stoicism'.[14]

The Countess of Pembroke, in response, removed the chapter divisions and their summaries, restored what Davis terms the pastoral element (chiefly the missing eclogues) and, in doing so, re-established 'her brother ... as an advocate of Neostoic ethics ... only insofar as the Sidney family itself embraced Neostoicism'. As such, she emphasised the *Arcadia*'s associations with the Sidney family, as opposed to 'its intellectual relationship to the writings of partisans of the earl of Essex'.[15]

Paradoxically, though I accept Davis's arguments about the differences between Greville and the countess, I wish to emphasise the continuities between Sidney Herbert's philosophical outlook and that of the Earl of Essex, in effect bypassing Greville's agenda as it is evident in his role as an editor of the *Arcadia*. Ironically, by publishing the *New Arcadia*, Greville put a text into the public domain that undermined his intention in doing so, not least because he prompted the Countess of Pembroke to publish what she believed to be a more Sidneian text. The approach here will shed light on the more optimistic and conciliatory aspects of Essex's career that are arguably part of Sidney's legacy, while also bringing to prominence the differences of emphasis and circumstance that produced a political culture that was peculiar to Essex.

The fact that Essex was the chief legatee of the political and cultural position established by Sidney has long been accepted. Both Essex and Sidney fought in the military campaign against Catholic Spain in the Low Countries that was led by Sidney's uncle, Essex's stepfather, Robert Dudley, the Earl of Leicester. This was a campaign, begun in 1585, that was intended to fulfil the political aims of Leicester and his party, who pursued a 'policy of Protestant activism' that, though barely realised,

> involved a European Protestant league, a larger investment of resources in the war with Spain, wider military commitments abroad, westward oceanic expansion, and an extended naval assault on the Spanish empire.[16]

Indeed, it is the tension between the activism of this party, to which Sidney and Essex belonged, and the more passive approach of Elizabeth and her closest aides, including the Cecils, William and Robert, that forms the background to this discussion of Sidney's legacy and Essex's inheritance. The death of Sidney, in October 1586, as part of the same war in the Low Countries, after receiving a wound at Zutphen, where he fought beside Essex, was a significant blow to the long-term project of Leicester's party. Not long after this loss of one of the cause's two bright young hopes, the other took his ally's place as one of the main challengers in the tilt held regularly on 17 November to celebrate the accession to the throne of Queen Elizabeth. Essex was bequeathed Sidney's sword, and later married his widow. In the years immediately following Sidney's demise, in both action and written word, Essex was both encouraging others and 'being encouraged to think of himself as Sidney's military and political heir'.[17] Essex's New Year's gift to Elizabeth in 1587 was a jewel that showed a rainbow above two pillars, one of which was cracked to represent Sidney, the other intact to represent himself.[18] In the dedicatory epistle to his *The Life and Death of Sir Phillip Sidney*, dedicated to Essex and published in 1587, John Philip asks, 'But is Sidney deade', and answers by addressing Essex directly:

> no he liveth, his virtues in this life have made a conquest of death, and in the world to come his faith hath obtained him the glorious presence of Jesus Christe in the kingdome of heaven. And to put you out of doubt, his virtues so revive him from the grave, that he in truth speaketh unto you.[19]

In 1589, George Peele addressed a pastoral work to Essex on the occasion of the earl's return from his unsanctioned participation in the forward-Protestant expedition to Spain and Portugal, under the command of Sir John Norris and Sir Francis Drake.[20] The full title of the work included a reference to Essex as the 'renowmed Shepheard of Albions Arcadia', and the text makes explicit this allusion to Essex as the inheritor of Sidney's symbolic role as the shepherd knight, Philisides, from the *Arcadia*, while acknowledging their shared military experiences and Essex's appearance at the Accession Day tilt dressed in black:

> Fellow in Armes he was, in their flowing deies,
> With that great *Shepherd* good P*hilisides*:
> And in sad sable did I see him dight,
> Moning the misse of P*allas* peereles Knight …
>
> With him he serv'd, and watcht and waited fate,
> To keepe the grim Wolfe from *Elizaes* gate:
> And for their *Mistresse* thoughten these two swains,
> They moughten never take too mickle paines …
>
> But, ah for griefe, that jolly groome is dead,
> For whome the *Muses* silver teares have shed:

> Yet in this lovelie swaine, source of our glee,
> Mun all his Vertues sweet reviven bee.[21]

Essex, here poetically characterised as the dutiful Arcadian shepherd of the nation's flock, keeping 'the grim Wolfe [of Catholic Spain] from *Elizaes* gate', was in reality also capable of behaviour reminiscent of the knights and princes from Sidney's romance. Sidney introduces the symbolic display and martial chivalry of the Elizabethan tiltyard into the conflicts represented in his fiction, and it has been argued that the 'military effectiveness [of Sidney and his like-minded party] may have been diminished by the fact that they were much more experienced in symbolic conflicts in the tiltyard than in real warfare'.[22]

In another ill-fated military campaign (begun in 1591) in the wider conflict with Spain, to aid the Protestant King of France, Henri IV, in his besieging of Rouen, Essex commanded an army of 4,000 men.[23] As the conflict progressed, Essex's forces became severely depleted and the earl came under severe criticism from Elizabeth for his own behaviour, which was typified by a 'sharp dash' to Compiègne to meet Henri, where Essex, with 'one hundred horsemen ... trimmed in the best Devereux tangerine', designed to produce an impressive display for the king, found himself and his men 'outflanked – and stranded', before taking a 'circuitous and hard-riding route to regain his companions' and losing a number of his soldiers in the process.[24] Yet, this did not dim Essex's fondness for the grand chivalric gesture. Just before returning to England for the final time during a sporadic and failing campaign, Essex challenged the governor of Rouen to 'personal combat, on foot or horse'. This again proved to be an empty deed when the governor politely declined the earl's offer 'on the grounds of his responsibility as governor'.[25]

Essex's chivalry, however, was not all about public display. It was also of serious political and cultural significance. The new chivalric romanticism, putatively inherited by Essex from Sidney, was, as Mervyn James observes, 'a synthesis of honour, humanism and religion' that was intended to fortify Elizabethan men such as Sidney and Essex against the vicissitudes of fickle Fortune. And, as Sidney's friend, Fulke Greville, outlines in his biography of Sidney, 'A Dedication to Sir Philip Sidney', the *Arcadia* could be seen as a guidebook to this new ethos:

> In which traverses [of the *Arcadia*] I know his [Sidney's] purpose was to limn out such exact pictures of every posture in the mind that any man, being forced in the strains of this life to pass through any straits or latitudes of good or ill fortune, might (as in a glass) see how to set a good countenance upon all the discountenances of adversity, and a stay upon the exorbitant smilings of chance.[26]

James's conception of Sidney's purpose in writing the *Arcadia* also relies on the suitability of Greville's 'A Dedication to Sir Philip Sidney' for reading the *Arcadia*. However, given that it was completed in the Jacobean (between

1610 and 1612) rather than the Elizabethan era, in a different political and philosophical climate, its suitability is open to doubt. Greville's early career under the reign of James I was marked by the loss of his position as treasurer of the navy, which he had gained with Essex's aid in 1599.[27] Indeed, Mervyn James acknowledges that during Greville's post-Elizabethan career, 'under the pressure of political disillusionment, his mind showed a progressive disintegration of the synthesis of wisdom, honour and religion which, under Sidney's influence, had sustained the idealism of his youth'.[28] Given this disintegration, it is debatable whether Greville's Jacobean articulation of Sidney's purpose in writing the *Arcadia* and the nature of the chivalric romanticism expressed in the romance, and passed on to Essex, are wholly the same.

James's formulation of the threefold nature of the *Arcadia* ('a synthesis of honour, humanism and religion') is derived from Greville's reading of the *Arcadia*, particularly as it may be applied to the careers of the romance's heroes, Pyrocles and Musidorus. It is these princes who must endure Greville's 'exorbitant smilings of chance', and 'pass through any straits or latitudes of good or ill fortune' they encounter, acquiring, according to James, 'first wisdom, then ... Christian "patience"' to add to their well-established magnanimity and honour. Through their love for the princesses, Philoclea and Pamela, which 'first reveals to the princes their own weaknesses and breaks down their heroic self-sufficiency', they attain 'a knowledge of the finite weakness of the fallen self, converting ... heroic self-sufficiency into a dependence on others, and on the divine order of things'. During the princes' later imprisonment, facing execution for the murder of the princesses' father, Basilius, they 'assert their completion of the full circuit of wisdom through the attainment of a religious fortitude, that of patience'.

As James notes, there is a strong influence in this synthesis of Platonic and Stoic philosophies, neither of which was wholeheartedly embraced by Sidney, who did not hold with their 'introverted unworldly emphasis'.[29] Greville, by contrast, seems to have adhered to a more stoical philosophy, at least after Sidney's death, when he became linked to a fashion for reading the Roman historian, Tacitus, associated with the circle of the Earl of Essex.[30] Alexandra Gajda, in Chapter 10 of this collection, examines how the reading of Tacitus, among other histories, was used by Essex and his contemporaries to understand the world of late Elizabethan politics, constructing images of the earl as either a hero or a traitor in the process. The reading of Tacitus, whose works contain numerous examples of high political factionalism, was associated with the polarisation of politics in the 1590s, as both a philosophical shield from the vagaries of court politicking and a source of a divisive and often passive political ethos. In the case of the military-minded Essex himself, as David Womersley notes, the attraction may also have been Tacitus' lessons for increasing the 'political gravity' of military office.[31] Sidney's activist attitude is famously expressed in his *Defence of Poesy*, where he endorses 'the end of well-doing and not of well-knowing only'.[32] Indeed, considering the epic adventures of Sidney's Arcadian heroes, it would be difficult to derive from their example a version of chivalric romanticism that was passive in nature. Yet, James's conception of this new style of honour remains strongly inflected with what he terms 'an acceptance in "patience" of a discipline of suffering', which appears to be derived more from Greville's mature, Jacobean 'Dedication' than from Sidney's romance of the 1580s.[33] Indeed, a 'discipline of suffering' hardly sounds like the kind of philosophical outlook that would sustain the idealism of youth, and, in his 'Dedication', Greville himself bemoans the passive effeminacy of the present [Jacobean] time, contrasting it with the late Elizabethan era: 'the real and large complexions of those active times'.[34]

It is here that I depart from James's account. On this issue, James is in danger of obscuring the optimistic aspects of Sidney's outlook, which are, I contend, discernible in his *Arcadia,* especially the revised version.[35] The vestiges of this ethos can be seen in Essex's career in the 1590s, even in the events leading to his fateful 'revolt' in 1601. The Earl of Essex is undoubtedly associated with the polarisation of Elizabethan politics in this later period of his career, but it is possible to see, in the midst of an era of division, the legacy of Sidney's own anti-divisive philosophy in the earl's attitudes and behaviour. Of vital importance to the polarisation of Elizabethan politics at that time was the issue of who was able to counsel the monarch and to what effect.

After returning from the Rouen campaign, in 1592, Essex 'sought to reinforce his special personal relationship with Elizabeth, which had been severely strained', not least because of his own wilful behaviour in the martial arena. To his prowess as a military man, Essex 'added the objective of becoming a formal participant in state affairs as a member of the privy council'. This he achieved in February 1593. In this new position, he hoped to influence the monarch, through counsel, to back the same 'forward-Protestant' policies that he had pursued in battle.[36] Unfortunately, as the decade proceeded he came up against similar resistance to that which had opposed his stepfather, the Earl of Leicester, in the form of a rival party headed by Elizabeth's Principal Secretary of State, Sir Robert Cecil. Most significantly, while Essex was away from the court, pursuing his cause by military means, he would often fall prey to the misrepresentation of his actions by his rivals. This was never more evident than during his campaign in Ireland in 1599, when Essex's inability to overcome the forces of the Earl of Tyrone led to mutual suspicions between Essex and his rivals, each side fostering the impression that the other's actions were traitorous with regard to the ongoing conflict with Spain. Eventually, on 28 September 1599, in an act of consiliary desperation, Essex returned from Ireland and burst into the queen's bedchamber when she was only partially dressed.[37] From this point onwards, Essex's precipitate 'revolt', begun in further desperation to recover his devastated political position, appears to have been inevitable. His subsequent execution seems, in this context, to have been a result of his failure to fortify himself against the vicissitudes of a factionalised polity, something his inheritance from Philip Sidney had the potential to achieve.

The work of historians like Simon Adams and Paul Hammer suggests that 'the Elizabethan polity was not characterized by persistent factionalism until the 1590s'.[38] For Adams, such a conclusion rests, in part, on his own 'narrow definition' of the term 'faction': 'a personal following employed in direct opposition to another personal following'.[39] On this basis, the rivalry between Robert Dudley, Earl of Leicester and William Cecil, Lord Burghley is not considered to be evidence of factionalism. As Adams notes, during the period prior to 1588 (the year of Leicester's death), Burghley's power was 'limited by the influence of Leicester', but a 'sustained struggle' was obviated by 'their similar outlook in religion and agreement on most matters of state, together with a mutual appreciation of their joint intimacy with the Queen'.[40] Such 'political homogeneity' was characteristic of both the Elizabethan court and council, not least due to successive events in the 1570s that necessitated a closing of Protestant ranks: the papal bull declaring Elizabeth a heretic in 1570; the Ridolfi Plot of 1571; and the St Bartholomew's Day Massacre in 1572.[41]

Arguably the most contentious issue of the period following these events and prior to the 1590s was the proposed marriage of Elizabeth to François, Duke of Anjou. This was linked to the similarly divisive question of whether to intervene in the Netherlands, where the Dutch Protestant rebellion against Spanish rule was undergoing a resurgence after 1572.[42] Burghley adopted a 'cautious role', shy of 'military overextension'; Leicester favoured intervention.[43] The proposed marriage to Anjou was also the occasion for John Stubbs to write *The Discoverie of a Gaping Gulf*, Edmund Spenser *The Shepheardes Calender* and Philip Sidney his *A Letter to Queen Elizabeth Touching her Marriage with Monsieur*, all either printed or circulated in manuscript in 1579, or 1580 at the latest in the case of Sidney's letter. The putative background to the production of these writings, that of debate about military intervention and the marriage to Anjou, but not specifically factional dispute, shapes Natalie Mears's case that Stubbs, Spenser and Sidney were not 'hired' by a particular court faction (Leicester and Walsingham) to push Elizabeth into intervention.[44]

This subtle distinction, between 'debate' and 'factionalism', has a bearing on the reading of Sidney's *Arcadia*, begun in the late 1570s and continued and revised in the early 1580s, but first published in the 1590s. Fulke Greville, Sidney's friend and the editor of the 1590 edition of the *Arcadia*, wished, as Joel Davis has shown,

> to represent Sidney and the *Arcadia* as intellectual precursors to the Tacitean political thought beginning to emerge at the same time in the circle of Robert Devereux, the earl of Essex, who had become Greville's patron.[45]

Greville was at pains to emphasise 'Sidney's treatments of constancy in the face of political oppression'.[46] Such an association is, indisputably, with a political faction in a time of factionalism; political divisions are seen to have widened after Essex's unsuccessful Rouen campaign, of 1591–92, and the earl's push towards statesmanship.[47] Nevertheless, the revised *Arcadia*, of which Greville's edition is a version, ought to be read in accordance with the alternative philosophy of Sidney's sister, Mary Sidney Herbert, the Countess of Pembroke, who shunned the factionalism and pessimistic Taciteanism of the Essex circle.[48] Sidney Herbert's edition of the *Arcadia*, of 1593, evidences a philosophy, also demonstrated in her translation of Philippe Duplessis-Mornay's *Discours de la mort et de la vie*; she shared Mornay's belief that corruption stems from the kind of political factionalism that was prevalent in Elizabeth's court in the 1590s. Such a reading has one advantage, among others, of being more in tune with the politics of the time in which the romance was composed, the pre-factional 1580s. Although Sidney Herbert's philosophy can be seen purely as a response to a later, truly factional polity, it is nonetheless an ethos more in keeping with the earlier reality than that of Fulke Greville. Significantly, in my reading of the *New Arcadia*, Sidney does not adhere to a form of stoicism in which the individual is cast as the passive victim of events. Indeed, it is a peculiar paradox of this interpretation that it is exemplified by the suffering of the princesses, Pamela and Philoclea, during their captivity in Book III of the revised version of Sidney's romance.

In associating the *New Arcadia* with an anti-factional ethos I do not wish to imply that Sidney, who died in 1586, was not conscious of the detrimental effects of political division, nor do I wish to suggest that the *Old Arcadia* does not display such a consciousness. On the contrary, Sidney, as heir to the title of his uncle, the Earl of Leicester, until June 1581 (when Leicester's son was born), was acutely aware of the political struggles at court and their significance for Elizabethan foreign policy. Indeed, the international consequences of the divisions at home were of great importance to both Sidney and his sister, and they were influenced in their less pessimistic philosophical outlooks by continental Protestant activists such as Hubert Languet and Philippe Duplessis-Mornay.

Furthermore, despite Mary Sidney Herbert's dislike for the Taciteanism associated with Essex and his circle, the Sidneys' international perspective was inherited by Essex, whose particular focus in the 1590s was the defence of the Protestant cause in France, in support of Henri IV. Paul Hammer sees in Essex a combination of religious piety and 'profound commitment to European affairs' rooted in 'his upbringing in the Protestant cause'; and this is the very same cause that the Sidneys shared with their continental allies, at least one of whom was still active during Essex's rise to prominence.[49] Philippe Duplessis-Mornay, who had been a friend and ally to Philip Sidney, was Henri IV's special envoy, and was sent to England in 1592, during the siege of Rouen, to ask Elizabeth for more aid in Essex's cherished campaign;

he was refused, however, and Essex returned to England soon afterwards. Mornay, in a notable display of loyalty to the earl, records in his *Mémoires et correspondance* that Elizabeth overlooked Essex for the chancellorship of Oxford soon after the earl's return from France as a punishment for his behaviour during the Rouen campaign.[50] While in England, Mornay is likely to have met Mary Sidney Herbert. Their probable meeting and the subsequent publication of Sidney Herbert's translation of Mornay's work have come to be seen, by scholars such as Victor Skretkowicz and Margaret P. Hannay, as part of the continuation of support for the long-standing, forward-Protestant cause, by then associated with both the Sidney and Essex circles.[51] Indeed, in November 1593, Robert Sidney – younger brother to Philip and Mary, and by then, like Greville, a member of the Essex circle – was ordered to go 'on an embassy to Henri IV of France, whose recent conversion to Catholicism had raised concerns in England'. And the 'same prudence and discretion that made [Robert] Sidney a successful ambassador helped him survive the treacherous cross-currents at court towards the end of Elizabeth's reign'.[52] Such characteristics, especially as displayed by a member of Essex's notorious faction, might also be considered a further testament to the enduring nature of the Sidney family's anti-factionalist philosophy.

If Robert Sidney's prudence enabled him to avoid the harshest consequences of having been in Essex's circle in the 1590s, a similar discretion may have saved Philip Sidney from the fate that befell John Stubbs after the publication of *The Discoverie of a Gaping Gulf* in 1579; in Philip's case, his abjuration of factionalism may be what saved him from severe punishment for his writing of *A Letter to Queen Elizabeth.* Indeed, Natalie Mears highlights a distinction between the different attitudes to counselling the monarch, revealed in the writings of Stubbs, Spenser and Sidney, that suggests that this is the case. *A Gaping Gulf,* written by a politically active citizen from beyond the legitimate circles of court counsel, 'suggests [for Mears] the existence of a lively public sphere',[53] but it clearly misjudged Elizabeth's acceptance of counsel as a 'necessary element of queenship',[54] and resulted in Stubbs's right hand being struck off as punishment. Spenser's *The Shepheardes Calender* 'emanated from the same milieu as *A Gaping Gulf*': 'the independent response of a politically active and aware man'. In contrast to both Stubbs and Spenser, Sidney's letter was 'rooted in the traditions of noble counsel (both humanist-classical … and feudal-baronial)' and conformed to the established court principle that 'counsel was advisory'.[55] It is also interesting to note that Stubbs's illegitimate contribution was discussed by Sidney's associates, Languet and Mornay, in terms that examine 'how best to devise – an eloquent and politically serviceable – means of writing that could enable the restoration of the true religion', avoiding 'polemicism', which 'can have no consequence except to exacerbate the very confessional divisions whose proliferation militates against the triumph of the church'.[56] This stance, by two of Sidney's closest philosophical allies, emphasises the anti-factional nature of their vision of the legitimate courtier. However, an interpretation of Sidney's position as that of a legitimate courtier, with leave to counsel the monarch, is complicated by the fact that he was rebuked by Elizabeth after his famous tennis-court argument with Edward de Vere, Earl of Oxford (protégé of Lord Burghley) in August 1579.[57] Pointedly, Elizabeth advised Sidney on 'the difference in degree between earls and gentlemen'.[58] As Leicester's heir, Sidney clearly believed he had a legitimate claim to counsel the queen. In reality, he seems to have been denied this privilege, but did not receive the severity of punishment meted out to Stubbs. Shortly after the period of the circulation of his *Letter to Queen Elizabeth* and the quarrel with Oxford, Sidney chose to retreat from his life as a courtier and appears to have spent a great deal of time at his sister's home, at Wilton, writing the *Arcadia*, which was ultimately dedicated to her. As will be shown, there are parallels between Sidney's retreat and Essex's own beleaguered position in the mid-1590s.

Sidney's status as a courtier, his employment of the conventions of consiliary rhetoric and his exclusion from an advisory role all suggest that during his time at Wilton (and at other times after 1579) he was writing from a social position both within and without the limits of 'noble counsel'. This paradoxical position has echoes of the status of Lady Mary Sidney, Philip's mother, who, was 'a gentlewoman "without wages" of Elizabeth I's privy chamber' for twenty years between 1559 and 1579, when finally ill health appears to have enforced her retirement.[59] As Natalie Mears observes, 'Elizabeth's network was male-dominated but not exclusively male. Parallel to the inner ring of counsellors was a group of female intimates often holding ... privy chamber posts'. Nevertheless, their roles appear to have been restricted to that of 'barometers of the queen's moods or channels of communication ... and as negotiators in marriage diplomacy'.[60] Lady Mary was one of this 'group of female intimates', though, apparently, excluded from an advisory role. On a notable occasion, Lady Mary was in touch with the Spanish ambassador responsible for Elizabeth's marriage negotiations with Charles, Archduke of Austria, but the queen fell short of explicitly sanctioning her in this quasi-ambassadorial position.[61]

In the revised *Arcadia*, more specifically in the captivity episode of Book III, Sidney was writing to an agenda, informed by his own retirement, but also participating in a discourse associated with the restricted political role of female members of the aristocracy, like his mother. Moreover, this literary stance, which has been characterised by Lisa Hopkins as 'writing to a woman's aesthetic agenda',[62] is not only reflected in his dedication of the *Arcadia* to his sister and his well-known narrative address to the 'fair ladies', but also in the peculiarly stoical activities of his female characters.[63] It is notable in this context that, as Chris Laoutaris explores in Chapter 9 of this collection, Essex's own sister, Penelope Rich (the inspiration behind Sidney's 'Stella'), through her roles as a patron, a linguist and a manipulator of romance narratives, forged her own political career in competition with her equally ambitious sibling.

In Book III of the revised *Arcadia,* the princesses, Pamela and Philoclea, are held captive by their aunt Cecropia, who wishes one of the princesses to marry her son, Amphialus, and gain control of her brother-in-law's (the princesses' father's) kingdom. In a famous scene, Cecropia approaches the solitary Pamela with the intention of persuading her into marriage. Much has been made of the ensuing philosophical contest between the Epicurean and atheistic arguments of Cecropia and the proto-Christian stoicism of Pamela. However, I wish to discuss that part of the text which precedes the verbal disputation, in which Pamela is described as 'working upon a purse certain roses and lilies'.[64] The reader is given a detailed portrait of Pamela, 'disdaining to keep company with any of the gentlewomen appointed to attend her, whom she accounted her jailers' (354/25–27), but rather 'borrow[ing] her wits of the sorrow that then owed them, and len[ding] them wholly to that exercise' (29–30). This may easily be seen as a situation closely analogous to Sidney's own: the composition of the *Arcadia* is to Sidney, in unwanted retirement, what the working of the flowers upon the purse is for Pamela. Both are, arguably, turning their 'wits', previously possessed by their enforced predicament, to a finely wrought creative piece of their own design. Indeed, this parallel is further enhanced by the description of Pamela's flowers as 'carr[ying] such life in them that the cunningest painter might have learned of her needle' (31–32). This echoes Sidney's own definition of the art of poetry as '*mimesis,* that is to say, a representing, counterfeiting, or figuring forth – to speak metaphorically, a speaking picture – with this end, to teach and delight'.[65] It is in such moments, in the face of her imprisonment and, elsewhere, cruel torment, that Pamela displays what Blair Worden terms 'the Stoic ... doctrine of fortitude'. It is, in Worden's analysis, a passive form of stoicism, distinct from the Ciceronian virtue, which is displayed elsewhere in the romance through dynamic action.[66] A similar point is made by Nancy Lindheim, who refers to the Aristotelian concept of 'complete virtue' as 'the exercise of virtue' in her discussion of the trial scene in the *Old Arcadia.*[67] Although critics such as Worden have identified episodes in the *Arcadia* when the princes, Musidorus and Pyrocles, and other male characters display a similar passive virtue, it is usually associated with the female characters and seen at its height during the captivity of the princesses in the revised version.[68] Of course, Pyrocles is also held captive, but, tellingly, he is disguised as the female Zelmane. If Sidney's project is seen as analogous to that of Pamela, he would appear to be participating in the pointedly gendered discourse of stoical retreat. Nevertheless, on the contrary, he, like Pamela, is adopting a stoical attitude as a means of strategically occupying a liminal social position, not unlike a gentlewoman of the queen's privy chamber, neither within nor without the circle of legitimate court counsel.

The significance of this for the Earl of Essex lies in his own compromised status, during the 1590s, as an embattled member of the privy council. It is possible to plot a career trajectory for Essex that is parallel to that of Sidney and identify where along that path the former's inheritance from the latter is evident. The most telling parallel is the possibility of the earl's retirement and the adoption of a literary career. This was suggested in the presentation to the earl of three alternative courses, those of soldier, secretary of state and hermit, as part of the symbolism of the Accession Day tilt devised by Essex in 1595;[69] the hermit invited Essex to eschew the active life and 'offer his service to the Muses'.[70] The temptation to withdraw from the court appears to have been attractive to Essex, who, according to Ray Heffner, 'withdrew himself into the country when his wishes were not granted by Elizabeth'.[71] Moreover, he did have a poetic aspect to his life that is often evocative of retreat, and he has been said to have 'produced a calculated poetics' with direct allusions to contemporary politics.[72] His 'Happy were Hee could finish foorth his Fate' meets all these criteria:

> Happy were Hee could finish foorth his Fate
> In some unhaunted Desert, most Obscure;
> From all Society, from Love, from Hate
> Of Worldly Folke! Then should Hee Sleepe Secure;
> Then Wake againe, and yield God ever Praise,
> Content with Hipps, and Hawes, and Brambleberry,
> In Contemplation passing still his Daies,
> And Change of Holy Thoughts to make him Merry;
> Who when Hee dies, his Tombe may bee a Bush,
> Where Harmeles Robin dwells with Gentle Thrush.
> Your Majesty's Exiled Servant
> Rob: Essex.[73]

This poem, with its evocation of escape from the 'love' and 'hate' of the 'worldly' court, was composed with his 'reluctance to undertake the Irish campaign' in mind.[74] The similarity between this poetically calculated retreat and Sidney's expedient consiliary position, as represented by his female characters, is notable, if, in literary terms, the quality and sophistication do not bear comparison.

Of course, Essex, like Sidney, was a man of action, and it is not immediately apparent how either of them may be properly represented by the passivity of an Arcadian princess. However, it is possible to free Pamela from her indolence, and both Elizabethan courtiers with her. The key to understanding Pamela as representing something other than the passive virtue of Blair Worden's analysis is the philosophical status of her refutation of Cecropia's atheism in the scene under consideration. D. P. Walker, in an article from 1955, describes Pamela's arguments as 'a bewildering display of sophistry'.[75] To summarise Walker's comprehensive examination of the theological and philosophical background to the Pamela–Cecropia episode,

Pamela demonstrates a broad knowledge of arguments from the school of Stoics, employed to pragmatically oppose the irredeemable Cecropia. In other words, Pamela's stoicism obviates Cecropia's response, but is not necessarily a sincerely held philosophical creed. There is a foreshadowing of the artificial nature of this dispute in the preliminary discussion between Cecropia and Pamela of the significance of the princess's purse. Cecropia suggests that the lucky man to whom Pamela is dedicating her skill in needlework, with a clear implication that it might be Amphialus, would be

> Full happy ... at least if he knew his own happiness ... in faith, he shall have cause to count it not as a purse for treasure but as a treasure itself worthy to be pursed up in the purse of his own heart. (355/32–33)

Pamela responds in a manner which punctures Cecropia's rhetorical affectation, and sets the tone for the exchange which follows:

> I promise you, I wrought it but to make some tedious hours believe that I thought not of them; for else, I valued it but even as a very purse. (355/38–356/2)

This passage has attracted the critical attention of Lisa Hopkins, who identifies Pamela's 'activity ... as having no meaning in itself', and argues that, more broadly, the princesses' incarceration represents the meaninglessness of the imprisonment of early modern women in general.[76] Hopkins equates the Arcadian detention of the princesses with the real case of Mary Stuart, and concludes that

> detention can serve only a spiritual function, humbling the patience of the proudly inclined Pamela, and not a political one. At best a stopgap ... it operates primarily as a ploy to gain time or in the hope of manipulating the outcome of future events.[77]

The function of this episode, as evident in Hopkins's reading, is suggestive of the motivations behind the circumstances of Sidney's own retirement and quiet industry at Wilton: 'a stopgap'; 'a ploy to gain time'; or 'in the hope of manipulating future events'. The lack of significance imputed by Pamela to her own creation echoes Sidney's reference, in the dedication of the *Arcadia*, to 'this idle work of mine' (506). Of greater importance is the sense of expediency implied by Pamela's refutation of Cecropia. She might be said, as Sidney said of his own apparent inactivity in a letter to his mentor, Hubert Languet, to be 'cleverly playing the stoic'.[78] Robert E. Stillman uses this pointed reference to bolster his argument that Sidney is not a true philosophical stoic, but someone with the necessary acquaintance with stoical doctrines to adapt them to his own purposes in the pastoral context of the *Arcadia*.[79] Sidney self-consciously puts on the garb of stoical passivity, without truly inhabiting the role of a Stoic. In such a mode, Sidney would appear to be conforming to a similar rhetorical model as he did with the humanist-classical tradition employed in his *Letter to Queen Elizabeth*. And yet, as in that instance, his status as a *bona fide* member of the school, or circle of counsel is in doubt, if not utterly compromised.

If Essex is adopting a similarly pragmatic approach to political counsel as suggested by my reading of the *Arcadia*, it would not be completely untypical of a man often otherwise characterised as 'hubristic'.[80] Indeed, he showed significant signs of taking to heart the strictures placed on court counsellors stressed by the likes of Languet and Mornay. An 'unusual willingness to accept constructive criticism' was on display when (during 1594–96) he received 'blunt cautions', from Lord Henry Howard and Francis Bacon, 'to be more subtle in his courting of public acclaim lest the queen come to see him as a political threat – and his rivals be able to exploit these fears against him'.[81] And, more significantly with respect to the issue of court counsel, Paul E. J. Hammer's account of the 'Essex Rising', in which the rebels are associated with the ideas of the publication *The State of Christendom*, is evidence of a greater appreciation of the delicacy of their relationship to monarchy than has often been attributed to Essex's party.[82] *The State of Christendom* is an unpublished work, of the mid-1590s, that may have been written by Anthony Bacon, Essex's 'chief intelligence gatherer'.[83] It was published in 1657 and attributed to Sir Henry Wotton, Essex's secretary. Its significance is in its cautious directions for 'petitioning a delinquent sovereign to save the state from oppression by corrupt and over-mighty councillors', which, as Hammer observes, represents a highly appropriate guide for Essex's party in their exploits on 8 February 1601.[84] Its language is one of humility, toleration and mitigation, in recognition of the gravity of the petitioners' act:

> Let the Subjects be therefore humble Petitioners unto the Princes to reform such abuses as are notoriously known to be abuses. Let them yeeld such measure unto their kings as they would desire for themselves; let them when neither their humble suits may prevail, nor their gentle connivence or toleration mitigate the wrath, or moderate the affections of their Soveraigns, humbly beseech the Peers of the Realm to be their Patrons and Protectors of their Innocency.[85]

This tract, like Sidney's romance and Essex's poetic works which were similarly the fruits of a humanistic education, were the kinds of text employed, if Francis Walsingham (Essex's father-in-law and Elizabeth's joint Principal Secretary of State) is to be believed, as 'better courses of action and counsel' to Walsingham and the privy council.[86] They were what Lorna Hutson terms a 'textualized intelligence service'.[87] It is this 'textualized intelligence' which Essex seems to have found most deleterious to his standing while in Ireland and at other times.[88] In effect, he lost the war of the counsellors, not of the soldiers.

To conclude, I suggest that such a reading of the *Arcadia* may have some significance for Sidney's reception in the 1590s, which is particularly significant for Robert Devereux, second Earl of Essex and his circle. As demonstrated here, there was a direct line of political and cultural inheritance between Sidney, the man and his works, and the Earl of Essex and his political ambitions, which culminated in the disastrous rebellion of 1601. Furthermore, by associating the *Arcadia* with a distinctly feminine discourse of pragmatic stoicism and principled anti-factionalism, it is possible that some of the usual literary-political boundaries of the 1590s could be redrawn. Gavin Alexander, in his examination of Sidney's reception, *Writing After Sidney*, describes how Samuel Daniel, who had dedicated his sonnet sequence, *Delia*, to Sidney's sister in 1592, later 'aligned himself with what [the Countess of] Pembroke would have seen as the wrong side – not Sidney's literary and biological heirs, but his chivalric and political heirs – Mountjoy, Greville, Essex'.[89] However, as argued in this chapter, Essex may be regarded as Sidney's literary (as well as chivalric and political) heir, at least with regard to the pragmatic stoicism handed down in Sidney's *Arcadia.* Rather than consider the divide to be between the literary-biological and the chivalric-political, it might be instructive to posit an alternative paradigm by which the politics of the 1590s could be judged, based on the gendered access to counsel and a concomitant philosophical attitude to factions. A shift in perspective of this kind, recognising the endurance of values such as humility, toleration and mitigation throughout a period of intense conflict, may contribute to what Paul E. J. Hammer describes as 'an attempt ... to re-contour our understanding of Elizabethan political life'.[90] Indeed, in the light of this suggestion, there is an interesting historical footnote in Margaret P. Hannay's study of the Countess of Pembroke, the definitive account of her role as patron and executor to her brother's literary and political legacy. In the mid- to late 1590s, during a protracted factional dispute between the Countess's husband the Earl of Pembroke and the Earl of Essex, which began over their interests in Wales, it is noted that 'the Sidney/Herbert women took no part in the quarrel and continued to treat Frances Walsingham, Sir Philip's widow and Countess of Essex, as a sister'.[91] Both Essex women were protected by Mary Sidney Herbert at the height of Essex's ill-fated revolt.[92] In the midst of such political schisms the discourse of principled anti-factionalism appears to have held, at least among the women.

Notes

1 Paul E. J. Hammer, *The Polarisation of Elizabethan Politics: the Political Career of Robert Devereux, Second Earl of Essex, 1585–1597* (Cambridge: Cambridge University Press, 1999; reprint, 2005).

2 Hammer, *Polarisation,* pp. 3–6. Such studies as Stephen Coote, *A Play of Passion: the Life of Sir Walter Ralegh* (London and Basingstoke: Macmillan, 1993), M. M. Reese, *The Royal Office of Master of the Horse* (London: Rowman & Littlefield, 1976) and L. B. Smith, *Treason in Tudor England: Politics and Paranoia* (London: Jonathan Cape, 1986, reprint Pimlico 2006) are cited by Hammer as examples of the perpetuation of the

negative image of Essex's career; he cites the work, conducted over several decades, of E. M. Tenison as evidence for the long-standing opposition to the caricatured view. E. M. Tenison, *Elizabethan England: being the history of this country 'in relation to all foreign princes'* (13 vols, Leamington Spa, 1933–61).

3 Sidney Lee, 'Devereux, Robert, second Earl of Essex (1566–1601)', in *Dictionary of National Biography*, eds Leslie Stephen and Sidney Lee (22 vols, London: Smith, Elder & Co., 1885–1900), XIV (1888); *ODNB online*, accessed 25 February 2010.

4 Paul E. J. Hammer, 'Devereux, Robert, second earl of Essex (1565–1601)', in *ODNB*; *ODNB online*, www.oxforddnb.com/view/article/7565, accessed 25 February 2010.

5 Mervyn James, *Society, Politics and Culture: Studies in Early Modern England* (Cambridge: Cambridge University Press, 1986), p. 416.

6 James delineates the nature of this 'Sidneian chivalric romanticism' in the preceding chapter of the same book, which is entitled 'English politics and the concept of honour, 1485–1642' (pp. 308–415); see pp. 387–391. This chapter first appeared with the same title as *Past and Present* Supplement no. 3 (1978).

7 James, *Society, Politics and Culture*, p. 391.

8 See Jean Robertson, 'General Introduction', in Sir Philip Sidney, *The Countess of Pembroke's Arcadia (The Old Arcadia)*, ed. Jean Robertson (Oxford: Clarendon Press, 1973), p. xv.

9 See Victor Skretkowicz, 'General Introduction', in Sir Philip Sidney, *The Countess of Pembroke's Arcadia (The New Arcadia)*, ed. Victor Skretkowicz (Oxford: Clarendon Press, 1987), p. xvii.

10 See H. R. Woudhuysen, *Sir Philip Sidney and the Circulation of Manuscripts, 1558–1640* (Oxford: Clarendon Press, 1996), pp. 299–355 and Heidi Brayman Hackel, *Reading Material in Early Modern England: Print, Gender, and Literacy* (Cambridge: Cambridge University Press, 2005), pp. 137–195.

11 Skretkowicz, 'General Introduction', p. xlvii.

12 Matthew Steggle, 'Markham, Gervase (1568?–1637)', in *ODNB*; *ODNB online*, www.oxforddnb.com/view/article/18065, accessed 25 February 2010.

13 Claire Preston, 'Arcadia', in *The Literary Encyclopedia*, www.litencyc.com/php/sworks.php?rec=true&UID=6542, accessed 11 July 2012.

14 Joel Davis, 'Multiple *Arcadias* and the Literary Quarrel between Fulke Greville and the Countess of Pembroke', *Studies in Philology* 101: 4 (Fall 2004), pp. 414–421. Davis enlarges on this theme in his book, *The Countesse of Pembrokes Arcadia and the Invention of English Literature* (Basingstoke and New York: Palgrave Macmillan, 2011), pp. 23–78, 145–178.

15 Davis, 'Multiple *Arcadias*', pp. 425–430.

16 James, *Society, Politics and Culture*, p. 391. The activist Protestant party associated with Leicester (and later with Essex) has been conveniently termed, by Blair Worden, as the 'forward-Protestants'; although they cannot be considered a 'party' in the modern sense, they were 'united in their diagnosis of the ills of Elizabethan policy ... and worked together in vain attempts to remedy them'; see Blair Worden, *The Sound of Virtue: Philip Sidney's* Arcadia *and Elizabethan Politics* (New Haven, CT: Yale University Press, 1996), p. xxii; Patrick Collinson's use of the same phrase to describe other groups of Protestants from different periods predates Worden's use; see, for example, Patrick Collinson, *Archbishop Grindal, 1519–1583: the Struggle for a Reformed Church* (Berkeley, CA: University of California Press, 1979), p. 61.

17 Gavin Alexander, *Writing After Sidney: The Literary Response to Sir Philip Sidney, 1586–1640* (Oxford: Oxford University Press, 2006), p. 61.

18 For discussions of contemporary allusions to Essex as Sidney's legatee see Alexander, *Writing After Sidney*, pp. 61–63 and Hammer, *Polarisation of Elizabethan Politics*, pp. 53–54.

19 John Philip, *The Life and Death of Sir Phillip Sidney, late Lord gouernour of Flushing: His funerals Solemnized in Paules Churche where he lyeth interred; with the whole order of the mournfull shewe, as they marched thorowe the citie of London, on Thursday the 16 of February, 1587* (London: Robert Waldegrave, 1587), sig. A2v.

20 This expedition is detailed by Hammer in *The Polarisation of Elizabethan Politics*, pp. 82–85 and *Elizabeth's Wars: War, Government and Society in Tudor England, 1544–1604* (Basingstoke: Palgrave, 2003), pp. 154–161.

21 George Peele, *An Eglogue Gratulatorie. Entituled: To the right honorable, and renowmed Shepheard of Albions Arcadia: Robert Earle of Essex and Ewe, for his welcome into England from Portugall* (London: J. Windet for Richard Jones, 1589), sigs A1r and A3v. For a detailed analysis of this and other poems occasioned by the expedition to Portugal see Hugh Gazzard, '"Many a Herdsman more disposde to morne": Peele, Campion, and the Portugal Expedition of 1589', *The Review of English Studies* 57 (2006), pp. 16–42.

22 David Norbrook, *Poetry and Politics in the English Renaissance* (London: Routledge and Kegan Paul, 1984), p. 108. Sidney's participation in the cult of honour was most publicly displayed during his involvement in numerous prestigious tilts, not least the entertainment that he devised (and in which he participated) for the occasion of the visit of the French Ambassadors to Elizabeth's court that began in April 1581, known as the *Four Foster Children of Desire*; see Malcolm William Wallace, *The Life of Sir Philip Sidney* (Cambridge: Cambridge University Press, 1915), pp. 263–267. For a discussion of (and guidance towards) the fictional parallels with Sidney's real-life tiltyard experience see Skretkowicz, 'General Introduction', pp. xiv–xv, xxi–xxii.

23 For accounts of this campaign see Hammer, *Polarisation of Elizabethan Politics*, pp. 97–108 and Chapter 6, as well as Howell A. Lloyd, *The Rouen Campaign 1590–1592: Politics, Warfare and the Early-Modern State* (Oxford: Clarendon Press, 1973).

24 Robert Lacey, *Robert, Earl of Essex: An Elizabethan Icarus* (London: Weidenfeld & Nicolson, 1971; reprint, London: Phoenix Press, 2001), pp. 84–85.

25 Lacey, *Robert, Earl of Essex*, p. 90. There are accounts of Essex's challenge to the governor in the memoirs of Maximilien de Béthune, duc de Sully (1559–1641), a minister of Henri IV, and in the *Essais historiques* of Saint-Foix; see *Memoirs of the Duke of Sully … a new edition, revised and corrected; with additional notes, and an historical introduction, attributed to Sir Walter Scott*, trans. Charlotte Lennox (London: H.G. Bohn, 1856), p. 274, and Monsieur de (Germain-François Poullain) Saint-Foix, *Essais historiques sur Paris*, Fifth Edition (Paris, Veuve Duchesne, 1776–77), p. 368.

26 Fulke Greville, 'A Dedication to Sir Philip Sidney', in *The Prose Works of Fulke Greville*, ed. John Gouws (Oxford: Clarendon Press, 1986), p. 11.

27 John Gouws, 'Greville, Fulke, first Baron Brooke of Beauchamps Court (1554–1628)', in *ODNB*; *ODNB online*, www.oxforddnb.com/view/article/11516, accessed 28 February 2010.

28 James, *Society, Politics and Culture*, p. 397.

29 James, *Society, Politics and Culture*, pp. 388–391.

30 Davis, 'Multiple *Arcadias*', pp. 401–430. For an examination of the complex response to the *Arcadia* by a Tacitus-reading associate of the Earl of Essex see Fred Schurink, '"Like a hand in the margine of a booke": William Blount's Marginalia and the Politics of Sidney's *Arcadia*', *The Review of English Studies* 59 (2008), pp. 1–24.

31 David Womersley, 'Sir Henry Savile's Translation of Tacitus and the Political Interpretation of Elizabethan Texts', *The Review of English Studies* 42: 167 (1991), p. 341.
32 Sir Philip Sidney, *An Apology for Poetry or The Defence of Poesy*, ed. Geoffrey Shepherd (London and Edinburgh: Thomas Nelson & Sons, 1965; reprint, Manchester: Manchester University Press, 1973), p. 104.
33 James, *Society, Politics and Culture*, p. 387.
34 Greville, 'A Dedication to Sir Philip Sidney', p. 7.
35 In his delineation of Sidney's romanticism, Mervyn James uses the composite *Arcadia* of 1593, which includes, broadly speaking, the revised books of the *New Arcadia* and the ending of the *Old Arcadia*. My reading makes use of the revised version, which, I contend, represents Sidney's ethos in its clearest and latest form.
36 Hammer, *The Polarisation of Elizabethan Politics*, pp. 111–120.
37 Paul E. J. Hammer, 'Shakespeare's *Richard II*, the Play of 7 February 1601, and the Essex Rising', *Shakespeare Quarterly* 59: 1 (Spring 2008), pp. 4–6.
38 Natalie Mears, 'Counsel, Public Debate, and Queenship: John Stubbs's *The Discoverie of a Gaping Gulf*, 1579', *The Historical Journal* 44: 3 (September 2001), p. 633.
39 Simon Adams, 'Faction, Clientage and Party: English Politics, 1550–1603', *History Today* 32 (December 1982), p. 34.
40 Adams, 'Eliza Enthroned? The Court and its Politics', in *The Reign of Elizabeth I*, ed. Christopher Haigh (Basingstoke and London: Macmillan, 1984; reprint 1994), p. 63.
41 Adams, 'Eliza Enthroned?', pp. 66–67.
42 The 'capture of Brielle and Flushing by William of Orange and the Sea Beggars signalled open but confused revolt (April 1572)'; see John Guy, *Tudor England* (Oxford: Oxford University Press, 1988), pp. 276–277. Susan Doran does regard such divisions as arose over the royal marriage proposal as being between factions. See Doran, *Monarchy and Matrimony: The Courtships of Elizabeth I* (London and New York: Routledge, 1996), pp. 174, 215–217.
43 Adams, 'Eliza Enthroned?', p. 67.
44 See Mears, 'Counsel, Public Debate, and Queenship'.
45 Davis, 'Multiple *Arcadias*', p. 404.
46 Davis, 'Multiple *Arcadias*', p. 420.
47 See Adams, 'Faction, Clientage and Party', p. 38.
48 See Richard Wood, '"The representing of so strange a power in love": Philip Sidney's Legacy of Anti-factionalism', *Early Modern Literary Studies* Special Issue 16 (October 2007), http://extra.shu.ac.uk/emls/si-16/woodsidn.htm, accessed 25 February 2010.
49 Hammer, *The Polarisation of Elizabethan Politics*, pp. 241–244.
50 Philippe de Mornay, *Mémoires et correspondance pour servir à l'histoire de la Réformation* (12 vols, Paris, 1824–25), vol. V, p. 170, cited in Hammer, *The Polarisation of Elizabethan Politics*, p. 108.
51 See Victor Skretkowicz, 'Mary Sidney Herbert's *Antonius*, English Philhellenism and the Protestant Cause', *Women's Writing* 6: 1 (March 1999), pp. 11–12 and Margaret P. Hannay, *Philip's Phoenix: Mary Sidney, Countess of Pembroke* (Oxford: Oxford University Press, 1990), pp. 60–63. Also, for the parallels between the lives of Philip Sidney and Philippe Duplessis-Mornay, including their similar educations under the guidance of Hubert Languet, see Roger Kuin, 'Sir Philip Sidney's Model of the Statesman', *Reformation* 4 (1999), pp. 93–117. For a discussion of the significance of Sidney's religious and philosophical inheritance for reading the *New Arcadia* see Richard Wood,

'"If an excellent man should err": Philip Sidney and Stoical Virtue', *Sidney Journal* 26: 2 (2008), pp. 33–48.

52 Robert Shephard, 'Sidney, Robert, first earl of Leicester (1563–1626)', in *ODNB*; *ODNB online* ed, www.oxforddnb.com/view/article/25524, accessed 31 May 2010.

53 Mears, 'Counsel, Public Debate, and Queenship', p. 650.

54 John Stubbs, *Gaping Gulf* (London, 1579; *STC* 23400), sigs F4, A5v–A6, E1v, cited in Mears, 'Counsel, Public Debate, and Queenship', p. 647.

55 Mears, 'Counsel, Public Debate, and Queenship', p. 646. For further discussions of the significance of the content of Stubbs's ill-advised publication see Jacqueline Vanhoutte, 'Queen and Country?: Female Monarchs and Feminized Nations in Elizabethan Political Pamphlets', in *Elizabeth I: Always Her Own Free Woman*, eds Carole Levin, Jo Eldridge Carney and Debra Barrett-Graves (Aldershot and Burlington, VT: Ashgate, 2003), pp. 7–19 and Leah S. Marcus, *Puzzling Shakespeare: Local Reading and Its Discontents* (Berkeley, CA: University of California Press, 1988), pp. 67–83. Vanhoutte highlights Stubbs's use of the rhetorical tropes of nationalism and motherhood, and Marcus places Stubbs's subversive use of Elizabeth's own 'male' rhetoric in a broader context of contemporary representations of the dominant woman, including Joan of Arc in Shakespeare's *1 Henry VI*.

56 Robert E. Stillman, *Philip Sidney and the Poetics of Renaissance Cosmopolitanism* (Aldershot and Burlington, VT: Ashgate, 2008), pp. 24–26.

57 H. R. Woudhuysen, 'Sidney, Sir Philip (1554–1586)', in *ODNB*; *ODNB online*, www.oxforddnb.com/view/article/25522, accessed 25 March 2008.

58 Greville, 'A Dedication to Sir Philip Sidney', p. 40.

59 Simon Adams, 'Sidney, Mary, Lady Sidney (1530x35–1586)', in *ODNB*; *ODNB online*, www.oxforddnb.com/view/article/69749, accessed 25 March 2008.

60 Natalie Mears, *Queenship and Political Discourse in the Elizabethan Realms* (Cambridge: Cambridge University Press, 2005), p. 54.

61 Mears, *Queenship and Political Discourse*, p. 55. See *Calendar of Letters and State Papers Relating to English Affairs, Preserved Principally in the Archives of Simancas*, vol. 1: Elizabeth 1558–1567, ed. Martin A. S. Hume (London: Eyre and Spottiswoode, for Her Majesty's Stationery Office, 1892), pp. 95–101, 106–107, 111–113, 115–16.

62 Lisa Hopkins, *Writing Renaissance Queens: Texts by and about Elizabeth I and Mary, Queen of Scots* (Newark, DE: University of Delaware Press; London: Associated University Presses, 2002), p. 56.

63 Sir Philip Sidney, *The Countess of Pembroke's Arcadia (The Old Arcadia)*, ed. Jean Robertson (Oxford: Clarendon Press, 1973), p. 27, line 21; among numerous others. For a discussion of Sidney's female audience see Mary Ellen Lamb, *Gender and Authorship in the Sidney Circle* (Madison, WI: University of Wisconsin Press, 1990), pp. 72–114. It should be noted that I am not suggesting that Sidney wrote the particular revisions to the *Arcadia* I discuss here during his initial retirement at Wilton. Rather, that such periods and their association with Sidney's marginalisation, in terms of court counsel, did inform his writing, and that this episode from the revised romance is particularly representative of this influence. Skretkowicz suggests that 'Sidney might have begun composition [of the *New Arcadia*] as early as 1582 and continued into 1584'; see Skretkowicz, 'General Introduction', pp. xiii–xvii.

64 Sir Philip Sidney, *The Countess of Pembroke's Arcadia (The New Arcadia)*, ed. Victor Skretkowicz (Oxford: Clarendon Press, 1987), p. 354; lines 27–28. Further references are contained within the text in the following form: 354/27–28.

65 Sir Philip Sidney, *An Apology for Poetry or The Defence of Poesy*, p. 101.

66 Worden, *The Sound of Virtue*, pp. 33, 25.

67 Aristotle, *Nicomachean Ethics*, trans. W. D. Ross, V.i.1129^{b}30; cited in Nancy Lindheim, *The Structures of Sidney's Arcadia* (Toronto: University of Toronto Press, 1982), p. 161.
68 Worden, *The Sound of Virtue*, p. 365.
69 Steven W. May, 'The Poems of Edward De Vere, Seventeenth Earl of Oxford and of Robert Devereux, Second Earl of Essex', *Studies in Philology* 77: 5 Texts and Studies (1980), p. 18.
70 John Nichols, *The Progresses and Public Processions of Queen Elizabeth* (3 vols, London, 1823), III, p. 373. Linda Shenk in her recent book, *Learned Queen: The Image of Elizabeth I in Politics and Poetry* (New York, NY: Palgrave Macmillan, 2010), sees Essex's entertainment as a notable example of the kind of literature that invoked 'Elizabeth's learned persona', in this case to further the earl's own 'military and transnational interests' (pp. 188, 159).
71 Ray Heffner, 'Essex, the Ideal Courtier', *English Literary History* 1.1 (1934), pp. 31–32.
72 May, 'The Poems of Edward De Vere, Seventeenth Earl of Oxford and of Robert Devereux, Second Earl of Essex', p. 21.
73 Robert Devereux, Second Earl of Essex, 'Poem No. 7', in May, 'The Poems of Edward De Vere, Seventeenth Earl of Oxford and of Robert Devereux, Second Earl of Essex', p. 47.
74 May, 'The Poems of Edward De Vere, Seventeenth Earl of Oxford and of Robert Devereux, Second Earl of Essex', p. 21.
75 D. P. Walker, 'Ways of Dealing with Atheists: A Background to Pamela's Refutation of Cecropia', *Bibliothèque d'Humanisme et Renaissance* 17: 2 (1955), p. 271.
76 Hopkins, *Writing Renaissance Queens*, pp. 64–66.
77 Hopkins, *Writing Renaissance Queens*, pp. 65–66.
78 A letter dated 1 March 1578, *The Correspondence of Philip Sidney and Hubert Languet*, ed. William Aspenwall Bradley (Boston, MA: The Merrymount Press, 1912), p. 159, cited in Robert E. Stillman, *Sidney's Poetic Justice:* The Old Arcadia, *Its Eclogues, and Renaissance Pastoral Traditions* (Lewisburg, PA: Bucknell University Press; London and Toronto: Associated University Presses, 1986), p. 73.
79 Stillman, *Sidney's Poetic Justice*, pp. 72–74.
80 Hammer, 'Shakespeare's *Richard II*', pp. 24–25.
81 Hammer, 'Shakespeare's *Richard II*', p. 23.
82 Hammer, 'Shakespeare's *Richard II*', pp. 12–13.
83 Alexandra Gajda, '*The State of Christendom*: History, Political Thought and the Essex Circle', *Historical Research* 81: 213 (August 2008), p. 425. Gajda shows that there is 'a body of evidence that firmly grounds the text in the scholarly and political interests of the associates of Robert Devereux, second earl of Essex, in the years 1594–5' (p. 425).
84 Hammer, 'Shakespeare's *Richard II*', p. 12.
85 *The State of Christendom, or, a Most Exact and Curious Discovery of Many Secret Passages and Hidden Mysteries of the Times* (London: Humphrey Moseley, 1657), sigs L13r–v.
86 Conyers Read, *Mr Secretary Walsingham*, 2 vols (Oxford: Clarendon Press, 1925), vol. I, 18, cited in Lorna Hutson, *The Usurer's Daughter: Male Friendship and Fictions of Women in Sixteenth-Century England* (London and New York: Routledge, 1994), p. 105.
87 Hutson, *The Usurer's Daughter*, p. 105.
88 Hammer, 'Shakespeare's *Richard II*', p. 4ff.
89 Alexander, *Writing After Sidney*, pp. 136, 140–141.
90 Hammer, *The Polarisation of Elizabethan Politics*, p. xi.
91 Hannay, *Philip's Phoenix*, p. 155.
92 Hannay, *Philip's Phoenix*, pp. 155–156.

2

Essexianism and the work of Gervase Markham

Matthew Steggle

> For thee ô *Essex* and thy noble line,
> Euer most great, yet greater then it was,
> Thou sun-shine, drying widdowes teared eyne,
> The Columb which supports a royall masse;
> Thou excellent, deriu'd from most diuine,
> The work *ELIZAS* power hath brought to passe:
> To thee am I deuote, and from thy deeds,
> I draw this breath, on which my spyrit feeds. [1]

Gervase Markham (?1568–1637) was one of the most prolific and successful writers of the seventeenth century, specialising in advice-books on subjects ranging from military tactics to cheesemaking. So influential were his farming manuals that one agricultural historian has called this period 'the age of Markham', but historians of horsemanship, cookery or home medicine could also with justice say much the same.[2] Best-selling throughout the seventeenth century, and in some cases reprinted into the eighteenth and even nineteenth centuries, those works are today recognised as important sources for cultural and social historians, giving a vivid and unusual insight into the practicalities of early modern life. They tell us how Renaissance people played tennis; chose a fishing rod; managed a forest; fired muskets; trained poodles as hunting dogs; designed a knot-garden; and stuffed sausages.[3] The factual manuals are only half of Markham's oeuvre. On the other hand – and this is the paradox this chapter will explore – Markham had enjoyed an earlier career as a writer of strongly romance-flavoured literature associated with the Earl of Essex. Indeed, in the 1590s Markham was one of the most committed, prolific, and successful of all Essexian writers.

This literary output is relatively little studied, and what scholarly critical attention Markham has received has tended to focus on the practical manuals.[4]

In this chapter it will be argued, firstly, that such an account of Markham under-emphasises the importance of the first part of his career. As one of the most prolific and engaged of Essexian writers, Markham has been described as 'the self-appointed laureate of the Essex group', and his copious writings from the 1590s offer an interesting and generally neglected case study of the whole world of what one might usefully term Essexianism.[5] Secondly, it will suggest that Markham's practical manuals are rooted fundamentally in those earlier military-chivalric writings. Markham's encyclopedia of everyday life should be thought of as a late and surprising flowering of Elizabethan Essexianism.

'Essexianism' is offered here as a coinage to describe the characteristic vocabulary, tropes, and even world-view of texts written in association with the Earl of Essex. The idea that followers of Essex might usefully be identified as 'Essexians' has been explored by a number of recent writers, including Margot Heinemann, who discusses 'the Essexians as a group'; Hugh Gazzard, who discusses Samuel Daniel's relationship with 'the leading Essexians'; and Paul Hammer, who identifies Cuffe and Southampton among a group of 'diehard Essexians'.[6] In such formulations 'Essexian' is already poised somewhere between a mere factional label, and something more like a *weltanschauung*, a cast of mind.

Moreover, there is seventeenth-century warrant for the idea that an Essexian position carried with it a belief system. Something of this sort is adumbrated in, for instance, the phrasing used by one former follower of Essex, Sir Henry Wotton:

> there were in Court two names of *Power,* and almost of *Affection,* the *Essexian* and the *Cecilian* with their Adherents, both well enough enjoying the present, and yet both looking to the future.

For Wotton, the 'Essextian side' [*sic*] are united primarily by pragmatic instincts of 'power', but also by something that goes beyond mere calculations of advantage to become almost, in the usual seventeenth-century meaning of 'affection', a mental state.[7]

In particular, the mental state of Essexians is marked by two distinct characteristics. The first, and most obvious, is that it is simultaneously contained within and defined against the dominant iconography of the era, that of Elizabeth herself. As an unmarried female monarch, and as one whose instincts tended towards deferring problems and avoiding wars, Elizabeth offered (of course) a stiff challenge to normal modes of representing valour and virtue. Imaginations of Essex, as a military and manly leader, are always defined and delimited by the fact that he is subservient to Elizabeth. Secondly, the Essexian mindset is defined by a sense of cultural belatedness, because by the 1590s the representational paradoxes thrown up by Elizabeth's continuing queenship had already been addressed in an entire generation's worth of figurations of masculine valour within a gynocracy: in texts such as *The Faerie Queene* and the works of Sir Philip Sidney. Essexians, writing in the 1590s, are thus troubled not merely by defining Essex within Elizabeth's continuing reign, but by the need to extend and outdo an entire pre-existing set of fictions about active male leaders under a queen's rule. In particular, for Essexians, one of the master-tropes, because of this sense of belatedness, is a value attached to acting things out: to translating pre-existing literary-chivalric tropes into practical action.

'Essexianism', then, can be thought of not just as a factional label, but also as a characteristic bundle of assumptions. As 'the greatest cultural patron of the 1590s', Essex's influence was wide indeed throughout the period. According to one estimate, more than sixty books of all sorts were dedicated to him during the 1590s.[8] 'Literary' writers including Spenser himself, Samuel Daniel, Jonson, and even Shakespeare all wrote to some extent within Essex's influence. Few, though, were as unreservedly and autobiographically Essexian as Markham.

Gervase Markham was the third son of Robert Markham of Cotham, a Nottinghamshire gentleman and MP and a staunchly militant Protestant who counted among his friends Sir Francis Walsingham, the Earl of Leicester, and Sir Henry Sidney. Growing up in the 1570s and 1580s, and inheriting their father's values, Gervase and his brothers were eager to take part in military action against the Catholic threat. At least one of the younger Markhams was involved in the Low Countries fighting of 1586–87, the campaign which saw the death of Sidney and the emergence of Essex as a leader of the militant Protestant cause. Gervase Markham's own biography is still poorly understood, but he seems to have served as a horseman in Essex's Rouen campaign of 1591, and gone from there to London, where – he later hints – he lived in Essex House for a while. There, Markham developed a career as a soldier-writer. He served on Essex's Azores voyage of 1597, and in the Irish disaster of 1599, producing in the same decade at least six books of poetry, two huge prose romances, three prose tracts, and probably one or more plays, until the fall of Essex in 1601 stopped his career in its tracks.[9]

Markham writes about this early section of his life in a late pamphlet, *Honour in his Perfection* (1624), in the course of biographies, founded on personal acquaintance, of both Essex and also the Earl of Southampton. In *Honour in his Perfection,* Markham attempts to encourage a new generation of militant Protestant leaders, including Essex's son the third Earl, as they embark on a campaign to reclaim Bohemia for the Elector Palatine. To do so, he recalls the deeds of Essex and other Elizabethan leaders a generation earlier. The book is not merely a biography of these leaders, but also, implicitly, an autobiography, guaranteeing its authenticity by drawing attention to Markham's own personal involvement in the wars it describes.

At the same time, the frame of reference for doing so is very much the world of Sidneyan and Spenserian literary romance. In describing the young Essex, for instance, Markham alludes explicitly to the world of Sidney's

Arcadia: 'for his youth and beauty he might, like *Pirocles*, haue made *Basilius* doat on his sweetnesse'. Equally, there is a Spenserian flavour to his description of Elizabeth's foreign policy.

> The poore King of *Portugale, Don Antonio* (held violently out of his right by the King of *Spaine* after the death of *Sebastian*) comes into England, fals at the feet of the great Queene *Elizabeth*; shewes his Iniury, and pleads to her mercy, for Succour: Shee who was altogether a plentifull Fountaine of pittie … presently vouchafes him aide, and sends away a Royall Army … [10]

The subdued image, here, is of course of Elizabeth as Faerie Queene. Compare Spenser's description in the *Letter to Raleigh*:

> Soone after entred a faire Ladye in mourning weedes … shee falling before the Queene of Faieries, complayned that her father and mother an ancient King and Queene, had bene by an huge dragon many years shut up in a brasen Castle, who thence suffred them not to yssew: and therefore besought the Faery Queene to assyne her some one of her knights to take on him that exployt.[11]

The Spenserian model is already so well established in the early modern imagination that the parallel does not even need to be spelt out explicitly. Essex and his comrades are cast not just as chivalric knights, but rather more specifically as Spenserian knights.

This pair of examples demonstrates in miniature some of the features that make Essexianism a distinctive, and slightly strange, subset of early militant protestant writing in general. The literary classics that define it are already in existence before it starts, and it sees itself as carrying out, for real, deeds previously only written about. Markham talks elsewhere about the literary legacy of

> the onely to be admired Sir Philip Sydney , whose like, though neuer age hath or shall present to memorie, yet shall it be renowne to the meanest that indeuour to liue by the crummes of his Table.[12]

and Markham, like the rest of the Essexians, never really escapes from Sidney's cultural shadow, even though Sidney is dead before Essex begins his rise. Markham works with (and indeed helps to develop) the highly mythologised, literary Sidney of the 1590s, a figure much discussed in recent work by scholars including Gavin Alexander, Joel B. Davis and Richard Wood.[13] Similarly, *The Faerie Queene* is centrally important to Markham's imagination of Essex, here and elsewhere, but the opening books are already in print by 1590, five years before Markham's earliest surviving poem and one year before the Rouen campaign which Markham treats as a founding moment in his own Essexian radicalization. Markham's Essexianism is always struggling against a sense of repetition and belatedness, a sense of being a rebirth rather than a new birth.

There are, of course, paradoxes in using, as one's templates for success, the examples of Sidney and of the generation of militant protestants celebrated by Spenser. Insofar as *The Faerie Queene* is about the actual events of the Irish campaigns of the 1580s, it is working with more defeats than victories. Sir Philip Sidney's own military career had been brief and, in the final analysis, far from glorious. And yet, both for Markham and other Essexians, Sidney and Spenser form the context through which to understand Essex.

Indeed, Markham insists that this slightly second-hand air of chivalric romance, used throughout *Honour in his Perfection,* is justified by autobiographical experience. A good example of this manoeuvre occurs a little further on in the pamphlet when it moves on to a description of Essex's first meeting with the King of France, in the course of the 1591 Rouen campaign. The carefully planted word 'yet' secures the connection between literary romance ('the flowers of England') and the authentic personal experience of an eye-witness:

> vnder the conduct of this most excellent Earle, *Robert* Earle of *Essex* (whom she made her Generall) she sent into *France* (number for number) the goodliest, the richest, and the most glorious Army that euer the Sunne shined on. O! yet me thinkes I see the enter-view, or first meeting betweene the King and this Earle, where the Flowers of England and the Flowers of *France* mixing together, gold so reflected vpon gold, that the Ayre and the Earth seemed all to be one flame, and the Sunne blushing, shrunke to see his glory ecclipsed.[14]

Similarly, in the biography of the Earl of Southampton which appears alongside that of Essex in *Honour in his Perfection,* Markham includes an account of Essex's Azores expedition of 1597. This expedition, an expensive failure, achieved nothing but a temporary English occupation of the unimportant town of Villa Franca. As they prepared to evacuate the town and return to their ships, they were menaced by a Spanish raiding party:

> the enemie taking aduantage of our rising, and finding that most of our men were gone aboard, & but only the *General,* the Earle of *Southampto~*, S^{r}. *Francis Vere,* & som few others left on Shoare, they came with their vtmost power vpon them, but were receiued with so hot an incounter, that many of the Spaniards were put to the sword, and the rest inforced to runne away: and in this skirmish no man had aduantage of safetie, for the number was (on our part) so few, that euery man had his hands imployment; and here the Earle of *Southampton* ere he could dry the sweat from his browes, or put his sword vp in the scaberd, receiued from the Noble *Generall, Robert* Earle of *Essex,* the order of Knighthood.[15]

It must be said that most other accounts make very little of the Villa Franca incident as a piece of military action. One observer, Sir Francis Vere, calls it a 'brave skirmish', but implies it was hardly more than a show of strength. Even Essex, in his own account of the campaign, describes it only as a stand-off. But it is important in Markham's mythology of the Essexian world, both for its obviously chivalric significance, and because Markham has earlier in the work planted the statement that he himself was present when Southampton received his knighthood: 'I ... haue seene him receiue the reward of a

Souldier (before the face of the Enemie) for the best act of a Souldier (done vpon the Enemie:)'.[16] Again, *Honour in his Perfection* makes a point of conflating first-hand reportage with the literary tropes of chivalric romance.

This odd mixture of second-hand, belated reference to the seminal texts of Elizabethan militant protestantism, together with first-hand personal experience, invites explanation in biographical terms: an old soldier looking back on his youth. And yet the combination of literary romance and personal experience is also the distinctive recipe of Markham's contemporary Essexianism nearly thirty years earlier, as can be seen by examination of his two long war poems, *Grenville* (1595) and *Devereux* (1597).

Each of these is Essexian by virtue of carrying multiple dedications to leading associates of Essex. *Grenville* is dedicated to Charles, Lord Mountjoy; Robert, Earl of Sussex; the Earl of Southampton; and Sir Edward Wingfield. *Devereux* is dedicated to the sisters Dorothy, Countess of Northumberland; and Penelope, Lady Rich, while also incorporating generous compliments to Sir John Norris; Sir Francis Vere, and to the Earl of Essex himself. The group as a whole are all allies and relatives, in one way or another. Lord Mountjoy is the lover, later husband, of Lady Penelope, who had herself been the lover, or at least the beloved, of Sir Philip Sidney. Robert Radclyffe, second Earl of Sussex, is related by marriage both to the Sidneys and to the Earl of Southampton.[17] Southampton, of course, is Essex's ally and perhaps his closest friend. [18] Sir Edward Wingfield of Kimbolton Castle, Huntingdonshire, was a soldier, literary patron and Member of Parliament. He took an active part in several of Essex's military adventures, including the expeditions to the Azores and to Ireland.[19] Thus, Markham's dedications define an interconnected cultural community.

As for the content of these poems: Markham's biographer, F. N. L. Poynter, calls *Devereux* 'almost pure Essex propaganda'. It is supposedly a 'paraphrastical' translation of a lost poem by a French Huguenot, Genevieve Petau.[20] Markham's version must be quite a loose paraphrase, as it almost ignores the eponymous Henri III, concentrating instead on the death in battle of Essex's younger brother Walter Devereux (the 'Devereux' of the title) at the siege of Rouen in 1591.[21]

Devereux is framed as a dream-vision in which the 'I' of the poem, moving through an unreal landscape, meets Aretea, the Spirit of Excellence, who explains that she ventured from war-torn France to fall at the feet of Queen Elizabeth and seek help from among her retinue of knights. She then describes how those knights took part in the Rouen campaign, laments the loss there of Walter Devereux, and ultimately conducts the narrator to Walter's diamond-encrusted tomb, to be found in the world of the Imagination. In this respect, it takes part in the expected conventions of dream-vision poems going back to Chaucer and Langland. However, it also has a flavour specifically of Elizabethan English romance. A particular example of this, and a particular similarity with the much later *Honour in his Perfection,* is the imagination of Elizabeth's foreign policy decisions in terms of *The Faerie Queene.* Aretea comes to the court of Eliza, and falls at her feet for help: Eliza graciously permits Aretea to select a knight to help her (thus somewhat rewriting history, since Essex had to beg and badger Elizabeth to obtain the Rouen command). As Markham explains:

> most almightie then
> Is he, whom her life-giuing grace endeares,
> And lends a leaue to search through Dangers den
> For all the praisefull Honours: or beside,
> What ought or should with Knighthoods fame abide.

Again, this phrase recalls *The Faerie Queene,* 1.1, in which the first trial faced by the Redcross Knight takes place in 'Error's Den'.[22] All the way through the poem, Markham negotiates the tricky problem of how to apportion praise for the mission between Elizabeth and 'princely Essex' himself (fol. 19r). The metaphor used here, in which Elizabeth grants 'leaue' for her knights to go and gain honour almost independent of her, is one which draws on *The Faerie Queene,* and also, in a sense, offers a way of writing Elizabeth out of the story once the expedition actually departs from court. After they do so, she is not mentioned again: Essex's forces are described in terms of 'England', not in terms of their monarch (e.g., fol. 28r). Only at the conclusion of the poem, where '*ELIZA,* Queene of harts and eyes' is among those invited to mourn (fol. 43v), is Elizabeth mentioned again in the poem, again in the manner of an absent Faerie Queene.

However, unlike *The Faerie Queene,* and again like *Honour in his Perfection, Devereux* is distinctive in overlaying the existing tropes of chivalric poetry with avowedly personal experience. The central section of the poem shifts subtly into an autobiographical first-person, repeatedly stressing, for instance, the fallibility of 'our harts', and of the speaker's own 'fainting Muse'.[23] The personal note comes back, too, in a thoughtful stanza within the poem on the question of eulogy in general. Although the speaker is still, notionally, the Spirit of Excellence, the voice is that of a mortal with first-hand experience, wondering whether a personal testimony is even of any use in an imperfect world.

> But what auailes it to say thys hee did,
> When twas but showes to that he would haue done?
> What better am I to say thus hee rid?
> Thus hee tryumph'd, thus did his foe-men runne?
> When what hee was, from present is, is hid,
> Remembraunce, by such memorie vndone;
> Who knew him, knew hee was the best of any,
> Who knew him not, may learne by mee and many.[24]

Thus, all of *Devereux,* including its praise of Essex as 'excellent, deriu'd from most diuine', is underpinned and guaranteed by the personal, eye-witness testimony of the speaker who was at Rouen. *Devereux*'s praise of Essex himself, such as the stanza quoted as the epigraph to this chapter, combines a frame of reference derived from literary romance with more local political referents, such as the column imagery, recalling the column symbolism used by Essex in his 1587 New Year's gift and discussed by Richard Wood in Chapter 1; with an insistence on personal experience. The author, in effect, is living out for real experiences previously read about in literary romance.

In Markham's other war poem from the period, this pattern of combining earlier Elizabethan romance with contemporary reportage is continued. In *Grenville*, a sister poem to *Devereux* narrating the death of Sir Richard Grenville at the hands of the Spanish navy in 1591, Sir Philip Sidney's ghost makes an appearance: a potent metaphor for the anxiety of influence felt by Essexian writing more widely in connection with Sidney, the pre-eminent soldier-poet. The poem is described as 'this labour of my Sunne-burnt braine', referencing as it does so the opening sonnet of *Astrophil and Stella* in which the speaker complains of a 'sun-burnt brain' that might be alleviated by 'fresh and fruitful showers' from others' influences. In claiming himself to possess a sun-burnt brain, Markham's speaker puts himself in a Sidneyan tradition. 'Sit on my hand', the narrator therefore asks Sidney's spirit, 'and teach me to indite', before relaying Grenville's story with lavish supernatural machinery.[25] A debt to Spenser is more implicit, in that Markham refers to Sir Richard Grenville throughout as 'our knight' – an appellation which is literally correct, but also once again enables the perspective of the *Faerie Queene*, in which the last fight of the *Revenge* becomes not merely a naval engagement but an episode in the global contest between good and evil. The Spanish, of course, embody the evil: their 'damned Nauie' destroying the Englishman in a one-sided encounter which should cause '*Englands* weeping ioy, and *Spaynes* disgrace'.[26]

Yet another Markham work which badges itself explicitly as a reinvention of the Elizabethan chivalric tradition is *The English Arcadia*, Markham's continuation of Sidney's *Arcadia*. This prose romance carries the adventures on with a new generation of heroes (including Pyrophilus, the son of Pyrocles and Philoclea) and in a new setting. This work was printed in two parts in 1607 and 1613, but, according to the work's own preface, was written in the decade of the 1590s. While much about the work remains mysterious, and while much of it seems to modern eyes to be a frantic, fan-fiction-like rehashing of the motifs and episodes of the *Arcadia*, we have seen that reference to Sidney, for Markham, is part of a world-view to do with Essexianism; and echoes of 1590s politics are certainly to be found within *The English Arcadia*. In the opening episode, for instance, an echoing of the opening of *The New Arcadia* so detailed that it might almost be called a reworking, two shepherds lament the unyieldingness of the mistress whom they serve and whom (they hasten to add) they both love entirely.

> hauing our hopes giuen ouer into the handes of Disdaine, our vowes inrespected; our loues fruitles, our torments pittiles, & our deaths Tomblesse) to vs I say these accidents of inhumane aduersitie, are but awaking thunders, or Night-Rauen cryes to our laboring remebrances, drawing in them and before them, the models of those mishappes where-with our owne soules are attainted. How oft haue thou and I (my *Carino*) from the top of yon Mountaine sent our eyes with the imbassage of our heartes, conueying in blood-drawing sighes (speedy messengers of dispaire) the occurrents of our dying hopes? How oft vpon this Plaine haue wee in darke *Eglogues* discoursed the pure intent of our honest seruices? How oft vpon these Sandes haue wee written her name with our Sheep-hookes, which the iealous Sea in loue with, hath greedily snacht into his bosome? And how oft from yon aspiring Rocke haue wee wisht (so she would beare witnes to our wish) to fal head-long into the Sea, as a scale to the great deed of our induring affection, and yet haue found neither hope in our desires, comfort in our loues, nor end in our dispaires?[27]

In case this rhetoric of service unrewarded is not clear enough, soon after we discover that their mistress is named Cynthia, that favourite literary alias of Elizabeth herself.[28] There are almost certainly more such moments in the work for committed Essexians to identify with. What, for instance, would a late Elizabethan reader have made of one shepherd's description of having once gone to court and seen there 'a God or man, or at least a moste Godly man, who with the shaking of his hand, ruling the sway of manye kingdomes … seemed better than *Numa*'?[29] This can't be a vision of Elizabeth, which is what one might expect at such a moment, because the gender is wrong. The word 'godly', too, seems strikingly loaded with meaning, and this man, whoever he is, is seen as acting on a distinctly international stage. Is this, for the initiated, a version of, or a fantasy based upon, Essex himself?[30]

Two more texts remain to be considered in this partial survey of Markham's political writing from the 1590s. Markham's play, *The Dumbe Knight*, features a valiant knight, Philocles, in love with a difficult mistress who sets him the task of not speaking for an entire year, a task which (as the play unfolds) she soon regrets. The play has been read by Lesel Dawson as an allegory of Essex's difficult relationship with Queen Elizabeth, and while one still cannot be certain whether the work is written after 1601 (as Dawson argues) or before that date (as I believe), the parallels between Essex and Philocles are impressive: a warrior, seemingly invincible in battle, and entirely loyal to his monarch, whose life is complicated by his capricious mistress. Even Philocles's name, a reference to the loyal general Philocles tortured by the tyrant Lysander, speaks to the idea of a loyal general.[31] The play's central theme, the problem of being honour bound to obey a mistress even when she is patently being unreasonable, is one which was dear to the hearts of Essexians.

Equally, Markham's three books of religious verse contain strong hints of political applicability, but here there is only space to discuss one: *Mary Magdalen's Lamentations for the Loss of Her Master Jesus.* Printed in summer 1601, the poem acquires inevitable political resonances with its theme of the fallen master, and the guilt of those left behind who feel they may have betrayed him. Here, for instance, Mary wonders whether there is any use or purpose in her weeping for Jesus:

> If they be teares of love to shew good will,
> As love is knowne, so let them be suppressed;
> If teares of wrath, denouncing anger still,
> To shed them here, thou shouldst not have addressed
> Here where all anger lately buried was,
> But none deserv'd, ah none deserv'd alas.[32]

It is not necessary to argue that the whole poem should be read as an allegory equating Essex to the Messiah. Such a reading of the poem would be absurd, and would not do justice to its religious complexity. Still, the very fact that it alludes to someone dead through undeserved anger, in a pamphlet printed in the summer of 1601, is obviously potentially risky.[33] Something of this sense of danger is suggested by the fact that the poem was published anonymously, with no dedication, and was Markham's last new publication of any sort for four years. The death of Essex marked the effective end of Markham's career as a poet.

Clearly, then, Essexianism, a political affiliation bringing with it a world-view, dominated Markham's creative writing in the 1590s. What one can now say, looking back to their origins in the 1590s, is that Markham's factual works – the suite of largely Jacobean publications upon which his reputation rests – also take much of their intellectual flavour and frame from this Essexianism.

For instance, the very first work in this sequence, *A Discourse of Horsemanship* (1593), even shares a publisher with Markham's poetry: both this and *Devereux* were published by the entrepreneur Richard Smith.[34] And the very opening sentence of the work puts this practical manual into the context of Spenserian romance, and specifically of *The Faerie Queene*, Book I, Canto I:

> It is but ignorance and selfe will (the vnwedded Parents of that vgly monster error) which hath blinded our English *Heroes*, from regarding in these latter times, that most excellent & prayse worthy gyft, the bréeding, ryding, and traynıng vppe of Horsses, which in all ages hath béene most commendable: because of all things most commodious, and of beastes in nature to man the neerest. The dead cynders of which famous quality, if my young experience (yet in the Midwifes armes, scarce readie for his first swathing cloutes) may reuiue againe, in the priuate mindes of those that shall viewe my labour, I shall holde my paine an eternall pleasure, and my selfe fully satisfied.[35]

In a later, Jacobean, work on horses, *Cavelarice, or the English Horseman*, these connections between horsemanship and Essex, personal experience and chivalric romance, are made more explicit. Markham is discussing how a very good horse can sometimes resist a bit:

> [F]or mine owne part, I once rid a blacke bastard Courser, which was afterwards giuen to the Earle of *Essex,* in whom I found that tractabilitie and sencablenesse, that before euer I put byt in his mouth, he would haue set a turne on both hands, either double or single, managed faire ... [36]

Elsewhere in *Cavelarice* he writes, in a similarly oblique fashion, about how his first-hand experiences in the Irish wars inform his understanding of horses:

> [F]or mine own part, I haue seene an Irish-Hobby which being shot cleane through the body, did bring his Maister safe from the fielde, and assoone as he was dismounted, the Horse dyed presently.[37]

Particularly telling here is the repeating formula, 'for mine own part': Markham has a characteristically Essexian compulsion to insist that he is personally involved in making a practical difference. And, again, writing about how to preserve one's horse's constitution by feeding it well at all times, Markham insists on the connection between this veterinary work and his lived, practical experience as a soldier for Essex.

> [O]ne Gentleman will both indure and bee seruisable, when a hundred Clownes will die like sheepe in a rotte yeare, because the straightnesse of their liues keept Nature euer leane and in weakenesse: and of this, when I was a poore commaunder in the warres, I euer tooke a principall notice, and held it for a maxime.[38]

All of these passages, in *Cavelarice,* draw attention to the continuity between Markham's Jacobean writing and the Essexian world of the 1590s.

From advice on horses, whose military-chivalric applicability is obvious, Markham diversified into *The Gentleman's Academy* (1595), a book of advice from late medieval sources on topics including hawking, hunting, and heraldry, dedicated to the gentlemen of England. *A Health to the Gentlemanly Profession of Servingmen* (1598) continues this celebration of English tradition, this time with particular reference to the servingman:

> the Maister calles to go on huntyng, haulkyng, fishyng, or fowlyng, in which he taketh most pleasure, or thinketh fit for the tyme. Then the Seruingman, or men, with all diligence prepare them selues to the feelde, euery one willing to shew his skil, to delight his Maister in which of these recreations he taketh most pleasure. Thus passing the day with these, or such lyke sportes, the nyght calleth them home.[39]

Markham's lifelong interest in the practical skills of hunting and fishing is bound up, in passages like these, with a sense that they serve the social order. For him, these skills stand for an entire way of life, one associated with Essexian values.

From these areas, still obviously connected to chivalry, and as well as frequently revisiting the topic of horses, Markham's factual writing spreads slowly and steadily in succeeding years towards estate management more generally and eventually to the more mundane topics of, for instance, gardening and cookery, for which his work is best known. But the underpinnings in personal experience of militant protestantism still come to the surface in the most unlikely places. At one point, for instance, Markham discusses different methods of storing grain, and refers back to the Azores campaign. In the Azores, he writes, grain is stored in underground pits, and 'for mine owne part, I have my self digged up many of these pits, and found great store of wheat'.[40]

Again and again, too the chivalric note re-emerges. For instance, *A Second Part to the Mother's Blessing* (1622) is a foray into the world of psychological medicine, in the form of a self-help book offering broadly neo-Stoic 'cures' for domestic grief from various causes. This is a diversification from Markham's previous book on home medicine, *Verus Pater*, itself diversifying from (and only lightly adapting) Markham's previous book on horse-medicine. But chivalry impinges even upon *A Second Part to the Mother's Blessing*. Markham explains that it is being written because of his personal experience of (unspecified) troubles:

> This experience of euils became unto me both a spurre to set mee forward in that *Cariere* which I haue now finisht (in this little Booke:) and also an Armor to defend me against the Bitings and Bitternesse both of Curiosity & Censure.[41]

Years after serving Essex in Rouen, the Azores, and Ireland, the imagery of knighthood never really relinquishes its grip on Markham's imagination.

All this is particularly interesting because Markham's later, Jacobean works are noted for their treatment of the idea of Englishness. Books such as *The English Horseman, The English Husbandman,* and *The English Housewife* promote a distinctly English identity even in King James's Britain. Indeed, it has been suggested that they explore the idea of a national English identity based not around loyalty to a monarch but instead around practices of husbandry. Wendy Wall writes of Markham's Jacobean output that:

> Early modern writers as disparate as Spenser and Markham negotiate what Benedict Anderson calls 'nation-ness' through stories of food, drink, swords, weather, the land, and labor; they created a conception of a cultural, if not political, national identity.

Drawing attention to Markham's wide readership, Wall adds that Markham was 'a critical part of a national-georgic revolution' in 'a mode deeply connected to the imperial national ideals of both Virgil and Spenser'.[42]

What we can now add to this is that Markham is not so disparate from Spenser after all, certainly not in the pre-1601 writing which is obsessed with the frame of reference provided by Elizabethan romance. And the theme in the factual manuals which Wall identifies, that of the idea of a national identity not based upon the monarch, arises quite directly from the Essexian world-view of Markham's earlier and more 'literary' output. The irony, then, of the whole project of Markham's later career – the description of and advice about everyday practice and lived experience, conducted on a huge and detailed scale – is that it emerges from an Essexian world-view which is all about acting out chivalric fictions. Despite its air of quotidian reality, it is linked to and originates from the purest Elizabethan romance. The Jacobean and Caroline Gervase Markham, writer of practical manuals, was, in a sense, England's last Essexian.

Appendix

Prose tracts

A Discource of Horsmanshippe (1593 and later editions)
The Gentlemans Academie (1595)*
A Health to the Gentlemanly Profession of seruingmen (1598)

Poetry

The Most Honorable Tragedie of Sir Richard Grinuile, Knight (1595)
The Poem of Poems (1596)*
Deuoreux (1597)
The Teares of the Beloued: or, The Lamentation of Saint Iohn (1600)
Marie Magdalens lamentations for the losse of her master Iesus (1601)
Rodomonths infernall, or The Diuell conquered (written before 1601, printed 1607)*

Prose romances

The English Arcadia (written before 1601, print publication 1607-1613)
Meruine (probably written before 1601, printed 1612)*

Plays

The Dumbe Knight (probably written before 1601, printed 1608)

Items marked with a * are translations or edited works. Dates of composition are mainly taken from Poynter, *Bibliography*.

Notes

1 Gervase Markham, *Deuoreux Vertues teares for the losse of the most christian King Henry* … (London: Thomas Millington, 1597), fol. 13r.
2 G. E. Fussell, quoted in Wendy Wall, 'Renaissance National Husbandry: Gervase Markham and the Publication of England', *Sixteenth Century Journal* 27 (1996), p. 767.

3 Wall, 'Renaissance National Husbandry', p. 767. The currently definitive guide to Markham's life and work is F. N. L. Poynter, *A Bibliography of Gervase Markham, 1568?–1637* (Oxford: Oxford Bibliographical Society, 1962). Poynter's biography of Markham can be supplemented with details from Robert Gittings, *Shakespeare's Rival: a Study in Three Parts* (London: Heinemann, 1960); Gervase Markham, *The English Housewife*, ed. Michael R. Best (Kingston, ON: McGill-Queen's University Press, 1986); and Markham's *ODNB* entry. This chapter arises from my own current work on Markham.

4 See Best (ed.), *The English Housewife*; Charles F. Mullett, 'Gervase Markham, Scientific Amateur', *Isis* 35 (1944), pp. 106–118.

5 Gittings, *Shakespeare's Rival*, p. 33. Among previous studies of Essexian literary culture, one might mention in particular Steven W. May (ed.), 'The Poems of Edward DeVere, Seventeenth Earl of Oxford and of Robert Devereux, Second Earl of Essex', *Studies in Philology* 77: 5 (1980); Robin Headlam Wells, *Shakespeare on Masculinity* (Cambridge: Cambridge University Press, 2005).

6 Margot Heinemann, 'Rebel Lords, Popular Playwrights, and Political Culture: Notes on the Jacobean Patronage of the Earl of Southampton', *Yearbook of English Studies* 21 (1991), pp. 63–86; Hugh Gazzard, '"Those Graue Presentments of Antiquitie": Samuel Daniel's *Philotas* and the Earl of Essex', *Review of English Studies* 51 (2000), pp. 423–450 ; Paul E. J. Hammer, 'Devereux, Robert, Second Earl of Essex (1565–1601)', *ODNB*.

7 Sir Henry Wotton, *A Parallel Betweene Robert late Earle of Essex, and George late Duke of Buckingham* (London, 1641), p. 5.

8 Estimate from Paul E. J. Hammer, *The Polarisation of Elizabethan Politics: the Political Career of Robert Devereux, Second Earl of Essex, 1585–1597* (Cambridge: Cambridge University Press, 1999), p. 212; quotation from Hammer, 'Devereux, Robert, Second Earl of Essex', *ODNB*; for Spenser's relationship with Essex, see John Pitcher, 'Essex, Robert Devereux, Second Earl of', in *The Spenser Encyclopedia*, ed. A. C. Hamilton (Toronto: University of Toronto Press, 1990), p. 535.

9 For the above details, see Poynter, 'Introduction', in *A Bibliography of Gervase Markham*; the allusion to Essex House is in Gervase Markham, *Honour in his perfection* (London: Benjamin Fisher, 1624), p. 21; biographies of Essex include Robert Lacey, *Robert, Earl of Essex: an Elizabethan Icarus* (London: Weidenfeld and Nicolson, 1971), and Hammer, *The Polarisation of Elizabethan Politics*.

10 Markham, *Honour in his Perfection*, pp. 27, 28.

11 Spenser, 'Letter to Raleigh', lines 56–61, in *The Faerie Queene*, ed. A. C. Hamilton, Hiroshi Yamashita and Toshiyuki Suzuki, 2nd edition (London: Pearson, 2001).

12 Gervase Markham, *The English Arcadia alluding his beginning from Sir Philip Sydneys ending* (London: Henrie Rocket, 1607), p. 3.

13 Gavin Alexander, *Writing After Sidney: The Literary Response to Sir Philip Sidney 1586–1640* (Oxford: Oxford University Press, 2006); Richard Wood, '"The representing of so strange a power in love": Philip Sidney's Legacy of Anti-factionalism', *Early Modern Literary Studies* Special Issue 16 (October, 2007) 4.1–20, http://purl.oclc.org/emls/si-16/woodsidn.htm; Joel B. Davis, *The Countesse of Pembrokes Arcadia and the Invention of English Literature* (Basingstoke: Palgrave Macmillan, 2011).

14 Markham, *Honour in his Perfection*, p. 29.

15 Markham, *Honour in his Perfection*, pp. 22–23.

16 Markham, *Honour in his Perfection*, p. 21; Francis Vere, *The Commentaries of Sr. Francis Vere being diverse pieces of service, wherein he had command* (Cambridge: John Field, 1657),

pp. 62–65; Samuel Purchas, *Purchas his Pilgrimes* (London: Henry Fetherstone, 1625), pp. 1937, 1966.

17 Victor Stater, 'Radcliffe, Robert, fifth earl of Sussex (1573–1629)', *ODNB*.

18 See G. P. V. Akrigg, *Shakespeare and the Earl of Southampton* (London: H. Hamilton, 1968).

19 P. W. Hasler, *The History of Parliament: The House of Commons, 1558–1603*, 3 vols (London: HMSO, 1981), 3.634–635; Wingfield's biography is explored more fully in my forthcoming study of Markham's life and works.

20 See F. N. L. Poynter. 'Gervase Markham and Genevieve Petau', *Times Literary Supplement* (16 October 1959), p. 600; for her husband see Alexander Gordon, 'Gordon, John (1544–1619)', in *ODNB*; *ODNB online*, www.oxforddnb.com/view/article/11061, accessed 5 March 2013.

21 For the historical background of the campaign see Lacey, *Robert, Earl of Essex*, and Hammer, *The Polarisation of Elizabethan Politics*; also Howell A. Lloyd, *The Rouen Campaign, 1590–1592: Politics, Warfare and the Early-Modern State* (Oxford: Clarendon Press, 1973).

22 Markham, *Devereux*, fol. 34v; Spenser, *The Faerie Queene*, 1.1.13.6.

23 Markham, *Devereux*, fols 21v, 19r.

24 Markham, *Devereux*, fol. 34v.

25 Gervase Markham, *The most honorable tragedie of Sir Richard Grinuile, Knight* (London: Richard Smith, 1595), sigs E3v, B2v; Sidney, *Astrophil and Stella* 1 cited in Sidney, *Sir Philip Sidney*, ed. Katherine Duncan-Jones (Oxford: Oxford University Press, 1989). On the connection to Tennyson's poem, see Clements R. Markham (ed.), *Markham Memorials* (London: Spottiswoode and Co, 1913), p. 66.

26 Markham, *The Most Honourable Tragedie of Sir Richard Grinuile*, sig. B2r.

27 Markham, *The English Arcadia*, 6; for one of the very few discussions of this work, see Alexander, *Writing After Sidney*.

28 See, for instance, Philippa Berry, *Of Chastity and Power: Elizabethan Literature and the Unmarried Queen* (London: Routledge, 1994), esp. pp. 137–166.

29 Markham, *The English Arcadia*, fol. 60r.

30 For instance, Hammer, *Polarisation of Elizabethan Politics*, p. 213, notes Essex's strategy of associating himself with the 'godly'.

31 Gervase Markham and Lewis Machin, *The Dumbe Knight*, ed. Kris Towse (2010), http://purl.org/emls/iemls/renplays/dumbknight.htm, accessed 5 March 2013; Lesel Dawson, 'The Earl of Essex and the Trials of History: Gervase Markham's *The Dumbe Knight*,' *Review of English Studies* 53 (2002), pp. 344–364.

32 Gervase Markham, *Marie Magdalens lamentations for the losse of her master Iesus* (London: Edward White, 1601), sig. D1v; for edition and discussion, see Gervase Markham, *The Teares of the Beloued (1600) and Marie Magdalene's Teares (1601)*, ed. A. B. Grosart ([Blackburn]: n.p., 1871); and Debora Kuller Shuger, *The Renaissance Bible: Scholarship, Sacrifice, and Subjectivity* (Berkeley, CA: University of California Press, 1994), p. 170.

33 As Hammer's *ODNB* entry notes, elegies on Essex only appeared in print once James had come to the throne.

34 On Smith's career, see Sidney Thomas, 'Richard Smith: "Foreign to the Company"', *Library* 5 (1948), pp. 186–192.

35 Gervase Markham, *A Discource of Horsmanshippe* (London: Richard Smith, 1593), sig. A1r.

36 Gervase Markham, *Cauelarice, or The English horseman contayning all the arte of horsemanship, as much as is necessary for any man to vnderstand* (London: Edward White, 1607), 2.37.

37 Markham, *Cavelarice,* 8.26.

38 Markham, *Cavelarice,* 5.18–19.

39 Gervase Markham, *A Health to the Gentlemanly Profession of Seruingmen; or, The seruingmans comforts* (London: W. W[hite], 1598), sig. A3v.

40 Gervase Markham, *Markhams farwell to husbandry* (London: Roger Jackson, 1620), pp. 113–114.

41 Gervase Markham, *A second part to the mothers blessing: or A cure against misfortunes. Divided into certain principal receipts, to cure the mind of man* (London: Thomas Dewe, 1622), sigs A2v–A3r.

42 Wall, 'Renaissance National Husbandry', pp. 776, 768.

3

Robert Devereux, 2nd Earl of Essex, and the practice of theatre

Grace Ioppolo

Literary critics and historians have primarily examined the relationship between Robert Devereux (1565–1601), 2nd Earl of Essex, and the early modern English stage in one of two possible ways. The first was to analyse plays that they thought were written *about* him, including William Shakespeare's *Henry V*, and the second was to historicise plays that they thought were staged *for* him, most notably that featuring the history of Richard II and performed on 7 February 1601, the eve of Essex's uprising, for some of his co-conspirators.[1] Either of these ways can allow scholars to attempt to achieve the same tantalisingly elusive goal of determining the precise nature of the relationship between Essex, the greatest courtier of the age, and Shakespeare, the greatest dramatist of the age. However, one further and much more constructive way exists to examine the extent of this relationship but surprisingly it has been rarely employed since the early nineteenth century: applying the methods of theatre historians to the study of Essex and the practice of theatre. While modern literary critics and historians have discussed Essex and stage business, modern theatre historians have not yet discussed Essex and the business of the stage. This latter relationship can, in fact, be examined by studying the patronage and support of Essex and his closest family members, friends and allies, of professional playing companies.

That this application of theatre history is necessary can be seen in the sometimes exceptionally ingenious ways in which scholars insist on finding Essex in as many early modern plays as possible while ignoring the standard conventions and conditions in which such plays were written by dramatists, censored by the Master of the Revels, and rehearsed and performed by players. Although these plays may have eventually circulated in print, and only occasionally in manuscript form,[2] they were then and remain primarily theatrical texts that were heard and seen in performance, which could be subject to revision or alteration when revived. These plays then are only latterly, and secondarily, fixed as literary or historical texts to be dissected for clues or codes by readers, as Essex would have undoubtedly known, given his family's long and significant history as patrons of playing companies. In addition, a wealth of theatre history documents can demonstrate that theatre had become by 1601 an externally and internally regulated business with a well-established set of practices and standards for dramatists, censors, actors and audiences. These documents include the printed volumes and online databases of the Records of Early English Drama (REED) series and hundreds of pages of Philip Henslowe's archives and those of his son-in-law Edward Alleyn, now available online at www.henslowe-alleyn.org.uk.[3]

Without some knowledge of these theatrical practices and conditions, and without investigation into Essex's artistic and financial support of players, rather than in plays, it is virtually impossible to define or determine Essex's relationship with theatre. As a young man, Essex became a supporter of a fledgling theatre profession that had become nearly an industry by the time of his death, and not only was he able to watch this industry grow and develop over the years, but he became as a patron a financial subsidiser of it. His returns may not have come in terms of money but in cultural status. Essex would have understood then that he did not need to be portrayed in one play to make his presence felt, nor is it likely that he based the future of his entire political career on a single performance of a play about Richard II. So, while many literary scholars and historians have used theatre to examine Essex in terms of his practices, strategies and cultural impact, they have not yet used Essex to examine theatre in terms of its practices, strategies and cultural impact.

This misdirection in the study of Essex and theatre probably rests on scholars' insistence that Essex was telling the truth in his letter of 12 May 1600 to Queen Elizabeth when he complained that he saw the stage as a source of his personal degradation. He comments specifically:

> I am gnawed on & torne by ye vilest & basest creatures vpon earth. The prating tavern hunter speaks of me what he list: the frantick libeller writes of me what he list; already they printe me, & make speak to ye world; and shortlye they will play me in what formes they list upon ye stage. The least of these is a thowsand tymes woorse then death.[4]

However, both the sources and the context of the letter need to be taken into consideration here before attempting to value Essex's comment about the stage. First, this letter survives only in scribal copies, including a contemporary copy by Essex's secretary Edward Reynolds. A comparison of extant letters in Essex's hand and extant copies of the same letters in the hand of secretaries, followers, or other copyists often shows some form of embellishment or exaggeration, reducing Essex's eloquent but terse writing style to a sentimental or maudlin one.[5] In fact, the comments above which move from 'tavern hunter' to 'frantick libeler' to printers and finally to players suggest not an author who is composing fluently but a reviser aiming for careful rhetorical balance. This type of revision is characteristic of secretaries eager to present their employer in particular ways. While it is possible to argue that Essex wrote all of these lines exactly as stated above, it is not certain that he did so.

Second, Essex wrote this letter, or some form of it, nearly eight months after he had last seen the queen in person, which was on 28 September 1599, the day he arrived uninvited at Nonesuch Palace after abandoning his post as Lord General in Ireland without her permission. According to a second-hand report, and thus subject to exaggeration, he arrived from his travels from Ireland at 10a.m. that day still so 'full of dirt and mire' that 'his very face was full of yt'. He 'made all hast up to the presence, and soe to the Privy Chamber, and staied not till he came to the queen's bed chamber, where he found the queen newly up, the heare about her face'. In an apparent attempt to apologise for this exceptionally rash and disrespectful behaviour, 'he kneeled unto her, kissed her handes and her faire neck, and had some privat speach with her, which seemed to give hym great contentment'. Elizabeth saw him two further times that day, but her 'contentment' with him seemed to wane significantly with each further encounter.[6]

The queen never allowed Essex into her presence again, although she sent eight of her physicians to treat him three months later when he appeared to be near death while under house arrest at York House, the home of the Lord Keeper, Sir Thomas Egerton. Essex's contrite and 'most humble letters' convinced Elizabeth to release him eventually to his nearby London home, Essex House.[7] From September 1599 and until his uprising seventeen months later, Essex wrote a series of increasingly desperate, and sometimes insulting, letters to the queen, some of which suggest that he was suffering from depression.[8] So, taken in context, his complaint above about being played 'shortlye … in what formes they list upon ye stage', even if it was written precisely as copied by Reynolds, is part of a general series of complaints, and should not be taken to represent the true or consistent value in which he held either the purpose or profession of playing.

In fact, from a young age, Essex must have been very familiar and comfortable with professional players and 'what formes they list upon ye stage', and with the duty or perhaps privilege of aristocratic patronage of theatre. A number of his ancestors in both the Bourchier and Devereux families had patronised companies of players during the late fifteenth and early sixteenth centuries.[9] By at least 1572, Walter Devereux (1541–1576), 1st Earl of Essex in the new creation and father of Robert Devereux, 2nd Earl of Essex, patronised a company of players, commonly called 'the Earl of Essex's Men', performing at least in Bath, Bristol, Gloucester and Nottingham in 1572 and 1573. Significantly, 1572 marks the first year that companies were required by the passage of the 'Act for the punishment of Vagabonds' to form into professional troupes supported by a royal or aristocratic patron or be subject to arrest.[10] In effect this Act signals to theatre historians the birth of professional

English theatre. Although Walter Devereux may not have taken up the role as patron of a company of players at this time precisely for this reason, he began his support of the theatrical profession in the first year in which it became a government-regulated business. From 1574 to 1576, the company travelled to Coventry, Lincoln, and York, and, according to E. K. Chambers, to Dover, Leicester and Nottingham.[11] As it is exceptionally difficult to trace the precise and complete performances of early modern playing companies and to build a full picture of their full composition or movements, these records, and those of other companies discussed later in this chapter, likely show the minimum and not the maximum extent of their careers. So there were probably many other undocumented performances by Essex's Men at a variety of venues during these years, including for holiday or other celebrations at Sir Walter's homes at which his children were present.

After the death of Walter Devereux in Ireland in 1576, his wife Lettice Knollys (1543–1634), a cousin of the queen through the Boleyn family, became the patron of the company, which can be recorded as performing under the name of 'the Countess of Essex's Men' in Coventry and Gloucester, and according to Chambers, in Oxford in 1576 and 1577.[12] Court rumour suggested that Lettice had engaged in an adulterous affair with Robert Dudley, Earl of Leicester, for at least the previous ten years and he had fathered one or more of her surviving Devereux children, and possibly one or two that died before birth. Gossip purportedly from the deathbed of Sir Walter in Ireland suggested that he had shared these suspicions about the paternity of some of his children, including his oldest son Robert. At some point between 1576 and late September 1578, Lettice and Leicester were secretly married, but her father, dissatisfied with this clandestine arrangement, insisted on another, formal marriage ceremony, which took place on 21 September 1578.[13]

Lettice's relationship with Leicester most likely explains why the Countess of Essex's Men took the place of the Earl of Leicester's more prestigious company of players at a court performance on 11 February 1578, although her company never performed there again. However, on 24 December 1578, the Privy Council included the company, under the name of the 'Earl of Essex's Men', in a list of those to be allowed by the Lord Mayor of London to play within the City during the Christmas period. The other companies in the list were three other adult companies patronised by the Lord Chamberlain, the Earl of Warwick and the Earl of Leicester, and two children's companies, Paul's and her Majesty's Chapel, 'and no companies els'.[14] Despite this formal approval, Essex's Men apparently did not play that winter but did perform at Coventry in 1577–78 and Ipswich in 1579–80, and then reverted to the title of the Countess of Essex's Men in performances at Oxford, Coventry and Stratford-on-Avon in 1578 and 1579 and at Oxford in 1579 and 1580.[15] As Chambers notes, the company would no longer have carried Lettice's name after her secret marriage to Leicester was revealed to the queen in August 1579.[16] Although Leicester worked his way back into Elizabeth's favour, Lettice never did, suffering the queen's displeasure for the rest of her life, despite the best efforts of her second husband and, later, her son Robert. Notably, the only other woman who served as patron of a company at this time or for the next twenty-four years was a Queen of England: Elizabeth I. That Lettice gave her husband's company her name, and was probably rebuked for it in the Privy Council's December 1578 entry under her late husband's name, suggests an audacious attempt at near-royal female support of the theatrical profession. At any rate, her patronage as a woman of an acting company marks her as a pioneer.

Although the timing of Essex's father's patronage of an acting company in 1572, the first year of professional playing, seems propitious, Essex's new stepfather Leicester had patronised his own company that performed from 1558 to 1564 as Lord Robert Dudley's Men and from 1564 to at least 1580 as the Earl of Leicester's Men.[17] In June 1559, Leicester sought permission from the Earl of Shrewsbury, Lord Lieutenant of Yorkshire, for the company to play in the north, calling them his 'servauntes' and 'plaiers of interludes', and describing them as 'honest men ... whereof some of them have bene herde here alredie before divers of my Lordis'.[18] This suggests that at least some of the actors were experienced professionals rather than young and amateur. Throughout his life, Leicester's support of his players appears to have been unusually generous,[19] and his company, most likely with a shifting set of players, had a long history of performing at such geographically diverse places as Norwich, Dartmouth, Plymouth, Rye, Cambridge, Gloucester, Bristol, Leicester, Lincoln, Nottingham, Coventry, Newcastle and Oxford.[20]

As Leicester was the queen's favourite, it is not surprising that his company performed at court for the Christmas holidays in 1560–61 and 1562–63. Although they are not recorded as playing there again for the next ten years, they undoubtedly would have performed at other events hosted for Elizabeth by Leicester, including during his series of entertainments for the queen at Kenilworth in 1575. The Earl of Leicester's Men also had a long history of performing in London, beginning in at least 1571, and returned to court in 1572–73, subsequently playing there at Christmas each year until 1583, while also touring throughout England for at least the next fifteen years, including to Stratford-upon-Avon in 1572–73, 1576–77, and 1587.[21] No doubt due to Leicester's influence with the queen, his company had been uniquely privileged in May 1574 with her royal patent to 'vse, exercise and occupie the arte and facultye of playenge Comedies, Tragedies, Enterludes, stage playes, and such other like' both at court for her 'solace and pleasure' and within the City of London, as well as throughout the 'Realme of England'. However the company's exclusive status did not release them from the demand that they, like other professional companies, had to submit their new play-texts to the queen's official censor, the Master of the Revels, for his approval.[22]

Due to the revival in 1572 of the statute requiring players to be retained as household servants, in response to the Act against Vagabonds, Leicester's

Men petitioned him for this purpose in 1572, naming themselves as James Burbage, John Perkin, John Laneham, William Johnson, Robert Wilson and Thomas Clark.[23] Four years later, Burbage became a theatre entrepreneur through the construction of the purpose-built Theatre in Shoreditch, London, which would be dismantled by his son Richard and other co-investors in 1599 after a dispute with the freeholder and rebuilt as the Globe on London's south bank. Leicester's Men, among many other companies, used Burbage's Shoreditch Theatre as their London base from the time of its construction in 1576.[24] At later points James Burbage became involved with the construction of the Curtain theatre and the refurbishment of Blackfriars Abbey as a playhouse, while his son Cuthbert also became a theatre entrepreneur and his other son Richard a foundational sharer, manager and leading actor of the Chamberlain's Men, the company in which Shakespeare became a co-sharer at its re-formation in 1594.

Three of Leicester's Men, including Robert Wilson, left the company in 1583 to join the newly formed Queen's Men. It was most likely a re-formed Leicester's Men that performed in 1586 at pageants in the Low Countries to celebrate Leicester's command of English troops there. One of the audience members was Leicester's nephew Sir Philip Sidney.[25] This re-formed company apparently included the comedian Will Kemp, who would later join the Chamberlain's Men. Before the company disbanded with the death of Leicester in 1588, some members of the players apparently moved to Lord Strange's (later the Earl of Derby's) Men, a company to which Shakespeare contributed plays at least in 1593 and 1594.[26] Robert Wilson was also later contracted by Henslowe to write plays for the Lord Admiral's Men, in one case at the express insistence of the assembled players in 1599.[27] This suggests that by this time he was a well-known and well-regarded theatrical colleague.

In short, at least these three members of Leicester's Men, Burbage, Kemp and Wilson, whose careers were personally subsidised for so long by Leicester, would become directly involved with the most prominent, successful and influential London professional companies of the 1590s and early 1600s. In addition, by the time of its dismantling in 1599, the Theatre had hosted many of the most famous and successful plays and players of the Elizabethan theatre. That the Theatre in Shoreditch's impact and original construction and design, carried over into the Globe in 1599 and used as the model for the Fortune theatre in 1600, was due to the financial support of the Earl of Leicester of Burbage's career emphasises Essex's family's foundational relationship to the business of theatre. Not only was the theatre profession small but it was interconnected and interrelated in a variety of ways, especially as so many personnel moved among so many companies over a long period of time. This implies that those including Burbage, Kemp and Wilson who had been subsidised and had financially profited by members of Essex's family would remain grateful to them and pass on this gratitude to their ever-shifting sets of companies and colleagues.

Given how widely players migrated among London playing companies, and these players' increasing investments in many aspects of the industry, the Essex family would then have had very wide influence by 1601. This significant aspect of Essex's relationship with professional theatre has clearly received almost no attention from previous scholars. Players may not have solely considered Essex to have been a nationally renowned hero and statesman, and later a reckless politician, whom they could celebrate or satirise on stage only as a distant, unapproachable figure. Instead he was their original benefactor's son or stepson before whom they had performed in his youth, a relationship similar to that of Hamlet and the provincial players whom he familiarly and warmly greets in Act 2, Scene 2 of *Hamlet* upon their return to Elsinore, exclaiming, 'Welcome, good friends'.[28] As theatrical patrons, Essex's father, the first Earl of Essex, his mother the Countess of Essex, his stepfather, the Earl of Leicester and many of their peers, including Lord Derby, the Lord Admiral, the Lord Chamberlain, the Earl of Pembroke and the queen herself served not just as theatrical benefactors but pioneering supporters of a profession that was at its peak in the early 1600s.

However, Essex's involvement in theatre was not only through patriarchal or matriarchal connections. Although no evidence survives on the repertories of these companies, we know that he supported his own provincial company, known alternatively as the Viscount of Hereford's or the Earl of Essex's Men, from 1575 to 1594 and, according to Chambers, as late as 1596. This company, which may have been formed or re-formed over the years from members of both his father's and stepfather's companies, travelled regularly to such places as Exeter, Chester, Shrewsbury, Ludlow, Hythe, Kendal, Lyme Regis, Leicester, Ipswich, Bath, Norwich, Coventry, Leicester, Oxford, York, Saffron Walden, Reading, Knowsley, Maldon, Faversham, and, in 1583–84 and 1587, Stratford-upon-Avon.[29] Like his father and stepfather, Essex also patronised troupes of minstrels, musicians and other types of performers,[30] and these personnel may have moved in and out of his playing company. A second company of the Earl of Essex's players performed in Coventry in 1600,[31] but as its patron was estranged from the queen in this year, the company may not have survived long and must have disbanded by the time of Essex's arrest in February 1601. That his early company did not appear to have performed in London or at court during the years in which Essex exerted great influence over Queen Elizabeth suggests that Essex had some affiliation with a separate London professional company. However, it remains likely that players in Essex's companies, particularly the earlier one, came to work in professional London playing companies at later periods, especially as it was common for provincial players to seek employment in London.

In fact, the date of the demise of the earlier company patronised by Essex coincides with the decline of companies that performed strictly in the provinces or at private performances. By the mid- to late 1590s, when Essex's fame and prestige were at their highest, the profession of playing, based on the repertory system,[32] became a major business being run by self-made entrepreneurs such as Henslowe, Alleyn and all three Burbages, who paid not only for the construction and maintenance of such public theatres as the Theatre, Curtain, Globe, Fortune, Rose and Swan, but managed or financed major playing companies. Two companies, the Lord Chamberlain's Men and the Admiral's Men, were eventually privileged as the exclusive companies who were allowed to act at court during such holidays as Christmastide and Shrovetide. In London at least, theatre was no longer an amateur form of entertainment supported only by rich aristocrats as a hobby, duty or even privilege but a profitable and nearly self-sustaining enterprise. Players, rather than nobles, became shareholders in their own companies and could receive good returns on their investments while accepting fees or payments from aristocrats who took no financial return on those investments.

In terms of status, companies that performed primarily in the provinces were relegated to a lower tier than London-based companies. By the mid-1590s, professionally established London companies toured the provinces, but provincial companies did not routinely perform in professional London playhouses. When London theatres were closed during various periods due to outbreaks of plague, the London companies toured provincially to stay financially solvent. This competition from companies with professional skills, costumes and playbooks may have contributed to the decline of companies that performed only in the provinces. Henslowe and Alleyn's manuscript archive especially records increasing commissions for the Admiral's Men from royals and aristocrats, some of whom had their own companies, for court or private performances by professional rather than provincial companies. Thus, that Essex's own playing company did not perform at court or in London does not mean that he had no interest or experience in the theatre. Instead it means that the theatre had no interest in companies like his which were considered non-professional. Whenever possible, London theatrical personnel strove to present to their audiences the best possible product, whether that was a play-text, a particular performance, a production, or a playhouse; provincial players simply could not compete in any of these aspects.[33]

After his father's death in 1576, Essex was sent to live in the household of his guardian William Cecil, Lord Burghley, and then to Cambridge University. Although he was not always physically resident at his own family's homes, there is no doubt that at least from 1572 to 1579 he had access to and was a member of the audience at performances by his parents' successive acting companies and from at least 1579 to 1588 by his stepfather's company. Leicester's Men was led by the highly industrious and influential actor and entrepreneur James Burbage, who died in 1597. Essex's link here with Burbage almost certainly extended to a link between Essex and Burbage's sons Richard and Cuthbert. If Essex had seen Leicester's Men perform at the Theatre in Shoreditch, it would not be surprising if he attended many more productions of the Chamberlain's Men at the same theatre. Each of his parents' and stepfather's companies had performed in Stratford-upon-Avon at various times in 1572–73, 1576–79, 1583 and 1587, but there remains no link with any of these companies and a youthful Shakespeare. His only connection to Essex would be at least from one remove through one or more of the Burbages or Will Kemp or through other players such as Robert Wilson who migrated to companies for whom Shakespeare worked before 1594. When not away on state business, Essex would also have attended at least some court performances in the Christmas holidays, at which the Chamberlain's Men performed, beginning in 1594–95 and at least until 1598–99, before he fell from Elizabeth's favour in September 1599.

Shakespearean editors and scholars, beginning with Edmond Malone and John Payne Collier, have sought to make a firmer connection between Shakespeare and Essex through the most convenient intermediary, Henry Wriothesley, 2nd Earl of Southampton, to whom Shakespeare dedicated *Venus and Adonis* and almost certainly the Sonnets. Southampton may have patronised an acting company for a brief period, as Thomas Heywood, dramatist, actor, theatre historian, London chronologer, translator and prose writer, calls himself Southampton's 'seruant once' in his 1625 'Funeral Elegy for James I'. Heywood portrays his relationship with Southampton as affectionate and cordial, and given Heywood's career history, if he did serve Heywood 'once' it was almost certainly as a player.[34] Southampton's support of an acting company may have begun in the mid- or late 1590s, and certainly before February 1601 when his implication in Essex's uprising against Elizabeth sent him to the Tower until James's accession to the throne in 1603.[35]

Margot Heinemann argues that Southampton's company most likely dates from after his restitution to his estate in 1603, particularly as Heywood would have encountered Southampton in a variety of official roles at James's court.[36] But it seems unlikely that Southampton would have waited so long to establish his own company, particularly as the vogue for such aristocratic patronage was in the 1590s, not the 1600s. In supporting a company in the 1590s, he would have been on a par with Essex and other allies as well as his court enemies, including Pembroke, all of whom had supported companies between the 1580s and 1590s. Nor would there have been much use for a fledgling company in 1603, given the prominence of such companies as the Chamberlain/King's Men and Admiral's/Prince Henry's Men at the time. Heywood's attachments to a succession of major London companies can be documented from at least 14 October 1596, when he sold a play to the Lord Admiral's Men, until his death in 1641, and there does not appear to be any period from 1603 in which Heywood could have worked for a newly formed company supported by Southampton. In addition, Henslowe had bound Heywood to a two-year exclusive playing contract on 25 March 1598,[37] suggesting that by that time Heywood had acquired enough experience and renown as a player to be worth Henslowe's clearly unusual investment in terms of players. Thus it is likely that Heywood began his career with Southampton's Men at some point prior to 1598, and that the company, like that of Robert Devereux, subsequently disbanded or remained in the provinces for a variety of reasons, including the increasing status and success of London-based companies.

While performances by professional playing companies at court can be documented by payments, patents or licences in State Papers, Calendars and Rolls, the records of performances financed at private venues for aristocrats who did directly patronise a company are much more difficult to find unless they appear in extant household papers, such as receipts, bills or expense lists, or local government records, or as anecdotes in letters, diaries or other documents. Of those few examples that are extant, some show an aristocracy that is comfortable and familiar with players. For example, in 1604, Sir Walter Cope wrote to his employer, Sir Robert Cecil, at that time Viscount Cranbourne, with Richard Burbage, for whom he has sent, at his side. Cope had been seeking 'players Iuglers & Such Creatures but fynde them harde to fynde', leaving notes for them to contact him. Finally Cope reports that

> burbage ys come & sayes ther ys no new playe that the quene hath not seene but they haue Revyvd an old one Cawled Loves Labour lost, wch for Wytt & mirth he sayes will please her exceedingly And Thys ys appointed to be playd to Morowe night at my Lord of Southamptons vnless you send a wyrtt to Remove the *Corpus Cum Causa* to yor house in [the] Strande.

It is unclear whether the legal joke about using a writ to move the 'body with cause' is Cope's or Burbage's. Cope concludes, 'Burbage ys my messenger Ready attendynge yor pleasure' in performing for Queen Anne.[38] Cope, in fact, miswrote the first word in the 'old' play's title and had to trace it over to get it right, suggesting that even though *Love's Labour's Lost* had been printed by 1598, and in performance for some time before that, he was evidently unfamiliar with it in 1604. That Burbage, a renowned player and a company-sharer in the Chamberlain's/King's Men and theatre-sharer in the Globe, served as a personal messenger to Cecil demonstrates both Burbage's ease and collaboration with the most powerful non-royal official in the kingdom, and his willingness to do anything to secure this financial commission. More simply, it could mean that Burbage considers Cecil an old friend or acquaintance. Cope had left numerous messages for Burbage and other company-managers, which in 1604 would have included those of the Lord Admiral's/Prince Henry's Men, to 'seek' him because he had been not been able to find enough actors to arrange this private performance. Presumably, as this performance was to be staged at the London home of Southampton, friend and patron of Shakespeare, the dramatist would also have joined the cast or been present in some other capacity.

Southampton was almost certainly an indirect intermediary in the link between Essex and Shakespeare, but he was probably a more direct link between Essex's sister, Penelope, and Shakespeare. During much of her unhappy marriage to Lord Robert Rich, Penelope carried on a long-term relationship with Sir Charles Blount, Lord Mountjoy, by whom she had several children. Although this relationship was adulterous, it came to be quietly accepted at court and among aristocrats, but by necessity it was not conducted at Penelope's homes with Rich. Instead she spent long periods living with Mountjoy in her brother's homes and those of her cousin Lady Elizabeth Vernon, who was the wife of Southampton. Penelope's letters can document long periods in the 1590s in which she was in residence at the Southampton homes. If Shakespeare, with or without the other Chamberlain's Men, came into regular social contact with Southampton, there is a good chance that Penelope was in Southampton's company. Although Penelope's coterie circle of poets, most notably Sidney, has been much studied, her possible connection to Shakespeare through the Southampton family deserves far more attention, as does that of her sister Dorothy, whose brother-in-law Sir Charles Percy was reported to have been the Essex conspirator who arranged the 'Richard II' performance at the Globe and was accompanied to the play by his brother Josceline.[39]

Essex hosted numerous private play performances at Essex House, almost certainly with London-based playing companies, but the precise records unfortunately are scarce or incomplete. For example, On 14 February 1598, Rowland White reported to his employer Sir Robert Sidney that after a banquet given at Essex House, Essex and his guests 'had 2 plaies which kept them up till 1 aclocke after midnight'.[40] Between 1594 and 1598 there is very little documentation of Essex's attendance at plays performed at private or at public venues. To celebrate the marriage, probably in 1595, of his sister Dorothy to Henry Percy, 9th Earl of Northumberland, Essex paid an unnamed company of players £10, a generous sum, to perform at the wedding reception,[41] most likely held at Essex House. No other record of this event appears to be extant. As Percy was already known as the 'Wizard Earl' due to his interest in alchemy and science, the play may have featured extravagant special effects in his honour. Shakespeare's play *Henry IV, Part I*, written no later than 1597, celebrates at length the heroism of Percy's ancestor Henry Percy, known as 'Hotspur', as well as the family of the Earls of Northumberland. Although it is tempting to argue that Shakespeare later wrote the play to dramatise the family history of Essex's brother-in-law, there is no extant evidence to tie this play to the Wizard Earl or Shakespeare to the play performed at the Percy marriage.

Essex's exploits at court, sea and on the battlefield were undoubtedly noted, celebrated, satirised or derided to a minor degree in plays performed by professional playing companies before or after his death. These plays may include at least the following: Shakespeare's *Henry V*, *Richard II* and *Julius Caesar*; Daniel's *Philotas*; Chapman's *Byron* plays; Dekker's *Old Fortunatus*; Heywood's *The Royal King and the Loyal Subject*; Markham's *The Dumbe Knight*; Ford's *The*

Queen; and a number of continental dramas.[42] However, the argument of some historians and literary critics that dramatists wrote plays with embedded clues, explicit references or consistent patterns of references to Essex cannot be supported because professional dramatists did not write plays in this manner.[43] To begin with, most plays of this period were based on existing sources available in print or manuscript, including history books, novellas, poems, prose romances, pamphlets, newsletters and plays. Such sources are routinely ignored by those attempting to find Essex's explicit words or actions embedded in plays by Shakespeare, Daniel, Chapman, Dekker, Markham, or Ford, for example. Second, professional dramatists considered themselves to be creative artists, not historians or chroniclers, with a strong command of what makes good theatre in terms of dialogue, setting, plot and structure. Dramatists were not willing to sacrifice these artistic skills simply to reproduce topical commentary at length.[44] So, while dramatists, who began plays by making clear outlines of each act, and sometimes, scene, may have been willing to include minor allusions to Essex's life or death, they would not have written or shaped their plays to feature him precisely.

In essence, although dramatists appreciated the value of flattering their patrons, they did not usually engage in writing made-to-order plays at their patrons' request, unless that play was a private 'entertainment', a short dramatic piece performed to celebrate particular events, such as 'Of Love and Self-Love', co-written by Essex and Sir Francis Bacon to celebrate the queen's Accession Day Tilts in November, 1595.[45] In fact this particular entertainment did not please Elizabeth in the slightest. However, an entertainment is not a professional play, and dramatists knew that writing made-to-order professional five-act dramas did not produce good plays, only bad theatre. That Essex was being represented publicly does not appear to be the source of his anger in his 1600 letter to Elizabeth. Instead it is that he is being represented in such low-class media as tavern gossip, tawdry pamphlets, and, especially, poor-quality theatre. What he does not complain of in his letter is the myriad public representations of him in the years before 1600 in others' poems, as well as elegant dedications to him of books of poems. In fact, Essex's attempt to court fame during the politically charged years of 1599 and 1600 would suggest that he valued such public representations in poems and books, if not the stage.

As to the source of most of the misinformation about Essex's connection to both theatre and Shakespeare, it comes in the seemingly endless discussion and irresolvable problem of whether Shakespeare helped to stage privately his play *Richard II* for the Essex conspirators in February 1601. From the beginning of the twentieth century the subject has been antagonistically debated among two camps: those who argue that the 'old play' of 'Richard iiiith' and the 'depoysing and kylling of Kyng Richard the Second' staged by the Chamberlain's Men for 40 shillings for the Essex faction was Shakespeare's play about Richard II; and those who argue for a version based on Sir John Hayward's contentious and controversial 1599 prose history of Henry IV, with its story of Richard II, which he dedicated to Essex. For example, the historian Blair Worden reopened the case for Hayward's text in an essay in the *London Review of Books* to be met with vehement objections by Frank Kermode.[46]

Put simply, this debate among literary critics and historians has not been worth the time, effort and vitriol it has produced because, as theatre historians know, much of it has been based on ignorance of the most basic practices and conditions of repertory companies. To begin with, hundreds of pages of archival records exist to prove that when a playing company referred to a play as 'old', they meant one thing only: the play had been in the repertory for a number of years. This was precisely the case when Cope wrote in 1604 to Cecil about the 'old' play of *Love's Labour's Lost*, which was at least six years old at that time. These archival records include not only anecdotes but Henslowe and Alleyn's papers, such as Henslowe's Diary, Alleyn's Diary, and their correspondence, bills, receipts, deed, leases and other documents, and the records and licences of the successive Masters of the Revels Edmund Tilney, George Buc and Herbert Henry. In the repertory system, in a six-week period, with performance usually six days a week, a play may have been performed only once.[47] That is, a play was not staged on successive nights or numerous times in a short period but occasionally over a period of several months. This meant that plays that had been staged occasionally over a period of two or so years were still active, and not 'old'. Shakespeare's *Richard II*, written no later than 1597, was indeed 'old' by February 1601. There is no evidence that Hayward's 1599 history book had been used to produce a play, and if it had, a play less than two years old would still have been considered active in the repertory and certainly would not be termed 'old'. That a play was 'old' produced a number of problems for a repertory company: it would need updating and possibly some measure of revision, for example in altering topical allusions or reshaping roles or passages that had not worked in the original performances. In addition, the play might require updating to suit players who had not originated the roles.

However, no matter the amount of revision, it was much more cost-efficient and common to alter an old play than to produce an entirely new one. As Henslowe's 'Diary' makes clear, companies did not routinely commission new plays on topics already covered by a play already in the repertory; that is, if the company already had Shakespeare's successful play on the topic of Richard II in the repertory, they would probably not have paid to commission another one on the same topic. Companies did commission plays on the same topics as those performed and still owned by other companies. For example, the Admiral's Men probably commissioned Jonson on 22 June 1602 to write 'Richard Crookback' to compete with the Chamberlain's Men play of *Richard III* written by Shakespeare, although Jonson does not appear to have completed his play.[48] In addition, companies did commission companion plays for those plays already in their own repertory, especially history plays, in order to form a cycle with the plays performed on successive days. Henslowe's 'Diary' especially suggests, and Shakespeare's canon demonstrates, that sequels were also commissioned once the original play proved popular.

Although plays were commodities that were purchased outright from dramatists who usually lost financial interest in them after submission to a company, as I have argued elsewhere, Shakespeare was the only dramatist of the age who was a financial investor in three different consortia, the sharers in the Chamberlain's/King's Men and the respective share-holders in the Globe and Blackfriars theatres. So Shakespeare sold his plays to *and* derived income in theory or in practice from consortia that included himself. This meant that he did not relinquish the artistic control or financial interest that non-sharer dramatists did in selling plays to a company.[49] Even though the play text of *Richard II* had been sold to printers in 1597, the Chamberlain's Men lost only the rights to sell it to another printer without buying it back from the previous printer. The company did not lose the rights to perform the play on stage. Shakespeare would have had great incentive to insist that his play about Richard II remain the company's main play on the topic, and its revival in February 1601 would have earned him income from sharing that part of the box office receipts that went to the company *and* that part of that went to the Globe consortium, in addition to the 40 shilling extra payment from the Essex conspirators. Even if Shakespeare wished to distance himself from this special performance of his play in 1601 at the Globe, it still is not possible to see a play written only two years previously as 'old'. So the idea of the Chamberlain's Men staging a play based on Hayward's history can be summarily dismissed on all counts.

In *Hamlet*, the title character asks the newly arrived provincial players if they can perform the play of *The Murder of Gonzago*; as Hamlet has not seen the players for some years the play must have been 'old' by this time. When they respond that they can play it, he asks, in the 1604 second Quarto text of the play, printed from Shakespeare's foul papers, 'You could for neede study a speech of some dosen lines, or sixteen lines, which I would set downe and insert in't, could you not?' In the 1623 First Folio text, printed from a theatrical manuscript showing Shakespeare's later revisions throughout, Hamlet asks, 'You could for a need study a speech of some dosen or sixteen lines, which I would set downe, and insert in't? Could ye not?' The 1603 first Quarto, printed from a reconstructed text that had been heavily cut for provincial playing, mostly follows the Folio text here: 'And could'st not thou for a neede study me / Some dozen or sixteene lines, / Which I would set downe and insert'.[50] The substantive and accidental variants in the second Quarto and First Folio texts about inserting lines suggest that Shakespeare the author felt free to revise Hamlet the character's revision. Hamlet's request demonstrates that he knows this play well enough to revise it by inserting into it some dozen or sixteen lines of his own composition. What Hamlet does not do in order to use theatre and drama for his own political ends is ask the players to write an entirely new play on the subject that is made to his order, or to revise substantially the old one.[51] Instead he asks their permission for him to add a relatively small insertion. Most importantly, these players, whom he has seen perform many times at his home, Elsinore Castle, in his youth, control the play's performance, structure and pace and Hamlet sees his role as a minor collaborator, not a major author or overseer. This is exactly the type of role that Essex would have undertaken with players and with plays throughout his tumultuous and short life.

As the son of theatre patrons Walter Devereux and Lettice Knollys and the stepson, or perhaps surrogate son, of Robert Dudley, Robert Devereux was immersed all his life in the world of theatrical make-believe and of fantastic tales on stage of history and myth featuring valiant but ultimately tragic heroes. That he staged his own life, playing it out first as the centre of a celebratory history or redemptive romance and then as an overwhelming tragedy, was not because plays were written *about* him or staged *for* him but because play-going was an intrinsic part of the culture of his life. Essex learned from the stage; the stage did not learn from him. He patronised theatre but, ironically, the theatre came to patronise him, for, as in *Hamlet*, the players moved on to their next plays and performances while their old 'friend' and patron became trapped and entombed by his own political ambition.

Notes

1 Paul E. J. Hammer builds a convincing case in 'Shakespeare's *Richard II*, the Play of 7 February 1601, and the Essex Rising', *Shakespeare Quarterly* 59 (2008), pp. 1–35 that Essex's purported 'rebellion' was in fact a last-minute uprising; Jonathan Bate reaches the same conclusion in 'Was Shakespeare an Essex Man?', *Proceedings of the British Academy*, p. 162 (The British Academy, 2009), 1–28. While *Henry V* may allude to Essex, there is no evidence that Shakespeare wrote the play about him. See for example Richard Dutton, '*The Famous Victories* and the 1600 Quarto of *Henry V*', in *Locating the Queen's Men, 1583–1603: Material Practices and Conditions of Playing*, eds H. Ostovich, H. S. Syme and A. Griffin (Surrey, England: Ashgate, 2009), pp. 135–144; and David Bevington, *Tudor Drama and Politics: A Critical Approach to Topical Meaning* (Cambridge, MA: Harvard University Press, 1968), p. 290.

2 For discussion on the ways texts circulated from author to censor to actor to audience, see Grace Ioppolo, *Dramatists and their Manuscripts in the Age of Shakespeare, Jonson, Middleton and Heywood: Authorship, Authority and the Playhouse* (London: Routledge, 2006).

3 The Records of Early English Drama series has been published in print form, with individual volumes for each city's records, by the University of Toronto Press beginning in 1979. REED records specifically about patrons are searchable online in a database called 'The Patrons and Performances Web Site' (hereafter known as REED online): http://link.library.utoronto.ca/reed/, from which this chapter draws extensively. The Henslowe-Alleyn website (www.henslowe-alleyn.org.uk) digitises over 2000 pages

of muniments, deeds, receipts, leases, accounts and correspondence, including: Henslowe's famous 'Diary', or account book, of managing theatre companies and the Rose and Fortune theatres; his bull- and bear-baiting records; Alleyn's 'Diary', or account book; the manuscript of the play *The Telltale,* the only surviving actor's 'part', or script, of the period (of Thomas Greene's play *Orlando Furioso*) and one of the few 'plots', or prompters' outlines, of the play *The Second Part of the Seven Deadly Sins.* In addition, other primary reference sources for provincial and London-based playing records are E. K. Chambers's *The Elizabethan Stage,* 4 vols (Oxford: Clarendon Press, 1923), and Glynne Wickham, Herbert Berry and William Ingram (eds), *English Professional Theatre, 1530–1660* (Cambridge: Cambridge University Press, 2001).

4 National Archives State Papers (hereafter SP) 274/138.

5 In transcribing all of Essex's autograph letters in the Hulton Collection (BL Additional MSS 74286) and collating some of them with later copies, I have noticed significant alterations and additions in non-autograph copies. See Grace Ioppolo, '"Y[ou]r Ma[jes]tie[s] most faithful servant": the Earl of Essex's Construction of Elizabeth in the Hulton Letters', in *Elizabeth I and the Culture of Writing,* eds Peter Beal and Grace Ioppolo (London: British Library Press, 2007), pp. 43–69.

6 *Historical Manuscripts Commission: Report on the Manuscripts of Lord De L'Isle & Dudley preserved at Penshurst Place,* 4 vols. (London: His Majesty's Stationery Office, 1925–42), vol. II, pp. 395–6. Hereafter cited as *HMC: De L'Isle.*

7 *HMC: De L'Isle,* II, 144, 407, 423; William Camden, *The Historie of the Most Renowned and Victorious Princesse Elizabeth* (London: 1630), IV, 165.

8 See for example some of his autograph letters discussed in Ioppolo, 'Y[ou]r Ma[jes]tie[s] most humble faythfullest and most affectionate seruant', pp. 43–69.

9 REED online, http://link.library.utoronto.ca/reed/ and Chambers, *The Elizabethan Stage,* vol. 2, p. 102. REED, both in print and online form, occasionally does not agree with Chambers's work, as in vol. 2, which concerns the troupes associated with Essex's family. In this chapter, I have cited both Chambers' book and REED online, even when such records do not entirely agree.

10 For a partial transcript, see Chambers, *The Elizabethan Stage,* vol. 4, p. 269.

11 REED online, http://link.library.utoronto.ca/reed/.

12 See REED online, http://link.library.utoronto.ca/reed/ and Chambers, *The Elizabethan Stage,* vol. 2, pp. 102–103.

13 For biographical information on Lettice Knollys, see Simon Adams, 'Dudley, Lettice, Countess of Essex and Countess of Leicester (1543–1634)', in *ODNB*; *ODNB online,* http://www.oxforddnb.com/view/article/8159, accessed 28 April 2013.

14 Chambers, *The Elizabethan Stage,* vol. 4, p. 278, Wickham, Berry and Ingram (eds), *English Professional Theatre, 1530–1660,* p. 310.

15 Chambers, *The Elizabethan Stage,* vol. 4, p. 278.

16 Chambers, *The Elizabethan Stage,* vol. 2, p. 103.

17 See REED online, http://link.library.utoronto.ca/reed/.

18 Chambers, *The Elizabethan Stage,* vol. 4, p. 264; Wickham, Berry and Ingram (eds), *English Professional Theatre, 1530–1660,* p. 206.

19 Wickham, Berry and Ingram (eds), *English Professional Theatre, 1530–1660,* p. 205.

20 See Chambers, *The Elizabethan Stage,* vol. 2, pp. 88–89 and REED online, http://link.library.utoronto.ca/reed/.

21 Chambers, *The Elizabethan Stage,* vol. 2, pp. 88–89.

22 Chambers, *The Elizabethan Stage,* vol. 2, p. 88.

23 Chambers, *The Elizabethan Stage,* vol. 2, p. 86.

24 Chambers, *The Elizabethan Stage,* vol. 2, pp. 88–89.

25 Chambers, *The Elizabethan Stage*, vol. 2, p. 90.
26 Chambers, *The Elizabethan Stage*, vol. 2, pp. 91, 126.
27 Dulwich College Alleyn Papers MSS 1, Article 26, 7: 65r, www.henslowe-alleyn.org.uk/images/MSS-1/Article–026/01r.html and www.henslowe-alleyn.org.uk/images/MSS-7/065r.html; *Henslowe's Diary*, eds R. A. Foakes and R. T. Rickert (Cambridge: Cambridge University Press, 1960; reprint 2002), pp. 126, 288.
28 Shakespeare, *Hamlet*, in *The Riverside Shakespeare*, ed. G Blakemore Evans (Boston, MA: Houghton Mifflin, 1974), 2.2.422.
29 REED online, http://link.library.utoronto.ca/reed/; Chambers, *The Elizabethan Stage*, vol. 2, p. 103.
30 See the entries on Essex and his family members in REED online, http://link.library.utoronto.ca/reed/.
31 Chambers, *The Elizabethan Stage*, vol. 2, p. 103.
32 On the repertory system, see Roslyn L. Knutson, *The Repertory of Shakespeare's Company, 1594–1613* (Fayetteville, AR: University of Arkansas Press, 1991).
33 On the success of such a company, see Scott McMillin and Sally-Beth MacLean, *The Queen's Men and their Plays* (Cambridge: Cambridge University Press, 1998).
34 Heywood, *A Funeral Elegie, vpon the much lamented death of the trespuissant and vnmatchable king, King Iames, King of Great Brittaine, France and Ireland, defender of the faith* (London: Thomas Harper, 1625), sigs B4v, C1r. Heywood states specifically: '*Henry, Southamptons* Earle, a Souldier proued; / Dreaded in warre, and in mild peace beloued. / Oh giue me leave a little to resound / His memory, as most in dutie bound, / Because his seruant once.' Heywood says that Southampton was 'in all things striuing / To gain a *Name*, by Arts, and Armes suruiuing / Beyond all Marble.'
35 Charles A. Rouse's suggestion in 'Was Heywood a Servant of the Earl of Southampton?', *PMLA* 45 (1930), p. 790, that Heywood may have belonged to the Earl of Southampton's Men between his departure from the Lord Admiral's Men in 1600 and his joining the Earl of Worcester's Men in 1602 can easily be dismissed given that Southampton was imprisoned in the Tower from 8 February 1601 to 10 April 1603 for his part in Essex's rebellion.
36 Margot Heinemann, 'Rebel Lords, Popular Playwrights, and Political Culture: Notes on the Jacobean Patronage of the Earl of Southampton', *The Yearbook of English Studies* 21 (1991), p. 72.
37 Dulwich College MS 7:23r, 231r, www.henslowe-alleyn.org.uk/images/MSS-7/023r.html and www.henslowe-alleyn.org.uk/images/MSS-7/231r.html, *Henslowe's Diary*, eds Foakes and Rickert, pp. 50, 241.
38 Hatfield House CP 189/95; for a transcript see *Historical Manuscripts Commission: Report on the Manuscripts of the Earl of Salisbury*, 24 vols (London: His Majesty's Stationery Office, 1883–1976), vol. 16, p. 415. Hereafter cited as *HMC: Salisbury*.
39 For brief summaries of the various reports in 1601 and 1602 of the investigation into the Essex, as well as the manuscript numbers of the original documents, see the *Calendar of State Papers, Domestic Series of the Reign of Elizabeth, 1601–1603*, ed. Mary Anne Everett Green, 12 vols (London: Longmans, Green and Co., 1856–72).
40 *HMC: De L'Isle*, vol. 2, p. 322.
41 Quoted in Sylvia Freedman, *Poor Penelope: Lady Penelope Rich, An Elizabethan Woman* (London: Kensal Press, 1983), p. 95.
42 On this point, see, for example, Hugh Gazzard, '"Those Graue Presentments of Antiquitie": Samuel Daniel's *Philotas* and the Earl of Essex', *Review of English Studies* 51: 203 (2000), pp. 423–450; Fredson Bowers, 'Essex's Rebellion and Dekker's *Old*

Fortunatus', *Review of English Studies* 3 (1952), pp. 365–366; Kevin Lindberg, 'Thomas Heywood's *The Royal King, and the Loyal Subject* and the Fall of Robert Devereux, Second Earl of Essex', *Comparative Drama* 39 (2005), pp. 31–53; Lesel Dawson, 'The Earl of Essex and the Trials of History: Gervase Markham's *The Dumbe Knight*', *Review of English Studies* 53 (2002), pp. 345–364 and Dawson, '"Dangerous misogyny": John Ford's *The Queen* and the Earl of Essex's 1601 Uprising', *Explorations in Renaissance Culture* 33 (2007), pp. 64–82; Wim Husken, 'Queen Elizabeth and Essex: A Dutch Rhetorician's Play', *Leeds Studies in English* 32 (2001), pp. 151–170.

43 In 'Was Shakespeare an Essex Man?' Bate reaches the same conclusion but does not elaborate (see p. 11).

44 An example of a reading of *Richard II* that depends on such a misdirected view of early modern plays is Chris Fitter's 'Historicising Shakespeare's *Richard II*: Current Events, Dating, and the Sabotage of Essex', *Early Modern Literary Studies* 11 (2005), pp. 1–47; see for example his argument that Richard's command in Act I, Scene 3, to stop the duel between Mowbray and Bullingbrook 'may have jolted audiences with recollection of Elizabeth's stop-go-stop policy at Calais' (p. 16).

45 On this topic, see, for example, Linda S. Shenk, '"To Love and Be Wise": the Earl of Essex, Humanist Court Culture, and England's Learned Queen', *Early Modern Literary Studies* 16 (2007), pp. 1–27.

46 For a discussion of this debate, see Hammer, 'Shakespeare's *Richard II*', especially p. 3, and Arthur F. Kinney, 'Shakespeare versus Hayward', *Shakespeare Quarterly* 44 (1993), pp. 464–466; Alzada J. Tipton, '"Lively Patterns ... For Affayres of State": Sir John Hayward's the *Life and Reigne of King Henrie IIII and the Earl of Essex*', *Sixteenth Century Journal* 33: 3 (2002), pp. 769–794.

47 In *The Shakespearean Stage, 1594–1642* (Cambridge: Cambridge University Press, 1980), p. 102, Andrew Gurr cites records from 1595–97 in Henslowe's *Diary* to argue that even the most popular plays 'would be put on stage not more often than once every month or so'. Roslyn Knutson notes in 'The Repertory' in *A New History of Early English Drama*, eds John D. Cox and David Scott Kastan (New York: Columbia University Press, 1997), p. 468, that 'a "typical" stage run, whether for a new play or a revival, appears to be one in which the play was performed eight to twelve times over four to six months'. However, the records vary enormously, with some plays performed more or less often than Gurr's and Knutson's typical runs. On possible Sunday performances, see 'Preface', in *Henslowe's Diary*, eds Foakes and Rickert, 1st edn, p. xiii.

48 See the entry in Henslowe's Diary: Dulwich College MS 7: 106v, www.henslowe-alleyn.org.uk/images/MSS-7/106v.html; *Henslowe's Diary*, eds Foakes and Rickert, p. 203.

49 See Ioppolo, *Dramatists and their Manuscripts*, pp. 140–141.

50 *The Tragicall Historie of Hamlet* (London: I. R. for N. L, 1604), sig. F4v; *Mr William Shakespeares Comedies, Histories, & Tragedies* (London: Isaac Jaggard and Ed. Blount, 1623); *The Tragicall Historie of Hamlet* (London: N. L and Iohn Trundell, 1603), sig. E4v.

51 Bate implausibly argues that Shakespeare 'dashed off' the deposition scene, omitted from early quartos of *Richard II*, specifically for this 1601 staging and 'gave it to his actors to learn overnight' (p. 8). The richness of the scene does not suggest it was 'dashed off', and there is no evidence that any of Shakespeare's own revisions to his other plays were made hastily.

4

Essex's international agenda in 1595 and his device of the Indian Prince

Linda Shenk

In the autumn of 1595, Robert Devereux, Earl of Essex, was poised to attain political greatness, and he knew it. The international political climate had become sufficiently precarious that a statesman with Essex's particular expertise in foreign intelligence and military matters possessed skills well-tailored to address England's current crises. Spain was once again preparing to invade, this time with an armada greater than in 1588; relations with England's key ally France were cooling; and the financial and military advantages of asserting a presence in the New World were becoming increasingly evident. Aware of this moment as opportune for his political career, Essex engaged in a period of intense personal campaigning during the latter half of 1595 – campaigning that, significantly, involved two theatrical entertainments produced for Queen Elizabeth I. These dramatic spectacles took place in the final weeks of 1595, and in both, Essex encouraged the queen to endorse his vision for a more internationally assertive England.

Essex sponsored the first of these two entertainments for Elizabeth on her Accession Day (17 November) with action that began on the tiltyard and continued after supper with a device scholars have titled *Of Love and Self-Love.* Using the language of love to portray Essex as a selflessly devoted pupil of his queen's wisdom, this interlude deftly acknowledged two of Elizabeth's recent displays of erudition that were steeped in international politics.[1] Essex used this device to present himself as the candidate whose expertise in foreign affairs made him the most qualified to serve as Elizabeth's next Principal Secretary – expertise that especially addressed England's current anxieties regarding France.

During this same period, Essex entertained the queen a second time with a piece that scholars often refer to as the device of the Indian prince. This interlude, again focused on love, is so clearly connected to *Of Love and Self-Love* in action and in references that the *Calendar of State Papers* assigns it also to 17 November 1595.[2] Steven W. May outlines the connections between the two devices and further suggests that the device of the Indian prince probably followed *Of Love and Self-Love.*[3] The exact relationship between these two entertainments remains a puzzle, however, largely because no textual evidence has surfaced either to verify when the device of the Indian prince was performed or to indicate who wrote the script. There is an eyewitness account suggesting that its companion piece, *Of Love and Self-Love*, was staged on Accession Day,[4] and we have evidence that traces its script to the pen of Francis Bacon. The author of the device of the Indian prince, however, remains a mystery. The *Calendar of State Papers* connects it to Essex, but who actually authored it remains unknown, even though Essex must have had a hand in its creation because its specifics align so closely with both his political agenda and, more concretely, with *Of Love and Self-Love*, in which he performed and was featured. Based on my work with both entertainments, I suggest that Essex was involved in the creation of the script for the device of the Indian prince – sufficiently connected that, even though he may not have been the primary author, he is part-creator. Thus, I will attribute to Essex a role in shaping the entertainment.

Essex's interest in creating, most likely also in commissioning, this device becomes even more probable through another, yet more speculative connection. The uncertainty surrounding its performance has left this fascinating entertainment largely unstudied, and some of the few scholars who do mention it wonder if it was performed at all.[5] This chapter will claim not only that it was performed but also that we have a visual representation of its action: the banqueting scene found on Sir Henry Unton's memorial portrait (c. 1596, see Figure 3). In early December 1595, Essex was urging Elizabeth to send Unton as her ambassador to the French king (which she did), and the specifics depicted in his memorial portrait closely resemble specifics in the entertainment. Indeed, featuring Unton's mission to France even in the banqueting scene on the portrait adds yet another visual emphasis on Unton's selfless service to the Crown in the painting because Unton died on the 1595–96 mission to France. This chapter will suggest how this image supports dating the entertainment to the first three weeks of December 1595 even as it further supports Essex playing a significant role in sponsoring the performance.

Because Essex's device of the Indian prince overtly acknowledges international contexts and directly involves the queen, it provides a remarkable window into how the earl sought to woo Elizabeth into accepting his transnational vision. Indeed, Essex and Elizabeth often had conflicting political approaches to foreign policy (to put it mildly), and their disagreements were driven by fundamentally different philosophies. Elizabeth and key statesmen such as William Cecil, Lord Burghley and his son Robert Cecil viewed international affairs through a domestic lens that was rooted in defensive tactics. Conversely, Essex and the Lord Admiral (Lord Howard of Effingham) adopted an approach more like that of Spain, which was amassing imperial power by systematically thinking offensively and transnationally.

Essex viewed England's ability to rival Spain as directly tied to relations with France and a greater presence in colonial outposts such as the West Indies. How he integrated these far-flung political arenas is evident when examining his device of the Indian prince alongside diplomatic correspondence produced from October to December 1595. From such analysis emerges an Essex who used the language of love to assert personal dedication to his queen while also seeking to negotiate common ground regarding foreign policy. He presents her as a figure who can – in a political sense – continue to be 'self-loving' (i.e. focused on preserving the defences of her own nation) while also accepting the offers of 'love' (political alliance) from other countries, particularly France. As a powerful and positive force at the centre of the global arena, Elizabeth could, Essex claims, reach out to other nations without compromising the strength of her own.

A study of Essex's device of the Indian prince not only sheds light on the earl's strategy of using his personal relationship with Elizabeth to promote transnational political action but also brings to the fore a larger trend in Elizabethan royal entertainment.[6] Throughout the reign, members of the Leicester-Sidney-Essex circle, in particular, repeatedly sponsored dramatic presentations as part of their efforts to urge the queen into greater international intervention.[7] Essex's entertainment is steeped in the same tropes (and their associated political interests) that underwrite such famous works as Robert Dudley, Earl of Leicester's Kenilworth entertainments (1575); Sir Philip Sidney's *The Lady of May* (1578); and Edward Seymour, Earl of Hertford's festivities at Elvetham (1591) even as they also suggest attention to court politics in plays such as John Lyly's *Endymion* and William Shakespeare's *A Midsummer Night's Dream*. These entertainments overall, this chapter argues, did not merely reflect political issues; they provided venues where Elizabeth's court figures actively coaxed the queen into pursuing specific political action. In light of this trend, studying Essex's device of the Indian prince allows us to synthesise seemingly disparate facets of the earl's political strategy. His rhetoric of love directly served his international agenda, revealing that the political and the poetical parts of Essex are two sides of the same coin.

The device of the Indian prince begins when the same squire who appeared in *Of Love and Self-Love* brings before the queen two individuals: a blind prince (purportedly from the Indies) and the prince's attendant. These two figures have insisted on meeting with Elizabeth because they, following the terms of a holy oracle, are seeking a fabled queen who will cure the Indian prince of his sole imperfection: blindness. Not surprisingly, Elizabeth is the queen described, and her mere presence provides the cure. The surprise occurs *after* this miracle: the attendant admits that the prince has been brought to Elizabeth under false pretences. The prince is not Indian royalty but rather 'seeing Loue; a prince indeed, but of greater territories then all the Indies; Armed after the Indian manner with bowe and arrows, and when he is in his ordinary habitt, an Indian naked, or attired with fethers, though nowe for semelynes clad'.[8] With clever wit, Essex uses the attributes of Indian dress (or lack thereof) – and the image of bows and arrows – to reveal that Elizabeth has, essentially, given sight to Cupid. The revelation of Love's true identity makes it clear that this device has really been about love all along, even though the opening context of Anglo-American contact remains important to Essex's strategies. In order to reflect the dominant theme, the entertainment will be referred to hereafter as *Seeing Love.*

Because Love is so grateful to have received his sight, he will place all his skills and authority under Elizabeth's direction. Furthermore, Love's ability to see has implications for Elizabeth, for now 'there can be no error in pollicie or dignitie to receiue him' (fol. 139v). In the past, the attendant states, Elizabeth had rejected Love's service and had adhered more to the words of Philautia, or Self-Love. Now that Love can see, however, even Philautia would endorse accepting his acts of homage. Elizabeth can remain self-loving yet also accept the love of others. Able to embrace both positions, she can presently do what has been attributed only to the gods – to love and be wise (*Amare et sapere*) simultaneously. Before asking the squire to show them the way out, the attendant gives him advice for his master (clearly Essex) on how best to demonstrate love for his sovereign-mistress.

Although the language of love is the dominant discourse in the second half of the entertainment, it is significant that the device opens with the exoticism of the Indies. In his first lines, the squire tells the queen that he has brought before her 'two wanderers, the one (as it should seme) some Indian youth, the other white of complexion and expert in language: to mee they will neither giue accompte whence they came, nor whether they would' (fol. 139r). The youth's attendant soon makes it clear why they have been so circumspect: the youth's situation involves the fate of an entire country. He explains:

> In the most retyred parte of that diuision wch those of Europe call the west Indias neare vnto the fountaine of the great river of the Amazons; there gouerneth at this day a mightie Monarche, whose rare happines in all things els, is onely eclipsed in the callamitie of his Sonne, this yong Prince who was borne blynde ... But yet no one thinge hath so much affected both his father and his people towards him, as an ancient prophecy, that it should be he that should expell the Castillians: a nation of strangers, wch as a scourge hath wounde it self about the bodie of that Continent, though it hath not pierced neare the harte thereof. (fol. 139r)

The attendant's opening claim that the prince is from the West Indies would have immediately sparked a chain of political associations pertaining to Spain. England's current presence in the West Indies was the most direct of these connections. At the very time that *Seeing Love* was performed for Elizabeth, it was hoped that Sir Francis Drake, Sir John Hawkins, and the men aboard their fleet of English ships were confiscating (or were about to begin confiscating) hoards of treasure from a Spanish galleon that had been stranded, mastless, off Puerto Rico. This act of plunder would have two main political benefits for England: it would help fund English military preparations against the impending invasion, and it would also keep that money out of Spanish coffers. Spain had garnered vast amounts of wealth from its colonial outposts in such places as the East and West Indies and was using these resources strategically to assume global dominance. Reminding Elizabeth of an act in the West Indies that she herself had sanctioned (although only after much royal delay), Essex was acknowledging an instance when the queen had asserted England's presence in the international arena to diminish Spain's power. It was a contemporary instance of her actions working in harmony with his goals.

In addition to the contemporary resonance of Spain lurking in Essex's reference to the Indies, Essex evokes this nation outright in the attendant's opening description of the prince as one destined to 'expell the Castillians' from his homeland. Using one of Spain's regions to represent it not only diminishes this nation's size (and therefore also its connection to an imperial presence) but also associates it with a specific geography. Now rooted pointedly to Castile, these individuals who are taking over the prince's West Indies are, indeed, 'strangers' and therefore have no right to force themselves on others, particularly (to a European mindset) on another monarchy. This subtext, in turn, allows Elizabeth, by 'curing' the prince, to become a righteous liberator who helpfully supports a fellow sovereign. Such a role reflected the queen's characteristic resistance to intervening abroad out of either expansionistic greed or potential threat to an existing monarch's authority.

Essex's approach to including the queen in the fate of the Indian prince is much in keeping with other royal entertainments produced to encourage Elizabeth's international intervention. Most recently in terms of *Seeing Love*, one of the pageants at Elvetham presents the queen as a life-giving force to 'gould-brested India'. The sea god Nereus directs Elizabeth's attention to 'See where her [India's] ship remaines, whose silkewouen takling / Is turnde to twigs, and threefold mast to trees, / Receiuing life from verdure of your lookes'.[9] Elizabeth's presence has magically transformed a galleon (associated with Spain that plunders India) into a growing space. Significantly, making Elizabeth a figure who unwittingly effects miracles gives the queen powers that require no action on her part; her virtue simply exudes a power of its own. Elizabeth's representation as a passively transnational figure participates in a long line of royal entertainments that extends back to Sidney's *The Lady of May* and back further still to a whole host of poems produced in the mid-1570s by Dutch diplomats campaigning to have Elizabeth assume sovereignty over the Protestant Dutch states. These poems and Sidney's entertainment depicted her as a radiant nymph whose virtuous beams cast peace on the continent.[10] Essex utilises the same strategy of presenting Elizabeth as a passive liberator, also with hopes of convincing her to assert transnational intervention.

In an immediate context related to the West Indies, Essex needed Elizabeth to send a ship to warn the English fleet that Spain had learned of its plans to raid the disabled galleon. Such action was crucial if the Indies expedition were to have any chance of success. But Essex had a second and much more urgent request: that Elizabeth help another monarchy withstand 'Castillian' pressure. The lynchpin of Spain's work to crush England as a political opponent in late 1595 was not the West Indies but rather France. Essex's use of 'Castillians' evokes this additional context.

Spain was focusing the majority of its political muscle on strong-arming France into a Franco-Spanish alliance – a situation that would tip the balance of power in Europe decidedly to Spain's advantage. When Essex refers to the Spanish as 'Castillians', he is most likely also evoking another 'Castile' related to Spanish threat: the Constable of Castile (Fernando de Velasco), one of Spain's key military officers. In the autumn of 1595, the Constable had been warring successfully against King Henri IV's forces in Franche-Comté. Antonio Pérez, Essex's close friend and informant at the French court, states explicitly that the Constable's successes were weighing heavily on the French king. Pérez emphasises that Henri is feeling great doubt and grief because Elizabeth had failed to provide aid and because the Spanish Philip II had ordered the Constable of Castile to take his forces to Flanders where he and Count Fuentes could launch a substantial attack on France.[11] Henri's expressions of anxiety about invasion were most likely overstated for Elizabeth's benefit; nonetheless, the Constable did play a vital role in Spain's strategies to intimidate France to the point where it would yield to an alliance.

The Constable was also involved in another tactic designed to erode Henri's military strength: he had been working to woo the powerful military figure, the Catholic Duke of Mayenne, back to the Spanish side. The Duke had recently declared fidelity to Henri, and his submission was crucial not only to Henri's forces but also to the king's public image as gaining support from former League members. As Sir Thomas Edmondes (England's resident ambassador in France) writes in a letter to Burghley on 5 November: 'The k: of Spayne hath vsed greate practises towardes Monsr de Mayne, to procure him to breake his composition wth the k: and by letters of his intercepted wrytten to the Conestable of Castile, hath geiuen him charge, to enterteine the said duke wth more kindnes then euer'.[12] Having Mayenne's support was essential because Henri's defences were vulnerable and his finances were rapidly dwindling. Thus, when the device refers to Spain specifically as Castile, it evokes a whole range of strategies used by Spain – strategies that integrate the far-flung political theatres of the West Indies, Spain and France and yet within an image of liberation that Elizabeth might find acceptable. In fact, Essex may have felt particularly assured that such dramatic images of international contexts would be amenable to Elizabeth because many of the same images surfaced in the Elvetham entertainments (1591), which took place in a political context similar to that of late 1595. Spain was threatening another armada; France was in great need of English assistance.

Even as Essex may have been echoing strategies from Elvetham, his choices in *Seeing Love* are tailored to the very specific context of 1595, particularly in his use of the rhetoric of love and self-love. Examining his language of love alongside contemporary diplomatic correspondence reveals that the device is steeped in up-to-the-minute Anglo-French relations. Throughout October and November 1595, Elizabeth had repeatedly refused to send Henri additional military aid or to agree to a formal alliance with France on the grounds that, with troops serving in Ireland and much of her fleet in the Indies, her defences were already overextended.[13] Elizabeth's language repeatedly stressed the issue of self-preservation, often framing it as self-love in order to justify her unwillingness to give Henri tangible aid or public gestures of a concrete alliance. Edmondes uses this language to defend Elizabeth's bait-and-switch tactics regarding her promise to send a high-ranking ambassador to Henri rather than provide the aid he had requested. In a letter to the English court on 24 November, Edmondes explains that Henri commented bitterly on the inadequacy of Elizabeth's offer, for,

> by the Amb^{r} wch she is sending to him, he [Henri] sayd that he could not hoape it, sith her ma^{tie} alleageth that she cannot helpe him for that she must conserue her meanes for her self. I tould him that I hoaped that reason was alloweable by howe much her owne interestes are dearest vnto her and charitie beginnng euer wth itself. He sayd that he must confesse it seing her ma^{tie} did avowe such necessitie, and so also that he was no lesse bound in his extremitie, to haue his preseruation in preference.[14]

Edmondes tries to represent Elizabeth's claims of self-preservation in terms of self-love and the positive notion that charity begins at home. But, as Henri demonstrates, two can play at this game. Employing the same logic, he responds that his own needs may prompt him to do what he must as well. Essentially, the cooling relations between France and England were articulated as entrenchment into self-love now that the English and French monarchs were beginning to adopt more independent positions out of their growing distrust of each other.

Diplomatic relations were frequently cloaked in the language of love during periods when decisions and official alliances were under consideration but not formalised. As Daniel Ménager has noted, ambassadors were often depicted as mediators of love, for they worked to nurture the overtures of political affection between nations.[15] Indeed, back in early October of 1595, Anglo-French relations were on a much better footing – and were described as such using the language of love. In this period, Robert de la Fontaine (Henri's *chargé d'affaires* in London) noted that Henri was, he thought, still planning to send the high-ranking ambassador Nicolas de Harlay, seigneur de Sancy to England and that Sancy would be coming with '*le coeur du Roi tout ouvert*'.[16] The claim of Henri's open and willing heart suggested that he was amenable to negotiations, but as October turned into November, such affection waned. After Elizabeth snubbed the French king through a series of refusals and a brusque response to his ambassador Antoine de Loménie, Henri decided not to send Sancy to England. By early December when *Seeing Love* was most probably performed, Essex was in despair over the Anglo-French state of affairs, worried that relations would cool to the point where France would yield to Spain.

In light of his frustration, Essex needed to soften Elizabeth's approach to France without dismissing her concerns regarding England's weakened defence. Working to find common ground with her, he used the current diplomatic language of love and self-love in the device. At the entertainment's pivotal moment – when it is revealed that the Indian prince is actually Love – the attendant presents a scenario in which Elizabeth can be both loving and self-loving. In a two-part quotation that is worth providing at length, he first explains that Love

> presents yor Matie with all that is his; His gifte and propertie to be euer yong; his winge of libertie to fly from one to another; his bowe and arrowes to wound where it pleasth yo^{w}; And withall humbly desireth that though Philautia hath hitherto so preuayled with yor Matie as yo^{w} would neuer accept of him while he was an vnperfect peece, yet nowe he is accomplished by yor Matie grace, and meanes, that yo^{w} will vouchsafe him enterteynment. (fol. 139v)

Then he includes the idea that Elizabeth, by accepting *Seeing Love,* can have the best of both worlds: she can adhere to self-love yet also accept love from others.

> But nowe that loue hath gotten posesyon of his sight, there can be no error in pollicie or dignitie to receiue him; Nay Philautia her self will subscribe to his admission. Then yor Matie shall first see yor owne vnualluable vallewe and therby descerne that the fauours yo^{w} vouchsafe are pure gifts, and no exchanges. And if any be so happie as to haue his affection accepted, yet yor prerogatiue is suche as they stande bounde and yor Matie is free. (fol. 139v)

Essex shifts the extent of Love's service; it is not limited to Cupid's homage to Elizabeth but rather expands to encompass a larger notion of other individuals seeking the queen's acceptance of their offers of affection. Quite interestingly, Essex emphasises that if Elizabeth accepts such offers, she nevertheless remains completely free from obligation.

Henri is a likely candidate for this reference to individuals who seek to have their affection accepted. This possibility becomes all the more feasible because the situation in the entertainment echoes the advice that Sir Robert Sidney gives Essex on 6 November. Sidney suggests how to approach Elizabeth regarding the recent difficulties in Anglo-French relations when he writes:

> For mine own opinion I know it will be some touch of resolution that the Queen should now, as it were, seek the French king, having so bravely refused him, but, my lord, she must not put *rumores ante salutem*, and if an error have been committed, not to think herself bound to make it good. For questionless the good of the State of England, and generally of all them that confess Religion, is by all means to keep the King of France in affection and in ability a balance against the greatness of Spain. But one point of that must be that, things standing as they do, the Queen may seem to doi t [*sic*] with her most honour, and that must be being again entreated and persuaded.[17]

As Sidney suggests, Elizabeth must be urged to make amends with Henri in a way that maintains her sense of blameless honour. This strategy mirrors what I see as the central approach in *Seeing Love*: Elizabeth is sought after – by Cupid himself as well as by others – but even in her willingness to accept love, she is pointedly in control of its terms.

As Sidney also emphasises, it is worth pleading with the queen because the good not only of England but of all Protestant states hangs in the balance. The situation in France is crucial to keeping Spain from amassing too much power in Europe. Sidney's representative at court, Rowland Whyte, notes that the Privy Council was indeed aware that Anglo-French relations were of the utmost importance. According to his letter to Sidney on 8 December, matters regarding France dominated the Council's activities:

> The Lords came of Purpose from the Court vnto hym [Burghley], and satt in Cownsell this after Noone, about *French* Busines, which indeed troubles them very much, for as I hear, the King [of France] answers, that as a Prince carefull of his Subiects; he must by some Meanes or other looke vnto their Safety, and keape his Cowntry from vtter Ruin, that is like to perish, if some Remedy be not found out to comfort it.[18]

In fact, the Lords are so focused on '*French* Busines' that Whyte is unable to act on Sidney's request to return to England for the birth of his child. All focus at court is devoted, instead, to preparing Sir Henry Unton to serve as the promised high-ranking ambassador to France. Whyte explains that Sidney's friends 'answer me, that now they are busy about Sir *Hen. Vmptons* Dispatch into *Fraunce*, that ended, they hope to fynd the Queen at better Leisure to be spoken vnto'.[19] Elizabeth had recently appointed Unton as envoy to Henri in an attempt to prevent relations between the two nations from disintegrating completely. This position of great responsibility made Unton the central figure in England's most pressing political crisis.

It is Unton's embassy that provides support for dating the performance of *Seeing Love*. I believe that the banquet scene famously depicted in his memorial portrait (Figure 3) might represent *Seeing Love*. This scene shows an attendant, followed by a masked, winged figure (Cupid). These two individuals are followed by a moon goddess (Cynthia) and then a procession of figures that includes ten pairs of naked cupids, of which one in each pair has a black complexion. Until now, scholars have been unable to identify the entertainment represented in the portrait, but elsewhere I provide detailed support for identifying it as Essex's device.[20] The portrait does contain added elements such as the figure of Cynthia with the moon on her headdress. This image may represent Elizabeth who, throughout the 1590s – such as at Elvetham – was frequently depicted as the moon (and often specifically as an imperial moon).[21] The text of a song thought to belong to this device and considered one of Essex's possible compositions also supports connecting Cynthia with the queen. Perhaps written to be performed at the moment when the queen grants Love his sight, its opening two stanzas associate her with this action:

> Behold a wonder here,
> Love hath receiv'd his sight,
> Which manie hundred years,
> Hath not beheld the light.
>
> Such beames infused be
> By *Cynthia* in his eyes,
> At first have made him see,
> And then have made him wise. [22]

Whether Essex composed these lines remains uncertain; however, the connection between these verses, Essex's device, and Unton's portrait supports the idea that this song was prepared in conjunction with *Seeing Love.* This possibility is further strengthened by the portrait's depiction of musicians playing while the masquers enter. Using Cynthia to symbolise Elizabeth may have been a way to acknowledge the queen's centrality in *Seeing Love* without detracting from her most important representation in the portrait. At the centre and primary section of the portrait, Unton is pointedly depicted as her ambassador – seated, ready to receive her instructions with pen in hand, and wearing the queen's image that he wore on his (fatal) embassy to France in 1595.[23] If the device depicted in his memorial portrait is *Seeing Love,* then the performance most probably occurred sometime during the first three weeks of December in the window of time between his official appointment as ambassador to France and his departure for that country on 22 December.[24]

Linking Essex's device with Unton's mission provides additional benefit beyond support for dating the piece. Examining the entertainment alongside the documents associated with Unton's dispatch adds valuable context to how Essex is trying to coax Elizabeth into acting as he hopes. Essex and Unton had worked closely on previous missions (France in 1591–92 and the Low Countries in 1585–86). Unton's assessment of the current situation was vitally important to Essex, and the earl trusted him so implicitly that he sent him secret instructions for the embassy. These instructions, in addition to Unton's official directions (which include repeated references to the West Indies, appropriately enough), provide key insight into Essex's strategies to involve Elizabeth in his plans for addressing England's precarious situation, especially with France.[25]

Unton's high rank and established connections in France positioned him to have individuals in and around the French court confide in him concerning Henri's inclination to ally with Spain. Repeatedly, Unton's official instructions direct him to ask numerous individuals about the king's disposition in this regard: he is to ask the king's (Protestant) sister and the Constable Montmorency, as well as other Protestants familiar with matters of state. In secret instructions, Essex stresses that Unton's assessment will be the key factor in determining England's tactics with France. Employing numeric codes to mask the identity of the figures he is discussing, Essex tells Unton that

> If, when he comes there, he discovers 99 [the French king] alienated from us, and treating openly or understand F. [Spain] he is warranted by his instructions to seek by all means to recover him, and upon 15 [Sir HENRY UNTON's] advertisements new overtures will be made to 99 [the French king] to please him, as treaty, and offer of good succours. If he find, at his coming over, that 99 [the French king] is no way looking to F. [Spain] nor so discontented with our courses, as he pretends, then upon this news we will leave all things as they were, and 99 [the French king] and his ministers shall be thought to be but men of words.[26]

Essex's secret instructions, like Unton's official ones, reveal the court's anxiety concerning Henri's disposition toward an alliance with Spain, but Essex goes on to give Unton advice not found in the official instructions. Essex tells Unton how to stage Henri's response in order to spur Elizabeth into assisting France.

Using the language of love to describe the interaction between the two monarchs, Essex explains that 'The soundest and surest way then is, to give us [i.e. Elizabeth] jealousy, and to awake us with matter of fact, and not with words and threatnings'.[27] Essex elaborates on this strategy, directing Unton (and through Unton, both Henri and Pérez) to express responses that are geared toward stirring the queen's emotions. He instructs Unton that once Henri realises that Unton

> brings nothing but words, he must seem to take this worse than all the rest, as either meant to do him a scorn, or else that he hath cause to think he hath some other secret design than is pretended, for on so idle a message he could not believe that we would have sent him. To conclude, he must so use the matter, as 15 [Sir HENRY UNTON] may send us thundering letters, whereby he [Henri] must drive us to propound and to offer. He must give some public shew of coldness at 15 [Sir H. UNTON'S] first coming, and of discontent after he hath heard him, but so as it be without offering him disgrace; and he must welcome him as 15 [Sir H. UNTON], tho' he do not as embassador. He must propound no treaty, nor make no request; for that will make us value him less than we do. He must cast out words, that either 100 [queen ELIZABETH] is

> carried to some secret treaty with F. [Spain]; the hope of which makes 100 [queen ELIZABETH] abandon him: or else that some of her ministers are corrupted to seal her eyes, and gnaw with their envious teeth the cards of amity betwixt B. [England] and A. [France] asunder. But all this without passion, for any shew of passion will make us think him destitute of all other remedy to his affairs.[28]

Essex hopes that such a cool reception in France will kindle Elizabeth's political affection – affection that Essex will fan, essentially, through high-drama reports. The earl is well-nigh desperate to get her to act, and Unton is distinctly reluctant about going to France, knowing that he goes empty-handed, without offer of tangible aid.[29] Both men need Elizabeth to lessen her resistance to helping the French king; thus, Essex urges Unton to embellish the description of the situation there and emphasises that a particularly appropriate venue for the greatest sense of drama is the letters that Pérez will send.[30] The strategy is therefore to vex Elizabeth by making Henri seem no longer in need of England's affection.

Essex's deep frustration and his expressed tactics in the secret instructions explain the motivation behind another depiction of Elizabeth in *Seeing Love.* He holds up a mirror to his queen that presents her – not as emotional – but as powerfully serene. She exudes love-in-moderation, and Essex claims that she is so wise that all her actions stem from a perspective of stability. This strategy adheres to the type of 'saving face' that Sidney advised Essex to pursue in his November letter. This image of royal serenity appears early in the device when the attendant states the oracle:

> Seated betweene the old world, and the newe,
> a land there is no other lande may touche;
> where reignes a Q: in peace & hono^{r} true
> storyes or fables doe describe noe suche
> Neuer did Atlas such a burthen beare,
> As she in holding vvp the world opprest.
> supplying with her vertue euery where,
> weaknes of frends, errors of servants best;
> No nation breeds a warmer bloud for warr,
> and yet she calmes them with her Matie,
> noe age hath euer witte refynd so farr,
> and yet she calmes them by her pollicie.
> To her thy sonne must mak his sacrifice
> if he will haue the morning of his eyes. (fol. 139r)

The final couplet brings the scenario back to the predicament of the prince, but it is actually the sequence of quatrains in this sonnet (an appropriate genre for Love) that is most significant to Essex's strategy. In the first quatrain, Elizabeth is poised between the Old and New Worlds but ruling solely over her untouchable nation. This opening image roots her in a self-loving position as a ruler who is, first and foremost, Queen of England. The second quatrain moves outward in scope to present her in the global role as an Atlas who supports oppressed nations, an image that resembles the influence her miracle for the prince will achieve. Then, in the third quatrain, the oracle returns to her national leadership but frames it within her responses to foreign policy and clever court figures. Twice in this last quatrain, Essex describes Elizabeth as the figure who calms. And it is her serenity that serves as the strength with which she rules both the warlike and the witty – individuals who represent, to a certain extent, figures (such as Essex) who embody the passion of war and the wisdom of wit.

The last sequence of the device returns to and expands on Elizabeth's control over these notions of wisdom and passion. Essex uses this combination to elevate Elizabeth's capacity for good judgment when he has the attendant explain to Elizabeth that, by accepting *Seeing Love,*

> Yo^r^ Matie shall obteyne the curious windowe into hartes of wch the Ancients speake; Thereby yo^w^ shall discerne protestacion from fulnes of harte, Ceremonys, and fashions from a habitt of mynde that can doe no other. Affection from affection. Yo^r^ Matie shall see the true proportion of yor owne fauours so as yo^w^ may deliuer them forth by measure, that they neither cause surfett or faintnes, and take as juiste a tribute of yor Commandments as yo^w^ vouchsafe an imparting of yor fauours, and so keepe them as well in breath, and exercise, as in strength and in harte. And to conclude yor Matie may be inuested in that wch the poet sayeth was neuer grannted *Amare & sapere.* (fol. 140r)

Elizabeth can exude the temperance of wise love while expressing this balance with utter moderation because she delivers everything 'by measure'. In *Of Love and Self-Love,* the self-aggrandising character of the Statesman included the maxim *Amare & sapere* but applied it to his own self-interested strategies that include feigning to be a scholar of the queen's wisdom (and indeed love was what Elizabeth asked for in her 1592 Latin oration at the University of Oxford).[31] In *Seeing Love,* Essex uses this maxim again but now gives its power to Elizabeth in a manner that echoes the sonnet-oracle and that prepares the way for Essex's intimation of the queen's divine perspective.

Essex subtly imbues Elizabeth with God-like perception when the attendant tells Elizabeth that, once she accepts *Seeing Love,*

> Then shall yor Matie rede the conditions of euery pretender, who it is that commeth manned out by the plotts and pollicies of others, and who commeth led only by his owne starre. Who is sent in vnto yo^w^ by the frownes of fortune, to haue some commendacion from yo^w^ to her againe. And who both lefte a favourable fortune when he came to yo^w^, and resolues neuer to establish a fortune because he will wholly depend vpon yo^w^. (fols. 139v–140r)

Through this series of generalised individuals who possess differing relationships with Fortune, the attendant is alluding to Elizabeth's translation of Boethius' *Consolation of Philosophy* (1593). In *Consolation,* Lady Philosophy teaches Boethius-prisoner that individuals must not base their happiness on

Fortune's whimsy but must rather look beyond external events to ground themselves in the constancy of the divine. In the group of 'pretenders' that the attendant describes, only the individuals who completely disregard Fortune are willing to leave even a favourable set of circumstances in order to come to Elizabeth and lead a life separate from any fortune at all. Knowing that Essex is referring to Lady Philosophy in this passage reveals not only which type of individual has the most enlightened perspective but also that Essex is pointedly placing Elizabeth in the position that Lady Philosophy gives to God.

No wonder Elizabeth is granted the depth of love and wisdom attributed only to the gods: she is already associated with divine presence. This connection further underscores her role as a constant figure who is centred on eternal principles and therefore not vulnerable to the weakness of changeable (Fortune-focused) emotion. In her serenity, she rests above the chaos of love in much the same way that Shakespeare's imperial vot'ress of the moon in *A Midsummer Night's Dream* (clearly a nod to Elizabeth) remains impervious to Cupid's potent love shaft. In fact, there is a good chance that Shakespeare may have been evoking Essex's device in *Dream*, which was most likely produced in late 1595 or early 1596. In this play, Shakespeare evokes an Indian boy, gives nods to the entertainment at Elvetham, and echoes the same two texts of Elizabeth's erudition that Essex does in this device as well as in *Of Love and Self-Love* (*Consolation* and 1 Corinthians 2:9 from Elizabeth's 1592 oration at Oxford).[32] Scholars have limited Essex's influence on Shakespeare largely to his actions at court and in warfare, but *Seeing Love* may demonstrate that Essex's literary ventures had an effect on Shakespeare's plays as well.

Perhaps Shakespeare's imperial vot'ress whose 'chaste beams' allowed her to remain impervious to 'young Cupid's fiery shaft' is part of the same strategy as Essex's efforts to represent Elizabeth as one who transcends the embarrassments of blinding, passionate love.[33] Most assuredly, Essex seeks to separate Elizabeth from the image of emotion – an image motivated by his hopes to prepare the way so that any decision she later makes (based on the dramatic reports coming from France) can be coloured as arising out of logic and strategy. What is more, Essex associates Elizabeth directly with the divine serenity that Lady Philosophy connects with God. This connection does more than merely elevate her perspective. It associates Elizabeth specifically with God who orders the cosmos through – appropriately enough – Love. Indeed, Essex is hoping that Elizabeth will also follow the Boethian principles she translated from *Consolation*: love orders the universe and creates harmony, even between nations.

Essex creates a literary piece that places Love in Elizabeth's service, but this love is not merely the intimacy of the heart. It includes the love between nations that arises lightly in *Consolation* and that arises repeatedly and pointedly in the correspondence directly surrounding Anglo-French relations in the autumn of 1595. Essex may have been a rogue of a courtier, but sometimes when working to entertain Elizabeth, he sought to cajole, to entreat, and to find common ground with her. His strategies may even have been so compelling and clever that they influenced other writers, including Shakespeare, to echo such literary ventures as *Seeing Love* in which Essex deftly bridged the arts of courtiership and the arts of international relations. He, like a cluster of famous court figures before him, used drama to place England's queen at the epicentre of the transnational world that so many of her court figures wanted her to embrace.

Notes

1 For my analysis of this entertainment, see Linda Shenk, *Learned Queen: The Image of Elizabeth I in Politics and Poetry* (New York: Palgrave Macmillan, 2010), pp. 159–188.

2 See the *Calendar of State Papers, Domestic Series of the Reign of Elizabeth, 1595–1597,* vol. 4 [Searchable text edition], ed. Mary Anne Everett Green (Burlington, ON: TannerRitchie Publishing in collaboration with the Library and Information Services of the University of St Andrews, 2005), pp. 130–133, item 67. In addition to the text found in *State Papers Foreign: France* two 'modern' editions contain the device as well: James Spedding's *The Works of Francis Bacon,* vol. 8, ed. James Spedding (London: Longman, Green, Longman, and Roberts, 1862), pp. 388–390 as well as Walter Bourchier's *Lives and Letters of the Devereux, Earls of Essex in the Reigns of Elizabeth, James I, and Charles I, 1540–1646,* vol. 2, ed. Walter Bourchier Devereux (London, 1853), pp. 501–505. For this essay, I quote from the text as found in *State Papers Foreign: France.*

3 Steven W. May, 'The Poems of Edward DeVere, Seventeenth Earl of Oxford and of Robert Devereux, Second Earl of Essex: An Edition and Commentary', *Studies in Philology* 77: 5 (1980), pp. 1–132; May discusses the device on pp. 89–90. Spedding, although he provides no evidence to confirm the date or the relationship between the two entertainments, notes that the text is produced 'in a hand belonging to the end of the sixteenth or the beginning of the seventeenth century' (*Works of Francis Bacon,* vol. 8, p. 387).

4 Rowland Whyte provides the eyewitness account for the performance of *Of Love and Self-Love* in his letter to Sir Robert Sidney on 22 November 1595. See Arthur Collins (ed.), *Letters and Memorials of State,* vol. 1, (1746; repr. New York: AMS Press, 1973), pp. 362–363.

5 Paul E. J. Hammer and James Spedding mention that some scholars have speculated that the device of the Indian prince was originally a section of the Accession Day festivities before Essex deleted it. Alan Young wonders if a different combatant used the entertainment instead. See Hammer, 'Upstaging the Queen: the Earl of Essex, Francis Bacon and the Accession Day Celebrations of 1595', in *The Politics of the Stuart Court Masque,* eds David Bevington and Peter Holbrook (Cambridge: Cambridge University Press, 1998), p. 46; Spedding, *Works of Francis Bacon,* vol. 8, p. 387; Alan Young, *Tudor and Jacobean Tournaments* (London: George Philip, 1987), p. 175. A few other scholars who discuss the device include E. K. Chambers and Timothy J. Reiss. (Reiss believes Bacon wrote it, and he links the device to Sir Walter Ralegh – a connection that may indeed be present based on Ralegh's current interest in returning to Guiana.) See E. K. Chambers, *The Elizabethan Stage,* vol. 3 (1923;

Oxford: Clarendon Press, 1967), p. 213 and Timothy J. Reiss, '"Seated Between the Old World and the New": Geopolitics, Natural Philosophy, and Proficient Method', in *Francis Bacon and the Refiguring of Early Modern Thought*, eds Julie Robin Solomon and Catherine Gimelli Martin (Aldershot: Ashgate, 2005), pp. 227–228 and p. 241.

6 Regarding Essex as a shrewd strategist, I am particularly indebted to the following studies: Paul E. J. Hammer, 'The Crucible of War: English Foreign Policy, 1589–1603', in *Tudor England and its Neighbours*, eds Susan Doran and Glenn Richardson (New York: Palgrave Macmillan, 2005), pp. 235–266; Paul E. J. Hammer, 'Essex and Europe: Evidence from Confidential Instructions by the Earl of Essex, 1595–6', *English Historical Review* 111 (April 1996), pp. 357–381; Paul E. J. Hammer, *The Polarisation of Elizabethan Politics: The Political Career of Robert Devereux, Second Earl of Essex, 1585–1597* (Cambridge: Cambridge University Press, 1999); L. W. Henry, 'The Earl of Essex as Strategist and Military Organizer (1596–7)', *English Historical Review* 68 (July 1953), pp. 363–393; R. B. Wernham, *The Return of the Armadas: The Last Years of the Elizabethan War Against Spain, 1595–1603* (Oxford: Clarendon Press, 1994).

7 See Shenk, *Learned Queen*, especially pp. 8–9 as well as Chapters 2 and 5.

8 All quotations from this device are taken from the *State Papers Foreign: France*, SP 78/254 (London: Swift, 1975), no. 67. This quotation is found on fol. 139v. Subsequent citations are given in the text.

9 Anon., *The Honorable Entertainement* ...(London: John Wolfe, 1591; *STC* 7583), sig. C3r.

10 Shenk, *Learned Queen*, pp. 68–73.

11 This passage in Pérez's letter reads: '[*S*]*atis dolens referebat et quasi confusus et ignarus, quid sibi deliberandum sit, praesertim cum major pars exercitus Condestabilis Hispaniae ex madato Philippi in Flandriam remittatur ad Comitem de Fuentes, vt majoribus cum viribus Gallia pre*[*mi*] *possit*'. This letter appears in Antonio Pérez, *A Spaniard in Elizabethan England: The Correspondence of Antonio Pérez's Exile*, vol. 1, ed. Gustav Ungerer (London: Tamesis Books, 1974), p. 362.

12 *The Edmondes Papers: A Selection from the Correspondence of Sir Thomas Edmondes, Envoy from Queen Elizabeth at the French Court*, ed. Geoffrey G. Butler (London: J. B. Nichols and Sons, 1913), p. 278.

13 For example, see *List and Analysis of State Papers, Foreign Series, Elizabeth I*, vol. 6, ed. Richard Bruce Wernham (London: HMSO, 1989), no. 226, p. 174.

14 *Edmondes Papers*, ed. Butler, p. 280.

15 See Daniel Ménager's Introduction to *Diplomatie et Théologie à la Renaissance* (Paris: Presses Universitaires de France, 2001).

16 *Calendar of the Manuscripts of the Most Hon. The Marquis of Salisbury, K.G., &c., Preserved at Hatfield House, Hertfordshire. Part V* (London: HMSO, 1894), p. 473. De la Fontaine turns out to be wrong: Henri had already decided to send Sancy to the Low Countries instead.

17 *Calendar of the Manuscripts, Salisbury*, p. 441.

18 *Letters and Memorials*, ed. Collins, p. 375.

19 *Letters and Memorials*, ed. Collins, p.376.

20 I am working on a full discussion of this portrait in my next book on Elizabethan drama and international relations in the 1590s. For other studies of this portrait, see, for example, Angela Cox, *Sir Henry Unton, Elizabethan Gentleman* (Cambridge: Cambridge University Press, 1982); Anthony Rowley, 'A Portrait of Sir Henry Unton', in *Companion to Medieval and Renaissance Music*, eds Tess Knighton and David Fallows (New York: Schirmer Books, 1992), pp. 85–92; and Roy Strong, *The Cult of Elizabeth:*

Elizabethan Portraiture and Pageantry (1977; reprint London: Pimlico, 1999), Chapter 3.

21 Donald Stump and Susan M. Felch (eds) provide a nice sampling of texts that depict Elizabeth as the moon in *Elizabeth I and Her Age* (New York: W. W. Norton, 2009), pp. 577–593.

22 Steven W. May includes the text of this song in *The Elizabethan Courtier Poets: The Poems and Their Contexts* (1991; reprint Asheville, NC: Pegasus Press, 1999), p. 266. For May's notes on these verses, see May, 'Poems', pp. 108–109.

23 For a description of this incident, see Cecil S. Emden, *Oriel Papers* (Oxford: Clarendon Press, 1948), pp. 2–3, 5.

24 Elizabeth's first choice to serve as ambassador to Henri was Sir Henry Killigrew, but he was too ill to serve.

25 A detailed description of Unton's official instructions is found in *List and Analysis*, ed. Wernham, vol. 6, no. 236, pp. 179–181. References to the West Indies appear on pp. 179 and 180.

26 Thomas Birch, *Memoirs of the Reign of Queen Elizabeth, From the Year 1581 till Her Death* ... vol. 1 (1754; reprint New York: AMS Press, 1970), p. 353. Birch provides the bracketed identification of the figures Essex mentions.

27 Birch, *Memoirs*, p. 353.

28 Birch, *Memoirs*, pp. 353–354.

29 Birch, *Memoirs*, p. 353. On 8 December, Whyte notes Unton's resistance to going on the mission (*Letters and Memorials*, ed. Collins, vol. 1, p. 375).

30 Birch, *Memoirs*, p. 354.

31 See Shenk, *Learned Queen*, Chapter 4 for a full discussion of Elizabeth's 1592 oration at the University of Oxford and her translation of Boethius' *Consolation of Philosophy*.

32 See Shenk, *Learned Queen*, pp. 189–195.

33 Shakespeare, *A Midsummer Night's Dream*, ed. Harold E. Brooks (1979; reprint London: Routledge, 1988), II.i.161–162.

PART II

Self-fashioning

5

'Achilles alter': the heroic lives and afterlives of Robert Devereux, 2nd Earl of Essex

Andrew Hiscock

> On the *3d.* of *Ianuary* at Night, there was a most honourable Presence of Great and Noble Personages, that came as invited to our Prince [of Purpool]; as namely, the Right Honourable the Lord Keeper, the Earls of *Shrewsbury, Cumberland, Northumberland, Sothampton* and *Essex*, the Lords *Buckhurst, Windsor, Mountjoy, Sheffield, Compton, Rich, Burleygh, Mounteagle,* and the Lord *Thomas Howard*; Sir *Thomas Henneage*, Sir *Robert Cecill*; with a great number of Knights, Ladies and very worshipful Personages: All which had convenient Places, and very good Entertainment, to their good Liking and Contentment.
>
> When they were all thus placed and setled in very good Order, the Prince came into the Hall with his wonted State, and ascended his Throne ... At the side of the Hall, behind a Curtain, was erected an Altar to the Goddess of Amity; her Arch-Flamen, ready to attend the Sacrifice and Incense that should, by her Servants, be offered unto her: Round about the same sate Nymphs and Fairies, with Instruments of Musick, and made very pleasant Melody with Viols and Voices, and sang Hymns and Praises to her Deity. Then issued forth of another Room the first pair of Friends, which were *Theseus* and *Perithous*; they came in Arm in Arm, and offered Incense upon the Altar to their Goddess ... Then likewise came *Achilles* and *Patroclus*; after them, *Pilades* and *Orestes*; then *Scipio* and *Lelius* ...
>
> 3rd January 1595, Gray's Inn Court[1]

This description relates to an evening's entertainment as part of the Inns of Court's Christmas celebrations for 1594–95. Such performances at the Inns of Court would clearly not have been unfamiliar to the elite society of Elizabethan England; and, as the narrative indicates, the dominant players in the political life of the realm were accustomed (like Elizabeth herself) to finding themselves in the company of deities and antique heroes when attending theatrical entertainments, viewing the visual arts, or indeed perusing reading matter petitioning for their patronage.

The notion that elusive demi-gods, often gifted with mysterious and extraordinary powers, might reside within the *sanctum sanctorum* of the court was a mythology that had been actively fostered by successive royal dynasties across early modern Europe. In many ways, such mythmaking was a very belated confection of knowledge that had survived from antiquity concerning the deification of rulers, and this *confection* was constantly being re-presented to tempt the palate of the last Tudor monarch – as may again be witnessed at the opening of Thomas Dekker's own Christmas entertainment for the court in 1599, *Old Fortunatus*. In Dekker's prologue, two old men enter as pilgrims seeking 'the temple of Eliza', advising the audience that, 'Some cal her Pandora: some Gloriana: some Cynthia: some Delphæbe: some Astraea: all by seuerall names express seuerall loues: Yet all those names make but one celestiall body, as all these loues meete to create but one soule.'[2] This chapter will explore the ways in which a pre-eminent courtier such as Essex might also be afforded frequent opportunities to enter the politically charged worlds of Tudor mythologising, and the diversity of ways in which acts of patronage and political heroism might be articulated in the textual cultures of Elizabeth's closing years. The strategic positioning of Essex from 1590 onwards in a proliferating number of antique and fabled settings demonstrates not only the complex variety of the cultural responses across Europe to this mighty subject, but often the astonishing breadth in ambition of the earl himself.

Keenly sensitive to the performative demands which her own sovereignty necessitated in an environment unsympathetic to female rule, Elizabeth drew upon the well-established practices of her royal forebears and seized every occasion to associate herself with an inviolable, transcendent authority. In the year following the Inns of Court entertainment, 1596, the Venetian envoy Francesco Gradenigo reported that he had arrived

> in England at the season when the Queen touches for scrofula ... She touched ten and then washed her hands, being served by the Lord Treasurer, the Lord Chancellor, and the Earl of Essex, all three on their knees, the Treasurer in the middle, opposite the Queen, holding a basin, the Chancellor on her right with a ewer of warm water, and on the left the Earl of Essex with a napkin which the Queen used to wipe her hands.[3]

The main participants in these public stagings of royalty were generally few, restricted to prominent royal servants and the peerage. The latter remained a relatively small community throughout the fifteenth and sixteenth centuries, no more than approximately sixty in number[4]; and it was at the age of twenty in 1585 that Robert Devereux, 2nd Earl of Essex, joined fully the high-ranking elite, the premier office-holders and the servants who made up Elizabeth I's court.[5] Years earlier, in 1577, Essex had entered Trinity College Cambridge and appears to have applied himself to his studies with remarkable industry. Later in life, he would refer to 'my contemplative retirednesse in *Wales*, & my bookishnesse from my very childhood',[6] but it is equally apparent that, even in his adolescent years, Devereux was also given to a showmanship which would characterise so much of his later adult life at court: he wrote to the family lawyer from Cambridge in 1581, at about sixteen years of age, pleading for 'one verie faire suite of apparel against St. George day; satten doublet, velvet hose, and jirkin of crimson laid on wth silver lace, wth my foote-cloth, my mens lyveries, etc.'[7]

From the mid-1580s the earl was exploring multiple routes by which he might showcase his very various talents in international conflicts. Nonetheless, if he was hailed as 'that flower of Chivalry'[8] by a fellow combatant, he may be found participating with a good measure of swagger in these years in the theatrics which were often used to quell the appetite for military combat at Elizabeth's court. In 1586 he first participated at the age of twenty-one in the Accession Day tilts and, in 1592, we learn that

> Uppon the coronation day at nyght ther cam two Knightes armed vpp into the pryvy chamber. Videlicet my L. of Essex and my L. of Cumberland and ther made a challenge that vppon the xxvjth of ffebruary next that they will runn wth all commers to mayntayne that ther M[istress] is the most worthyest and most fayrest Amadis of Gaule.[9]

By 1595, reaching the zenith of his power as a Privy Councillor, the earl was assuming a governing role in such festivities: 'his Senate robes shall beautyfie his armes/his chivallrie nobilitate his name'.[10] If the pageantry on this occasion fêted the 'faire Queene of Brutes New Troie', Essex positioned himself centre-stage as one Erophilus, receiving symbolic visitations before the onlooking crowds from a Hermit, a Secretary of State and a Soldier, who presented gifts in celebration of Elizabeth's magical realm. Virgil had originally hailed the inhabitants of these western isles in his First Eclogue as 'penitus toto divisos orbe Britannos',[11] and the 1595 Accession Day celebrations now renewed the charmed, liminal identity of the latter-day Hesperides, locating the Tudor realm as 'Seated between the olde world and the newe,/A Land there is no other lande may touche'.[12]

The potent and well-worn political mythologies conjured up in such entertainments had been strategically exploited since the beginning of Elizabeth's reign, but were affirmed more urgently and with greater frequency in its final decade as the court's fictions of chivalric heroes offering their devotion to an ageless sovereign became increasingly unpersuasive.[13] Looking back at the Elizabethan *fin-de-siècle* from the vantage point of the Caroline period, Godfrey Goodman, Bishop of Gloucester, observed that 'The people were very generally weary of an old woman's government'.[14] However, it might be noted that even during the reign of the last Tudor monarch herself, Essex's sister, Penelope, Lady Rich, was writing tactically to James VI across the border, limning her brother as 'excedinge wery, accomptinge it a thrale he lyves nowe in and wysshes the change'.[15]

Heroic patron

The 1590s witnessed enormous political success for the earl as he rose progressively from being a leading royal favourite and courtier, to military command in Europe (with admittedly varying success), to the Privy Council, and then to the title of Earl Marshall in 1597 and the Chancellorship of Cambridge University in 1598.[16] These (seemingly) unceasing good fortunes inevitably rendered the young aristocrat increasingly attractive to those seeking patronage, and he found himself the dedicatee of a vast array of texts – indeed, it has been estimated that they exceed the number dedicated to Elizabeth herself in this period.[17] Many of these publications were religious in focus or, like Roger Williams' *A Briefe Discourse of Warre* (1590), William Garrard's *The Arte of Warre* (1591), Matthew Sutcliffe's *The Practice, Proceedings and Lawes of Armes* (1593), or John Norden's *The Mirror of Honor wherein euerie professor of armes … may see the necessitie of the feare and seruice of God* (1597), treated directly a subject close to the heart of this 'Paterne to all men', military combat.[18]

Like the courtly entertainments described at the beginning of this discussion, these dedicatory texts became a frequent means through which Essex was inscribed within a superlative world of human experience. Thus, at the beginning of the decade, if Spenser hailed his 'Magnificke Lord' in the 1590 publication of *The Faerie Queene*, and Barnabe Barnes his 'thrise valiant Lord' in one of the prefatory sonnets to *Parthenophil and Parthenophe* (1593),[19] they would quickly find themselves significantly outmatched by the obeisance and grandiloquence being deployed by their rivals as the years wore on. The historian John Hayward called upon the 'Illustrissimo & honoratissimo Roberto Comiti Essexiae & Ewe', trusting that his *First Part of the Life and Raigne of King Henrie the IV* (1599) would find protection 'sub nominis tui vmbra (tanquam sub *Aiacis* clipio *Teucer* ille *Homericus*)'.[20] In the dedications to his own multiple legal commentaries upon the practices of war, Alberico Gentili, Regius Professor of Civil Law at Oxford, variously invoked the 'Comes Excellentissime', 'nobilissime Essexi' and 'Illustrissimo Comiti Essexio'.[21] The dramatist William Gager honoured this 'Illustrissimo ac Nobilissimo Heroi', and George Carleton hailed him as a 'novum … Phœbum'. However, William Covell attended most fully to his prospective patron with a greeting to the 'thrise honorable, & worthilie-worthie-honored-noble *Essex*'.[22]

In direct comparison with his prominent military and political profiles, Devereux's learning was widely appreciated; and, indeed, Gervase Markham, whose textual relations to Essex are discussed in illuminating detail by Matthew Steggle in Chapter 2, submitted of the earl's university days that he applied himself 'with such a carefull (yet Noble) severitie that the Vniversity wherein he liued will and must confesse, that not the porest Pentioner or House-scholler whatsoeuer kept his acts or disputations more duly, freely, and out of his owne knowledge and readings, then this Earle did'.[23] Moreover, like many of his contemporaries, Essex did not fail to proffer public demonstrations of his erudition. He underlined, for example, to the Lords of the Privy Council that times past had confirmed the wisdom that one should 'rather to attempt and do something in another country than to attend an enemy'. This, he argued, was widely held true 'among the ancients' and the case was not altered, 'for we have, as the Athenians had with that ancient usurping Philip, *praelium facile, bellum difficile*,[24] therefore it is our disadvantage to draw the wars into length'.[25] Elsewhere, he drew upon his classical learning in a response to Lady Bacon who had informed him that the court suspected his involvement in an adulterous affair. He replied swiftly, contending that 'Plutarch taught me long since to make profit of my enemies; but God teacheth it me much better now. Worthy Lady, think me a weak man, full of imperfections; but be assured I do endeavour to be good, and had rather mend my faults than cover them'.[26] Rather more playfully, he wrote to Anthony Bacon – regarding what is thought to have been a riding accident – that 'Medea had not more sympathy of those which felt the same evils which herself did, than I have of my friend that is lame'.[27]

Thus, at the heart of Elizabeth's court in the 1590s, Essex moved in aristocratic and intellectual milieux which enjoyed a well-established and frequent acquaintance with the writings and visual representations of antiquity, and it was hoped by those seeking favour that such mighty figures would respond benignly to finding themselves reborn in the narratives of the ancients. Annaliese Connolly and Lisa Hopkins highlight in the Introduction, for example, that Francis Davison presented his 'Worthily famous lord' with a New Year's gift of 1596–97 in the form of copies of the Roman histories of Caesar and Tacitus. Here, Davison argues that his patron's 'Sword with enuy imitates/Great Caesars Sword in all his deeds victorious,/So your learn'd Pen would striue to be glorious'.[28] Furthermore, as this volume clearly indicates, Essex's circle was repeatedly associated in the 1590s with the reading of Tacitus: the publication of the *Annales of Cornelius Tacitus. The Description of Germanie* (1598), for example, included a submission from the translator Richard Grenewey:

> I present [Tacitus] therfore to your Honors fauourable protection … no otherwise then as a glasse, representing in liuely colours of prowesse, magnanimitie and counsell, not onely woorthie personages of ages past and gone, but also your L[ordship's] owne honorable vertues, wherof the world is both wit[n]es & iudge.[29]

A Greekish earl

Essex's acquaintance with the writings of Ancient Greece was not simply restricted to his years at Cambridge. Evidence points to the bookish earl supplementing his earlier studies with a sustained educational programme during his adult years. There were a number of lively scholars within his secretariat such as Robert Naunton, Henry Wotton and Henry Cuffe – the latter, for example, was Regius Professor of Greek at Oxford.[30] Indeed, in an attempt to clear his name from the suspicion of being part of Essex's revolt, Sir Thomas Arundel later gave an account of Essex's intellectual circle in a letter submitted to Robert Cecil

> Theare is one Cuffe a certayne purytane skoller one of the hottest heades of my lo: of Essex his followers. This Cuffe was sente by my lo: of Essex to reade to my lo: of Southampton in Paris where hee redd Aristotle's polyticks to hym wth sutch exposytions as, I doubt, did hym but lyttle good.[31]

Given the intellectual accomplishments and boundless political ambition of this potential patron, it is not surprising that he was repeatedly cast by contemporary writers in the garb of the heroic empire-builders of the first ages. In *Euphues his Censure* (1587), Robert Greene begged that the earl might accept the dedication 'as Alexander did vouchsafe of Misons rude & vnpolished picture of Mars'; and working a similar vein, Richard Harvey honoured the dedicatee of his *Theologicall Discourse of the Lamb of God* (1590) as one who had distinguished himself at the gates of Lisbon in England's revenge attack after the Armada in 1589 with '*more felicitie ... then euer* Alexander *himself did his valiancy at the cittie* Malla'.[32] These Hellenic associations would culminate in Samuel Daniel's *Philotas* (1605) which directly treated the political fall of Alexander's general – in part, owing to the machinations of the scheming Craterus. Daniel (who moved within the Sidney and Essex circles) had begun writing his narrative in the later 1590s, years before the earl's execution. However, as Fritz Levy has demonstrated, the discussion of Philotas was certainly circulating in the correspondence of the Essex entourage by 1597.[33] In any event, with the performance and publication of *Philotas* the analogies with the collapse in the fortunes of the earl became apparent to a much wider public (Sostratus – 'is it to be belieud/That great *Philotas* whom we all beheld/In grace last night should be arraignd to day [?]'),[34] and Daniel was called to answer for himself before the Privy Council: 'when called in question for the tragedy of Philotas, [he admitted] that he had read part of it to the earl [Charles Blount, Lord Mountjoy];[35] had no other friend in power to help him; knows he shall live "inter historiam temporis";[36] and will vindicate his innocence'.[37]

However, rather than the world of Alexandrian triumphs and vicissitudes, Essex was most characteristically held up for compare with the military feats of wholly mythological heroes. The famous taking of Cadiz in 1596 became the *locus classicus* for such panegyrics. A contemporary verse declared, 'Vere Dux, Devereux, et verior Hercule Gades/Nam semel hic vidit: vicit ac ille simul';[38] and the celebration of a latter-day Hercules would be taken up in the first dedicatory verse entered into a huge Psalter looted from Cadiz, and in Latin verses by Andrew Melvin, for example.[39] This strain of Essex's heroic identity found its fullest expression in George Carleton's epic *Devoraxeidos Liber Unus* (1603), in which the earl was hailed as 'Hectoreis animis & viribus Herculis', the 'maior ... Iason'. Indeed, the poem concluded with the celebration of 'Hercule ... Britanno'.[40] The referencing of Hector in Carleton's poem links directly with what appears to have been the most famous backdrop for celebrating Essex, namely, Troy. In his *Philadelphus or A Defence of Brutes, and the Brutans History* (1593), Robert Harvey confided to his dedicatee that he saw 'nothing even in *Vlisses* or *Achilles*, but it may be seen ... in another', and recalling the storming of Cadiz in *Troia Britannica* (1609), Thomas Heywood proclaimed that the English commanders led their forces to victory on the Spanish port, 'As *Greece* did *Troy*, great *Essex* and bold *Drake*'.[41] The swordsman Vincentio Saviolo honoured this commander, 'whose valour inforceth all soldiers to acknowledge you the English *Achilles*', one of Essex's agents (Antonio Pérez) greeted him as 'Achilles alter',[42] and Gabriel Harvey arrived at precisely the same conclusion in his identification of Tudor statesmen in terms of classical heroes – 'Essexius, Achilles'.[43]

Nonetheless, even for contemporaries, it seems, the most influential dedication to '*most true* Achilles' was that of Chapman's *Seauen Bookes of the Iliades of Homere, prince of poets* (1598): 'To the most Honoured now liuing instance of the Achilleian virtues' – Chapman also dedicated his *Achilles Shield Translated as the other seuen bookes of Homer, out of his eighteenth booke of Iliades* (1598) to the earl, '*humbly presenting your Achilleian vertues with* Achilles *Shield*'.[44] Yet, as would be amply demonstrated in Shakespeare's later *Troilus and Cressida*, the age nourished competing interpretations of Homer's rather unclubbable warrior.[45] Depending upon the narrative selections made, Achilles might appear noble, invincible, heroic, vulnerable, foolhardy, vain, devious, implacable in his resentments, and given to weakness of judgement and action. Thus, if the analogy always warranted fuller scrutiny, the evocations of this *Achilles alter* might have remained memorable for early modern minds because, in their multifarious connotations, these allusions communicated the anxiety-ridden responses which Essex so often elicited in both life and death.[46]

Equally interestingly, given some notable instances of adversarial politicking between Essex and his former guardian William Cecil, Lord Burghley, in the 1590s when the earl continually sought to be *primus inter pares* and the Lord Treasurer was energetically working to secure key offices for his son Robert, it is not surprising that the chief minister might wish to oust Essex from this heroic Greek world altogether. In his coded diplomatic correspondence to the French ambassador Sir Henry Unton and the military commander Sir John Norris, Burghley disarmingly adopted the cipher of the meditative 'Aurelius' for himself, but graced Essex with the title of 'Cyrus'.[47] Similarly minded to snuff out the insatiable appetite for Grecian myth-making, Francis Bacon (acting for the prosecution at the trial in 1601) likened his former patron to the contemptible conduct of 'one Pisistratus, in Athens, who, coming ... with the purpose to procure the subversion of the Kingdom

… entered the city, having cut his body with a knife, to the end [the citizens] might conjecture he had been in danger of his life'.[48]

Essex and the Roman Pantheon

When positioned in Ancient Greece, Essex was mostly characterised in terms of political heroism and aspiration. However, when his contemporaries turned their attentions to the Roman world, these emphases were not only extended further, but complemented by a much wider scheme of analogy. As was indicated in the case of *Troilus and Cressida*, it has long been suspected that Essex might be figured forth variously in Shakespearean dramatic narrative as an unbiddable subject, an aristocrat of overweening ambition, a testy adult male devoid of emotional intelligence, or even as a rather truculent *miles gloriosus.* On the eve of the revolt, when a company of Essex's followers assisted at a performance of the fall of Richard II, did anyone present consider the imminent advent of a latter-day Bolingbroke, living up to the Hereford title and marching through the streets of London?[49] Moreover, in the years after the earl's death, was he being revived on stage as a petulant Achilles, or as an inexorable, war-crazed hero in Shakespeare's *Coriolanus*? Certainly, William Barlow, whom the authorities had instructed to preach at St Paul's Cross upon the Sunday directly following Essex's execution, informed the assembled masses that '*Coriolanus*, a gallant young, but a discontented Romane … might make a fit parallel, for the late Earle'.[50] As Chris Butler and Willy Maley discuss in Chapter 6, *Henry V* may also have conjured up the earl (or, alternatively, his more notably triumphant successor in command of the Irish campaign, Lord Mountjoy) as one 'from Ireland coming' and greeted adoringly by London dignitaries: 'Like to the senators of th' antique Rome,/With the plebians swarming at their heels', they welcome 'their conqu'ring Caesar in' (V.Prol.26–28).[51] Intriguingly, echoing the very leadership qualities which are emphasised in Shakespeare's history play, Barnabe Barnes would later submit that he had seen the earl 'in the French warres to communicate in sports and sometimes in serious matters with men of meane condition and place, their fortunes and parentage valued … even as *Salust* describeth *Sylla*, so did he become precious in presence of his souldiers'.[52]

On the death of his father, Essex inherited an estate riddled with debts (owed mostly to the Crown), and he himself acknowledged in later life, 'I sawe no way of merite lie so open as by seruice in the warres'.[53] When not actively employed in military campaigns, his mind appears often to have been exercised by the ancient arts of war. Paul E. J. Hammer has drawn attention importantly to the vigorous learning programme unfolding in the earl's household, whereby 'Lord Henry Howard, himself a former Cambridge don, wrote advices for Essex on political conduct studded with quotes and references from Thucydides and Livy. With Cuffe and Savile, Essex scrutinised ancient history for insight into war and politics'.[54] Indeed, the extensive library of the earl clearly attracted the attentions of the most powerful in the land, for it was noted that 'at the time of his conviction [the earl] had in a certain room *vocat*[55] his "Studdy" in the aforesaid house called Essex House, divers printed books of divers kinds and languages; and our aforesaid Most Serene Lady Elizabeth was pleased to remove these books for herself' – even his enemy Lord Cobham sought to borrow 'a paper boke of my lord of Essex notations of Cornelius Tacitus' two years after his execution.[56]

In the prefatory materials to Savile's *The Ende of Nero and Beginning of Galba. Fower Bookes of the Histories of Cornelius Tacitus. The Life of Agricola* (1591), one A. B. underlined that

> There is no treasure so much enriches the minde of man as learning; there is no learning so proper for the direction of the life of man as Historie; there is no historie (I speake onelie of profane) so well worth the reading as Tacitus ... In Galba thou maiest learne, that a good Prince gouerned by euill ministers is as dangerous as if hee were euill himselfe. By Otho, that the fortune of a rash man is *Torrenti similis*[57], which rises at an instant, and falles in a moment.[58]

The conviction of some early modern voices, such as those of Ben Jonson and Edmund Bolton, that this 'A. B.' was Devereux himself might certainly give these prefatory thoughts added piquancy for those Elizabethans who subscribed to such doctrines.[59] More generally, if Essex was often to be discovered in the company of Romans in the literatures of the period, it could be for good or ill. When Camden came to describe the earl's fateful return from Ireland in 1600, he contended that Essex

> had not any more deadly enemies, than (as was said in old times of *Germanicus,*) his own ornaments; and that those which were his adversaries, had nothing to complaine of him more than his greatnesse. With whom notwithstanding, they despaired not to returne into favour, seeing that he as well as *Pompey*, was not sharpe to his adversaries, and to such as yeelded, placable.[60]

Elizabeth herself was well versed in ancient histories and would not have failed to appreciate the allusiveness of such passages, if they had been brought to her attention.[61] Indeed, in the months directly following her death, John Clapham recalled that the late queen 'took pleasure in reading of the best and wisest histories, and some part of Tacitus' *Annals* she herself turned into English for her private exercise'.[62]

Roman historical narratives clearly continued to enjoy particular currency with reference to Essex and at the beginning of his trial in 1600, the Queen's Sergeant, Yelverton, pursued an analogy at length for the edification of the assembled company:

> the sedition of Catiline was in the city of Rome, and consequently England is in no less danger; for as Catiline entertained the most seditious persons about all Rome to join with him in his conspiracy, so the Earl of Essex entertained none

> but Papists, Recusants, and Atheists for his abettors in this his capital rebellion against the whole estate of England.[63]

Jonson's tales of political conspiracy and rebellion from Tacitus and Sallust for his tragedies *Sejanus* and *Catiline* failed to earn him ovations in the playhouse, but the former generated sufficient concern in 1603 for him to be summoned before the Privy Council to account for himself.[64] Nonetheless, Essex was far from being uniformly associated with political subversives from Roman history. Exploring new permutations for Devereux's identity in 1601, one Abraham Colfe had the temerity to deliver an oration on the late earl at Oxford University, and found himself in Newgate prison for his pains. He went on to plead his innocence in a letter to Robert Cecil:

> I thought to praise the virtues of the Earl, and darkly to point at his death under the history of Cicero; but not to grieve at the sentence of his condemnation, for I was never yet disloyal to Her Majesty. I confess I said he had enemies some of whom I call Piso, Catiline, and Anthony, who were enemies of Cicero. Pray pardon this offence, and make me rather a pattern of mercy than of justice.[65]

From the very beginning of his political career, Essex had been widely perceived and, indeed, perceived himself to be the successor of Sir Philip Sidney, exploiting strategically for his own ends, as Richard Wood argues persuasively in Chapter 1, a marked strain of 'Sidneian chivalric romanticism'.[66] Sidney famously bequeathed his sword to his kinsman, and the earl subsequently married the widow of the fallen knight, Frances Walsingham. The translation of Francesco Colonna's *Hypnerotomachia* (1592) was not unrepresentative in counterpointing a lament for the loss of 'that matchlesse Knight Syr *Phillip Sydney*' with an affirmation that there were no 'more Noble personage ... to patronize, shield, and defende [the author's] duties to the deade then your Honour'.[67] James VI of Scotland had contributed lyrics to the Cambridge collection *Lachrymae* recalling Sidney's passing, yet he noted in a communication to Essex (via Anthony Bacon) that he was 'bien aise d'avoir recouvert en sa person Sire Philipe Sydnay'.[68] Furthermore, George Peele's panegyric *An Ecglogve Gratvlatorie* (1589) echoed precisely these sentiments. Welcoming Essex back from his military exploits in Portugal, he mourned the loss three years earlier of 'that great *Shepherd* good *Philisides*', yet honoured 'this louelie swaine' in '*Nue reared Troy*': 'his dread aduentures here sing I,/Equiuolent with the *Punic Chiualrie*'.[69] Equally interestingly, Sir Thomas Smith recalled that even after his execution, the earl was being inscribed within Sidneian narratives: 'that Noble but vnfortunate *E.* of *Essex*, of whom many through the world, do make in diuers kinds, but (as that learned and heroycall Poet *Sir Phil. Sidney* speaks of *Prince Plangus*') neuer any can make but honorable mention'.[70]

During his own lifetime Sidney had excited heroic comparisons between himself and the Roman General Scipio Africanus (conqueror of Spain and of Hannibal in the Punic wars), even though the poet's military experience had not been extensive. From the early 1590s onwards, Essex began to be figured in this way in a growing number of publications. If, in the rather prophetically titled *Polimanteia, or, The meanes lawfull and vnlawfull, to iudge of the fall of a common-wealth* (1595), William Covell hailed 'Englands *Scipio*', in the following year, the Oxford academic John Rainolds similarly honoured this latter-day Scipio in the dedication to his *De Romanae Ecclesiae Idololatria* (1596).[71] Most arrestingly, in his *Fortunate Farewell to the most forward and noble Earle of Essex* (1599), Thomas Churchyard proclaimed

> Now Scipio sails, to Affrick far from ho[me] ...
> On Irish seas, ELIZAS ships shall ri[de] ...
> The sword is drawn, TYROENS dispatch draws ny
> A traitor must, be taught to know his king,
> When MARS shal march, with shining sword in hand.[72]

In the years between Essex's execution and Elizabeth's death, the only publications which officially addressed the earl's passing were William Barlow's *Sermon Preached at Paules Crosse* (1601) and Bacon's state-commissioned offering, *A Declaration of the Practises & Treasons attempted and committed by Robert late Earle of Essex and his complices, against her Maiestie and her kingdoms* (1601). However, with the advent of the new reign and James VI/I's swift return of the family estate to the fatherless twelve-year-old Robert, the 3rd Earl of Essex, it was altogether safer to laud Elizabeth's fallen courtier and return to the wonted eulogies of the 1590s. In his *Devoraxeidos* (1603) George Carleton commemorated the martial prowess of this Scipio with his god-like strength, Barnabe Barnes's *Foure Bookes of Offices* (1606) recalled the taking of Cadiz where that 'noble (though vnfortunate)' Essex performed 'like a true Scipio both in valour and discipline', and W. H.'s *Englands Sorrowe or, A Farewell to Essex* (1606) affirmed that 'The forraigne spoiles and conquests which [Essex] wan/Were like to those of Scipio African'.[73]

Given Essex's eminent status at Elizabeth's court in the 1590s it is unsurprising that he should also have been identified as a latter-day Maecenas by those willing to be named as his distinguished protegés.[74] Interestingly, the earl does indeed appear on occasions to have fulfilled this protective role, for, as Camden underlined, Spenser 'dyed, and was interred at *Westminster*, neere to *Chavcer*, at the charges of the Earle of *Essex*'.[75] In his betrothal lyric 'Prothalamion', Spenser (clearly in search of the earl's patronage in the mid-1590s) had fashioned the 'noble Peer' as 'Radiant Hesper' recalling Book VIII of the *Aeneid*: here, Spenser's 'noble Lord' descends like the morning star from the 'high Towers' of Essex (formerly Leicester) House to greet the prospective brides before the onlooking crowds.[76] Yet the *Aeneid* was also being exploited for equally creative purposes in this period by the Essex entourage. Devereux was overseeing an extensive network of spies and 'intelligencers' across Europe from 1592 onwards which came to supersede that of Burghley in this period. It is clear, for example, that the ambassador in

Paris, Sir Henry Unton, did not appreciate being landed with one of Essex's men (the Spaniard Antonio Pérez), and wrote to Elizabeth's minister that 'the Earle doth not deall so kyndlye with me as I expected': for, he declared, Pérez would 'imparte nothynge vnto me but such genneralytyes as the lackyes doe know; so as I feare hee would bee a spy vppon me'.[77] Given his participation in Henri IV's Normandy campaign in 1591 and continued interest in the fortunes of the House of Navarre, it is not surprising that Essex believed that 'ffraunce is at thys daye the theater and stage wheron the greatest actions are acted'.[78] He sent another of his agents, Robert Naunton, across the Channel in 1595, underlining that 'To attayne the Frenche quickly you must converse with ffrenche', but stressed equally characteristically that the 'rules and patternes of pollecy, are as well learned out of olde Greeke and Romayne storyes, as out of states which are at thys daye'.[79]

In the atmosphere of fear and suspicion between factions and nations in late sixteenth-century Europe, ciphers continued to be resorted to in all manner of communications circulating across the Continent. In his correspondence with Pérez, Essex was repeatedly identified in the guise of Aeneas attempting to prepare the way for a new empire, but often thwarted by the contrary forces of the Queen of Olympus and the ministrations of her factotum, Aeolus or Cecil. In 1595, Pérez writes to his master, 'Sed, Mylorde, quid de isto tempestuoso mari? Quid de Junone, quae Æolum et ventos contra te convocat et commouet?'[80] Later in the correspondence, a direct quotation from Virgil is integrated into a communication from Essex to Pérez, evoking the enraged Juno: 'Flectere si nequeo superos, Acheronta movebo'.[81] Furthermore, Pérez writes from Paris that he wishes to outdo his master in faithfulness to their great mission – 'etiamsi fides mea plus quam Ænea sit'.[82] Tellingly, in direct comparison with the Essex–Achilles analogy discussed earlier, this mythological coding appears to have enjoyed wider currency beyond the Essex spy network. In the secret correspondence between Essex and James VI (via intermediaries such as Essex's sister, Penelope), Elizabeth was designated as 'Pallas';[83] and in the aftermath of the taking of Cadiz, Francis Davison wrote to his father from Italy lamenting Essex's court battles with the hunchbacked Secretary of State, Robert Cecil:

> my Lord's fortune is hard, and his enemies' estate most fortunate. If my Lord break their necks as nature hath broken their backs, they may comfort their fall with the nobleness of the author, and his arch enemy may glory in himself that *Æneae magna dextra cadit.*[84] *But what glory shall it be to him, that hath so notably beaten the greatest Monarch of the world at his own door, to cut off such a viper's tail, or being a Hercules to beat a Pigmy?*[85]

By way of a postscript to these encounters with the earl's Roman selves, it remains evident that there were those during his lifetime who sought to veil their political satire of him with a lightly archaised narrative. Thus, Edward Guilpin's 'Skialetheia' (1598), for example, mocked the overweening ambition and war-mongering of Essex (or 'Felix'), comparing him to the Roman Sulla and ridiculing his wooing of 'the people's love': 'great *Fœlix* passing through the street,/Vayleth his cap to each one he doth meet, / ... Like a Swartrutters hose his puff thoughts swell,/With yeastie ambition'.[86]

Alternative heroes, alternative selves

Continuing to seek military assistance from Elizabeth's favourite, Henri IV had his ambassador assure her Majesty in 1592 that the earl was 'plein de valleur et de courage'.[87] However, if she generally surpassed her advisers in political caution and parsimony, Elizabeth remained a match for any of her favourites in terms of vanity – and the queen was not accustomed to finding herself eclipsed by her subjects in the eyes of Europe. A rather animated Philippe Duplessis-Mornay shortly reported back to his master that the speeches of the queen were 'entrecoupées de digressions de courroux[,] d'injures et de menaces contre le comte d'Essex, qu'elle le feroit le plus petit compagnon d'Angleterre; qu'il faisoit accroire au roy qu'il gouvernoit tout, et qu'elle lui feroit bien voir que non'.[88] As we have seen, in his various military engagements, the attention-seeking Essex certainly sought to brandish his chivalric and military prowess. Indeed, the earl had an irrepressible penchant for histrionics, as John Speed later related in his account of the 1589 assault on Lisbon:

> the noble *Essex* in the courage of his Martiall bloud, ranne his speare and brake it against the Gates of that City: demanding alowde, if any *Spaniard* mewed therein, durst aduenture forth in fauour of his Mistresse to break a staffe with him. But those Gallants thought it safer to court their Ladies with amorous discourses, then to haue their loues written on their breasts with the point of his English Speare.[89]

Similarly minded in the Normandy campaign of 1592, he threw down the challenge to the Governor of Rouen, proclaiming 'Si vous voulez combattre vous-même à cheval ou à pied, je maintiendrai que la querelle du Roi est plus juste que celle de la Ligue, et que ma Maîtresse est plus belle que la vôtre'.[90] The potential for glorifying Essex's exploits in the service of the House of Navarre was not lost on contemporary writers. It would not have taken a supersubtle reader at the time of the 1596 publication of *The Faerie Queene* to identify Essex as a possible reading for Sir Artegall in Book Five, for example, who goes forward to rescue Burbon (or Henri IV), 'a Knight in daungerous distresse' (V.xi.44). Burbon had earlier been dubbed a knight for his valour by the Protestant warrior Redcrosse (V.xi.53), but thus far he has been unable to win back his damsel, Flourdelis (or France), from the countless forces ('a swarme of flyes' V.xi.58) of the tyrant Grandtorto. If Artegall eventually restores a rather truculent Flourdelis to her swain and tempers the latter's taste for slaughter at the close of Book Five, canto eleven, in 1597 another of Henri's ambassadors to Elizabeth's court, André Hurault de Maisse, remained curmudgeonly in his praise of Elizabeth's knight errant: Essex 'believes no counsel save his own ... He is a good Englishman and Frenchman all the more as he thinks that it sorts with his designs ... He is entirely given to arms and the war, and is the only man in England who has won any renown thereby ... I believe that, so far as an Englishman can, he covets glory'.[91]

These concerns with a national allegiance and a national experience were articulated elsewhere in the textual celebrations of Essex by his fellow countrymen. The patronage of Essex was actively sought by writers of British chronicle history in the 1590s, as has already been evidenced in the dedications of Robert Harvey's *Philadelphus or A Defence of Brutes, and the Brutans History* (1593) and John Hayward's *First Part of the Life and Raigne of King Henrie the IV* (1599). However, in his *Devoraxeidos*, George Carleton not only honoured a latter-day Jason and Achilles in terms familiar from the publications of earlier contemporaries, for the taking of Cadiz he wittily unveiled his hero as Ostrosaxonides (descendant of the East Saxons) in a remarkably detailed account of the maritime assault:

> Crescit, & antiqui surgit nova gloria sæcli
> Ostrosaxonides: nostroq: illustrior orbi
> Maiorum virtus collecta relucet in vno.[92]

Moreover, if in the 'Prothalamion' Spenser had hailed 'Great Englands glory and the Worlds wide wonder' (146), other writers sought to strike an even more patriotic note in yoking the earl together in various ways with the nation's patron saint. When Richard Williams turned his attention to the taking of Cadiz, the patriotic emphasis is unmistakeable: '"Saynt George and Essex:" at *wh*ich name/It Ioyed so eache Englishe Harte,/The spanyards felte bothe woe and smarte'.[93] An earlier *ballade of the tryump[h]es kept in Ireland uppon Saint Georg's day last, by the noble Earle of Essex and his followers, with their resolution againe there* (1599) similarly offered a rousing finale: having demonised at length 'the Traytor, base *Terone*', the closing lines constructed an energetic rallying call of support for the 'noble *Essex of England*':

> Therefore, let all true English men,
> With every faythful subiect then,
> Vnto my prayers say Amen!
> Now God and Saint George for England!.[94]

It has been commonplace down the centuries to stress the ways in which Essex might be compared to Icarus, drawing principally upon the figurative language of Francis Bacon.[95] Nevertheless, it should be underlined that the most critically neglected heroic representation of Essex by his contemporaries exploits this ongoing concern with Devereux's role in the national destiny, yet marks a significant departure from the narratives of Graeco-Roman culture which so often shaped his cultural reception in the early modern period. In the same way that Elizabeth was frequently associated with the Old Testament heroines such as Deborah, Judith and Esther,[96] late sixteenth-century writers might also choose to align Essex with the triumphs and adversities of Hebrew leaders in Scripture. In *Ecclesiastes* (1597), for example, Henry Lok contended, 'Not Neptunes child or Triton I you name,/ Not Mars, not Perseus, though a Pere to all', it was more fitting for the age to celebrate 'Englands ioy … vices scourge … To Church a shield, to Antichrist a barre', for Essex was one of 'heauens elect'.[97] Striking a similar note, the cleric George Gyfford likened the wars with Spain to the apocalyptic battles envisaged in the Book of Revelation, and so Essex was to 'put on that fine white linnen and pure, ride upon that white horse among this blessed company, and follow this high captaine'.[98] In 1597, he was urged in a communication by a 'well-wisher' to be 'like wise Mordecai [and] prevent the wicked purposes and desires of proud Haman' [or Cecil].[99] Essex himself is reported in 1596 as declaring to Anthony Bacon that 'yf I be not tyed by the handes, I know God hath a greatt worke to worke by me',[100] and numerous commentators down the centuries have stressed the religious urgency with which Essex frequently perceived the need for English participation in foreign wars. It has become evident that the earl certainly had an appetite for military feats of derring-do (such as at the sieges of Lisbon (1589) and Rouen (1591), yet he also knew how to nuance his responses for an exhausted England in the closing years of Elizabeth's reign. The meditations contained in his *Apologie of the Earle of Essex, Against those which iealously, and maliciously, tax him to the Hinderer of the Peace and Quite of his Country … penned by himself. Anno 1598* clearly indicate a mind strategically seeking to engage with a war-weary society of the 1590s:

> I have thought, *Excellent mindes should come to the warres, as Surgeons doe to their Cauteries,* when no other easie or ordinarie remedie will serve … But, though warres be diseases, yet I thinke it better to endure some sicknesse, then to venture upon every medecine.[101]

As is apparent throughout this volume, the earl's temperament was one given to violent passions: an insatiable appetite to distinguish himself internationally as a military commander; an irrepressible desire to surpass all other royal advisers in the management of national policy; and when thwarted, a grand staging of the classical pursuit of *otium,* of cultural withdrawal, for the purposes of political critique, retrospection and resistance. In 1598, in the face of the growing rebellion led by the mighty Tyrone, Essex was appointed by Elizabeth to undertake what he himself perceived to be 'the hardest task that ever gentleman was sent about'.[102] After the event, those of his affinity proved themselves similarly minded: Barnabe Barnes cursed the 'pestilent and inauspicious expedition to Ireland', and Henry Wotton wrote that the earl's 'blackest [employment] was that to *Ireland*, ordained to be the Sepulcher of his Father, and the Gulph of his owne Fortunes'.[103]

However, a number of contemporary authors referencing this Irish campaign sought to identify Essex explicitly as an instrument of God: Thomas Churchyard, for example, found the expedition to recall that campaign when 'IOAB went, to war in DAVIDS right'.[104] Barnabe Barnes also contended that the wavering fortunes of great men of state such as Essex might recall those of David, 'who (though protected by the great prouidence of God) … [was] in danger to lose his life, by many treacherous conspiracies'.[105] Equally interestingly, Camden's *Annales* (1615) related how, after the unexpected return from Ireland, Elizabeth and Essex might both be found to renew Old Testament cycles of human experience for a Jacobean readership. By means of Lord Henry Howard, the penitent Earl communicated to the queen that he must

> *say with* Nabuchodonozor, My dwelling is with the beasts of the field, to eat grasse as an Oxe, and to be wet with the dew of heaven, *till it shall please the Queene to restore my understanding unto me.* The Queene reioyced at these words, saying, … *My father would not have endured such perversnes. But I will not look behind me, lest with Lots wife I be turned into a Pillar of Salt. All is not gold that glistereth. If this could bee brought to passe with the furnace, I should be more favourable to the profession of Alchimy.*[106]

In this later, Jacobean period, Fulke Greville also remained exercised by the ways in which Biblical rhetoric might be allowed to articulate such crises of state: 'though I lament the fall of this great man in Israel, nevertheless the truth enforceth me to confesse that … [these kinds of high justice may] prove … mercy to many by example … Thus you see how our famous *Iudith* dispersed the terrour of this *Holofernes*'.[107] In reality, Elizabeth seems to have found little source for comfort in these final years of her reign. In the aftermath of the Essex revolt, her godson Sir John Harington wrote that 'the dangers are over, and yet she always keeps a sword by her table', and Sir Robert Sidney, that 'I do see the Queen often; she doth wax weak since the late troubles'.[108]

Essex was executed on Ash Wednesday, 25 February 1601, at the age of thirty-four and may have suffered as many as three strokes of the axe before his head was severed from its body. Camden's *Annales* had him repeating the first verses of Psalm 51 before kneeling at the block 'in humilitie and obedience', and David Lindsay concurred that the 'noble and valorous Earle, ROBERT DEVEREUX, Earle of ESSEX, who suffred in the yeare 1601 for his rebellion … died verie Christianlie, as Historians report'.[109] If the state-commissioned preacher and confessor, William Barlow, insisted that at the end of his life the earl pondered the 'constancie of Martyrs at their death', concluding 'that they died in a good cause, but he should dye in a BAD CAUSE', this did not prevent a number of early modern voices from investing deeply in the religiously charged language of sacrifice in relating his death.[110] Richard Williams, for example, described the condemned man at the block 'yet as a lambe hee quyett laye'.[111]

Such unwonted meekness on the earl's part also found expression in his own correspondence during the period of confinement after the revolt: he apparently wrote to his fellow-rebel, the Earl of Southampton, 'As neither Nature nor Custom ever made me a Man of Compliment, so now I shall have less will than ever to sue such Ceremonies when I have left, with *Martha*, to be *sollicitus circa multa*, and believe, with *Mary*, *unum sufficit*'.[112] And many in his society required little coaxing to fashion a sacrificial victim out of an aristocrat's execution. The Earl of Northumberland wrote to Dudley Carleton referring to 'my Lo: of Essex marterdowm', and there was a story circulating of 'a certayne man [who] weares a litell neck-bone of his, which the giddie executioner of the first unluckie stroake forcst from the rebound of his valiant and hardie neck'.[113] Indeed, the post-Reformation generations remained eager to secure alternative, secular sites of veneration and the realm of politics continued to offer rich pickings: it was reported that on the spot in the Tower grounds where Essex was executed there was 'a bloudie circle ... in which ... no grasse springs up ... as if they were loathe to runne their blades through his blood that suffered once alreadie'.[114]

Postscript: the afterlives of Essex

Years later, in his poetic collection *Idea* (1619), Michael Drayton lamented to his Jacobean readers, 'Lastly mine Eyes amazedly haue seene/ESSEX great fall, TYRONE his Peace to gaine'.[115] Clearly subscribing to such sentiments in the mid-seventeenth century, Francis Osbourne argued that there was 'no act' of Elizabeth's which 'registred so contrary to the grain of her own people, as the death of this man', yet he added that 'if *Essex* had been try'd by a *Peerage* of *Angels,* they would have passed a like *sentence* upon him, or exposed *Monarchy* to contempt'.[116] Indeed, the ambition of the earl had never been in question. At the arraignment of Essex, the government's attorney, Sir Edward Coke, had argued in his customary inflammatory manner that the earl '*affected to be* Robert *the first of that name King of England*'. With a little more moderation, Gervase Markham later honoured 'Robert (surnamed the Great) Earle of *Essex*, a man of whom it behoueth euery man to be carefull how to write'.[117]

The dual themes of Essex's political ambition and Elizabeth's *penchant* for royal favourites offered an irresistible narrative resource for a great number of authors throughout Europe in the seventeenth century (and beyond). In an illuminating study, Wim Husken has drawn attention to the little known Dutch rhetoricians' play from the province of Zeeland which survives in 1629 and 1694 scribal versions, but would appear to have been written very close to the date of the earl's execution. Here, much is made of the collapse of Essex's heroic potential (Ralegh – 'Like Darius and Julius Caesar, the earl has finally fallen into disgrace'),[118] and at the end of the play a regretful Elizabeth rehearses a *de casibus* narrative which stretches back to antiquity.[119] In general, however, what is remarkable about the literary (rather than historiographical) afterlives of Essex is how frequently he becomes locked for succeeding generations in a narrative of erotic defeat, rather than one of overweening pride, or political aspiration. Phineas Fletcher's poetic narrative *The Purple Island* (1633), for example, pauses not to contemplate an abortive *coup d'état*, but an anguished separation between a sovereign and her most favourite subject: 'But (ah!) no joy her dying heart contented,/Since she a deare Deers side unwilling rented;/Whose death she all too late, too soon, too much, repented'.[120] Thomas Heywood's political romance *The Royall King and Loyall Subject* (written c. 1600?, first pub. 1637?) has its protagonist, the Lord Martiall, feasting foreign dignitaries, and beset by court emnities (in the same manner as Daniel's Philotas). However, if, in the midst of multiple marital wrangles, the jealous king ousts the Lord Martiall from his court ('Since he a Subject would precede his Prince'),[121] the play ends pondering the precarious fate of those who become too involved with sovereigns.

Barnabe Barnes's wish that 'it had so pleased God, that [Essex] might have died in the warres upon the enemies of his countrey, that I might heroically with good cheere have registred his death', was taken up a year later across the Channel in the *Histoire de la Vie et Mort dv Comte d'Essex avec vn Discours Grave et Eloquent de la Royne d'Angleterre au Duc de Biron sur ce subiect* (1607).[122] The latter remains strikingly supportive of Elizabeth's actions, and of the royal prerogative in general: 'Il vaudroit mieux mourir après quelque glorieuse action, que de commettre quelque chose au surplus de la vie qui en dès-honore la mémoire'.[123] The Spanish play *Dar la Vida por su Dama. El Conde de Sex* (1600?)[124] has been variously attributed down the centuries to Antonio Coello, and to Luis Velez de Guevara, for example. However, this 'Comedia Famosa ... De un ingenio de esta corte'[125] is much more representative of a narrative tradition, which would be established for centuries to come, in detailing the love wrangles, in this case, between 'El Conde de Sex' and 'La Reyna Doña Isabel'.[126]

Nonetheless, it was writers in France who remained most seduced by this possibility of yoking together a *tragédie d'amour* with a *tragédie d'état.* Recent British history had earlier been presented to French audiences in the shape of Antoine de Montchrestien's *L'Ecossaise* (1601).[127] For his *Le Comte dEssex. Tragedie* (1650), la Calprenède made the rather surprising claim (at least to modern eyes) that he had invented nothing whatsoever: 'ie n'ay rien escrit que sur de bonnes memoires que i'en avois receuës de personnes de condition'.[128] At the opening of the drama, the anguished 'reine Elisabeth', like so many later Racinian heroines, discovers that her soul 'Esleve dans son sein le serpent qui la tuë',[129] but (to complicate matters even further) she has a rival in Madame Cecile! Essex has plotted with Tyrone to seize the throne, but now in captivity he faces the constant possibility of a death sentence from his irresolute sovereign: Elisabeth – 'il se faut perdre, &. ie veux qu'auiourd'huy/Le traitre perissait ie perisse avec luy'.[130] Enforcing a political dimension to the intrigue, a rather fatalistic Comte de Soubtantonne (or Southampton) confirms to the hero that

> La puissance des Rois ne peut estre bornée,
> ... Nous sommes leur ioüet, & l'inconstante main
> Qui nous hausse auiourd'huwy nous rabaisse demain.[131]

However, the potential for fully fledged neo-classical drama dissipates as all attentions become focused upon whether or not Madame Cecile will pass on a ring from the earl to the queen (as a symbolic petition for clemency).[132] Later in the century, Thomas Corneille's *Le Comte D'Essex* (1678) does away with any need at all for a political backdrop, and transports us into the middle of a *crise passionnelle* in which Essex is in love with the queen's lady-in-waiting, and a jealous Elizabeth is determined to marry her off to the Duc d'Irton. Essex's acts of resistance are interpreted as political in tenor, and so the imperious queen seeks her revenge:

> Elisabeth (to the Duchesse d'Irton)
> Non, il faut qu'il périsse, et que je suis vangée,
> Je dois ce coup funeste à ma flamme outragée,
> Il a trop merité l'Arrest qui le punit,
> Innocent ou coupable, il vous aime, il suffit.[133]

As John Florio *helpfully* reminded his early modern readers, 'Wordes they are women, and deeds they are men',[134] and in many ways the textual remembering of the Elizabeth-and-Essex narrative constituted repeated attempts to dissolve their political identities and to contain them within a less troubling, affective world of foiled desire. The prose narrative *Le Comte D'Essex. Histoire Angloise* (1678) described another *histoire d'amour royale*, and responded very much to the tastes of an audience which was enjoying the publication of Madame de Lafayette's *La Princesse de Clèves* in the same year. Here, Elisabeth has as her confidante the Comtesse de Nottingham, and is principally significant for her anguished feelings of attraction for her unruly subject: 'il n'y a point de consolation pour moy, si le Comte d'Essex perit. Par l'état où sa prison me met, iugez de celuy où sa perte povrroit me reduire'.[135] Such was the success of the prose romance that it was published in English at the beginning of the next century as *The History of the Most Renowned Queen Elizabeth and her Great Favourite, the Earl of Essex. In Two Parts. A Romance* (1700): 'But the Queen could not forbear Loving, yet she used all imaginable Caution to prevent the Discovery of that Passion it was not in her Power to conceal'.[136]

The fascination with this intrigue continued in England into the Restoration and beyond into the eighteenth century. John Banks's *The Unhappy Favourite, or, The Earl of Essex a Tragedy* (1682) clearly presents a thwarted hero ('The

World had not a Favourite so great,/So lov'd as I'),[137] and establishes definitively the templates of theme and intrigue for the English stage, with a spurned Countess of Nottingham pressing Burleigh to bring about Essex's downfall after his return from Ireland:

> Now famous *Cecil, England* owes to thee
> More than *Rome's* State did once to *Cicero* pay,
> That crusht the vast Designs of *Cataline.*[138]

There is a good deal of classicising allusion throughout which recalls the eulogies of Essex's contemporaries, but the inanities of the verse did nothing to impair its rapturous reception in the London theatre, as *The Tatler* acknowledged: '*The Earl of Essex* is a Tragedy in which there is not one good Line, and yet was never seen without drawing Tears from some part of the Audience ... it is impossible, for one unprejudiced, to see it untouched with pity'.[139]

Theatrical success inevitably bred imitation, and in the next century Ralph James's *The Fall of the Earl of Essex ... Alter'd from the Unhappy Favourite of Mr. Banks* (1731) was followed by Henry Jones's *The Earl of Essex. A Tragedy* (1753). Here again, we discover Essex held in the Tower, bereft of his sovereign lady and victim to the factional struggles led by a Burleigh and/or a Ralegh, and sometimes a jealous woman, such as a Countess of Nottingham: Burleigh – ''Tis gone too far, he dies – proud Essex now,/Or Cecil falls'.[140] In turn, Jones's dramatic narrative maps out much of Henry Brooke's *The Earl of Essex. A Tragedy* (1761); interestingly, however, there is a much greater patriotic note being struck here in a manner not untypical of mid-Georgian 'historical' drama. In Brooke's Prologue read by 'Mrs. Sheridan', we learn that rather than the 'new Electras and new Phaedras' of Athens, or the 'Theban monarchs' of French tragedy, 'Much more a British story should impart/The warmest feelings to each British heart'.[141]

By way of conclusion, it is fitting to return to the place where this discussion began, late Elizabethan England. Some six months after Essex's execution, the queen played host to the Duke of Byron, and Camden later reported that at this meeting she 'sharply accused the Earle of *Essex* of ingratitude, rash counsailes and wilfull disdaining to aske pardon'. Nonetheless, Camden gave short shrift to 'certaine French writers' who affirmed that 'shee shewed [Essex's] skull in her priuate Chappell, or (as others write) fastned vpon a pole, to *Byron* and the Frenchmen, it is a ridiculous vanity, for it was buried together with his body'.[142] From his final captivity, the earl had complained to his sovereign that 'The prating tavern haunter speaks of me what he lists; the frantic libeller writes of me what he lists; already they print me and make me speak to the world, and shortly they will play me in what forms they list upon the stage'.[143] The truth of this matter is not in doubt; as we have seen, Europe itself lost no time in staging his travails, and Essex continued to be fashioned in an increasing number of guises for seventeenth-century consumption. When Philip Julius, Duke of Stettin-Pomerania, visited the realm of the ageing queen in 1602, the earl had already become a tourist attraction at the Tower of London:

> Als wir hinunter auf den Platz kommen ward uns der Ort gezeiget, da der tapfere Held Graf von Essex enthauptet und in der nächst dabei leigenden Kapelle begraben worden. Wie lieb und werth dieser Graf in dem ganzen Reich gehalten, stehet genugsam daraus zu ersehen, dass sein Lied darinnen er der Königin und dem ganzen Lande valediciret, und auch die Ursache seines Unglücks anzeignet, hin und wieder im Reiche, ja in dem königl. Hoflager sebsten in unserer Gegenwart ist gesungen und auf Instrumenten gespielet worden, da doch seine Memoria als eines rei majestatis publico judico damniret.[144]

Ironically, like Ralegh, Essex would become significant for many, as the century unfolded, for his cultural capital as a royal victim, and his name continued to be exploited for political purposes by anti-royalist writers: the year 1624, for example, saw the publication of the pamphlet *Robert Earle of Essex his Ghost; Sent from Elizian: To the Nobility, Gentry, and Communaltie of England.*

Over the course of his lifetime, the mythologies of Essex (in which writers *and* the earl himself deeply invested) were both numerous and diverse. At Elizabeth's court, he began his career having a particular affection for the identities of knight errant and courtly lover, though these were displaced increasingly as the 1590s wore on: he strove tirelessly for national, nay international recognition as a man of state, a spymaster and as a distinguished military commander. The cultural mediation of all of these various *personae* was shaped in one way or another by his reputation for intellectual pursuits, most especially classical study. He and his affinity sought confirmation of the extraordinary nature of the Essex destiny by constantly invoking the names of heroes and warriors from Greece, Rome, Israel and the Judaea of antiquity. George Carleton's unveiling of Ostrosaxonides, hero of the East Saxons, in the years directly after the earl's execution remains perhaps the most arresting, most imaginative fashioning of a national hero for early modern consumption. Thereafter, he was all too often reduced to the principal role of anguished lover, of romantic lead on European stages during the seventeenth and eighteenth centuries – and indeed into the nineteenth century with *Roberto Devereux* (1837), Donizetti's opera or *tragedia lirica*, in which the by now very familiar love triangle of Elizabeth, Essex and the Duchess of Nottingham was given yet another airing for a willing audience.

However, it is perhaps timely to remember at the end of this discussion that we may not need to travel quite so far from the closing years of the Tudor century to discover striking incarnations of Elizabeth's last favourite. In fact, it would take no longer than a couple of weeks after the earl's execution for him to be accommodated into the narratives of myths and legends which had haunted him throughout his adult life.

> Strange rumours are noised about of three rainbows seen in the Tower, and of a spectre appearing in the place where the Earl of Essex was beheaded. Others

tell of a bloody block, seen by the guards, falling from heaven to earth upon that spot.[145]

Notes

1 See *Gesta Grayorum, or, The history of the high and mighty prince, Henry Prince of Purpoole* (London: W. Canning, 1688), pp. 25–26. Perithous, king of Thessaly, was the closest friend of the mythical hero Theseus. Patroclus, son of the Argonaut Menoetius, went into exile into the realm of Phitia, met the royal prince Achilles there and they remained the closest of friends. Pilades, or Pylades, was the cousin (and perhaps lover) of the doomed prince Orestes in Greek myth. The general Lelius, or Gaius Laelius, had been the closest friend of the Roman military commander Scipio Africanus since childhood.

2 Thomas Dekker, *Old Fortunatus* (London: William Apsley, 1600), sig. A1v.

3 (18th?) August 1596. Francesco Gradenigo to Venetian ambassador in France. CSP Venetian ix.505. quoted in G. B. Harrison (ed.), *Elizabethan and Jacobean Journals 1591–1610*, vol. II, *A Second Elizabethan Journal* (London/New York: Routledge, 1931, reprint 2001), p. 130.

4 For further discussion here, see Simon Adams, 'The Patronage of the Crown in Elizabethan Politics: the 1590s in Perspective', in *The Reign of Elizabeth I: Court and Culture in the Last Decade*, ed. John Guy (Cambridge: Cambridge University Press, 1995), p. 26.

5 However, it should be noted that even as a young boy, Essex had been taught to consider the illustrious destiny which awaited him. See the dedicatory epistle to Richard Davies, *A funerall sermon preached the xxvi. day of Nouember in the yeare of our Lord M.D.LXXVI. in the parishe church of Caermerthyn, by the Reuerende Father in God, Richard by the permission of God, Bishoppe of Saint Dauys, at the buriall of the Right Honourable Walter Earle of Essex and Ewe* (London: Henry Denham, 1577), sig. ¶2v–¶3r. As Cecil's ward, the young earl had been first introduced to this exclusive world at the Christmas festivities of 1577–78.

6 Robert Devereux, 2nd Earl of Essex, *An Apologie of the Earle of Essex, Against those which iealously, and maliciously, tax him to the Hinderer of the Peace and Quite of his Country … penned by himself. Anno 1598* (London: J. Smethwick?, 1603), sig. A2v. Devereux spent the winter of 1584–85 at his uncle's house in Lamphey in Pembrokeshire.

7 See Henry Elliot Malden (ed.), 'Devereux Papers, with Richard Broughton's *Memoranda* (1575–1601)', *Camden Miscellany* xiii, 1923, p. 22. Richard Broughton was brother to the leading Hebraist, Hugh Broughton. Essex was at Trinity College during the years 1577–81.

8 Thomas Moffett (1553–1604), *Healths Improvement* (1655), p. 60: 'whilst I lay there in Camp with that flower of Chivalry the Earl of *Essex*'.

9 Philip Gawdy to his Brother, 8 December 1592. See Philip Gawdy, *Letters of Philip Gawdy of West Harling, Norfolk, and of London to Various Members of his Family 1579–1616*, ed. Isaac Herbert Jeayes (London: J.B. Nichols & Sons, 1906), p. 67. For an account of Essex's profile at the Accession Day tilts, see R. McCoy, '"A dangerous image": the Earl of Essex and Elizabethan Chivalry', *Journal of Medieval and Renaissance Studies* 13 (1983), pp. 313–329.

10 'Anglorum Feriae' (Accession Day, 17 November 1595), in George Peele, *The Life and Minor Works of George Peele*, 3 vols, ed. David H. Horne (New Haven, CT: Yale University Press, 1952), vol. I, p. 271.

11 'the Britons, wholly sundered from all the world'. See Virgil, *Eclogues, Georgics, Aeneid I–VI*, English trans. H. Rushton Fairclough, revised G. P. Goold (Cambridge, MA: Harvard University Press – Loeb Classical Library, 1999), pp. 28–29. Unless indicated otherwise (as is the case above), the translations which follow in the notes are my own.

12 See Steven W. May, 'The Poems of Edward de Vere, Seventeenth Earl of Oxford and of Robert Devereux, Second Earl of Essex', *Studies in Philology* 77: 5 (1980), p. 44. For further discussion here, see Paul E. J. Hammer, 'Upstaging the Queen: the Earl of Essex, Francis Bacon, and the Accession Day Celebrations of 1595', in *The Politics of the Stuart Court Masque.* eds David Bevington and Peter Holbrook (Cambridge: Cambridge University Press, 1998), pp. 41–66.

13 For critical discussions here, see: Annaliese Connolly and Lisa Hopkins, *Goddesses and Queens: the Iconography of Elizabeth* (Manchester: Manchester University Press, 2007); Susan Frye, *Elizabeth I: the Competition for Representation* (Oxford: Oxford University Press, 1993); Helen Hackett, *Virgin Mother, Maiden Queen: Elizabeth I and the Cult of the Virgin Mary* (Houndmills: Macmillan, 1995); Louis Montrose, *The Subject of Elizabeth. Authority, Gender and Representation* (Chicago: Chicago University Press, 2006); Julia M. Walker (ed.), *Dissing Elizabeth: Negative Representations of Gloriana* (Durham, NC: Duke University Press, 1998).

14 Quoted in Guy, *The Reign of Elizabeth* I, p. 17.

15 Quoted in Paul E. J. Hammer, *The Polarisation of Elizabethan Politics: The Political Career of Robert Devereux, 2nd Earl of Essex, 1585–1597* (Cambridge: Cambridge University Press, 1999), p. 92. This cross-border correspondence appears to have had its beginnings in 1589.

16 Indeed, at the end of the 1580s Essex already warranted attention. He had attracted the eye of the queen, enjoyed positions of command during Leicester's campaign in the Netherlands in 1585 and at the time of the defensive measures against the Armada. He was made a Knight of the Garter in 1588 and was awarded the lucrative right to the levy on sweet wines in 1589 (which he enjoyed for the next ten years).

17 For further discussion here, see Hammer, *The Polarisation of Elizabethan Politics*, p. 212ff.

18 Thomas Bradshaw, *The Shepherds Starre* (London: William Jones, 1591), sig. ¶3r. This publication is dedicated to Essex. However, such publications by no means monopolised the petitions for Essex's attention: they ranged widely in tenor from the translation of Henry Holland's *Treatise Against VVitchcraft* (1590), Simon Kellwaye's *A Defensatiue Against the Plague* (1593), to Thomas Middleton's *The Wisdome of Solomon Paraphrased* (1597).

19 See respectively: Edmund Spenser, *The Faerie Queene* (London: William Ponsonby, 1590), p. 601; Barnabe Barnes, *Parthenophil and Parthenophe* (London: John Wolfe, 1593), p. 147. Barnes's epithet would find its counterweight in Robert Pricket's *Honors Fame in Triumph Riding* (London: Roger Jackson, 1604) in which Devereux's enemies were referred to: 'There are certain polititians in this age, not vnlike the Grecian Orators, which Diogenes called … thrise double men' (p. 3).

20 Respectively: 'most illustrious and most honourable Robert Earl of Essex & Ewe'; 'under the shade of your name (as that Homeric Teucer under the shield of Ajax)' – Sir John Hayward, *The First Part of the Life and Raigne of King Henrie the* [IV] *Extending to the end of the first yeare of his raigne* (London: John Wolfe, 1599), sig. A2r. Teucer,

the half-brother of Ajax, fired his arrows during the Trojan siege while protected by Ajax's shield. I am particularly grateful here and throughout this discussion for the illuminating glosses and commentaries which the classicist Dr Judith Owen, Bangor University, has shared with me during the preparation of this research.

21 Respectively: 'most excellent Earl' Alberico Gentili, *De Iure Belli, Commentatio secunda* (London: John Wolfe, 1589), sig. A2r; 'most noble Essex', *De Iure Belli, Commentatio tertia* (London: John Wolfe, 1589), sig. A2r; 'most illustrious Earl of Essex', *De Iniustitia Bellica Romanorum Actio* (Oxford: Joseph Barnes, 1590), sig. ¶3r.

22 Respectively: 'to the most illustrious and most noble hero', William Gager, *Meleager Tragoedia noua* (Oxford: Joseph Barnes, 1592), sig. A2r; 'new-born Phoebus', George Carleton, *Heroici Characteres* (Oxford: Joseph Barnes, 1603), p. 19; William Covell, *Polimanteia* (Cambridge and London: John Legate and J. Orwin, 1595), sig. Q3r.

23 Gervase Markham, *Honour in his Perfection* (London: Benjamin Fisher, 1624), p. 27. Interestingly, if the adolescent Essex is reported in 1578 as referring to Cambridge as 'Ithacam meam', Markham adds wistfully that such were the adult Earl's seductive charms that 'his youth and beauty he might, like *Pirocles,* have made *Basilius* doat on his sweetnesse' (ibid. p. 27). For further discussion of *Honour in his Perfection,* see Chapter 2.

24 'an easy battle, a difficult war'.

25 Letter dated May 1596 addressed to the Lords of the Council. See Walter Bourchier Devereux, *Lives and Letters of the Devereux, Earls of Essex in the Reigns of Elizabeth, James I and Charles I, 1540–1646* (London: John Murray, 1853), vol. I, p. 350.

26 Quoted in E. M. Tenison, *Elizabethan England: Being the history of this Country 'In Relation to all foreign Princes' ... From Original Manuscripts, many hitherto unpublished,* 13 vols, vol. X (1953), pp. 166–167.

27 Letter to Anthony Bacon (1594?), see Devereux, *Lives and Letters,* vol. I, p. 292.

28 Published after Essex's execution in Francis Davison, *A Poeticall Rapsodie ...* (1602), sig. E9r. See also 'Introduction' in this volume.

29 Richard Grenewey, 'To the Right Honorable Robert Earle of Essex and Ewe', in *Annales of Cornelius Tacitus. The Description of Germanie,* ed. J. R. Tanner (1598), pp. 2–3.

30 For a full and illuminating discussion of Essex's secretariat, see Paul E. J. Hammer, 'The Earl of Essex, Fulke Greville, and the Employment of Scholars', *Studies in Philology* 91: 2 (Spring 1994), pp. 167–180.

31 Bodleian Library, Ashmolean MS. 1729 fo. 189, quoted in Lisa Jardine and Anthony Grafton, '"Studied for Action": How Gabriel Harvey read his Livy', *Past and Present* 11: 129 (1990), p. 33. It is later reported by Camden that the condemned Essex said to Cuffe, 'Aske pardon of God and the Queenes Maiesty, and see you deserue it. For my part, my minde is wholly fixed vpon another life, I haue resolued to deale sincerely before God and men: and I cannot but tell you this plainely, you were the principall man that moued mee to this perfidiousnesse'. See William Camden, *The Historie of the Life and Reigne of the most renowmed and victorious Princesse Elizabeth, late Queene of England* (1630), year 1601, p. 187.

32 Richard Harvey, *A Theologicall Discourse of the Lamb of God and his enemies* (London: W. Ponsonby, 1590), sig. A2v.

33 Fritz Levy, 'The Theatre and the Court in the 1590s', in *The Reign of Elizabeth I,* ed. Guy, p. 299.

34 IV.i. See Samuel Daniel, *Certaine Small Poems lately printed with the tragedie of Philotas* (London: Simon Waterson and Edward Blount, 1605), sig. D5v.

35 Created Earl of Devonshire by James I.

36 '[caught] in the history of the time'.

37 Cal. S. P.: Dom. James I, vol. xi (1604?), quoted in Samuel Daniel, *The Tragedy of Philotas by Samuel Daniel*, ed. Laurence Michel (New Haven, CT: Yale University Press, 1949), p. 37. Michel also establishes illuminating parallels between the language of Daniel's dramatic narrative and that of Essex's trial record (p. 50ff). The play is recorded as having been acted by the Children of the Queen's Revels in January 1605.

38 'True leader, Devereux, and more true than Hercules, for he [Hercules] once saw Cadiz, [whereas] he [Essex] also conquered it at the same time'. See Devereux, *Lives and Letters,* I, note 1, p. 379.

39 See respectively: G. W. Groos (ed.), *The Diary of Baron Waldstein. A Traveller in Elizabethan England* (London: Thames and Hudson, 1981), pp. 105–7; 'Ad Essexium Comitis Illustrissimus' (1599) in Bodleian MS. 990 Les Proverbes de Saloman. This manuscript contains, amongst others, three Latin poems dedicated to Essex by Andrew Melvin, Robert Pollock and John Johnstone. Melvin's 'Ad Essexium Comitis Illustrissimus' includes the phrase (in translation) 'Thine is the right hand Hercules'. See Tenison, *Elizabethan England,* vol. XI (1956), p. 2.

40 Respectively: 'the spirit of Hector and might of Hercules'; 'the greater Jason'; 'the British Hercules'. See Carleton, *Heroici Characteres,* pp. 20, 42. Analogies with Achilles and Jason also occur, for example, at p. 22.

41 See respectively: Robert Harvey, *Philadelphus or A defence of Brutes, and the Brutans History* (London: John Wolfe, 1593), p. 106; Thomas Heywood, *Troia Britanica: or, Great Britaines Troy* (London: William Jaggard, 1609), p. 163.

42 'another (latter-day) Achilles'.

43 See respectively: 'Epistle Dedicatorie', in Vincentio Saviolo, *His Practise in two Bookes. The first intreating of the vse of the Rapier and Dagger. The second, of Honor and honorable Quarrels* (1595), N. pag.; letter from Pérez to Essex, 26 November 1595, in *A Spaniard in Elizabethan England: The Correspondence of Antonio Pérez's Exile,* ed. Gustav Ungerer (London: Tamesis, 1974), vol. 1, p. 368; Virginia F. Stern, *Gabriel Harvey. His Life, Marginalia and Library* (Oxford: Clarendon Press, 1979), p. 153.

44 See respectively: George Chapman, *Seauen Bookes of the Iliades of Homere, Prince of poets* (London: John Windet, 1598), sig. A4r, A3r; George Chapman, *Achilles Shield Translated as the Other Seuen Bookes of Homer, out of his eighteenth booke of Iliades* (London: John Windet, 1598), sig. B1r.

45 For easily accessible and important critical reviews of this cultural association of Essex and Achilles in the early modern period, see: 'Introduction', to Shakespeare, *Troilus and Cressida,* ed. David Bevington (London: Arden/Cengage, 1998), pp. 11–19; 'Introduction', in William Shakespeare, *Troilus and Cressida,* ed. Jonathan V. Crewe (Harmondsworth: Penguin/Pelican Shakespeare, 2000), p. xxiff.

46 Furthermore, after the deaths of both Essex and his sovereign, Robert Pricket intriguingly styled Elizabeth as Thetis, mother to Achilles. See Pricket, *Honors Fame in Triumph Riding* (Londno: Roger Jackson, 1604), p. 16.

47 PRO, SP 78/25, fols. 88v, 99V; PRO, SP 106/2, fol. 141r, quoted in Hammer, *Polarisation of Elizabethan Politics,* p. 101.

48 David Jardine (ed.), *Criminal Trials,* 2 vols (London: Charles Knight, 1832), vol. I, p. 351.

49 The robust critical debate surrounding which playtext was performed on this occasion continues, as indeed the present collection bears witness. Challenges to the view that the performance commissioned by the Essex entourage was indeed that of Shakespeare's *Richard II* have been put forward, for example, by: Leeds Barroll, 'A

New History for Shakespeare and his Time', *Shakespeare Quarterly* 39 (1988), pp. 441–464; and in Blair Worden's correspondence with Frank Kermode in *The London Review of Books,* beginning 10 July 2003, p. 23. For more recent contributions to this debate, see Chris Fitter, 'Historicising Shakespeare's *Richard II*: Current Events, Dating and the Sabotage of Essex', *Early Modern Literary Studies* 11: 2 (September 2005); and Paul E. J. Hammer, 'Shakespeare's *Richard II,* the Play of 7 February 1601, and the Essex Rising', *Shakespeare Quarterly* 59: 1 (Spring 2008), pp. 1–35.

50 William Barlow, *A Sermon Preached at Paules Crosse* (London: Matthew Law, 1601), sig. C3v. Fearing censure in the same manner as Daniel for praising the fallen earl, Fulke Greville's version of the Antony and Cleopatra story was consigned to the flames: 'This sudden descent of such greatnesse, together with the quality of the Actors in every Scene, stir'd up the Authors second thoughts, to bee carefull (in his own case) of leaving faire weather behind him.' See Fulke Greville, *The Life of the Renowned Sr Philip Sidney* (London: Henry Seile, 1652), p. 179.

51 See Chapter 6, esp. pp. 143–145ff. Critical discussions have continued to propose Mountjoy as the possible focus for this celebratory passage. See, for example: Warrren D. Smith, 'The *Henry V* Choruses in the First Folio', *Journal of English and Germanic Philology* 53 (1954), pp. 38–57; David Bevington, *Tudor Drama and Politics: A Critical Approach to Topical Meaning* (Cambridge, MA: Harvard University Press, 1968), p. 290; Christopher Highley, 'Wales, Ireland, and 1 Henry IV', *Renaissance Drama* 21 (1990), pp. 108–109; Richard Dutton, '"Methinks the Truth Should Live from Age to Age": The Dating and Contexts of *Henry V*', *Huntington Library Quarterly* 68: 1 & 2 (2005), pp. 173–204. I am indebted here and elsewhere in this discussion to the editors for their recommendations of additional critical sources.

52 Barnabe Barnes, *Foure Bookes of Offices, enabling privat persons for the speciall seruice of all good princes and policies* (London: Adam Islip, 1606), p. 180. The Roman military commander and dictator Sylla is described at length by the first century B.C. Roman historian Sallust in his history of the Jugurthine War, *Bellum Iugurthinum.*

53 Devereux, *An Apologie of the Earle of Essex,* sig. A3v.

54 Hammer, *Polarisation of Elizabethan Politics,* p. 307. See also Hammer, 'The Uses of Scholarship: the Secretariat of Robert Devereux, Second Earl of Essex, c. 1585–1601', *English Historical Review* 109: 430 (February 1994), pp. 26–51.

55 'he calls'.

56 See respectively: inventory of Essex House after execution excerpted in Tenison, *Elizabethan England,* vol. XI (1956), p. xl; BL, Cotton MS Vespasian FXIII, fol. 290r, quoted in Hammer, *Polarisation,* p. 308, note 204.

57 'like a torrent'.

58 'A. B. to the Reader', in Henry Savile, *The Ende of Nero and Beginning of Galba Fower bookes of the Histories of Cornelius Tacitus. The life of Agricola* (Oxford: Joseph Barnes, 1591), sig. ¶3r.

59 See respectively: 'Conversations with William Drummond, ll. 372–373, in Ben Jonson, *The Complete Poems,* ed. George Parfitt (Harmondsworth: Penguin, 1975, reprint 1996), p. 471; Ben Jonson, *Ben Jonson,* vol. I 'The Man and his Work', ed. C. H. Herford and Percy and Evelyn Simpson (Oxford: Clarendon Press, 1925), p. 167, note 368. Frances A. Yates also discussed the oblique referencing of A.B. as Essex from the *Worlde of Wordes* (1598) in *John Florio: The Life of an Italian in Shakespeare's England,* ed. Yates (Cambridge: Cambridge University Press, 1934), p. 198.

60 William Camden, *Annales or, The History of the Most Renowned and Victorious Princesse Elizabeth, Late Queen of England … Written in Latin by the Learned Mr William Camden. Translated into English by R. N. Gent* (3rd edn 1635), p. 532.

61 Camden's work was, of course, published after her death.

62 Clapham continues, 'She also translated Boethius, *De Consolatione Philosophiae,* and a treatise of Plutarch, *De Curiositate,* with diverse others.' See John Clapham, *Elizabeth of England. Certain Observations concerning the Life and Reign of Queen Elizabeth by John Clapham,* eds Evelyn Plummer Read and Conyers Read (Oxford: Oxford University Press, 1951), p. 89.

63 Jardine, *Criminal Trials,* vol. 1, p. 315. Francis Bacon also affirmed that, during the trial, Queen's Counsel declared the accomplices ('Sir Christopher Blunt, Sir Charles Davers, Sir John Davies, Sir Gillie Mericke, and Henry Cuffe'), 'were but like the president of the protestation vsed by *Manlius* the Lieutenant of *Catiline,* that conspired against the State of Rome'. See Bacon, *A Declaration of the Practises & Treasons attempted and committed by Robert late Earle of Essex and his complices* (London: Robert Barker, 1601), sig. I4v.

64 See Jonson, *Ben Jonson,* vol. I, p. 37.

65 See Tenison, *Elizabethan England,* vol. XI (1956), p. 526.

66 See Chapter 1, pp. 26–32ff.

67 Francesco Colonna, *Hypnerotomachia = The Strife of Loue in a Dreame* (London: Simon Waterson, 1592), sig. A2r.

68 'most pleased to have Sir Philip Sidney restored in him [i.e. Essex]'. See respectively: *Academiae Cantabrigiensis lachrymae tumulo nobilissimi equitis, D. Philippi Sidneij* (1587); British Library MS Additional 4125 f. 164r, quoted in Maureen Claire King, '"Essex, that could vary himself into all shapes for a time": The Second Earl of Essex in Jacobean England', PhD thesis, University of Alberta, 2000, p. 17. Moreover, King's discussion of James VI/I's responses to Essex (and of Carleton's *Devoraxeidos* in particular) is meticulous and illuminating throughout this thesis.

69 George Peele, *An Eglogve Gratvlatorie* (London: Richard Jones, 1589), sig. A3v, A4r, B1r. In this context, see Hugh Gazzard, '"Many a Herdsman More Disposde to Mourn": Peele, Campion and the Portugal Expedition of 1589', *Review of English Studies* 57 (2006), 16–42.

70 Sir Thomas Smith, *Sir Thomas Smithes Voiage and Entertainment in Rushia* (1605), sig. D3v–D4r.

71 See respectively: Covell, *Polimanteia,* sig. Q3r; John Rainolds, *De Romanae Ecclesiae Idololatria* (Oxford: Joseph Barnes, 1596), sig. 4v.

72 Thomas Churchyard, *Fortunate Farewell to the most forward and noble Earle of Essex* (London: William Wood, 1599), sig. A2r.

73 See respectively: Carleton, *Heroici Characteres,* p. 20; Barnes, *Foure Bookes,* p. 179; W. H., *Englands Sorrowe or, A Farewell to Essex* (London: Henry Ricket, 1606), sig. B2v.

74 See, for example, Vincentio Saviolo, *His Practise in Two Bookes* (London: John Wolfe, 1595), sig. A3v; letter of Antonio Pérez to Essex dated 1 December 1595, in Ungerer, *A Spaniard,* 1.376.

75 William Camden, *Annales* (3rd edn 1635), p. 501.

76 See respectively: *Aeneid,* 8, p. 590ff; Edmund Spenser, 'Prothalamion', ll. 145, 163–167.

77 Ungerer, *A Spaniard,* II, p. 77.

78 See Paul E. J. Hammer, 'Essex and Europe: Evidence from Confidential Instructions by the Earl of Essex, 1595–6', *English Historical Review* 111: 441 (April 1996), p. 379.

79 See Hammer, 'Essex and Europe', p. 378.

80 'But, my lord, why do you find yourself in this sea-tempest? What about Juno who summons Aeolus and the winds and stirs them against you?' For the Latin text, see Ungerer, *A Spaniard,* I, p. 329. The association of Elizabeth with Juno is not without

precedent in this period. In his posthumously published *The Life of the Renowned Sr Philip Sidney* (1652), Fulke Greville unveils Elizabeth at close of her reign as a wrathful goddess resembling Virgil's Juno who calls upon the forces of the underworld (VII, p. 285ff.) to challenge Aeneas and his forces when her own endeavours have come to nothing: 'I discerned my Gracious Soveraigne to bee every way so invironed with these, not *Iupiter's*, but *Pluto's* thunder-workers; as it was impossible for Her to see any light, that might lead to grace, or mercy: but many encouraging Meteors of severity, as against an unthankfull favourite, and traiterous Subject'. In this case, however, the disoriented 'Soveraigne' is 'invironed' by Pluto's forces rather than controlling them (p. 181). See also Erasmus's examination of this passage from the *Aeneid* as the basis for an exercise in letters of request: *Collected Works of Erasmus*, ed. J. K. Sowards (Toronto: University of Toronto Press, 1985), vol. XXV, p. 172.

81 See Ungerer, *A Spaniard*, I, p. 354. This line (VII.312) is rendered in English as 'If Heaven I cannot bend, then Hell I will arouse!', in Virgil, *Aeneid VII–XII*, trans. H. Rushton Fairclough (Cambridge, MA: Harvard University Press, Loeb Classical Library, 2000), p. 25. Interestingly, this very quotation is taken up in the tricksy correspondence between James VI and Elizabeth in this period, although a wrathful English queen forces her cousin in a subsequent communication to stress that he had been earlier casting himself as Juno: 'I am Juno, ye are the rest of the gods, Bothwell is Aeneas, and other foreign princes are Acheron; Juno seeking aid of Acheron, then, was only for the wrack of Aeneas and no ways either for the invading or threatening of the rest of the gods.' See James VI/I, *Letters of King James VI & I*, ed. G. P. V. Akrigg (Berkeley, CA: University of California Press, 1984), pp. 131, 133.

82 'although my faith is greater than [that of] Aeneas'. For Latin text, see Ungerer, *A Spaniard*, I, p. 367.

83 In this correspondence, Essex is 'Ernestus' and James VI, 'Victor', HMC *Calendar of the Manuscripts of the Marquis of Salisbury*, 3.435. For a lively discussion here, see King, 'Essex, that could vary himself', p. 11. James himself was not averse to epic similes: he writes to Elizabeth, 'Now, madame, I have refuge to you at this time as my only pilot to guide me safely betwixt these Charybdis and Scylla'. See letter dated 13 April 1594, in *Letters*, ed. Akrigg, p. 128.

84 'was felled by the mighty right hand of Aeneas'.

85 Tenison, *Elizabethan England*, vol. XI (1956), p. 392.

86 See Edward Guilpin, *Skialetheia. Or, A shadowe of truth, in certaine epigrams and satyres* (London: Nicholas Ling, 1598), sig. C3v.

87 'full of valour and courage' – For the French text, see Philippe de Mornay, *Mémoires et correspondance pour servir a l'histoire de la Reformation*, 12 vols (Paris: Treuttel, 1824–25), V, p. 148, 'Lettre du Roy à M. De Beauvoir, ambassadeur pour sa majesté en Angleterre, janvier 1592'.

88 'interrupted by angry outbursts, insults and threats towards the Earl of Essex, that she would reduce him to the lowest rank in England, that he was making the [French] King believe that he was managed everything, and that she would show him how wrong he was'. For the French text, see Mornay, *Mémoires et correspondance*, V, p. 155, 'De M. Duplessis en Angleterre, en janvier 1592'. Essex himself acknowledged to Duplessis-Mornay that 'l'humeur de la royne a esté si amere, qu'il est impossible devant vostre partement de recevoir quelque aultre response' (p. 198) – 'the queen has been so choleric that it is impossible to obtain an alternative answer before your departure'.

89 John Speed, *The theatre of the empire of Great Britaine* (London: John Sudbury and George Humble, 1612), p. 865.

90 'If you are seek combat on horseback or on foot, I will declare that the King's cause is more just than that of the [Catholic] League, and that my Mistress is more beautiful than your own'. For the French text, see Devereux, *Lives and Letters*, I, p. 273.

91 André Hurault de Maisse, *A Journal of all that was Accomplished by Monsieur de Maisse, Ambassador of England from Henri IV to Queen Elizabeth anno domini 1597*, trans. and ed. G. B. Harrison and R. A. Jones (London: Nonesuch, 1931), pp. 7, 33–34.

92 'a new glory of these times appears and stands great, He of the East Saxons, brought together in this one man of ours the greater virtues of our forebears blaze forth'. See Carleton, *Heroici Characteres*, p. 20.

93 See Richard Williams, 'A Poore Man's Pittance', Part II: 'The Life and Death of Essex', in *Ballads from Manuscripts*, vol. II, ed. F. J. Furnivall and W. R. Morfill (Hertford: Ballad Society/Stephen Austin & Sons, 1873), stanza xv, p. 27.

94 See Andrew Clark (ed.), *The Shirburn Ballads 1585–1616* (Oxford: Clarendon, 1907), p. 326.

95 Bacon had written to his erstwhile patron that he 'was ever sorry, that your lordship should fly with waxen wings, doubting Icarus' fortune.' Indeed, Bacon later acknowledged in print that 'I would further say vnto him: My Lord, stand upon two feet, and fly not vpon two wings. The two feet are the two kinds of *Justice*, commutative and distributive'. See respectively: *The Letters and the Life of Francis Bacon including all his Occasional Works*, ed. James Spedding (London: Longman, 1862), vol. II, p. 191; vol. III, p. 145. Pursuing the same theme some five years later, John Speed relates that Essex found himself held in confinement after his return from Ireland so that he might 'somewhat to decline his lofty soaring, lest in mounting too high, he should melt his waxen wings against the hot Sunne' (Speed, *Great Britain*, p. 877). Interestingly, this image is also taken up (with reference to the author) in the Prologue to Henry Jones's *The Earl of Essex. A Tragedy* (1753),in *The British Theatre, or a Collection of Plays*, ed. Elizabeth Inchbald (London: Hurst, Robinson and Co., 1824), vol. I, p. vii.

96 See, for example, Richard Mulcaster's *The Passage of Most Dread Sovereign* (1558), in A. F. Pollard, *Tudor Tracts* (Westminster: A. Constable, 1903), p. 387. For modern critical discussions here, see: John N. King, *Tudor Royal Iconography: Literature and Art in an Age of Religious Crisis* (Princeton, NJ: Princeton University Press, 1989); Michele Osherow, '"A poore shepherde and his sling": A Biblical Model for a Renaissance Queen', in *Elizabeth I: Always Her Own Free Woman*, eds Carole Levin, Jo Eldridge Carney and Debra Barrett-Graves (Aldershot: Ashgate, 2003), p.122; Alexandra Walsham, '"A very Deborah?": The Myth of Elizabeth I as a Providential Monarch', in *The Myth of Elizabeth*, eds Susan Doran and Thomas S. Freeman (Houndmills: Palgrave MacMillan, 2003), pp. 143–168.

97 'To the Ri: Ho: the Earle of Essex, Great Master of the Horse', in Henry Lok, *Ecclesiastes or The Preacher* (London: Richard Field, 1597), p. 176.

98 Dedicatory epistle to Essex, in George Gyfford, *Sermons vpon the whole Booke of the Reuelation* (1596), sig. A5v. Quoted in Hammer, *Polarisation of Elizabethan Politics*, p. 213.

99 See Tenison, *Elizabethan England*, vol. X (1953), p. 299. There is some doubt whether Essex ever received this letter.

100 LPL, MS 657, fol. 134r. Quoted in Hammer, *Polarisation of Elizabethan Politics*, p. 141.

101 Devereux, *An Apologie* (1603), sigs A3r–A3v. See Chapter 7, esp. pp. 156–157ff. and Chapter 8, for fuller discussion of this publication.

102 Essex writing to Fulke Greville in 1599, quoted in Tenison, *Elizabethan England*, Vol. XI (1956), p. 1.

103 See respectively: Barnes, *Foure Bookes*, p. 180; Sir Henry Wotton, *A Parallel betweene Robert late Earle of Essex, and George late Duke of Buckingham* (London, 1641), p. 11.

104 Churchyard, *The Fortunate Farewell*, sig. A4r. Other contemporary sources also exploited biblical analogies in their account of the Irish campaign. See, for example: Lancelot Andrewes, *Sermon Preached before Queene Elizabeth, at Richmond, on the 21st February A. D. 1599 being Ash Wednesday* (London: D. Smith, 1629), p. 183; John Norden, *A Prayer for the Prosperous Proceedings and Good Successe of the Earle of Essex and His Companies* (London: E. Alde, 1599), sig. A3r. See also Paul E. J. Hammer, 'Myth-making: Politics, Propaganda and the capture of Cadiz in 1596', *The Historical Journal* 40 (1997), pp. 621–642.

105 Barnes, *Foure Bookes*, p. 179.

106 William Camden, *Annales* (3rd edn 1635), pp. 533–534.

107 Greville, *The Life of the Renowned Sr Philip Sidney*, pp. 185, 231.

108 Respectively: Sir John Harington to Sir Hugh Portman, Knight, 9 October 1601, Kelston Castle; Sir Robert Sidney to Sir John Harrington, 1600. See Sir John Harington, *Nugae Antiquae*, 2 vols (London: Vernor and Hood, 1769), vol. I, pp. 47, 121.

109 See respectively: Camden, *Annales* (1635), p. 551; David Lindsay, *Funerals of a right reuerend father in God Patrick Forbes of Corse, Bishop of Aberdfne* (Aberdeen: Edward Raban, 1631), p. 57. At Ralegh's trial, Edward Coke would contend that Essex died 'the child of God, and God honoured him at his death'. See Jardine, *Criminal Trials*, vol. I, p. 446.

110 Barlow, *A Sermon Preached at Paules Crosse*, sigs E2r–E2v.

111 Richard Williams, 'A Poore Mans Pittance', stanza xlvi, p. 33.

112 Respectively: 'worried about many things'; 'one thing is sufficient'. See: Anon, *Memoirs of the Life of Robert Devereux, Earl of Essex* (London: M. Cooper, 1753), p. 36. Steven W. May attributes the long poetic narrative 'The Passion of a Discontented Minde' to the pen of Essex as he awaited execution in the Tower of London. The text had been formerly attributed to Nicholas Breton. Here, the sinful but repentant voice draws upon a wide repertoire of Biblical figures. He fears to lose 'everlasting blisse … To live like cursed Caine, base, vile, abjected' (stanza 14), invokes Mary Magdalene (stanza 33) and the prodigal son (stanza 56), for example. See May, 'The Poems of Edward de Vere … and of Robert Devereux', esp. pp. 48–59.

113 See respectively: PRO SP 12/279 no. 59 f. 98r. quoted in King, 'Essex, that could vary himself', p. 35; from 'a manuscript of the time', in John Hutchins, *The History and Antiquities of the County of Dorset*, vol. IV (Dorchester: Dorset County Library, 1973 [1870]) note a, p. 219. This is also discussed in an illuminating manner in King, 'Essex, that could vary himself', p. 240.

114 Hutchins, *History and Antiquities*, IV, p. 219, note a. Drawing upon this widespread appetite for heroic veneration, *A Lamentable new ballad vpon the Earle of Essex death* concluded with a pious Earl affirming: 'I nere worshipt Saint, nor Angell in heauen/ Nor to the Uirgin Mary I,/But to Christ which for my sinnes did dye,/Trickling with sad teares in his sight:/Spreading my armes to God on high,/Lord Jesus, receiue my soule this night.' See Anon, *A lamentable new ballad vpon the Earle of Essex his death To the tune of, Essex last goodnight* (London: E. A., 1620).

115 Sonnet 51 in the collection 'Idea'. See Michael Drayton, *Poems* (London: John Smethwick, 1619), p. 270.

116 Francis Osborne, *A miscellany of sundry essayes, paradoxes, and problematicall discourses, letters and characters; together with politicall deductions from the history of the Earl of Essex, executed under Queen Elizabeth* (London: S. Royston, 1659), p. 229.

117 See respectively: Camden, *Annales* (3rd edn, 1635), p. 544; Markham, *Honour in his Perfection*, p. 26.

118 Wim Husken, 'Queen Elizabeth and Essex: A Dutch Rhetoricians' Play', *Leeds Studies in English*, vol. 32 (2001), p. 154.

119 Husken, 'Queen Elizabeth and Essex', p. 155.

120 Phineas Fletcher, *The Purple Island* (Cambridge: Thomas Buck and Roger Daniell, 1633), p. 36.

121 Thomas Heywood, *The Royall King and Loyall Subject* (London: James Becket, 1637), Act III, sig. F1r.

122 See respectively: Barnes, *Foure Bookes of Offices*, p. 181; Anon, *Histoire de la Vie et Mort dv Comte d'Essex avec vn Discours Grave et Eloquent de la Royne d'Angleterre au Duc de Biron sur ce subiect* (Paris, 1607), p. 17.

123 'It would be better to die in the wake of some great action, than to perform some unnecessary deed which besmirches one's memory.' For the French text, see Anon., *Histoire* (1607), pp. 16–17.

124 'To Give One's Life for One's Mistress. The Earl of Essex'. In this drama, the queen not only suspects that the Earl is in love with Blanca but that he has conspired to have her killed. In the aftermath of his execution, she comes across his last letter to Blanca in which he declares he would never harm the queen, but was desperate to rescue her from all danger. In the analysis of this text, I am very grateful to Dr Helena Miguelez-Carballeira, Bangor University, for kindly sharing her knowledge with me.

125 'celebrated drama ... based on the account of a wit at this court'.

126 This text is later published in Barcelona in 1638 as *Una, de Las Meiores Comedias, que hasta oy han salido*, 'One of the best dramas that has so far appeared'.

127 This austere Senecan drama progresses (often inexplicably, given the events related on stage) from Elizabeth's pardon to Mary's execution. However, it concentrates principally upon the anguished emotions of both women, related at some rhetorical length in the company of 'conseillères' or the 'choeur'.

128 'I have only written that which has been founded on the sound accounts which I have received from persons of quality'. For the French text, see 'Au Lecteur', in Gautier de Costes de la Calprenède, *Le Comte dEssex. Tragedie* (Paris, 1650), n. p.

129 'Nurtures in its breast the serpent which is killing her'.

130 'He must die, and I am resolved that on this day/The death of the traitor will be accompanied by my own.' For the French text, see la Calprenède, *Le Comte dEssex*, see respectively: I.i and I.iv, pp. 3, 11.

131 'There are no limits to the power of Kings/ ... We are their plaything, and the fickle hand/ Raises us up one day and throws us down on the next'. For the French text, see la Calprenède, *Le Comte dEssex*, I.v, p. 14.

132 The detail will come to play an increasing role in dramatic narratives down the generations and has its roots in an account circulating in the early seventeenth century that an English noblewoman on her deathbed confessed that she had failed to pass on a ring from Essex as a plea for mercy.

133 'No, he must die, and I must be avenged,/This deadly act is owed to my scorned passion,/He has only too well deserved the punishment of arrest,/It matters not whether he is guilty or innocent, it is enough that he loves you'. For the French text, see Thomas Corneille, *Le Comte D'Essex*, ed. Wendy Gibson (Exeter: University of Exeter Press, 2000), III.iv.1029–32, p. 48. Gibson also underlines that there is another 'Essex' play written in 1678 by de Boyer.

134 'Epistle Dedicatorie', in John Florio, *A Worlde of Wordes* (London: Edward Blount, 1598), sig. a4r.

135 'There is no consolation whatsoever for me if the Earl of Essex dies. Given the effect which his imprisonment has upon me, imagine in what state you would find me in at the news of his death'. For the French text, see Anon, *Le Comte D'Essex. Histoire Angloise* (Paris: Claude Barbin, 1678), p. 15.

136 Anon, *The History of the Most Renowned Queen Elizabeth and her Great Favourite, the Earl of Essex. In Two Parts. A Romance* (London, 1700), p. 3.

137 II.i, in John Banks, *The Unhappy Favourite, or, The Earl of Essex a Tragedy* (1682), p. 23.

138 III.i, in Banks, *The Unhappy Favourite*, p. 28.

139 See *The Tatler: or, Lucubrations of Isaac Bickerstaff, Esq.*, 4 vols (Dublin, 1777), vol. I, p. 90.

140 Act II, in Jones, *The Earl of Essex* (1753), p. 16.

141 Henry Brooke, *The Earl of Essex. A Tragedy* (Edinburgh, 1761), sig. A2v.

142 William Camden, *The historie of the most renowned and victorious princesse Elizabeth, late Queene of England* (1630), p. 199. In the next century, the rendering of Voltaire into English would make the very same point, together with a quite different conclusion: 'Several persons in France still imagine that Elizabeth put the earl of Essex to death merely from a fit of jealousy; and found their belief on a tragedy and a novel. But those who have read any thing know, that the queen was at that time seventy-eight years of age, and that the earl of Essex, finding the queen grown old, and hoping that her authority would decline with her years, had been guilty of an act of open rebellion, for which he was afterwards tried by his peers, who passed sentence of death upon him and his accomplices. Elizabeth would have enjoyed an unblemished fame, had she not sullied a reign, in other respects so glorious, by the murder which she ventured to perpetrate with the sacred sword of justice'. See Voltaire, *The works of M. de Voltaire. Translated from the French. With notes, historical and critical. By T. Smollett, M.D. T. Francklin, M.A. and others*, 34 vols (London: J. Newbery, 1762): vol. 5, ch. CXL, p. 24.

143 Devereux, *Lives and Letters*, vol. II, p. 99. For fuller discussion of the context of this letter, see Chapter 3, pp. 64–65ff.

144 'On descending to the courtyard, the spot was shown to us where the brave hero the Earl of Essex was beheaded, and lay buried in the chapel close by. How beloved and admired this Earl was throughout the kingdom, may be judged from the circumstance that his song, in which he takes leave of the Queen and the whole country, and in which also he shows the reason of his unlucky fate, is sung and played on musical instruments all over the country, even in our presence at the royal court, though his memory is condemned as that of a man having committed high treason.' Translated in Gottfried von Bülow (ed.), 'Diary of the Journey of Philip Julius, duke of Stettin-Pomerania, through England in the year 1602', *Transactions of Royal Historical Society*, 2ndseries 6 (1892), p. 15.

145 Richard Smith, *Rerum vulgatorum nota*, f. 55v (British Library, Sloan, 414, ff. 50–61), quoted in G. B. Harrison (ed.), *A Last Elizabethan Journal … 1599–1603* (London: Routledge & Kegan Paul, 1933, reprint 1974), p. 174.

6

'Bringing rebellion broached on his sword': Essex and Ireland

Chris Butler and Willy Maley

The short tenure of Robert Devereux, 2nd Earl of Essex, as Lieutenant of Ireland from 15 April to 25 September 1599 involved a complex web of connections, linking senior political figures, such as Robert Cecil and Hugh O'Neill, the 'rebel' Earl of Tyrone; persons from then-recent history, such as Robert's father, Walter Devereux; canonical literary heavyweights, including Shakespeare, Spenser and Marlowe; and now-neglected authors like Thomas Churchyard and Barnaby Rich. This tangled congeries unloops to some extent with Essex's disastrous campaign against Tyrone. Exploring the knots and threads of the Essex–Ireland web, drawing heavily on contemporary literary texts to supplement and complicate the contradictory assertions of 'factual' documents, this chapter links Irish involvement with challenges to royal authority, revealing the extent to which colonial context doubled as site of anti-courtly resistance. As Barnaby Rich put it in one of his last works, unpublished in his lifetime: 'thos wordes that in Englande would be brought wythin the compasse of treason, they are accounted wyth us in Ireland for ordynary table taulke'.[1] It is now commonly understood that Essex's Irish commission was a poisoned chalice; this chapter will assemble evidence confirming that understanding, but will also indicate the degree to which Essex was privy and party to seditious 'table taulke'.[2]

Given his known animus towards Lord Burghley, Spenser's political dialogue *A View of the Present State of Ireland* presumably circulated among appropriate anti-Cecilian English statesmen in 1596–97. It may well have been addressed to the Earl of Essex in particular. After all, in a dedicatory sonnet to Essex in the first edition of *The Faerie Queene* Books 1–3 (1590), Spenser anticipates the earl becoming his patron in the final stages of Elizabeth's reign.[3] Essex is known to have possessed a manuscript copy of *A View*, so it is conceivable that Spenser, to secure receipt of his text, delivered his work in person.[4] There would have been need for discretion. The criticisms of common law in *A View* might have passed for 'table taulke' in Ireland but they would have been 'intolerable to Lord Burghley or to Sir Edward Coke as they were to Elizabeth'.[5]

In both *A View* and *The Faerie Queene,* Ireland figures as a place where militant Protestantism, which Essex was perceived to champion, could confirm the justice of its cause. In *The Faerie Queene* Book VI, Artegall informs Calidore that the object of his heroic quest, the blatant beast, may be found in 'the salvage Island' (1.9.1). This location plausibly implies Ireland given Eudoxus's explicit reference at the outset of *A View* to 'that salvage nation'. Eudoxus's interlocutor Irenius suggests Ireland may prove pivotal in England's destiny, for either

> Almighty god hath not yet appointed the time of her reformation, or ... hee reserveth her in this unquiet state still for some *secret scourge,* which shall by her come unto England.[6]

Arguably, this passage alludes to Essex's conception of himself as God's scourge, a special instrument for England's deliverance. A haze of ambivalence is conjured by Irenius's artful circumlocutions. One might expect an English champion to scourge Ireland, but Irenius's scourge is heading for England *via* Ireland. Possibly Irenius hints that Ireland's dreadful destiny is to provide the means whereby, say, a Spanish force will attack England and, as God's indirect agent, punish the latter nation's failure to complete its own reformation. By contrast, Thomas Churchyard's pamphlet *A Scourge for Rebels* (1584) calls straightforwardly for an English scourge to cleanse Ireland of rebellion. The image retained its potency. Fifteen years later, in *The Fortunate Farewel to the Earle of Essex,* a poem written to commemorate Essex's departure for Ireland, Churchyard insists that 'tyrants ... damnable deeds, craves vengeance every day / Which God doth scourge, by his own blessed will'.[7] The poet seems to identify Essex as the vehicle for God's justice, in Ireland and wherever tyrants reign. Read closely, though, these lines say that God scourges tyrants' *deeds* not the tyrants themselves. Tyrone was referred to as Elizabeth's 'creature', in a sense her 'deed', but other persons nearer to home, raised to high office (i.e. 'made' by the queen), might also be alluded to.[8]

From *Richard II* to 'Lycidas' the passage to Ireland betokened ruination – Ireland being both convenient dumping ground for rebellious English spirits, and springboard for anti-English attacks. The younger Mortimer in Marlowe's *Edward II* rehearses both senses, first expressing relief that the king's favourite has been posted to the pale:

> I mean that vile torpedo, Gaveston,
> That now, I hope, floats on the Irish seas.[9]

Then, persuaded by the queen that having Gaveston within striking distance makes more sense, he about-turns, declaring:

> Know you not Gaveston hath store of gold,
> Which may in Ireland purchase him such friends
> As he will front the mightiest of us? (4.258–260)

Giving Gaveston his commission, Edward had suggested it would prove a useful staging post for a return to favour:

> Be Governor of Ireland in my stead,
> And there abide till fortune call thee home. (4.125–126)

Clearly, Ireland was where subversive energies could be earthed, recharged and, most importantly, in a culture obsessed with ethical props, primed for virtuous ends. In John Donne's epistle to his friend Henry Wotton, Irish conquest engenders self-conquest:

> Went you to conquer? and have so much lost
> Yourself, that what in you was best and most,
> Respective friendship, should so quickly die?[10]

Even when writing jingoistically at the height of Essex–Ireland mania, Churchyard is aware of the need for ethical assurance: 'A warlike band of worthy knights, *I hope*, / Are armed for fight'. That is an arresting 'I hope': does the speaker hope the knights are 'armed'? that they *are* a band of *knights*, and not mercenary rabble? That, if they are knighted, it is *worthily* so? (Essex, of course, was notorious for knighting troops by the shipload.) This note of uncertainty leads one to look more closely at the lines that follow: 'With rebels shall, both might and manhoed coep'.[11] Early modern authors linking near-synonyms by 'and' invariably stressed a conjunction in such a way as to draw attention to a possible distinction.[12] That is, Churchyard anticipates Donne's appeal for self-control. 'Rebels' are both internal and external to the self; physical 'might' may cope with the latter sort, but 'manhood' (a synonym of virtue) is required to defeat the former kind. Only by subduing both kinds of rebel may 'Our contreis right, and quarrell ... be tried'.[13] Again, the terms are doubled: the 'country's right' to Ireland must be proved, and the domestic 'quarrell' will be determined by Essex's conduct during the campaign. Seeing the matter in this light, it is clear why Essex's domestic enemies would want him to fail in Ireland.

Relevant to this issue of self-justification are Spenser's criticisms of common law in *A View*. For the Cecils, common law legitimised the Tudor settlement (its purported immemorial origins and global applicability obscured the violence of the specific moment of institution). This ideological position promoted lineal succession as the 'natural' (divinely-sanctioned) means of negotiating a succession open to dispute. Spenser hints that 'common law', originating in violent seizure (the Norman Conquest), is human, not divine. Alternative methods of deciding succession may, therefore, be justifiably sought. James VI's lineal claim to the English throne is insufficient and debatable, presumably by parliament. Force may be needed to secure this process. In this way, *A View*, which discusses alternative methods of determining succession, such as the Irish tanist system, implies that Essex (positioned as the text's ideal reader) should orchestrate his campaign to acquire the military means to broker the succession.[14]

As well as veiled allusions to the threat of a troubled succession – 'the Tanist is alwayes ready knowne, if it should happen the Captaine suddenly to dye, or to be slaine in battell, or to be out of the countrey, to defend and kepe it from all such doubts and dangers'[15] – *A View* contains warnings about Scottish anti-Englishness, observing that the Scottish and Irish 'are all one and the same'.[16] Irenius recommends a Lord Lieutenant be appointed to oversee Irish affairs, referring to 'such a one I could name, upon whom the eye of all England is fixed, and our last hopes now rest'.[17] Most probably, Spenser's Irenius looked to Essex, who assumed office within two months of paying for the poet's funeral in 1599.

Irenius's citation of Machiavelli, following the allusion to Essex as candidate for the top job, implies Spenser's perception of the extensive authority required and the stakes involved should Essex obtain it:

> Machiavel in his discourses upon Livie ... commendeth the manner of the Romans government, in giving absolute power to all their Councellors and Governours, which if they abused, they should afterwards dearely answere.[18]

This refers to Machiavelli's praise of Cesare Borgia 'for bestowing power on his general, Remiro de Orco, letting him take the blame for the harsh rule imposed in Romagna, before having him put to death in the square'.[19]

Notwithstanding the ominous precedent, Spenser wished Essex to understand that gaining proper control of Ireland, and establishing a standing army there, would help him to secure an authentically mixed polity for England. That a succession of viceroys had met their doom in the colony, whether through apparent illness (Walter Devereux), debt (Henry Sidney), or treason (John Perrot), did not diminish its potential as a power-base.

One problem for Spenser, while writing *A View*, though, is that Essex at that time had his sights set not on Ireland but on wars in France, Spain and the Netherlands. Book 5 of *The Faerie Queene* touches on Essex's commitment to the French situation. In canto 11 Burbon (a transparent figure for Henri IV) attempts to justify his conversion to Catholicism as politically necessary temporisation (56.1–5). Artegall (representing Essex (see 43.6–65n)) will have none of it ('Fie on such forgerie' (56.6)) but aids Burbon anyway (57.7–9). Spenser apparently endorses this chivalric action. By placing the Burbon incident here, though, digressing from the pressing need to rescue Irena, Spenser arguably steers Essex's political course (ultimately) Irelandwards, implying that however commendable efforts on behalf of the Low Countries, France and Henri IV are, the real battleground is Ireland.

Some commentators, however, assume the Irish posting never appealed to Essex. Paul Hammer argues that Devereux 'sought to avoid more direct entanglement', citing the earl's description of the Irish conflict in his *Apologie*

(1598) as 'a miserable beggarly … war'.[20] Conversely, during the mid-1590s, 'more and more of the officers being sent to Ireland … had previously served with Essex'.[21] Whatever his protestations in pamphlets or letters to Elizabeth, Essex was preparing for an Irish campaign as early as 1596, from which year dates a list of captains drawn up in the earl's handwriting.[22] A thousand veterans of the Islands expedition were dispatched by Essex in companies to Portsmouth, Plymouth and Falmouth to be drilled until the following August, when they were sent to Ireland.[23]

In any case, Essex was steeped in Irish politics long before his official appointment as Viceroy on 12 March 1599. His father, Walter Devereux, the first Earl, who died in Dublin in 1576, served as Governor of Ulster from 1573. Indeed, Robert might take his father's Irish experience as augury of his own fate should he accept the commission. Walter Devereux knew while he served in Ireland that individuals at court – particularly Leicester – strove to hinder his success. Before embarking for Ireland, in a letter dated 22 June 1573, Walter told Burghley: 'I look for to find enemies enough to this enterprise, and I feel some of them already'.[24] Sir William Fitzwilliam, then Lord Deputy of Ireland, saw 'prospective colonists [such as Walter Devereux] as provoking needless political chaos [and so] gave little assistance'.[25] Fitzwilliam was perceived to cause the failure of an expedition planned by Essex 'partly through a want of supply of victuals'.[26] So obvious was Fitzwilliam's lack of cooperation that the English council discussed replacing him. Essex coveted the job himself, as it would afford him the authority to prosecute his intended measures (and personal projects). Sir Francis Knollys wrote to Burghley, however, remarking that 'Her majesty hath said that in no wise she will allow my Lord of Essex shall be Deputy in Ireland, because she would have no man that hath lands of inheritance there to be Deputy'.[27] As Knollys observes, the queen's resolve would probably result in Essex being so hampered that his Irish expedition 'will be undone'.[28] Elizabeth preferred to lose expenditure and honour in a failed expedition than allow an ambitious noble to establish a rival power-base in Ireland. Why, then, was Devereux appointed if the queen did not care to achieve anything? The obvious answer is that it was a useful place for disposing of Essex, leading him to deplete his resources in fruitless projects. Ireland was viewed variously as unprofitable zone for attempted cultivation, handling device for refuse matter, convenient repository for rebellious elements, and site of potential resistance to Crown rule, from Irish and English sources alike.

Impeded by Fitzwilliam, Walter concluded a truce with the Irish rebel Tirlogh Lenoghe on 16 March 1574. Elizabeth responded relatively favourably, of which fact the second earl would have been cognisant. Indeed, Robert Devereux might have been predisposed to consider Hugh O'Neill (later Earl of Tyrone) – the rebel leader he was sent to defeat in 1599 – as a possible ally, based on his father's experiences. O'Neill served under Walter Devereux in his campaign against the Irish rebel Brian McPhelim. In a letter dated

20 October 1573, Walter tells Burghley that 'the Baron of Dungannon [i.e. O'Neill, created Earl of Tyrone, 1587] … is the only man of Ulster that is, in my opinion, meet to be trusted and used'.[29] There were reasons why O'Neill would ally himself with Walter Devereux. The Ulster colonial enterprise conducted chiefly by Sir Thomas Smith and the first Earl of Essex had sought 'to keep out the Scots' and reduce the power of the O'Neills.[30] Though an O'Neill himself, Dungannon supported the colonists. Walter Devereux recognised that Dungannon's 'loyalty might be accounted for by the fact of Tirlogh Lenoghe having usurped the title of O'Neill, which the Baron claimed'.[31] As Earl of Tyrone, Dungannon visited the English court in 1587 and 1590, establishing links with Leicester and Robert Devereux. By this stage, Essex had fixed assets to protect in Ireland following the 1591 land settlement regarding the barony of Donamayne. In March 1594 Essex supported an isolated Tyrone at the English court.[32] Presumably this relationship encouraged Cecil to suppose that sending Essex to fight Tyrone would compromise the English earl. Certainly, Tyrone may be viewed as Essex's natural ally, committed to a counter-absolutist (and counter-*centralist*) ethos. Once Tyrone became a declared rebel, though, Essex was obliged to oppose him. However, Tyrone, on securing a parley with his former friend, would argue that he was no rebel. The later sixteenth-century wars in Ireland had resulted from 'attempted centralization', an effort 'to abolish the Gaelic institution of lordship'. Such lordships were '"ancient liberties" which the English crown had deigned to recognize in the past'. Thus, the loyalty of the Irish lords 'never became the absolute loyalty of the subject but remained the self-serving and conditional support of the tribal lord'. The Irish confederates, therefore, were exactly equivalent to Dutch opponents of Spanish rule in the legitimacy of their claims.[33]

This sort of Irish 'table taulk' may have enjoyed currency in England. Spenser's Eudoxus beseeches Irenius to resolve whether Tyrone's claim to the North is valid. Irenius bluntly says Tyrone's claim is 'surely none at all', following oaths obtained from the Irish lords acknowledging Henry VIII as sovereign.[34] However, earlier in the dialogue, Irenius had stressed that Henry VIII needed no such oaths, given that English authority was established by conquest.[35] By requiring a new oath, needlessly questioning the right of conquest, Henry 'did great hurt unto his title'.[36] Furthermore, Irenius implies, Henry VIII inadvertently confirmed that the Tudor dynasty was consequent upon an act of usurpation. And if Tyrone were a usurper, what real difference obtained between his claim and Elizabeth's?

Walter Devereux died in Dublin in 1576, allegedly poisoned via the machinations of Leicester.[37] Despite such warnings from his family's history, Walter's son Robert eventually accepted charge of the 1599 Irish campaign. Why do so if he recalled his father's fate, and understood that his own enemies desired precisely this outcome? Presumably, Essex felt that, given sufficient authority and means, he could turn the appointment to his advantage.

Writing to his Spanish agent Antonio Perez on 14 September 1596, Essex appears determined 'to stay at court unless he should be permitted to go to Ireland with such a fleet and forces as he should choose on his own terms'.[38] Open to question is what Essex intended to do once installed in Ireland. He certainly devised an adequate plan for defeating Tyrone. A long letter to Elizabeth from Waterford outlines 'most of the principal means by which the war was to be successfully concluded' later by Mountjoy.[39] From this it has been concluded that Essex never intended to treat with Tyrone. However, if his father's experiences are taken into account, Essex might have anticipated his enemies at court would deliberately thwart his efforts.

Walter Devereux had been convinced the Irish rebels would be defeated more rapidly if the fort at Lough Foyle was taken, for their Scottish reinforcements usually landed there. This became a key objective for his son Robert, but in the latter's case it might have been to facilitate the arrival of Scottish forces intended to aid him in marching on the English court. Essex admitted at his trial he had agreed to launch an immediate attack on Tyrone upon arriving in Ireland. Later in 1599, however, 'Nottingham taxed Essex with "holding to a project of your own"'. This alternative project was probably Essex's plan to secure Lough Foyle.[40] Curiously, in Essex's Waterford letter to Elizabeth no mention is made of any plan to establish a base at Lough Foyle. It was, however, no great secret. The Irish Council had insisted that establishing a fort there was essential. Nonetheless, Elizabeth advocated an 'isolated frontal attack'.[41] By September, when the time for such an attack had passed, Elizabeth angrily acknowledged that Essex had 'often resolved us, until Lough Foyle and Bealsliman were planted, there could be no hope of doing service on the capital rebels'.[42] Did the English government calculatedly strive to prevent Essex securing this base? L. W. Henry emphasises lack of transport: 'Notwithstanding urgent personal directives from Essex [to the Privy Council], dated 26th February ... orders for horses went unheeded until after 6th April'. Nothing can 'wholly account for [this] inactivity, given the queen's warrant [issued] in mid-January'. Without the promised carriage-horses, Essex's troops were immobilised. Sir William Knollys prudently 'warned Cecil in May of the possibility that Essex "could show necessary reason touching the carriage-horses which are not there to be had and without which he will not be able to march"'. Perhaps as a result, 'the Privy Council levied a further proportion of 200 carriage-horses ... ready to be dispatched ... on 9th July'.[43] In addition, some mystery surrounds the supply of the flyboats promised to support Essex's Ulster campaign. Given these problems, the Irish Council agreed Essex was in no position to march north. This decision was 'approved by the English government'.[44] Yet Essex's failure to attack Tyrone featured prominently among accusations of treachery at his trial. The Irish Council relied on a specious quibble to claim they had not prevented Essex from going north.[45] Essex was specifically criticised for marching west from Munster in a manner resembling a royal progress. Yet when he returned from southern manoeuvres after two months, the promised shipping remained unavailable.[46]

Taking the foregoing into account, it appears that certain parties sought to frame Essex as a traitor, and/or prevent him from establishing a power-base while 'banished' to Ireland. Certainly, Essex believed Cecil's faction had obstructed the dispatch of supplies needed to win the Irish campaign. The establishment of the Lough Foyle fort was prevented by supply problems arising from central acts of omission. The building of this fort enabled Mountjoy's subsequent success – when, of course, Scottish forces were no longer a threat to Cecil (the latter having cemented his relationship with James once Essex was removed). Mountjoy's operation *did* receive adequate material support from the Crown.[47]

Nonetheless, despite lack of supplies and other circumstances preventing Essex from implementing his plan against Tyrone, it remains possible to suppose Essex had no appetite for the encounter, a view Elizabeth intimates in her angry letter of 14 September 1599: 'we require you to consider whether we have not great cause to think that your purpose is not to end the war'.[48]

All things considered, Essex might have adjudged it against his interests to attack Tyrone. A convincing victory would probably have provoked an order for the rapid dismantling of Essex's military forces, cementing the absolutist imperial regime under construction by Burghley, Cecil, Elizabeth and others. This set of circumstances obliged Essex to adopt a prevaricating strategy, one that recalls Prince Hamlet's distaste for the wrong kind of war – despite his embodying 'the soldier's ... eye, tongue, sword' (3.1.150).[49] The war conducted in Poland by Fortinbras in order, as the Danish captain explains, 'to gain a little patch of ground / That hath in it no profit but the name ... I would not farm it', recalls the Irish expedition. Despite this lack of worth, the land 'is already garrisoned' (Q2, 4.4.9.8–10, 9.14). Essex, this comparison implies, though committed to endless activity, was rendered incapable of conclusive action.

Essex and the city: a chorus of (dis)approval?

Shakespeare, like Spenser, possibly regarded Essex as a means to effect regime change. This would explain why play after play contains figures available to be read as policy indicators for Essex.[50] Thus Shakespeare's Richard II offers (according to political taste and/or a given production's slant) a veiled representation of, say, Elizabeth I as deposable tyrant or, indeed, Essex as emotionally unstable bungler.[51] Historically, Richard II had been the last English monarch to personally undertake an Irish expedition, with results ruinous enough to discourage any sovereign from following in his footsteps for nearly three centuries. Michael Neill speculates that 'the play's Irish dimension may have been one of the things that commended it to the Essex plotters in 1601'.[52]

Similarly, aspects of the usurper Bolingbroke recall Essex: 'Both left dangers at home when they went to war, besieged Rouen, sacked foreign towns, were taken to represent a revival of chivalry and national purpose'.[53] Furthermore, 'the noble lineage of "banished Hereford" traced by York in the play is the actual line of descent through which Essex's claim to the throne must be traced'.[54] Essex's Hereford title features prominently in the *Lawes and Orders of Warre* (1599) issued to his troops in Ireland, while the tradition of viceroys assuming – usurping – royal style goes back at least to John Derricke's woodcuts depicting Henry Sidney enthroned in Dublin in *The Image of Irelande* (1581). Scandal broke out in London in early February 1599 when copies of Thomas Cockson's engraving of Essex-on-horseback started selling like hot cakes. One of the captions to the image called Essex 'God's elected'.[55]

Clearly, whether or not Essex sought the throne, he was perceived as desiring it. At the earl's trial, Cecil claimed that 'Essex had been devising five or six years to be king of England'.[56] Individuals accompanying Essex on his Irish campaign understood their leader's objective as being a throne: 'To gain a country was his hunting sport', remarks a sonnet by Richard Mynshall. The poem is copied in a book of lute music containing a draft of Essex's letter to Elizabeth of 30 August 1599. Mynshall's sonnet may postdate the letter draft, for it continues: 'soldiers may be kings – / Kings in conceit I mean … / To aspire to crowns we see it danger brings'.[57]

Keeping in mind the possible heights Essex aspired to in his ambition, it is worth stressing that Shakespeare's Essex-fashioning campaign was not restricted to the histories. As Richard McCoy observes, chivalric romances were 'ideologically important' in stressing the role and responsibility of the aristocrat. The seminal resistance theory manual *Vindiciae Contra Tyrannos* warns against regarding chivalric ceremonies as trivial. Its author (presumed to be Henry of Navarre's counsellor Philippe de Mornay) tells 'electors, palatines [and] peers' that chivalric pageants are not just occasions for dressing up as 'Roland [and] Oliver'. The reciprocal relations elaborated by such performances declare the commonwealth to be 'entrusted to the king ... and yet to [the electors, palatines, peers] also, as its co-protectors'.[58] To Elizabethan audiences, chivalric texts such as *As You Like It* were privileged sites of constitutionally charged discourse. No doubt Sir John Harington understood this when presenting Tyrone with a copy of his translation of *Orlando Furioso* during truce negotiations in 1599.[59]

Juliet Dusinberre's recent argument for a first performance date of 14 February 1599 for *As You Like It* alters the play's place in a sequence of works (partly) addressed to Essex.[60] The play's hero Orlando shares traits with the earl: both figures are (almost) universally loved, possessed of inborn grace, capable of provoking intense envy, prone to violent responses where gentle speech would better serve, and given to protecting their honour for egotistical reasons. Like Bolingbroke, Orlando seems a cautionary figure, blended of positives and negatives, for Essex to emulate and be instructed by.

The February 1599 dating recasts the play's relationship with Ireland. Orlando learns not to assume everything is savage in Arden. Bursting upon Duke Senior and company in the Forest, wielding a sword and demanding food, Orlando is told he had only to ask. 'Pardon me,' the young man apologises, 'I pray you. / I thought that all things had been savage here' (2.7.105–106).[61] Ideological forces produce Orlando's aggressive manner. At the play's moment of composition, Ireland for Elizabethans was a savage wilderness. The poet-veteran of Henry Sidney's Irish campaign, Barnaby Rich, who returned to the island in 1599 with Essex, decries it in *Anothomy of Ireland* (1615) as 'more barbarous and more brutysh in [its] costomes and demeanures then ... any other parte of the world that is knowne'.[62] Essex considered Ireland especially wretched, complaining to Elizabeth on 30 August 1599 that 'my service past deserves no more than banishment and proscription into the most cursed of all countries'.[63] Conversely, Fynes Morison found the Irish civilised, tacitly admitting 'his perceptions of the Irish may owe much to false propaganda'.[64]

Of course, the conspicuous reference to 'the howling of Irish wolves at the moon' (5.2.105–106) becomes more intriguing if Dusinberre's dating is allowed. In the play's source, Thomas Lodge's *Rosalynd*, the howling wolves are Syrian. Protestant propaganda would consider Ireland and Syria idolatrous, deserving of conquest by 'Christian' armies. In Melanchthon's *Carion's Chronicle* (translated in 1550), the Syrian empire, last in the list of empires in the Book of Daniel, is equated with that of the Turk, which 'stands allegorically for the Roman Church'.[65] The link to Daniel gives the blurring of Syria and Ireland an eschatological edge, recalling Spenser's representation of Ireland as predestined site of the scourge that will finally reform England.

In *As You Like It*, moreover, the court's multi-stage invasion of the Forest of Arden may be related to the attempted colonisation of the Ards peninsula, 'the most eligible district of Ulster', in which Walter Devereux and his son Robert engaged.[66] Fleeing court corruption, a starving Orlando is received with civility by rebel figure Duke Senior, who, according to the satirist Jaques, is a usurper of the natives in the forest, i.e. a colonist (2.1.60–63). The poet who accompanied Essex to Ireland, Barnaby Rich, shares many of Jaques's attitudes. Jaques 'most invectively ... pierceth through / The body of country, city, court' (58–59) and wishes to 'Cleanse the foul body of th'infected world' (2.7.60). Rich, too, sees moral disease corrupting 'Cytty towne & cuntry'.[67] Jaques is a sceptical observer among the entourage of Duke Senior. Rich, likewise, may have been a spy in Essex's Irish camp, acting on behalf of Robert Cecil.[68] In any case, such encounters between banished political leaders and wretched fugitives as Shakespeare's play shows between Duke Senior and Orlando are described by Rich's *Anothomy*; the text nominates Ireland as 'the place for *Rende vous*, for traytors ... for papystes, for runegates ... that fly out of *England* ... wher all thes may have lyberty to conspyre'.[69]

In the final act of *As You Like It*, Shakespeare makes another signal departure from Lodge's text. In *Rosalynd*, the usurping tyrant Torismond leads an army to exterminate his brother Gerismond (the legitimate king) and his growing retinue of rebels, but is defeated in battle. In *As You Like It*, the usurper Frederick

> Addressed a mighty power, which were on foot
> In his own conduct, purposely to take
> His brother here, and put him to the sword.
> And to the skirts of the wild wood he came
> Where, meeting with an old religious man,
> After some question with him was converted
> Both from his enterprise and from the world. (5.4.145–151)

The 'mighty power' gathered under Essex represented the largest single army mobilised by Elizabeth. Sent to 'put him to the sword', Essex met Tyrone at the 'skirts' of a wood, holding their notorious parley at the ford of Bellaclynthe, six miles north of the town of *Ardee*. The parallels work so neatly a need is felt either to question Dusinberre's pre-Ireland campaign date, or assume the text (first printed in the 1623 Folio) incorporates additions for unrecorded Stuart era productions. This would explain the tacked-on aspect of Jacques de Boys' eleventh-hour appearance to deliver these revelations.[70] Duke Frederick shares few distinguishing characteristics with Essex, but again, the emotionally unstable usurper of Act 1 might figure a moral and political warning for Essex, pending his possible return from Ireland leading a revolt.

Most famously, the Chorus in Shakespeare's *Henry V* 5.0 compares the king's return to London with the repatriation of another heroic figure. Henry's homecoming is first compared with Caesar's to Rome, then with Essex's anticipated arrival from Ireland. After describing Henry's triumphant return from France in the prologue to Act 5, the Chorus ruminates:

> As, by a lower but high-loving likelihood,
> Were now the General of our gracious Empress –
> As in good time he may – from Ireland coming,
> Bringing rebellion broachèd on his sword,
> How many would the peaceful city quit
> To welcome him! Much more, and much more cause,
> Did they this Harry. (29–35).

Christopher Highley doubts how pro-Essex the dramatist's intention is: 'The Chorus's syntactically ambivalent lines about Henry convey the exact sense of uncertainty, the mixture of danger and excitement surrounding Essex in Ireland'.[71] But is the ambivalence aimed at 'the General' or the 'Empress'? A real empress, after all, possessed an empire, not an underfunded colony up in arms. The words 'lower' and 'much more cause' undermine the worthiness of the Irish expedition. Rebellion indeed is broached, but whose? And which 'General'?

According to Gary Taylor, 'though the allusion to Essex is unquestionably complimentary, the sting in its tale ("much more, *and much more cause, /* Did they this Harry") deserves more attention than it seems to have attracted'.[72] Highley suggests that 'Shakespeare's misgivings about Essex together with an awareness of burgeoning public alarm at the war in Ireland produce a skeptical counter-discourse about English expansionism'.[73] Opposition to the 1598–99 Irish campaign need not mean opposition to Essex. As noted, those in favour of the earl's Irish appointment may not have had his interests at heart. The Lord Deputyship was a double-edged sword, as Richard II found when he assumed the role personally.

The type of patient to be operated upon by the sword's second edge, though, was open to contest. The Chorus's vision of the general bringing 'rebellion broachèd on his sword' (5.0.32) possibly warns that Essex, having settled with Tyrone, and overcome his own rebellious (read: ambitious) nature may shortly return from Ireland, at the head of a well-disciplined army, brandishing the sword of justice in the character of God's scourge. His intention, in that case, would be to remove Cecil and his faction from Elizabeth's council and secure James VI the English throne. Patricia Parker notes that the Chorus's choice of word ('broachèd') 'might also be interpreted in relation to the imagery of breaching in the play'.[74] Curiously, Thomas Churchyard's *Farewel* not only says that Irish rebels have 'woluish minds' but also observes that 'liek breetchles beares they goe ... that knoes ne ruel nor lawe'.[75] Essex *had* promulgated strict laws to his troops, in the pamphlet *Lawes and Orders of Warre established for the good conduct of the service in Ireland*, issued 25 February 1599.

Whether Essex planned rebellion with Tyrone or not, the apparent deletion in the 1600 *Henry V* quarto of the long genealogical argument in 1.1 raises eyebrows. These sixty-two heavy-going lines on Henry's lineage were presumably of 'special interest' to a particular audience, perhaps Essex and his supporters. Evelyn May Albright notes that the earl's claim to the English throne, albeit tenuous, followed the line of Henry's, via the daughters of Bohuns. This explains the emphasis on descent through the female.[76] However, the scene could support other claimants reliant on female lines (most pertinently James VI). As with Robert Persons's *A Conference About The Next Succession to the Crowne of Ingland* (1594), apparent endorsement of Essex might aim to stir trouble, not to incriminate the earl specifically but make matters regarding the succession damagingly divisive.

Other allusions to the Irish situation may be found in *Henry V*. Shakespeare's chorus, in the prologue to Act 1, makes a pointed (if oblique) allusion to supply problems, offset by imaginary powers: 'Think, when we talk of horses, that you see them ... For 'tis your thoughts that now must deck our kings'

(26, 28). In the Prologue to Act 3, the Chorus asks the audience to 'Play with your fancies' and 'Suppose that you have seen / The well-appointed king … and his brave fleet' (3.0.7; 2–5). In the real theatre of war, a lack of horses and ships prevented Essex's northern expedition to tackle Tyrone.

How 'well-appointed' this imaginary Essex would be to kingship depended on the beholder. In the 1587 edition of Holinshed:

> The first Earl of Essex's abortive plans to colonize various parts of Ulster are praised on the grounds that 'he was ... of so heroicall a mind, that if his abilitie had answered his good will, he had not bin a second, neither to Lacie, nor to Courcie, nor to anie the first conquerors of Ulster to the crowne of England'.[77]

A failed Essex attempt at Irish subjection, bound up with O'Neill, predating Shakespeare's play, is prominently placed in the dramatist's major historical source; Holinshed registers Walter Devereux's defeat, but also acknowledges his heroism. Note, also, the subtle elision allowing a suggestion that Walter Devereux is second to none with regard to 'the crowne of England'.

Between Holinshed and *Henry V* lies *Edward II* (1592?), where Marlowe has Lancaster warn the king:

> Look for rebellion, look to be deposed:
> Thy garrisons are beaten out of France,
> And, lame and poor, lie groaning at the gates;
> The wild O'Neill, with swarms of Irish kerns,
> Lives uncontrolled within the English pale. (6.158–62)

Clearly sending Gaveston was not a good idea. Spencer Junior later gives Edward the advice the king gave Gaveston:

> Fly, fly, my lord! The Queen is over-strong;
> Her friends do multiply and yours do fail.
> Shape we our course to Ireland, there to breathe. (18.1–3)

Breathing space, bolt-hole, and base camp, Ireland was a staging post for fugitive figures.

If Ireland was key to Essex's fortunes and history, so was Wales, but the Cecils, despite their Welsh provenance, plotted a Scottish succession.[78] For his Cadiz expedition in 1596, Essex had Welsh officers (including known recusants) raise and lead his forces. To Ireland, Essex took 'most of the … Welshmen who had been at Cadiz', including Owen and John Salusbury and Gelly Meyrick.[79] The Welsh gentry warned the Privy Council in January 1599 of Tyrone's popularity in Wales, advising that 'no Welshmen … should be used in service against the Irish men'. This may have been an attempt to reduce Welsh conscription.[80] Nonetheless, the Essex Rebellion of 1601 had a pronounced Welsh dimension, alongside a wider sense of Celtic encirclement: 'As developed by Essex, Southampton, and Mountjoy, [the Essex plan] involved the use of joint forces of Scotland, Wales, and Ireland, along with the English'.[81] This offers one way of reading the four captains scene in *Henry V*. Fluellen's criticisms of Irish methods echo Essex's own comments on rebel methods in letters of 20 May and 25 June, saying the Irish do not 'fight in order'.[82] As has been noted, the record preserved in poetic texts indicates how vital the notion of self-discipline was to Essex's project as righteous scourge. In any case, Jamy's stance in the four captains scene replicates the cautious manner of King James.[83] Southampton's confession shows that 'he and Mountjoy and Essex all knew this attitude of James'.[84] Going to colony and back, intent on purging court corruption, Essex would have been unwise to bank too much on James VI. If, as A. H. Dodd suggests, Essex's projected *coup* was a 'Celtic rising', the Scots (in the metonymic guise of their monarch at least) were not onboard.[85]

Since no Welsh or Irish claimant could expect to succeed Elizabeth, Essex's Welsh and Irish supporters gained more in supporting an attempt to broker the succession on pan-Celtic rather than nationalist terms. However, Essex's attempt to take control of the situation was hampered by the concept of obedience to his monarch, bred in sixteenth-century aristocrats by Tudor ideological apparatuses.[86] Loyalty to the monarch featured strongly in Essex's Welsh background.[87] Arriving at court without their rebel army, Essex and his circle dithered between adopting the petitionary strategy of Sir Henry Wotton, or the abstract theories of key secretarial advisers such as Henry Cuffe, which failed to communicate the inevitability of their conclusions to the popular forces Essex needed to muster.[88]

Admittedly, one risks losing a sense of Essex as historical figure beneath the foregoing welter of literary allusions and tendentious records. Nonetheless, the 'table taulke' of Essex's time was where the attitudes preserved in poems, pamphlets and plays would have been most passionately expounded. Analysing these documents and literary works allows one to imagine the outrageous, shocking, and exciting notions Essex listened to and uttered while at table with his contemporaries. As far as Essex himself was concerned, all that argument and chatter led to a pathetic denouement. Nonetheless, the issues brought to prominence by Essex's political endeavours continued to reverberate in the Stuart era. Hence, scepticism about the motives behind sending a prominent figure to Ireland surfaces again in Shakespeare's last history, *Henry VIII* (1613), where two gentlemen discuss Buckingham's treason trial, blaming Cardinal Wolsey:

> FIRST GENTLEMAN ... first, Kildare's attainder.
> Then deputy of Ireland, who, removed,
> Earl Surrey was sent thither – and in haste, too,
> Lest he should help his father.
> SECOND GENTLEMAN That trick of state
> Was a deep envious one.
> FIRST GENTLEMAN At his return
> No doubt he will requite it. This is noted,

And generally: whoever the king favours,
The Card'nal instantly will find employment –
And far enough from court, too. (2.1.42–49)

For King read Queen, for Cardinal read Cecil, for Surrey read Essex. The 'trick of state' played throughout Shakespeare's histories – and English history – uses Ireland as cover for anti-courtly criticism and convenient posting for potential troublemakers, a source of rebellion in a double sense. The idea that Ireland was a form of exile is here related specifically to faction and court intrigue. Surrey returns from Ireland to confront Wolsey, accusing the Cardinal of bringing down 'noble Buckingham, my father-in-law':

Plague of your policy,
You sent me deputy for Ireland,
Far from his succour, from the King, from all
That might have mercy on the fault thou gav'st him. (3.2.260–263)

Plague of policy or trick of state, the use of Ireland as last post for troublesome subjects is a recurring feature of the histories, and of the criticism they have attracted. Five years after *Henry VIII,* as Paul Hammer informs us, another trick of state was alluded to: 'Sir Walter Ralegh was awaiting his own execution and ... asked about his role in the death of Essex ... said "that my Lord of Essex was fetcht off by a trick, which he privately told me of"'.[89] That trick, as Hammer speculates, was probably the rumour that Ralegh was on his way to kill Essex, prompting the latter to his ill-fated rebellion, but the larger trick was arguably the disappearing act that wafted Essex to Ireland in the first place. Like father, like son, two Devereux dispatched by the same courtly conjurors.

The afterlife of Essex and Ireland

In 1753 Henry Jones's *The Earl of Essex: A Tragedy in Five Acts* was performed in London, showing 'Burleigh', Robert Cecil, as a schemer viewing Ireland as exile for Essex but also spawning ground for rebellion and invasion.[90] Burleigh tells the queen that Essex married Lady Rutland in secret the night before he sailed, informing her:

Tyrone embarks six thousand men
To land at Milford, and to march where Essex
Shall join them with his friends.

Essex pleads with Elizabeth that 'loyalty misled, and duty extreme ... drove me from my high command in Ireland'.[91] His plea takes a comic turn in poet Micki Myers' rendition, where the earl says his mission failed because '"Everybody was king-fu fighting, your Majesty"'.[92] Not only martial arts but, as Myers' pun suggests, monarchical arts and political games surrounding two successions impinged on Essex's Irish expedition – the handing on of England's throne and the earl's own accession to his father's fate. In this sense it is fitting that the successful overthrow of a monarch fifty years later should have its origins in another Irish rebellion, and the execution of another chief governor there, but this time the usurper, Oliver Cromwell, would lead his Irish expedition only after assuming the highest office.[93]

Notes

1 Edward M. Hinton, 'Rych's "Anothomy of Ireland" [1615], with an account of the author', *PMLA*, 55: 1 (1940), p. 91.

2 For Essex's Irish campaign as 'poisoned chalice', see James Shapiro, *1599: A Year in the Life of William Shakespeare* (London: Faber & Faber, 2005), pp. 88–96 and Paul E. J. Hammer, 'Robert Devereux, 2nd Earl of Essex (1565–1601), Soldier and Politician'. *ODNB*.

3 *Edmund Spenser: The Faerie Queene*, eds A. C. Hamilton, H. Yamashita and T. Suzuki, revised 2nd edn (Harlow: Pearson, 2007), *Dedicatory Sonnet 6*, p. 729. All further references will be given in the text.

4 Rudolf B. Gottfried, 'Spenser's *View* and Essex', *PMLA* 52: 3 (1937), p. 646.

5 Ciaran Brady, 'The Road to the *View*: On the Decline of Reform Thought in Tudor Ireland', in *Spenser and Ireland: An Interdisciplinary Perspective*, ed. Patricia Coughlan (Cork: Cork University Press, 1989), p. 42.

6 *Edmund Spenser, A View of the State of Ireland (1633): from the first printed edition*, Andrew Hadfield and Willy Maley (eds) (Oxford: Blackwell, 1997), p. 11; emphasis added.

7 Thomas Churchyard, *The Fortunate Farewel to the Earle of Essex* (London: William Wood, 1599).

8 Nicholas Canny, 'O'Neill, Hugh, 2nd Earl of Tyrone (c.1550–1616), Magnate and Rebel', *ODNB*. For further discussion of Churchyard's *Farewel* see Shapiro, *1599: A Year in the Life of William Shakespeare*, p. 107; see also the chapter on Churchyard in Adam N. McKeown, *English Mercuries: Soldier Poets in the Age of Shakespeare* (Nashville, TN: Vanderbilt University Press, 2009) and Raphael Lyne, 'Thomas Churchyard (1523?–1604), writer and soldier', *ODNB*.

9 *Christopher Marlowe: Edward II*, eds Martin Wiggins and Robert Lindsey, 2nd edn (London: A. & C. Black, 1997), 4, pp. 223–224. All further references will be given in the text.

10 A. J. Smith, ed. *John Donne: The Complete English Poems* (London: Penguin, 1996), pp. 217–218; Andrew Murphy, 'Gold Lace and a Frozen Snake: Donne, Wotton and the Nine Years War', *Irish Studies Review* 2: 8 (1994), pp. 9–11.

11 Churchyard, *The Fortunate Farewel to the Earle of Essex*, sig. A2.

12 See Sir Francis Hastings' accusation that Robert Persons had distinguished 'faith and belief' in writing 'there was then one faith and belief in Christendom before Luther', in *The Other Face: Catholic Life under Elizabeth I*, ed. Philip Caraman (London: Longmans, 1960), p. 154.

13 Churchyard, *The Fortunate Farewel to the Earle of Essex*, sig. A2.

14 Hadfield and Maley (eds), *Edmund Spenser, A View of the State of Ireland (1633)*, pp. 16–18.

15 Hadfield and Maley (eds), *Edmund Spenser, A View of the State of Ireland (1633)*, p. 17.

16 Hadfield and Maley (eds), *Edmund Spenser, A View of the State of Ireland (1633)*, p. 45.

17 Hadfield and Maley (eds), *Edmund Spenser, A View of the State of Ireland (1633)*, p. 159.
18 Hadfield and Maley (eds), *Edmund Spenser, A View of the State of Ireland (1633)*, p. 160.
19 Andrew Hadfield, *Spenser's Irish Experience: Wilde Fruit and Salvage Soyl* (Oxford: Clarendon Press, 1997), p. 78.
20 Paul E. J. Hammer, *The Polarisation of Elizabethan Politics* (Cambridge: Cambridge University Press, 1999) p. 137.
21 Hammer, *Polarisation of Elizabethan Politics*, p. 133.
22 Gottfried, 'Spenser's *View* and Essex', p. 645.
23 L. W. Henry, 'The Earl of Essex as Strategist and Military Organizer (1596–7)', *English Historical Review* 68: 268 (1953), p. 388.
24 Walter Bourchier Devereux, *Lives and Letters of the Devereux, Earls of Essex in the Reigns of Elizabeth, James I, and Charles I, 1540–1646*), 2 vols. (London: John Murray, 1853), vol. I, pp. 30–31.
25 Hiram Morgan, *Tyrone's Rebellion: The Outbreak of the Nine Years War in Tudor Ireland* (Woodbridge: Boydell, 1993), p. 21.
26 Morgan, *Tyrone's Rebellion*, p. 53.
27 Morgan, *Tyrone's Rebellion*, p. 51.
28 Morgan, *Tyrone's Rebellion*, p. 52.
29 Devereux, *Lives and Letters of the Devereux*, vol. I, p. 40.
30 Morgan, *Tyrone's Rebellion*, p. 20.
31 Devereux, *Lives and Letters of the Devereux*, vol. I, p. 48.
32 Morgan, *Tyrone's Rebellion*, p. 68.
33 Morgan, *Tyrone's Rebellion*, p. 219.
34 Hadfield and Maley (eds), *Edmund Spenser, A View of the State of Ireland (1633)*, p. 111.
35 Hadfield and Maley (eds), *Edmund Spenser, A View of the State of Ireland (1633)*, p. 18.
36 Hadfield and Maley (eds), *Edmund Spenser, A View of the State of Ireland (1633)*, p. 19.
37 See D. C. Peck (ed.), *Leicester's Commonwealth: The Copy of a Letter Written by a Master of Art of Cambridge (1584) and Related Documents* (Athens, OH: Ohio University Press, 1985), pp. 267–269.
38 Ray Heffner, 'Essex and Book Five of *The Faerie Queene*', *English Literary History* 3: 1 (1936), p. 79.
39 L. W. Henry, 'The Earl of Essex and Ireland, 1599', *Bulletin of the Institute of Historical Research* 32: 85 (1959), p. 14.
40 Henry, 'The Earl of Essex and Ireland, 1599', pp. 4–5.
41 Henry, 'The Earl of Essex and Ireland, 1599', pp. 14, 17.
42 Devereux, *Lives and Letters of the Devereux*, vol. II, p. 63.
43 Henry, 'The Earl of Essex and Ireland, 1599', p. 8.
44 Henry, 'The Earl of Essex and Ireland, 1599', pp. 10–11.
45 Devereux, *Lives and Letters of the Devereux*, vol. II, p. 87.
46 Henry, 'The Earl of Essex and Ireland, 1599', p. 11.
47 Henry, 'The Earl of Essex and Ireland, 1599', p. 22.
48 Devereux, *Lives and Letters of the Devereux*, vol. II, p. 63.
49 All quotations from Shakespeare, except from *As You Like It*, are from Stephen Greenblatt, Walter Cohen, Jean E. Howard and Katharine Eisaman Maus (eds), *The Norton Shakespeare* (London: Norton, 1997).
50 See Alzada J. Tipton, '"Lively Patterns … for Affayres of State": Sir John Hayward's *The Life and Reigne of King Henrie IIII* and the Earl of Essex', *Sixteenth Century Journal*

33:3 (2002), pp. 769–794.

51 Debora Shuger, '"In a Christian Climate": Religion and Honor in *Richard II*', in *Shakespeare and Religious Change*, eds Kenneth J. E. Graham and Philip D. Collington (Basingstoke: Palgrave Macmillan, 2009), p. 51.

52 Michael Neill, 'Broken English and Broken Irish: Nation, Language, and the Optic of Power in Shakespeare's Histories', *Shakespeare Quarterly* 45: 1 (1994), p.13 note 50.

53 Jonathan Dollimore and Alan Sinfield, 'History and Ideology: The Instance of *Henry V*', in *Alternative Shakespeares*, ed. John Drakakis (London: Methuen, 1985), p. 219.

54 Evelyn May Albright, 'Shakespeare's *Richard II* and the Essex Conspiracy', *PMLA* 42: 3 (1927), p. 695.

55 Hammer, 'Robert Devereux, 2nd Earl of Essex'; see also Paul E. J. Hammer, 'Myth-Making: Politics, Propaganda and the Capture of Cadiz in 1596', *The Historical Journal* 40: 3 (1997), pp. 621–642.

56 Albright, 'Shakespeare's *Richard II* and the Essex Conspiracy', p. 699.

57 Robert Spencer, 'Three English Lute Manuscripts', *Early Music*, 3:2 (1975), p. 121. It is not known how Richard Mynshall, a schoolboy of Nantwich, acquired the lute-book, embossed with Elizabeth's coat-of-arms. Spencer concludes that Mynshall served under Essex in Ireland.

58 Richard McCoy, *The Rites of Knighthood: The Literature and Politics of Elizabethan Chivalry* (Berkeley, CA: University of California Press, 1989), pp. 19, 26.

59 See Jason Scott-Warren, *Sir John Harington and the Book as Gift* (Oxford: Oxford University Press, 2001), p. 179.

60 Juliet Dusinberre, 'Pancakes and a date for *As You Like It*', *Shakespeare Quarterly* 54: 4 (2003), pp. 371–405. Dusinberre discusses links between *As You Like It*, Essex and Ireland in '*As You Like It*' in Richard Dutton and Jean E. Howard, eds. *A Companion to Shakespeare's Works, Volume III: The Comedies Blackwell Companions to Literature and Culture* (Oxford and Malden: Blackwell, 2003), pp. 411–428, and in her edition of *As You Like It* (London: Thomson Learning, 2006), pp. 56, 72–77, 96–97, 102–106, 124, 167, 193, 216, 231, 321. Alan Brissenden, in his edition of *As You Like It* (Oxford: Oxford University Press, 1993), links the play to Essex's political fortunes and the removal of the choruses from the *Henry V* quarto (pp. 3–4). Other scholars associating *As You Like It* with Essex include Geoffrey Bullough, *Narrative and Dramatic Sources of Shakespeare* (London: Routledge & Kegan Paul, 1968), vol. II. p. 142; and A. Stuart Daley, 'To Moralize a Spectacle: *As You Like It*, Act 2, Scene 1', *Philological Quarterly* 65: 2 (1986), pp. 149–150.

61 All quotations from *As You Like It* are from Dusinberre (ed.), *As You Like It.*

62 Hinton, 'Rych's "Anothomy of Ireland"', p. 82.

63 Spencer, 'Three English Lute Manuscripts', p. 120.

64 Hadfield, *Spenser's Irish Experience*, pp. 27–28.

65 Clare Carroll, 'The Text, its Sources, and Traditions', in *Solon his Follie, or a Politique Discourse Touching the Reformation of Common-weales Conquered, Declined or Corrupted* by Richard Beacon, eds Clare Carroll and Vincent Carey, Medieval and Renaissance Texts and Studies (Binghamton, NY: Centre for Medieval and Early Renaissance Studies, 1996), p. xl.

66 A. L. Rowse, *The Expansion of Elizabethan England* (London: Cardinal, 1955), p. 154.

67 Hinton, 'Rych's "Anothomy of Ireland"', p. 84.

68 Hinton, 'Rych's "Anothomy of Ireland"', p. 78.

69 Hinton, 'Rych's "Anothomy of Ireland"', p. 84.

70 Dusinberre, in her edition of *As You Like It*, notes the parallels between a song partly censored from Dekker's *Old Fortunatus* (1600) ('a leaf was torn out a third of the ... copies') and Amiens' song in *As You Like It* 2.5. The song in Dekker's play 'contained a verse referring to the ambition nurtured in courts ... possibly seen as a reference to Essex'. Amiens' song invites 'Who doth ambition shun' (2.5.33) to join him 'Under the greenwood tree' (1). This scene was cut from the Douai manuscript version of *As You Like It* (copied 1694–95), which 'may indicate ... an early theatrical tradition of excision' (p. 74). Similarly, if Jaques de Boys is taken to function as a choric figure, his speech may represent a section of the play to be added, removed or altered to suit political circumstances, as with the choruses of *Henry V*.

71 Christopher Highley, *Shakespeare, Spenser, and the Crisis in Ireland* (Cambridge: Cambridge University Press, 1997), p. 158.

72 William Shakespeare, *Henry V*, ed. Gary Taylor (Oxford: Clarendon Press, 1982), p. 7.

73 Highley, *Shakespeare, Spenser, and the Crisis in Ireland*, pp. 135–136.

74 Patricia Parker, *Shakespeare from the Margins: Language, Culture, Context* (Chicago: The University of Chicago Press, 1996), p. 332, note 37.

75 Churchyard, *The Fortunate Farewel to the Earle of Essex*, sig. A3.

76 Evelyn May Albright, 'The Folio Version of *Henry V* in Relation to Shakespeare's Times', *PMLA* 43:3 (1928), pp. 738–739. Albright bases her overall argument on some questionable datings. However, she offers an extensive and plausible treatment of the possible deletions from the *Henry V* quarto. More recent discussion of the removal of the choruses from the quarto of *Henry V* may be found in *Henry V*, ed. Taylor, pp. 4–7, 20–21; Andrew Murphy, '"'Tish ill done": *Henry the Fift* and the Politics of Editing', in *Shakespeare and Ireland: History, Politics, Culture*, eds Mark Thornton-Burnett and Ramona Wray (Basingstoke: Macmillan, 1997), pp. 213–234; and James P. Bednarz, 'When did Shakespeare Write the Choruses of *Henry V*?', *Notes and Queries* 53 (2006), pp. 486–489. For the argument that the choruses date from 1602, see Richard Dutton, '"Methinks the Truth Should Live from Age to Age": The Dating and Contexts of *Henry V*', *Huntington Library Quarterly* 68 (2005), pp. 173–204, and '*The Famous Victories* and the 1600 Quarto of *Henry V*', in *Locating the Queen's Men, 1583–1603: Material Practices and Conditions of Playing*, eds Helen Ostovich, Helger Schott Syme and Andrew Griffin (Farnham: Ashgate, 2009), pp. 135–144.

77 Richard A. McCabe, 'Making History: Holinshed's Irish *Chronicles*, 1577 and 1587', in *British Identities and English Renaissance Literature*, eds David J. Baker and Willy Maley (Cambridge: Cambridge University Press, 2002), pp. 59–60.

78 A. H. Dodd, 'Wales and the Scottish Succession', *Transactions of the Honourable Society of Cymmrodorion*, Session 1937 (1938), pp. 201–225.

79 A. H. Dodd, 'North Wales in the Essex Revolt', *The English Historical Review* 59: 235 (1944), p. 361.

80 Highley, *Shakespeare, Spenser, and the Crisis in Ireland*, p. 86.

81 Albright, 'The Folio Version of *Henry V* in Relation to Shakespeare's Times', p. 743.

82 Albright, 'The Folio Version of *Henry V* in Relation to Shakespeare's Times', p. 743.

83 See Willy Maley, 'The Irish Text and Subtext of Shakespeare's English Histories', in *A Companion to Shakespeares Works, Volume II: The Histories, Blackwell Companions to Literature and Culture*, eds Richard Dutton and Jean Howard (Oxford and Malden: Blackwell, 2003), pp. 94–124.

84 Albright, 'The Folio Version of *Henry V* in Relation to Shakespeare's Times', p. 744.

85 Dodd, 'North Wales in the Essex Revolt', p. 361.

86 John Bossy, *Christianity in the West, 1400–1700* (Oxford: Oxford University Press, 1985), p. 135.
87 David Mathew, *The Celtic Peoples and Renaissance Europe: A Study of the Celtic and Spanish Influences on Elizabethan History* (London: Sheed and Ward, 1933), p. 30.
88 For Wotton, see Paul E. J. Hammer, 'Shakespeare's *Richard II*, the Play of 7 February 1601, and the Essex Rising', *Shakespeare Quarterly* 59: 1 (2008), p. 12; for Cuffe, see David Womersley, 'Sir John Hayward's Tacitism', *Renaissance Studies* 6: 1 (1992), p. 59.
89 Hammer, 'Shakespeare's *Richard II*, the Play of 7 February 1601, and the Essex Rising', p. 15.
90 Henry Jones, *The Earl of Essex: A Tragedy in Five Acts* (1753), in *The British Theatre, or, A Collection of Plays*, ed. E. Inchbald, 20 vols, vol. 1 (London: Hurst, Robinson & Co., 1824).
91 Jones, *The Earl of Essex*, pp. 13, 21, 39.
92 Micki Myers, 'The Earl of Essex Unsuccessfully Defends his Return from Ireland Before the Privy Council, 29 September 1599', *Critical Quarterly* 49: 4 (2007), p. 123.
93 On the downfall of Thomas Wentworth, Earl of Strafford, Charles I's Irish viceroy, see Hugh Kearney, *Strafford in Ireland, 1633–41: A Study in Absolutism* (Manchester: Manchester University Press, 1959, reprint 1989).

7

Essex's last campaign: the fall of the Earl of Essex and manuscript circulation

Andrew Gordon

The Earl of Essex was one of the most prominent courtiers of Elizabeth's reign but in the later 1590s he was increasingly absent from the court itself, the central venue of power politics. At a time when access to the monarch was both a vital mark of favour and a key means of exercising influence, these episodes away from presence chamber and council table had a significant effect upon his fortunes, and a defining influence upon his engagement with court politics. Essex's service as a military commander entailed lengthy periods abroad: the Cadiz expedition of 1596, the islands voyage of 1597, and the ill-fated Irish campaign of 1599 all drew him from England and from the company of his sovereign in his final years. These exploits assured Essex a voice in questions of military strategy but they also reduced his immediate ability to shape policy and affect the decision-making process. Bouts of illness, periods of disfavour, and the sudden fits of pique to which he was sometimes prone further limited the earl's attendance at court. Absence from court increasingly shaped the textual output of Essex and his followers. It also informed the use of manuscript circulation in cultivating a textual following for the earl that continued to flourish throughout the seventeenth century.

A decisive moment in Essex's courtly career came at the end of June 1598 when disagreements over strategy in Ireland erupted into a major incident between the earl and the queen resulting in his self-imposed exile from the court. According to William Camden's later account Essex had offered an affront to royal authority by turning his back upon the monarch, and when Elizabeth responded by striking the earl he stormed out, incensed at the indignity, and refused to return.[1] Despite the dishonour incurred by Essex, many of his closest dependants found his deliberate absence from court difficult to fathom. His mother, who had suffered royal disfavour since her re-marriage to the earl of Leicester, wrote to him 'I cannot be quyet tyll I know the trew caus of your absence and dyscontentment'.[2] Essex's failure to repair the damage swiftly was an obstacle to advancement for his sister

Dorothy, now married to the Duke of Northumberland, Henry Percy, whose recusant father had died in the Tower. Essex had protected Dorothy when her first husband was executed for treason, and following her remarriage she had frequent recourse to Essex to help restore the Percy family fortunes.[3] News of an apparent illness prolonging the earl's seclusion elicited a letter from Dorothy that suggests her frustration: 'Dear brother', she wrote, 'I haue harkened after your coming backe to the courte, and euen now harde more then I desiered, of your not being well'.[4] For these family members, the earl's non-attendance deprived them of their principal means for obtaining their suits, but it was not only family interests that suffered by his absence. Essex's devoted secretary, Edward Reynolds, was well aware of the personal and political fallout from his exile, and confided his regret that 'we wear absent from ye Court 12 weeks in discontentm^{t}', in a letter to his future wife.[5] Mindful of the political disadvantages of absence Reynolds would warn Essex when he left for Ireland in 1599 that 'her Ma.[jesty's] eares are too open to suggestinge tonges'.[6] Sir William Knollys, the earl's uncle and one of his few allies on the Privy Council, was equally sensitive to the politics of occasion at court and recognised the death of Lord Burghley in August 1598 as a crucial opportunity to influence the direction of rule. He wrote to Essex that 'your <Lo:^{shipps}> being ffrom court at this tyme ys in my opinion verye unseasonable … ffor the comon good' and urged his return 'that ther be no disposyng off offyce or place wthout your Lo:^{shipps} allowance'.[7]

The withdrawal from court in 1598 was a watershed moment that challenged the faith of those who depended upon Essex for influence and advancement and those who looked to him for political leadership. Although he was back at court by the end of September doubts over his disposition persisted. The remaining months before he left for Ireland in the spring would represent his last season as a courtier in regular attendance upon the queen. Thereafter he would return to court only once more, in September 1599, when he broke off from a failing Irish campaign hampered by over-expectation, under-resourcing and poor health, to ride suddenly for England in hope of convincing the queen in person to address the problems besetting his commission. Catching the court and the sovereign unawares, he obtained the immediate audience he sought, but the meetings he had with the queen that day were to be his last. After abandoning his Irish command the last year and a half of his life was spent in confinement and house arrest. This was a pivotal moment in the earl's relationship with court and queen and its significance for the understanding of Essex's fortunes was recognised by a contemporary reader of Stow's *Annales* who annotated the account of this sudden interview: 'he could neuer spek wth hear, nor se: hear mor'.[8] As this anonymous reader recognised, in the court-centric world of Elizabethan England to be deprived of speech with the queen, and to be denied her presence, was an exclusion both practical and symbolic from the influence of intimacy.

Support for the earl within the council had dwindled with his deepening detachment from the court while Cecil's monopolisation of political patronage had grown and Essex turned increasingly to other avenues to exert his influence.[9] His martial exploits had always played better to the gallery than the council chamber and he enjoyed widespread popular support beyond the confines of the court. A reputation for valour established early with acts of sometimes reckless bravery was confirmed in the popular imagination by the capture of Cadiz, which brought widespread acclaim to the earl but few of the promised riches to Elizabeth's treasury.[10] Essex cultivated his martial charisma at home with prominent participation in the Accession Day tournaments and stage-managed other public appearances to maximum effect. Departing for Ireland he set off from Seething Lane in order to show himself to best advantage in the city processing 'through Fenchurch streete, Grace streete, Cornehille, Cheape, &c' with 'a great traine of Noble men, and gentlemen, on horsebacke before him, to accompany him on his iourney'.[11] Essex's use of highly visible public performance and cultivation of a common popularity did not endear him to fellow members of Elizabeth's council and his attempt to 'challeng[e] the monopoly which a sovereign supposedly enjoyed over their subjects' "love"' was seen as dangerously destabilising.[12]

The gestural economy of public appearances was a useful tool in establishing Essex in the popular imagination but the earl sought to address his absence from the centres of influence by developing a more expressive voice in political culture. To this end from the late 1590s Essex and his associates made use of a strategy of textual production and circulation in which letters, verse and other textual forms were deployed to shape his popular image and to articulate his conception of service to the crown. Essex was already a prominent figure within the literary culture of the period as one of its leading patrons. More printed works were dedicated to him than to any other figure in the 1590s, throwing up some unexpected and controversial associations which played into contemporary perceptions of the earl.[13] Chapman's *Seaven Bookes of the Iliades*, with its dedication to Essex as the 'now living instance of the Achileian vertues', appeared in mid-1598, in time to resonate with the modern military hero's withdrawal from court.[14] The dedication to Essex of Hayward's Tacitean history *The Life and Reigne of King Henrie IIII* attracted much comment for the potential parallels between Richard II and Elizabeth, although repeated investigation could demonstrate no link with Essex nor specific seditious intent on Hayward's behalf.[15] In addition to the associations produced by patronage and dedications, Essex had also made his own use of the written word in propaganda campaigns. In the wake of the Cadiz voyage he had contended with Ralegh, that master of self-promotion, in seeking to disseminate his own accounts of the expedition and have them printed under fake initials.[16] Letters of advice to the Earl of Rutland had also been circulated in manuscript to present the earl's credentials as a wise counsellor.[17] Essex was thus alive to the potential of both print and manuscript to help manage his public persona and shape understanding of current events. In 1598 however he turned from self-promotion to policy with the text known as *Essex's Apologie*, the context and dissemination of which is the subject of Chapter 8. With this text, Essex took the arguments he had made unsuccessfully in the council chamber for an aggressive interventionist policy against Spain to a new constituency beyond the court. Appealing to an audience outside the immediate circle of court and counsellors as a way of influencing policy was a radical manoeuvre resembling the textual strategies of opponents during the Exclusion crisis whose appeal to a broader textual audience has been associated by Peter Lake with the emergence of an Elizabethan precursor to the public sphere. In common with so many of the texts identified by Lake as simultaneously invoking and bringing into being a space of political consciousness and debate, Essex delivered his commentary upon foreign policy in the form of a letter.[18] The letter form provided a pretext for discussion of political strategy between members of an elite group of statesmen and counsellors concerned for the common good. The chosen vehicle in the *Apologie* was a letter to Anthony Bacon, one of the earl's closest advisers, but its common heading in manuscript copies as *An Apologie of the Earle of Essex against those which falsly and maliciouslye taxe him to bee thonely hinderaunce of the peace and quiet of his country* announces the engagement with a broader community within an inherently political culture of circulating opinion.[19]

The appropriation of the letter form in the *Apologie* is thus a manifest fiction intended not to deceive but to license an exercise in political persuasion. In parallel to this, many of Essex's writings of the period occupy themselves with the symbolic construction of a textual voice, and incorporate complaints about Essex's personal situation that have an implicitly political resonance. The widely circulated letters between Essex and Egerton dating from the earl's self-imposed exile of mid-1598 provide a prominent example. Essex's letter came close to accusing Elizabeth of tyranny in rejecting the Lord Keeper's explication of his duty to submit to the queen, the earl countering with a more conditional model of service in which he explicitly rejected the obligation to wait upon his sovereign: 'the duty of attendance ys noe indissoluble diuty' Essex affirmed.[20] In this notorious text Essex appropriated the discourse of justice to complain of being condemned 'without tryall or hearing' and made the refusal to 'forsake myne owne iust defence' the premise for his discordant letter.[21] Essex's rhetorical construction of a textual voice in this text is predicated upon a literary re-imagining of exclusion that dramatises his textual act as defiant resistance to injustice. In so doing Essex transforms the occasion for submission presented by Egerton, into a platform for complaint against oppression. Essex also makes use of conventional modes of anti-court complaint in a number of widely copied texts epitomised by the letter to the queen in which he refashions his absence from court in the language of melancholic withdrawal, announcing 'I Choose in this wearysome Corse, rather to be retyred, then tyred', while carefully attributing the cause of his grief to those who 'take advantage of my absence'.[22] Essex characteristically transposes his melancholy into a figure for the deprivation of voice and makes this the pretext for taking up the pen: 'greife Cannot speake, and this greife hath made me wright'. This letter would swiftly become a mainstay of manuscript letter compilations in the seventeenth century, but it is also extant in early examples datable to around the time of Essex's troubles.[23] Essex frequently appropriated a Petrarchan poetics in some of his more lyrical letters addressed to Elizabeth and where he represents absence from the court in terms of exile from the favour of his mistress in such widely circulating letters as that sent from Ireland beginning 'From a mind delighting in sorrow' where he 'figur[es] lack of resources and support in the cruelty of Elizabeth'.[24] A politically resonant Petrarchanism was equally prominent in the poetry of and about Essex as well as among the many libellous verses centring on courtly corruption in which he often heads the cast list of those persecuted by a Cecilian faction.[25] Despite the deployment of a variety of modes and a range of textual forms, suppression of voice and exclusion from the queen's presence remain the twin poles of a common discursive strategy traceable in the Essex works circulating beyond the court. The political resonance of these twin topoi is perhaps best illustrated by some of the letters from Essex to Elizabeth written during 1600 that do not circulate. In a number of direct appeals to Elizabeth written as hope of rehabilitation receded, Essex recognised the need to address the threatening symbolism of voice which figured so prominently within his circulated letters and verses. A letter of February 1600 offers Elizabeth the testimony of his tongue envisaging 'how much more it will agre wth yor princely & angel-like nature, to haue yor mrcye blazed by ye tongue of yor Mats once happy but now most sorrowful creature'.[26] By September, with financial ruin hanging over him as Elizabeth demurred on the renewal of his principal source of revenue, the farm on sweet wines, his tone is wholly abject. No longer offering the service of his tongue, he gives up all claim to speech affirming that 'my uttermost ambicon is to be a mute ꝑson in that presence, where joy & wonder would bar speech'.[27] The extreme attenuation of voice in these letters can be read in conjunction with his persistent reference to the repression of voice in the circulating texts as a measure of the political potency of this theme.

Essex's strategic deployment of voice and absence within his letters and other writings is matched by indications of a circulation strategy calculated to attract a greater readership while preserving an outward commitment to a highly exclusive textual community. The association of Essex with the circulation of libels and letters was raised in Star Chamber in November 1599 and featured prominently in the York House Hearing of June 1600.[28] The *Apologie* is dealt with more fully in Chapter 8 but Essex's response in May 1600, when he was called upon to answer for its appearance in a printed edition, offers an insight into the poetics of manuscript circulation. Pleading ignorance, he attributed the text's coming abroad to 'the corruption of some of my seruants thatt had accesse to my chamber who might take and copy owt my loose papers wch lay euer sheete by sheete under my beds head'.[29] Here the earl exploits contemporary anxiety over the trustworthiness of servants and draws attention to the vulnerability of his 'loose papers' to unscrupulous misuse. His denial of direct involvement in the printing is extended to organised manuscript circulation and he claims never to have 'sent any [copies] to the presse or to skriueners shopp' but the studied negligence over his papers opens a rhetorical window of opportunity.[30] Dissociating himself from direct involvement in textual circulation he nevertheless acknowledges the accommodation of a privileged readership: 'I was so farr from geuing copyes of yt as I chardged my man thatt kepes my papers not to lett any of my frends see yt butt in his hand or att least in his presence'. By confining legitimate access to intimate associates Essex looks to represent the text's limited dissemination as the embodiment of its textual form: the sharing of ideas among his immediate circle of advisers – an explanation imitative of conciliar practice that seeks to pass off his actions as those of a dutiful statesman. But this account is deeply disingenuous, for while a readership of friends might be used to downplay the extent of access to this sensitive text, part of the appeal of such texts in manuscript, and particularly those adopting the letter form, lay in their capacity to inculcate in the reader a sense of intimate association. The loosely defined category of 'friends' here could as well describe one of the textual effects through which manuscript circulation of Essex texts was able to generate allegiance. Scribal circulation itself, as Harold Love has suggested, functions to 'bond … groups of like-minded individuals into a community, sect or political faction, with the exchange of texts in manuscript serving to nourish a shared set of values and to enrich personal allegiances'.[31] David Colclough has argued that the material engagement of textual agents itself stimulates political engagement since 'the very practices of transcription or annotation are acts that place [the individual] in a critical and active relationship to the civic world'.[32] Love identified a predisposition for scribal communities to map onto existing social groups but he also acknowledged the potential of manuscript circulation to bring communities into being. Building upon this work, Jason Scott-Warren has proposed the concept of the manuscript network to describe the dynamic practices of manuscript communities and address the tendency to 'over-emphasise closure and exclusivity' within models of circulation.[33] The need to embrace a broad range of circulation practices is integral to Love's conception of scribal publication which incorporates both professionally produced texts and diverse forms of 'user publication' that cover the actions of individuals in making their own copies of a circulating text. User publication of this kind is always social in nature – from the obtaining of texts to their use after copying since 'individuals who assembled large numbers of scribally published documents were also likely to be active transmitters of texts'.[34] Despite Essex's protestations of innocence in matters of scribal publication, the material evidence illustrates both the organisation of scribally produced texts, and the social breadth of transmission via user publication.

One of the challenges in tracing the circulation of Essex-related material is the very success of its dissemination in manuscript form. The corpus of Essex texts remained a cornerstone of manuscript compilation through much of the seventeenth century. 'Letters of all sorts. especially by ye late E. of Essex' topped the list of 'Manuscripts to gett' drawn up by the sometime Essex follower Francis Davison, whose manuscript library was obtained by the archivist-collector Ralph Starkey.[35] The sustained appeal of these texts cannot be confined to a desire for model letters or a general historical interest. Chapter 10 in this volume examines the contrasting lessons drawn from his actions amongst contemporaries schooled in politic history but the ongoing presence of his texts in manuscript continued to provide a touchstone for political reflection in debates over tyranny and royal authority after his death, supplied the grounds for comparative analysis of topical issues such as Buckingham's revival of a politics of popularity in the 1620s as well as registering within the conceptualisation of an oppositional politics more generally.[36] Proving early circulation is complicated by the difficulty of identifying specific contexts of production and interpretation for individual manuscript copies. In the case of the letter of Essex to Egerton, however, the considerable number of scribal copies extant in the format of a separate, generally the earliest type of copy to emerge, provide evidence of organised contemporary circulation.[37] Of these, two copies in the same scribal hand include a list of 'Articles where upon the earle of Essex was accused in the Starchamber. 29. Nouember: 1599'.[38] That the letter was paired with this text rather than any of the numerous materials generated by the earl's uprising and subsequent trial of February 1601 suggests that these duplicate separates were produced for circulation during the period of the earl's imprisonment in 1599–1600.[39]

If these scribal separates indicate organised production, two remarkable manuscript copies provide an opportunity to explore the response of readers to Essex's textual output, illustrating the dynamic operation of manuscript transmission in cultivating a textual following for the Earl of Essex. The first example is a copy of Essex's August 1599 letter to the queen from Ireland ('from a mind delighting in sorrow'). It is found in a contemporary manuscript lute book and sheds light upon a rich culture of manuscript transmission. The manuscript was compiled by the adolescent Richard Mynshall, a native of Nantwich in Cheshire, and contains the tablature for a sequence of forty-one lute pieces, one of which is annotated with the date 1597, when Mynshall was fifteen.[40] As a pedagogical lute book, the manuscript would have been compiled under the guidance of a teacher and analysis of the hands in the volume has shown that the pupil was responsible for copying thirty-nine of the items, with errors indicative of his lack of knowledge, while two other hands contribute an item each.[41] The copy of the earl's letter appears at the end of the book beneath a recipe for toothache embellished with Mynshall's signature and is copied in a neat secretary hand that differs from the other items (f.98v; Figure 5). Mynshall has carefully written out the first three words of the letter in the top right hand corner of the page indicating that the text is not an extraneous addition but part of the composite work over which he asserts his propriety. Although the copy of the letter contains a number of insertions in the hand of the copyist, including a missing line, the text itself corresponds closely to the holograph original, containing the correct date in contrast to other textual witnesses, and lacking the principal variants found in other copies.[42]

The appearance of the earl's letter in this context illustrates a series of cultural and material connections which inform the circulation of Essex-related material in the period. Although Essex was a prominent musical patron and a number of instrumental pieces were produced in his honour along with lute settings of various Essex-attributed poems by John Dowland, Daniel Bacheler and others, the musical contents themselves do not point to any clear agenda.[43] Recent work by Kirsten Gibson has persuasively identified the Essex associations of the politicised trope of banishment and exile within Dowland's repertoire yet while Dowland is the most prominent composer in the Mynshall lute book, the only one of the pieces with an overt Essex connection is the William Hewes composition titled here 'the earl of Essikes dumpte'.[44] More illuminating is the social profile of lutenists in the period. The 1590s has been seen as a high point within the golden age of the lute in England. Its popularity extended across social groups, connecting amateur and professional, and linking diverse geographical and cultural locations, including some of the key centres of manuscript production. Its principal exponents comprised 'wealthy amateurs (often women) with gentry or noble backgrounds; professional male musicians of a lower social status; and young men at court, the universities, and Inns of court'.[45] Teaching and performance granted social access and recent research has demonstrated the mobility of the contemporary musician, with those in the service of noble families as well as the waits employed by various civic corporations, touring extensively around the country.[46] The practitioners of music exerted influence as teachers and performers and were also the agents of personalised manuscript transmission in a field where professional scribes were a rarity.[47] Professional lutenists who gained positions in noble households or at court 'were marked out [from other servants] by their literacy'.[48] Since lute tablature, in contrast to notation, is scriptural in basis, the overlap between musical and textual copyist was significant.

The frequent travel as well as the national and continental contacts of lutenists led to their employment as messengers in the delivery of letters. The accounts of Sir John Stanhope, Treasurer of the Chamber, reveal payments to the lutenist and composer Antony Holborne to deliver letters to the Estates General in January 1599.[49] At the same time lutenists figured within clandestine networks, as with the boy lutenist brought over from Brussels in 1599 to serve as the 'trustie Messinger' delivering letters between the exiled Earl of Westmorland's connections.[50] Closer to Essex himself the skilled lutenist and composer Daniel Bacheler, who set to music Essex's poem 'To plead my faith', was also employed in the delivery of letters.[51] Bacheler had formerly been in the service of the Walsingham family and Sir Philip Sidney before joining Essex's household upon his marriage to Sidney's widow, Frances Walsingham. Stanhope's accounts record payment on a warrant of 10 August 1599 when Bacheler was 'sent wth lres for her ma^{ts} specyall seruice to the Lo Lewtenante and Councell of Ireland'.[52] Henry Cuffe, Essex's secretary accompanying him in Ireland wrote from Dublin to the London-based Edward Reynolds on 19 August recording the arrival of 'Daniell', as he was known, 'muche besides of expectation because the wynde hathe bene of late almost euer contrary'.[53] The evidence thus puts Bacheler in Ireland some eleven days before the date of the letter from Arbracken and it is not unlikely that he may have carried letters in return, passing through Nantwich itself, a stopping point on the royal post route from Ireland.[54] The chances of a servant such as Bacheler breaking open a letter to the queen are surely remote, but the cultural connections of musicians and lutenists nevertheless represented a ready and available network for manuscript transmission if deliberate circulation of Essex's letter to Elizabeth was sought.[55] As a professional instructor influencing the formation of young minds, a trafficker in manuscripts circulating a repertoire with discernible patronage links, a performer with access to court and noble households, and a textual agent entrusted with the highly sensitive role of letter bearer, the lutenist was particularly well placed to execute this function. While the Mynshall lute book cannot be linked to a specific instructor, the material form of the manuscript itself betrays its connections to the court. From the evidence of its extravagant binding embossed with the royal arms, and analysis of watermarks, Spencer has argued that before coming into the hands of Richard Mynshall the volume was 'issued as a blank manuscript book to one of Elizabeth's lutenists'.[56]

In the evidence of this artefact then we see the operation of a manuscript network through which the culture of the court provides the material site for an individual's formative exercises in political positioning. The pedagogical structure of the Mynshall lute book as a whole associates it with a series of imitative textual transactions as the pupil mastered both the tablature and the performance of a simplified lute repertoire drawn from older standards and pieces from prominent composers of the day. Yet the multiple hands which annotate the volume on the non-musical pages, in the signatures of Hugh Allan, Thomas Crockett and Mynshall himself, also point to the manuscript as an example of the kind of 'quasi public environment' of the page Jason Scott Warren has identified in the marking up of early modern books.[57] This provides a wider context for understanding the extent of Mynshall's engagement with Essex's letter, shown by a verse in Mynshall's hand inscribed on the recto (f.98r; see Figure 6).

> Souldiers are like the Armo^{r} that the waiere
> All gay at firste, newe faire & ffurbishede
> But after showers & stromes & blowes the baire
> Broken disarmde & all soe hargabushed [arquebussed]
> Some throwne aside some hanged againste the walls
> Soe after wars souldiers to Ruine falls
> The gallent Courtier wch for his mistris gloue
> Dare breeke a bullrushe against annothers strawe
> And bandie baules for luker & for loue
> And dance a galliard none a better sawe
> & sette a bataile wth a pare of cardst
> these be the ladds that liue & haue rewards
>
> But the gallente worne & untrimmde man
> That wth a tree Encounters dare a thee
> & bides the brunts of bulletts nowe & then
> Treadinge the grounde where Rampte aduentures lie
> & in that ground Intrenchte wth battaile pike
> These bee the ladds may sterue & die in dicke [dyke]
>
> Couragius Caesar made his campte his courte
> His captaines kings Inferior laiders lords
> To gaine a countre was his huntinge sporte
> & as the huntsman to his houndes afordes
> The entreals of the ^< beasts> that he hath slaine
> Soe what he got rewa^<r>ded souldiers paine
> Well, tyme may come that souldiers ~~my~~ may bee kinges
> Kings in conseate I meane not other wise
> To aspire to crounes wee see it daunger brings
> to bee inspired wth crownes shall us suffise,
> But ^<not> for this since Avorice cannot hould
> When Midas' cheists are chockte wth towe much gould.
> finis finis
> Rich. Mynshall (f.98r)

The poem is a soldier's complaint, resoundingly anti-court in its stance, which juxtaposes the graphically evoked brutality of the soldier's lot against the rich rewards available to the courtier and represents a generalised poetic statement of the argument put in passionate and personalised terms in Essex's letter. Lamenting contemporary disregard for the virtues of military service Mynshall looks back to the example of 'Couragius Caesar' who 'made his campe his courte'. This image of inversion carries with it a threatening resonance as Mynshall acknowledges in a qualification that alludes to the Earl of Essex's troubles:

Well, tyme may come that souldiers ~~my~~ may bee kinges
Kings in conseate I meane not other wise
To aspire to crownes wee see it daunger bringes (f.98r)

The lines strongly evoke the earl's failed uprising of 1601 and indicate the author's empathy with the discontent of the fallen martial statesman – there may even be a faint echo of Essex's memorable qualifier in the text of his letter on the verso ('to ransome my selfe my soule I meane'). Even the apparent condemnation of dangerous aspiration is undermined by the substitution of a dishonourable alternative course 'to bee inspired wth crownes'.

The connections between the earl's letter and Mynshall's poem illustrate the impact of Essex texts in circulation. They point to the compilation of the manuscript in this example of user publication as a dynamic process giving form to allegiance. The effects of a textual encounter with Essex's words can be further demonstrated in a remarkable scribal copy of the two Egerton–Essex letters where we find another adolescent pen at work a generation after Mynshall providing evidence of another kind of identification. The manuscript is a bifolio separate amongst the papers of William Sancroft, the non-juror who became Archbishop of Canterbury after a long academic career as scholar and master at Emmanuel College, Cambridge. Sancroft, from Fressingfield in Suffolk, was one of the most assiduous collectors and compilers of manuscripts in the period, amassing a vast collection that included Bod Tanner MS 76, an important group of assorted Essex-related materials which he collated and annotated extensively.[58] The bibliographical annotations of Sancroft, however, are markedly different in kind from those which adorn BL Harley MS 3787, ff.177–178. Figure 7 illustrates the conclusion of the earl's letter and the extensive annotation beneath it with the repeated rehearsals of the signature 'Anthony Grenlinge'. The author of these annotations is almost certainly Sancroft's brother-in-law, Anthony Grenlinge, from the neighbouring Suffolk village of Stradbroke, who matriculated at Emmanuel College in Easter 1637 just as William Sancroft the elder, the Master of the college and father of his future wife, lay dying.[59] The multiple versions of the signature are a common feature of adolescent manuscript annotation shared by Mynshall's lute book, and given the thriving manuscript culture at the universities Grenlinge may well have come into contact with the separate during his time at Emmanuel.[60] Differences in ink and nib suggest more than one occasion of writing. The variant forms of Grenlinge's name show the working out of a signature in italic, developing a flourish linking A and G through repeated practice. Beneath this on the page we find his rehearsal of another signature, this time in a mixed secretary hand. The two signatures in contrasting hands allow us to glimpse Grenlinge imaginatively inscribing himself on the one (italic) hand, within a humanist, courtly context and on the other, within a form of scribal service represented by the secretary script; exercises in the process of 'character formation' explored by Jonathan Goldberg.[61] Grenlinge's rehearsals are more than mere pen-trials, however, they are undertaken in dialogue with the copied Essex letter, the text of which includes a bitter meditation upon service of the monarch where the earl recalled 'I haue bene content to doe her the seruice of a Clarke'. Grenlinge's penmanship includes imitating the valediction and the scribal version of Essex's signature in which the 'Ess' and the elaborate flourish above the capitalised 'L' recall elements of the studied flourish in Grenlinge's name. Nor is the engagement with Essex limited to the valedictory elements. The overlap of imitation with articulation of the self is at its most intense where Grenlinge copies a line from the letter 'since you doe but see and I doe suffer', and adds to it an extravagant italic signature. In this manoeuvre Grenlinge both inhabits and appropriates the experience of the earl – a moment of identification made all the more powerful by the dramatic insistence upon individuated experience in the quoted lines. In both a physical and an imaginative sense Grenlinge identifies himself as an Essex follower in this moment, but his act of enscription does not yield easily to precise political interpretation. Essex's writings certainly provided a discursive model of opposition that could find ready application within contemporary resistance theory and the gathering storm clouds of the late 1630s had triggered increased interest in resistance topoi. Nevertheless part of Essex's ongoing appeal which translated itself particularly well to the embodied materiality of manuscript culture was the potential for the personal history of his troubles to embody manifold forms of complaint. Grenlinge's enigmatic mark of allegiance is a product of the simultaneous intimacy and sociability of manuscript circulation. From the fragile scribal separate produced for ease of circulation and annotated by Grenlinge, to the lavish court volume in which Mynshall's sympathies with the copied Essex letter are evidenced in his verse, we find in these manuscript witnesses a vivid illustration of how Essex's cultivation of a textual community could continue to generate diverse articulations of allegiance even beyond the grave.

Notes

1 William Camden, *Annales or the History of the most Renowned and Victorious Princesse Elizabeth* trans. Robert Norton (London: Benjamin Fisher, 1635), p. 493.
2 Undated letter endorsed 'July 98', *Devereux Letter Book*, Warwickshire Record Office MI229, f. 38.
3 Paul Hammer, *The Polarisation of Elizabethan Politics: The Political Career of Robert Devereux, 2nd Earl of Essex, 1585–1597* (Cambridge: Cambridge University Press, 1999), p. 274 note 33.
4 Undated letter, *Devereux Letter Book*, f. 22.
5 Letter of 15 Jan 1599, National Archive (NA) SP 12/270, f. 47.
6 Letter of 1 March 1599, BL Harley MS 292, f. 163.
7 Letter endorsed "August 98", *Devereux Letter Book*, f. 44.
8 The marginal annotation is in the Folger copy of John Stow, *The Annales of England* (London, 1601) Shelf mark cs309, p. 1305. That this was a contemporary reader is

shown by dated annotations such as the note on p. 1240 'Mr watts was then bot a power man and now is a Riche alder man 1602'.

9 Natalie Mears, '*Regnum Cecilianum*? A perspective of the Court', in *The Reign of Elizabeth*, ed. J. Guy (Cambridge: Cambridge University Press, 1995), pp. 46–63.

10 Paul Hammer, *Elizabeth's Wars: War, Government and Society in Tudor England 1544–1604* (Basingstoke: Palgrave 2003), pp. 197–198.

11 John Stow, *The Annales of England* (London, 1601), p. 1304.

12 Paul Hammer, 'The Smiling Crocodile: the Earl of Essex and Later Elizabethan "Popularity"' in *The Politics of the Public Sphere in Early Modern England*, eds Peter Lake and Steven Pincus (Manchester: Manchester University Press, 2008), p. 105.

13 Alastair Fox, 'The Complaint of Poetry for the Death of Liberality; the Decline of Literary Patronage in the 1590s', in *The Reign of Elizabeth: Court and culture in the 1590s*, ed. J. Guy (Cambridge: Cambridge University Press 1995), p. 231.

14 George Chapman, *Seaven Bookes of the Iliades* (London, 1598), sig. A3. The translation was registered with the Stationers prior to Essex's withdrawal, in April 1598.At the end of that year his dedication to Essex of *Achilles Shield* more deliberately exploited Essex's martial prestige during preparations for the Irish campaign. John Channing Briggs, 'Chapman's *Seaven Bookes of the Iliades*: Mirror for Essex', *SEL* 21 (1981), pp. 59–73.

15 The connection between Essex and Hayward has been extensively investigated in recent scholarship, see *The Life and Raigne of King Henrie IIII*, ed. John Manning, Camden Society, 4th series, no. 42 (London: Camden Society, 1991), pp. 1–55; Leeds Barroll, 'A New History for Shakespeare and His Time', *Shakespeare Quarterly* 39 (1988), pp. 441–464; Rebecca Lemon, 'The Faulty Verdict in "The Crown v. John Hayward"', *Studies in English Literature 1500–1900* 41 (2001), pp. 109–132; Alzada Tipton, '"Lively patterns … for affayres of state": Sir John Hayward's *The Life and Reigne of King Henrie IIII* and the Earl of Essex', *Sixteenth-Century Journal* 33: 3 (2002), pp. 769–794; Chapter 10 provides an important new contribution to this list.

16 Paul Hammer, 'Myth-Making: Politics, Propaganda and the Capture of Cadiz in 1596,' *The Historical Journal* 40: 3 (1997), pp. 621–642.

17 Paul Hammer, 'The Earl of Essex, Fulke Greville, and the Employment of Scholars', *Studies in Philology* 91 (1994), pp. 167–180; on the dating and authorship of these letters see also Alan Stewart (ed.) with Harriet Knight, *The Oxford Francis Bacon vol 1: Early Writings 1584 to 1596* (Oxford: Oxford University Press, 2012).

18 Peter Lake, 'The Politics of "Popularity" and the Public Sphere: the "Monarchical Republic" of Elizabeth I Defends Itself', in *The Politics of the Public Sphere*, eds Lake and Pincus, pp. 59–94. See also David Randall, 'Epistolary Rhetoric, the Newspaper, and the Public Sphere', *Past and Present* 198 (2008), 3–32.

19 Bodleian Tanner MS 76, f. 12.

20 BL Lansdowne MS 87, f. 191. See Andrew Gordon, '"A Fortune of Paper Walls": the Letters of Francis Bacon and the Earl of Essex', *English Literary Renaissance* 37: 3 (2007), pp. 319–336.

21 BL Lansdowne MS 87, f. 191.

22 BL Royal MS 17 BL, f. 16v.

23 There is no known holograph of this letter which has an opening prone to variation in the copying process ('My dutiful affection to your Majesty always so overweighed all other worldly respects'). The earliest definitively dateable example is in Folger MS V. b. 214, f. 106, part of a volume belonging to Richard Greene inscribed with the date of 1st July 1601. Two early copies in the forms of separates are BL Add MS 4106, f. 72 which also contains Bacon's 1599 letter to Henry Howard and reply, and

BL Harley MS 3786, f. 49. A number of the Essex-focused collections containing copies are likely to date from the early 1600s e.g.: Bod Rawlinson MS C744, f. 61; BL Royal MS 17 B. L. ff. 14v–17; NLS Adv MS 34.2.10 ff. 95–96v. The copy in Folger MS V. a. 321, ff. 5v–6, is part of a collection associated with Peter Ferryman which Braunmuller suggests may date from 1614 in his critical edition, *A Seventeenth-Century Letter-Book* (Newark, DE: University of Delaware Press, 1983), p. 33. Examples in the large general letter collections such as Bodleian Tanner MS 82, ff. 25–26v; BL Add MS 44848, ff. 23v–25; BL Add MS 4108, f. 6; Bod Eng Hist MS c272, pp. 37–39; Yale Beinecke Osborn fb220; Folger v a 239 ff. 50–54; and Folger V b 234, pp. 38–41, are likely to date from the 1620s at the earliest while one copy, BL Harley MS 1323, ff. 246–247v, is part of a collection of state tracts and letters identified as in the hand of the Feathery Scribe (fl. c. 1628–c.1641) in Peter Beal's *In Praise of Scribes: Manuscripts and their Makers in Seventeenth-Century England* (Oxford: Clarendon Press, 1998) Appendix II, p. 244.

24 Andrew Gordon, '*Copycopia*, or the Place of Copied Correspondence in Manuscript Culture: a Case Study', in *Material Readings of Early Modern Culture: Texts and Social Practices, 1580–1700*, eds James Daybell and Peter Hinds (Palgrave, 2010), p. 77. A holograph of the letter survives among the Hulton papers dated from Arbracken 30 August [1599] BL Add MS 74286 f. 127. It also appears in the following collections BL Add MS 44848, ff. 25v; BL Add MS 4108, f. 6v; Bod Ashmole MS 781, f. 83; Bod Rawlinson MS C744 f. 59v; Bod Tanner MS 82 f. 27r; NLS Adv MS 34.2.10, f. 93r; BL Royal MS 17 B L f. 17r-v; Folger v a 239 f. 55; Folger V b 234, pp. 41–42, Chetham Library MS A. 4. 15, f. 30v and in Royal Academy MS 601, f. 98v. Grace Ioppolo lists some MS witnesses in '"Your Majesties most humble faythfullest and most affectionate seruant": The Earl of Essex Constructs Himself and his Queen in the Hulton Letters', in *Elizabeth I and the Culture of Writing*, eds Peter Beal and Grace Ioppolo (London: British Library, 2007), p. 55 n 34.

25 Steven M. May,'The Poems of Edward De Vere, Seventeenth Earl of Oxford and of Robert Devereux, Second Earl of Essex.' *Studies in Philology Texts and Studies* 77:5 (1980). Texts of various Essex-centred libels in circulation are given in Section A of Alastair Bellany and Andrew McRae (eds), 'Early Stuart Libels: an Edition of Poetry from Manuscript Sources', *Early Modern Literary Studies* Text Series I (2005), http://purl.oclc.org/emls/texts/libels.

26 Letter of 11 February 1600, NA SP 12/274 f. 52.

27 Letter of 9 September 1600, NA SP 12/275, f. 104

28 Gordon, '*Copycopia*', pp. 70–74.

29 Undated letter endorsed 'ꝑtestacon of my L. conc'ning his apology', Cecil Papers 67/38. A letter of Sir Richard Barkeley to Cecil dated 23 May 1600 repeating the precise details of Essex's explanation confirms the occasion of its composition, Cecil Papers 79/74.

30 Cecil Papers 67/38.

31 Harold Love, *Scribal Publication in Seventeenth-Century England* (Amherst, MA: University of Massachusetts Press, 1993), p. 177.

32 David Colclough, *Freedom of Speech in Early Stuart England* (Cambridge: Cambridge University Press, 2005), p. 199.

33 Jason Scott-Warren, 'Reconstructing manuscript networks: the textual transactions of Sir Stephen Powle' in *Communities in Early Modern England: Networks, Place, Rhetoric*, eds Alexandra Shepard and Phil Withington (Manchester: Manchester University Press, 2000), p. 19.

34 Love, *Scribal Publication*, pp. 79–80.

35 BL Harley MS 298, f. 159v. The leaf is reproduced as fig. 2 in Lara M. Crowley, 'Donne, not Davison: Reconsidering the Authorship of "Psalme 137"', *Modern Philology* 105:4 (2008), pp. 603–636. On Davison and the potential Essex allegiances of his print miscellany *Poetical Rhapsody* see Richard C. McCoy, 'Lord of Liberty: Francis Davison and the cult of Elizabeth' in *The Reign of Elizabeth*, ed. J. Guy, pp. 212–228. On the manuscript collections of Davison and his father see Beal, *In Praise of Scribes*, pp. 88–92.

36 Arthur Marotti, *Manuscript, Print, and the English Renaissance Lyric* (Ithaca, NY: Cornell University Press, 1995), pp. 95–98; Thomas Cogswell, 'The People's Love: The Duke of Buckingham and Popularity', in *Politics, Religion and Popularity in Early Stuart Britain*, eds Thomas Cogswell, Peter Lake and Richard Cust (Cambridge: Cambridge University Press 2002), pp. 210–234; Colclough, *Freedom of Speech in Early Stuart England*, pp. 238–250.

37 BL Lansdowne MS 87 ff. 45–46; BL Lansdowne MS 87 ff. 191–192; BL Harley MS 3787, ff. 177–178; NA SP 12/268 ff. 73–74 (pencil pagination ff.45–6); NA SP 12/268 ff. 75–76. This supplements the list of manuscript witnesses in all formats given in Gordon, '"A Fortune of Paper Walls"', p. 327 note 29.

38 NA SP 12/268 ff. 73–74; NA SP 12/268 ff. 75–76.

39 The compiler of Folger V a 321 was almost certainly working from a separate from this group, since s/he includes the same list of accusations after the earl's letter (ff. 4v–5). Comparison of the principal variants in the letter text supports the textual connection.

40 The Mynshall Lute Book, Royal Academy of Music, MS 601. The date annotation appears on f. 5v. A facsimile edition was produced by the former owner of the manuscript Robert Spencer, *The Mynshall Lute Book* (Leeds: Boethius Press, 1975).

41 Julia Craig-McFeely, 'English Lute Manuscripts and Scribes 1530–1630', University of Oxford DPhil 1993, www.ramesescats.co.uk/thesis, pp. 222–229.

42 Hence in the first sentence the order of 'trauell care & greefe' found here and in the holograph, differs from the 'care, grief and travel' found in Bod Rawlinson MS C 744, f. 59v; Bod Tanner MS 82, f. 27; Bod Ashmole MS 781, f. 83; NLS Adv MS 34. 2. 10, f. 93r; Chetham Library MS A. 4. 15, f.30v; or the variant 'Care grefe and sorowe' found in BL Royal MS 17 B L f. 17r. The Mynshall copy differs from the holograph in the obvious misreading of 'passinge' for 'passion', a variation I have not encountered in the transcriptions collated for this chapter.

43 On settings of Essex-related verses see Diana Poulton, *John Dowland* (London: Faber and Faber, 1982), pp. 229, 285–286; Edward Doughtie, 'Sidney, Tessier, Batchelar and *A Musicall Banquet*: Two Notes', *Renaissance News* 18: 2 (1965), pp. 123–126. The claim of Ruff and Wilson that 'the madrigal and lutenist composers from 1598 to 1600 were overwhelmingly of Essex sympathies' is overstated, Lillian M. Ruff and D. Arnold Wilson, 'The Madrigal, the Lute Song and Elizabethan Politics', *Past & Present* 44 (1969), p. 23.

44 Kirsten Gibson, '"So to the wood went I": Politicizing the Greenwood in Two Songs by John Dowland', *Journal of the Royal Musical Association* 132: 2 (2007), pp. 221–251. On the Mynshall repertoire see Craig-McFeely, 'English Lute Manuscripts and Scribes 1530–1630', Appendix 1, pp. 502–507. Matthew Spring, *The Lute in Britain* (Oxford: Oxford University Press 2001), pp. 112, 131. The earl evoked in the title is Essex's father.

45 Spring, *The Lute in Britain*, p. 102.

46 Mark Brayshay, 'Waits, Musicians, Bearwards and Players: the Inter-Urban Road Travel and Performances of Itinerant Entertainers in Sixteenth and Seventeenth Century England', *Journal of Historical Geography* 31 (2005), pp. 430–458.

47 Craig-McFeely, 'English Lute Manuscripts and Scribes 1530–1630', p. 82.

48 Spring, *The Lute in Britain*, p. 104.

49 NA E 351/543, f.40. See Brian Jeffery, 'Anthony Holborne', *Musica Disciplina* 22 (1968), pp. 136–137.

50 According to information given by William Bowes at the Marshalsea in July 1599. Cecil Papers 71/71 f. 1.

51 On Bacheler's career See Anne Batchelor, 'Daniel Bacheler: The Right Perfect Musician', *The Lute* 28 (1988), pp. 3–12.

52 NA E 351/543 f. 43.

53 Cuffe to Reynolds, 19 August 1599, Cecil Papers 72/105.

54 Mark Brayshay, 'Royal Post-Horse Routes in England and Wales: the Evolution of the Network in the Later-Sixteenth and Early-Seventeenth Century', *Journal of Historical Geography* 17:4 (1991), pp. 382–384.

55 From comparison with Bacheler's mature hand in his extant 1606 letter to Cecil, he is not the copyist of the Mynshall text. Cecil Papers 118/134.

56 Spencer, *The Mynshall Lute Book*, unpaginated introduction.

57 Jason Scott-Warren, 'Reading Graffiti in the Early Modern Book', *Huntington Library Quarterly* (2010) 73: 3, p. 375.

58 On Sancroft's book collecting see Helen Carron, 'William Sancroft (1617–93): a Seventeenth-Century Collector and his Library', *The Library* 7th ser., 1: 3 (2000) pp. 290–307.

59 J. A. and John Venn, *Alumni Cantabrigienses* (Cambridge: Cambridge University Press, 1922), p.260. Grenlinge died aged thirty-three in 1654 and remembered his esteemed brother-in-law with a gift of 40s in his will. NA Prob/11/236. Given Sancroft's extensive collecting activities and the adolescent nature of the annotations it is probable that Sancroft acquired the manuscript from Grenlinge or his widow, rather than lending them to the young man.

60 On student life and intellectual culture at Emmanuel in this period see Sarah Bush, Christopher Brooke and Patrick Collinson, *A History of Emmanuel College Cambridge* (Woodbridge: The Boydell Press, 1999), pp. 56–90 and 177–256.

61 Jonathan Goldberg, *Writing Matter: From the Hands of the English Renaissance* (Stanford, CA: Stanford University Press, 1990), p. 117.

Illustrations

1 'Young Man among the roses'. Miniature by Nicholas Hilliard, c. 1588. Victoria and Albert Museum, London.

2 'Interview between Queen Elizabeth and the Earl of Essex'. Line engraving by Thomas Milton, after Robert Smirke, published 1806. © National Portrait Gallery, London.

3 'Sir Henry Unton'. Portrait by unknown artist, oil on panel, c. 1596. © National Portrait Gallery, London.

4 'Robert Devereux, 2nd Earl of Essex'. Portrait by Marcus Gheeraerts the Younger, 1596–97. Reproduced by kind permission of his Grace the Duke of Bedford and the Trustees of the Bedford Estates.

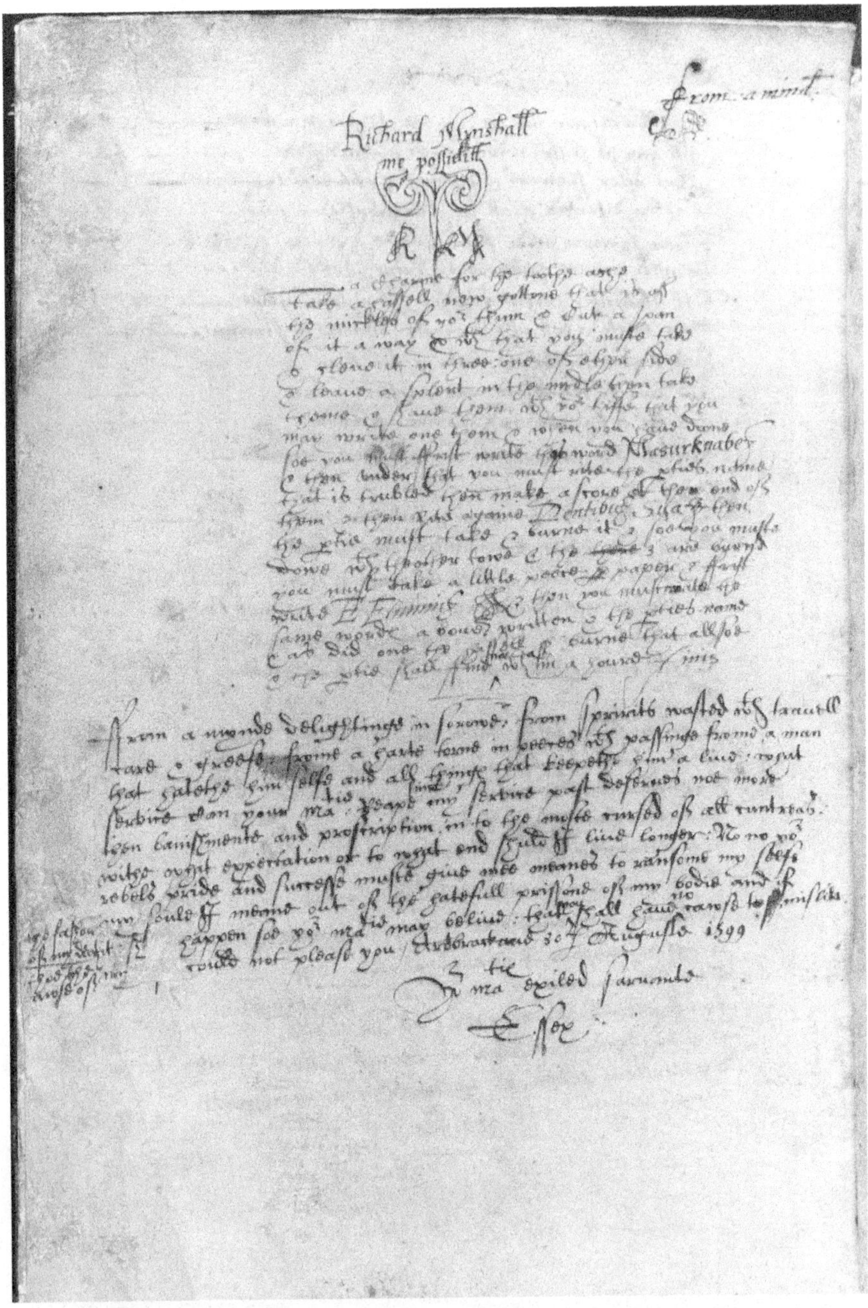

5 Letter from Essex to Elizabeth, August 1599, copied in Richard Mynshall's Lute Book. Royal Academy of Music MS 601 f.98v. Reproduced by kind permission of the Royal Academy of Music, Robert Spencer Collection.

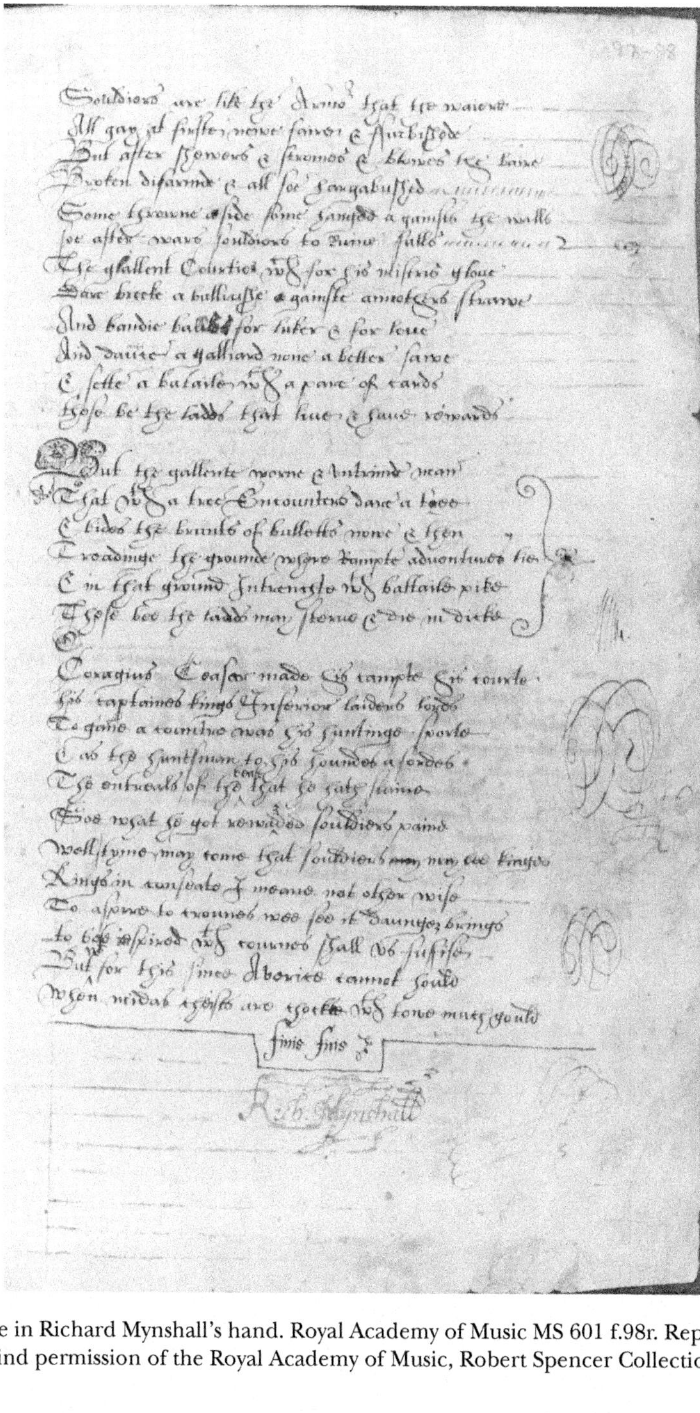

6 Verse in Richard Mynshall's hand. Royal Academy of Music MS 601 f.98r. Reproduced by kind permission of the Royal Academy of Music, Robert Spencer Collection.

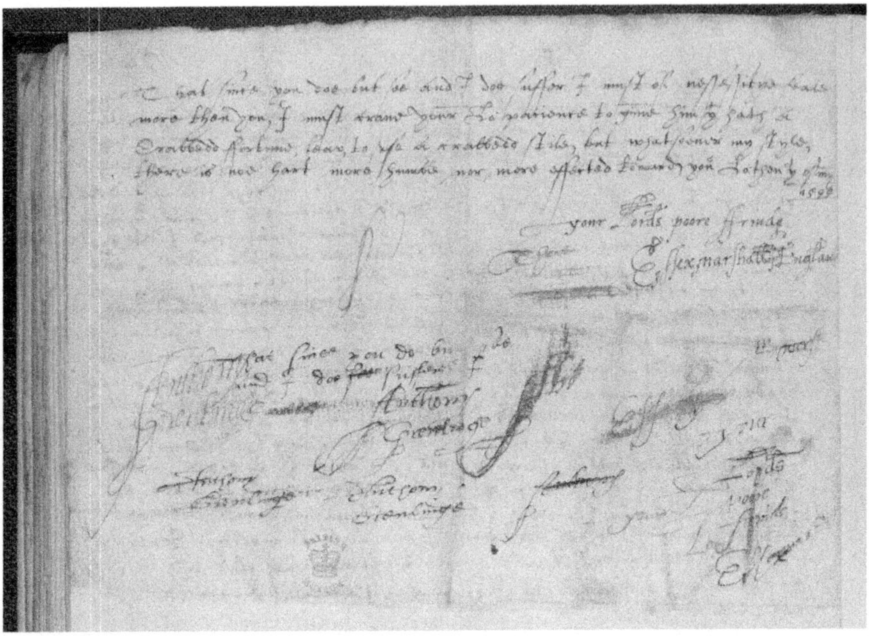

7 Scribal copy of the letter from Essex to Egerton with Antony Grenlinge's annotations. BL Harley MS 3787, f.178v. Reproduced by kind permission of the British Library.

8 'Lady Penelope Rich?' c. 1589. Miniature portrait by Nicholas Hilliard. Royal Collection Trust. Supplied by Royal Collection Trust. © HM Queen Elizabeth II 2012.

9 Essex meets Elizabeth for the last time. Bette Davis and Errol Flynn in Michael Curtiz's *The Private Lives of Elizabeth and Essex*, Warner Brothers, 1939. Courtesy of the Wisconsin Center for Film and Theater Research, University of Wisconsin-Madison.

8

'Idle papers': *An Apology of the Earl of Essex*

Hugh Gazzard

By May 1600 the Earl of Essex had been under house arrest – first at York House, and latterly at Essex House, in the custody of Sir Richard Berkeley – ever since his unauthorised return from Ireland the previous September. Ahead lay the quasi-judicial hearings on his actions at York House, and the stripping of his offices; the months of diminishing prospects for reintegration into royal favour; and the prospect of total financial and political collapse. But this last May all perhaps was still in the balance; at least, some sort of reconciliation with the queen and with the now-ascendant Cecil faction at court seemed still a possibility.

On 9 May, in the morning, someone browsing on a bookseller's stall in Paul's Churchyard might have spotted – perhaps displayed in prime place on the trestle by an over-confident bookseller – a new title-page announcing (in effect; the title-page of this edition is lost) *An Apology of the Earl of Essex, against those which Falsely and Maliciously Tax Him to Be the Only Hinderer of the Peace and Quiet of his Country.*[1] The title-page would probably not have carried any more information; the *Apology* was the earl's dissentient, impassioned personal testimonial and appeal for a renewed war effort against Spain – a tract too controversial, we shall see, for any save surreptitious publication. Annexed to it, just as audaciously, was the text, in bifolium, of a letter to the queen from the earl's sister, Penelope, Lady Rich, appealing for clemency and renewed favour for her brother.

Somehow word of the publication reached Essex, and the promptness with which he raised the alarm argues his good faith in, at least, the matter of this print publication.[2] He wrote to his brother-in-law, Lord Rich – why him, is not clear, although the two seem to have remained on reasonable terms despite Rich's difficult relations with his wife. Essex's letter is undated but, it will be seen, must have been written on 9 May:

My L. I vnderstood this morning thatt ther weare some new libells come abroade and thatt a printed pamflet was seene vnder the name of myne Apology. I was so moued wth yt as att the instant desired Sr Rich. Barkley to p*ro*cure conueyance of a lr of myne to the LL^{s}. butt first wished him to aduertise Mr Secretary of yt. I sent y^{r} l by Renolds a copy of the lr wch I ment to send thatt y^{w} might before hand acquaint Mr Sec wth yt. I now must add this thatt y^{r} l. will tell Mr Sec I know this is some practise of some such fellow as Cornwallys against the time thatt by his [i.e. Secretary Cecil's] good endeuours I looke for an end of my tedious trobles. and though I assure myself he [Cecil] wold answer for me and satisfy her Matie. how giltlesse I am of these libelling courses. yett I haue written my lr to the LL^{s}. to geue him the better ground to pleade myne iñocency both in this and in the like heretofore. y^{r} lp. knoweth thatt more then 2 yeares agoe I wrote some idle papers wch I comitted to the handes of Ed Renolds and did beleeue as my creede thatt they had bene buried in eternall obliuion. this published pamphelett nether agrees wth thatt I wrote nor hath any thing of myne butt by stelth. for I resolued yt shold neuer see the light. I am very much moued wth this cowrse of practise and therfore I pray y^{r}. L. conferr wth o^{r} honorabel frend how right may be done ... [3]

The syntax is knotty, but the defensive drift is clear. Essex is desperate to disavow the printed *Apology* – contacting both Robert Cecil and the Privy Council, the former also through Rich. (The 'libels' are very probably new vituperative verse satires posted up and passed around – like those attacking Cecil after Essex's downfall.) How has the *Apology* found its way into print? Is 'Cornwallys' Sir William Cornwallis, the essayist (c. 1579–1614)? Sir William was a follower of Essex, knighted by him in Ireland. How imprecise is the accusation of 'some such fellow' intended to be, and how was it taken? Was Essex right, or was Cornwallis just the easiest fall guy? Although Essex's disavowal of his own complicity in the print edition is convincing (his alacrity in raising the alarm is probably evidence enough), his account of the earlier fate of his 'idle papers' is disingenuous. 'Idle papers' cannot possibly hide the importance to him of the *Apology*. His longest-serving secretary, Edward Reynoldes, is damned by implication for these papers' circulation which, we shall see, the earl must have encouraged. It is surprising that there is no mention here of the printed addition of Penelope Rich's letter, overlooked in much of the documentary evidence about this affair; despite his claim about the inaccuracy of the printed text, it is doubtful that Essex had actually at this stage seen a copy of the book.

In a letter also dated 9 May Berkeley wrote to Cecil requesting that Essex might have leave to write to the Privy Council.[4] Evidently this was allowed, because a letter survives, presumably also 9 May, from Essex to the Council:

My very good LL^{s}. Though I haue bene many tymes and deeply woonded by practising libellers who since my cõmittment haue shadowed ther intended mischeefe to me vnder pretended greefe or passion for me, yett I haue bene silent till now, thatt I heare they do nott only renew ther former practises butt haue conspired wth a printer to sett out a pamphilett in my name. Butt now

> since I see thatt the malice of these conspirators doth not decrease butt thatt ther desperate boldnes increaseth. I do beseach yr llpš be so honorable and iust vnto me as to beleeue thatt my name is vsed wthout my liking or priuity. thatt I hold them no wellwishers to me butt my secrett enemyes thatt thus abuse my name. and thatt next the recouring of the pretious fauor of my gracious Souuerayn no worldly thing can bring me greater comfort then to see these practisers receaue such punishment as they deserue ... [5]

Here is a self-defence in more general terms, taking the moral high ground, but perhaps betraying the paranoia which his predicament was breeding. Here is a shift in the defence, also: the book appears without his authorisation, but there is no disclaiming his authorship. Perhaps he had by now seen a copy.

On 10 May Archbishop Whitgift, in his capacity as the principal press censor, sent a copy of the printed *Apology* to Cecil; Essex's secretary Henry Cuffe had the day before told Whitgift of Essex's knowledge of the printing. The Archbishop had then instigated inquiry after the printer, through the Stationers' Company. Evidently with ease, they found it was from one Dawson's press,

> the Printers, two of Dawsons servants, whom I sent for yesternight and examined so farrefurth as the tyme then served, and cõmitted them to close Custodie in severall prisons. And all this fore-noone I haue bestowed in th'examinacõn of some others allso towching that matter. They confess, that they haue printed .292. Copies, whereof I haue gotten into my hand*es* .210. or thereaboutes, and am in good hope to recover moste of the rest some tyme this daye. Their examinacõns I purpose to bring wt mee to morrowe to the Cowrte, because they are not yet finished. [6]

Here is the Elizabethan press censorship system (insofar as it was a system) working thoroughly, although it had taken a tip-off to set it in motion – and in fact Berkeley had written to Cecil to say that (probably on the evening of 9 May) Essex's own servants had found out the printer.[7] But the rigour with which the matter was pursued is imposing, involving the immediate close attention of the Archbishop. How the 210 copies had been recovered is not clear, although the Star Chamber order of 1586 regulating the press provided for the Stationers' Company wardens themselves, or their two nominees, to search for and seize offending books and to arrest stationers, both routinely and as need arose.[8] '292' is very precise; were 82 copies, ahead of the complete run, perhaps already distributed to the trade – and some sold? Was this standard practice, or speedy circulation a result of the book's topical vendibility? The figures differ on 13 May, when Rowland Whyte sends Sir Robert Sidney an update on the suppression: 'The Queen is offended that this Apology of peace is printed; for of 200 copies only 8 is hard of. Yt is sayd that my Lady Riches letter to her Majesty is alsoe printed, which is an exceeding wrong donne to the Earle of Essex'.[9] Does *heard of* necessarily mean *recovered*? Whitgift must in any case be regarded as authoritative on numbers.

It is clear that the search and suppression were thorough – and indeed only one copy of this edition is known to survive, now in the Huntington Library (STC 6787.7).

Probably it was Dawson, as the master named in the official documents, who bore the brunt of the Council's enquiries, rather than the two servants, who disappear from the record. The printer is named in the first Privy Council warrant as Thomas Dawson.[10] Having gained the freedom of the Stationers' Company in 1568, Dawson is recorded as active in printing from 1576 until his death in 1620. For some time he acted as deputy or assignee to others in the printing of New Testaments (Bishops' Version) and broadside almanacs. *STC* suggests that the 'apparent drop in his productivity after 1585 may mask what was a specialized and highly perishable part of his later output … His unusual career deserves further study'. This output also included catechisms and school textbooks. Although he is not known to have printed anything further in 1600, the trouble seems not to have done any lasting or even immediate damage to Dawson's livelihood: indeed, from 3 July 1600 he was a Warden of the Stationers' Company (one of several stints), and he was appointed Master in 1609 and 1615. It is probable that there was a bookseller/publisher, communicating copy of the *Apology* and commissioning its printing, and that this was John Smethwick (see below, p. 190). There is, though, no report of any action against Smethwick, and there seems to be nothing unusual in the detention of a printer, rather than a bookseller/publisher, in the case of an offending publication; on the other hand, it seems to have been generally a rather infrequent occurrence – ten printers are on record as having been imprisoned in the years 1576 to 1602.[11]

John Chamberlain's report to Dudley Carleton, on 28 May, is probably right about motives: '[Essex's] apologie was lately printed with the Lady Riches letter in the end, and some few of them sold, but they were presently suppressed, and upon search found not to be don somuch upon frendship or faction as upon hope of gaine: the poore Lady is like to have the worst of yt, being sent for and come up to aunswer and interpret her riddles'.[12] Chamberlain assumes Carleton's familiarity with the *Apology*, as Essex had done in writing to Lord Rich.

Essex himself apparently persuaded the Council of his innocence in this publication. Certainly he protested it as much as he could, complaining to the queen in a letter of 12 May that 'they print me and make me speak to the world' – this pain is from the 'stigma of print', no less than from the political damage done.[13] Apparently his last word on the matter is reported in a letter from Berkeley to Cecil on 23 May:

> the erle of Essex hys awnswer to the matter conteyned yn yowr ho. Letter to me [untraced] ys thus: hys lo. Dothe protest hym sellff free from all thought or purpose to haue the booke publyshed eyther yn writing or prynt. & that hys lo. was so farr from giving copyes off yt, as he charged hys man that kept hys papers, not to lett any of hys lo. Frendes see yt but yn hys hand or at least yn

hys presence. hys lo. can not gesse how yt shulde come abroade, but by the corrupcyon of some of hys servantes that had accesse to hys chamber who myght take A wrytt owt hys loose papers, wch lay ever sheete by sheete vnder hys lo. beds heade tyll he had leysure to fynyshe the whole. & sayeth he hathe had the papers of hym, whom hys lo. hathe cause to suspect, browght to hym by the lyke yndyrect meanes. But never sent any to the presse or to skryveners shopp. thys ys as moche as hys lo. hathe sayed to me ... [14]

Content, context, and composition

The *Apology* is Essex's confession of his personal principles, a defence of his conduct in the campaigns against Spain, and a prospectus for the policy of continued prosecution, indeed escalation, of that war against 'an Idolatrous and irreligious Nation'.[15] The *apologia* was an established form for the Renaissance; its typical rhetorical strategies would repay further study. Both Prince William of Orange (a pattern for the Protestant potentate) and Dom António, Prior of Crato (whose cause Essex pursued in the 1589 expedition to Portugal) had written, or had written for them, an *Apology*. Essex's is also cast as an epistle, to Anthony Bacon, Francis's brother: an intimate of the earl's from the 1590s, a kind of special advisor to him, and indeed resident at Essex House for a few years. What must have been the most contentious part of the work comprises Essex's political arguments concerning the prospect of peace. The *Apology* reaches a climactic, hortatory passage in which classical and biblical exempla are cited to urge the nation to provide adequately for war and to revive 'that auncient vertue' of martial valour. Essex's peroration emphasises that 'Now, now is the fittest time to make warre vpon the Spaniard', and elaborates the future dangers of an ill-founded peace.[16]

The title-page of the 1603 edition – and, substantially, the titles of many of the surviving manuscript copies – state that Essex's *Apology* was *Penned by himselfe in Anno 1598.* In his first letter to Lord Rich Essex speaks of it as having been written more than two years earlier. Textual evidence dates the work more closely. Essex writes that Spain's 'first attempt against *England* was in 88. From that time to this present it is full 10. yeares'.[17] This suggests composition some time in the second half of 1598, but passages elsewhere show that the work's inception, at least, came some months before that – early in 1598 (reckoning the year as beginning 1 January). Essex, who refers to the Azores expedition of 1597 as 'this last Sommer', sets himself to defend his 'crossing of the Treatie in hand', and writes that his opponents allege that his 'doubtes' and 'Arguments' 'doe shew I would not haue her Maiesties Commissioners sent ouer'.[18] These references, and indeed the entire drift of Essex's case against a negotiated peace with Spain (presented, as it is, as an immediate prospect), confirm that the *Apology* was written in the context of the Cecil diplomatic mission to France which ran in February and March 1598.

The Cecil mission was the English response to overtures for peace negotiations made by the Archduke Albert in autumn 1597.[19] The English commissioners, including Sir Robert Cecil, landed at Dieppe on 18 February 1598. Essex must have started writing when their departure was immediately in prospect. Other evidence from the text indicates that Essex was initially responding to the European political situation as it stood in winter 1597–98. Essex refers to the planned marriage of the Infanta Isabella to the Archduke Albert and their joint rule of the Spanish Netherlands; the Archduke had made the plans public by early December 1597.[20] And Essex refers to the victory of the Papal States over Ferrara; the Governor of Dieppe wrote to Essex on 17 January 1598 communicating this news.[21]

It is also clear that the *Apology*, relatively short though it is, must have been composed and revised piecemeal over the space of some weeks, and that as it progressed it was adapted in response to the changing political scene. Essex does not directly answer at length the charge of opposing himself to the dispatch of the mission, but instead insists upon the bad faith of Spanish negotiation. This would accord with the situation a few weeks after January, by when the Cecil mission had become a hard fact to be argued around, rather than a proposal to be opposed. Essex alludes to 'the intercepted Letters and instructions' of the Archduke, which were in government hands by March.[22] Among the revelations was the fact that Spain stood poised to conclude a peace with France, the terms of which would not include England. Early in April 1598 Cecil wrested from Henri an admission that this peace had indeed been concluded; this spelt the end of the Cecil mission, and the English commissioners left France on 15 April. Seven days later the Treaty of Vervins, formalising peace between France and Spain, was signed. Passages in the *Apology* show that it was finished in at least a first form in the light of these developments. Essex writes of Spain having 'so lately assayled *England*, *Fraunce*, & the lowe Countryes at once, hauing now broken the band of our League, and diuided *Fraunce* from the other two'. Spain 'shall now by the peace with *France* haue as much as he list'. 'Restitution of places wee cannot demaund as *Fraunce* did'.[23] And '*Fraunce* hath left vs'.[24]

Essex, then, began his *Apology* in January 1598. He added to it over the ensuing weeks of the Cecil mission, and had most likely completed a full version by late April. It might well have been begun as a short manifesto or memorandum, perhaps not even intended for circulation, but as an instrument for organising its author's thoughts, and then it might have been expanded and adapted as the prospect of negotiated peace took shape. We know that about this time the earl was propounding in Privy Council his arguments against peace; moreover, as Alexandra Gajda has shown, Essex's is just one of a set of manuscript considerations of the terms of war and peace which were (with greater or lesser readerships) circulating at this tense and controverted time.[25] The 'imputations' of Essex's war-mongering were being made around now at the highest level. Camden reports that Burghley said of Essex, perhaps at the Council table, 'that he breathed nothing but warre, slaughter, and bloud, and after an hot disputation about this matter, I know not with what presaging minde, he reached forth a Psalme booke, and silently pointed to this verse: *Men of bloud shall not live out halfe their dayes*': which was indeed prophetic.[26] Clients of the earl's, too, might have voiced caution over his support for belligerency: we shall see that Francis Bacon claimed to have sown the seed for the *Apology*.

It is no surprise that his tract's composition took weeks rather than days, for during Cecil's absence the earl, in addition to the customary press of his own affairs, was undertaking the responsibilities of the Secretaryship. There is, finally, some evidence of revision – disagreements of detail, wording, and fact which are apparent across the range of states of the text, some of which were made after spring 1598. The copy-text of the 1603 edition must have been written before definite news of the death of the Philip II had reached London in late September or early October 1598, or at least not revised in the light of that news. It is the earlier, 1600 printing which contains the later, revised reference to the now deceased King Philip. (Cf. the revision of a reference to the Archduke Albert to 'brother-in-law', from 'son-in-law'. It is of course just possible that both or either change was scribal and not authorial, down the chains of transmission.)[27] The great degree of variance in many substantives across the manuscripts suggests that copying might have been started while composition, or revision, was ongoing, as well as showing a range of scribal mistakes, sophistications and editorial interventions.

The *Apology* encapsulates Essex's favoured image of himself as naturally 'more inflamed with the loue of knowledge, thē with the loue of Fame', but also his sense of his military vocation, offering a defence of soldiery in general.[28] It engages in detail with factional politics and strategic planning at home and the trend of current events abroad; it offers a reasoned defence of what had proved to be contentious past actions in his successive military commands; it promotes the earl's personal ethic and political colours, definitively. This was material far too combustible to set out openly. Contemporaries, it will be shown, admired its prose, and it is easy to see how its lucid, forceful cadences – which, with their repetitions, with their suspended constructions, with their oratorical 'finish', tend towards the Ciceronian – won admirers. Its lexis is relaxed enough to admit what, trusting *OED*, were new or newish usages ('embarge', for *embargo*; 'elbow-room'; 'babes' for 'pictures in books'). A scattering of Latin tags, chiefly from or adapted from Tacitus (an author of great importance for the Essex circle)[29] – and including a quotation from the expatriate jurist, Alberico Gentili, a client of the earl's – strengthens the authoritative tone.[30] The epistolary address, which Essex brings back into focus at the peroration, is handled with great skill, to enhance but harness the tone of vehemence and confidence. But however powerfully put, history ran counter to Essex's argument. Peace was concluded six years later, and truce for the United Provinces five years after that, calamitous in neither case.

Scribal publication

On 10 June 1599 (New Style; Old Style 31 May), John Petit, half-English, intelligencing, a canon at Liège, wrote from that city, in the latest of his newsletters to 'Peter Halins' in London – actually the English intelligence-gatherer and decipherer Thomas Phelippes:[31]

> I had the sight of a long discours wrytten in English agaynst the peace babtised [*sic*] to be thearle of Essex ^doyng and sent from hym to one mr. Bacon. the same ys translated into french & by manie much myslyked especiallie Spaniards & others yt are the K: subiect*es* in respect of the vnmodest mannr of layng downe his mynd . rayling agaynst the king of Spa & the nation in general in certayne termes not fyt for an earl of essex esteemyd to be so complet a cauallero as he ys to vtter agaynst a king & whole nation.

Petit had been in company with Italians, Spaniards, and Spanish Netherlanders. 'I tould them I thought yt my l. of essex wold neuer wryte such a thing for yt I hard hym esteemyd by such as knew hym to be verey modest & discreet in his behauiouer to al men much more to kings and princes'. A Spaniard there understood Essex to be 'a gallant cauollero', from whom one would expect fitting words; he marvelled that the queen should allow 'such libels ^ to be wrytten and some to be printed & put out'; he would send the discourse to King Philip, who will give Essex the lie-in-the-throat, should Essex avow 'this heire to be wrytten by hymself or by his consent to be published'. Everyone there agreed, refused to believe it Essex's, rather than the work of some diabolical impostor.

So, within a short time of its composition, manuscript copies of the *Apology* had gained sufficiently wide circulation to have reached the Spanish Netherlands. Probably in 1598 Tobie Matthew, then a young courtier on the fringes of the Essex circle, wrote (presumably from England) to the diplomat Dudley Carleton. The *Apology*, or news of it, seems to have reached Carleton, probably then at Ostend, who evidently had raised some question about its circulation. Matthew replies that

> I … do allow of your iudgement in the obseruation of this discourse. To the later part of your exception only, I thincke an awnswrer may be made, as thus, that it was only ment for him to whom it was directed [i.e. Anthony Bacon]; who in knowledge of our state is little inferiour to many counsaillours, and in obseruation of others excellinge any of them in merit as much, as he is excelled by them in fortune. And I haue heard it mainly stood vpon how contrary the publishing of it hath been to my Lordes desire; and yt he hath censured *Fulke Greuill* with much displeasure, whom he holdes to haue been the spreadder of it.[32]

But there is every reason to think that all this was but strategic deniability, and that, at home, circulation was being orchestrated by the earl personally, and his closest associates. The *Apology* survives in at least forty-nine manuscript copies (see Appendix), evidently the product of concerted and sustained scribal publication. Sir Henry Wotton, who had been in a position to know, was later unequivocal about Essex's role: in the 'managing' of his reputation, 'the Earle proceeded by way of Apology which hee Wrot and dispersed with his owne hands at large, though till his going to *Ireland* they [criticisms of him] were but ayery objections'.[33] John Petit, who registers some sense of the original polemical shock of the tract, was probably being politic, knew the *Apology* to be Essex's, and perhaps suspected the source of its circulation. One other testimony, it is true, is less downright. Camden reports Cecil as urging, at Essex's trial, '*Hinc edita tua contram pacem Apologia*'; this passive construction is mistranslated (tendentiously?) by Camden's first translator as, '*And hence was it that you set forth an Apologie against the Peace*'.[34] If Cecil's phrasing was as noncommittal as Camden has it, Essex might have covered his tracks well, and perhaps the Cecilians could not prove the earl's complicity.

The proliferation of copies looks closest to Harold Love's category of *user publication*, in effect ongoing, and his category of *strong* publication. Some of the surviving manuscripts are separates (three or fewer bifolia), some are copied into compilations, some are separates included in aggregations.[35] The separates are in fact like Petit's description of the one he saw:

> The discours contayned thre great sheets of pap*er* wrytten in a smal secreatarie hand verey near togethr yt was over long and a tediouse peece of work to copie otherwise I wold haue sent y^{u} one y^{t} y^{u} might se the good stuff yt conteyned.

Love notes that some 'political separates ... can still be found in fifty or more contemporary copies', and, even, that probably 'the loss rate has been considerable'.[36] Purposeful this half-disavowable, half-secret publication most surely was: the *Apology* was a work meant to *persuade*, on matters of international importance at a crucial – and, indeed, unfolding – time. Very often the aggregates or compilations including the *Apology* comprise copies, made at once or over quite long spells of time, of other Essex-related material, from different times: letters, especially to and from Lord Keeper Ellesmere; lists of the knights he made, and materials relating to his military ventures; accounts of his insurrection, and trial, and speech at execution, and the names of those arrested; pro-Essexian verse 'libels'; miscellaneous texts variously concerned with his clients and followers, including Penelope Rich's letter; sometimes also with some anonymous policy papers on the war and peace. Perhaps at least as many copies of some of these, as of the *Apology*, survive.

What fraction of other, lost, copies the survivals represent is impossible to say, but the production of more than a hundred copies is not implausible. I have not found Essex's hand in any manuscript, nor that of his secretary Edward Reynoldes, who was usually closely involved with the earl's most guarded projects; indeed I have not been able to identify any hands. Folger MS V. a. 158 is dated at the end, evidently by the copyist, 'April 8, 1600' further illustrating the tract's widespread dissemination before the suppressed print-run of May 1600. Some of the titles of the manuscripts render the year, in the description 'penned' or 'written by himself in *anno* 1598', as '*anno* 1599', which may well register the year of their copying rather than its composition.[37] There would have been the utmost interest in Essex's words across the political elite – first of course from those closest in his faction and circle; then, in London, from fellow courtiers, potential parliamentarians, leading lawyers, senior soldiers; at the universities, scholars; across the country, the landed interest. On 18 August 1599 Rowland Whyte wryly reported to Sir Robert Sidney that 'I saw an Apologie he [Essex] made of his own Doings; and then your Lordship may iudge in what State a Man stands, that is forced to doe that'.[38] We have seen that Essex assumed Lord Rich's familiarity with the *Apology* – no very close ally, at that.

Even given the painstaking investigations of early modern scribal culture by, especially, Peter Beal, Grace Ioppolo, Harold Love and Henry Woudhuysen, it is hard to say precisely how, where, when, or by whom this work was transmitted. Love quotes a brief, vivid vignette, by a contemporary, of 'dyuers stationers' (which might include professional scribes and scriveners), who scramble after interdicted books, arrange their transcription by 'some younge Fellowes', and sell them 'to such Nuefangle persons as will not spare anie charges for acqueiringe such trashe'.[39] That might describe the further reaches of the transmission; closer to the source, Henry Best of Temple Bar was a scrivener known to have undertaken work for Essex.[40] Some copies were very probably produced by secretaries of interested parties, and might not materially differ from the work of professional scribes or scriveners who must also have produced some, and whose handiwork might feature frames around text, marginalia, different hands for miscellaneous purposes, dropped catchwords, and calligraphic titling and flourishes. All these can be found across the whole range of manuscripts of the *Apology*.

British Library MS Add. 30662, ff. 26ᵃ–60ᵃ, is a French translation in manuscript of the *Apology*, but it is an eighteenth-century copy. The one manuscript of the *Apology* in a continental European collection which I have traced was perhaps made for Louis Verreycken, envoy to England from the Spanish Netherlands in 1600.[41] It is clear, though, that this very wide scribal publication continued even after the 1603 edition, and presumably using that edition sometimes as copy. British Library MS Harley 405, for example, is dated 1616, seemingly integrally. Some of the compilations, however and whenever assembled, contain later, Jacobean items. In this political culture lines of communication might still be tenuous, and information at a premium: 'En[quire] whether printed', Bodleian MS Jesus College 83 has noted at its top.

Essex and his circle were alert to the uses of print and, especially, scribal publication. 'It is remarkable testimony to Essex's frustration and the scale of his political ambition that he should have adopted this strategy when he remained at the very centre of politics'.[42] Andrew Gordon's Chapter 7 has shed some new light on this scribal activity. There were divulged communications, disseminated doubtless in such a way as to allow disavowal: letters of counsel and of self-explanation, to the Earl of Rutland, to Lord Ellesmere, perhaps that to Fulke Greville; the scribal publication of the Accession Day Tilt 'device' of 1595.[43] After Essex's departure on the Cadiz expedition in 1596, a letter directed (with tactical tardiness) to the Privy Council, outlining his intentions to put his strategic vision into practice, was circulated also among a number of allies.[44] At the ambiguous end of that venture, and 'both to stopp all vagrant Rumors, and to enforme those that are well affected of the truth of the whole', Essex directed Henry Cuffe, the Oxford intellectual now in his secretariat, and with him on the voyage, to compose a 'True Relacion' of the campaign. Cuffe sent directions to Edward Reynoldes to arrange for its print publication in the popular guise of a letter 'sent to a gentleman in Court from one that served there in good place', the text 'to be deliuered to some good printer in good Characters'; specifying a title-page; and proposing initials for pseudonymous authorship and ('F. G.', for Fulke Greville) for receipt.[45] In the event, details of the publication project were leaked, and this, as with other accounts of the expedition, rigorously debarred the press – at the very least down to the suppression of an account of Cadiz in the 1598 edition of Hakluyt's collection. Undeterred, the Essex circle turned to the scriptorium, and also sought an international aspect to their promotion of their hero. Reynoldes 'imparted' the manuscript 'Relacion' to a well-affected courtier. Anthony Bacon 'resoulued to give it passage to greater honour by sending abrode copies' (to Scotland, for one), where they would proliferate. Sir Thomas Bodley (diplomat and Essex ally) dispatched it to the Netherlands. Fontaine, the minister of the French Church in London, sent a translation to France. Henry Hawkins, Essex's agent and intelligencer in Venice, had a copy, and pursued the possibility of its inclusion in Cesare Campana's forthcoming universal history – without success. It is surprising that only six copies, in English, have been traced – rather, six versions, since there was revision manifestly bolstering the Essexian partisanship.[46]

To fill out the picture further, in a climate where claim and counter-claim ran wild, and contemporaries must have mused at the lack of a centrally authorised, triumphal commemoration of the expedition in any medium, the Essex camp circulated (though perhaps not very widely) the exculpatory 'Omissions' and celebratory 'Advantages of the Cadiz Voyage' , surviving in several copies. These were excerpted from a longer, unfinished, military treatise, apparently near-private but probably intended for circulation once finished, written by Essex after Cadiz; the holograph is in British Library Add. MS 74286. This was an important seed of the *Apology*, outlining Essex's strategic vision of war with Spain, developing his favourite theme of the possibility of occupying some Spanish territory and of blockading trade out of Spain and bullion inwards.[47] The discourse is again cast as an epistle, to an unspecified recipient. Essex's thinking on these themes simply deepened and intensified; by August 1597 he was pressing the queen 'to give ear to those plain and easie courses which your poor servant shall lay down' – still more tractate projection – and 'in the mean time I will digest and set down my own projects to make them more clearly understood, when I shall deliver them'.[48]

Another edition and a translation

Controversy of a less clear kind than in 1600 attended the work's second appearance in print, in 1603. On 8 June the *Apology* was entered in the Stationers' Register to Cuthbert Burby, the bookseller, with the usual fee, but with the proviso, 'not to be printed till he bringe Aucthoritie for the same' – a sign of continuing political sensitivity.[49] The title-page of the 1603 edition bears the imprint of 'Richard Bradocke', as well as a device identified by McKerrow as Bradock's, but no statement that it was printed 'for' Burby, or anyone else.[50] The publication followed closely upon the death of Elizabeth, manifesting continued interest in Essex, under the new and, for penalised Essexians, rehabilitative regime. Whoever arranged for this publication procured sounder manuscript copy than was used in 1600; there is no evidence that the earlier edition was used in setting the later. However instigated, the work's reappearance marks an important intervention in the debate that was intensifying about the imminent prospect of negotiations with Spain, although in the end its cautionary note was ignored by the peace-makers.

The publication history is complicated by the proceedings recorded in the Court of the Stationers' Company. On 6 August 1604, on the authority of the wardens,

> Vppon the hearing of the matter in Controu'sie betweene them about the book of the Erle of Essexes Apologie by the*m* submitted to a court holden this day. yt is Ordered for the endinge of all thing*es* touching this matter: That Ric Bradock shall pay vnto Jo. Smythick V^{li}. the one half at Christmas next And thother half at our Lady day in Lent next And herevnto bothe the seid p*ar*ties doo agree/.[51]

Both parties signed the record. On the strength of this entry *STC* surmises that John Smethwick, a bookseller, might have been the publisher (not the printer) of the 1600 edition, and was asserting his prior claim to the title. This may be so, but no other evidence suggests it; Smethwick does not seem to have had trade connections with Thomas Dawson; the assertion of a claim to a suppressed book seems unlikely; and Smethwick's dispute was with the printer, Bradock, not with the publisher, Burby. Bradock printed two other books for Burby in 1603: STC 7120 and 12988. They seem not to have worked together before 1603. There is a further twist to the 1604 dispute: Bradock had probably also undertaken work for Smethwick (STC 3666 in 1600 and 3685 in 1603). Although the triangle of a work entered to one party being printed by another and contested by a third is not unusually complicated for the early modern book trade, nothing has emerged to qualify Jackson's conclusion that 'it is not possible to know what the controversy was about' – save for money.

Any important tract promoting the campaign against Spain might find a captive readership in the crucible of conflict, the Low Countries, so it is no surprise to find a translation of the *Apology* into Dutch: *Apologie oft verantwoordinge vanden Grave van Essex*, expressly translated from the text of the Bradock edition, and printed at Middelburg 'Voor Bernaert Langhenesse' in 1603.[52] There is an easy means of transmission here, for the only printer active in Middelburg in 1603, and who had undertaken work for Langenese, was Richard Schilders, the radical repatriate Dutch refugee.[53] The translator, 'C. C.' on the title-page, may have been Caspar Coolhaes, a controversial preacher and pamphleteer who changed through his career from ex-Carthusian Protestant convertite to proto-Arminian apologist.[54]

Reception

Essex enjoyed a high reputation as a prose and, especially, epistolary stylist (also as a courtly poet, though his *oeuvre* is uncertain): 'for his writings', reckoned Wotton, 'they are beyond example ... his Stile was an elegant perspicuity, rich of praise, but seldome any bold Metaphors, and so farre from Tumor [turgidity of language, style, or deportment – first *OED* citation] that it rather wanted a little Elevation'.[55] A generation after publication, the *Apology* was still valued. Edmund Bolton, in a note in *Hypercritica* of 'Prime gardens for gathering English; according to the true gage, & common standard of the tongue, about 15. or 16. yeares past' coupled it with Essex's letter to Rutland as work 'then which nothing almost can bee more honorablie vttred, nor more to the writers praise, so farr as beelongs to a noble English Orator'.[56]

In 1604 Francis Bacon, client of Essex in the 1590s, made public his own, much-needed, if not entirely convincing attempt to clear his reputation in his dealings with the earl. With some front, he styled it (all the more pointedly, given his brother's recipience of Essex's) as an epistolary *Apology*, addressed to Charles Blount, Earl of Devonshire. Bacon, not one to understate his own impact on affairs, averred that:

> Nay, I remember I was thus plaine with him [Essex] vpon his voyage to the Ilands [i.e., the Azores voyage of summer 1597], when I saw euery spring put foorth such actions of charge and prouocation, that I said to him: My Lord, when I came first vnto you, I tooke you for a Phisition that desired to cure the

> diseases of the State; but now I doubt you will be like those Phisitions, which can be content to keepe their patients low, because they would alwaies be in request: which plainenesse he neuerthelesse tooke very well, as he had an excellent eare, and was *patientissimus veri*, and assured me the case of the Realme required it: and I thinke this speech of mine, and the like renewed afterwards, pricked him to write that Apologie which is in many mens hands.[57]

In women's hands, also: the binding of Pierpont Morgan MS M.A. 1159 is stamped with the crest and badge of Lucy Russell, Countless of Bedford. And Lady Margaret Hoby, in her diary entry for 16 July 1600, records, with characteristic brevity, having a local minister read to her 'a book that was mad[e], as it was saied, by my lord of Essex in defence of his owne Causes'.[58] Lady Margaret naturally took a special interest in the *Apology*, for she had been Essex's sister-in-law, married first to Walter Devereux, who was killed at the siege of Rouen in 1591. The book was perhaps in manuscript, given the thoroughness of its recent suppression in print.

There are later scattered traces of the *Apology*. In one of the belated commemorations of Essex which had to await the reign of James, 'W. H.', detected in the book the lineaments of a moderate hero for popular celebration – the professedly peaceable hero of the *via media*:

> This was a man, the world shall never see
> So faire a mirror made of glories glasse,
> A Captaine true of note and name was hee;
> What was he not? no lover of the Masse,
> Nor over pure, as some supposde he was:
> He vsde a meane, Experience said t'was best,
> Nor was he prone to warre, but bent to rest.

This point is amplified with the marginal note, '*The protestation of his owne Apologie*'.[59] Again, from an unknown date which might have been around Ralegh's execution, in an unattributed manuscript verse, in Ralegh's voice – 'The disparinge complainte of wretched Rawleighe for his treacheries wrought against the worthie Essex' – there is the claim that, beset by enemies, 'envie wrought that nothinge might availe thee, / Though truthe thy iust Apologie did make'.[60] The earl's memory stayed live for the political elite, not least as his son grew into public life. In 1622/23 Sir Simonds D'Ewes bought 'The Earle of Essex Apologie a rare booke' for a shilling (a lot for a pamphlet): perhaps the 1603 edition, once 'in many mens hands', was already rare (although many copies – thirty or more – survive today).[61] Rarity in print is also suggested by the indications that scribal transmission persisted even after print publication (British Library MS Harley 405 is dated, apparently integrally, '1616'). In a list made in 1634 of books and papers in the study of Archbishop Laud is a note of 'An Apologie of the Earle of Essex'.[62]

The three most interesting uses to which the book was put involved quoting or excerpting its text – once very much in passing, and twice extensively.

Elsewhere I have shown how the recollection of a phrase from the *Apology* – Essex's description of his dead brother Walter as 'the half-arch of my house' – seals the case for regarding Samuel Daniel's tragedy *Philotas* as its opprobrious government audience saw it: as a more or less consistently allegorical treatment of the earl's downfall.[63] Keeping an eye out for sources or analogues for this striking image, I have only spotted 'Main arch of my house' (*The Roaring Girl*: probably derivative), and of course 'The noble Duke my master, / My worthy arch and patron' (*King Lear*, 2.1.57–8).

Interest in the memory of Essex, and its political usefulness, persisted. Thomas Scott, radical Protestant divine and polemicist (d. 1626), invoked Essex's shade at a time when the issues were being stirred anew during the run-in to another war. Prompted by the prospect of the 'Spanish Match', Scott's anti-Hispanic polemic, *Robert Earle of Essex His Ghost, Sent from Elizian: to the Nobility, Gentry and Communaltie of England* (1624, 'Printed in PARADISE', STC 22084), includes, separately titled, 'A Post-script, or, a second part of Robert Earle of Essex his ghost'.[64] It is a turgid recital of Spanish plots and practices against England under Elizabeth, purportedly dictated by the revenant earl, including extended excerpts from the *Apology*, the wording often a little altered or paraphrased – principally, Essex's defensive account of his service, his polemic against Spain, and his exhortation of a war-effort. The excerpts are introduced:

> I ... could doe no lesse then giue you this my Sacred *Declaration* and *Admonishment* which I send you, by this my *Blessed Genius*, written with a pen made of an *Angels* Pinion; and agreeing with my *Apology* which I left behind me on Earth, in mine owne defence, and for the good of my Country, after my discease. (A2^{a}–^{b})

The excerpts do not seem to come from printed copy, and not from any authoritative manuscript.[65] There is no record of any government action against Scot's book, but its disguised imprint sufficiently shows its controversial cast.

Certaine Choise and Remarkable Observations Selected out of a Discourse Written Long Since by the Late and Ever Famous Earle of Essex, Very Usefull for these Times (London, 1642, Wing H1096A; the title's advertisement for Essex was toned down in another issue, Wing H1096) comprises Hugh Peter's biographical notice of Sir Edward Harwood, a career soldier fighting the Spanish Netherlands, with the text of Harwood's recovered manuscript 'Discourse on the rumour of the French Kings Preparation at Sea', enjoining practical defensiveness, and with 'The Late Earl of Essex His Instructions for Englands Safetie'. Sir Edward's brother George Harwood here transcribed and paraphrased extracts from the *Apology*'s rousing affirmation ('read ... long since, in a little Treatise') of Essex's sovereign, his soldiery, his nation, his religion, and his reasoned readiness for war. In 1642, in a nation febrile with foreign and domestic alarms, this was part of the rhetorical attempt to figure impending struggle by way of the appeal to a supposedly common heritage of heroic Protestant militancy.

No further seventeenth-century printing of the *Apology* is recorded, despite the earl's strong afterlife, evident in the revival of assorted Essexiana in print: editions of the letters to Rutland (STC 6789) and Southampton (Wing E3305–8). But there was one more lease of life for the work. In 1729 it was printed as *The Earl of Essex's Vindication of the War with Spain. In an Apology to Mr. Anthony Bacon* (London: J. Roberts), the text from a derivative manuscript and not authoritative. There was yet another war with Spain to vindicate, and which obviously gave the publication its topical point, and served the agenda of some unknown party who arranged its publication: the Anglo-Spanish War of 1727–29. And again history was against the earl: a formal peace was concluded by the Treaty of Seville in November 1729.

I have set out here as many details as possible about the troubled history of this important work, partly in the hope that this might be of value for anyone undertaking a critical edition (something I had once projected). Schrickx, who edited the Brussels fragment, cites an edition of the 1603 text by Christine Remmery (University of Ghent dissertation, 1981): this I have been unable to find.[66] My sense is that there is still more to say about this strident, reflective, and well-styled piece of political and personal advocacy, and especially about its scribal publication. Any book which commanded the attention of so many should command our attention – the more so given the dazzling and disastrous life of its author.

Appendix

Manuscript copies of the Apology: a census

Birmingham University Special Collections

MS 342

Brussels: General Archives

Audiences, Register 366 (*Miscellanées*), ff. 24[a]–31[a] (imperfect).

Cambridge: Emmanuel College Library

MS 3.1.13 (James 181), ff. 1[a]–13[b].

Cambridge: Gonville and Caius College Library

MS (James 73), ff. 141–156 (imperfect).

Cambridge: Trinity College Library

MS R. 5. 18 (James 713), ff. 107[a]–116[b].

Cambridge University Library

MS K. k. I. 3 (2) (1937), ff. 2^{a}–12^{b}.
MS M. m. IV. 24 (2372), ff. 36^{a}–50^{a}.
MS Add. 72, ff. 16^{b}–39^{b}.

Cambridge, MA: Harvard University, Houghton Library

MS Eng. 1266.2, ff. 159^{a}–165^{a}.

Dublin: Trinity College Library

MS 545 (E. 2. 36), pp. 147–169.

Durham Cathedral Library

MS Hunter, art. 4.
MS Hunter 26, art. 7.

Gloucester: Gloucestershire Archives

D7115/1 (Old ref. 7) (imperfect).

London: British Library

MS Add. 4128, ff. 29^{a}–42^{b} (imperfect).
MS Add. 4129, 1^{a}–15^{a}.
MS Add. 5495, ff. 8^{a}–15^{b}.
MS Add. 38137, 161^{a}–172^{b}.
MS Add. 48063, ff. 238^{a}–251^{b}.
MS Add. 72411, ff. 1–14.
MS Harley 405, ff. 36^{a}–41^{a}.
MS Sloane 1132, ff. 15^{a}–25^{b}.
MS Stowe 275, ff. 2^{a}–12^{a}.

London: Inner Temple Library, London

MS 538, ff. 385^{a}–398^{b}.

London: Lambeth Palace Library

MS 250, ff. 185^{a}–191^{a}.
MS 841, art. 13.
MS 933, art. 4.
MS 2872, ff. 59^{a}–73^{a}.

London: National Archives

SP 12/269/71.

New York City: Pierpont Morgan Library

MS M.A. 1159 (V.10. B.), ff. 2^{a}–28^{b}.

Oxford: Bodleian Library

Ms Ashmole 767, ff. 10^{a}–43^{a}.
MS Eng. hist. c. 120, ff. 8^{a}–19^{b}.
MS Jesus College 83, ff. 5^{a}–18^{a},
MS Malone 24, ff. 3^{a}–26^{a}.
MS e. Mus. 55, ff. 73^{a}–81^{a}.
MS Rawlinson d. 1048, ff. 3^{a}–24^{b}.
MS Rawlinson d. 1062, ff. 1^{a}–16^{a}.
MS Tanner 76, ff. 12^{a}–19^{a}.
MS Tanner 79, ff. 17^{a}–19^{b} (imperfect).
MS Tanner 237, ff. 31^{b}–54^{b}.
MS Willis 58, ff. 386^{a}–423^{a}.

Philadelphia, PA: Rosenbach Museum and Library

MS 444/27.

San Marino, CA: Henry E. Huntington Library

HM 102, ff. 17^{a}–34^{b}.
HM 971

Washington DC: Folger Shakespeare Library

MS V. a. 158, ff. 1^{a}–38^{a}.
MS V. a. 177, ff. 1^{a}–12^{b}.
MS V. b. 41, p. 263–280.
MS V. b. 142, ff. 32^{a}–39^{b}.
MS V. b. 214, ff. 213^{a}–225^{b}.

Woking: Surrey History Centre

LM/1331/9

Notes

1 The title-page of the 1603 printed edition is unusual in reading *Jealously* rather than *Falsely*.

2 A case in some ways comparable to that of the *Apology* is recounted and analysed by Richard Serjeantson and Thomas Woolford, 'The Scribal Publication of a Printed Book: Francis Bacon's *Certaine Considerations Touching… the Church of England* (1604)', *The Library*, 7th ser. 10 (2009), pp. 119–156, who speculate (pp. 151–152) – but do

not firmly conclude – that Bacon himself might have instigated the suppression of the printed *Considerations.*

3 Hatfield House, Cecil Papers (hereafter CP), 83/9. The Cecil Papers cited in this essay are available on microfilm at the British Library.

4 CP 79/37.

5 CP 80/2.

6 CP 79/40.

7 CP 79/41.

8 W. W. Greg (ed.), *A Companion to Arber: Being a Calendar of Documents in Edward Arber's Transcript of the Registers of the Company of Stationers of London, 1554–1640* (Oxford: Clarendon Press, 1967), p. 41; for this order as codifying existing practice, p. 17.

9 *Letters and Memorials of State*, ed. Arthur Collins, 2 vols (London, 1746), vol. II, p. 194. (I have not been able to consult the manuscript letter, at Kent Archives – also on microfilm at the British Library – to verify the numeral reading.) On 10 May Whyte had informed Sidney of the print publication, 'donne without [Essex's] Knowledge or Procurement', and that Essex had 'sent ... to the Stationers to suppress them' (p. 193).

10 *Acts of the Privy Council of England*, NS vol. 30, *1599–1600*, ed. John Roche Dasent (London: HMSO, 1905), p. 317; mistakenly as Robert Dawson at p. 324. On Dawson, see R. B. McKerrow (gen. ed.), *A Dictionary of Printers and Booksellers in England, Scotland and Ireland, and of Foreign Printers of English books 1557–1640* (London: Bibliographical Society, 1910), p. 86, and Katharine F. Pantzer (ed.), *A Short-Title Catalogue*, 3 vols (London, 1976–91), vol. III, p. 51. The picture is confused by the fact that McKerrow (p. 86), lists a second Thomas Dawson, identified by him as a London stationer active 1597–1600, on the strength of five entries in Arber's transcripts referring to a Thomas Dawson *junior. A Transcript of the Registers of the Company of Stationers of London, 1554–1640 A.D.*, ed. Edward Arber, 5 vols (London, 1875–94), vol. II, p. 28, lists him amongst stationers but gives no further information. The other Arber citations to Dawson junior record apprenticeships: vol. II, pp. 222, 240, 249, 720. The entry at p. 240 refers to him as 'Thomas Dawson the younger Citizen and Stacioner of London'. If this Dawson printed anything it has not been distinguished from the output of Dawson senior.

11 Serjeantson and Woolford, 'Scribal Publication', 144 n. 94. But cf. the detention in 1568 of two expatriate Dutch stationers (for one of whom, in fact, Dawson had done some printing) for 'causing it [the French original of STC 25708?] to be printed': *Companion to Arber*, ed. Greg, p. 11; and the provision for action against 'partyes offendinge in pryntinge, sellinge, vtteringe, byndinge, stytchinge, or sowinge' books: *Transcript*, ed. Arber, vol. II, p. 811.

12 *The Letters of John Chamberlain*, ed. Norman Egbert McClure, 2 vols (Philadelphia, PA: 1939), vol. I, p. 96.

13 National Archives, Kew (hereafter NA), SP 12/274/138.

14 Cecil Papers 79/74.

15 Robert Devereux, 2nd Earl of Essex, *An Apologie of the Earle of Essex* (London: Richard Bradocke, 1603, STC 6788), E3^{b}.

16 Devereux, *Apologie* (1603), E4^{b}, F1^{b}.

17 Devereux, *Apologie* (1603), C2^{b}.

18 Devereux, *Apologie* (1603), C1^{a}, C2^{a}, C3^{b}.

19 On the conduct and context of the Cecil mission, see R. B. Wernham, *The Return of the Armadas: The Last Years of the Elizabethan War against Spain, 1595–1603* (Oxford: Oxford University Press, 1994), pp. 210–232, and Wallace T. MacCaffrey, *Elizabeth I:*

War and Politics, 1588–1603 (Princeton, NJ, 1992), pp. 196–219.

20 Devereux, *Apologie* (1603), D2^{b}; Wernham, *Return of the Armadas*, 198.

21 Devereux, *Apologie* (1603), F2^{a} (mistakenly rendered '*Tenera*'); CP 49/27.

22 Devereux, *Apologie* (1603), E2^{a}; Wernham, *Return of the Armadas*, 222.

23 Devereux, *Apologie* (1603), C4^{b}, D1^{a}, E1^{b}.

24 Robert Devereux, 2nd Earl of Essex, [*An Apologie of the Earle of Essex*] ([London: J. Smethwick?, 1600], STC 6787.7), D3^{a}; the text of the 1603 edition is corrupt here.

25 'The Journal of Sir Roger Wilbraham ... 1593–1616', ed. Harold Spencer, *The Camden Miscellany*, 10, Camden Society 3rd ser., 4 (London, 1902), pp. 27–30. Alexandra Gajda, 'Debating War and Peace in Late Elizabethan England', *The Historical Journal* 52 (2009), pp. 851–878 analyses and contextualises Essex's arguments; I cannot agree with her dating of the *Apology* (p. 858) to July 1598.

26 William Camden, *Annals, or, The Historie of the Most Renowned and Victorious Princesse Elizabeth, Late Queene of England*, trans. Robert Norton (London: Benjamin Fisher, 1635, STC 4501), p. 493. Camden summarises the contending arguments of the factions for and against peace with Spain, and in the same passage as the psalm-book anecdote he mentions the *Apology*, noting that it exemplified the arguments of the pro-war party.

27 Devereux, *Apologie* (1600), C3^{b}.

28 Devereux, *Apologie* (1603), A2^{b}.

29 On which, see Paul E. J. Hammer, *The Polarisation of Elizabethan Politics: The Political Career of Robert Devereux, 2nd Earl of Essex, 1585–1597* (Cambridge, 1999), 307ff.

30 Gajda, 'Debating War and Peace', p. 868 note 92, locates the quotation.

31 NA SP 77/6//f.21^{a}–^{b}; contractions expanded in italics, interlineations as in original. For Petit see Wernham, *Return of the Armadas*, pp. 223–224.

32 NA SP 12/261/f.114^{a}. The letter is unsigned, undated, with no location. The *Calendar of State Papers Domestic* identified Matthew as the writer; a (nineteenth-century?) endorsement on the document reads '1598' (deleted) and '96?'. Perhaps the endorser was led by the involvement of Greville into thinking that this letter relates to the Cadiz 'True Relation' (p. 189 above) – which is unlikely, given the arrangements for that work's transmission, its much narrower circulation, and that the commendation of the recipient of the 'discourse' rings true of contemporary estimates of Anthony Bacon (and of Matthew's subsequent commendations of Francis Bacon). More information about the whereabouts and activities of Matthew and Carleton might conclusively settle the matter. Paul E. J. Hammer, 'The Earl of Essex, Fulke Greville and the Employment of Scholars', *Studies in Philology*, 91 (1994), p. 174, takes the letter (on whose remaining portion, not transcribed here, I can shed no light) to refer to the *Apology*.

33 Sir Henry Wotton, *A Parallel betweene Robert Late Earle of Essex, and George Late Duke of Buckingham* (London, 1641, Wing W3647), B2^{b}.

34 William Camden, *Annales rerum Anglicarum, et Hibernicarum, regnante Elizabetha* (London: Simon Waterson, 1615, STC 4496), 2H1^{b}; William Camden, *The Historie of the Life and Reigne of that Famous Princess Elizabeth*, trans. Thomas Browne (London: William Webbe, 1634, STC 4499), 2Q3^{b}.

35 For these terms see Harold Love, *The Culture and Commerce of Texts: Scribal Publication in the Seventeenth Century* (Amherst, MA: University of Massachusetts Press, 1998), p. 13 and notes 34, 36, 44.

36 Love, *Culture and Commerce*, p. 13.

37 The front pastedown of Folger MS V. b. 214, a compilation, has the note 'Die veneris Iuly . 1^{8}. 1601 . per me Richardũ Greeneũ'; the back, 'Iacob Silver' and '1599'.

38 *Letters and Memorials*, ed. Collins, vol. II, p. 118.
39 Love, *Culture and Commerce*, p. 96.
40 H. R. Woudhuysen, *Sir Philip Sidney and the Circulation of Manuscripts, 1558–1640* (Oxford: Clarendon Press, 1996), p. 57.
41 Willem Schrickx, *Foreign Envoys and Travelling Players in the Age of Shakespeare and Jonson* (Ghent: State University of Ghent, 1986), p. 36.
42 Hammer, *Polarisation of Elizabethan Politics*, p. 315.
43 See Hammer, 'Essex, Greville and Scholars', pp. 167–180, esp. p. 173; Hammer, 'Letters of Travel Advice from the Earl of Essex to the Earl of Rutland: Some Comments', *Philological Quarterly* 74 (1995), pp. 317–325, and Hammer, *Polarisation of Elizabethan Politics*, pp. 149–151, 339 and note 99; Hammer, 'Upstaging the Queen: the Earl of Essex, Francis Bacon, and the Accession Day Celebrations of 1595', in *The Politics of the Stuart Court Masque*, eds in David Bevington and Peter Holbrook (Cambridge, 1998), pp. 41–66.
44 Paul E. J. Hammer, 'Myth-making: Politics, Propaganda and the Capture of Cadiz in 1596', *The Historical Journal*, 40 (1997), pp. 621–642; reference at p. 630, citing Warwick County Record Office, TD 69/6(ii), item 80; and, for a census of copies, note 50. See also Bodleian Library, MS Tanner 79, f. 93[b].
45 Lambeth Palace Library, MS 658, f. 88[a]; and see Hammer, 'Myth-making', p. 631, and *Polarisation of Elizabethan Politics*, pp. 252–253.
46 See Hammer, 'Myth-making', pp. 631–635.
47 See L. W. Henry, 'The Earl of Essex as Strategist and Military Organizer (1596–7)', *English Historical Review* 68 (1953), pp. 363–393, esp. pp. 363–372, 391–393, and Hammer, *Polarisation of Elizabethan Politics*, pp. 255–257.
48 Quoted in Henry, 'Essex as Strategist', p. 387.
49 *Transcript*, ed. Arber, vol. III, p. 236.
50 R. B. McKerrow, *Printers' and Publishers' Devices in England and Scotland, 1485–1640* (London: The Bibliographical Society, 1913), p.108, no. 280.
51 *Records of the Court of the Stationers' Company, 1602 to 1640*, ed. William A. Jackson (London: Bibliographical Society, 1957), p. 9; my italicised expansions.
52 For fuller title-page transcription see Anna E. C. Simoni, *Catalogue of Books from the Low Countries 1601–1621 in the British Library* (London: British Library, 1990).
53 On Schilders, see J. Dover Wilson, 'Richard Schilders and the English Puritans', *Transactions of the Bibliographical Society*, 1st ser. 11 (1909–11), pp. 65–134. Dover Wilson does not attribute the *Apologie*, but its title-page device is one used by Schilders around this time (ill. 61), and the ornamental initial 'G' on A2[a] is part of a Schilders alphabet set (ills 38–48). During his time in England Schilders had on one occasion been ordered by the Stationers' Company to complete a print job as journeyman to Thomas Dawson (pp. 72–73).
54 Neither H. C. Rogge, *Caspar Janszoon Coolhaes, de Voorlooper van Arminius en der Remonstraten*, 2 vols (Amsterdam, 1856–8), nor P. C. Molhuysen and P.J. Blok (eds), *Nieuw Nederlandsch biografisch Woordenboek*, 10 vols (Leiden 1911–37), vol. I, pp. 631–636, mentions the *Apologie*. The attribution seems first to have been made, on unspecified authority, by J. I. van Doorninck, *Vermomde en naamlooze schrijvers opgespoord op het gebied der Nederlandsche en Vlaamsche letteren*, 2 vols (Leiden, 1883–5), vol. I, p. 90.
55 Wotton, *A Parallel*, B1[b].
56 Bodleian Library, MS Wood F. 9, f. 21[a]. Thomas H. Blackburn, 'The Date and Evolution of Edmund Bolton's *Hypercritica*', *Studies in Philology*, 63 (1966), pp. 196–202, dates its distillation to something like fixed form to 1621.

57 Francis Bacon, *Sir Francis Bacon His Apologie, in Certaine Imputations* (London: Felix Norton, 1604, STC 1111), B3[a–b].

58 *The Private Life of an Elizabethan Lady: The Diary of Lady Margaret Hoby 1599–1605*, ed. Joanna Moody (Stroud: Sutton, 1998), p. 99.

59 W[illiam]. H[arbert], *Englands Sorrowe or, A Farewell to Essex* (London: Henry Rocket, 1606), B3[a].

60 *Ballads from Manuscripts*, ed. W. R. Morfill, 2 vols (London, 1868–73), ii. 254; from BL Add. MS 15226, f. 6[b].

61 Andrew G. Watson, *The Library of Sir Simonds D'Ewes* (London: British Museum, 1966), p. 235.

62 Bodleian Library MS Tanner 88, f. 25[b].

63 Hugh Gazzard, '"Those Graue Presentments of Antiquitie": Samuel Daniel's *Philotas* and the Earl of Essex', *The Review of English Studies* NS 51: 203 (2000), pp. 423–450.

64 For an account of more works, and context, see Louis B. Wright, 'Propaganda against James I's "Appeasement" of Spain', *Huntington Library Quarterly* 6 (1943), pp. 149–172. The front pastedown and f. 271[b] of Folger MS V. b. 214 show penmanship trials including variations around 'Thomas Scott', but the inscription 'Thomas Scott of Eggerton Gent.', deleted on the contents page, shows that this is the parliamentary diarist, Thomas Scott (*c.* 1566–1635: *ODNB*), whose family owned Egerton manor (Peter Clark, 'Thomas Scott and the Growth of Urban Opposition to the Early Stuart Regime', *The Historical Journal* 21 (1978), p. 3).

65 A marginal citation of one paraphrased passage to '*Apol. page* 19' (B3[a]) correlates with neither early edition.

66 Schrickx, *Foreign Envoys*, pp. 300–312.

9

'Toucht with bolt of Treason': the Earl of Essex and Lady Penelope Rich

Chris Laoutaris

> Of foule rebellion then I do appeach thee now;
> Rebell by *Nature*'s law, rebell by law of reason,
> Thou, sweetest subject, wert borne in the realme of *Love*.
> And yet against thy Prince thy force dost dayly prove:
> No vertue merits praise, once toucht with bolt of Treason.
>
> Sir Philip Sidney, *Astrophe and Stella*, ll. 62–66.

Muse, adulteress, rebel: Penelope Rich, sister of Robert Devereux, 2nd Earl of Essex, was one of the most notorious women of her generation. A captivating beauty, she was the subject of some of the finest poetry ever composed, the patroness of England's most lauded authors and artists, and the focus of sexual scandal during two royal reigns. King James I called her 'a fair woman with a black soul' and in the final days before his execution Essex, in an astonishing confession, accused her of being the catalyst for the coup which was to cost him his head.[1] In the tense time following Essex's death, Rowland White warned his friends that she was still the centre of a 'storm [which] ... depends upon my Lady *Riches* being, or not being, amongst you', yet she was the only one of the rebels listed in connection with the Essex conspiracy who escaped punishment.[2] Could Penelope Rich really have been the chief instigator of the Essex rebellion?

Immersing herself in a culture of encryption and espionage, Lady Rich had a direct line of communication to Elizabeth I; conducted a secret correspondence with James VI of Scotland; courted some of the most notorious spies and intelligence operatives in Europe; and cultivated an identity as political advisor to royalty. This chapter will explore the ways in which the woman who came to be known as Sidney's 'Stella' involved herself in the seismic power struggles of her age, intervening in the court factionalism which shaped one of the most volatile periods in Queen Elizabeth's reign. Lady Rich was a highly active member of the coterie of scholars and politicians who became closely associated with her brother, contributing decisively to the intellectual and cultural ethos which emerged from the Essex circle. Employing her great learning and proficiency in languages, while conducting an international correspondence in English, Spanish and French, she manipulated resonant literary and iconographic traditions in ways which were to prove explosive. The Romance mode, the aristocratic and courtly postures linked to melancholy, and the discourses of Aristotelianism and Tacitism which informed theoretical models of civil government, provided her with topoi which she appropriated and skilfully transformed for political ends. Ambitious and persuasive, Lady Rich did not merely live in Essex's shadow. She was fully capable of, and often intent on, realising her own agenda, with sometimes tragic results.

Lady Rich's 'devised terms': the art of encryption and the Rialta conspiracy

In October 1589 the poet Henry Constable undertook a mission of the utmost sensitivity. His destination was the court of James VI of Scotland. With him he carried a sought-after gift for his royal host, a sumptuous miniature painted by Nicholas Hilliard. The portrait's illustrious sitter was the Lady Penelope Rich who, along with her husband, Lord Robert Rich, and her brother, Robert Devereux, 2nd Earl of Essex, had dispatched Constable on a 'com[m]issyon' which would result in the poet's having 'secret conference sundry tymes' with the king.[3] Constable was unaware that his movements were being traced by one of Lord Burghley's spies, Thomas Fowler, who, despite facing 'great trooble and daunger of lyffe', had succeeded in alerting his employer to the existence of 'an alphabet of sipher [cipher]' which contained the 'nykname [nickname] for every one that is partaker in the matter'. This was a list of code-names for those involved in this intriguing episode of Elizabethan espionage, and it was devised by Lady Rich herself.[4]

On 7 October Fowler informed Burghley that he had infiltrated a covert operation by Richard Douglas, alias 'Robert Dalle', and one Mr Ottoman, code-name 'Orlando'. Their purpose was to initiate a correspondence between James VI and the mysterious 'Ryalta' and 'Ernestus', the names Lady Rich had invented for herself and the Earl of Essex. Ottoman, or Dr Jean Hotman, was a Huguenot refugee once in the service of the King of Navarre.[5] He appears in a list of the Earl of Leicester's servants, compiled 21 July 1587, which records those who had taken an oath to 'faythe fullye kepe secret all suche things as secrettly by worde or writing, shalbe from tyme to tyme, by his Exc[ellency, the Earl of Leicester] or others in his name com[m]itted to me' and to report 'any thinge tendinge directly, or indirectly, to the hurt or p[re]judice of her Maj[es]ties person, and dignitye'.[6] Hotman's involvement in the Rialta affair indicates that the young Devereux, whose mother, Lettice Knollys, had married the Earl of Leicester on 21 September 1578, had begun to take over their step-father's secretariat following his death in 1588.[7] If Lady Rich and her brother were acting entirely independently, and not on the orders of William Cecil,[8] then Fowler's missive to Burghley suggests that Hotman had broken his oath of 'true allegiaunce to o[u]r soveraigne ladye Elizabeth', for Lady Rich's mediators were conducting negotiations which could be construed as treasonous.[9]

Penelope Devereux was born just after the New Year of 1563 and became wife to Lord Robert Rich in 1581.[10] According to her future lover, Lord Mountjoy, the spirited young bride was 'married ag[ain]st her will unto one ag[ain]st whom she did protest at the very solemnity, and ever after, between whom from the first day there ensued continual discord'. Mountjoy's description of Lord Rich as a Machiavellian figure, who 'Instead of a Comforter' became his wife's persecutor and 'did study in all things to torment her',[11] should be read in context as a means of justifying his own marriage to Lady Rich. James was happy to tolerate Mountjoy's open affair with the famed Devereux beauty but expressly forbade the marriage which, when it was finally solemnised in December 1605, following Lord and Lady Rich's divorce, brought disgrace upon the newlyweds.[12] Mountjoy's account should therefore be approached with some caution. Early in the marriage Essex appeared to have been close to Lord Rich, whom he praised in a Latin letter to Lord Burghley, and Lord Rich himself was introduced to his bride's family as 'a propper gentleman and one in yeares verry fytte for my Ladye Penelope Devereux'.[13] As late as May 1600, as Hugh Gazzard has indicated, it was to his brother-in-law that Essex first turned for support when his name became attached to an inflammatory printed pamphlet, *An Apology of the Earl of Essex*.[14] Throughout much of their marriage, Lord Rich certainly seems to have relied on his wife's sharp intellect and competence in handling legal matters. In a letter to the Earl of Southampton, Lady Rich revealed that her husband had 'importune[d] me dayly' to serve him as his 'soliseter' and 'to beare parte of his trobles' in a dispute which had resulted in his being 'persecuted for his Lande, as he is in feare, to loose the greatest parte he hath'.[15]

Lady Rich's conduct throughout the Rialta correspondence also suggests that her husband trusted her enough to allow her to take the lead in the negotiations with James VI, and to act as spokeswoman for the Rich household in order to 'assuer' the Scottish King of their combined loyalty as well as of 'the erles [i.e. her brother's] service and fydelite'.[16] On 7 October 1589 Fowler had reported that there had been 'no wrytyngs frome the Lord [Rich], yet, tho[ugh] severall letters frome the Lady [the name 'Ryalta' is inserted in Lord Burghley's hand above the line here] Riche' who had been writing 'almost every weeke'. More surprising still, Lady Rich had been particularly instrumental in securing Fowler's cooperation as an agent, and after being sent word that she was 'especyally' solicitous for his welfare, he was urged to write to her directly. Lady Rich was quick to respond, said Fowler, with 'a letter frome her to me in short tyme, w[hi]ch letter contayned but curteowse promes [promise] of her frendshyp and the erles when I wyll in p[ar]tycular let them know how they may stand me in stede'. She closed with an encouraging post-script assuring Fowler of the love and support of Richard Douglas, the man code-named 'Robert Dalle'.[17] To find a married woman of this period commandeering a politically sensitive operation of this nature is highly unusual. The 'devised termes'[18] of Lady Rich's letters allowed her to negotiate with James VI on a political forum to which her involvement in networks of patronage gave her access. This was facilitated by her employment of the two men who had come to epitomise the courtly sophistication of their respective arts: Hilliard and Constable.[19]

The miniature of 'Rialtas Picture'[20] which Constable presented to the King appears to have been one of two Hilliard had executed of Lady Penelope Rich. One of these may well survive in the Royal Collection (Figure 8), a full-length miniature portrait of a woman standing before an architectural backdrop, the geometrical Palladian elegance of which seems almost to echo the Italianate resonances of Lady Rich's chosen *nom de plume*, 'Ryalta'. The figure in Hilliard's miniature bears the striking black eyes and fair hair which became Lady Rich's most celebrated features, clearly visible in the arresting double-portrait in which she appears with her sister Dorothy Devereux, displayed at Longleat House in Wiltshire.[21] There is a possibility that Lady Rich also commissioned a later miniature, for similarly diplomatic purposes, in 1590. This was delivered by Dr Hotman, as revealed in a letter from Lady Rich to his wife, Jeanne de Saint-Martin, who was one of her ladies in attendance. Its intended recipient was a 'monsieur l'ambasadeure', who Michele Margetts surmises may have been Henri IV's ambassador from August 1589, Jean de La Fin, Seigneur de Beauvoir-la-Nocle, with whom the Earl of Essex had forged ties.[22] The reason for this lies with the Devereux' interest in courting the favour of the French king, and it was in 1590 that Essex wrote to him requesting that he act as godfather to Lady Rich's child.[23] By assenting to the manipulation of her body's biological and representational capabilities, Essex's ambitious young sister commanded a potent tool for consolidating such crucial political alliances on an international stage. The authority which Lady Rich could derive from the careful projection and control of her image can be gleaned in a sonnet by Constable, probably inspired by the very miniature which he delivered into the hands of James VI of Scotland:

> If Michaell the arch-painter now did live,
> Because that Michaell he angell hight,
> As partial for his fellow-angels, might
> To Raphael's skill much prayse and honour give.
>
> But if in secreat I his judgment shrive,
> It would confesse that no man knew aright
> To give to stones and pearles true die and light,
> Till first youre art with orient nature strive.

But thinke not yet yow did that art devise;
Nay, thank my Ladie that such skil you have;
For often sprinckling her black sparckling eyes,
Her lips and breast, taught you the [form you gave]
To diamonds, rubies, pearles, the worth of which
Doth make the jewell which you paynt seeme Rich.[24]

In a witty reversal of the customary polarities of the patron–artist relationship, Constable attributes the 'devis[ing]' of the miniature to its mysterious subject, whose 'black sparckling eyes' have 'taught' the artist how to execute his wondrous craft. This revelation is coterminous with the unveiling of the woman behind the illusion, whose identity is disclosed in the sonnet's riddling word-play. The textual game draws attention to the fact that the skill of the miniaturist as well as the sonneteer inheres in techniques of encrypted brevity and contraction, decipherable only to the initiated few.[25] For Lady Rich this acquired particular resonance in what we might term a culture of encryption with which she became associated and which was to last her entire life. This is evident in the works of numerous poets of her generation who had set pen to paper in praise – and, towards the end of her life, in condemnation – of her.[26] A late manuscript epigram for example, composed after the death of her lover Lord Mountjoy, is indicative of the less flattering allusions to her scandalous life:

The Divell men say in Devonshyre dyed of late
but Devonshyre lately lived in Riche estate
till Riches Toyes did Devonshyre soe bewitche
as Devonshyre died & lefte the Divell Riche.[27]

During more favourable times, the coterie of courtiers who had access to the poetic output of the Devereux-Sidney circle could derive particular pleasure from decoding the identity of Sir Philip Sidney's enigmatic Stella, 'Rich in the riches of a royall hart, ... / Who though most rich in these and everie part, ... / Hath no misfortune, but that Rich she is'.[28] In his own sonnet, Constable exploits the possibilities for encryption afforded by Lady Rich's name in order to turn the usually passive subject of the artist's gaze into the active 'devise[r]' of the ensuing masterpiece. Combining the formal diplomacies of gift-giving with the self-authoring potential of the courtly arts, Lady Rich's presentation of her own image to the Scottish king performs a similar function, demanding of its recipient that he *visualise* its sitter as the absent centre and instigator of the unfolding consultations. Bringing together art and espionage in potentially subversive ways, she adapts the models of encryption available to her as a wealthy patron in order to cultivate an identity as political advisor to royalty.

In the absence of Lady Rich's original Rialta letters, we can never be certain how much of Fowler's report is an accurate reflection of the extent of her involvement in the conspiracy. The Cecil Papers, however, provide us with tantalising glimpses of an operation which appears to have been sustained through a framing narrative of her own composition. 'She is very plesant in her letters', wrote Fowler, 'and wryghtes the most part thereof in her brothers behalffe'. These letters, which were 'shewed to the Kinge', were clearly challenging and resistant to easy interpretation, requiring explication, for 'the darke partes thereof [were] expownded to him [James VI]'. Impressed with Lady Rich's epistolary style, the letters' royal recipient 'com[m]ended muche the fyn[n]es of her wit[,] the invencyon and well wrytynge', his delight in the textual game deriving from his privileged access to the meaning of the inventive word-play as much as from his recognition that his correspondent was a skilled manipulator of Romance fictions. Scripted into a narrative reminiscent of Arthurian legend and Arcadian Romance, the latter form popularised by Sir Philip Sidney, the king is assigned the flattering and heroic pseudonym 'Victor', while 'the Quenes ma[jes]tie is Venus [here the word 'Pallas' is written in Lord Burghley's hand above the line], and the erle [of Essex] the wery [i.e. weary] knight'.[29] As Helen Hackett has demonstrated, Sidney had appropriated the iconography of Venus 'as a figure of [Queen] Elizabeth' in the *New Arcadia*, in a manner which was 'strategically ambiguous, voicing criticism under the cover of praise'.[30] Lady Rich appears to be doing nothing less and, as far as Fowler was concerned, her decision to place James in antagonistic relation to the Queen constituted a flirtation with treasonous fantasies:

> ... the erle ... allwayes that he is excedinge wery[,] accomptyng it a thrale [i.e. thrall] he lyves nowe in and wysshes the change ... But I knowe sum of them went too far in p[er]swadinge the powre Kinge to hope for hap shortly and that Her Ma[jes]tie cowld not lyve above a yere or ij by reson of sum imp[er]fecyon[.] I know not that.[31]

These sentiments were penned in the shadow of Elizabeth I's Second Treasons Act of 1571, which greatly strengthened the role of the imagination in cases of suspected treason. This made it an offence to 'compass, imagine, invent, devise, or intend the death' of the queen and included 'such compasses, imaginations, inventions, devices, or intentions ... utter[ed] or declare[d]' in 'ciphering'. This was reinforced in 1585 by the Act of Surety of the Queen's Person, which increased the law's severity against the 'aiders, comforters, and abettors' of those who 'compassed or imagined' the queen's demise.[32] In the amendments made to Elizabethan legal statutes in the years leading up to the Rialta conspiracy, the realms of fantasy could become highly politically charged counters in prosecutions for treason.

To understand the subversive nature of Lady Rich's 'cipher' it is useful to consider another image which may have emerged from the Devereux patronage. Roy Strong convincingly argues that Hilliard's exquisite miniature of the *Young Man Among Roses* depicts the Earl of Essex and was composed shortly before the Rialta affair, during 1587–88 (Figure 1).[33] Surrounded by eglantine roses, a courtier leans against a tree in a melancholy pose, his hand pressed to his heart. Above him is the inscription '*Dat poenas laudata fides*', from Lucan's *De Bello Civili* which, in its original rendering, continues with the words '*dum sustinet inquit, / Quos fortuna permit*'. The allusion, which can be translated as 'admired faithfulness punishes itself, when it maintains the condition of those whom fortune debases',[34] transforms the portrait into a vignette of unrewarded love and fidelity. The emblematic eglantine rose, associated with both Venus and Elizabeth I, indicates that the queen is the object of the melancholic's unrequited desire. Indeed, in Renaissance iconography the roses of Venus could be interpreted negatively as symbols of 'the pleasing delights and outward faire shews and colours of love'.[35] Whether or not Essex is the miniature's subject, its vocabulary of disappointed service to an indifferent mistress can help us clarify the daring nature of Lady Rich's own re-interpretation of Elizabethan iconography. While Hilliard's forlorn lover is passive and stubbornly maintains his 'admired faithfulness' despite his lack of 'fortune', Lady Rich's 'weary knight' more actively 'wysshes … change', calling for an end to his 'thrale'. If the arresting miniature is indeed a portrait of the Earl of Essex, then it may be useful to view it as part of a larger emblematic programme instigated at this time by the Devereux, one which includes the Rialta correspondence and which Lady Rich took an active role in shaping.

Making his first appearance in Malory's *Morte D'Arthur*, the figure of the 'weary knight' becomes a common trope in Renaissance Romance fiction.[36] When he returns in Matteo Maria Boiardo's *Orlando Inamorato* (1495), translated into English in 1598, the 'wearied Knight' is Orlando's warrior-cousin Rinaldo whose adventures in love form a subplot of the main story. Slumbering beside the 'BROOK of LOVE', whose 'cristall Streame' runs beneath the shadows of 'The Beechen tree, the Pine, and Olive greene',[37] Rinaldo recapitulates the posture of the disillusioned or melancholy courtier which would later find expression in Shakespeare's *As You Like It*, in which the 'melancholy Jaques … / … lay along / Under an oak, whose antic root peeps out / Upon the brook'.[38] This play, which boasts its own Orlando character, may have been inspired by John Harington's translation of Ludovico Ariosto's *Orlando Furioso*, this Italian prototype itself intended originally as a continuation of the unfinished *Orlando Inamorato*. Harington's version was published in 1591, just two years after the Rialta conspiracy, replete with flattering allusions to 'the gallant' and 'noble Earle of Essex'.[39] It is perhaps no coincidence that the narrative which Lady Rich fashioned during her encounter with James VI also features an 'Orlando', the persona devised for Ottoman/Hotman. As well as a friend of the Devereux and Sidney families, Harington was close to both Constable and Hilliard, praising the latter's talents in his commentary to the *Orlando Furioso*, and it is not unlikely that the Essex circle may have known about his translation, and even read all or parts of it in manuscript form.[40]

Intriguingly, Andrea Cambini's *Two Very Notable Commentaries ... of the House of Ottomanno*, translated by John Shute in 1562, praises 'th[e] moste rare force of Orlando, and Rynaldo, with other famous Knyghtes of the mightye kinge Charles'.[41] We may never know if 'Ottomanno' sparked in Lady Rich the idea of using 'Orlando' as the alter ego of Ottoman/Hotman, or if the name 'Rynaldo' influenced that of the close-sounding Italianate 'Ryalta'. The contexts for her choice of suggestive intertexts, however, may indicate a deliberate desire to evoke histories involving large-scale national conflict. Ariosto's *Orlando Furioso*, for instance, delineates the crisis faced by Christendom as it struggles to free itself from the Saracens, while another name in Lady Rich's cipher, that of 'Robert Dalle', also turns up in a text which has been noted for its role in the revival of chivalric culture in both France and England, Jean Froissart's *Cronycles*; a work which may have been known to the Devereux because it was translated in 1523 by an ancestor of theirs, John Bourchier. Providing the historical background to the events which culminated in the Hundred Years' War, the *Cronycles* reveal Robert Dalle's role in the siege of Antwerp.[42] The names Lady Rich assigned to the characters in her own intertextual drama, with their chivalric and martial connotations, may have therefore recalled the kind of seismic political events which resulted in a form of regime change; the very fantasy which the Rialta narrative seems to place tantalisingly before the Scottish King. While Essex's alter ego 'Ernestus' suggests the Earl is sincere in his fidelity to James, his role of 'we[a]ry knight' under an ailing Queen presents him as the discontented young gallant looking forward to a new, more vigorous, reign, one amenable to his desire for military glory. In Lady Rich's hands the world-weariness which animates conventional renderings of the melancholy courtier or lovelorn hero of Romance fiction becomes a stimulus to pointed political agitation.

These appeals to James may have been intended to secure the Devereux' own place at the heart of what they believed would be the new royal establishment following the death of Elizabeth I. The ambitious reach of these endeavours is perhaps embodied in Lady Rich's own pseudonym. The 'Ryalta' refers most consistently in texts of the period to Venice's financial and mercantile Exchange.[43] The name may also have some relation to the word 'Rialty', an early source for 'Royalty'.[44] Could Lady Rich be defining herself as a conduit for international exchange, an enabler of royalty, bringing together the realms of England and Scotland? Whatever its exact import, the ambiguity of 'Ryalta' boldly invites speculation and, presented for the interpretative delectation of James VI, plays with notions of royalty and service to the Crown in a manner which binds Lady Rich's encrypted identity to the political intrigues enacted across two royal courts. William Cecil's interest in Lady Rich's 'cipher' taps into a reservoir of anxiety surrounding the royal aspirations of the Devereux and their extended family. The King of Spain's ambassador had reported, in the early 1580s, that the Earl of Leicester had been working to arrange a marriage between Essex's sister Dorothy and James VI. Upon hearing this news, Elizabeth I was said to have exclaimed indignantly:

> that she would rather allow the King to take her crown away than see him married to the daughter of such a she-wolf and, if she could find no other way to repress her ambition and that of the traitor Leicester, she would proclaim her all over Christendom for the bad woman she was, and prove that her husband was a cuckold.[45]

The 'she-wolf' was Lettice Knollys, whose ambitions were the subject of close scrutiny by the queen's chief courtiers. When Essex and Leicester were engaged in the Netherlands, it was rumoured that Lady Knollys had resolved to join them 'with such a train of ladies and gentlewomen and such rich coaches, litters and side saddles as Her Majesty had none such; and that there should be such a court of ladies as should pass Her Majesty's Court here'.[46] There may have been a very good reason for the Crown's fears, one which added a further impetus to Cecil's interest in the Rialta conspiracy, since there is a strong possibility that the grandmother of the Devereux siblings, Katherine, Lady Knollys, was the illegitimate daughter of Henry VIII and Mary Boleyn; a scion of the royal blood.[47]

It was with some relief therefore that Fowler reported from Edinburgh on 8 November 1589, 'the best is, Victor regardes not theyre offers muche, and the instrumentes ar[e] worst rewarded of all that ever cam[e] here of that nacyon, w[hi]ch discourages sumwhat theyre p[ro]cedinges'.[48] This crushing blow had followed a previous failure to convince the Scottish king to write to Lady Rich directly.[49] However, this did not deter Essex's intrepid sister, who would continue to dabble in the world of Elizabethan secret intelligence, cementing associations with some of the most notorious men in Europe, and taking the arts of encryption to an even more dangerous level. Her activities would land her in a formal investigation during which she would be called upon by the authorities to 'interpret her riddles'.[50]

The book of secrets: Lady Rich and her monster of fortune

On 3 May 1595 Lady Penelope Rich attended a supper at Essex House. Among the diners present at this occasion were the King of Spain's former Secretary of State, Antonio Pérez, and the Catholic agent, Anthony Standen, who had once been in the service of Mary Queen of Scots.[51] These men entered the Earl of Essex's circle at a time when his private secretariat was expanding to such a degree that it rivalled the queen's official intelligence network, then managed by Lord Burghley (who had long served his royal mistress as Lord High Treasurer and principal Secretary) and his son, Sir Robert Cecil. By the end of 1595 Essex employed at least four secretaries

– Edward Reynoldes, Henry Wotton, William Temple and Henry Cuffe – and was considering making further appointments.[52] For those close enough to the Elizabethan secret services to be privy to the knowledge that Pérez and Standen were two of the most notorious men in Europe, this would have been an intimidating gathering.[53] Not long into the proceedings, however, Lady Rich would demonstrate that this was not a concern she shared.

The dinner-table conversation at Essex House was interrupted by the sudden entrance of the Earl of Essex and Sir Robert Sidney. Just three days before, King Henri IV had signed a summons requesting the immediate return of Pérez, who had been in the employ of the French Crown since 1593, after defecting from the King of Spain's intelligence service. It is from November of this year that Pérez is registered in Essex's extant record of expenses, with a monthly allowance of £20. In addition to a regular stipend, payments were made for extravagant gifts of 'Plate', and for travel and subsistence costs, until July of 1595.[54] Lady Rich, who was fluent in Spanish, also became part of the scheme to entice him from the French king, and was soon dispatching regular letters and presents to him.[55] Pérez's usefulness to the Devereux is summarised by Camden, who reported that 'the earle of Essex gave him entertainment and supplied him with great cost, making use of him (as an Oracle) that was so well skilled in the secrets of the Spanish Court'. The volatility and eccentricity of the exiled Spaniard's character are aptly encapsulated in Camden's grandiloquent summary of his adventures, since he was 'so tossed up and down by fortune that he bestowed upon his Picture nothing but this Motto: THE MONSTER OF FORTUNE'.[56]

Essex was not above dining with monsters if it meant increasing the effectiveness of his burgeoning secret service. He had resolved therefore to take Pérez to the queen the following morning in the hope of securing an extension to his commission in England. This was to be followed by a meeting at Walsingham House, at which Sir Anthony Bacon would be in attendance.[57] Formerly in the service of Sir Francis Walsingham, Bacon had returned to England in 1592, following a thirteen-year sojourn on the Continent.[58] Now Essex's chief spymaster, the vast store of contacts he had accumulated while abroad made him an indispensable conduit for foreign intelligence to the Essex secretariat, and his presence at Walsingham House would ensure that his role in managing the influential, yet wayward, Pérez would continue to be a pivotal one. For Essex's sister there was one problem with this plan: she was not on the guest-list.

Not content with inviting herself to the Walsingham House conference alone, Lady Rich proceeded to commandeer the arrangements for the following day. She demanded that Essex be taken to Bacon's house in Bishopsgate Street while Sidney escorted her in a coach to their appointed meeting-place, before returning to collect Essex and Bacon. A woman travelling in the company of men, without her husband, could draw unwanted attention and Standen was alarmed enough by the level of independence Lady Rich was showing to write to Anthony Bacon 'by waye of advise to thende you be not taken unarmed', warning him that 'womens determynations beinge uncertayne, ytt maye be she wyll not dysmount'. Essex was also worried and asked Pérez to keep a close watch on his sister, as Standen jocularly proclaimed: 'my Lorde [of Essex] hathe provided hym [Pérez] here of the same office those Eunuches or Enuckes have in Turkye whiche ys to have the custodye of the fayrest dames'.[59]

The collective anxieties of Essex and his associates bespeak the potential reach of Lady Rich's influence. Her dealings with her friends and kinsmen suggest that she was used to getting her own way. Before the year was out Sir Robert Sidney would have an intimate understanding of this. A close friend of Sidney's wife, Barbara Gamage, Lady Rich had agreed to be godmother to their first son and became involved in the preparations for the christening which took place on New Year's Eve 1595. Her conduct at this time made an impression on Rowland White, who had written to Sidney informing him that 'My Lady *Riches* Desires are obeyed as Commandment'. This included shaping the child's future identity for 'They named hym *Robert*, by my Lady *Riches* Desire'.[60] Robert Sidney's realisation that Essex was susceptible to his sister's petitions would lead him to employ her in an attempt to acquire the post of Warden of the Cinque Ports, an office which the earl had aimed at for himself. 'Lady Rich has undertaken to appease the Earl of Essex', wrote White, informing Sidney that she was more than willing to deliver a letter from him to the queen which, when presented to Essex's sister, 'she kissed yt, and tooke yt, and told me, that you had never a Frend in Court, wold be more ready then her self, to doe you any Pleasure'.[61] Other male contemporaries similarly exploited Lady Rich's position of influence, including Sir Humphrey Ferrers, who petitioned for her support when seeking a Barony.[62] Essex was no doubt aware that his sister could prove a powerful mediatrix, and seems to have sought her aid during moments of crisis. In a tantalising, undated, letter Essex's request that his sister join him urgently at court early in the morning is answered with a concern for secrecy. 'I am here scarse well and in my night clothes, having nothing else here', she writes, 'but yet I will come and desire not to be seene by any but him selfe', asking the letter's recipient, Essex's servant William Downhall, to 'devise how I may come in very privately'. Such was her haste to come to her brother's rescue that she 'would have come in the night, to have kept my selfe from any others eyes', had she not feared disturbing 'my brothers rest'.[63] The drama of the letter suggests that her mission was a sensitive and potentially dangerous one. Essex's own surviving letters to Lady Rich reveal that he trusted her and nurtured a desire to please her. Rhetorical show-pieces, these epistolary exchanges anticipate the connoisseurship and wit of their female recipient, indicating that her opinion was genuinely valued. In one instance he writes 'I am melancholy, merry, sometimes happy and often unfortunate. The court is of as many humours as the rainbow hath colours, the time wherein we live more inconstant than women's thoughts ... breeding both people and occasions like to itself that is violent, desperate and fantastical'.[64] Beneath the commonplaces that shimmer over the surface of these statements there is a nod towards Essex's growing disillusionment, perhaps due, as another letter may imply, to his ongoing feud with the Cecils:

> To Hope for that w[hi]ch I have not, is a vaine expectation, to delight in that w[hi]ch I have, is a deceiving pleasure ... I will ne[i]ther bragg of my good happ nor complaine of my ill ... I do not envy, because I will do no man that honor to thinke he hath that w[hi]ch I want, nor yet am I not contented because I know some thinges that I have not.[65]

The letter reveals that Essex's relationship with his sister is based on a meeting of minds and an expectation that she will share his sense of frustration at 'some thinges that I have not', a possible complaint at his lack of preferment at court. By the time Lady Rich had become involved with Pérez and Standen, Essex had much to grumble about, after repeated failures to secure the advancement of the Bacon brothers, which included his fruitless attempts at acquiring the influential posts of Attorney-General and Master of the Rolls, for Francis.[66] Essex's patronage of Francis' brother was more troubling to the Cecils, who attempted to draw Anthony away from the earl through the intercessions of the learned Cooke sisters, Elizabeth Russell and Anne Bacon.[67] By the end of August 1595 Anthony had taken up permanent residence in Essex House, a course of action which his mother, Anne, had warned him against, insisting that it would bring 'some increase of suspicion and disagreement, which may hurt you privately if not publicly'.[68] Her sister, Lady Elizabeth Russell, in a rigorous interrogation of her nephew which took place in September 1596, made the even more daring insinuation that Anthony was 'factious and busie' with 'matters above yo[u]r reach, as forraine intelligences, and intertainment of spies', dubious practices which allowed him to conduct 'ill offices ... w[i]the the Earl [of Essex]' and 'oppose yo[u]r self more directlie, then annie noble man in Englande durst doe howe great soever'.[69]

It was in this highly charged atmosphere that Lady Rich decided to occupy apartments in Essex House, placing herself at the heart of what was fast becoming a satellite court. Her intimacy with Pérez also provided her with a conduit for information on the intrigues of these intelligencing men rarely available to women of the time. In 1594 he was writing to Lady Rich about Elizabeth I's physician, Dr Roderigo Lopez, who was accused of attempting to assassinate his royal patron and arrange for the murder of Pérez himself, who was probably involved in helping Essex uncover the 'dangerous ... treason'.[70] Essex's apparent success in unravelling what he claimed was a plot which immediately threatened the throne, and which would eventually lead to the execution of Lopez, allowed him to stake a claim for the utility of his own intelligence networks when pressed to the queen's service and Lady

Rich's interest in the case demonstrates her support of these endeavours. In continual fear of assassination during this scandal, Pérez wrote to Essex's sister in typically flamboyant terms:

> Whoever gave your ladyship the power to give life, gave you the prudence to use his remedy on the [right] occasion. When they try to kill me in England, your ladyship arrives with your favour, like those of your letter, one of them sufficient as a strong antidote against the poisons and human violence ... What offends your ladyship and affrights you? Is there a fiercer lioness nor crueller beast than a beautiful lady? Your ladyship knows well from whom I flee in a garden with this fear. So, what if after being mortally wounded she looks on displeased? The wounded man is finished. There is no remedy or spell that thus cures and resuscitates by a miracle as she herself, if she looks and acts mercifully.[71]

There is a suggestion that, behind these hyperbolic compliments, Lady Rich's mediation was an essential means of securing the Spanish courtier's fortune. Pérez's letters frequently play with the notion that a woman of her standing possesses a kind of power to confer life or death through the offering or withholding of her patronage. In another ingenious epistle, probably composed around May 1594, he offers an elaborate conceit structured around the various uses of 'skin', writing 'God fell in love with earthly creatures and in their flesh dressed himself', and since 'through their coat divinity was seen' all created beings are therefore both 'known' and 'esteemed' through their skins. In a characteristically artful rhetorical flourish, Pérez shifts the focus onto his patroness's own skin and presents himself as 'one dead', awaiting her miraculous intercessions, for 'skin is powerful enough to give life to one dead only by gazing upon it'. A near blasphemous implication that Lady Rich is a deity whose willing incarnation has the power to resurrect the dead underlies her suppliant's insistence that if he is abandoned and left to 'proceed forth' in life without her divine aid then 'no bone or skin will be left ... and a dead man will die, which will be a novel mode of punishment'.[72]

This obsession with skin returns in a more sexually provocative fashion in another letter in which Pérez apologises for the delay in sending Lady Rich a gift of gloves made from dog-skin. As a gruesome compromise he offers instead 'to sacrifice myself for your service and flay a piece of my hide, the most delicate part that I can', for 'love and the desire to serve can achieve this, that a person flay himself for his Lady and make gloves out of himself', signing off with a closing salutation in which he calls himself the 'Flayed dog of your ladyship'.[73] Other letters are more conventionally romantic, turning the patron at whose 'hands' great 'benefit [was] received', into 'a visible and palpable Angel'.[74] There may even be an allusion to Lady Rich's literary identity as Sidney's 'Stella' in a letter which seems to distinguish 'A great planet' (*planeta mayor*) from 'other stars' (*estrellas*), outdoing even Sidney by defining her as 'the Sun for it is light and guides' (*luz y guya*).[75] There was, however, a more sinister side to the verbal sparring between Pérez and Lady Rich. In a letter of 26 March 1596, surviving in a contemporary translation among the Bacon papers, he addressed the 'three systers and Godesses', Lady Rich, her sister Dorothy, and Frances Walsingham, Countess of Essex. Praising these 'Gardners' for nurturing 'buds of those divine bewties' and wishing them 'so good tyllage of their grounds', Pérez's quips indicate that the three women were probably all pregnant at the time. This, however, serves as the prelude to a more disturbing claim:

> O what a booke I have full of secretes of the lyke tillage and trymmynge of gardens. If I retourne agayne to Englande I shall have no nede to seke my lyvinge of any bodye for my booke will serve my tourne, but I will not be so good chepe this seconde tyme, my [the word 'secrets' is struck through here] receytes will cost dearer; wherfore lett ev[r]y[one] provyde.[76]

Could this have been a veiled threat? Could Pérez have been so inward with Lady Rich that he knew that the child she was carrying may have been fathered by her lover, Lord Mounjoy?[77] The fact that this letter was copied and translated suggests that Anthony Bacon and Essex may have begun to have doubts about Pérez at this time, and felt he needed to be watched. His constant demands for money, his penchant for fulsome sexual innuendo, and his dubious past had already drawn the suspicions of Lady Bacon who warned Anthony about Francis' relationship with him, requesting, in a letter of 27 April 1594, that he abandon 'that Bloody Peerez as I so tolde him then, yea as a co[a]ch co[m]panion & Bed companion[.] A prowde prophane [this word is added above the line] costly fellow, whose being abowt him I verely feare [this word is also added above the line] the Lord God doth mislyke'.[78] Worse still, the Spanish defected agent had grown rather loose-tongued of late for, as Lady Bacon observed, the 'owlde Dooted pollinge[s]t [most thieving or cheating, *OED*] papist' was using 'discources owt of season', and her sons' association with him merely compounded suspicions directed at anyone attached to the Essex faction: 'some do think that yo[u]r Broth[er] & yow make to[o] great a note of the Earles favo[u]r'.[79]

By the spring of 1596, Anthony Bacon was beginning to share his mother's feelings about Pérez. Writing from Twickenham around 24 May, where he fled to escape the former Spanish Secretary's constant petitions, he complained to Francis that his 'patience being at t[h]e last ov[er]chargd', he felt a 'just anger' that he could 'not obteine me t[h]e priviledge of rest at Sig[no]r Perez his hand but t[ha]t I must daylie [here the words '& howerlie' are struck through] heare my deare Lords honour hamerd upo[n] both by him & the Ffrench & serve as it were [here the words 'daylie &' are struck through] howerlie in steed of a cesterne to receave his Spa[nish] exclamations & scallding co[m]plaints'.[80] His blood was still boiling by 27 May when he wrote to his brother with the ominous suggestion that 'I dare assure yow t[ha]t w[i]thout my watchfullnes & painefull patience he [Pérez] would have chaunced upo[n] some blott wherby to have made an after game'.[81] Essex and the Bacons had stopped trusting him and began to distance themselves. Despite this, Lady Rich remained interested in Pérez's activities, for she had written to Anthony Bacon on 13 May 1596 requesting news of 'French affaires' and of her brother's involvement in the campaign for the relief of Calais, taking the opportunity to add a post-script asking: 'I would faine hear what becomes of your wandering nayghbore', a reference to Pérez's alias, Raphael Peregrino or 'Pilgrim'.[82] Catching the hint, Anthony Bacon wrote back two days later with a stern warning: 'your La[dyshi]pp may well call my neighbour wandring if you knew as I doe against my will what strange bypathes his thoughts walke in w[hi]ch fester ev[er]y day more & more in his mind by my Lords silence & the continuall alarums t[ha]t sounds in his eares of t[h]e Queenes displesure'.[83]

Lady Rich's desire to persist in her relations with the Spanish agent runs counter to the actions of the Essex circle at this time, and indicates that she was capable of pursuing her own agenda. Indeed there is evidence that she and Lord Mounjoy continued to court the favours of Lady Rich's 'monster of fortune' as late as 1604.[84] While Essex had managed largely to detach himself from Pérez by the close of the 1590s, Lady Rich's most controversial act of political intervention was, as will be argued later in this chapter, influenced in part by her own encounters with the literary wanderings of 'Raphael Peregrino'.

War against heaven: Lady Rich and the battle behind the throne

On 5 June 1600, the Earl of Essex entered the great chamber of York House and approached the long council table around which were seated the eighteen men who had been summoned to hear the charges against him. These were made up of the queen's Privy Councillors and four Judges of the law. A further two hundred spectators watched as the earl kneeled before the assembly on the cold bare floor, where he remained until the Archbishop of Canterbury, John Whitgift, asked for a cushion to be fetched for the prisoner to rest his knees upon. The private hearing was chaired by the Lord Keeper, Thomas Egerton, who had been Essex's jailor during the eight months that he had been confined to York House.[85] Along with an investigation into the earl's handling of the crisis in Ireland and his brokering of an unauthorised truce with the rebel Tyrone, the interrogations focused on his role in the circulation of 'a le[tte]r presumed to be written to her Ma[jes]tie herself, by a la[dy] to whome though neerest in blood to my Lo[rd] it apperteined little to inetermedle in matters of this nature'. The letter concerned the queen greatly, since it 'nourished' rumours which 'had gott to[o] great a he[a]d to be rep[re]ssed w[i]thout some hearing of the cause and calling my Lo[rd] to Answere'. Bold and uncompromising, the epistle was penned in a style in which no other woman had dared address her sovereign before:

> ... in w[hi]ch le[tte]r in a certaine violent and minerall spiritt of bitternes, remonstrance and representac[i]on is made to her Ma[jes]tie, as if my Lo[rd of Essex] suffred under passion, and faction, and not under justice mixed w[i]th mercye, w[hi]ch le[tte]r though written to her sacred Ma[jes]tie, and therfore unfitt to passe in vulgare handes, yet was first divulged by copies everie where (that being as it seemeth t[h]e newest and finest forme of libelling) and since comitted to the pr[e]sse ...[86]

This explosive letter was written by Lady Penelope Rich.[87] Her insistence that Essex was the victim of a 'faction' meant this document concealed one of the most outspoken contemporary claims that there was an ongoing battle behind the queen's throne; that between the earl and the supporters of Sir Robert Cecil, who had by this time become the Secretary of State and probably the most powerful man in England. In the period leading up to its composition, its author became embroiled in events which severely dented the relationship between Essex and the queen. Lady Rich herself may have once more come under surveillance, for at least two of her letters ended up on Robert Cecil's desk. Both of these were addressed to Henry Wriothesley, Earl of Southampton.[88] The reason for Cecil's piqued interest may have been the queen's fury at the Devereux' involvement in the clandestine marriage of Southampton and one of her maids of honour, Elizabeth Vernon, which Essex and his sister arranged at Essex House in the summer of 1598. Lady Rich was Lady Vernon's cousin and became her confidante and helper during the birth, on 8 November, of the daughter to whom she would shortly become godmother.[89] One of the letters which fell into Cecil's hands closes with a touching post-script, probably alluding to this child and Lady Rich's hopes for Southampton's future offspring: 'Your L[ordship's] Daughter is exseeding faire and well and I hope by your sonn to winn my wager'.[90] With evidence like this, Cecil would have been in no doubt that Lady Rich had disobeyed royal edict by facilitating this prohibited union. Things went from bad to worse the following year when Essex, against the express orders of the queen, promoted Southampton to Master of the Horse during his disastrous campaign in Ireland. Worried about his reputation at court, he took the decision to explain his actions to the queen personally and on the morning of Friday 28 September, having abandoned his commission in Ireland without royal leave, he stormed back to Nonsuch Palace, bursting in on the queen in her private apartments while she was still undressed.[91] Within a few hours he was under house arrest and on 2 October was confined to York House where his health began to deteriorate rapidly.[92] During his imprisonment, his sister became his most active defender and Essex House, now under her stewardship, began to attract sympathisers and agitators for the earl's release.

On 11 October 1599 Rowland White informed Sir Robert Sidney that 'my Lord of Essex's disgrace' had put the spot-light of suspicion on his associates, and his 'very Servants are affrayed to meet in any place to make merry, lest yt might be ill taken'. Lady Rich and Lady Southampton became aware that they could be viewed as galvanising forces for Essex's supporters and decided to vacate Essex House for 'the Country, to shunne the Company that daily were wont to visit them in Town, because yt gave Offence to the Court'. In their place remained Lady Scrope to petition the queen on the earl's behalf. 'She weares all Black', wrote White, 'she mournes and is pensive, and joies in nothing'. This was a demeanour which, he insisted, provided her with some license to speak, for 'Tis thought she saies much, that few wold venture to say but her self'.[93] Before long, however, Lady Rich and her sister Dorothy returned to Essex House, and on 4 November White reported that they had come to court to act as 'Sutors' to the queen. At this time Lady Essex had taken to wearing black garments of the lowest price and quality she could find, and was determined to take 'no comfort in any thing'.[94] Essex's female champions must have formed a striking community, for Lady Rich and her sister had also begun to follow Ladies Scrope and Essex in appearing, by 8 December, 'all in Blacke', clad in the habiliments of mourning and requesting that 'the Earle [be] removed to a better Ayre ... for where he is, he is somewhat straitly lodged'.[95] As she had done over a decade before, during the Rialta correspondence, Lady Rich was quick to adopt the postures of melancholy for political ends. The collective efforts of these loyal women may have been partially responsible for the false report of Essex's demise, the bells of St Clement Danes tolling for his death on a cold December day towards the end of 1599.[96]

During this period Lady Rich and the women who followed her lead in campaigning for the earl were also targeting the highest officials in the land, among them the Secretary of State, Sir Robert Cecil; the Lord Treasurer Buckhurst, Thomas Sackville; and the Chancellor of the Exchequer, Sir John Fortescue.[97] It was probably around early January of 1600 that Lady Rich herself wrote directly to Cecil as a 'very importunate suter unto her Ma[jes]ty ... in so distressed a tyme'[98] and, in another letter, requested that he 'speke ernestly for me, to her Ma[jes]ty for my leve to visit my brother', insisting that she should enjoy this right 'before others, because I have humbly and ernestly made the first sute [suit]'.[99] Costly gifts were also winging their way to the court. On 12 January 1600 White told Robert Sidney that Lady Leicester had sent 'a rich New Years gift' and Lady Rich, not to be outdone, 'writes to her Majestie many Letters, sends many Jewels, many Presents' in the hope of being granted leave at least to speak to her brother in person. 'Her Letters are read, her Presents receved', lamented White, 'but no Leave granted'.[100] It was in one of these letters, however, that lady Rich would overstep the mark. The document which would spark the queen's fury is audacious, erudite, and rich in allusion. It also bears the traces of the more subversive reading practices of the Essex circle. In order to understand how a letter by a female courtier could become so compelling and talismanic an artefact as to result in its being copied many times and sensationally circulated in both manuscript and printed form,[101] it is necessary first to explore the literary and political culture to which it is directly related.

The Earl of Essex had cultivated a learned secretariat, encouraging those in his service to apply theoretical models of governance to the more practical problems of realpolitik. In his private instructions to Robert Naunton, for example, he insisted that 'rules and patternes of pollecy are aswell learned out of olde Greeke and Romayne storyes as out of states which are at thys day'.[102] Two such sources appear to have been particularly central to the Essex community of scholars: Tacitus and Aristotle. When the Essex conspiracy came to a head, the potentially inflammatory nature of some of these texts became of interest to the earl's prosecutors.[103] Antonio Pérez was one of Europe's premier Tacitean scholars and was naturally attracted to Essex's friends and associates, Henry Savile, Henry Cuffe, Henry Wotton and the Bacon brothers, all of whom were equally devoted to this classical historian. Tacitus became more widely available to an English readership in 1591 when Savile translated the *Fower Bookes of the Histories of Cornelius Tacitus* and the *Life of Agricola.* These were supplemented with his own account of *The Ende of Nero and the Beginning of Galba,* which carried a preface to the reader by a mysterious A.B., whom Ben Jonson would later identify as the Earl of Essex.[104] This was followed in 1594 by Richard Field's publication of the London edition of Pérez's Tacitean autobiography, the *Relaciones.* Characterised by terse *sententiae* which, according to Gustav Ungerer, delivered their controversial author's 'observation for the education of monarchs and statesmen', the *Relaciones* was composed in imitation of the Tacitean model whose 'obscurity of style' harmonised with 'the necessity of political secrecy or dissimulation'.[105] Francis Bacon, in his essay *Of Simulation and Dissimulation,* explicitly associated Tacitus with the 'arts of state' demonstrated by those who had the skill to 'discern what things are to be laid open, and what to be secreted, and what to be shewed at half lights, and to whom and when'.[106] Lady Rich's letter should be read in relation to this literary tradition of encrypted political advice. In doing so it will be possible to explain why the queen was so enraged by it and why it may have been seen as a potentially dangerous document.

Essex had set the wheels in motion for an English translation of Perez's Spanish text and Arthur Atey was assigned the task, though it was one that would remain incomplete. It is likely, however, that Lady Rich had read the *Relaciones* in Spanish, for Pérez had sent her a copy along with a letter, composed in a suitably Tacitean aphoristic style, in which he drew her attention to what 'Raphael Peregrino says there', echoing his own tempestuous fate, in contrast to 'stories of good fortune', in a striking natural image: 'the calm and gentle sea is not so admirable to sight and consideration as a brave and rough one that shows forth the grandeur of its Element'.[107] This elemental motif is specifically related to the strong ruler's ability to control the vagaries of fortune in Atey's translation of Pérez's dedicatory letter to Catherine of Bourbon, in which the *Relaciones,* standing in for the author himself, is jocularly defined as 'a monster of fortune' seeking royal protection. Those 'princes' with weaker stomachs eschew nature's elemental and congenital monstrosities, while those who 'practise on earthe the nature of the Elementes' have the ability to safeguard those with whom 'fortune hathe so strived and raged' because they have an 'admiracion' for 'effects of more violent causes'.[108] There is a double edge to Pérez's observation here, given the *Relaciones*' treatment of those monarchs too given to violent means and ends. This can be gleaned from a review of the *Relaciones*, completed in the early part of 1595 but not published until 1657 as a supplement to *The State of Christendom*. This has traditionally been attributed to Henry Wotton, though Alexandra Gajda argues that it is a 'collaborative operation by members of Essex's circle'.[109] When reflecting on the *Relactiones*' implications for the lawfulness of deposing a corrupt monarch, this text dwells on the dangers of fostering factions within the royal court:

> [A] good Prince should procure his subjects peace, quiet, and tranquillity; to impoverish subjects is simply most unlawful, for that the wealth of their subjects is the riches of good Princes; and good Kings will rather labour to enrich them then to impoverish them, to comfort then to afflict them, to succour then to leave them succourless ... lastly, to destroy one faction by another is of all actions the most inhumane of all inhumanity, because it behoveth a Prince to preserve his subjects at home and abroad, in time of peace, and in time of wars, against open adversaries and secret enemies.

Under the pseudonym Raphael Peregrino, Pérez composed the *Relaciones* as a means of attacking the Spanish king who, as Wotton summarises, 'may be lawfully excommunicated and deposed, because all these crimes concur in him together'.[110] That this may have been considered an inflammatory text, carrying subversive implications for the English royal constitution, is indicated in the limited circulation of Field's London edition. By 1604 there were only four known copies, with Sir Robert Cecil owning one of them.[111] By the late 1590s the Essex faction had become synonymous with the flowering of the Tacitean aphoristic style in England and the proximity of the earl and his circle to the royal court may have prompted some uncomfortable interpretations of the texts issuing from this group.

In 1598 Savile's second edition of Tacitus' *Histories* was published with Richard Greenway's *Annales of Cornelius Tacitus*. The latter work carried a fulsome dedication to the Earl of Essex in which the Tacitean interpretation of history was transformed into a 'true and lively pattern of things to come'.[112] The author who identified himself only as A.B. in the preface to *The Ende of Nero and the Beginning of Galba*, had already underscored the relevance of Savile's text to contemporary court politics and internal factional strife, writing 'In Galba thou maiest learne, that a good Prince governed by evill ministers is as dangerous as if hee were evill himselfe'. In praising Savile's labours as a Tacitean translator, he goes on to offer a curious reinterpretation of '*vertù*', insisting that 'he that hath no vertue can never bee happy: for by his owne basenesse hee will loose all, which eyther fortune or other mens labours have cast upon him'. This is not as straightforward a statement as it may appear. Virtue here is not a purely private moral attribute, a quashing of one's personal sins, ultimately rewarded by a benevolent deity. It inheres rather in the conquering of both fortune and one's enemies. This definition, potentially highlighted in the text's prefatorial machinery by Essex himself (if we are to believe Ben Jonson), is taken up and vividly elaborated on by Savile in his essay outlining the demise of the tyrant Nero:

> Nero, a Prince in life contemptible and hatefull in government, ... disarmed himself both of the love and feare of his subjects ... at the First having ruled the estate with reasonable liking ... but after breaking forth into all infamous behaviour, and detestable oppressions and cruelties, and being withal a Prince weake in action, not of virtue sufficient to upholde his vices by might, he was at length thus overthrowen.[113]

As David Womersley has demonstrated, this opposition of virtue to fortune applies 'novel criteria' to Savile's reinterpretation of political history, making Tacitean discourse a vehicle for the Machiavellian observation that 'there is no necessary continuity between private and political morality'.[114] Tyranny in a prince is redefined as *weakness*, a failure to act with the adequate 'virtue', the appropriate 'might', when eradicating competing political factions. This allows us to re-read Pérez's *Relaciones*, and the Tacitean works of the Essex circle, in a new light. The monarch may display an 'admiracion' of 'violent causes' yet be neither a 'weake' ruler nor a tyrant, provided his or her power is manifested in the right way: in order to ensure the swift and uncompromising eradication of the factionalism which threatens the coherence and security of the kingdom. These ideas reappear in a manuscript text attributed to Henry Cuffe, which includes a liberal sprinkling of aphorisms deriving from Tacitus, condemning the 'ulcerous' nature of tyrants' 'cruelltye'. In particular, attention is paid to enumerating the corrosive activities of the fawning courtier who is allowed to flourish by a weak monarch: 'The greatnes of princes is the object of flattery ... The greatness of Favouritts the object of accusation'.[115] This statement is here applied retrospectively to Essex's own fate and draws on a connection between the earl and Tacitus which was recognised by his contemporaries. When John Hayward published his contentious book on *The First Part of the Life and Raigne of Henry IV* with an incriminating dedication to Essex in 1599, he may have done this because of this well-publicised literary association. This is likely, given that Hayward's work borrows extensively from Savile's translations.[116] Indeed, during Hayward's interrogation Francis Bacon informed the queen, with more than a hint of sniping wit, that the suspect's most heinous crime was to plagiarise most of the book from Tacitus.[117]

It was not only Essex's reading of Tacitus which concerned the Cecil faction. In 1601 Cuffe was accused of initiating clandestine readings of commentaries on Aristotle's *Politics*, the purpose of which was to draw the Earls of Southampton and Rutland into a more activist stance against the queen. Between December 1597 and January 1598, Cuffe was keeping his eye on the activities of the latest translators and interpreters of the *Politics*,[118] and it was in 1598 that the French commentary on this work was published in English as *Aristotles politiques, or Discourses of government.* This text elaborated on the constitution of the ideal *polis* in cosmic terms, the formation of which is 'agreeable to God', and whose 'governours and preservers ... as they first descended from heaven, so shall they returne thither again'. The citizen who is not 'deprived of justice' is able, through contemplation of the 'law Naturall or Civill' which underpins the human 'inclination' towards the creation of structured societies, to 'mount up even unto heaven, by retiring himself in contemplation from this world to Godward'.[119] Published in the same year as the combined edition of Savile's and Greenway's Tacitus, *Aristotles Politiques* provides a gloss on the philosophical text which is infused with the more radical Machiavellian precepts which informed the reinterpretation of the Roman historian's political theory. In a chapter concerning 'The changing, marring, and overturning of Monarchies', the anonymous commentator of Aristotle defines the tyrannical ruler as one who 'hath no respect to the publicke commodity', but allows those who are most 'familiar with them, and men of great credite about them' to 'conspire' against them, 'provoked ... by reason of too many benefits & good turns which they have received' or by 'revenge of outrage ... receaved'. If the ruler is to 'keep himself fro[m] conspiracie', therefore, he 'ought more to fear the[m] who[m] he raised to great preferment' and act more decisively to curtail their ambitions for the 'Prince is despised when he sheweth himself variable, light, efeminat, cowardly, and not well staied'.[120] It is no coincidence that this work was dedicated to Sir Robert Sidney, prominent member of the Essex circle at this time.

The Tacitean colouring of *Aristotles Politiques* may have appealed to Sidney, who owned his own copy of Tacitus' works which he had annotated copiously. Close to the beginning of this book, we read of the Roman historian's interest in the political uses of '*obscura verba*', a phrase which Sidney underlines and supplements with the marginal note 'obscure maner of speaking'.[121] As well as jottings highlighting Sidney's definition of a Prince's 'Vertu' as resting on public opinion rather than personal probity,[122] there is a note which places an emphasis on the threat posed by corrupt councillors: 'How many things under a weake prince are done by his greate councelors w[i]thout his knowledg: and if they come to light justified by theyr authorit[i]e'.[123] It is telling that this note appears directly beside another which explicitly relates the lessons drawn from Tacitus to contemporary court factionalism, lamenting the 'fashion now in our court when a great man wil do one harm to cover his malice'.[124]

Lady Rich's letter contains striking similarities to both these Tacitean and Aristotelian models. An appeal for 'justice and favou[r]', it offers political advice to the queen through a series of powerful and allusive *sententiae* which mirror the aphoristic style closely. It also alludes to, while dismantling, the divine teleology of the Aristotelian state to stunning rhetorical effect. The epistle opens with Lady Rich casting herself as the central protagonist of a narrative of thwarted ascension, a humble suitor hoping to have her 'eyes blessed w[i]th yo[u]r Maj[es]tie's beauties' but who finds instead that the desired object of her contemplation is suddenly withdrawn as 'the sunne depart[s] into a cloud'. Receiving only a 'doubtfull answeare' from 'the hyghe *Majestie* and devine Oracle', the devastated suppliant encounters 'spirits that did presage by the wheeles of the[i]r charyottes some thunder in the ayer'. Unable to move the queen in person she decides in writing 'to importune heaven' with 'wordes ... deliv[er]ed for my unfortunat brother whom all men have libertie to defame as if his offence weare capitall'. Condemning those 'p[ar]siall [i.e. partial] judges or those combyned enemyes who labour (upon false groundes) *to build* his ruine', Essex's female champion draws the queen's attention to the precarious nature of an Elizabethan *polis* in which such 'enemyes' are allowed to thrive:

> I have reasson to app[re]hend that if yo[u]r fayer handes do not checke the course of theire unbridell[ed] *hate*, the[i]r last course wilbe his last [the word 'last' is added above the line] breath since the evill Instruments that w[i]th the[i]re *office and cunning* p[ro]vid[e] for the feast have sufficient poyson in their hartes to infect[.] [T]he service w[hi]ch they serve shalbe esie to digest untill yt be tasted & then yt will p[ro]ve a bitter p[re]p[ar]ative to great mischeefe [the published *Apologie* has '*preparation for greater mischiefes*'] consealed among such crafty workemen ...[125]

Lady Rich's potent imagery recapitulates that of the commentary in *Aristotles Politiques,* in which the lawless citizen who practises 'great mischiefes' is compared to the 'child that as yet hath not attained to the fountain of perfect prudence' and who 'therefore should be kept under as it were with a bridle'. The 'evill education' which has produced this 'deceitfull and wanton creature' is expressed in alimentary terms as the replacement of adequate 'nourishment' with poisonous provisions and a breach in the sacred decorums of hospitality. These cankers of the state, the text warns, conceal the 'beastly crueltie' of a Diomedes, 'who killed his guests, and made them meate and provender for his horses'.[126] In her letter Lady Rich implies, in not dissimilar fashion to its Tacitean and Aristotelian forbears, that the queen is under immediate threat from those obsequious courtiers whose minds are bent on treasonous deeds. Condemning those who sustain factions by 'buyld[ing] the wall of the[i]r owne fortunes ... more dangerously highe then is yet discov[er]ed', Elizabeth I's petitioner urges her to demonstrate an 'unstained vertue' by 'not suffer[ing] those to take advantage that lie in Amboush'. These enemies, who think it 'heaven to blaspheme heaven', are working through 'the[i]r p[ar]tic[u]l[ar] malice and counselles' to 'g[l]utt them selves in their privat revenge' and must be dealt with swiftly. Forming a clandestine community, these conspirators have successfully concealed themselves from the queen but 'under stand one another to[o] well'.[127] Lady Rich's oblique references to formal 'office' and the machinations of 'counselles' may have been intended as allusions to prominent members of the Privy Council. As we will see, this was certainly the interpretation of the Council's foremost representative, Sir Robert Cecil.

Like her Tacitean forebears, Lady Rich brings to light the dark and secret intrigues of those dissimulators who thrive under royal protection. Not content with this, she makes the even more shocking insinuation that if these seditious men are not flushed out they 'will not onely pull downe all obstackles of the[i]r greatnes[,] but when they are in the[i]r full strength *like the Giants* make warre against heaven yt selfe'.[128] These '*Giants*' are the Titans, who waged a fierce uprising against their father, Uranus (literally 'heaven'), in an attempt to depose him. Having established the identity of Elizabeth I as Heaven, through her deft handling of the intertexts of Aristotelian and Tacitean political theory, Lady Rich implies that Essex's enemies are aiming at nothing less than the royal throne. Her apparently flattering appeals for 'mercie' and 'sacred clemency' for the fortune-tossed Essex, but speedy punishment for any 'faction' – a word Lady Rich uses in her letter – which might threaten the Devereux' safety, mirrors the Tacitean reinterpretation of princely *vertù* closely. Essex's sister is, however, walking on a tight-rope. As we have seen, according to the Tacitean political theory cultivated by the Essex circle at this time, a failure to conform to this ideal can provide justification for the deposition of a monarch, where the ruler's *weakness* becomes synonymous with tyranny. This may account for the queen's strong reaction to the 'violent and minerall spiritt' of this epistolary address, despite its apparent observation of the proprieties of deference in its obsequious diction. As with her Rialta correspondence, Lady Rich politicises, in heart-stopping fashion, the arts of interpretative reading and fiction-making by entering into a dynamic dialogue with texts generated by, and circulated amongst, her closest allies.

While Essex was beginning to recover his health by 2 February 1600, his sister found herself at the centre of a formal investigation because of her letter. This prompted her less than a week later to write once more to the queen, as Dudley Carleton reported to Sir Edward Norris, 'but in other kind of language'.[129] Her attempts to appease her sovereign failed for on 22 February John Chamberlain broke the news to Dudley Carlton (in terms redolent of Lady Rich's own scandalous letter) that the expectation of Essex's friends, that they 'shold se him a cockhorse again' in the near future, 'was but a kinde of dreame, and false paradise ... for the bright sunshine that seemed so to dasell then ... was sodainly overshadowed again, and the skie as full of cloudes as before'. With no 'reconciliation twixt him and Mr Secretarie [Sir Robert Cecil] (wherupon they built many false fancies and liberall discorsings)', the noose was beginning to tighten around Lady Rich and she was 'called coram [i.e. publicly] again about her letter'. Perhaps sensing the growing seriousness of the situation, 'she excused her self by sicknes'.[130] Before the month was out, however, she was placed under house arrest when copies of the offending document were, it was mooted, 'by her Means ... published Abroad'. Her cause was not helped by Lady Leicester who, with some of Essex's other supporters, had drawn the attention of the authorities after commandeering a property which backed onto the garden of York House so that they could have unhindered conference with the earl 'out of a Window'. Essex's mother attempted to bribe the queen with a sumptuous gown costing £100, but her gesture was returned with the royal opinion that 'yt was not fitt for her to desire what she did'. That the machinations of Lady Rich and her fellow female activists were taken seriously is indicated by an event which came to Rowland White's ears on 8 March. Once again a rumour had been circulated that Essex's release was imminent. An excited Lady Rich, along with her sister Dorothy, the Lady Southampton, and Lady Leicester, 'assembled themselves, at Essex House, to receve hym'. Their collective presence, however, set alarm bells ringing at court and this 'hyndred' the earl's liberation.[131] It was not until 22 March that Essex was permitted to return to his own home under guard. Attention now focused on Lady Rich who had, according to a sceptical Dudley Carleton, feigned sickness and 'stolen into the country' in order to evade the authorities.[132]

Worse was to come for Lady Rich. By the end of May copies of her letter began issuing from the press appended to one of the Earl of Essex's former propagandist pamphlets, *An Apologie* addressed to Anthony Bacon and offering a rebuttal to the Cecils' foreign policy.[133] This text solidified in print the connection between Lady Rich and Essex's ongoing factional squabbles with Cecil and, on 28 May, John Chamberlain confirmed that 'the poore Lady is like to have the worst of yt, being sent for and come to aunswer and interpret her riddles'.[134] This emphasis on the riddling nature of her letter became a sticking-point for Sir Robert Cecil when Lady Rich was finally tracked down and questioned in early August. Her interrogator was the Lord Treasurer Buckhurst and he had received detailed letters from Cecil on the manner in which he was to conduct the investigation. Lady Rich had clearly worked her charms on him for he immediately accepted, without further quibbles, her assurances that 'she acknowledged ... her folies & faultes comitted, & ... that this shold be a warning to her for ever not to comit the like'.[135]

The ease with which Lady Rich drew the sympathies of Buckhurst worried Elizabeth I, who took it upon herself to study her answers closely before appraising Cecil of the response she wished him to return to the Treasurer. Cecil duly informed him of the queen's 'mislike' of the fact that 'you were still so apt to excuse my ladyes course in her former answeres by imputing that to fe[a]re only in her, of giving furth[er] offence, w[hi]ch rather shewed a proud disposition & not much bett[er] ... then a plaine contempt of her

M[ajest]y'. Warming to his theme, he asked Buckhurst to deliver a searing message to the Lady Rich from the queen herself:

> [I]t is true her Ma[jes]tie was displeased as she had cause, to see that she beinge a lady to whom it did not appertayne so to meddle in such matters, would be so bold, to write in such a style to her, especially when the best interpretacions w[hi]ch she doth make can not free her from stomach and presumptio[n] when she writ and when her form[er] careless and dry answers shewed how little she valued her M[ajesty']s comandments.

While the queen was willing to 'free her from direct desyre or purpose to have it printed', the apparent reprieve carried a further sting in the tale since 'her err[or] was not so excusable but th[a]t shreud [i.e. shrewd] circu[m]staunces might be infered uppon such a voluntary negligence'. Lady Rich may not have commandeered the publication of her explosive letter but, the queen implied, had deliberately turned a blind eye when she could have prevented it from reaching a public readership. Cecil closed by informing Lady Rich that he had been made aware that she had sent a sealed cipher meant for royal eyes only (as she had done during the Rialta affair), containing the names of all those involved in the 'faction' against her brother. The Queen had burned this letter without divulging its contents to Cecil who now exclaimed bitterly, 'I doubt not but I was and am in her L[adyshi]ps contemplac[i]on the person on whom all the figures of th[a]t l[et]re [i.e. letter] did principally play'.[136] Cecil's own response to the letter accords with its Tacitean character, a text providing coded political advice to the monarch delivered in aphoristic 'figures'; a masterly instance of '*obscura verba*'.

After the catastrophic events of 8 February 1601, Lady Rich's role as political advisor again came under consideration when the Earl of Essex sensationally identified his sister as the mastermind behind the failed coup. The Lord High Admiral Nottingham, in a letter to Lady Rich's lover, Lord Mountjoy, reported that after his arrest Essex had said: 'I must accuse one who is most nearest to me, my sister, who did continually urge me on with telling me how all my friends and followers thought me a coward and that I had lost all my valour', adding ominously 'she must be looked to, for she had a proud spirit'. Mountjoy would not have been pleased with the cryptic warning that accompanied news of Essex's supposed confession: 'I think Her Majesty would be most glad to look upon your black eyes here so she was sure you would not look with too much respect on other black eyes'.[137] The reference is unmistakably to the renowned dark eyes of Lady Rich, and indicates that as far as the queen was concerned, no friend of the Lady Rich was a friend of hers. In the immediate aftermath of Essex's disastrous campaign against the Cecil faction, it must have seemed as if his sister would be charged with treason. Her name appeared on the list of principal conspirators with a note that 'the ladie Riche is w[i]th Mr Sackforde', having been placed under arrest at the home of the Keeper of the Privy Purse.[138] Once the testimonies of witnesses were collated, a picture began to emerge of Lady Rich's involvement in the events of that fateful day.

Essex had not planned a meticulously prepared coup. As Paul E. J. Hammer reveals, the catalyst for the doomed venture was probably the earl's panicked response to what he perceived to be a direct threat to his life.[139] As a means of stimulating an uprising, the surviving witness statements suggest, Lady Rich took it upon herself to ensure that these fears were made known to Essex's supporters. After dining with her brother, the Earl of Southampton, and other conspirators, on the eve of the failed coup, she sent a messenger to Henry Bromley requesting a 'secret conference' at Walsingham House during which, as Bromley's brother Edward confessed under interrogation on 2 March, she repeated Essex's belief that a summons he had received to appear at court was a trap.[140] When the Earl of Bedford was interviewed for his part in the conspiracy on 11 February 1601, he revealed that Lady Rich had been forceful in her insistence that the earl's life was in danger.[141] Three days later he wrote to the Privy Council with further explanations, stating that on Sunday 8 February, just after 10a.m. prayers, 'the Lady Riche came into my house, desyring to speke with me spiedelie'. While the sermon was being read, she spoke to him in secret 'in the next ro[o]me' and urged him to accompany her to a meeting with Essex, 'whereupon I went p[re]sently w[i]th her in her coche, none of my famylie following me owt of the sermon roome, and so departed w[i]th her unknowne to my said famylie'.[142] Lady Rich had done all she could to secure the loyalty of Essex's associates, but the venture quickly deteriorated when the conspirators kidnapped four members of the Queen's Privy Council who had been sent to Essex House to negotiate with them, including the Lord Chief Justice Popham. Once again Lady Rich allegedly took centre stage in the unfolding events, according to the testimony given at the examination of Sir John Davies on 10 February 1601, after Essex demanded that she and the Countess of Essex be 'brought down ... into the chamber where the lordes were the better as he sayth to contente them to passe the tyme', believing that their presence would calm a situation becoming increasingly volatile.[143] It was later reported, however, that Lady Rich refused to take on the role her brother had assigned for her and began taunting the armed men who had gathered in the courtyard in readiness for Essex's further instructions, goading them that 'if they were true gentlemen they would throw her down the head of that old fellow [Popham]'.[144]

Damning as these accusations were, Lady Rich escaped without punishment. The Queen may have thought it unwise to risk enraging Lord Mountjoy who, having been sent to Ireland to deal with the crisis which Essex was unable to resolve, was now in command of a substantial army. It would also have been unclear how much Lady Rich really knew about her brother's personal grievances against the Cecils. On 18 February 1601, Sir John Peyton sent a letter, which Robert Cecil had read, containing a further enclosure which revealed that, just before he was arrested, Essex had burnt a 'booke of his trobles all wryten w[i]th his owne hande'; a mysterious paper of 'nott abowe vi or vii lynes' which contained 'an advertyseme[n]t sent unto him & not of his owne hande' by a mysterious unknown man; and a tantalising 'cathaloge of divers names all wryten w[i]th his owne hand'. While Peyton's account stressed that Essex's 'divers private papers and letters' were seen by 'no mans Ii [eye] ... but his owne', these were destroyed 'in the presence of my lady his wife [and] the lady Riche'.[145] Did Essex's sister know anything of their contents? Since both Essex and Lady Rich had made claims about the corruptions of the Cecil 'faction' in the years leading up to the failed coup, their intimacy may have led Sir Robert to ask this very question. She had proved herself adept at gathering and conveying sensitive intelligence in the past, and this may have been troubling to the Crown's chief servants.[146] Lady Rich's ability to evade her brother's fate may also have been due to her considerable charms, which had previously allowed her to avoid the harsher penalties which could have attended her provocative letter to the Queen. Writing to the Lord High Admiral, she passionately protested her innocence in a poignant and highly affecting manner:

> For my desartes towards him that is gon, it is knowen that I have bine more like a slave then a sister, which proceeded out of my exceeding love, rather then his authority. What I have lost, or suffered, besides hir Mag[es]tys displeasure, I will not mention: yet so strangly have I bine wronged, as may well be an argument to make one dispise the worlde, finding the smoke of envy, where affection should be clearest.

If Essex had indeed accused Lady Rich of being the catalyst for the abortive uprising that was to lead him to the chopping-block, this must have been a particularly cruel blow for his ever-loyal sister. It is tempting therefore to read a deeply felt sense of personal betrayal in her dismissal of the charges against her as the fruits of 'malitious tonges'.[147] From the very earliest years of Essex's career, Lady Rich had employed her undeniable gifts as a patron, linguist, re-interpreter of chivalric and romance narratives, political advisor, and manipulator of the arts of encryption, in the service of the Devereux. Her extraordinary activities reveal that the intense, and ultimately destructive, relationship between these ambitious siblings was, in part at least, responsible for the crisis which nearly obliterated the great Gloriana's court. The story of Essex's daring uprising is not simply that of the actions of the great men of the Elizabethan constitution. It is also the story of the women who, working alongside and supporting the redoubtable Lady Rich, played a role in writing this remarkable chapter in English history.

Acknowledgements

I would like to thank the British Academy for their invaluable support during much of the research for this chapter. I am immensely grateful to

Yasmin Arshad for her feedback and expertise in Tacitean discourses in the Renaissance, and owe a huge debt to Alexander Samson for his tremendous translations of Pérez's Spanish letters to Lady Rich. I have also drawn inspiration from discussions on Renaissance women's writing from Helen Hackett, Shona McNeill, Patricia Phillippy, Yewande Okuleye and Sasha Garwood. The staff at the British Library, Lambeth Palace Library, and Hatfield House have been particularly helpful. Annaliese F. Connolly and Lisa Hopkins deserve a special mention for their hard work, endless stores of patience, and tireless devotion to this project.

Notes

1 Cyril Falls, *Mountjoy: Elizabethan General* (London: Odhams Press, 1955), p. 180; John S. Brewer (ed.), *The Court of King James the First; by Dr Godfrey Goodman*, vol. 2 (London: Richard Bentley, 1839), p. 17. Throughout I have modernised all i/j and u/v orthographical constructions and indicated expanded elisions or additions to quotations in square brackets for all manuscripts and early printed books.

2 Letter from Rowland White to Sir Robert Sidney, 28 December 1602, in *Letters and Memorials of State ... Written and Collected by Sir Henry Sidney, Sir Philip Sidney, Sir Robert Sidney*, vol. 2, ed. A. Collins (London: T. Osborne, 1746), p. 262.

3 Letter from Thomas Fowler to Lord Burghley, 20 October 1589, Hatfield House, Cecil Papers, 18/55.

4 Letter from Thomas Fowler to Lord Burghley, 7 October 1589, Hatfield House, Cecil Papers, 18/50.

5 For a biography of Hotman see *Household Accounts and Disbursement Books of Robert Dudley, Earl of Leicester, 1558–1581, 1584–1586*, vol. 6, ed. Simon Adams (Cambridge: Cambridge University Press, 1995), pp. 475–476.

6 British Library, Cotton MS Galba C VIII, f. 102.

7 The wedding of Elizabeth I's favourite, the Earl of Leicester, was initially kept a secret from the queen, but sparked an investigation when it became public knowledge. For the interrogations into the matter see entry for 13 March 1581 in *Calendar of State Papers, Domestic Series, of the Reign of Elizabeth* (hereafter CSP Dom), 1581–90, vol. 148, ed. Robert Lemon (London: Longman, 1865), no. 24, p. 11.

8 Sally Varlow suggests that the Rialta affair may have been engineered by Lord Burghley as a means of implicating Essex in a conspiracy against the queen's life. There is no evidence for this, though it cannot be entirely ruled out. See, Varlow, *The Lady Penelope: The Lost Tale of Love and Politics in the Court of Elizabeth I* (London: André Deutsch, 2007), p. 115.

9 British Library, Cotton MS Galba C VIII, f. 102.

10 Alison Wall, 'Rich, Penelope, Lady Rich (1563–1607)', *ODNB*. For the marriage see Lisle C. John, 'The Date of the Marriage of Penelope Devereux', *PMLA* 49:3 (1934), pp. 961–962. The marriage negotiations are outlined in a letter by Henry Hastings, Earl of Huntingdon, of 1581, British Library, Lansdowne MS 31, f. 105.

11 Charles Blount, Lord Mountjoy, 'Discourse written by the Earl of Devonshire in defense of his marriage w[i]th the Lady Rich', British Library, Lansdowne MS 885, f. 86^{v}.

12 For an account of the potential literary impact of Lady Rich's marriage to Lord

Mountjoy see Katherine Duncan-Jones, 'Ford and the Earl of Devonshire', *Review of English Studies* 29: 116 (November 1978), pp. 447–452. For a detailed treatment of Lady Rich's long-standing affair with Lord Mountjoy see Johanna Rickman, *Love, Lust, and License in Early Modern England: Illicit Sex and the Nobility* (Aldershot: Ashgate, 2008), pp. 111–140.

13 Letter from the Earl of Essex to Lord Burghley, British Library, Lansdowne MS 33/10, f. 20, and letter from Henry Hastings, Earl of Huntingdon, British Library, Lansdowne MS 31, f. 105, respectively.

14 See Chapter 8.

15 Penelope Rich, letter to Earl of Southampton, Hatfield House, Cecil Papers, 101/205. This letter is dated to 1603 in the *Calendar of the Manuscripts of the Most Hon. the Marquis of Salisbury, Preserved at Hatfield House, Hertfordshire* (hereafter HMC, Hatfield), 1603, vol. 15, ed. M.S. Giuseppi, Historical Manuscripts Commission (London: His Majesty's Stationery Office, 1930), no. 419, p. 179. This date is clearly incorrect since Lady Rich asks the Earl of Southampton to 'speeke with my brother', who was still alive when the letter was composed.

16 Letter from Thomas Fowler to Lord Burghley, Hatfield House, Cecil Papers, 18/50. A letter written by Lord Rich, with playful emendations and post-script by Lady Rich, mostly consisting of sexual innuendos, compounds the uncertainties surrounding their marriage. It could indicate jovial collusion or Lady Rich's attempt to undermine her husband. Where Lord Rich writes he is 'a poor man of no language only in the French', Lady Rich adds the word 'disease' after 'French', suggesting syphilis, see Sylvia Freedman, *Poor Penelope: Lady Penelope Rich, An Elizabethan Woman* (London: The Kensal Press, 1983), pp. 120–121.

17 Hatfield House, Cecil Papers, 18/50.

18 Hatfield House, Cecil Papers, 18/50.

19 For Lady Rich's involvement in musical patronage see John M. Ward, 'Tessier and the Essex Circle', *Renaissance Quarterly* 29, no. 3 (Autumn, 1976), pp. 378–384.

20 Thomas Fowler, letter to Lord Burghley, Hatfield House, Cecil Papers, 18/55. This phrase appears to have been underlined by Lord Burghley in this document.

21 The Longleat portrait can be seen in Varlow, *The Lady Penelope*. For another portrait miniature, which Roy Strong suggests may be related to Lady Rich or the Essex circle, see Strong, *The English Renaissance Miniature* (London: Thames and Hudson, 1983), p. 166.

22 Michele Margetts, 'Lady Penelope Rich: Hilliard's Lost Miniatures and a Surviving Portrait', *Burlington Magazine* 130: 1027 (October 1988), pp. 758–761. Once under the patronage of the Earl of Leicester, Hilliard had a previous association with Lady Rich's grandfather, and between 1583 and 1586 both Lady Rich and her mother, Lettice Knollys, may have become godmothers to two of Hilliard's children; see Varlow, *The Lady Penelope*, pp. 114 and 298. Jean Hotman would go on to write a treatise, translated into English as *The Ambassador* (1603), outlining the function of 'cyphers' in international political relations, see Alan Stewart, 'Francis Bacon's Bilateral Cipher and the Materiality of Early Modern Diplomatic Writing', in *Diplomacy and Early Modern Culture*, eds Robyn Adams and Rosanna Cox (Houndmills: Palgrave, 2011), pp. 120–137.

23 Robert Devereux, letter to Henri IV, British Library, Egerton MS 6, f. 71. See also Paul E. J. Hammer, *The Polarisation of Elizabethan Politics: The Political Career of Robert Devereux, 2nd Earl of Essex, 1585–1597* (Cambridge: Cambridge University Press, 1999), p. 93.

24 'To Mr Hilliard, upon occasion of a picture he made of my Ladie Rich', reproduced in Roy Strong, 'Queen Elizabeth, The Earl of Essex and Nicholas Hilliard', *Burlington Magazine* 101: 673 (April 1959), pp. 145–149. I have incorporated Strong's conjectural addition to the elided portion of the sonnet in square brackets.

25 For a study of the relationship between Renaissance poetry and the exchanging of finely wrought works of art see Pamela S. Hammons, *Gender, Sexuality, and Material Objects in English Renaissance Verse* (Aldershot: Ashgate, 2010).

26 For a survey of the many poets who have composed works either dedicated or alluding to Lady Rich see Hoyt. H. Hudson, 'Penelope Devereux as Sidney's Stella', *Huntington Library Bulletin* 7 (April 1935), pp. 89–129.

27 Poems about Penelope Rich, British Library, Additional MS 25303, f. 98.

28 Sir Philip Sidney, *Astrophil and Stella*, sonnet 37, *Defence of Poesie, Astrophil and Stella, and Other Writings*, ed. Elizabeth Porges Watson (London: Everyman, 1997), p. 37. A later example is Alexander Craig's *The Amorose Songes, Sonets, and Elegies* (London: William White, 1606): 'If curious heades to know her name do crave, / She is a Lady Rich, it needes no more', sig. C3[v]. For an interesting approach to the biographical problems of Astrophil and Stella see Alan Sinfield, 'Sidney and Astrophil', *Studies in English Literature 1500–1900* 20: 1 (Winter 1980), pp. 25–41.

29 Hatfield House, Cecil Papers, 18/50.

30 Helen Hackett, *Virgin Mother, Maiden Queen: Elizabeth I and the Cult of the Virgin Mary* (Houndmills: Macmillan, 1995), pp. 115 and 125. The passage in question, as cited by Hackett, is Sir Philip Sidney, *The Countess of Pembroke's Arcadia*, ed. Maurice Evans (Harmondsworth: Penguin, 1977), book 2, ch. 21, p. 352. Hackett also explores literary instances of Elizabeth I as Pallas on pp. 97, 101, 104–105, and 120–121 of *Virgin Mother, Maiden Queen*. For a reading of the Earl of Essex's association with the literary and chivalric culture surrounding Sidney's *Arcadia* see Chapter 1 in this volume.

31 Hatfield House, Cecil Papers, 18/50.

32 *Tudor Constitutional Documents, A.D. 1485–1603*, ed. J. R. Tanner (Cambridge: Cambridge University Press, 1951), pp. 413–421.

33 Roy Strong, *The Cult of Elizabeth: Elizabethan Portraiture and Pageantry* (London: Pimlico, 1977), pp. 56–83. See also David Piper, 'The 1590 Lumley Inventory: Hilliard, Segar and the Earl of Essex-II', *The Burlington Magazine* 99: 654 (September 1957), pp. 298–303.

34 The translation is my own. The Latin is transcribed from Strong, *The Cult of Elizabeth*, which also includes an account of the significance of the eglantine in Elizabethan culture and portraiture, pp. 68–78.

35 Richard Linche, *The Fountaine of Ancient Fiction* (London: Adam Islip, 1599), sig. Cciii[v]; a translation of Vincenzo Cartari's *Imagini de i Dei* (1571).

36 Thomas Malory, *Le Morte D'Arthur* (London : William Caxton? 1485), Capitulum xxxiij. See also William Warner, *Albions England or historicall map of the same island* (London: Joan Broome, 1586), p. 19.

37 R. T., *Orlando Inamorato* (London: Valentine Sims, 1598), Book III, sig. H[v].

38 *As You Like It*, ed. Alan Brissenden (Oxford: Oxford University Press, 1993), 2.1.26–32.

39 John Harington, *Orlando Furioso* (London: John Norton and Simon Waterson, 1607 [1591]), pp. 78 and 111.

40 'I think our countryman (I mean M[aster] *Hilliard*) is inferiour to none that lives at this day', writes Harington in his *Orlando Furioso*, p. 278. For more on the culture of manuscript exchange which existed between Harington, the Sidneys and the Devereux, particularly as it pertained to Lady Rich, see Henry Woudhuysen, *Sir Philip*

Sidney and the Circulation of Manuscripts 1558–1640 (Oxford: Clarendon Press, 1996), pp. 234, 246, 252–254, and 290.

41 Andrea Cambini, *Two Very Notable Commentaries … of the House of Ottomanno*, trans. John Shute (London: Humfrey Toye, 1562), p. 42.

42 John Bourchier, *The First Volum of Sir Iohan Froyssart of the Cronycles of Englande, Fraunce, Spayne, Portyngale, Scotlande, Bretayne, Flau[n]ders … Tra[n]slated out of Frenche into our maternall englysshe tonge, by Iohan Bourchier knight lorde Berners* (London: Richard Pinson, 1523), p. 231.

43 'Rialto' in William Shakespeare, *The Merchant of Venice*, ed. John Russell Brown (Walton-on-Thames: Arden, 1955), 1.3.17; Quarto and Folio spell this 'Ryalta'. See also Thomas Dekker, *The Cold Yeare* (London: Thomas Langley, 1615), sig. C4.

44 'Royalty; regal state or dignity; royal pomp or splendour', deriving from Anglo-Norman 'Rialté', *OED*.

45 Entry for 13 June 1583 in *Calendar of letters, dispatches, and state Papers, relating to negotiations between England and Spain, preserved in the archives at Simancas and elsewhere*, 1550–1586, vol. 3, ed. Martin A. S. Hume (London: Longman, 1896), no. 343, p. 477.

46 *Correspondence of Robert Dudley, Earl of Leycester, during his government of the Low Countries, in the years 1585 and 1586*, ed. John Bruce (London: J. B. Nicols and Son, 1844), p. 47.

47 This is very much Varlow's contention, see *The Lady Penelope*, pp. 7, 16, 19, and 21–24.

48 Thomas Fowler, letter to Lord Burghley, 8 November 1589, Hatfield House, Cecil Papers, 18/59.

49 Thomas Fowler, letter to Lord Burghley, Hatfield House, Cecil Papers, 18/55. There is some evidence that Essex was reprimanded for his role in the Rialta affair, see Hammer, *The Polarization of Elizabethan Politics*, p. 91.

50 *The Letters of John Chamberlain*, vol.1, ed. Norman Egbert McClure (Philadelphia, PA: American Philosophical Society, 1939), p. 96.

51 Letter from Anthony Standen to Anthony Bacon, Lambeth Palace, MS 651, no. 68, f. 111.

52 See Paul E. J. Hammer, 'The Uses of Scholarship: The Secretariat of Robert Devereux, Second Earl of Essex, c. 1585–1601', *English Historical Review* 109: 430 (February 1994), pp. 26–51.

53 For Standen's career see Kathleen M. Lea, 'Sir Anthony Standen and Some Anglo-Italian Letters', *English Historical Review* 47: 187 (July 1932), pp. 461–477. Pérez's controversial life is recorded in Gustav Ungerer, *A Spaniard in Elizabethan England: The Correspondence of Antonio Pérez's Exile*, 2 vols (London: Thamesis Books, 1974–76).

54 Lambeth Palace, MS 651, no. 68, f. 111. For a printed version of the 'Expenses of the Earl of Essex for the Maintenance of Antonio Pérez', see Ungerer, *A Spaniard in Elizabethan England*, vol. 1, pp. 295–296.

55 Hammer, *The Polarization of Elizabethan Politics*, p. 310; Ungerer, *A Spaniard in Elizabethan England*, p. 82, n. 4.

56 William Camden, *Annales … or The Historie of the Life and Death and Reigne of that Famous Princesse, Elizabeth* (London: Thomas Harper, 1629), pp. 103–106.

57 Lambeth Palace, MS 651, no. 68, f. 111.

58 G. B. Harrison, *The Life and Death of Robert Devereux, Earl of Essex* (Bath: Cedric Chivers, 1970 [1937]), p. 71. For an account of the life of Anthony Bacon see Daphne Du Maurier, *Golden Lads: A Study of Anthony Bacon, Francis and Their Friends* (London: Virago, 2007 [1975]).

59 Lambeth Palace, MS 651, no. 68, f. 111–111^{v}.

60 Collins, *Letters and Memorials of State,* vol. 1, pp. 371–373 and 385–386.

61 Letter from Rowland White to Sir Robert Sidney, dated 19 March 1596, Collins, *Letters and Memorials of State,* vol. 2, p. 32. See also Freedman, *Poor Penelope,* pp. 113–114.

62 Letter from Humphrey Ferrers to Lady Rich, British Library, Stowe MS 150, ff. 192–193^{v}. Lady Rich also offered her support to Dr Julius Caesar, see British Library, Additional MS 12506, f. 421.

63 Letter from Penelope Rich to William Downhall, Hatfield House, Cecil Papers, 206/95.

64 Bodleian Library, Misc. MS Don.c.188; this is one of the so-called 'fantastical letters' both of which are printed in A. Freedman, 'Essex to Stella: two letters from the earl of Essex to Penelope Rich', *English Literary Renaissance* 3 (1973), p. 248ff.

65 Letter from Robert Devereux to Penelope Rich, British Library, Additional MS 64081, f. 1.

66 Bourchier Devereux, *Lives and Letters of the Devereux Earls of Essex,* vol. 1 (London: John Murray, 1853), pp. 282–296.

67 For the political and literary activities of the Cooke sisters see Chris Laoutaris, 'Translation/Historical Writing', in *The History of British Women's Writing: 1500–1610,* eds Caroline Bicks and Jennifer Summit (Houndmills: Palgrave, 2010), pp. 296–327. For Elizabeth Russell (aunt to Sir Robert Cecil as well as the Bacon brothers) and her role as an agent for her brother-in-law, Sir William Cecil, see Lambeth Palace, MSS 659, no. 21, ff. 23–26^{v}; 659, no. 75, ff. 104–105; and 659, no. 76, f. 106. See also Chris Laoutaris, 'The Radical Pedagogies of Lady Elizabeth Russell', in *Performing Pedagogy in Early Modern England: Gender, Instruction, and Performance,* eds Kathryn M. Moncrief and Kathryn R. McPherson (Aldershot: Ashgate, 2011), pp. 65–86.

68 Du Maurier, *Golden Lads,* p. 155.

69 Lambeth Palace, MS 659, no. 21, f. 24.

70 Letter from Robert Devereux pertaining to the case of Dr Lopez, Lambeth Palace, MS 653, no. 171, f. 312 (Essex's letter identifying Lopez as the queen's would-be 'executioner'). For more on the Lopez plot see Devereux, *Lives and Letters,* vol. 1, pp. 307–310; and Conyers Read, *Lord Burghley and Queen Elizabeth* (London: Jonathan Cape, 1960), pp. 497–499.

71 Translation by Alexander Samson from the Spanish published in Ungerer, *A Spaniard in Elizabethan England,* vol. 1, no. 48, pp. 87–89. I am immensely grateful to Alexander Samson for translating Pérez's letters to Lady Rich for me.

72 Ungerer, *A Spaniard in Elizabethan England,* vol. 1, no. 45, pp. 82–83, trans. Alexander Samson.

73 Ungerer, *A Spaniard in Elizabethan England,* vol. 1, no. 42, pp. 79–80, trans. Alexander Samson.

74 Ungerer, *A Spaniard in Elizabethan England,* vol. 1, no. 41, p. 79, trans. Alexander Samson.

75 Ungerer, *A Spaniard in Elizabethan England,* vol. 1, no. 44, p. 82, trans. Alexander Samson. Samson also suggests a possible allusion to Garcilaso de la Vega's Sonnet 1 in Pérez's letter no. 48, Ungerer, *Spaniard,* pp. 87–89.

76 Copy of letter from Antonio Pérez to Penelope Rich, Lambeth Palace, MS 653, no. 74, f. 145. The original Spanish letter, which is MS 653, no. 73, f. 144, does not contain the crossed-out word 'secrets', but reads 'mis receptas' ['my receipts'].

77 Lady Rich had five children by Lord Rich and five by Lord Mountjoy, see the family tree in Varlow, *The Lady Penelope,* p. 276. Lord Mountjoy would later acknowledge his children, see Rickman, *Love, Lust, and License in Early Modern England,* pp. 111–40.

78 Letter from Anne Bacon to Anthony Bacon, Lambeth Palace, MS 653, no. 175, f. 318.

79 Letter from Anne Bacon to Anthony Bacon, Lambeth Palace, MS 653, no. 177, f. 320.

80 Letter from Anthony Bacon to Francis Bacon, Lambeth Palace, MS 657, no. 9, f. 12.

81 Letter from Anthony Bacon to Francis Bacon, Lambeth Palace, MS 657, no. 8, f. 11.

82 Letter from Penelope Rich to Anthony Bacon, Lambeth Palace, MS 657, no. 46, f. 61.

83 Letter from Anthony Bacon to Penelope Rich, Lambeth Palace, MS 657, no. 88, ff. 133–133^{v}.

84 Ungerer, *A Spaniard in Elizabethan England*, vol. 2, p. 238.

85 Robert Lacey, *Robert, Earl of Essex, An Elizabethan Icarus* (London: Phoenix Press, 1971), pp. 253–256; Harrison, *The Life and Death of Robert Devereux*, pp. 262–275.

86 'The procedinges of the Erle of Essex', an account of the York House interrogations, British Library, Harley MS 6854, f. 179.

87 The letter survives in multiple manuscript copies. I will be using the British Library manuscript, 'A coppie of the La[dy] Riches letter to the Queene', dated I January 1599 [old-style dating], Stowe MS 150, f. 140, as my base text, with small additions and emendations made using the printed version of the letter in Devereux, *An Apologie of the Earle of Essex* (London: J. Smethwick?, 1600), sigs A2–A3. While most critics use the British Library's Stowe MS 150 as the basis of their analyses because of a general agreement with the letter's dating as found in this document, James Daybell, in his thorough study of Lady Rich's controversial epistle, convincingly argues for a date of late January 1600 for its composition, see his 'Women, Politics and Domesticity: The Scribal Publication of Lady Rich's Letter to Elizabeth I', in *Women and Writing c. 1340-c.1650: The Domestication of Print Culture*, eds Anne Lawrence-Mathers and Phillipa Hardman (York: York Medieval Press, 2010), pp. 111–130, espec. p. 119.

88 Letters from Penelope Rich to Earl of Southampton, Hatfield House, Cecil Papers, 99/167 and 101/205.

89 Bourchier Devereux, *Lives and Letters of the Devereux Earls of Essex*, vol. 1, p. 474.

90 Hatfield House, Cecil Papers, 99/167, dated May 10 but without indication of year.

91 Harrison, *The Life and Death of Robert Devereux*, pp. 248–249.

92 Bourchier Devereux, *Lives and Letters of the Devereux Earls of Essex*, vol. 2, pp. 88–89. Essex was still ill on 22 December 1599, Collins, *Letters and Memorials of State*, vol. 2, p. 153.

93 Collins, *Letters and Memorials of State*, vol. 2, p. 132.

94 Collins, *Letters and Memorials of State*, vol. 2, p. 139.

95 Collins, *Letters and Memorials of State*, vol. 2, p. 149.

96 Entry for 29 December 1599 in CSP Dom 1598–1601, vol. 273, ed. Mary Anne Everett Green (1869), no. 59, p. 365.

97 Penelope's letters to Robert Cecil are: Hatfield House, Cecil Papers, 68/10, 75/83, and 178/117. Having been forbidden from entering court, Lady Essex rose 'almost every Day, by Day light, to goe to my Lord Treasurers, and Sir John Fortescue' to petition on her husband's behalf, see Collins, *Letters and Memorials of State*, vol. 2, p. 149.

98 Hatfield House, Cecil Papers, 75/83.

99 Hatfield House, Cecil Papers, 68/10.

100 Collins, *Letters and Memorials of State*, vol. 2, pp. 158–159.

101 For an account of the circulation of the differing versions of Lady Rich's letter see Daybell, 'Women, Politics and Domesticity...', pp. 111–130.

102 Robert Devereux to Robert Naunton, University of London, MS 187, f. 13[v]. For more on this MS see Paul E. J. Hammer, 'Evidence from Confidential Instructions by the Earl of Essex, 1595–6', *English Historical Review* 111: 441 (April 1996), pp. 357–81.
103 See Hammer, 'The Uses of Scholarship', pp. 43–49.
104 *Notes of Ben Jonson's Conversations with William Drummond of Hawthornden*, ed. David Laing (London: The Shakespeare Society, 1842), p. 25.
105 Ungerer, *A Spaniard in Elizabethan England*, vol. 2, pp. 371–377.
106 *Francis Bacon: A Critical Edition of the Major Works*, ed. Brian Vickers (Oxford: Oxford University Press, 1996), p. 349. See also Edwin B. Benjamin, 'Bacon and Tacitus', *Classical Philology* 60: 2 (April 1965), pp. 102–110.
107 Ungerer, *A Spaniard in Elizabethan England*, vol. 1, letter no. 48, pp. 87–89, trans. Alexander Samson.
108 The quote from Atey's translation of Pérez's letter to Catherine of Bourbon is taken from Ungerer, *Spaniard*, vol. 2, pp. 373–374.
109 See Chapter 10 for the authorship of *The State of Christendom*, for further readings of the role of the *Relaciones* among the Essex circle, and the Earl's promotion of the 'didactic utility of history' in politically charged contexts. See also Alexandra Gajda's article '*The State of Christendom*: History, Political Thought and the Essex Circle', *Historical Research* 81: 213 (2008), pp. 423–446.
110 *The state of Christendom, or, A most exact and curious discovery of many secret passages and hidden mysteries of the times* (London: Humphrey Moseley, 1657), p. 32.
111 Letter from Henry Brooke, Lord Cobham, to Sir Robert Cecil, Hatfield House, Cecil Papers 106/36.
112 *The Annales of Cornelius Tacitus*, trans. Richard Greenway (London: Banham and John Norton, 1598), dedication to the Earl of Essex.
113 Henry Savile, *The Ende of Nero and the Beginning of Galba. Fower Bookes of the Histories of Cornelius Tacitus. The Life of Agricola* (Oxford: Joseph Barnes, 1591), 'A.B. to the reader' and p. 11 respectively.
114 See David Womersley, 'Sir Henry Savile's Translation of Tacitus and the Political Interpretation of Elizabethan Texts', *Review of English Studies* 42: 167 (August 1991), pp. 313–342.
115 'Aphorismes gathered out of the life and end of that most noble Robert Earle of Essex ... ', British Library, Harley MS 1327, ff. 58–60. For the erroneous attribution of this text to Cuffe, see Chapter 10.
116 Edwin B. Benjamin, 'Sir John Hayward and Tacitus', *Review of English Studies* 8: 31 (August 1957), pp. 275–276.
117 Alzada J. Tipton, ' "Lively Patterns ... For Affayres of State": Sir John Hayward's *The Life and Reigne of King Henrie IIII* and the Earl of Essex', *Sixteenth Century Journal* 33: 3 (Autumn 2002), pp. 769–794, esp. pp. 772–773; Alison Weir, *Elizabeth the Queen* (London: Vintage, 1998), p. 441.
118 See HMC, Hatfield, vol. 7, p. 525, for the activities of 'Signor Montecatino, secretary to the late Duke Alphonso (the author of the treatise on Aristotle's three first books of Politics)', who had 'secretly stolen to Rome ... and [was] fed with hope of a Cardinal's hat', an act which Cuffe described as 'very dishonourable'. See also Hammer, 'The Uses of Scholarship', p. 49 and n. 7.
119 *Aristotles Politiques, or Discourses of Government* (London: Adam Islip, 1598), pp. 16–17.
120 *Aristotles Politiques*, pp. 310, 318 and 317 respectively.
121 *C. Cornelii Taciti Opera Quae Extant* (Antwerp, 1585), p. 4. This book is signed by Robert Sidney with a date of 1588 and is located in the British Library, Shelfmark

C.142.e.13. I would like to thank Yasmin Arshad for drawing my attention to this text and for her comments on works relating to Tacitus.

122 *C. Cornelii Taciti*, pp. 19 and 34 (in the case of the latter Sidney muses on the dangers of a discontented populace who 'wil take hold of every small thing' when 'offended').

123 *C. Cornelii Taciti*, p. 76. I owe knowledge of this particular note to Yasmin Arshad.

124 *C. Cornelii Taciti*, p. 76.

125 British Library, Stowe MS 150, f. 140. Additions from the printed version of the letter in the *Apologie* (1600) have been added in italics. See British Library, Additional MSS 40838, 25707, 34218 for further versions of Lady Rich's letter.

126 *Aristotles politiques*, pp. 19–20.

127 British Library, Stowe MS 150, f. 140.

128 British Library, Stowe MS 150, f. 140.

129 Entry for 8 February 1600 in CSP Dom 1598–1601, vol. 274, ed. Mary Anne Everett Greene (1869), no. 37, p. 391; National Archives, Kew, State Papers, 12, no. 274, f. 49.

130 National Archives, Kew, State Papers, 12, no. 274, f. 67.

131 Collins, *Letters and Memorials of State*, vol. 2, letters from Rowland White to Sir Robert Sidney, between 25 February and 8 March, pp. 171–176.

132 Entry for 29 March 1600 in CSP Dom 1598–1601, vol. 274, ed. Mary Anne Everett Greene (1869), no. 86, p. 414.

133 For a detailed analysis of the circulation of the *Apology*, to which Lady Rich's controversial letter became attached, see Chapter 8. Hugh Gazzard reveals that the *Apology* was itself informed by Tacitean discourse and that it is likely that its 'circulation was being orchestrated by the earl personally, and his closest associates'. On the significance of the *Apology*'s use of epistolary form see Chapter 7.

134 *The Letters of John Chamberlain*, ed. Norman Egbert McClure (Philadelphia, PA: American Philosophical Society, 1939), vol. 1, p. 96.

135 National Archives, Kew, State Papers, 63, no. 207/4, f. 161. Dated 13 August 1600 in Calendar of State Papers, Ireland, 1600, vol. 207, part 4, ed. Ernest George Atkinson (1903), no. 67, p. 346.

136 Letter from Robert Cecil to Thomas Sackville, Hatfield House, Cecil Papers, 181/62. This manuscript appears to be Cecil's original draft, and contains numerous dense deletions, corrections and annotations. For the sake of clarity I have not reproduced these, but have broadly followed the reconstructed transcription found in HMC, Hatfield, vol. 10, p. 167 (dated May or June 1600), supplementing this with small changes from my own transcription of the manuscript.

137 Brewer, *The Court of King James the First*, pp. 14–20.

138 National Archives, Kew, State Papers, 12, no. 270, f. 57. A second document, recording fewer conspirators' names, is State Papers, 12, no. 278, f. 55. Both of these are given a conjectural date of 10 February 1601 in the CSP.

139 Hammer, 'Shakespeare's *Richard II*, the Play of 7 February 1601, and the Essex Rising', *Shakespeare Quarterly* 59: 1 (2008), pp. 1–35. Hammer also reveals that many of Essex's co-conspirators were Catholic. In his diary, John Gerard had reported that Lady Rich had considered converting to Catholicism and asked 'to see a priest provided he could come without anyone knowing'. It is not clear how far her actions, if we are to believe Gerard's claims, were intended to draw further support for Essex's cause from the Catholic community. Lady Rich did not become Catholic during her lifetime, though Gerard boasted she had converted on her 'death-bed', *John Gerard: The*

Autobiography of an Elizabethan, trans. Philip Caraman (London: Longmans, 1951), pp. 34–36.

140 National Archives, Kew, State Papers, 12, no. 279, f. 13.
141 National Archives, Kew, State Papers, 12, no. 278, f. 71.
142 The Earl of Bedford to the Privy Council, Hatfield House, Cecil Papers, 76/67, dated 14 February 1601.
143 National Archives, Kew, State Papers, 12, no. 278, f. 65.
144 Quoted in Varlow, *The Lady Penelope*, p. 210.
145 Letter from John Peyton, Hatfield House, Cecil Papers, 83/86, with enclosure 83/85.
146 Cecil may also have been aware that James VI of Scotland, whose passage to the throne he was secretly involved in smoothing during the final years of the Elizabethan establishment, was fond of Lady Rich. Before the scandal of her divorce and marriage to Lord Mountjoy, she was shown great favour by the new King and Queen of England after Elizabeth I's death. See Anne Clifford, *The Memoir of 1603 and The Diary of 1616–1619*, ed. Katherine O. Acheson (Plymouth and Ontario: Broadview, 2007), pp. 50 and 57 ('Now was my Lady Rich grown great with the Queen insomuch as my Lady of Bedford was something out with her ... ').
147 Letter from Penelope Rich to Lord High Admiral, Bodleian Library, Tanner MS 114, f. 139.

10

The Earl of Essex and 'politic history'

Alexandra Gajda

Few aspects of Essex's extraordinary career have fired more debate than his association with political history.[1] The play staged at the Globe Theatre about 'Kyng Henry the iiiith, and of the kyllyng of Kyng Richard the Second', commissioned and watched by a handful of Essex's supporters on the eve of his revolt, continues to fascinate scholars with its tantalising association of text, stage and political event.[2] Almost as notorious is the censorship of John Hayward's *The First Part of the Life and Raigne of King Henrie the IIII*, published in February 1599 and dedicated to 'the most illustrious Earl ... great indeed, both in present judgment and in expectation of future times'.[3] For Elizabeth's government this history was a powerful steer to Essex's ambitions to 'become an other Henry the 4th'.[4]

Essex's circle has also been strongly associated with the English manifestation of broader intellectual trends: the political thought associated with Roman history, especially Tacitus, which electrified European literati in the later sixteenth century, and the directed reading of history with a serious political purpose.[5] Given this rich range of associations between the earl and the interpretation of history in various literary forms, the revolt of 8 February 1601 promised to be one of the most significant examples of 'studying for action', the particular belief that history unlocked a deeper understanding of the world.

Essex's career, though, was also defined by contemporaries through a thick weave of competing historical narratives. After the rising, Essex was condemned at trial and in propaganda as an archetypal traitor, a would-be Bullingbrook, or a popular demagogue like the Roman aristocrat Catiline.[6] For the earl's ardent admirers, though, Essex, the hero of Cadiz, remained the embodiment of classical heroism, cut down by malicious rivals. Shortly after Essex's execution, the Oxford scholar Abraham Colfe was imprisoned for delivering an ill-considered oration which 'thought to prayse the vertues of the Earle ... & darkely to poynt at his death under the historie of Cicero', ruined by Piso, Catiline and Anthony, easily recognisable as Essex's enemies, Sir Robert Cecil, Sir Walter Ralegh and Lord Cobham.[7]

This inclination of Elizabethans to explain their own political circumstances through historical analogies reduces Essex's career to a series of positive or negative paradigms, which threaten to obscure rather than illuminate his complicated behaviour. Most obviously, a range of knotty problems continue to shroud our understanding of the performance of the play at the Globe on 7 February (at which Essex was not present) and the rising. From the same opaque evidence, scholars are still chewing over the identity of the play itself – refuting and asserting Shakespeare's authorship – and making imaginative attempts to reconstruct the playgoers' interpretation of the performance. Did the earl's followers watch the play to incentivise revolt? Or did they, as Paul Hammer has argued, view Richard II's deposition as a parable of the perils of rebellion, the dangers of misconceived aristocratic interventions?[8]

This chapter is not going to retread these familiar paths by attempting a close reading of a particular literary or historical text associated with Essex. Rather, it will consider the broader construction of competing narratives of Essex's behaviour that defined the earl as a hero or a traitor, according to particular historical typologies, and argue that the political divisions of late Elizabethan England were intensely sharpened by the historical frameworks used by contemporaries to describe and understand the world around them. Patterns from history – ancient, medieval and contemporary – exacerbated the earl's acute sensitivity to the 'deformities' of the realm, and his public role as a man of virtue, whose fate was intrinsically linked to the health of the state. The negative critique of the earl, though, was rooted in the tangible correspondences between Essex's behaviour and historical accounts of the paradigmatic behaviour of traitors and rebels. Both narratives embodied the baroque anxiety that underpinned late sixteenth-century political culture: a deep uncertainty about the future of the realm after Elizabeth's death.

History and Essex's circle

A string of texts associated with Essex emphasised the didactic utility of history. Pedagogic instruction written either by Essex or in Essex's name by Francis Bacon urged the recipient, the young Earl of Rutland: 'Above all other books be conversant in the Histories, for they will best instruct you in matter moral, military, and politic, by which and in which you must ripen and settle your judgment'.[9] Most famously, the author of the anonymous 'A.B.' introduction to Sir Henry Savile's English translation of four books of Tacitus' *Histories* and the *Life of Agricola* – attributed to Essex himself – insisted: 'there is no learning so proper for the direction of the life of man as Historie'.[10]

Conventionally, Essex commended the reading of historical texts for exemplarity. A letter on scholarly techniques written to Fulke Greville (again written by either Francis Bacon or Essex, or both), advised on the 'gathering' of information from histories, under 'heads or commonplaces', carefully chosen to impart the greatest 'profit and use'.[11] In particular Essex's Latin correspondence with Antonio Pérez, the former Secretary of State of Philip II turned traitor and rebel, who lived at Essex House in 1594–95, is riddled with historical, classical and biblical exempla. Essex is figured as Aeneas or Achilles; the Lord Treasurer, William Cecil, as Aeolus, a malign windbag; Philip II, the Spanish tyrant, is a modern Tiberius.[12]

Although he was a prominent patron of scholars, evidence of Essex's own reading of English history is elusive.[13] Scholars rue the sibylline lack of context in Sir Walter Ralegh's remark to Sir Robert Cecil in July 1597 reporting Essex's considerable amusement 'at the consait of Richard the 2'.[14] According to Gabriel Harvey, Essex enjoyed William Warner's popular *Albions England*, a poetic account of formidable length of England's history that drew indiscriminately on myth, scripture and chronicle sources.[15] The earl was also the recipient of flattering verses in Samuel Daniel's 1595 and 1599 editions of *The Civile Wars*, a quasi-epic poem on the baronial conflicts of the later medieval period, inspired by Lucan's *Pharsalia*.[16] Intriguingly, Essex signalled his awareness of printed English chronicles in perhaps his final extant letter, written on Christmas Day 1600 to warn James VI that his title to the throne was imperilled. As a covert response, Essex suggested that James write a breezy reply enquiring after 'Stowes Chronicle which I heare is newly reprinted and enlarged'.[17]

Essex's scholarly associates have also been linked to the development of 'politic history' or 'civic' history (the latter Francis Bacon's term). Eschewing the messy annalistic form of the chronicles, writers emulated classical-humanist prose genres, shunning providentialism for analysis of the human causation of historical events based essentially on the morality of political actors.[18] The only example of the genre written in Elizabeth's reign on an English subject-matter is Hayward's *Life and Raigne of King Henrie the IIII*.[19] Despite its title, the famous *First Part* (the only section to be published) narrates the reign and dethroning of Richard II, a bleak dissection of the manifold acts of misgovernment of a prince 'absolute in power, resolute in will, and dissolute in life'.[20] As Andrew Gordon notes in Chapter 7, though, this history's connections to Essex himself are almost impossible to determine. Accusations of treason against the earl drawn up over the course of 1600 and 1601 alleged his complicity in the 'underhand permitting of that most treasonous booke of Henry the fourth to be printed and published', as well as his 'being so often present at the playing thereof' – an opaque reference that has suggested to some scholars that Essex enjoyed a play based on Hayward's history.[21] Whether or not these allegations were true, the Privy Council's interrogation of the author uncovered no personal links to Essex: it was John Wolfe, the publisher, who appears to have persuaded Hayward to add the troublesome dedication, typically to boost sales.[22] As Cyndia Clegg reminds us, Essex initiated the official interrogation of the history himself, when the book's wild popularity became apparent.[23]

An important work of 'politic' history' that certainly emanated from the heart of Essex's circle, though, was neither about English history or written by an English author, but by Antonio Pérez, Essex's voluminous, controversial correspondent and advisor on foreign affairs, whose significant contribution to political discussion amongst Essex's advisors and friends is discussed by Chris Laoutaris in Chapter 9. The earl's circle organised the London publication of the 1594 version of Pérez's *Pedaços de Historia o Relaciones* (pieces of history, or relations), a racy account of tyranny and murder at the court of Philip II, justifying Pérez's own murky behaviour and relating his crucial role in the Aragonese revolt of 1590–91.[24] This memoir fitted the definition of Francis Bacon's third category of 'Just and Perfect History' – 'Narrations or Relations'.[25] Pérez dedicated the *Relaciones* fondly to Essex, while Anthony Bacon, Pérez's great friend, who orchestrated Essex's intelligence service, commissioned an English translation.[26] A detailed commentary on Pérez's *Relaciones* also formed the supplement to the anonymous treatise, *The State of Christendom*, written by collaborative operation by members of Essex's circle in 1594–95. Compiled like a giant commonplace book, the main body of the treatise forged exempla 'gathered' from classical, medieval and recent history into a rich analysis of European politics.[27]

Pérez was also a representative of the particular interest in Tacitus that in England, as Laoutaris notes, has been identified as almost synonymous with the intellectual culture of the 'Essex circle'. The *Relaciones* styles itself as work of 'politic history', edifying the reader's grasp of the 'affections and naturall inclinacions of Princes'.[28] Hayward's *Life and Raigne* was self-consciously a work of Tacitean history – a bravura collage of myriad quotation from literary texts, but especially Henry Savile's edition of Tacitus' *Histories* and *The Life of Agricola*.[29] The earl's close relationship with Savile probably prompted Richard Greneway to dedicate his 1598 translation of the *Annals* to Essex, while the translation of Justus Lipsius' *Sixe Bookes of Politickes*, the foremost interpretation of Tacitus in the sixteenth century, was published by William Jones, also a follower of the earl.[30] In death, Essex became the object of Tacitean analysis himself, his story inspiring sets of maxims and aphorisms that exemplified the dangerous workings of the court.[31]

Tacitus' bleak account of the origins and early history of the principate, though, was notoriously malleable in the hands of sixteenth- and seventeenth-century readers. Lipsius' *Sixe bookes of politickes*, which had a significant impact on Francis Bacon's developing political thought, stipulated the techniques of government, or *raison d'état*, through which rulers should enhance the power of the state. Although the investigation of the Attorney General Edward Coke and Lord Chief Justice Popham charged Hayward with endorsing the theory of subjects' resistance, recent close readings have argued this was a wilful misreading of the orthodox, providentialist warning about the sins of rebellion preached in the *Life and Raigne*: as in any conventional mirror-for-princes, the authorial voice excoriates Richard's misgovernment, but prophetically denounces Henry's usurpation of the throne as an unjust action, which visits God's punishment on the House of Lancaster.[32] In stark contrast, though, Pérez's *Relaciones* contained one of the more radical interpretations of Tacitus of the late sixteenth century. In quite the opposite sense to Lipsius, Pérez explained that the admirable aim of Tacitus had been to magnify the flawed humanity of rulers to their subjects, so 'that men should not believe that [princes] were any thinge ells but men'. The metier of the historian, he argued, was to puncture the carapace of sacred monarchy, which blinded subjects to their natural liberties: that they might 'deminishe parte of that love and confidence which they have in princes. The parte I meane which is to muche, and draweth men to Idolatrye … [whereby subjects] make themselves slaves and are manacled with their owne handes'.[33]

Essex and the critique of the Elizabethan polity

But what was the impact of all of this interest in the forensic analysis of power? The interrogators of Hayward's *Life and Raigne* alleged that the history was intended as a parable of the current 'deformities of state', covertly condemning Elizabeth's prerogative taxation, the military crisis in Ireland, and her choice of counsellors. Most strikingly, Coke read Hayward's emphasis on Richard's childlessness as a warning about the unsettled succession.[34] If Essex had pored over the *Life and Raigne*, as his accusers insisted he had, would he have shared Coke's interpretation?

The answer is almost certainly yes. In his letter to James VI of Scotland, written just before the rising, Essex defines England as a kingdom on the precipice of disaster. A 'raigning faction' has grown 'so potent in a state as they could oppress innocencie, cancel merit, justify conspiracy, make lawe … bury freedome, usurpe sovereignty for the present, and prepare a way for an unjust succession hereafter'. Elizabeth is virtually impotent, 'led blindfold into hir owne extreme danger'. Now 'their speaking to suppress all noble vertuous and heroicall spirits', 'their juggling with our enemies, their practise for the Infanta of Spaine' demands action: 'Now am I summoned of all sides … to releeve my poore cuntry that grones under hir burthen'.[35] Some six weeks later, Essex would process into London, exhorting the citizens to join him in defence of his life and the protection of the queen from the murderous faction who had sold the Crown to Isabella Clara Eugenia, the Spanish Infanta.[36]

This vision was the product of Essex's bitter alienation from the regime that had swiftly followed the high point of his career, the storming of Cadiz in 1596. By the late 1590s, Essex regarded himself as the wronged victim of a range of misfortunes: lack of due recognition for his military achievements, high-profile slights to his role as a patronage broker, a slackening grip over the direction of the war. Writing to James, Essex was in the frozen winter of his career. Formally stripped of political office in June 1600 on charges of misconduct during campaign in Ireland, Essex's inability to regain access to the court was proof to the earl and his followers that Elizabeth was enslaved by an antagonistic faction of his personal enemies, led by the Principal Secretary of the Privy Council, Sir Robert Cecil. Crucially, Essex's appeal to James VI rested on the identification of his own rivals as foes of James and of the realm itself – as opponents of the Scottish succession.

The tangible foundations of this 'succession plot' lay in Essex's hostility to the willingness exhibited by councillors and courtiers to find common ground for pacification with Spain. These suspicions had been hardened in 1599 and 1600 by Robert Cecil's development of friendly contacts between England and the Habsburg Netherlands, where the Infanta and her husband, Albert, ruled as joint sovereigns.[37]

Widespread fears that England was acutely vulnerable to a succession crisis, though, were also deeply etched in the literary and historical culture of the 1590s, in the efflorescence of plays and poems about the baronial wars for the Crown in late medieval England, or the internecine civil conflict that precipitated the structural transformations of the Roman state from Republic to Imperial rule.[38] In the letter to Greville, Bacon or Essex recommends that scholars of history make notes on 'Periods or revolutions of state' caused by 'the uncertainty of succession', which might 'ruin the greatest monarchy'.[39] Even more pointed were the literary interests of Charles Blount, Lord Mountjoy, Essex's most powerful political ally, who initially shared the opinion that the earl's fall from grace was evidence of a wider succession plot.[40] On 7 September 1601, some months after Essex's execution, Mountjoy watched a performance of the old Elizabethan play *Gorboduc*, the famous drama of succession crisis and civil war set in Britain's mythical past.[41] Mountjoy was also a patron of Samuel Daniel, and the dedicatee of the early editions of Daniel's *Civile Wars*: tellingly Gabriel Harvey wrote that Mountjoy greatly esteemed 'Daniel's peece of the Chronicle touching the usurpation of Henrie of Bullingbrooke'.[42]

In fact, as Coke's interrogation of the *Life and Raigne* indicates, the history of Richard II's deposition had wide currency in the 1590s as a cautionary tale about the succession. The firebrand Puritan parliamentarian Peter Wentworth warned the queen that Richard II's subjects had preferred the rule of a usurper who would 'preserve the crowne & them, then a rightfull king, that would perill the crowne and state'.[43] At the other end of the religious spectrum, *A Conference about the Next Succession to the Crown of Ingland* (1594/5) – almost certainly written by the Hispanophile Jesuit Robert Parsons – magnified the most powerful nightmare of Elizabethan Protestants, the possibility that England's next ruler might be female, Catholic – and Spanish. To justify the hereditary claim of the Infanta, who was descended from the House of

Lancaster, Parsons argued at length that Bullingbrook's usurpation of the throne was a just and legitimate action, undertaken for the 'reformation of his realme against so potent a tyrant, as King Richard'.[44]

Parsons' *Conference*, with its radical endorsement of subjects' right to resist and depose an anointed monarch, cast Essex into a maze of paranoid suspicion. Intending to cause ruptures in the earl's relationship with Elizabeth and James VI, Parsons notoriously dedicated the text to Essex, heaping poisonous praise on his noble lineage and extraordinary virtues, and horribly lauding Essex's ambition to 'have a greater part or sway in deciding of this great affaire' of the succession.[45] As scholars have often noted, the laudatory dedications of the *Conference* and Hayward's *Life and Raigne* are strikingly similar in vocabulary and conceit. Wolfe and/or Hayward may have hoped that *their* dedication would perform a positive service for Essex, expunging Parsons' smear by attaching Essex's name to a history that countered the arguments of the *Conference* by emphasising the sinfulness of Bullingbrook's actions, thus obliquely endorsing the succession of James VI.[46]

The deep impact of Parsons' devilish dedication, though, was to sensitise Essex's tender antennae to the synchronisation of the deceitful strategies that his political enemies would use to undermine him with conspiracies focused on Spain and the Infanta. In his *Apologie* of 1598, Essex vituperated those who advocated a peace with Spain as 'Iniurious ... to the Country that hath bredde them', by dangerously enhancing the likely succession of Isabella, 'the same person, whose tytle to the Crowne of *England, Parsons* so laboureth to prove'.[47] The centrality of Parsons to the succession plot that gripped Essex's mind by the end of 1600 resurfaced at his treason trial on 19 February 1601, when he dramatically revealed that the foundations of his conviction that the Crown was sold to Spain were grounded in rumours of Sir Robert Cecil's favourable reading of the *Conference*.[48]

The wider literary culture also girded Essex's inclination to demonise his personal rivals as amoral machiavels and nascent kingmakers. As Blair Worden notes, it was from the early 1590s that the evil counsellor and the corrupt favourite became a stock feature of political and historical drama.[49] The enchantment of Edward II by low-born favourites in Marlowe's eponymous play had also featured prominently in Catholic polemic, which likened the influence of Protestant councillors – most recently Lord Burghley – to that of Piers Gaveston and the Despensers, perpetuating a '*regnum Cecilianum*', where the queen was in thrall to Cecilian power.[50] Although they play a surprisingly small role in Shakespeare's *Richard II*, corrupt counsellors and hateful favourites are a dominating factor in the alienation of the king from his subjects in Daniel's *Civile Wars* and Hayward's *Life and Raigne*.

The most influential literary model of the evil counsellor, though, was Tacitus' brilliant psychological portrait of Aelius Sejanus, the head of the praetorian guard, who for a time had seemed more powerful in Rome than the emperor Tiberius himself. For the author/s of *The State of Christendom*, the career of Sejanus had been exactly mirrored in recent years by Henry Duke of Guise, who had tyrannised over Henry III of France. Guise's example was particularly chilling to those inclined to believe that an English faction plotted a Spanish succession. As the author/s of *The State of Christendom* warned, Guise had attempted to thwart the claim of the true heir, Henry of Navarre, by harnessing the military backing of Philip II – 'a step and Ladder to climb up to the Kingdom'.[51]

Almost inevitably, then, Essex and his supporters turned to these same conceptual parameters to define their Elizabethan dystopia, where his courtly rivals, Sir Walter Ralegh and Lord Cobham, were poisonous acolytes to Secretary Cecil, heir to 'Burghley's Commonwealth'. In a bitter libelling campaign in late 1599 and 1600, the hunchbacked Cecil was vilified as this type of overreaching counsellor, and (perhaps inevitably) compared to the ultimate historical machiavel, Richard III: a 'Crookeback spider', a 'Proude and ambitious wretch', 'Poison to the state and Comons'.[52]

The final 'proof' that Essex offered of this conspiracy theory to James was his interpretation of his own political disgrace – the suppression of 'all noble vertuous and heroicall spirits' – as a synecdoche for the state of the realm itself. Even in the mid-1590s, while the political relationship between Essex and the Cecils had functioned in outward harmony, the private correspondence of the earl and his friends defined politics in terms of this dichotomised moral universe, where Essex's noble courses were inevitably hindered by rivals, envious of his virtue. On 4 January 1599, as he prepared for the Irish campaign, Essex gloomily predicted to his friend, Lord Willoughby of Eresby, that even victory against the rebel would entrench the position of his 'practising enemies', who 'passionately urge' his command so that he might be defamed to the queen: 'I will never forswear virtue for fear of ostracism'.[53] Essex's followers also relentlessly insisted that his virtue imbued him with the moral legitimacy to assume his indispensability in public affairs. For Anthony Bacon, Essex's 'noble active minde' was constantly at work 'for the publique good which stands now in need of diligent Arquitecks'.[54] After the rising, Sir Ferdinando Gorges, one of the inner circle of conspirators, explained that the 'cause that bounde mee so inseperably to [Essex]' had been 'observation of his worthe and vertue' who made every effort 'by any meanes hee coulde get for the publick good of his country'.[55]

This habit of conceptualising the world in terms of enemies and followers, men of virtue and vice-ridden courtiers and counsellors, was of course an extraordinarily reductive understanding of politics that destroyed Essex's ability to compromise with rivals for Elizabeth's favour. But yet again, these stereotypes derived from the very serious 'politic' histories that claimed to illuminate the world of the court, and the psychological motivation of the powerful.

In particular, the notion that the virtuous man in politics is vulnerable to the schemes of immoral enemies is repeatedly emphasised in Henry Savile's interpretation of Tacitus, in his notes to his translation of the *Histories* and especially on the *Life of Agricola,* which develop into a commentary on the operation of virtue and vice at princely courts. Tacitus depicts Agricola, his father-in-law, as a valorous military leader and a just administrator, impeccably loyal to his emperor, Domitian, and to Rome itself. Agricola's career foundered, though, 'partly through his owne vertues, and partlie the vices of others' which incurred implacable 'spite and envy' from unmilitary creatures of the court. In a long note, Savile marks up the danger of 'commenders', who removed Agricola from the centre of power by hypocritically recommending his virtues to a suspicious Domitian.[56] This was, of course, exactly how, eight years later, Essex would denounce the conduct of those 'practising enemies' who recommended him for service in Ireland. The author of a set of Tacitean aphorisms on Essex's life sees in the earl the best illustration of this *arcana domus,* this secret of the palace: one of the darkest 'Rules of state' is to 'hurt with praise', 'impoverish with tytles of honor', and 'banish with offices of imployment'.[57]

As Pérez insisted, though, the lens of history was to be tuned to magnify the human fallibility of the prince as well as the prince's servants. Evil counsel could only flourish if the prince were weak and inadequate, unable to judge the true appearance of virtue, or susceptible to the flattery of devious courtiers.

Once more, Savile's notes explore this conundrum extensively: 'The efficacy of 'commendation' only works upon weak princes who are especially jealous of estimable qualities in their subjects, particularly 'militar renowne, magnanimity, patronage of justice against al oppressions & wronges, magnificence, & other Heroical vertues properly belonging, or chiefly beseeming the Princes person', virtues which breed 'admiration also generally among the mean people'. Agricola is a classic exemplum for Savile of a militaristic, virtuous hero, feted by popular acclaim, who ought to be the chief subject of a strong and capable ruler. But the weak tyranny of Domitian is far more prevalent in the dark world of the Tacitean Principate. Tacitus strongly insinuates that the emperor, 'umbrageous & fearefull' of his subject's exceptional character, was deeply implicated in the suspicious circumstances that governed Agricola's death.[58]

The theme of princely jealousy of virtue pulsed through Tacitean literature connected to Essex and the Elizabethan court. John Hayward borrowed busily from Savile to describe the relationship of Richard and Bullingbrook. Richard was suspicious of military virtue, especially when 'a cunning kinde of enemies, *commenders* [my emphasis]' persuaded the king 'that to be a discreet and valiant commander in the fielde [is] a virtue peculiar to a prince'. The king's 'eternall jealousy' of Bullingbrook was the 'generall favour & love [of] the people'.[59] The Tacitean aphorisms on Essex's life are bleaker still: 'the settled Jealousye of a prince is uncurable'.[60]

And Essex assuredly employed these analytical frames to make sense of his own deteriorating relationship with Elizabeth. Savile's list of 'Heroical virtues' defines the qualities that Essex would come to most value in himself over the next meteoric years of his career. In October 1596, Francis Bacon issued a stern warning to Essex that his sense of his own virtue, his adherence to militarism, popularity, his pursuit of 'honourable commonwealth causes' inflamed the queen's own jealousy of his 'suspected greatness', with portentous implications for the earl's future.[61] Departing for Ireland, Essex bemoaned 'the construction of princes under whom *magna fama* is more dangerous than *mala*'.[62]

The reconstruction of Essex's attitude to Elizabeth's authority in the final years of his life is complex. In a sustained campaign of florid letters designed to wheedle his way back into the queen's affections, Essex larded his letters to Elizabeth with flattering expressions of devotion to her service, and his reverence for her 'princely and angel-lik nature'.[63] The earl and his co-rebels justified the rising itself as an act of political loyalism, an action taken in defence of the queen as well as the safety of the realm.[64]

But readers of history knew that monarchs who were swayed by evil counsel were traditionally weak rulers like Edward II, or wilful and bloodthirsty tyrants, such as Nero and Domitian, ruling through passions rather than rational analysis of the needs of the public good. The 'A.B.' introduction to Savile's translation of the *Histories* argues that to forge a distinction between the prince who listens to evil counsel and the prince who is tyrannical is not only conceptually problematic, but in practical terms, pointless: 'In Galba thou maiest learne, that a good Prince governed by evill ministers is as dangerous as if hee were evill himselfe'. This is an adage reused by Hayward to explain the discontent of Richard's subjects: 'it is oftentimes as daungerous to a prince to have evil and odious adherents as to bee evil and odious himselfe'.[65] Finally, the set of Tacitean aphorisms taken from Essex's life is even more radically emphatic that the culpability for the acts of evil counsellors lies firmly at the door of the prince: 'Except the prince be odious it ys noe policy for State to move against odious counsellors'.[66]

Another Bullingbrook?

While Essex's admirers viewed their hero as a maligned man of virtue, critics defined his behaviour as conforming to another historical bogeyman just as prominent as the evil counsellor – the over-mighty noble who uses the rhetoric of political reform to conceal his darker designs.

For some years before the rising, this mantle threatened to fit Essex's frame. Parsons' dedication, of course, was an arrow fired straight at the fleshy heel of this aspirant Achilles, encouraging readers to identify sinister motivation into the earl's obsession with virtue, statecraft and his aristocratic lineage. From

1598, as Essex grew increasingly estranged from the court, fears of his unstable conduct deepened. In August 1599, John Chamberlain reported gossip that the Council's over-zealous reaction to the so-called 'Invisible Armada' was instead a display of military strength, aimed at showing Essex that the country could mobilise quickly to arms.[67] After his return from Ireland in September 1599, reports filtered back that the unauthorised truce struck by Essex with Hugh O'Neill, Earl of Tyrone, had been accompanied by a secret deal between the earls to divide power in England and Ireland between them. Although he had been cleared of charges of treason and disloyalty the following summer, the festering presence of Essex in London, attracting hordes of well-wishers to Essex House, was a looming threat to his rivals. Should Elizabeth die, the action that Essex would surely take to enthrone his preferred candidate, James, would certainly encompass the destruction of his antagonists. Ralegh's advice to Cecil was brutal: 'to relent towards this tyrant yow will repent it when it shalbe to late. His malice is fixt'.[68]

Negative comment on Essex's behaviour – the skeleton of later narratives of his treachery – had a growing currency before the disaster of the Irish campaign. In Everard Guilpin's 1598 satire, *Skialetheia*, Essex was ominously lampooned as Bullingbrook reborn – 'Great *Foelix*', who 'Vayleth his cap to each one he doth meet', as his 'thoughts swell/With yeastie ambition'.[69] The following April, in the wake of the earl's rapturous reception by Londoners as he departed for Ireland, the French ambassador revealed extraordinarily ambiguous attitudes to Essex's loyalty, when he reported that Elizabeth and some courtiers had openly compared the earl's popularity with the love of Parisians for the Duke of Guise.[70] While Essex sweated in political disgrace, in 1600 and 1601, the Privy Council forged a charge of treason from disparate evidences of the earl's seditious behaviour, the brokering of power with Tyrone, his mingling with suspicious Catholics, as well as his enjoyment of Hayward's *Life and Raigne*. Underscoring the charge was the allegation that Essex was aspiring 'and Settling to himself, Aswell the Crowne of England, as of the kingdome of Ireland'.[71]

Essex's rising was the product of the cumulative clash of these competing narratives of conspiracy. Through the earl's spectacles, evil counsellors intended to perpetuate their usurpation of power by subverting the succession to Spain. From the perspective of the Council, Essex was a malcontented nobleman, feeding his rampant ambition through the reading of seditious histories. In early February 1601, now desperate, the inner ring of Essex's circle analysed various strategies to force their way to court, where the queen could be petitioned, and the earl's enemies arrested and tried. The merits of a direct attack on the court were compared with the seizure of the Tower, or an appeal to the city itself – the latter most favoured by Essex who was 'assured the Citizens would take armes in his behalfe'.[72] But the sally into London on 8 February was prompted when the Privy Council, worried by the massing of followers at Essex House, summoned the earl to appear before them. Fearing that he would be charged with treason, or even assassinated, Essex led his followers into London, launching an appeal to the citizens and civic elite to join the defence of his person and of the realm.

How, then, are we to make final sense of the patterns of history and the earl's rising? For the government, the answers could clearly be interpreted from a long range of precedents. Fulfilling the prophecy of the treason charge, Essex had launched an attempt to realise his long-held designs to be a usurper. A 'Memoriall about the Insurrection of the E. of Essex' in Cecil's hand is in itself a series of historical notes comparing the earl to all kinds of rebellious traitors who had pretended to reform the commonwealth: Richard Duke of York had made false 'humble petitions' to Henry VI, while plotting usurpation; identical justifications had been used by the earls of Northumberland and Westmorland, Catholic nobles who had led the last rebellion against Elizabeth's government in 1569; they had also been employed by the 'family and faction of Guise'.[73]

This definition of Essex as a would-be usurper was fiercely opposed by Essex and his followers, who insisted at first on their innocence of charges of treason. Even when it was revealed to the earl that his co-conspirators had confessed the substance of his post-rising plotting, Essex continued to argue that the ends of all of his actions had been virtuous, aimed at the reform of the state. The rising, such as it was, had been intended as a peaceful procession to the court, where his enemies would be overcome and Elizabeth petitioned to try pestilent creatures of court and council, with the minimum shedding of blood. The rebels were the queen's loyal subjects, even if their actions had been misconceived.[74]

It is this misplaced emphasis on the earl's alleged designs on the crown, argues Paul Hammer, which has confused our understanding of the meaning of a history and/or a play about Richard II to Essex and his followers. It seems obvious that the audience at the Globe would have interpreted a drama about Richard II as a mirror-for-princes enacted of current dangers to the realm. Hammer also plausibly argues that the play's resonance may have resided in the scorched memory of Parsons' *Conference*, with its endorsement of the claim of the Infanta and the House of Lancaster. Rather than a blueprint for revolt, though, the story of Richard's deposition was to Essex's supporters a cautionary tale about the worst perils of a succession crisis. If he were to make a physical intervention, they envisaged that Essex should, in Hammer's words, 'do it *properly*' – to maintain and *reform* Elizabeth's queenship – and to save the kingdom from the turmoil of revolt, deposition, illegitimate kingship and civil war. This interpretation requires that we understand the rising on Essex's own terms, as a loyalist action, to cleanse the realm of evil counsellors, but to protect the queen herself.[75]

Hammer also suggests that the remedies for tyranny proposed in *The State of Christendom* are a far more likely blueprint for the earl's intended courses.[76] The author/s argue that in the instance of gross misgovernment, 'Peers and

Nobility' might take positive action, restraining misgoverning princes before the Commons ignite in rebellious anarchy. The legitimacy of such behaviour can be found in historical precedent: the 'Colledge of Cardinals and the States of the Empire have ... used a certain Right both over the Pope and over the Emperor'; the power of Henry III was restrained after the battle of Lewes by a baronial council; so too 'Prelates, Earls and Barons made Ordinances for the State and Government of the Realm' in Edward II's reign. Offending princes might even be 'chastened according to the nature and quality of their offences' in a Parliament, 'from whence all or most Laws have their beginning, their foundation, their strength'. This passage has very clear correspondences with the ways that Essex appears to have conceptualised his rising, as an extraordinary public action, legitimised by his identification as a virtuous nobleman.[77]

There seems little doubt that Essex did not envisage wearing the crown himself: his sincere end, as future kingmaker, was to secure a parliament to legally verify James' title and, perhaps, to try his enemies.[78] But Essex's protestation of the legitimacy of his actions was easily dismantled by the government in the propaganda that followed the rising, and forensically at his trial. The prosecution could easily argue that, humble petitioning aside, an attempt to force access to the queen's presence and to attack her chosen ministers was to usurp the monarch's sovereign powers, if not the Crown itself; a manifest act of treason according to contemporary interpretations of statutory law, as the rebels must have known.[79] Moreover, no orthodox theory of divine right monarchy in the late sixteenth century viewed as legitimate the kind of autonomous noble intervention recommended by the author of *The State of Christendom*, or planned and abortively attempted by Essex, irrespective of whether or not that subject had designs on the throne. By assuming public authority – 'summoned of all sides to stop the malice ... to releeve my poore country' – by appealing to the civil elites and citizens of London for support, and by taking autonomous action to defend the succession, Essex was claiming the extraordinary authority of a subaltern magistrate with power to reform the state.

The constitutional restraints on tyranny discussed in *The State of Christendom* were in fact advocated by sixteenth-century resistance theorists, Catholic and Protestant, who defined monarchy as a public office, bound by the latent agency of lesser magistrates and/or institutions, or by solemn contracts. The German electors' capacity to bridle the power of the Holy Roman Emperor, and the conciliar authority of cardinals over the pope, were standard *topoi* of more radical theories of limited monarchy that sometimes advocated the deposition of tyrannical princes by magistrates and representative bodies.[80] In an exceptionally careful manner, the author of *The State of Christendom* tentatively discusses the legitimacy of such an extreme action. Listing a roll call of the depositions of princes removed 'for their insufficiency' the author admits that '*the most part of them* will be found scant lawful' [my emphasis];

the crimes of the majority of these princes, 'in *private* men, are not capital' [my emphasis], and thus cannot be a just treatment of a crowned monarch. Richard II, though, is sandwiched into this list as the exemplum of a king deposed 'for not tendring the Weal, and *public* Welfare of their Subjects' [my emphasis]. By this subtle use of the language of private and public acts of misgovernment, the careful reader is invited to infer that Richard's removal may have been lawful after all.[81]

Finally, the similarities between Essex and Bullingbrook's predicaments – *and their actions* – were so pressingly acute that it seems strained to read these historical interests as a pattern of how not to behave. If Essex had read any literary portrait of Richard's deposition – Hayward's, Shakespeare's, Daniel's, even Stowe's *Chronicle* – he would have recognised that the decision to try to effect a bloodless intervention, at the head of a group of noblemen, was hardly dissimilar to the coup successfully achieved by Bullingbrook in 1399. The decision to turn to the citizens – a decision taken by Essex himself, against the better judgement of his advisors – must have been sharpened by historical accounts of the responsiveness of London to a charismatic nobleman of ostensible virtues. In Hayward's *Life and Raigne*, Bullingbrook uses 'all other complements of popular behaviour' to secure the allegiance of London as his 'seat of the warre'.[82]

Rather than avoiding emulation of Bullingbrook, then, Essex appeared to have motored down the 'beaten path of Traytours, turning their imputation upon Counsellours, and persons of credit with their Soveraigne', as Francis Bacon's official printed report of the rising alleged.[83] Even the earl's presentation of himself as the instrument of reform of the commonwealth was denounced by the government as the seditious rhetoric typically used by rebels; as Robert Cecil noted, 'Jack Cade termed him self John Amend all'; 'Watt Tyler cried out for the King and Commons as you dyd for the Q. and the Erl of Essex'.[84] And at Essex's trial Francis Bacon (now counsel for the prosecution), pointed to the extraordinary similarities between Essex's actions and the Day of the Barricades in 1588, when Guise, the malleable Machiavel, had raised Paris, to make himself the foremost power in the kingdom. Like Essex, Guise's rising had been at the head of a small clique of nobles; like Essex, Guise proclaimed his peaceful intentions, and his desire for reconciliation with the king. [85]

Even – perhaps especially – the earl's main point of defence; his presentation of his rising as a mere attack on enemies, separable from his absolute loyalty to Elizabeth, was in itself defined as incontrovertible *proof* that Essex meant more radical actions than he had admitted to. In his notes for the trials of the rebels, Edward Coke remarked that Edward II's queen, Isabel, assembled the nobility ostensibly 'to remove councellors' as a precursor to the king's deposition.[86] And Bullingbrook, of course, had initially launched his own campaign through an attack on evil counsel, rather than as an assault on the Crown itself. In Shakespeare's play, the Duke of York is won round to Henry's cause when he is assured that his nephew returns only to claim his inheritance, and to 'weed and pluck away' the 'caterpillars of the commonwealth'.[87] Coke posed the unanswerable question at the trials of the lesser conspirators: 'How long liveth Richard the 2 after he was surprised in the same waie?'[88] How could anyone with any faith in the patterns of history expect that the relationship of queen and subject could be restored once Essex had gained power over the court and his enemies?

With extraordinary irony, the ways that Essex legitimised his protest were most characteristic of Parsons' account of Bullingbrook's rising in the *Conference*. As Essex claimed that he was 'summoned' to action, Parsons' Henry was 'called home by expresse letters of the more and better part of al the realme'. Lightly armed, Essex appealed to the London citizens to join in his non-violent petition to Elizabeth. Parsons' Bullingbrook 'came wholy (in a manner) unarmed', at the head of 'only threescore men in al', meeting with such great 'concourse of al people' that 'he achieved the matter, and that without any battaile or bloodshed at al'. For Parsons, this was a limited intervention done 'properly': 'it could not be executed in better nor more convenient order'. But when the king's offences were brought before parliament – as recommended in *The State of Christendom* – Richard was 'by act of parlament' lawfully deposed.[89] These correspondences were too strong to be missed by the government's propagandists. Preaching the public sermon after the earl's execution, William Barlow insisted that the *Conference* was 'a principal, if not the originall poyson of the late Earles hart'.[90]

The government's prosecution and propaganda, then, had an achingly valid argument: if the earl was so sensitive to the lessons of history, how could he not have known that the autonomous intervention of noblemen had resulted in the deposition of monarchs in the past? To assure a different fate for Elizabeth, the earl would have to ignore rather than learn from 'politic' history to ensure that James VI inherited the throne in non-violent circumstances.

These clashing conspiracy theories arose from the claustrophobia of court politics, stoked by fear of succession crisis, and the long unsettling reach of Parsons' *Conference*. They were energised by the inclination of the 'politic' historian to search for the secret springs of action and 'ridels' of state from accounts of the past, which encouraged Elizabethans to turn a deeply negative lens on their own world. The narrative of Essex's treasons also calls pointed attention to the very real difficulties that we face in understanding the earl's apparently volatile attitude to Queen and state. Essex's insistence that his attack on Elizabeth's ministers and courtiers was separable from his loyalty to the queen characterised the tenor of his letters and public expressions of devotion to Elizabeth. It is necessarily undermined, though, in the light of contemporary critiques of evil counsel that queried the foundation of the relationship between the counsellor and the monarch, and by historical frameworks that implied that the queen's weakness of character and judgement were indicative of her burgeoning tyranny. History provided a very dark mirror for understanding the operation of monarchical power in late Elizabethan England. But studying histories did not provide any easy guides or patterns for positive action for aggrieved subjects that had a less than radical end.

Notes

1 This chapter condenses a more detailed discussion of the scholarly culture of Essex's circle and its relation to the earl's rising in my monograph, *The Earl of Essex and Late Elizabethan Political Culture* (Oxford: Oxford University Press, 2012). For Essex's career see P. E. J. Hammer, *The Polarisation of Elizabethan Politics: The Political Career of Robert Devereux, 2nd Earl of Essex, 1585–1597* (Cambridge: Cambridge University Press, 1999); Janet Dickinson, *Court Politics and the Earl of Essex, 1589–1601* (London: Pickering and Chatto, 2012); G. B. Harrison, *The Life and Death of Robert Devereux, Earl of Essex* (London: Holt & Company, 1937); Robert Lacey, *Robert, Earl of Essex. An Elizabethan Icarus* (London: Weidenfeld & Nicolson, 1971).

2 The National Archives, SP 12/278/78, fol. 130r, examination of Sir Gelly Merrick. Also see SP 12/278/72, fol. 122r, examination of Sir William Constable. The literature on the performance is enormous: but for the most recent discussion see P. E. J. Hammer, 'Shakespeare's *Richard II*, the Play of 7 February 1601, and the Essex Rising', *Shakespeare Quarterly*, 59: 1 (2008), pp. 1–35; Blair Worden, 'Which Play was Performed at the Globe Theatre on 7 February 1601?', *London Review of Books* 25: 13 (2003), pp. 22–24; Leeds Barroll, 'A New History for Shakespeare and His Time', *Shakespeare Quarterly*, 39: 4 (1988), pp. 441–464.

3 *The First and Second Parts of John Hayward's* The Life and Raigne of King Henrie IIII, ed. John Manning, Camden Society, fourth series, 42 (London, 1991), p. 61, translation of the Latin dedication by the editor. Details of the publication and suppression of *The First Part* between 1599 and 1601 are given pp. 17–32.

4 NA, SP 12/278/63, fol. 108v, 'Directions for the preachers', circulated by the Privy Council immediately after the rising on 14 February to publicise the earl's treasons.

5 See the famous article by Lisa Jardine and Anthony Grafton, '"Studied for Action": How Gabriel Harvey read his Livy,' *Past and Present*, 129 (1990), pp. 30–78; Lisa Jardine and William Sherman, 'Pragmatic Readers: Knowledge Transactions and Scholarly Services in Late Elizabethan England', in *Religion, Culture and Society in Early Modern Britain: Essays in Honour of Patrick Collinson*, eds Anthony Fletcher and Peter Roberts (Cambridge: Cambridge University Press, 1994), pp. 102–124. For Essex's patronage of scholars, and association with Tacitism see Paulina Kewes, 'Henry Savile's Tacitus and the Politics of Roman History in Late Elizabethan England', *Huntington Library Quarterly* 74: 4 (2011), pp. 515–551; Hammer, *Polarisation of Elizabethan Politics*, pp. 298–315; Hammer, 'The Uses of Scholarship: the Secretariat of Robert Devereux, Second Earl of Essex, c. 1585–1601', *The English Historical Review* 109: 430 (1994), pp. 26–51; R. Malcolm Smuts, 'Court-Centred Politics and the Uses of Roman Historians, c. 1590–1630', in *Culture and Politics in Early Stuart England*, eds Kevin Sharpe and Peter Lake (London: Macmillan, 1994), pp. 21–43; David Womersley, 'Sir Henry Savile's Translation of Tacitus and the Political Interpretation of Elizabethan Texts', *The Review of English Studies* 42:1 67 (1991), pp. 313–342; J. H. M. Salmon, 'Stoicism and Roman Example: Seneca and Tacitus in Jacobean England', *Journal of*

the History of Ideas 50: 2 (1989), pp. 209–214; Richard Tuck, *Philosophy and Government 1572–1651* (Cambridge: Cambridge University Press, 1993), pp. 104–119; Hugh Gazzard, 'The Patronage of Robert Devereux, Second Earl of Essex, *c.* 1577–1596' (DPhil, University of Oxford, 2000); Gajda, *Earl of Essex*, pp. 216–254.

6 On 21 March 1601, Sir Robert Cecil wrote to the English envoy in Scotland, George Nicolson, that this 'Catelyn Army' would have sought the destruction of Elizabeth but also 'of the successor', ie. James: *Historical Manuscripts Comission Calendar of the Manuscripts of the Most Hon. The Marquis of Salisbury, K.G., etc., Preserved at Hatfield House, Hertfordshire*, 24 vols (1883–1976), XI, 138.

7 TNA, SP 12/279/67, I, fol. 120[r-v] notes from Colfe's speech, 23 April 1601; and SP 12/279/89, fol. 167[r], Colfe's apologetic letter of explanation to Sir Robert Cecil from Newgate prison written on 21 May; William Hunt, 'Colfe, Abraham (1580–1657)', rev. Vivienne Larminie, *ODNB*; *ODNB online*, www.oxforddnb.com/view/article/5900, accessed 3 September 2010. Little is known of Colfe's precise connections to Essex, but the earl had extensive patronage connections in Oxford: Hammer, 'Uses of Scholarship'; Penry Williams, 'Elizabethan Oxford: State, Church and University, 1558–1603', in *A History of the University of Oxford. Volume 3. The Collegiate University*, ed. James McConica (Oxford: Clarendon Press, 1986), pp. 437–438.

8 Hammer, 'Shakespeare's *Richard II*'.

9 Brian Vickers (ed.), *Francis Bacon: A Critical Edition of the Major Works* (Oxford: Oxford University Press, 1996), p. 73. The authorship of letters of travel advice written to Rutland in the winter of 1595–6 has been the subject of disagreement between Vickers, who attributes them to Bacon, and Paul Hammer, who argues for Essex's own authorship of two of them, including the letter containing advice on reading history; see Hammer, 'Letters of Travel Advice from the Earl of Essex to the Earl of Rutland: Some Comments', *Philological Quarterly*, 74: 3 (1995), pp. 317–325, and Vickers, 'The Authenticity of Bacon's Earliest Writings', *Studies in Philology*, 94: 2 (1997), pp. 248–296. A direct attribution is probably unnecessary; in his biography of Essex, Hammer admits that the letters were probably a joint project of the earl's scholarly associates: Hammer, *Polarisation of Elizabethan Politics*, pp. 149–150 and note 200.

10 Henry Savile, *The Ende of Nero and the Beginning of Galba*, in Cornelius P. Tacitus, trans. Savile, *Fower bookes of the Histories of Cornelius Tacitus. The Life of Agricola* (1591), sig. ¶ 3[r]. See also the epistle 'A.P. to the Reader', which argues that history affords 'lively patterns, both for private directions and for affayers of state': Hayward, *Life and Raigne*, 62.

11 Vickers, *Francis Bacon*, p. 105. Again Hammer and Vickers dispute the authorship; see P. E. J. Hammer, 'The Earl of Essex, Fulke Greville and the Employment of Scholars', *Studies in Philology* 91: 2 (1994), pp. 167–180, which argues that the letter was written c. 1600 by Essex, and Vickers, who attributes the letter to Bacon, printing it in his edition of Bacon's works.

12 See Gustav Ungerer (ed.), *A Spaniard in Elizabethan England. The Correspondence of Antonio Pérez's exile*, 2 vols (London: Tamesis Books, 1974–76), vol. I, pp. 329, 336, 353–354, 368, 466.

13 When besieged at Essex House following his failure to raise London, Essex destroyed papers and books before surrendering himself to the government. His library was dispersed after the rising.

14 Agnes Latham and Joyce Youings (eds.), *The Letters of Sir Walter Ralegh* (Exeter: University of Exeter Press, 1999), p. 160.

15 *Albions England. Or a Historicall Map of the Same Island* (1586) reprinted in expanded editions in 1589, 1592, 1596, 1597, 1602, 1606, 1612; G.C. Moore Smith (ed.), *Gabriel Harvey's Marginalia* (Stratford-upon-Avon: Shakespeare Head Press, 1913), p. 232.

16 Samuel Daniel, *The First Fowre Bookes of the civile wars between the two houses of Lancaster and Yorke* (London: Simon Waterson, 1595), 2.126, 127, reprinted in *The Poeticall Essayes of Sam. Danyel* (1599). The lines were removed from the 1601 edition printed in *The Works of Samuel Daniel newly augmented.* For excellent recent studies of *The Civile Wars* see Gillian Wright, 'Samuel Daniel's use of sources in "The Civil Wars"', *Studies in Philology* 101: 1 (2004), pp. 59–87; Wright, 'The Politics of Revision in Samuel Daniel's The Civil Wars', *English Literary Renaissance* 38: 3 (2008), pp. 461–482.

17 B[ritish] L[ibrary], Add[itional] Manuscript 31022, fol. 108^{r}.

18 F. J. Levy, *Tudor Historical Thought* (The Huntington Library: San Marino, CA, 1967), pp. 237–285; also see D. R. Woolf, *The Idea of History in Early Stuart England* (Toronto: University of Toronto Press, 1990), pp. 33–44. Paulina Kewes (ed.), *The Uses of History in Early Modern England* (The Huntington Library: San Marino, CA, 2006); Patrick Collinson 'One of Us? William Camden and the Making of History', *Transactions of the Royal Historical Society,* 6th ser. 8 (1998), pp. 139–163. The definition of history by Henry Savile is typical: 'The commendation of an history consisteth not in reporting bare events, but in discovering the causes of those events, without which the reader can picke but small profit out of a simple register booke'; Savile, 'Annotations on the first booke of Tacitus', in *Ende of Nero,* second pagination, 5.

19 The first edition of the *First Part* only survives; a second, revised edition, was burned before sale on 27/28 May; F. J. Levy, 'Hayward, Daniel, and the Beginning of Politic History in England', *Huntington Library Quarterly* 50 (1987), pp. 1–34.

20 Hayward, *Life and Raigne,* 167.

21 SP 12/275/33, fols 55^{r}–57^{r}, from 'An Abstract of the Erl of Essex his Treasons'. Dated July 1600, the treason charge was apparently drawn up from material collated by the Privy Council between July 1600 and January 1601. The interrogation of Hayward's history is complicated. On 27/28 May, when the second edition of the *First Part* was seized and burned, Essex was already on campaign in Ireland. It became controversial again only in the aftermath of Essex's political disgrace, in 1600, in July, when Hayward was brought to the Tower and interrogated. On 22 January 1601, Hayward was once again interrogated about the book. The documentation is in the State Papers: NA, SP 12/ 274/58, 59, 60, 61, 62, SP 12/ 275/25, 25 I, 28, SP 12/278/17.

22 See Wolfe's examination on 13 July 1600, NA, SP 12/275/28, fols 45^{r}–46^{r}.

23 Cyndia Susan Clegg, *Press Censorship in Elizabethan England* (Cambridge: Cambridge University Press, 1997), pp. 203–210.

24 The work, written under the pseudonym 'Raphael Peregrino' was printed by Richard Field in 1594 apparently for distribution in the Netherlands. For a discussion of Pérez's *Relaciones,* and the uses made of it by Essex's circle see Ungerer, *A Spaniard in Elizabethan England,* vol. I, pp. 202–215, vol. II, pp. 249–250, 280–230; Alexandra Gajda, '*The State of Christendom*: History, Political Thought and the Essex Circle', *Historical Research* 81: 213 (2008), pp. 423–446.

25 Francis Bacon, *The Advancement of Learning,* Book 2, in Vickers, *Francis Bacon,* p. 179.

26 Bodleian Library, Manuscript English History, C 239. The manuscript contains a preface and has a note to printer at the end, fol. 108^{r}, indicating that the work was initially intended for publication.

27 *The State of Christendom. Or, A most exact and curious discovery of many secret passages and hidden mysteries of the times* was published in 1657 and posthumously attributed to Sir

Henry Wotton, who joined Essex's secretariat in 1595. Chris Laoutaris accepts the traditional attribution in Chapter 9; I have argued elsewhere that Wotton's sole authorship seems unlikely, and that the treatise was a collaborative work by members of the Essex circle coordinated by Anthony Bacon, as head of Essex's intelligence service: for further discussion of authorship see Gajda, '*State of Christendom*'.

28 Bod., Manuscript Eng. Hist. C 239, fol. 20[v].

29 Francis Bacon joked about Hayward's theft of Tacitus' prose in his explanation of his own involvement in the investigation of the *Life and Raigne*. *Sir Francis Bacon his apologie, in certaine imputations concerning the late Earle of Essex* (1604), pp. 36–37; Lisa Richardson has discovered that 72 per cent of the *First Part* is translated directly from sources, 18 per cent from Savile's Tacitus; L. J. Richardson, 'Sir John Hayward and early Stuart historiography', 2 vols (PhD thesis, Cambridge University, 1999).

30 Greneway explains his dedication because 'the woorthines of this Author well knowen vnto your honour, putteth me in some hope of pardon for my presumption', *The Annales of Cornelius Tacitus. The description of Germanie* (1598), [unpaginated]; Justus Lipsius, *Sixe Bookes of Politickes or ciuil doctrine,* ed. and trans. William Jones (London: William Ponsonby, 1594). The *Sixe Bookes* is also a work that organises its political arguments around extracted quotation, where '*Cornelius Tacitus* hath the prehemi-nence, being recited extraordinarily, because he alone affoordeth more matter, then all the rest', sig. [A5[v]]; for Jones see Gazzard, 'Patronage of Robert Devereux', pp. 208–211, 230–231.

31 Most significantly, 'Aphorisms gathered out of the life and end of that most noble Robert Earle of Essex in the life tyme of Queene Eliza:', attributed to Henry Cuffe, BL, Harley Manuscript 1327, fols 58[r]–59[r]; the attribution to Cuffe, Essex's secretary, who was executed with a handful of Essex's lower-born followers and Catholics is almost certainly wrong, because the aphorisms appear to have been written after the rising. Also see 'Observacions in the Earle of Essex's Example that it is exceeding dangerous to a Favorite to bee long absent from his Prince', BL, Egerton Manuscript 2026, fols 32[r]–33[v]. After the earl's death, Lord Cobham asked Robert Cotton to borrow the 'paper boke of my Lord of Essex notations of Cornelius Tacitus': BL, Cotton Vespasian Manuscript F XIII, fol. 290[r].

32 Manning argues that Hayward 'conveys unmistakable disapproval of the Bolingbroke insurgency': Hayward, *Life and Raigne,* p. 41. See also, Rebecca Lemon, 'The Faulty Verdict in "The Crown v. John Hayward"', *Studies in English Literature, 1500–1900* 41: 1 (2001), pp. 109–132; Richard Dutton, 'Buggeswords: Samuel Harsnett and the Licensing, Suppression and Afterlife of Dr. John Hayward's *The First Part of the Life and Reign of King Henry IV*', *Criticism* 35: 3 (1993), pp. 305–339.

33 Bod. Manuscript Eng. Hist. C. 239, fols 20[v], 24[r].

34 Coke's notes single out Hayward's striking phrase: 'For neyther armyes nor strong-holds are so greate defences to a prince as the multitude of children', NA, SP 12/274/61, fol. 107[r]; see 'Hayward, *Life and Raigne,* p. 67.

35 BL, Additional Manuscript 31022, f. 107[r–v].

36 The best account of Essex's revolt remains M.E. James, 'At a crossroads of the political culture: the Essex revolt, 1601', in his *Society, Politics and Culture: Studies in Early Modern England* (Cambridge: Cambridge University Press, 1986), pp. 416–465; also see Hammer, 'Shakespeare's *Richard II*'; Gajda, *Earl of Essex,* ch.1.; Dickinson, *Court Politics,* ch. 3.

37 Leo Hicks, S.I., 'Sir Robert Cecil, Father Persons and the Succession, 1600–1601' in *Archivum Historicum Societatis Iesu* 24 (1955), pp. 95–139; Pauline Croft, '*Rex Pacificus,* Robert Cecil, and the 1604 Peace with Spain', in *The Accession of James I. Historical*

and Cultural Consequences, eds Glenn Burgess, Rowland Wymer and Jason Lawrence (Basingstoke: Macmillan, 2006), pp. 140–154; Alexandra Gajda, 'Debating war and peace in late Elizabethan England', *The Historical Journal* 52 (2009), pp. 851–878.

38 Andrew Hadfield, 'The Political Significance of the First Tertralogy', in *The Monarchical Republic of Early Modern England*, ed. John McDiarmid (Aldershot: Ashgate, 2007), pp. 149–164, especially pp. 149–150.

39 Vickers, *Francis Bacon*, p. 104.

40 Before his departure as Lord Deputy of Ireland – as Essex's replacement – in February 1600, Mountjoy had engaged James in treasonous correspondence, asking the Scottish king to send an army to restore Essex's political fortunes and confirm the succession. The transcripts of the confessions of Essex's inner circle of conspirators are printed in John Bruce (ed.), *Correspondence of James VI of Scotland with Sir Robert Cecil, and others in England, during the reign of Queen Elizabeth* ..., Camden Society, 78 (London, 1861), pp. 86–87, 96–101, and passim; see Helen Georgia Stafford, *James VI and the Throne of England* (New York and London: D. Appleton-Century Company, 1940), pp. 198–221.

41 Christopher Morash, *A History of Irish Theatre, 1601–2000* (Cambridge: Cambridge University Press, 2002), pp. 2–3; Henry James and Greg Walker, 'The Politics of *Gorboduc*', *The English Historical Review* 110: 435 (1995), pp. 109–121.

42 Moore Smith, *Gabriel Harvey's Marginalia*, p. 232.

43 Peter Wentworth, *A Pithie Exhortation to her Maiestie for establishing her successor to the crowne. Whereunto is added a discourse containing the authors opinion of the true and lawfull successor to her Maiestie* (Edinburgh: Robert Waldegrave, 1598), pp. 79–80.

44 [R. Doleman, ie. Robert Parsons], *A Conference about the Next Succession to the Crowne of Ingland* (Antwerp, 1594/95), Part 2, Cap. IV, 67. Despite the pseudonym the authorship of Parsons is widely accepted; Peter Holmes, 'The Authorship and Early Reception of *A Conference about the Next Succession to the Crown of England*', *Historical Journal* 23 (1980), pp. 415–429; for Parsons more generally see Victor Houliston, *Catholic Resistance in Elizabethan England. Robert Persons's Jesuit Polemic, 1580–1610* (Aldershot: Ashgate, 2007), pp. 47–70.

45 [Parsons], *Conference*, sig. *2^{r}–[*3^{r}].

46 In James's reign, Hayward wrote his own refutation of the *Conference*, insisting that this had been his aim: 'I here present unto your Majesty this defence, both of the present authority of Princes, and of succession according to proximitie of bloud: wherein is maintained that the people have no lawfull power, to remove the one, or repell the other: In which two points I have heretofore also declared my opinion, by publishing the tragicall events which ensued the deposition of King *Richard*, and usurpation of King *Henrie* the fourth', Hayward, *An answer to the first part of a certaine conference, concerning succession* (1603) sig. A3^{r-v}; see also Lily B. Campbell, *Shakespeare's* 'Histories'*: Mirrors of Elizabethan Policy* (San Marino, California: The Huntington Library, 1947), pp. 173–211, a reading endorsed by Lemon, 'Crown's Faulty Verdict'.

47 Robert Devereux, 2nd Earl of Essex, *An Apologie of the Earle of Essex, against those which jealously and maliciously, tax him to be the hinderer of the peace and quiet of his country* (1603), sigs D3^{r}, E3^{r}. The treatise, which circulated in manuscript, was published in 1600 and 1603: see Chapter 8 in this volume.

48 NA, SP 12/278/101, fols 175^{r}–177^{v}. It should be noted that various accounts of the trial of Essex and Southampton survive, based around two (broadly similar) manuscripts that had widespread circulation in the early seventeenth-century; the version printed in Howell's *State Trials* is similar to this, fuller account from the State Papers; another version is SP 12/278/102, fols 183–198^{r}.

49 Blair Worden, 'Favourites on the English stage', in Laurence W. B. Brockliss and John H. Elliot (eds), *The World of the Favourite* (New Haven, CT and London: Yale University Press, 1999), pp. 159–183.

50 [Richard Verstegan], A *Declaration of the True Causes of the Great Troubles, presupposed to be intended against the realme of England...* (Antwerp: J. Trognesius?, 1592), p. 68; and see the brilliant treatment in Curtis Perry, *Literature and Favoritism in Early Modern England* (Cambridge: Cambridge University Press, 2006), p. 187, and passim, especially pp. 2–24, 185–232.

51 *The State of Christendom*, pp. 23–28, at p. 21.

52 Bod, Manuscript Don. C 54, f. 20^{r}; The arachnid imagery was, of course, Shakespeare's. The association of Cecil and Richard III was perpetuated well into James I's reign; see P. Croft, 'The Reputation of Robert Cecil: Libels, Political Opinion and Popular Awareness in the Early Seventeenth Century', *Transactions of the Royal Historical Society*, 6th ser. 1 (1991), pp. 43–69.

53 *HMC Salisbury*, IX, 10.

54 Lambeth Palace Library, MS 654, fol. 149^{r}.

55 BL, Manuscript Cotton Julius VI F, fols 451^{v}–452^{r}.

56 Savile, 'The Life of Iulius Agricola' and 'Annotations upon the life of Agricola', in *Ende of Nero*, 263, second pagination, pp. 46–48. For Essex and Tacitus see in particular, Kewes, 'Henry Savile's Tacitus'; Smuts, 'Court-Centred Politics'; Womersley', 'Sir Henry Savile's Tacitus'. Savile himself defines the *arcana domus* as a subsidiary of the *arcana imperii*, secrets of state.

57 BL, Harley MS 1327, fols 58^{r-v}.

58 Savile, 'Annotations upon the life of Agricola', p. 47.

59 Hayward, *Life and Raigne*, pp. 107, 116.

60 BL, Harley MS 1327, fol. 58^{r}.

61 James Spedding (ed.), *The Letters and Life of Francis Bacon, Including all his Occasional Works*, 7 vols (London: Longmans, Green, Reader and Dyer, 1861–74) vol. II, pp. 40–45, at p. 43 .

62 *HMC Salisbury*, IX, 10.

63 NA, SP 12/274/39, fol. 52^{r}, draft of a letter by Essex's secretary, Edward Reynolds, written to Elizabeth on 11 February 1600 to thank her for cancelling a prospective trial in Star Chamber.

64 See *HMC. The Manuscripts of the Marquis of Bath Preserved at Longleat, Wiltshire. Volume V. Talbot, Dudley and Devereux Papers, 1553–1569* (1980), pp. 277–281, an eyewitness account of the rising.

65 Savile, *Ende of Nero*, sig. ¶3^{r}; Hayward uses the conceit twice: 'it falleth out to be as dangerous to a prince to have hurtfull and hateful officers in place and services of weight, as to be hurtfull and hatefull himself' (Hayward, *Life and Raigne*, pp. 70, 121).

66 BL, Harley MS 1327, fol. 58^{v}.

67 N. E. McClure, *The Letters of John Chamberlain*, 2 vols (Philadelphia, PA: The American Philosophical Society, 1939) vol. I, p. 83.

68 Latham and Youings, *Letters of Walter Ralegh, p.* 185.

69 Everard Guilpin, *Skialetheia. Or, A Shadowe of Truth, in certaine Epigrams and satyres* (London: Nicholas Ling, 1598), sig. C3^{r-v}. The Bishops' Ban of 1 June 1599 with prohibition of the publication of unlicensed histories and satires called in Guilpin's work, around the time that the second edition of Hayward's *Life and Raigne* was burned: Clegg, *Press Censorship*, pp. 198–217.

70 Pierre Paul Laffleur de Kermaingant, *L'Ambassade de France en Angleterre sous Henri IV. Mission de Jean de Thumery, Sieur de Boussise, 1598–1602* (Paris, 1886), 483. The famous comparison between Henry V, Julius Caesar and the heroic general lauded by Londoners as he departs on his climacteric military campaign in Shakespeare's *Henry V*, is traditionally thought to be a reference to the earl's departure for Ireland; however, Richard Dutton has queried the parallel with a redating of the play, arguing that the parallel is intended instead with Essex's successor, Lord Mountjoy; see Dutton, 'Methinks the truth should live from age to age': The Dating and Contexts of *Henry V*', in Kewes, ed., *Uses of History*, pp. 169–199.

71 NA, SP 12/275/33, fols 55^{r}–57^{r}. For the dating of the treason charge, which is misleadingly labeled July 1600, see above, n. 21; Hammer, 'Shakespeare's *Richard II*', pp. 21–23.

72 BL, MS Cotton, Julius FVI, fol. 450^{v}, from Sir Ferdinando Gorges's statement of his involvement in the rising. Details of the plotting at Drury House are to be found in fols 449^{r}–450^{v}, and the examinations and confessions Sir Charles Danvers, and (although they were not present) Henry Cuffe and Sir Christopher Blount: see Bruce, *Correspondence of James VI and I with Sir Robert Cecil*, pp. 85–110; also see TNA, SP 12/279/11 fol. 17^{r-v}, from the statement of Sir Henry Neville.

73 NA, SP 12/278/127, fol. 252^{r}.

74 At trial, Essex refused to admit that he was guilty of treason, although he allegedly confessed in the Tower and made a penitent execution speech; TNA, SP 12/278/104, fol. 207^{r}, 'An abstract out of the Earle of Essex's confession under his owne hand'; also see NA, SP 12/278/113, f. 227^{r}, one contemporary account of Essex's execution on 25 February. Abdias Ashton, Essex's chaplain, who helped procure the earl's admission of guilt, insisted that Essex had not admitted to entertaining thoughts of usurpation or murder, despite certain imputations that were glossed from his confession and execution speech; see Fritz Levy, 'The Theatre and the Court in the 1590s,' in *The Reign of Elizabeth I: Court and Culture in the Last Decade*, ed. John Guy (Cambridge: Cambridge University Press, 1995), pp. 292–294.

75 Hammer, 'Shakespeare's *Richard II*', p. 34 and passim.

76 Hammer, 'Shakespeare's *Richard II*', pp. 12–23, 34.

77 *The State of Christendom*, pp. 203–208.

78 See, for example, the anonymous letter written to Anthony Bacon, written by a supporter of the earl just after the rising, explaining that the earl had acted for the removal of 'evil instruments' from about Elizabeth's person, and the settling of the succession in parliament upon the King of Scots: Bod., Manuscript Rawlinson, D 1175, 198–209 at 104–105.

79 See John Bellamy, *The Tudor Law of Treason: an Introduction* (London: Routledge, 1979), pp. 9–82; Alan Orr, *Treason and the State: Law, Politics and Ideology in the English Civil War* (Cambridge: Cambridge University Press, 2002), pp. 1–35.

80 Francis Oakely, 'Almain and Major: Conciliar Theory on the Eve of the Reformation', *American Historical Review*, 70:3 (1965), pp. 673–690; Quentin Skinner, *The Foundations of Modern Political Thought*, 2 vols (Cambridge: Cambridge University Press, 1978), vol. II, pp. 36–47, 59, 114, 227–228, 235, 321, 344. In fact, the whole treatise is deeply engaged with contemporary theories of resistance and contractual monarchy; the Supplement, a commentary on Pérez's *Relaciones*, is modelled on the structure of the *Vindiciae Contra Tyrannos* and contains an argument that also allows the resistance of princes by inferior magistrates, or lesser members of the nobility; see Gajda, '*State of Christendom*'.

81 *The State of Christendom*, p. 203.
82 Hayward, *Life and Raigne*, pp. 118–120.
83 Francis Bacon, *A Declaration of the Practices and Treasons attempted and committed by Robert late Earle of Essex and his complices* (1601), sig. [E4^{r}].
84 NA, SP 12/278/127, fol. 252^{r}.
85 NA, SP 12/278/101, fol. 179^{r}.
86 NA, SP 12/278/98, fol. 159^{v}.
87 William Shakespeare, *King Richard II*, 2.4.2, 165–6, ed. Andrew Gurr (Cambridge: Cambridge University Press, 1984), p. 111.
88 Thomas Bayley Howell (ed.), *Cobbett's Complete Collection of State Trials and Proceedings for High Treason and Other Crimes and Misdemeanors* ..., 33 vols (London: T.C. Hansard, 1809–26), vol. I, pp. 1421–1422.
89 [Parsons], *Conference*, Part II Cap IV, 66–67.
90 William Barlow, *A Sermon Preached at Paules Crosse, on the first Sunday in Lent* (London: Matthew Law, 1601) sig. [B5^{v}].

PART III

Afterlives

11

Prodigality and the Earl of Essex[1]

Mary Partridge

In the aftermath of his abortive Irish campaign of 1599, the Earl of Essex brooded bitterly on the damage that the whole sorry episode was doing to his reputation. After several months in deep disgrace, he complained that Elizabeth's continued displeasure had made him an object of ridicule, pity and scorn. 'The prating tavern haunter speaks of me what he lists', he groused, 'the frantic libeller writes of me what he lists; already they print me and make me speak to the world, and shortly they will play me in what forms they list upon the stage.'[2] Fritz Levy considered this prediction 'a little overwrought'. 'If we may judge by what happened to the *Play of Sir Thomas More*,' he wrote, 'it is reasonably certain that fear of public disturbance would have kept the censor from allowing such a play on the boards.'[3] Levy is right to suggest that a direct impersonation of Essex on the public stage would probably have taxed the nerves and patience of the authorities. However, as scholars such as Gazzard have argued, contemporary playwrights were well versed in the arts of oblique characterisation.[4] Literary critics – including Grace Ioppolo - have cautioned against viewing every drama of the early 1600s through the distorting prism of Essex's spectacular implosion.[5] They have analysed the theatre as a commercial enterprise, rather than focusing exclusively on its role as a vehicle for political commentary. Historians should, of course, be wary of straitjacketing plays into neat political allegories without reference to contemporary cultural conventions. Nonetheless, it is worth exploring the resonance that a particular play might have had for a particular audience at a particular juncture. Returning to Essex's alleged (and rather implausible) fear of being portrayed on the public stage, we should remember that material deemed too sensitive for general dissemination was sometimes granted an audience in more rarefied circles. The earl's misfortunes may not have been considered 'off-limits' by court dramatists.

The year 1602 witnessed the publication of *A Pleasant Comedie, Shewing the Contention Betweene Liberalitie and Prodigalitie: As it was Playd Before her Maiestie.*

A number of twentieth-century scholars noted that this was a somewhat old-fashioned entertainment for sophisticated courtiers at the end of Elizabeth's reign.[6] Its costuming and characterisation are those of a traditional moral interlude. The principal characters personify virtues or vices, and (judging from the stage directions) were symbolically attired as such. The setting is semi-realistic, to the extent that the characters occasionally refer to locations in and around London. However, as much of the action takes place at the allegorical courts of Fortune and Virtue, the play can hardly be described as a modish city comedy. Scholars consequently tend to treat *Liberality and Prodigality* as an interesting specimen of a dying dramatic tradition.[7] Most subscribe to the view that the late Elizabethan production was a revival.[8] This hypothesis rests upon two pieces of evidence. Firstly, there is a document authorising the settlement of debts incurred by the Office of the Revels between 14 July 1567 and 3 March 1567/8. Among the items of expenditure listed is a play 'callede prodigallitie'.[9] W. W. Greg thought that this was probably the original version of the comedy published in 1602.[10] Secondly, the Revels accounts for 1575 mention a payment to 'the ffethermaker' for a rather distinctive costume, to be worn by a character called 'vanytie in sebastians playe'. It comprised 'A Cote, A hatt, & Buskins all ouer covered with ffethers of cvllers'. At the same time, 6d. was paid for 'A ffelt *tha*t was covered wi*th* mony'.[11] The 1602 edition of *Liberality and Prodigality* begins with the entrance of Vanity 'all in feathers', and features a character called Money. According to H. N. Hillebrand, 'sebastians play' may have been a revival of 'prodigallitie' - which would mean that the script was dusted down for a third time in the early seventeenth century.[12] Such recycling was by no means uncommon in the last years of Elizabeth's reign. The children's acting troupes resumed performances at court during the season of 1600/01, after a decade-long hiatus.[13] Lacking an up-to-date repertoire, they were forced to rely upon a back-catalogue of 'mustie fopperies'.[14] *Liberality and Prodigality* was almost certainly written for a children's company; the prologue warns the audience that they can expect no 'quirkes of sage Philosophie', because such matter is 'for childish yeeres too rare'.[15] The play's stylistic archaisms, the circumstantial evidence from the Revels documents, and contemporary complaints about the 'antiquitie' of the child actors' offerings, all suggest that the 1602 script was not the original version of the play.[16]

However, to dismiss *Liberality and Prodigality* as a literary dodo may be unfair. At the risk of mixing zoological metaphors too bizarrely, it is possible to suggest that the dodo had a sting in its tail. The play posits two rival queens, Fortune and Virtue. The former is attended by Vanity; the latter by Liberality. The swashbuckling Prodigality and the comically rustic Tenacity make their way to Fortune's court, in the hope of securing custody of her son, Money. Having heard both suits, Fortune capriciously awards Money to Prodigality. Prodigality immediately goes roistering, and his spending attracts a crowd of fellow revellers. Soon, however, Money is exhausted. Naked and starved, he makes his way home to Fortune's court, where Tenacity successfully sues for his guardianship. Lacking Money, Prodigality becomes desperate. He, too, returns to court, and is enraged when Fortune will neither admit him nor return his Money. He threatens the queen: 'charge her in the name of Prodigality, / That [Money] be restored to me incontinently, / Lest she repent it').[17] Following the advice of his ruffian followers, he attempts to scale a wall and force his way into the court. Fortune ensnares him with a halter round the neck, but he escapes. He and his friends then chase after Tenacity, whom they rob and kill. Prodigality is picked up by the hue and cry, and brought to Virtue's court. He is indicted and arraigned by Equity for 'a robbery, murther, and felonie, against the lawes'. Having been found guilty, he is sentenced to death. He confesses his culpability, and declares himself 'heartily sorrie'.[18] He is advised to throw himself upon Virtue's mercy: 'The Prince is mercifull'. He agrees to do so. Virtue then acknowledges the real queen in the audience, declaring herself Elizabeth's 'humble vassal'. The play concludes.[19] It is unclear whether Prodigality's sentence has been commuted or not.

Far from regarding *Liberality and Prodigality* as outmoded, contemporaries may well have been struck by its topical relevance. Prodigality's experience of hubris and nemesis is comparable to that of Essex. Prodigality's first trip to court is a resounding success; he wins Fortune's favour, and receives her bounty. Essex's early court career was similarly auspicious. After his return from active service in the Low Countries in 1586, Elizabeth embraced him as her favourite. She granted him two important sources of revenue: the office of Master of the Horse (1587), and his late stepfather's farm of customs duties on sweet wines (1589).[20] Essex, however, was jealous of Elizabeth's favour, and particularly resented having to share it with his rival, Sir Walter Ralegh. The contempt that Prodigality displays for his competitor Tenacity - 'villaine, traitour, theefe, pickpurse, / Thou penurious knaue, caterpiller, and what's worse?' - recalls Essex's more extravagant outbursts against the 'Knaue' Ralegh.[21] It is perhaps worth noting that Tenacity speaks in a pronounced south-western accent, strikingly similar to that of 'the Deuenshyre man' Oliver in *The London Prodigal* (published in 1605).[22] Ralegh came from Devon, and John Aubrey recorded that 'he spake broad Devonshire to his dying day'.[23] However, the grumpy old miser Tenacity bears little resemblance to the glamorous Ralegh. The significance of the rivalry between Prodigality and Tenacity is that it highlights the strongly possessive attitude of the former towards the fruits of favour – an attitude characteristic of Essex throughout his career.

Prodigality's relationship with Money is interesting. In the heyday of his fortune, he lavishes Money on a band of followers.[24] Essex was similarly generous to his friends. He aspired to give them more than he could actually deliver, as demonstrated by his failure to secure the Attorney or Solicitor Generalship for Francis Bacon (1593–95), the Secretaryship for Thomas

Bodley (1595), and the Wardenship of the Cinque Ports for Robert Sidney (1597).[25] Yet no one could accuse him of stinginess towards his supporters. When Thomas Fleming secured the post of Solicitor General in 1595, Essex insisted that the disappointed Bacon 'accept a piece of land' as a compensatory gift.[26] Like Prodigality, Essex could only afford such acts of largesse while his creditworthiness was underpinned by royal favour. When he finally lost Elizabeth's confidence after the Irish debacle of 1599, the effect on his finances was catastrophic. The queen declined to renew his lease on 'that gainfull Farme of Sweet Wines'.[27] This punishment left Essex facing bankruptcy.[28] He was convinced 'that the Queene, the Councell, and his aduersaries, had purposely resolued to beggar him quite, to make him liue on the Almes-basket'. He railed against Elizabeth, declaring 'that the Queene being growne old, was now as ill-fauoured in her minde, as her body'.[29] The newly impoverished Prodigality abuses Queen Fortune in even more colourful terms: 'thou iniurous dame … vile, ill-fauoured, crow-troden, pye-pecked'.[30] These epithets, with their connotations of ugliness, old age and spite, are reminiscent of Essex's embittered attacks on Elizabeth in the last months of his life.

The confrontation between Prodigality and Fortune recalls several unfortunate episodes in Essex's career. When Prodigality first realises that Money has returned to Fortune, he shouts:

> Thou, Fortune, hearest thou? by faire meanes I aduise thee,
> Restore my Money to me agane, deale plainely and wisely:
> Or by this sharpe-edge sword, shalt see me play a proud part.[31]

It seems clear that at this point, the actor playing Prodigality drew his sword.[32] Prodigality reiterates his warning to Fortune, and is reproved ('These be sore and cruell threatnings, marry').[33] The action evokes – and underscores the outrageousness of – Essex's disastrous encounter with Elizabeth in 1598, as reported by Camden. The earl and the queen quarrelled over the appointment of a new lord deputy for Ireland: 'The Queene growne very impatient thereupon, gaue him a box on the eare, and bid him be gone with a vengeance. He forthwith layes his hand vpon his pummell: the Admirall stepping into him, he vowed and swore that he would not put vp so great an indignity'.[34] The spectacle of Prodigality threatening Queen Fortune with his sword must have revived memories of this shocking event. Moreover, Prodigality subsequently demands that Fortune 'Restore vnto me my money quietly / Else looke for warres'.[35] Elizabeth and some of her advisers feared that Essex would seek a military solution to his perceived grievances. As early as 1596, Francis Bacon warned the earl that his 'popular reputation' and 'military dependence' were liable to alienate any monarch – especially 'a lady, and of her Majesty's apprehension'.[36] This warning was validated in 1597, when Monsieur de Maisse, special ambassador from Henri IV of France, recorded that 'The Queen is put in fear of [Essex], and they tell her that he wishes to be always in arms'.[37] In the summer of 1599, when the Irish campaign was imploding, Bacon advised the Queen to recall her hapless general and give him honourable employment at home: 'For to discontent him as you do, and yet to put arms and power into his hands, may be a kind of temptation to make him prove combersome and unruly'.[38] Acting as government spokesman, Bacon later affirmed that Essex had, indeed, intended to bring a private army over from Ireland, '*as hee should be able to march with his power to* London, *and make his own conditions as he thought good*'.[39] At the time, he was dissuaded from this violent course of action; but in 1600, balked of the queen's forgiveness and his sweet wines farm, his thoughts turned once again to arms. During his final months, he 'brought together the boldest men of the sword, whom he secretly lodged in his own neighbourhood'.[40] Prodigality's blustering promise to let slip the dogs of war thus encapsulated some of the darkest misgivings that Essex inspired in the last years of his life. The fact that Prodigality tries to force his way into the queen's presence in order to remonstrate with her is also suggestive. In 1599, Essex notoriously burst into Elizabeth's chamber uninvited, determined to exculpate himself after his military failure in Ireland.[41] On 8 February 1601, he marched through the city of London with a band of armed followers. He later admitted 'his purpose *of surprising the court', and his intention* 'to possesse the priuie chamber'.[42] His botched rebellion was characterised by the same aggrieved incompetence as Prodigality's clumsy assault on Fortune's court.

The trial scene in *Liberality and Prodigality* is also evocative of Essex's last days. The first confession that Judge Equity obtains from Prodigality is rather grudging:

> Well, since there is no other remedie,
> And that my fact falles out so apparantly,
> I will confesse, that in deed I am guilty.[43]

Essex was tried for treason on 19 February 1601. In response to the inevitable guilty verdict, he initially offered a similarly guarded admission of culpability: 'Since I have committed that which hath brought me within the compass of the law, I may be counted the law's Traitor in offending the law'.[44] However, while awaiting execution in the Tower, Essex was famously 'councelled into a conscience by the Minister that was with him' (Abdias Ashton). On the morning of his death, he gave thanks 'That God had enlightened him to see his sinnes, it being to him a great cause now of his sorrow, that he had so strongly defended his so vnjust a cause'.[45] Prodigality performs a similar *volte face* at the end of the interlude. After his condemnation, he shows signs of genuine repentance: 'I haue runne a wanton wicked race, / Which now hath brought me to this wofull wretched case'.[46] Like Essex, he abandons any serious attempt at self-justification, and assumes the role of a scaffold penitent.[47]

Essex was beheaded in the Tower of London on 25 February 1601. Prodigality's fate is not specified in the 1602 edition of *Liberality and*

Prodigality. This is slightly unusual; most sixteenth-century 'prodigal son' plays conclude unambiguously with the pardoning or punishment of the prodigal.[48] Prodigality was, presumably, 'pardoned' by Elizabeth when the interlude was played at court. However, the element of ambiguity raises intriguing questions about the timing of the performance. In the trial scene, the court clerk indicts Prodigality for crimes committed 'the fourth day of February, in the three & fortie yeere of the prosperous raigne of Elizabeth our dreade Soueraigne'.[49] In other words, Prodigality's felonies were perpetrated on 4 February 1601, four days before Essex attempted his coup. W. W. Greg took the indictment to mean that 'The performance [of *Liberality and Prodigality*] may originally have been planned for 4 February'.[50] However, there is no record of a court entertainment on this date. According to the Chamber accounts, there was only one performance by a children's company in February 1601. Nathaniel Giles, master of the Chapel Children, was paid £10 'for a play' enacted on 22 February as part of the Shrovetide festivities.[51] Greg concluded 'that Liberality and Prodigality is the play performed at court by the Children of the Chapel Royal on 22 February 1601'.[52] In 1601, Shrove Tuesday fell on 24 February. The Chamberlain's Men provided the customary entertainment for the queen and her entourage.[53] 25 February, Ash Wednesday, marked the end of the revelling season. The next recorded court performance by a children's company did not take place until Twelfth Night 1602.[54] Greg's proposed performance date seems the most plausible, given the evidence available.

On 22 February 1601, many courtiers were unsure when or whether the sentence of death passed on Essex three days previously would be carried out. On 24 February, John Chamberlain reported that 'His execution was expected on Saturday, then yesterday, now to-morrow or Thursday'.[55] Camden suggested that Elizabeth vacillated over the fate of her fallen favourite: 'The Queene, by reason of her good will alwaies to him, somewhat now mooued in mind, commanded that he should not die, by *Sir Edward Cary*. But then, on the other side, weighing his contumacy and stubbornnesse, that scorned to aske her pardon ... she altered her resolution, and by Darcy commanded the execution to proceed.'[56] According to this account, Essex would have been well advised to follow Prodigality's example and 'appeale to the Princes mercy'.[57] It is intriguing to think that a child actor may have invited Elizabeth to confirm or commute Prodigality's sentence before the assembled court, at precisely the moment when Essex's fate hung in the balance. The extent to which this precise scenario could have been planned in advance is, of course, open to question. Events moved swiftly after the Essex rebellion, and it would have required an exceptionally prescient individual to predict exactly where matters would stand on 22 February. Equally, though, only a very insensitive person would have failed to appreciate the topical resonance of *Liberality and Prodigality*. It seems inconceivable that the Chapel Children could have performed that particular play, at that particular time, without recognising the potential for their interlude to be interpreted as a commentary on Essex's fall.

Presenting plays that appeared to engage with highly sensitive political issues was a risky business. The Essex rebellion and its aftermath was a minefield into which early seventeenth-century dramatists strayed at their peril.[58] However, as a juvenile acting troupe, the Chapel Children were accustomed to handle potentially explosive material. Children's companies were traditionally granted more licence than their adult counterparts. Michael Shapiro identified this phenomenon as a legacy from the period when choirboys enacted inversion rituals at festival times.[59] The culture of permissiveness was certainly entrenched by the start of the seventeenth century. In 1612, the dramatist Thomas Heywood felt obliged to disavow 'The liberty which some arrogate to themselues, committing their bitternesse, and liberall inuectiues against all estates, to the mouthes of children, supposing their juniority to be a priuiledge for any rayling'.[60] The 'priuiledge' conferred by juniority was often underscored in the prologues to children's plays. The prologue to *Liberality and prodigality* contains - in fact, consists of - a lengthy disclaimer:

> To pulpits we referre Diuinitie:
> And matters of Estate, to Councill boords.
> As for the quirkes' of sage Philosophie,
> Or points of squirgliting scurrilitie;
> The one we shunne, for childish yeeres too rare,
> Th'other vnfit, for such as present are.[61]

Perhaps this ostentatious protestation of infantile innocence succeeded in drawing the sting from their allegory. The likelihood that *Liberality and prodigality* was a recycled play may also have emboldened the actors. In 1639, the players of the Fortune used 'an old play revived' as a vehicle for an attack on Laudian worship. The ploy was unsuccessful, as 'it was apparent that this play was revived on purpose in contempt of the ceremonies of the Church'.[62] Nonetheless, it is possible that the antiquity of *Liberality and Prodigality* afforded a degree of protection to the company that performed it in 1601.

Even if *Liberality and Prodigality* was not performed on 22 February 1601, the similarities between Essex and Prodigality would have been striking. Let us suppose, for the sake of argument, that the interlude was actually presented at court before the Essex rebellion. The dramatisation of Prodigality's hubris and nemesis would still have mirrored the trajectory of Essex's career. Prodigality's aggressive sense of entitlement, harassment of his Queen, and threats of war would still have prompted comparisons with Essex. Elizabeth kept Essex suspended between rehabilitation and ruin from September 1599 onwards.[63] The appeal to her judgment at the end of *Liberality and Prodigality* could have highlighted her power over the earl, and the crippling uncertainty of his prospects, months before the events of February 1601. Whatever the precise date of the court performance, Essex would surely have been justified in exclaiming: 'I am Prodigality: know ye not that?'.

The characterisation of Essex as a prodigal was consistent with the criticism he attracted throughout his career. Whenever he irritated the queen, she was wont to berate him as a headstrong, ungovernable youth. When Elizabeth heard of his celebrated duel with Charles Blount, later Lord Mountjoy, 'she swore by Gods death, it was fit that some one or other should take him down, and teach him better manners, otherwise there would be no rule with him'.[64] When he first accused her physician, Dr Lopez, of a plot against her life in 1594, she dismissed him as a 'rash and temerarious youth'.[65] In 1596, she used an audience with Essex's friend, the Duke of Bouillon, 'to accuse the earl of *opiniastreté*, of wilfulnes and rashness, alledging, that he would not be ruled; but that she would bridle and stay him'.[66] In February 1597, during the anticlimactic period following his return from Cadiz, Essex retreated to his chamber for two weeks. Rowland Whyte reported to Robert Sidney that 'Her Majesty ... resolved to break him of his will, and pull down his great heart; who found it a thing impossible, and says he holds it from his mother's side'.[67] Wilfulness and rashness were signature characteristics of the prodigal son. Even when Essex was in his thirties, Elizabeth evidently found it convenient to cast him in this adolescent role.

Like most of his peers, Essex had always been vulnerable to charges of prodigal consumption. In 1582, aged seventeen, he sought to excuse the extent of his expenditure to his guardian, Lord Burghley, by assuming the persona of a penitent young prodigal: 'I hope your L. in courtesy will pardon my youth, if I have, through want of experience, in some sort passed the bounds of frugality'.[68] Three years later, Essex's costly preparations for war in the Netherlands provoked a stern reprimand from his maternal grandfather, Francis Knollys: 'you must give me leave to say unto you, that wasteful prodigality hath devoured and will consume all noble men that be wilful in expenses before they have of their own ordinary living to bear out such wasteful and wilful expenses'. Knollys concluded with a pious exhortation to God 'to assist you with His heavenly grace, that youthful wilfulness and wasteful youth do not consume you, before experienced wisdom shall have reformed you'.[69] As Paul Hammer pointed out, Knollys' strictures were perhaps unfair. Noblemen who aspired to military greatness were more or less required to pour vast sums of money, borrowed if necessary, into the maw of Mars.[70] The costs of living as an aristocrat, and pursuing a court career, were also formidable.[71] In certain respects, Essex appears to have behaved more frugally than some of his colleagues. For example, Henry Wotton did 'not remember that my Lord of *Essex* in all his life time did build or adorn any house, the Queen perchance spending his time, and himself his means'.[72] Nonetheless, fairly or otherwise, Essex's critics were able to link his expenditure to the prodigal vices of wilfulness and profligacy.

The fact that profligacy was a fault to which the nobility were peculiarly, indeed almost unavoidably, prone may have facilitated the characterisation of Essex as Prodigality – especially after the 1601 rebellion. As Lacey Baldwin Smith observed, early modern commentators 'assumed that traitors were basically unthrifty types', who wasted their own substance in riotous living, then sought to recoup their losses through violent, illegitimate means.[73] To this extent, the anti-hero of *Liberality and Prodigality* was a text-book traitor. Baldwin Smith argued that such behaviour was typically ascribed to restless, rootless social climbers, rather than members of the ancient nobility.[74] Yet Aristotle identified prodigality as a perversion of liberality – a virtue ideally associated with the upper echelons of society.[75] Furthermore, prodigality was not considered too base a fault to impute to a nobleman. Echoing Aristotle's *Ethics*, William Vaughan observed that prodigal conduct 'for the most part, issueth from a generous spirit, and hath some tokens of grace and repentance'. Vaughan added that 'the prodigall man doth good vnto many, by his lauish gifts, & by wise counsels may be brought to the square of liberalitie'.[76] The prodigal, in other words, was not an entirely unsympathetic character. He might possess the instincts of a noble and munificent man, and merely lack self-discipline. The role of Prodigality thus suited Essex nicely. The earl was popular, and none of his critics suggested he lacked redeeming qualities. Even after his treason, the government did not attempt to blacken his name completely. As William Barlow observed at Paul's Cross on the Sunday after Essex's execution,

> who grieues not that a man so noble by birth, so honourable in office, so gratious with his prince, so witty by nature, so learned by conference and study, so religious in profession, so valiant in warre, so beloued of the commons, so followed and honoured by men of all sortes, should not vse those great fauours of God and his soueraigne to gods glory and his countries good? for could he in any moderation haue carried himselfe, and haue béene contented with his great state, what good might he haue done to this church and realme, to men of state, of religion, of learning, of war?[77]

Essex could not credibly be cast as a villain. It was easier to package his implosion as a prodigal narrative – the story of a great man whose grandiose pretensions o'erflowed the measure, with disastrous consequences.

The identification of Essex as a prodigal also allowed a substantial proportion of the blame for his rebellion to be sloughed off onto the shoulders of his cronies. As Baldwin Smith observed, the government chose to explain Essex's treason through reference to low-born friends and evil counsellors.[78] Camden blamed the crisis upon the self-interested scheming of 'turbulent spirits' in the Essex circle. He claimed that Henry Cuffe, Gelly Merrick and other 'vndiscreet Counsellours' exploited the earl's generosity, inflated his sense of entitlement, and urged him on to reckless self-destruction in the hope of personal gain. Camden wrote that, in the months preceding the rebellion, 'the Earle kept open house, Mericke his Steward entertaining at boord all kinde of Souldiers, audacious, and discontented persons, that would not care whom they wounded with their tongues'.[79]

Robert Naunton similarly attributed 'none of the least of [Essex's] blame, on those that stood Sentinels about him, who might have advised him better, but that like men intoxicated with hopes, they likewise had suckt in with the most, and of their Lords receipt, and so like *Caesars* would have all or none'.[80] This was precisely the kind of company that prodigals were known to keep. A prodigal could expect to attract a horde of greedy, feckless friends, who would encourage his irresponsibility and accelerate his self-destruction. In *Liberality and Prodigality*, the initiative for Prodigality's outrageous schemes comes from the riotous companions who attach themselves to him like leeches. When Prodigality wonders how to set about regaining Money, Dick Dicer advises him to storm Fortune's palace: 'Marry, sir, be rul'd by me, Ile shew you a tricke / How you may haue him quickly'. Dick helpfully provides the ladder with which Prodigality attempts to scale the palace walls, although he refrains from participating in the assault. He also goads his patron into escalating the conflict with Fortune, insisting that the queen's steward is treating him contemptuously: 'Swounds, sir, he mocks you'.[81] Dick's role in *Liberality and Prodigality* resembles that assigned to Henry Cuffe, Essex's secretary, in early modern accounts of the 1601 rebellion. Cuffe was the government's principal scapegoat – the upstart who profited handsomely from his association with Essex, played expertly upon his master's sensibilities, and offered an attractive solution to his financial difficulties.[82] According to this analysis, Essex was ruined by his sidekick in the time-honoured fashion of a prodigal.

Another advantage of the prodigal son story as a frame for interpreting Essex's actions was its implicit exculpation of Elizabeth. It cast the queen as the loving parent of an incurable ingrate, neatly deflecting speculation that her treatment of Essex pushed the earl to breaking point. After the 1601 rebellion, the government insisted that Elizabeth had always been extraordinarily generous to her favourite. According to Bacon,

> The most partiall will not denie, but that *Robert* late Earle of *Essex* was by her Maiesties manifold benefits and graces, besides oath and allegeance, as much tied to her Maiestie, as the subiect could be to the souereigne, her Maiesty hauing heaped vpon him both dignities, offices, and gifts in such measure, as within the circle of twelue yeres or more, there was scarcely a yeere of rest, in which he did not obteine at her Maiesties hands some notable addition either of honour or profit.

Essex, however, was incapable of receiving these favours in a spirit of thankful humility, 'looking vpon them, not as her benefits, but as his aduauntages, supposing that to be his owne mettall which was but her marke and impression'.[83] The prodigal son was similarly arrogant and discontented, scorning the provision his father made for him, and insisting on receiving what he considered to be his due (Luke 15. 11–12). Bacon implied that, like the prodigal's father, Elizabeth had done everything she could for her wayward protégé. It was not her fault that Essex could never be satisfied. Adherents of the Cecil faction had previously accused the earl of gross ingratitude towards his adoptive father, Lord Burghley.[84] It was easy to suggest that Essex replicated this behaviour in his relationship with another quasi-parental figure: the queen.

The father in Jesus' parable restores his errant son to the bosom of his family at the first sign of penitence (Luke 15. 20–24). Essex and Elizabeth enjoyed no such reconciliation. Yet the identification of Essex as a prodigal implied that forgiveness would have been possible, had the earl not despaired of it and committed 'his great sinne, his bloudy sinne, his crying sinne, his infectious sinne' of rebellion.[85] Essex was accused of wasting the queen's army and treasure in Ireland – just as the prodigal son consumed his patrimony in a foreign land.[86] Upon his return, the earl chose to interpret his disgrace as a temporary punishment, inflicted by a benevolent monarch, who would ultimately follow the forgiving example of the Prodigal's father. In March 1600, he wrote to thank Elizabeth for allowing him to leave the custody of Lord Keeper Egerton and return to Essex House. He claimed, somewhat optimistically, that the concession 'doth sound in mine ears, as if your Majesty spake these words, *Die not,* Essex*; for tho' I punish thine offence, and humble thee for thy good, yet I will one day be served again by thee*'. In May, he reminded Elizabeth that 'At sundry times and by several messengers, I received these words, as your majesty's own, that you meant to correct, but not to ruin'.[87] Elizabeth colluded with this interpretation of her agenda. She ordered Essex's house arrest 'protesting, that these her punishments were not entended for his ouerthrow, but for his amendment'.[88] She assured Francis Bacon that 'whatever she should do, should be towards [Essex] *ad castigatiorem,* and not *ad destructionem*'.[89] After the York House trial, she 'often repeated and reminded mr. Bacon, that she had ever said, that her proceeding with regard to the earl should be *ad reparationem,* and not *ad ruinem*'.[90] If Elizabeth's protestations were sincere, then Essex's Irish escapade had not taken him beyond the pale in anything other than a literal, geographical sense. The bountiful queen was preparing to welcome a suitably chastened Essex back into the fold.

It suited the authorities to extol the magnanimity of Elizabeth's behaviour towards her errant earl. If *Liberality and Prodigality* was performed before 8 February 1601, it might have seemed to dangle the prospect of Essex's rehabilitation before the audience. It would thus have paid tribute to Elizabeth's capacity for forgiveness, assigning her the parental part in the prodigal son story. If the performance took place after the 8 February, the implications would have been different. For Essex, a full restoration to his former estate was out of the question. The most that he could hope for was a reprieve from execution. Under these circumstances, Elizabeth could still be presented as a model mistress, who had done everything within her power to rescue her servant from the consequences of his personal failings. Essex, however, assumed the persona of a prodigal who had rejected redemption while weltering in the slough of despond. Camden suggested that, during his imprisonment in York House, Essex prepared to receive the queen's forgiveness in a spirit of true humility. Tragically, his penitent progress was derailed when he accepted Cuffe and Merrick back into his confidence. These mischief-makers 'suggested to him all that was naught', and persuaded him that only the most desperate of measures could redeem his situation.[91] Abandoning hope, Essex became utterly reckless, and embarked upon his suicidal venture. In *Liberality and prodigality*, there is a strong suggestion that Prodigality also succumbs to despair. When he attempts to storm Fortune's palace, the queen throws a halter around his neck.[92] As Samuel Chew observed, in medieval iconography, the halter symbolised despair.[93] The audience of a traditional moral interlude would certainly have registered the significance of the emblem. Snared by despair, Prodigality proceeds to commit a desperate crime (the murder of Tenacity), for which he is subsequently sentenced to death. In this respect, as in so many others, his descent into depravity resembles that of Essex.

Essex's story is usually treated as the stuff of tragedy. The earl has been identified as the model for George Chapman's Byron and Samuel Daniel's Philotas, not to mention a possible source of inspiration for Shakespeare's Coriolanus.[94] His downfall is unlikely subject matter for 'a pleasant comedie'. Yet *Liberality and Prodigality* lends itself surprisingly well to an analysis of the crisis that engulfed both Essex and the late Elizabethan regime in 1601. The authorities held Essex and his cronies personally responsible for the rebellion, insisting that the fault was not in their stars, or circumstances, but in themselves. As a moral interlude, *Liberality and Prodigality* was not ostensibly concerned with messy politics; its function was simply to delineate virtues and vices. It could thus highlight the vices that undermined Essex - both his own and those of his friends - with impressive clarity. This emphasis on individual culpability would have rendered the play more acceptable than (for example) *Cynthia's Revels*, which blamed the problems of the regime upon its corrupt political culture.[95] The archaic format of the entertainment may also have forestalled objections to its topical resonance. Furthermore, as a prodigal play, *Liberality and Prodigality* explored the themes of punishment, forgiveness and rehabilitation. These issues dominated the final months of Essex's life, raising a plethora of questions. Was Essex punished justly for his actions in Ireland, and for his abortive march through London? Did Elizabeth ever intend to forgive him? Who was responsible for his implosion? In *Liberality and Prodigality*, Prodigality is held accountable for his actions – yet the queen is invited to show mercy. This may have reflected the widespread hope that Elizabeth would treat Essex leniently, despite his manifold faults.[96] Finally, the role of Prodigality suited Essex in various ways. From boyhood onwards, the earl had been criticised for prodigal behaviour. The Queen repeatedly castigated him as a headstrong, wilful youth – even after his salad days were well behind him. Yet to characterise Essex as a prodigal was not to demonise him. This was important, because the earl maintained his popularity. The citizens of London may not have heeded his call to arms on 8 February 1601, but the rebellion failed to drain a long-standing reservoir of sympathy for him.[97] A prodigal can be likeable; indeed, his faults can be presented as the misguided excesses of noble virtues. Moreover, his cronies can share, or assume, responsibility for his behaviour. After the 1601 rising, a consensus emerged that Essex was (to a certain extent) the victim of his confederates – just as Prodigality was exploited by his acolytes, Dick Dicer and Tom Tosse.

Prodigality was thus a convenient caricature of Essex. His antics invited comparison with Essex's most injudicious outbursts and actions. On 22 February 1601, the parallels would have been particularly hard to miss. Perhaps Essex was not simply being hysterical when he predicted that 'shortly they will play me in what forms they list upon the stage'.

Notes

1 I would like to thank Richard Cust and Blair Worden for their comments on various versions of this paper.

2 Walter Bourchier Devereux, *Lives and Letters of the Devereux, Earls of Essex*, 2 vols (London: John Murray, 1853), vol. II, p. 9.

3 Fritz Levy, 'The Theatre and the Court in the 1590s', in *The Reign of Elizabeth I: Court and Culture in the Last Decade*, ed. John Guy (Cambridge: Cambridge University Press, 1995; reprint 1999), p. 286.

4 Hugh Gazzard, '"Those Graue Presentments of Antiquitie": Samuel Daniel's *Philotas* and the Earl of Essex', *Review of English Studies* new ser. 51: 203 (August 2000), pp. 423–450.

5 See Chapter 3, pp. 63–65.

6 C. F. Tucker Brooke, *The Tudor Drama: A History of English National Drama to the Retirement of Shakespeare* (Boston, MA: Houghton Mifflin, 1911), pp. 122–123.

7 Arthur Bivins Stonex, 'The Sources of Jonson's the Staple of News', *PMLA* 30: 4 (1915), p. 825. M. C. Bradbrook, 'Authority, Truth, and Justice in Measure For Measure', *Review of English Studies* 17: 68 (October 1941), p. 392.

8 Although widely held, this theory has not attracted universal consensus; see Samuel S. Chew, 'Time and Fortune', *English Literary History* 6: 2 (June 1939), p. 91.

9 British Library, Harleian MS 146, fol. 15r; *Documents Relating to the Office of the Revels in the Time of Queen Elizabeth*, ed. Albert Feuillerat (Louvain: A. Uystpruyst, 1908; reprint Vaduz: Kraus Reprint Ltd, 1963), p. 119.

10 W. W. Greg (ed.), *The Contention Between Liberality and Prodigality* (Oxford: Oxford University Press, 1913), pp. v–vi.

11 Feuillerat, *Documents Relating to the Office of the Revels*, p. 241.

12 Harold Newcomb Hillebrand, 'The Child Actors', *University of Illinois Studies in Language and Literature* 11: 1–2 (February 1926), pp. 1–356.

13 Michael Shapiro, *The Children of the Revels: The Boy Companies of Shakespeare's Time and their Plays* (New York: Columbia University Press, 1977), pp. 17–18.

14 John Marston, *Jacke Drums Entertainment* (London: Thomas Creede for Richard Olive, 1601), sig. H3v.
15 Anon., *A Pleasant Comedie Shewing the Contention Betweene Liberalitie and Prodigalitie: As it was Playd Before her Maiestie* (London: Simon Stafford for George Vincent, 1602), sig. A3r.
16 Marston, *Jack Drum*, sig. H3v.
17 Anon, *Liberalitie and Prodigalitie*, sig. Ev.
18 Anon, *Liberalitie and Prodigaliti*, sig. F3v.
19 Anon, *Liberalitie and Prodigaliti*, sig. F4r.
20 See Paul Hammer, *The Polarisation of Elizabethan Politics: The Political Career of Robert Devereux, Second Earl of Essex, 1585–97* (Cambridge: Cambridge University Press, 1999), pp. 55–57, 60, 77.
21 'Essex to Mr. Dior, 28 July 1587', Bodleian Library Tanner MS 76, fol. 29^{r}–^{v}; Bourchier Devereux, *Lives and Letters of the Devereux*, vol. I, pp. 187–188.
22 Anon, *The London Prodigall* (London: T[homas] C[reede] for Nathaniel Butter, 1605), sig. C3v. See Helge Kökeritz, 'Elizabethan che vore ye "I warrant you"', *Modern Language Notes* 57: 2 (February 1942), pp. 98–103.
23 John Aubrey, *Brief Lives*, ed. Oliver Lawson Dick (London: Secker and Warburg, 1949), p. 255.
24 Anon., *Liberalitie and Prodigalitie*, sig. Dr.
25 Thomas Birch, *Memoirs of the Reign of Queen Elizabeth, from the Year 1581 until her Death*, 2 vols (London: A Millar, 1754), vol. I, pp. 65; 272, vol. II, p. 296; Thomas Bodley, *The Life of Sir Thomas Bodley* (Oxford: Henry Hall, 1647), pp. 9–11.
26 Birch, *Memoirs*, vol. II, p. 272.
27 William Camden, *The Historie of the Life and Reigne of that Famous Princesse Elizabeth*, trans. Thomas Browne (London: William Webbe, 1634), p. 295.
28 J. E. Neale, 'The Elizabethan political scene', in *The Age of Catherine de Medici and Essays in Elizabethan History* (London: Jonathan Cape, 1963; reprint 1965), p. 170.
29 Camden, *Historie*, pp. 295, 299.
30 Anon., *Liberalitie and Prodigaltie*, sigs Ev–E2r.
31 Anon., *Liberalitie and Prodigaltie*, sig. Er.
32 Prodigality subsequently describes himself as 'he that will not put vp such a foyle'. Anon., *Liberalitie and Prodigalitie*, sig. Er.
33 Anon., *Liberalitie and Prodigaltie*, sig. Er–v.
34 Camden, *Historie*, p. 219.
35 Anon., *Liberalitie and Prodigalitie*, sig. Ev.
36 'Francis Bacon to the Earl of Essex', in *The Letters and Life of Francis Bacon*, ed. James Spedding, 7 vols (London: Longman, Green, Longman and Roberts, 1861–74), vol. II (1862), p. 41.
37 Andre Hurault, Monsieur de Maisse, *De Maisse: A Journal of all that was Accomplished by Monsieur de Maisse Ambassador in England from King Henri IV to Queen Elizabeth, Anno Domini*, trans. G. B. Harrison and R. A. Jones (Nonesuch: London, 1931), p. 17.
38 Birch, *Memoirs*, vol. II, p. 432.
39 Francis Bacon, *A Declaration of the Practises & Treasons Attempted and Committed by Robert late Earle of Essex and his Complices, against her Maiestie and her Kingdoms* (London: Robert Barker, 1601), sig. C3v.
40 Birch, *Memoirs*, vol. II, p. 463.
41 Camden, *Historie*, p. 245; Birch, *Memoirs*, vol. II, p. 433.
42 William Barlow, *A Sermon Preached at Paules Crosse, on the First Sunday in Lent: Martij 1. 1600* (London: [R. Read] for Matthew Law, 1601), sig. Dv.

43 Anon, *Liberalitie and Prodigalitie*, sig. F3v.
44 Cobbett, William, T. B. Howell and T. J. Howell (eds), *A Complete Collection of State Trials and Proceedings for High Treason and Other Crimes and Misdemeanors*, 33 vols (London: R. Bagshaw and Longman *et al.*, 1809-26).
45 Camden, *Historie*, pp. 323–324.
46 Anon, *Liberalitie and Prodigalitie*, sig. F3v.
47 Levy, 'Theatre and Court', 287–295.
48 John Doebler, 'Beaumont's *The Knight of the Burning Pestle* and the Prodigal Son Plays', *Studies in English Literature, 1500–1900* 5: 2 (Spring 1965), p. 334.
49 Anon, *Liberalitie and Prodigalitie*, sig. F3r.
50 Greg (ed.), *Liberality and Prodigality*, v.
51 E. K. Chambers, *The Elizabethan Stage*, 4 vols (Oxford: Clarendon Press, 1923; reprint 1951), vol. IV, p. 166.
52 Greg (ed.), *Liberality and Prodigality*, vol. V. If 'sebastians play' was *Liberality and Prodigality*, the script may have passed from the Paul's Boys (led by Sebastian Westcote from 1547–82) to the Chapel Children during the brief merger of the two companies from 1582–4. The merger was engineered by Henry Evans, who later ran the Chapel Children, alongside the choirmaster Nathaniel Giles. See Shapiro, *Children of the Revels*, p. 16. Other plays changed hands between the children's companies; see F. G. Fleay, 'On the History of Theatres in London, from their First Opening in 1576 to their Closing in 1642', *Transactions of the Royal Historical Society* 10 (1882), p. 125.
53 Chambers, *Elizabethan Stage*, vol. IV, p. 166.
54 Shapiro, *Children of the Revels*, p. 259.
55 *Calendar of State Papers Domestic Series of the Reign of Elizabeth*, ed. Mary Everett Green, 12 vols (London: Longmans & Green, 1856–72), vol. V: 1598–1601 (1869), no. 110 (589–590).
56 Camden, *Historie*, p. 324.
57 Anon., *Liberalitie and Prodigalitie*, sig. F3v.
58 See, for example, Hugh Gazzard, '"Those Graue Presentments of Antiquitie".
59 Shapiro, *Children of the Revels*, pp. 4–14.
60 Thomas Heywood, *An Apology for Actors* (London: Nicholas Okes, 1612), sig. G3v.
61 Anon., *Liberalitie and Prodigalitie*, sig. A3r.
62 Edmund Rossingham to Edward Viscount Conway and Killultagh, 8 May 1639, in the *Calendar of State Papers, Domestic Series, of the Reign of Charles I*, ed. John Bruce, William Douglas Hamilton & S. C. Lomas, 23 vols (London: Longman, Brown, Green, Longmans, & Roberts, 1858–1897), vol. XIV: 1639 (1873), no. 109, 140. I owe this reference to Annaliese Connolly and Matt Steggle.
63 Camden, *Historie*, pp. 245–246, 287–299.
64 Robert Naunton, *Fragmenta regalia* (London: s. n., 1641), p. 34.
65 Devereux, *Lives and Letters,*, vol. I, p. 303.
66 Birch, *Memoirs*, vol. II, p. 5.
67 Devereux, *Lives and Letters*, vol. I, p. 404.
68 Devereux, *Lives and Letters*, vol. I, p. 171.
69 Devereux, *Lives and Letters*, vol. I, p. 178–179.
70 Hammer, *Polarisation of Elizabethan Politics*, p. 47.
71 Lawrence Stone, *The Crisis of the Aristocracy, 1558–1641* (Oxford: Clarendon Press, 1965), pp. 449–463, 547–586.
72 Henry Wotton, *Reliquiae Wottonianae*, 3rd edn (London: T. Roycroft for R. Marriott, F. Tyton, T. Collins and J. Ford, 1672), p. 174.
73 Lacey Baldwin Smith, *Treason in Tudor England* (London: Jonathan Cape, 1986;

reprint Pimlico, 2006), p. 3.

74 Baldwin Smith, *Treason in Tudor England*, p. 21.

75 Aristotle, *The Nicomachean Ethics of Aristotle*, trans. David Ross (Oxford: Clarendon Press, 1925; reprint London: Oxford University Press, 1954), pp. 79–85.

76 William Vaughan, *The Golden Grove* (London: Simon Stafford, 1600), sigs Iv– I2r.

77 Barlow, *Sermon*, sigs C2v – C3r.

78 Smith, *Treason*, pp. 248–254.

79 Camden, *Historie*, pp. 287–296.

80 Naunton, *Fragmenta Regalia*, p. 33.

81 Anon, *Liberality and Prodigality*, sigs Ev–E2r.

82 Smith, *Treason*, pp. 250–254.

83 Bacon, *Declaration of Treasons*, sig. A4v.

84 Bourchier Devereux, *Lives and Letters*, vol. I, pp. 18–19.

85 Barlow, *Sermon*, sig. D4v.

86 HMC, *Calendar of the Manuscripts of the Most Honourable the Marquess of Bath Preserved at Longleat*, eds J. J. Cartwright, J. M. Rigg, S. C. Lomas, Marjorie Blatcher and G. Dyfnallt Owen, 5 vols (London: HMSO, 1904–1980), vol. V: *The Talbot, Dudley and Devereux papers, 1533–1659*, ed. G. Dyfnallt Owen (1980), p. 270.

87 Birch, *Memoirs*, vol. II, pp. 443–444.

88 Camden, *Historie*, p. 287.

89 Birch, *Memoirs*, vol. II, p. 446.

90 Birch, *Memoirs*, vol. II, p. 455.

91 Camden, *Historie*, p. 287, 294–295.

92 Anon., *Liberalitie and Prodigalitie*, sig. E2r.

93 Chew, 'Time and Fortune', pp. 93–94.

94 Levy, 'Theatre and court', pp. 295–299; Buchanan Sharp, 'Shakespeare's Coriolanus and the crisis of the 1590s', in *Law and Authority in Early Modern England: Essays Presented to Thomas Garden Barnes*, ed. Buchanan Sharp and Mark Charles Fissel (Newark, DE: University of Delaware Press, 2007), p. 55.

95 See Leah S. Marcus, 'Jonson and the Court', in *The Cambridge Companion to Ben Jonson*, ed. Richard Harp and Stanley Stewart (Cambridge: Cambridge University Press, 2000), pp. 31–33.

96 Camden reports that, after Essex's trial at York House, 'many notwithstanding [the censure incurred by the earl] conceiued great hope of his recouery and restoring to the Queenes fauour'. Even after the 1601 rebellion, the citizens of London were reluctant to believe that Essex was guilty of treason. Camden, *Historie*, pp. 289, 309–310.

97 If sympathy for Essex had evaporated, Barlow would not have deemed it necessary to tell the Londoners how Essex had come to disdain them in his last days. Barlow, *Sermon*, sigs D5v–D6r.

12

The Earl of Essex and the Duke of Windsor: Elizabeth and Essex on film

Lisa Hopkins

The Private Lives of Elizabeth and Essex (dir. Michael Curtiz, 1939) is usually described as an adaptation of Maxwell Anderson's 1930 play *Elizabeth the Queen*, and there are certainly similarities. In Anderson's play, Raleigh wears ostentatious silver armour and Essex buys some exactly like it for the rest of the guard, as happens in the fim. The Essex of the film says as the Essex of the play does, 'I come of better blood than Elizabeth. / My name was among the earls around King John / Under the oak'; later, he adds, as his counterpart in the play does, 'If she were my mother's kitchen hag, / Toothless and wooden-legged, she'd make all others / Colorless', and finally 'I tell you she's a witch – / And has a witch's brain. I love her, I fear her, / I hate her. I adore her'.[1] Anderson's Elizabeth herself says as she does in the film that 'I had bad bringing up. / I was never sure who my mother was going to be / Next day, and it shook my nerves' (p. 32) and 'I am my mother's daughter. / I, too, can walk the path my mother walked' (p. 91). As also happens in the film, Elizabeth and Burghley discuss the fact that Burghley has forbidden a performance of *Richard II* (pp. 76–77), and when he and the queen have their climactic quarrel, Essex breaks his sword (p. 95). However, there are also some notable differences between the two. There is no mention or equivalent of Margaret Ratcliffe in Anderson's play, and Essex is not such an isolated figure as in the film: he says 'If we face Tyrone again it's because Southampton / Has gone my surety' (p. 52), suggesting that, as was in fact the case, he has friends and political allies.

This reference to Southampton, Shakespeare's patron, in turn also alerts us to another notable aspect of the play, which is the prominence of allusions to poetry and literature in general and to Shakespeare in particular. Elizabeth says to Essex 'I have kept the peace / And kept my people happy and prosperous. They / Have had time for music and poetry' (p. 30) and tells him 'you're more a poet than a general' (p. 33). She quotes *A Midsummer Night's Dream* when she says 'When we met last it was, as I remember, / Ill-met by moonlight, sirrah' (p. 24), while Penelope echoes Beatrice in *Much Ado About Nothing* when she says 'I will eat all that Sir Walter kills' (p. 74). Like King Lear, the queen has a Fool, who tells truth, and who quotes Hotspur when he says to one of the maids of honour: 'I've heard that you are perfect at lying down' (p. 97). Towards the end of the play, Burbage and Hemmings act some of *Henry IV*, although Elizabeth finds it tedious (p. 103), and Essex finally admits that

> You govern England better than I should.
> I'd lead her into wars, make a great name,
> Perhaps, like Henry Fifth, and leave a legacy
> Of debts and bloodshed after me. You will leave
> Peace, happiness, something secure. A woman governs
> Better than a man, being a natural coward.
> A coward rules best.(pp. 110–11)

Shakespeare's contemporary Marlowe is also alluded to when Elizabeth says 'if Christ his blood / Ran streaming from the heavens for a sign / That I should stay my hand' (p. 112), echoing the closing scene of *Doctor Faustus*, and there is another literary allusion when the Fool refers to the Penelope of the *Odyssey* (p. 58). The only survival of any of this in the film is a double-entendre chess game which might perhaps recall Middleton's *Women Beware Women*.

Conversely, some aspects of the film seem to derive ultimately not from Anderson's play but from Lytton Strachey's 1928 dual biography of Elizabeth and Essex: as Barbara Hodgdon observes, 'however much his play gave the film a high-culture gloss, most cinema-goers probably knew less about Anderson's Theatre Guild production than Strachey's *Elizabeth and Essex*, which resonates throughout the film', and 'throughout Davis's performance ... a series of mannerisms visualize Strachey's demonizing tropes of sexual pathology: moodily restless eyes, twitching elbows, and heavily ringed hands clenching and unclenching as she picks at her skirts belie the anxiety and emotion beneath her brusque demeanor'.[2] In both book and film, both the Cecils are pitched against Essex from the outset, Bacon is his close but unreliable advisor, and Ralegh is a strangely sinister and unlikeable figure (he is played by a young Vincent Price) rather than the ultimately negligible character that he is in the play. The book's account of Elizabeth's reception of Essex on his return from Cadiz is very similar to that in the film, down to the use of the same language, with the book speaking of 'Essex, who had good reason to expect a very different reception',[3] and the Essex of the film saying that as a soldier he understands but that 'The man had hoped for a different kind of reception'. In both, Elizabeth's granting of an earldom to Lord Howard is mentioned and its consequences explained (p. 97); in both, the defeat and death of Sir Henry Bagenal in Ireland are noted (p. 108); and the film's Essex calls Elizabeth 'The great-granddaughter of a Welsh pantryman', closely echoing Strachey's in his aristocratic dismissal of the pretensions of the Tudors, 'why should the heir of the ancient aristocracy of England bow down before the descendant of some Bishop's butler in Wales?' (pp. 112–113), which is not found in the Anderson play. When the scene shifts to Ireland, both book and film give us a vignette of English soldiers ambushed while crossing a bog – 'Clifford, caught by the enemy on a causeway crossing a bog, was set upon, defeated, and killed' (p. 132) – while on Essex's return from Ireland the Elizabeths of book and film go through very similar thought processes: 'What kind of following had the man brought with him from Ireland and where was it? What had happened? Was it possible that at this very moment she was in his power? Completely in the dark, she at once sought refuge in the dissimulation which was her second nature' (p. 135).

Curtiz's film does part company from Strachey in its treatment of the famous story of the ring which Elizabeth was supposed to have given to Essex with the instruction that if he was ever in disgrace he should send it to her and she would forgive him. Strachey dismisses the ring story, saying Essex would have known an appeal would be useless (p. 163), but as Michael Dobson and Nicola J. Watson point out, 'Maxwell Anderson's script returns to the ring plot's earliest traces, though this is not to say that his own twist on it is any less unhistorical than the *Secret History*'.[4] The play's Elizabeth says

> My father gave me this ring – and told me if ever
> He lost his temper with me, to bring it to him
> And he'd forgive me. And so it saved my life –
> Long after, when he'd forgotten, long after, when
> One time he was angry. (p. 48)

This story is also found in the film, and there too Essex will not give her the ring because he wants power.[5] What both the film and Strachey's book have in common, though, is an underlying faith in the usefulness and validity of a Freudian paradigm for understanding the story of Elizabeth and Essex, something which is not an emphasis in Anderson's play. Michael Holroyd notes in his introduction to the Oxford edition of *Elizabeth and Essex* that 'Strachey dedicated *Elizabeth and Essex* to his younger brother and sister-in-law, James and Alix Strachey, who were then pupils of Sigmund Freud and became his authorized translators into English' (p. ix) and suggests that 'In particular, he implemented Freud's theories concerning father-daughter relationships to account for the probable underlying attitude of Elizabeth to Essex's execution' (p. ix). (Holroyd points out that there are several allusions to castration (p. xiii), and Freud wrote to congratulate Strachey on the book (p. x).) Thomas Betteridge notes of the film that

> in *The Private Lives of Elizabeth and Essex* Errol Flynn is constantly moving through the feminine space of Elizabeth's court, taking the audience with him, in a search for Elizabeth the woman. Ultimately, however, this search is bound to fail and for this reason the film is marked by narrative failure.[6]

For Strachey, however, it is not Elizabeth but Essex who will imitate Elizabeth's mother – 'it was supremely fitting that Robert Devereux should follow Anne Boleyn to the block' (p. 162). Renée Pigeon suggests of the first scene to show Elizabeth and Essex alone that 'Their dialogue suggests that Elizabeth, with her deepened voice and abrupt, "masculine" manner of speaking, is trying too hard to mimic her father; it also alludes to a possible psychoanalytic interpretation of her character, that she is overcompensating for her insecure childhood, a woman trying to do a man's job and doing it, so Essex freely tells her, quite poorly'.[7] Elizabeth is masculinised in other ways too. Greg Walker, commenting on the huge success of *The Private Life of Henry VIII* and the resulting blossoming of interest in all things Tudor, observes that 'Merle Oberon (in her Anne Boleyn costume) made the cover of *Film Weekly* on 16 February 1934, and she and her fellow "queens" were suddenly in great demand for product endorsements and other advertising work'.[8] Both the title of Curtiz's film and Elizabeth's reference to her mother remind audiences of the earlier film, which opens on the morning of Anne Boleyn's execution, forcing a structural equation between the king and his daughter, an echo reinforced by the fact that Katherine Howard cradles Thomas Culpeper as Elizabeth does Essex, Henry's declaration that 'Elizabeth will never learn to rule so much as a kitchen', and that we actually glimpse the young Elizabeth towards the end of Korda's film; indeed Paul Hammer notes that 'When Charles Laughton, who had famously played the title role in *The Private Life of Henry VIII* (1933), visited the set, she greeted him "Hi, Pop", to which Laughton replied, "Ah! It's my favourite daughter!"'.[9] In addition, Elizabeth is first seen in silhouette, a tactic which Curtiz would generally reserve for male characters: James C. Robertson comments that 'stars Bette Davis, William Powell, and John Wayne are introduced to the audience in shadow in *The Private Lives of Elizabeth and Essex*, *Life With Father*, and *The Comancheros* respectively, covering a period from 1939 to 1961'.[10]

In fact, where the film differs most sharply from both book and play is in the fact that, despite 'Flynn's insistence that the film's title, originally *Elizabeth, the Queen*, be changed to reflect his costarring role',[11] Elizabeth is a more central and compelling character than her nominal co-star; Holroyd observes that 'It is as a play, a five-act Elizabethan drama, that Strachey constructed this biography. *Elizabeth and Essex* is his *Antony and Cleopatra*' (p. xi), and the film, though not Shakespearean in other ways, is certainly like *Antony and Cleopatra* in this respect, with the female lead a notably more dynamic and magnetic character than the male. Despite his title, which identifies Elizabeth and Essex as twin points of interest, Strachey is in fact interested in many of his characters. There is, for instance, detailed analysis of the motives and mentality attributed to Bacon (pp. 154–155), and indeed Strachey's own authorial sense of identification with his characters was curiously diluted:

> It was Maynard Keynes who first detected the interaction between Strachey's life and that of his subjects. 'You seem, on the whole, to imagine yourself as

> Elizabeth,[‘] Keynes suggested, ‘but I see from the pictures that it is Essex whom you have got up as yourself. But I expect you have managed to get the best of both worlds.’ (p. viii)

Similarly in the play the Fool becomes an intriguing character in his own right as well as a commentator on events. In the film, however, only Elizabeth has a subjectivity to speak of (she quotes the court jester on Ireland but we never see him), and she is also significantly strengthened in comparison with the model provided by Strachey: he dwells on her supposed appearance *en déshabille* before the French ambassador (p. 100) and recounts the traditional story of Essex on his return surprising her before she was dressed, but, *pace* Dobson and Watson’s view that of her first appearance in silhouette that she ‘is, by implication at least, *en déshabille*’,[12] we never see her anything other than gorgeously clad and looking anything but vulnerable; in fact Bette Davis, who ‘had campaigned for years to play the role of Elizabeth’, was only thirty,[13] which was exactly the same age as Flynn.

Equally she has no love rival, whereas in Strachey Essex’s extramarital amours are mentioned, especially the story of his alleged intrigue with Lady Mary Howard (p. 104). The film also introduces a character not found in either Strachey or Anderson, Mistress Margaret Ratcliffe, who is clearly there partly to provide a contrast with Lady Penelope Gray and partly to provide an emotional surrogate for Elizabeth herself. This is a role which is in fact particularly interesting because recent scholarship on the Caroline playwright John Ford has made Margaret Ratcliffe something of a minor celebrity: Michael Neill points to the congruence between Ford’s obsessive interest in the interior quality of hearts, particularly but not exclusively in *’Tis Pity She’s a Whore*, and the autopsy conducted on Margaret Ratcliffe, which apparently found ‘certaine stringes striped all over her harte’, which was taken as proof that the cause of death was her grief over the loss of her brother Sir Alexander Ratcliffe on active service in Ireland;[14] here that lost brother becomes a lover, Sir Peter Finchley. The autopsy on Margaret Ratcliffe’s heart is mentioned in Philip Gawdy’s letters, which were published in 1906, so the knowledge was available, and her story is also discussed in some detail in Violet A. Wilson’s 1922 book *Queen Elizabeth’s Maids of Honour and Ladies of the Privy Chamber*, where we are told that she was in love with Lord Cobham but became mortally ill with grief at the death of her brother in Ireland; Wilson’s book also reprints Gaudy’s account of the state of her heart.[15] In the film, however, there is no hint of any of this: Margaret Ratcliffe is evoked as an emblem of love, and though we are not told that she dies, whoever decided to include her – most probably one of the scriptwriters, Norman Reilly Raine and Aeneas MacKenzie – was presumably aware of her ultimate fate, since there is evidence of a decent amount of background research having been undertaken: for instance, Ralegh’s name is pronounced ‘Rawly’, something which is presumably informed by knowledge of King James’s pun that ‘I have heard but rawly on thee’. However, the Margaret Ratcliffe of the film simply disappears, leaving the focus on Elizabeth. Nor is there a word said about Elizabeth's successor; indeed the sense at the end of the film is not that Elizabeth will now proceed to sink down to a lonely death but that she is free to go on to raise England to still greater glory.

Essex, by contrast, is a curiously denuded figure. There is no mention of either of his parents, nor of his sister Penelope (here transformed into a rather thinly delineated love interest, Lady Penelope Gray, whose existence Essex seems hardly to notice, despite the fact that she is played by Olivia de Havilland, an emerging star in her own right who was 'simultaneously playing in David O. Selznick's *Gone With The Wind*'),[16] and there is no sense of the friends, the patronage circle, or the interest in history and literature of the historical figure. Bacon tells Essex that 'The old order is dead. You and your house will die with it if you're not careful', but the audience might well wonder what house, since although we briefly hear the names of Mountjoy and Knollys mentioned, we have no idea who they are; Bacon is his only companion and is not trustworthy. This is a diminished Essex, who is outfought and outthought in Ireland and in the council chamber with equal ease, and who has no credible political programme except for a vague and poorly defined sense of class- and gender-based entitlement. There is not even any mention of the farm of sweet wines, which would have made clear that he had a financial motive, let alone of any other substantial figures who might agree with his view of things, and indeed Paul Hammer laments that 'In the case of the Earl of Essex, whose place in modern historical consciousness is less prominent than that of Queen Elizabeth, the dramatic liberties which *Private Lives* takes with historical events has [*sic*] been a positive hindrance to a realistic understanding of the past'.[17] Dobson and Watson suggest that

> As the unconventional relative positioning of the stars Davis and Errol Flynn in … the ring-giving scene suggests … this film regards Elizabeth's reign as a time when a woman was, improperly but excitingly, in a superior position to a man: tellingly, the studio, Warner Brothers, vetoed the use of this shot as a publicity still and instead chose another picture in which the composition is inverted, with Flynn cradling Davis on his manly breast.[18]

To some extent, the inadequacies of Flynn's Essex can be blamed on the circumstances of his performance: Roy Kinnard and R. J. Vitone comment that 'Taking direction from a man he had come to dislike and acting with a woman he despised, Flynn merely walks through the film. He appears disinterested [*sic*] in most of his scenes, and is barely able to keep from laughing as he proclaims unending love for the pinch-faced Davis'.[19] However, in this, as in some other respects, Curtiz's film resembles William K. Howard's 1937 film *Fire Over England*, in which the hero, Michael (Laurence Olivier), is, like Essex, an idiot: Michael completely fails to understand what the Inquisition will do with his father, and when his identity is discovered while he is on a mission to the Spanish court, he escapes only because the entire Spanish guard is collectively about as effectual as the Marx Brothers. Michael though at least gets some fight scenes. Essex by contrast is not heroic, and not swashbuckling; indeed unusually for an Errol Flynn character, he never gets to fight in the film. He once puts his hand to his sword and is prevented by Bacon; finally, he breaks his sword across his knee. In short, he is diminished.

The only respect in which *The Private Lives of Elizabeth and Essex* does not enfeeble its Essex is that it suppresses all mention of the many illnesses of his to which the book refers, and which even in Anderson's play are mentioned jocularly, as when he tells Raleigh that 'News came of your silver / Even in my retreat! I was ill, and I swear it cured me!':[20] Flynn's Essex is at least a magnificent physical specimen, and he is also spared the indignity of Elizabeth boxing his ears, as she does in Strachey (p. 107). She does slap his face, but although this is something which must have given her considerable personal satisfaction in view of the fact that she (and indeed Michael Curtiz)[21] had comprehensively fallen out with Errol Flynn,[22] this is an action associated with a man–woman relationship rather than the adult–child one implied by boxing ears.

By contrast, the Elizabeth of both *Fire Over England* and *The Private Lives* knows perfectly well what they think of her, and she is certainly the more compelling character: in both films the sight of her is initially withheld, piquing our interest in her. Indeed *Fire Over England* presents its queen as quite simply magnificent: at the outset we are told that 'A woman guides and inspires them – Elizabeth the Queen'; later, Elizabeth says 'I am England' and claims to have the 'heart and valour of a king' rather than the more prosaic 'stomach of a king', and Leicester says to Michael 'the greatest joy of my lifetime has been to serve her – and so will you find it'. There is certainly a striking contrast between the queen of these films and the queens of *The Private Life of Henry VIII,* where Jane Seymour is a ninny, Katherine Howard a cheap and ambitious flirt, and Katherine Parr a nag.

While Carole Levin and Jo Eldridge Carney compare *The Private Lives of Elizabeth and Essex* with *Queen Elizabeth* (1912), which stars Sarah Bernhardt, in that both focus on her relationship with Essex,[23] Thomas Betteridge has suggested reading Curtiz's film as being in deliberate opposition to *Fire Over England*:

> *Fire over England* ... embodies a positive model of the past in arguing that its lessons are relevant to the present. Indeed, the basic narrative motivation of this film is the desire to collapse the present into the past ... In particular, it constantly incites its audience to make political and historical connections between Michael's words and the state of 1930s Europe. For example, when Michael claims that 'Spain is a land of ghosts', or later when he is in Spain and proposes a toast to the 'prudent' people of Spain 'who think as the State thinks', it is clear what parallels we as an audience are expected to draw.

Betteridge suggests that 'The implication of *Fire over England* is that the coming struggle with Fascism will return England to a historical moment when it first took on a transnational or European role', and that Curtiz's film, by contrast,

> can be seen as a direct response to *Fire over England.* At one level it is a radically a- (almost anti-) political film. Although it opens with the usual historical titles, its first substantial piece of dialogue is a conversation between the court's women, including Olivia de Havilland, over Essex's attractiveness. This opening sequence immediately sets up the film's main focus, the problems caused by Elizabeth's gender ... The idea of a female ruler being able to command love, to collapse her public and private roles in order to benefit the latter, reverses the relationship between these two worlds constructed in *Fire over England.*[24]

Hodgdon, on the other hand, suggests that 'At a national level, the relations between Essex and Elizabeth glance at those between Franklin Delano Roosevelt and Eleanor Roosevelt'.[25] However, I want to read *The Private Lives of Elizabeth and Essex* rather differently from either, and suggest that it is in fact acutely aware of contemporary politics. To a certain extent this is already present in the Anderson play, where the First Lady asks 'Is it true, Sir Francis, that we are at war?' (p. 74) and Essex says 'if this were a freer time, / If there were elections' (p. 89) (in the film, this becomes 'If this had been a freer time – if the people could elect – I'd have swept the city before me'), but I think it is a feature much more strongly marked in Curtiz's film.

Specifically, I suggest that the reason for the prioritisation of the domestic sphere over the political in *The Private Lives of Elizabeth and Essex* is that its paradigm is debate about and response to the Abdication of Edward VIII, which precisely privileged the personal over the political. A number of small but significant indications point in this direction. Almost at the outset Lady Penelope says that Essex 'Carries himself like a king'; later, Essex calls Elizabeth 'a king in petticoats' (the Elizabeth of *The Sea Hawk* [1940], also directed by Curtiz and also starring Errol Flynn, is also called 'A king in petticoats').[26] Neither Elizabeth nor Essex had any claim to the title king, but these phrases make the word ring in the audience's ears. When Essex returns from Ireland, he is specifically said to have come through Wales, though there is no mention of Wales in Strachey (p. 133); Edward VIII had of course been Prince of Wales before his accession and subsequent abdication, and the month before the Abdication the king toured 'the distressed areas' of South Wales, where he made a huge impression; J. Lincoln White observes in his 1937 account of the Abdication that

> This tour was generally regarded as the most important ever undertaken by a British Monarch. In the grim misery of these derelict valleys he was greeted on all sides by the populace as a harbinger of hope, a promise of better times. All the newspapers emphasized the impression he made on the people and the no less profound impression their conditions made on him.[27]

Susan Williams notes that as well as being covered in the papers, 'Through newsreels ... people all over Britain were made aware of Edward's visit to

South Wales'; indeed she considers it of crucial importance that 'Edward had been a dominant figure in the newsreels ever since the end of the Great War', and that at the height of the crisis 'Cinema-goers were still showing their support for the King' during the national anthem and by applauding his image whenever it appeared. In America, too, 'Cinema-goers ... made their feelings known';[28] J. Lincoln White noted at the time that there was massive press coverage in America, because of Mrs Simpson's nationality, and in Europe, particularly Curtiz's native Hungary: 'In Vienna and in Budapest the king and the girl were seen dancing together'. White observes that 'No wonder the American visitor to our shores smiled a little contemptuously at the poor Britisher who had yet to know of this great story. Into England poured the star reporters and the sob-sisters of America. Nothing could satisfy the palates of their readers'.[29] Curtiz's audiences would, therefore, have been both familiar with the story of Edward VIII and accustomed to seeing film act as a medium for telling it.

A number of aspects of the film chime with the story of the Abdication. The prominence of the Cecils in the film echoes the fact that, as Susan Williams notes, the pro-Abdication thinkers met amongst other places 'at Hatfield House in Hertfordshire, the seat of the influential Cecil family and home of the current Lord Salisbury'. Edward's Private Secretary Alexander Hardinge, who might be said to have spied on him for the pro-Abdication movement, was married to the daughter of Lord Edward Cecil. Essex thinks he has been born out of time, and George Bernard Shaw wrote a satire for the *Evening Standard* in which he referred to those opposed to the marriage as 'some two or three centuries behind the times',[30] while Col. Josiah Wedgwood lamented in Parliament that

> I could have wished that the King had been allowed to live here married, happy, and King, but he has wished otherwise. A thousand years hence, perhaps, we shall be liberal enough to allow such a thing; it is too early now ... there were really only two alternatives – to continue lonely, disappointed, bitter, ruling the Empire, or else to do what he has done, to throw up royalty and remain a man.[31]

Ireland features prominently in the film, and though this was of course part of the story of the historical Essex, it also chimes with the fact that 'De Valera sent a telegram to the King ... stressing that abdication could not take place without the authority of the Irish Free State ... In other words, Edward would continue to be King in Ireland until his abdication was accepted'.[32] (It may also be pertinent to the film's own historical moment that the Irish shoot arrows in English backs, since Ireland was to be neutral during the war; it was for this reason that Olivier's *Henry V* was filmed there.) A post-hoc link between Curtiz's film and the Abdication is also created by virtue of the fact that Penelope Gray and Margaret Ratcliffe sing 'The Passionate Shepherd to his Love' and Ralegh's reply; a sung setting of the same poem opens Richard Loncraine's *Richard III*, which certainly references the Abdication.[33]

Perhaps above all the paradigm of the Abdication makes sense of the treatment of Essex in the film. Susan Williams observes of the correspondence from the public at the time of the Abdication crisis that 'Some of the letters were hostile to Edward, others were written by cranks, but overwhelmingly they offered loyal and heartfelt support to the King'. In particular, 'To many Americans who supported the Democrats, King Edward VIII seemed to display the same qualities as their President. "You & Roosevelt. What a Democratic combination! What a team!" wrote a man living in Birmingham, Alabama, to the King' (indeed that Edward might go into politics was a real fear for those who had insisted on Abdication: Williams notes that 'by giving Edward a royal style, the new King made sure that Edward would never at any time be able to take part in British politics').[34] However, not everyone was so enthusiastic. The trades unionist MP James Maxton declared that 'in the very nature of the monarchical institutions on an hereditary basis, circumstances of this kind were bound to arise'; he therefore suggested that 'the monarchical institution has now outlived its usefulness'. Even sterner words came in a speech which became famous in its own right and whose first seven words formed the title of a separately published booklet of parliamentary speeches on the Abdication by members of the Independent Labour Party: George Buchanan, Independent Labour Party Member for Glasgow Gorbals, declared that 'I have listened to more cant and humbug than I have ever listened to in my life. I have heard praise of the King which was not felt sincerely in any quarter of the House ... you know he is a weak creature'.[35] Certainly Edward's official biographer, Philip Ziegler, is quite confident that Edward VIII lied to both George VI and Churchill about the true state of his finances in order to extract more money from his brother (it was partly on account of this that relations between the new and the former king deteriorated rapidly after the Abdication), and it is also a striking fact that none of the former king's servants would accompany him into exile; he professed himself astonished at 'their amazing disloyalty to me'.[36]

A particular source of criticism was that Edward VIII was perceived as having pro-German sympathies.[37] His first destination on leaving England was Austria, and at the height of the Abdication Crisis the Independent Labour Party MP William Gallacher thundered in Parliament that

> we have here not an issue between the King and Parliament, for Parliament has never been consulted from beginning to end – interviews, secret and otherwise, but Parliament not consulted and the forces operating, two forces fighting with one another on this issue, as they have been fighting continually on every important issue that has come on foreign policy ...
>
> I want to draw attention to the fact that Mrs. Simpson has a social set, and every Member of the Cabinet knows that the social set of Mrs. Simpson is

closely identified with a certain foreign Government and the Ambassador of that foreign Government.[38]

The ambassador to whom Gallacher referred was the German Ambassador, Von Ribbentrop, and his accusation seems to have been not entirely without foundation. Ziegler remarks that 'There seems little doubt that one of the reasons Hitler sent Von Ribbentrop to London as ambassador was his belief that Von Ribbentrop enjoyed a special relationship with the King and Mrs Simpson' and that those around Edward VIII were concerned that he was showing confidential government documents to Mrs Simpson and that she in turn was 'in the pocket of the German Ambassador'. In October 1937 Edward made a singularly ill-advised visit to Germany, of which Ziegler observes that 'The image lingers, as from a flickering newsreel, of his dry smile as he shook hands with the Führer, of the half-sketched and aborted fascist salute, of glowing words in praise of workers' housing and the miracle of full employment'.[39] In a sense, this visit to Germany bookends the visit to Wales a year before, with one seen as wholly positive and the other as wholly negative. This was also something of which those working in the film would be likely to be well aware: the composer of its score, Erich Wolfgang Korngold, had moved his family from Austria after the Anschluss and swore not to compose any further concert works until Hitler was removed from power. Korngold was part of a long tradition of émigré workers putting British history on screen: Greg Walker remarks that '*Henry VIII* was … shot by the influx of German artists and technicians fleeing from the newly established Nazi regime', and that 'Korda's decision to have Laughton's Henry VIII call for the fortification of Dover … was an active intervention in the debates conducted in Parliament and Cabinet, and in the wider forum of the popular press, in favour of the line argued by Churchill and the anti-German die-hards'.[40]

The Essex of Curtiz's film shares both the strengths and the weaknesses of Edward VIII. He says 'I'll go, and I'll return too', echoing Edward's description of his willingness to abdicate as being prepared to 'go'. He says he has been insulted, as Edward did, and Bacon says he is 'too popular', something which those courtiers who pushed for abdication seem also to have felt about Edward. Indeed in the film, without warrant from the play, the younger Cecil says of Essex that 'Something's got to be done to tarnish him', echoing Edward's celebrated response to the poverty he saw in South Wales, 'Something must be done'. Those who pushed for abdication did so because they saw Edward as weak and selfish. In this they are echoed by the Elizabeth of the film, who thinks Essex is putting himself before 'the English people' and tells him that he 'Put Essex first and England second'; she, by contrast, says that 'My personal feelings must not enter into this – God help me'. Indeed in a number of crucial scenes, the film is at pains to present its Essex as weak and its Elizabeth as correspondingly strong. Her treatment of the courtier from Ireland is much more reasonable than that of Essex in a similar situation, and in the scene in which Essex enters the throne room on his return from Ireland she has complete authority. Essex, though, values love above everything, telling Bacon that 'I have never yet loved nor hated for a policy nor a purpose. And I'll burn for eternity before I attempt it', and he does not think ahead. When Elizabeth asks him 'What are your plans?', he says 'I have none'; she replies incredulously that 'You could hardly take a queen prisoner and have no thought of her destiny', but actually that is exactly what he has done.

One direct consequence of the Abdication was that England's new queen consort was a Queen Elizabeth, who was generally popular (Sir Archibald Sinclair, leader of the Opposition Liberals, declared in Parliament that there was great sympathy and support for the Duke of York and 'all will welcome to the Throne that gracious lady his wife, who was born a commoner but has won the hearts of the British people by showing a clear and just conception of Royal duty and opportunity in a democratic country')[41] and that the next monarch would almost certainly be another Queen Elizabeth. When King George VI replaced his brother in 1936, his two daughters, Elizabeth and Margaret, were aged ten and six respectively, and the new Queen was thirty-six years old. Although it was not impossible that she would bear more children, the young Princess Elizabeth was clearly heir presumptive, and probably likely to succeed in due course. (Dobson and Watson point out that in a neat coincidence, 'The last important statement of Strachey's story of the old Queen and Essex came in the shape of Benjamin Britten's opera *Gloriana* [1953], commissioned to mark the coronation of the young Queen Elizabeth II',[42] and Susan Doran notes that '*The Private Lives of Elizabeth and Essex* was reissued in 1953').[43] While Edward VIII was still making up his mind, Virginia Woolf commented that in the papers 'Pictures of D of York & the Princesses fill every cranny',[44] while in J. Lincoln White's 1937 account of the Abdication the narrative proper is preceded by a family tree which makes it obvious that Princess Elizabeth is next in line to the throne; White also notes that the Archbishops of Canterbury and York issued a joint statement requesting that the order of prayer on Sunday should be for the King followed by 'our gracious Queen Elizabeth, Mary the Queen Mother, the Princess Elizabeth, and all the Royal Family'.[45] In fact Susan Williams observes that in Japan 'Edward's behaviour towards Wallis was seen as reflecting an increase in the independence and freedom of women' in general,[46] since he had insisted on making her his wife rather than keeping her as his mistress.

It was also clear that it had been a considerable personal sacrifice for the York family, as they formally were, to renounce their previous relatively private existence and step into the limelight, not least because the new king had a serious stammer and found public appearances purgatorial. It is in this context that Herbert Wilcox directed *Victoria the Great* for RKO in 1937 and followed it with *Sixty Glorious Years* in 1938,[47] and that *The Private Lives of Elizabeth and Essex* presents its own heroic queen, who lives to serve England and seeks to transcend the personal, and who at the end of the film remains above while Essex goes down to his cell (although he is subsequently allowed to be elevated again as he walks up to the block) and who is also further glorified when lightning flashes outside as she sits on her throne, recapitulating the iconography of the iconic Ditchley Portrait. Finally, even Essex agrees that 'I'd have made a sorry king' and 'You and England must live'.

The association between the two queens is present again in *Elizabeth I*, dir. Tom Hooper (2005), since it was already known that Helen Mirren, who played Elizabeth I in this, would also be playing Elizabeth II in *The Queen* (dir. Stephen Frears, 2006). The Internet Movie Database lists the working title of this as 'Elizabeth and Essex', and Hugh Dancy's Essex is certainly a prominent character. We first see him as a rather unprepossessing child shortly after the death of his father the first Earl, though the queen hints that his real father may in fact be Jeremy Irons' Earl of Leicester, and it is very much as the dead Leicester's surrogate if not actual son that Elizabeth initially responds to him, although this later develops into a passion which she can only just control. This Essex is a fuller, more rounded figure than Flynn's – much is made of his propensity for elaborate tilting costumes, and we hear of the farm of sweet wines and its loss and see his friends, including a nicely observed Southampton (Ben Pullen), though there is no mention of the fact that his wife Frances is Sidney's widow – but he is also entirely lacking in the insight and self-control which the queen displays, even if he is at least more straighforward than the fickle Bacon and the cringing Southampton prove to be. For Mirren's Elizabeth, though, Essex is only one of two significant men, as we see when, dying, she says 'There was a man …' and Robert Cecil asks 'Does your majesty mean the Earl of Essex?' and, getting no response, tries again: 'Does your majesty mean the Earl of Leicester?' For Davis's Elizabeth, there is only Essex, who becomes the ultimate paradigm of an aristocracy seen as doomed to self-destruction in much the same way in both 1600 and 1936.

Acknowledgements

I would like to thank John Baxendale and Chris Hopkins for help with the political backgrounds of those involved in the Abdication debate.

Notes

1 Maxwell Anderson, *Elizabeth the Queen: A Play in Three Acts* (London: Kessinger, 2004), pp. 20–21. All further quotations from the play will be taken from this edition and reference will be given in the text.

2 Barbara Hodgdon, *The Shakespeare Trade: Performances and Appropriations* (Philadelphia, PA: University of Pennsylvania Press, 1998), pp. 131 and 126. Paul Hammer also traces the film's debts to Anderson and Strachey; Paul E. J. Hammer, '*The Private*

Lives of Elizabeth and Essex and the Romanticization of Elizabethan Politics', in *Tudors and Stuarts on Film: Historical Perspectives*, eds Susan Doran and Thomas S. Freeman (Basingstoke: Palgrave Macmillan, 2009), pp. 192–3).

3 Lytton Strachey, *Elizabeth and Essex* (London: Chatto and Windus, 1928), p. 71.

4 Michael Dobson and Nicola J. Watson, *England's Elizabeth: An Afterlife in Fame and Fantasy* (Oxford: Oxford University Press, 2002), p. 277.

5 Paul Hammer also comments on the treatment of the ring story in book, play and film. He suggests that 'Although rings appeared in plays about Essex as early as the 1620s, the first appearance of a ring that would guarantee Essex's safety seems to have been in France in the late 1630s', '*The Private Lives of Elizabeth and Essex*', p. 201, though Leonora in Webster's *The Devil's Law Case* hints at *something* which would have saved Essex if it had been brought to the queen but does not specify a ring; John Webster, *The Duchess of Malfi and Other Plays*, ed. René Weis (Oxford: Oxford University Press, 1996), 3.3.270–275).

6 Thomas Betteridge, 'A Queen for All Seasons: Elizabeth I on Film', in *The Myth of Elizabeth*, eds Susan Doran and Thomas S. Freeman (Basingstoke: Palgrave Macmillan, 2003), p. 251.

7 Renée Pigeon, 'Gloriana Goes Hollywood: Elizabeth I on Film, 1937–1940', in *Reinventing the Middle Ages and the Renaissance: Constructions of the Medieval and Early Modern Periods*, ed. William F. Gentrup (Turnhout: Brepols, 1998), p. 118.

8 Greg Walker, *The Private Life of Henry VIII* (London: I. B. Tauris & Co., 2003), pp. 5–6.

9 Paul Hammer, '*The Private Lives of Elizabeth and Essex*', p. 199.

10 James C. Robertson, *The Casablanca Man: The Cinema of Michael Curtiz* (London: Routledge, 1993), p. 138.

11 Hodgdon, *The Shakespeare Trade*, p. 131.

12 Dobson and Watson, *England's Elizabeth*, p. 277.

13 Pigeon, 'Gloriana Goes Hollywood', p. 116.

14 See Michael Neill, '"What Strange Riddle's This?": Deciphering *'Tis Pity She's a Whore*', in *John Ford: Critical Revisions*, ed. Michael Neill (Cambridge: Cambridge University Press, 1988), p. 156.

15 Violet A. Wilson, *Queen Elizabeth's Maids of Honour and Ladies of the Privy Chamber* (London; John Lane, The Bodley Head, 1922), pp. 232, 244–245 and 248.

16 Robertson, *The Casablanca Man*, p. 51.

17 Paul Hammer, '*The Private Lives of Elizabeth and Essex*', p. 190.

18 Dobson and Watson, *England's Elizabeth*, p. 275.

19 Roy Kinnard and R. J. Vitone, *The American Films of Michael Curtiz* (Metuchen, NJ: The Scarecrow Press, 1986), p. 62.

20 Anderson, *Elizabeth the Queen*, p. 16.

21 Kingsley Canham, *The Hollywood Professionals: Michael Curtiz, Raoul Walsh and Henry Hathaway* (London: The Tantivy Press, 1973), p. 18.

22 Pigeon, 'Gloriana Goes Hollywood', p. 110.

23 Carole Levin and Jo Eldridge Carney, 'Young Elizabeth in Peril: from Seventeenth-Century Drama to Modern Movies', in *Elizabeth I: Always Her Own Free Woman*, eds Carole Levin, Jo Eldridge Carney and Debra Barrett-Graves (Aldershot: Ashgate, 2003), p. 232.

24 Betteridge, 'A Queen for All Seasons: Elizabeth I on Film', pp. 250–251.

25 Hodgdon, *The Shakespeare Trade*, p. 132.

26 Pigeon, 'Gloriana Goes Hollywood', p. 114.

27 J. Lincoln White, *The Abdication of Edward VIII: A Record with all the Published Documents* (London: George Routledge & Sons, 1937), pp. 35–36.
28 Susan Williams, *The People's King: The True Story of the Abdication* (London: Penguin, 2004 [2003]), pp. 48, 214 and 267.
29 White, *The Abdication of Edward VIII*, pp. 28–29.
30 Williams, *The People's King*, pp. 76 and 167.
31 White, *The Abdication of Edward VIII*, p. 122.
32 Williams, *The People's King*, p. 245.
33 See Lisa Hopkins, 'How very like the home life of our own dear queen: McKellen's *Richard III*', in *Spectacular Shakespeare: Critical Theory and Popular Cinema*, edited by Lisa Starks and Courtney Lehmann (Madison, NJ: Fairleigh Dickinson University Press, 2002), pp. 47–61.
34 Williams, *The People's King*, Introduction, p. xviii, pp. 50 and 236.
35 White, *The Abdication of Edward VIII*, pp. 120–121 and 126–127.
36 Philip Ziegler, *King Edward VIII* (London: Fontana, 1991 [1990]), pp. 327, 333 and 348–349.
37 For an account of this perception and its possible bearing on the Abdication, see Richard Griffiths, *Fellow Travellers of the Rught: British Enthusiasts for Nazi Germany, 1933–9* (London: Constable, 1980), pp. 240–244.
38 White, *The Abdication of Edward VIII*, pp. 124–125.
39 Ziegler, *King Edward VIII*, pp. 271, 276 and 386.
40 Walker, *The Private Life of Henry VIII*, pp. 28 and 57.
41 White, *The Abdication of Edward VIII*, p. 113.
42 Dobson and Watson, *England's Elizabeth*, p. 227.
43 Susan Doran, 'From Hatfield to Hollywood: Elizabeth I on Film', in *Tudors and Stuarts on Film*, eds Susan Doran and Thomas S. Freeman (Basingstoke: Palgrave Macmillan, 2009), p. 100.
44 Williams, *The People's King*, p. 137.
45 White, *The Abdication of Edward VIII*, p. 149.
46 Williams, *The People's King*, p. 235.
47 Walker, *The Private Life of Henry VIII*, p. 34.

Select bibliography

Manuscripts

Bodleian Library
——MS Don. c. 54.
——Misc. MS Don. c. 188.
——MS English History c. 239.
——MS Rawlinson D 1175.
——MS Tanner 76.
——MS Tanner 88.
——MS Tanner 114.
——MS Wood F 9.
——MS 990.
British Library
——Add. MS 12506.
——Add. MS 25303.
——Add. MS 25348.
——Add. MS 25707.
——Add. MS 31022.
——Add. MS 34218.
——Add. MS 40838.
——Add. MS 64081.
——Cotton MS Vespasian F. XIII.
——Cotton MS Galba C. VIII.
——Egerton MS 6.
——Egerton MS 2026.
——Harley MS 146.
——Harley MS 292.
——Harley MS 298.
——Harley MS 1327.
——Harley MS 6854.
——Lansdowne MS 31.
——Lansdowne MS 33/10.
——Lansdowne MS 87.
——Lansdowne MS 885.
——Royal MS 17 B.L.

——Stowe MS 150.
Dulwich College
——Alleyn Papers, MS 1/26.
——Alleyn Papers, MS 7.
Hatfield House
——Cecil Papers 18/50.
——Cecil Papers 18/55.
——Cecil Papers 18/59.
——Cecil Papers 40.
——Cecil Papers 41.
——Cecil Papers 67/38.
——Cecil Papers 68/10.
——Cecil Papers 71/71.
——Cecil Papers 72/105.
——Cecil Papers 74.
——Cecil Papers 75/83.
——Cecil Papers 76/67.
——Cecil Papers 79/37.
——Cecil Papers 79/74.
——Cecil Papers 82/2.
——Cecil Papers 83/9.
——Cecil Papers 83/85.
——Cecil Papers 83/86.
——Cecil Papers 99/167.
——Cecil Papers 101/205.
——Cecil Papers 106/36.
——Cecil Papers 178/117.
——Cecil Papers 181/62.
——Cecil Papers 206/95.
Lambeth Palace
——MS 651, no. 68.
——MS 653, no. 73.
——MS 653, no. 74.
——MS 653, no.171.
——MS 653, no. 175.
——MS 653, no. 177.
——MS 654.
——MS 657, no. 8.
——MS 657, no. 9.
——MS 657, no. 46.
——MS 657, no. 88.
——MS 659, no.21.
——MS 659, no. 75.
——MS 659, no. 76.
National Archives, Kew
——SP 12/261.
——SP 12/268.
——SP 12/270.
——SP 12/274.
——SP 12/275.

——SP 12/278.
——SP 12/279.
——SP 77/6.
——SP 78/254
——E 351/543.
Royal Academy of Music
——MS 601, Richard Mynshall's Lute Book.
University of London
——MS 187.
Warwickshire Record Office
——M1229, Devereux Letter Book.

Primary sources

Adams, Simon (ed.), *Household Accounts and Disbursement Books of Robert Dudley, Earl of Leicester, 1558–1581, 1584–1586*, vol. 6 (Cambridge: Cambridge University Press, 1995).

Anderson, Maxwell, *Elizabeth the Queen: A Play in Three Acts* (London: Kessinger, 2004).

Andrewes, Lancelot, *Sermon Preached before Queene Elizabeth, at Richmond, on the 21st February A. D. 1599 being Ash Wednesday* (London: D. Smith, 1629).

Anon. *Aristotles politiques, or Discourses of government* (London: Adam Islip, 1598).

——, *Le Comte D'Essex. Histoire Angloise* (Paris: Claude Barbin, 1678).

——, *Gesta Grayorum, or, The history of the high and mighty prince, Henry Prince of Purpoole* (London: W. Canning, 1688).

——, *Histoire de la Vie et Mort dv Comte d'Essex avec vn Discours Grave et Eloquent de la Royne d'Angleterre au Duc de Biron sur ce subiect* (Paris, 1607).

——, *The History of the Most Renowned Queen Elizabeth and her Great Favourite, the Earl of Essex. In Two Parts. A Romance* (London, 1700).

——, *The Honorable Entertainement …* (London: John Wolfe, 1591).

——, *A lamentable new ballad vpon the Earle of Essex his death To the tune of, Essex last goodnight* (London: E. A., 1620).

——, *The London Prodigall* (London: T[homas] C[reede] for Nathaniel Butter, 1605).

——, *Memoirs of the life of Robert Devereux, Earl of Essex* (London: M. Cooper *et al.*, 1753).

——, *A Pleasant Comedie Shewing the Contention Betweene Liberalitie and Prodigalitie: As it was Playd Before her Maiestie* (London: Simon Stafford for George Vincent, 1602).

——, [ie. Richard Verstegan] A *declaration of the true causes of the great troubles, presupposed to be intended against the realme of England …* (Antwerp: J. Trognesius?, 1592).

——, [attrib. Sir Henry Wotton] *The State of Christendom. Or, A most exact and curious discovery of many secret passages and hidden mysteries of the times* (London: Humphrey Moseley, 1657).

Arber, Edward, ed., *A Transcript of the Registers of the Company of Stationers of London, 1554–1640 A.D.*, 5 vols (London, 1875–94).

Aristotle, *The Nicomachean Ethics of Aristotle*, trans. David Ross (Oxford: Clarendon Press, 1925; reprint London: Oxford University Press, 1954).

Aubrey, John, *Brief Lives*, ed. Oliver Lawson Dick (London: Secker and Warburg, 1949).

Bacon, Francis, *Apologie, in certaine imputations concerning the late Earl of Essex* (London: Richard Field for Felix Norton, 1604).

——, *A declaration of the practices and treasons attempted and committed by Robert late Earle of Essex and his complices* (London: Robert Barker, 1601).
——, *Francis Bacon: A Critical Edition of the Major Works*, ed. Brian Vickers (Oxford: Oxford University Press, 1996).
Banks, John, *The unhappy favourite, or, The Earl of Essex a tragedy* (London: Richard Bentley, 1682).
Barlow, William, *A Sermon Preached at Paules Crosse, on the first Sunday in Lent* (London: [R. Read] for Matthew Law, 1601).
Barnes, Barnabe, *Foure Bookes of Offices, enabling privat persons for the speciall seruice of all good princes and policies* (London: Adam Islip, 1606).
——, *Parthenophil and Parthenophe* (London: John Wolfe, 1593).
Bellany, Alastair and Andrew McRae (eds), 'Early Stuart Libels: an edition of poetry from manuscript sources', *Early Modern Literary Studies* Text Series I (2005), http://purl.oclc.org/emls/texts/libels/, accessed 29 April 2013.
Birch, Thomas, *Memoirs of the Reign of Queen Elizabeth, from the Year 1581 until her Death*, 2 vols (London: A Millar, 1754; reprint New York: AMS Press, 1970).
Bodley, Thomas, *The Life of Sir Thomas Bodley* (Oxford: Henry Hall, 1647).
Bourchier, John, *The first volum of sir Iohan Froyssart of the cronycles of Englande, Fraunce, Spayne, Portyngale, Scotlande, Bretayne, Flau[n]ders … Tra[n]slated out of Frenche into our maternall englysshe tonge, by Iohan Bourchier knight lorde Berners* (London: Richard Pinson, 1523).
Bradshaw, Thomas, *The Shepherds Starre* (London: Robert Robinson for William Jones, 1591).
Braunmuller, A. R. (ed.), *A Seventeenth-Century Letter-Book: A Facsimile Edition of Folger MS V.a. 321* (Newark, DE: University of Delaware Press, 1983).
Brewer, John S. (ed.), *The Court of King James the First; by Dr Godfrey Goodman*, vol. 2 (London: Richard Bentley, 1839).
Brooke, Henry, *The Earl of Essex. A Tragedy* (Edinburgh, 1761).
Bruce, John (ed.), *Correspondence of James VI of Scotland with Sir Robert Cecil, and others in England, during the reign of Queen Elizabeth …* (London: Camden Society, 1861).
——, William Douglas Hamilton and S. C. Lomas (eds), *Calendar of State Papers, Domestic Series, of the Reign of Charles I* (London: Longman, Brown, Green, Longmans, & Roberts, 1858–97).
Bülow, Gottfried von (ed.), 'Diary of the Journey of Philip Julius, duke of Stettin-Pomerania, through England in the year 1602', *Transactions of Royal Historical Society*, 2nd series, 6 (1892), pp. 1–67.
Calprenède Gautier de Costes de la, *Le Comte dEssex. Tragedie* (Paris, 1650).
Cambini, Andrea, *Two very notable commentaries … of the house of Ottomanno*, trans. John Shute (London: Rouland Hall for Humfrey Toye, 1562).
Camden, William, *Annales rerum Anglicarum, et Hibernicarum, regnante Elizabetha* (London: William Stansby for Simon Waterson, 1615).
——, *Annales … or The Historie of the Life and Death and Reigne of that Famous Princesse, Elizabeth* (London: Thomas Harper for William Web and Roger Daniell, 1629).
——, *The Historie of the Most Renowned and Victorious Princesse Elizabeth* (London, 1630).
——, *The Historie of the Life and Reigne of that Famous Princess Elizabeth*, trans. Thomas Browne (London: William Webbe, 1634).
——, *Annals, or, The Historie of the Most Renowned and Victorious Princesse Elizabeth, Late Queene of England*, trans. Robert Norton (London: Thomas Harper for Benjamin Fisher, 1635).
Carleton, George, *Heroici Characteres* (Oxford: Joseph Barnes, 1603).

Cartwright, J. J., J. M. Rigg, S. C. Lomas, Marjorie Blatcher and G. Dyfnallt Owen (eds), *Calendar of the Manuscripts of the Most Honourable the Marquess of Bath Preserved at Longleat*, 5 vols (London: HMSO, 1904–80).

Chamberlain, John, *The Letters of John Chamberlain*, vol. 1, ed. Norman Egbert McClure (Philadelphia, PA: American Philosophical Society, 1939).

Chapman, George, *Achilles Shield Translated as the other seuen bookes of Homer, out of his eighteenth booke of Iliades* (London: John Windet, 1598).

——, *Seauen bookes of the Iliades of Homere, prince of poets* (London: John Windet, 1598).

Churchyard, Thomas, *A Scourge for Rebels* (London: Thomas Dawson for Thomas Cadman, 1584).

——, *The Fortunate Farewel to the most forward and noble Earle of Essex* (London: Edmund Bollifant for William Wood, 1599).

Clapham, John, *Elizabeth of England. Certain Observations concerning the Life and Reign of Queen Elizabeth by John Clapham*, eds Evelyn Plummer Read and Conyers Read (Oxford: Oxford University Press, 1951).

Clark, Andrew (ed.), *The Shirburn Ballads 1585–1616* (Oxford: Clarendon Press, 1907).

Clifford, Anne, *The Memoir of 1603 and The Diary of 1616–1619*, ed. Katherine O. Acheson (Plymouth and Ontario: Broadview, 2007).

Cobbett, William, T. B. Howell and T. J. Howell (eds), *A Complete Collection of State Trials and Proceedings for High Treason and Other Crimes and Misdemeanors*, 33 vols (London: R. Bagshaw and Longman *et al.*, 1809–26).

Collins, Arthur, ed., *Letters and Memorials of State*, 2 vols (London: T. Osborne, 1746; reprint New York: AMS Press, 1973).

Colonna, Francesco, *Hypnerotomachia – The strife of loue in a dreame* (London: Abell Jeffes *et al.* for Simon Waterson, 1592).

Corneille, Thomas, *Le Comte D'Essex*, ed. Wendy Gibson (Exeter: University of Exeter Press, 2000).

Covell, William, *Polimanteia* (Cambridge and London: John Legate and J. Orwin, 1595).

Craig, Alexander, *The Amorose Songes, Sonets, and Elegies* (London: William White, 1606).

Daniel, Samuel, *The first fowre bookes of the civile wars between the two houses of Lancaster and Yorke* (London: P. Short for Simon Waterson, 1595).

——, *Certaine small poems lately printed with the tragedie of Philotas* (London: G. Eld for Simon Waterson and Edward Blount, 1605).

——, *The Tragedy of Philotas by Samuel Daniel*, ed. Laurence Michel (New Haven: Yale University Press, 1949).

Dasent, John Roche (ed.), *Acts of the Privy Council of England*, NS vol. 30, *1599–1600* (London: HMSO, 1905).

Davies, Richard, *A funerall sermon preached the xxvi. day of Nouember in the yeare of our Lord M.D.LXXVI. in the parishe church of Caermerthyn, by the Reuerende Father in God, Richard by the permission of God, Bishoppe of Saint Dauys, at the buriall of the Right Honourable Walter Earle of Essex and Ewe* (London: Henry Denham, 1577).

Davison, Francis, *A poetical rapsody containing, diuerse sonnets, odes, elegies, madrigalls, and other poesies, both in rime, and measured verse. Neuer yet published. The bee and spider by a diuerse power, sucke hony' & poyson from the selfe same flower.* (London: John Baily, 1602).

Dekker, Thomas, *Old Fortunatus* (London: S. Stafford for William Apsley, 1600).

——, *The Cold Yeare* (London: W. White for Thomas Langley, 1615).

Devereux, Robert, 2nd Earl of Essex, *Lawes and Orders of Warre, established for the good conduct of the service in Ireland* (London: Christopher Barker?, 1599).

——, [*An Apologie of the Earle of Essex*] [London: J. Smethwick?, 1600].

——, *An Apologie of the earle of Essex, against those which jealously and maliciously, tax him to be the hinderer of the peace and quiet of his country* (London: Richard Bradocke, 1603).

Devereux, Walter B., *Lives and Letters of the Devereux, Earls of Essex in the Reigns of Elizabeth, James I, and Charles I, 1540–1646*, 2 vols (London: John Murray, 1853).

Doleman, R. [ie. Robert Parsons], *A Conference about the next succession to the crowne of Ingland* (Antwerp, 1594/5).

Drayton, Michael, *Poems* (London: W. Stansby for John Smethwick, 1619).

Dudley, Robert, Earl of Leicester, *Correspondence of Robert Dudley, Earl of Leycester, during his government of the Low Countries, in the years 1585 and 1586*, ed. John Bruce (London: J. B. Nicols and Son, 1844).

Edmondes, Sir Thomas, *The Edmondes Papers: A Selection from the Correspondence of Sir Thomas Edmondes, Envoy from Queen Elizabeth at the French Court*, ed. Geoffrey G. Butler (London: J. B. Nichols and Sons, 1913).

Emden, Cecil S, *Oriel Papers* (Oxford: Clarendon Press, 1948).

Erasmus, *Collected Works of Erasmus*, ed. J. K. Sowards (Toronto: University of Toronto Press, 1974–2011).

Feuillerat, Albert (ed.), *Documents Relating to the Office of the Revels in the Time of Queen Elizabeth* (Louvain: A. Uystpruyst, 1908; reprint Vaduz: Kraus Reprint Ltd, 1963).

Fletcher, Phineas, *The purple island* (Cambridge: Thomas Buck and Roger Daniell, 1633).

Florio, John, *A Worlde of Wordes* (London: Arnold Hatfield for Edward Blount, 1598)

Gager, William, *Meleager Tragoedia noua* (Oxford: Joseph Barnes, 1592).

Gawdy, Philip, *Letters of Philip Gawdy, 1579–1616*, ed. I. H. Jeayes (London: J. B. Nichols and Sons, 1906).

Gentili, Alberico, *De Iure Belli, Commentatio secunda* (London: John Wolfe, 1589).

——, *De Iure Belli, Commentatio tertia* (London: John Wolfe, 1589).

——, *De Iniustitia Bellica Romanorum Actio* (Oxford: Joseph Barnes, 1590).

Gerard, John, *John Gerard: The Autobiography of an Elizabethan*, trans. Philip Caraman (London: Longmans, 1951).

Green, Mary Everett (ed.), *Calendar of State Papers Domestic Series of the Reign of Elizabeth*, 12 vols (London: Longmans & Green, 1856–72).

——, *Calendar of State Papers, Domestic Series of the Reign of Elizabeth, 1595–1597*, vol. 4 (searchable text edition). (Burlington, ON: TannerRitchie Publishing in collaboration with the Library and Information Services of the University of St. Andrews, 2005).

Greenblatt, Stephen *et al.* (eds), *The Norton Shakespeare* (London: Norton, 1997).

Greg, W. W. (ed.), *The Contention Between Liberality and Prodigality* (Oxford: Oxford University Press, 1913).

——, *A Companion to Arber: Being a Calendar of Documents in Edward Arber's Transcript of the Registers of the Company of Stationers of London, 1554–1640* (Oxford: Clarendon Press, 1967).

Greville, Fulke, *The life of the renowned Sr Philip Sidney* (London: Henry Seile, 1652).

——, 'A Dedication to Sir Philip Sidney', in *The Prose Works of Fulke Greville*, ed. John Gouws (Oxford: Clarendon Press, 1986).

Groos G. W. (ed.), *The Diary of Baron Waldstein: A Traveller in Elizabethan England* (London: Thames and Hudson, 1981).

Grosart, A. B. (ed.), *The Dr. Farmer Chetham MS being a common-place book in the Chetham Library Manchester temp. Elizabeth, James I , Charles I* (Manchester: Chetham Society 1873).

Guilpin, Everard, *Skialetheia. Or, A Shadowe of Truth, in certaine Epigrams and satyres* (London: James Roberts for Nicholas Ling, 1598).

H[arbert], W[illiam], *Englands Sorrowe or, A Farewell to Essex* (London: Valentine Sims for Henry Rocket, 1606).

Harington, John, *Orlando Furioso* [1591] (London: Richard Field for John Norton and Simon Waterson, 1607).

——, *Nugae Antiquae*, 2 vols (London: Vernor and Hood, 1769).

Harrison, G. B. (ed.), *Elizabethan and Jacobean Journals 1591–1610*, vol. II – *A Second Elizabethan Journal* (London: Routledge, 1931, reprint 2001).

Harvey, Richard, *A Theologicall Discourse of the Lamb of God and his Enemies* (London: John Windet for W. Ponsonby, 1590).

——, *Philadelphus or A Defence of Brutes, and the Brutans History* (London: John Wolfe, 1593).

Hasler, P. W., *The History of Parliament: The House of Commons, 1558–1603*, 3 vols (London: HMSO, 1981).

Hayward, John, *The First Part of the Life and Raigne of King Henrie the* [IV] *Extending to the end of the first yeare of his raigne* (London: E. Allde and T. Judson for John Wolfe, 1599).

——, *An answer to the first part of a certaine conference, concerning succession* (London: Eliot's Court Press for Simon Waterson and Cuthbert Burbie, 1603).

——, *The First and Second Parts of… The Life and Raigne of King Henrie IIII*, ed. John Manning, Camden Society, fourth series, 42 (London: Camden Society, 1991).

Henslowe-Alleyn Digitisation Project, www.henslowe-alleyn.org.uk.

Henslowe, Philip, *Henslowe's Diary*, ed. R. A. Foakes and R. T. Rickert (Cambridge: Cambridge University Press, 1960; reprint 2002).

Heywood, Thomas, *Troia Britanica: or, Great Britaines Troy* (London: William Jaggard, 1609).

——, *An Apology for Actors* (London: Nicholas Okes, 1612).

——, *A Funeral Elegie, vpon the much lamented death of the trespuissant and vnmatchable king, King Iames, King of Great Brittaine, France and Ireland, defender of the faith* London: Thomas Harper, 1625).

——, *The royall king and loyall subject* (London: Nicholas and John Okes for James Becket, 1637).

Historical Manuscripts Commission, *Calendar of the Manuscripts of the Most Hon. The Marquis of Salisbury, K.G., etc. Preserved at Hatfield House, Hertfordshire*, 24 vols (1883–1976).

——, *Report on the Manuscripts of the Earl of Salisbury*, 24 vols (London: 1883–1976).

——, *Report on the Manuscripts of Lord De L'Isle & Dudley preserved at Penshurst Place*, 4 vols (London: 1925–42).

——, *The Manuscripts of the Marquis of Bath Preserved at Longleat, Wiltshire. Volume V. Talbot, Dudley and Devereux Papers, 1553–1569* (1980).

Hoby, Margaret. *The Private Life of an Elizabethan Lady: The Diary of Lady Margaret Hoby 1599–1605*, ed. Joanna Moody (Stroud: Sutton, 1998).

Holland, Henry, *treatise against vvitchcraft* (Cambridge: John Legatt, 1590).

Howell, T. B., *Cobbett's Complete Collection of State Trials and Proceedings for High Treason and Other Crimes and Misdemeanors …* , 33 vols (London: T.C. Hansard, 1809–26).

Hume, Martin A. S. (ed.), *Calendar of Letters and State Papers Relating to English Affairs, Preserved Principally in the Archives of Simancas.* Volume 1: *Elizabeth 1558–1567.* (London: Eyre and Spottiswoode, for Her Majesty's Stationery Office, 1892).

Hurault, André, Monsieur de Maisse, *De Maisse: A Journal of all that was Accomplished by Monsieur de Maisse Ambassador in England from King Henri IV to Queen Elizabeth, Anno Domini 1597*, trans. G. B. Harrison and R. A. Jones (London: Nonesuch, 1931).

Jackson, William A. (ed.), *Records of the Court of the Stationers' Company, 1602 to 1640* (London: Bibliographical Society, 1957).

Jones, Henry, *The Earl of Essex: A Tragedy in Five Acts* (1753), in *The British Theatre, or, A Collection of Plays*, ed. Elizabeth Inchbald, 20 vols, 1 (London: Hurst, Robinson, & Co., 1824).

Jonson, Ben, *Notes of Ben Jonson's Conversations with William Drummond of Hawthornden*, ed. David Laing (London: The Shakespeare Society, 1842).

——, *Ben Jonson*, eds C. H. Herford, Percy Simpson and Evelyn Simpson, 4 vols (Oxford: Clarendon Press, 1925–52).

——, *The Complete Poems*, ed. George Parfitt (Harmondsworth: Penguin, 1975, reprint. 1996).

Kellawaye, Simon, *A Defensatiue against the Plague* (London: John Windet, 1593).

Laffleur de Kermaingant, Pierre Paul, *L'Ambassade de France en Angleterre sous Henri IV. Mission de Jean de Thumery, Sieur de Boussise, 1598–1602* (Paris, 1886).

Latham, Agnes and Joyce Youings, *The Letters of Walter Ralegh* (Exeter: University of Exeter Press, 1999).

Linche, Richard, *The Fountaine of Ancient Fiction* (London: Adam Islip, 1599).

Lindsay, David, *Funerals of a Right Reuerend Father in God Patrick Forbes of Corse, Bishop of Aberdfne* (Aberdeen: Edward Raban, 1631).

Lipsius, Justus, *Sixe Bookes of Politickes or ciuil doctrine*, ed. and trans. William Jones (London: Richard Field for William Ponsonby, 1594).

Lok, Henry, *Ecclesiastes or The preacher* (London: Richard Field, 1597).

Malden, Henry Elliot (ed.), 'Devereux Papers, with Richard Broughton's *Memoranda* (1575–1601)', *Camden Miscellany*, xiii (1923).

Malory, Thomas, *Le Morte D'Arthur* (London: William Caxton?, 1485).

Markham, Gervase, *Cauelarice, or The English Horseman contayning all the arte of horse-manship, as much as is necessary for any man to vnderstand* (London: Edward White, 1607).

——, *Deuoreux Vertues Teares for the losse of the most christian King Henry …* (London: Thomas Millington, 1597).

——, *A Discource of Horsmanshippe* (London: Richard Smith, 1593).

——, *The English Arcadia alluding his beginning from Sir Philip Sydneys ending* (London: Henrie Rocket, 1607).

——, *The English Housewife*, ed. Michael R. Best (Kingston: McGill-Queen's University Press, 1986).

——, *A Health to the Gentlemanly Profession of Seruingmen; or, The seruingmans comforts.* (London: W. W[hite], 1598).

——, *Honour in his Perfection* (London: B. Alsop for Benjamin Fisher, 1624).

——, *Marie Magdalens lamentations for the losse of her master Iesus* (London: Edward White, 1601).

——, *Markhams Farwell to Husbandry* (London: Roger Jackson, 1620).

——, *The Most Honorable Tragedie of Sir Richard Grinuile, Knight* (London: Richard Smith, 1595).

——, *A Second Part to the Mothers Blessing: or A cure against misfortunes. Divided into certain principal receipts, to cure the mind of man* (London: Thomas Dewe, 1622).

——, *The Teares of the Beloued: (1600) and Marie Magdalene's Teares: (1601)*, ed. A.B. Grosart ([Blackburn]: n.p., 1871).

——, and Lewis Machin, *The Dumbe Knight, 1608*, ed. Kris Towse (2009), http://purl.org/emls/iemls/renplays/dumbknight.htm, accessed 29 April 2013.

Marlowe, Christopher, *Edward II*, eds Robert Lindsey and Martin Wiggins (London: A. & C. Black, 1997).

Marston, John, *Jacke Drums Entertainment* (London: [Thomas Creede] for Richard Olive, 1601).

May, Steven W. (ed.),'The Poems of Edward De Vere, Seventeenth Earl of Oxford and of Robert Devereux, Second Earl of Essex: An Edition and Commentary', *Studies in Philology* 77.5 Texts and Studies (1980), pp. 1–132.

——, *The Elizabethan Courtier Poets: The Poems and Their Contexts* [1991] (Asheville, NC: Pegasus Press, 1999).

Middleton, Thomas, *The wisdome of Solomon paraphrased* (London: Valentine Sims, 1597).

Moffett, Thomas, *Healths improvement* (London: Thomas Newcomb for Samuel Thomson, 1655).

Moore Smith, G. C. (ed.), *Gabriel Harvey's Marginalia* (Stratford-upon-Avon: Shakespeare Head Press, 1913).

W. R. Morfill (eds), *Ballads from Manuscripts*, 2 vols (Hertford: Ballad Society/Stephen Austin & Sons, 1873).

Mornay, Philippe de, *Mémoires et correspondance pour servir a l'histoire de la Reformation*, XII vols (Paris: Treuttel, 1824–25).

Naunton, Robert, *Fragmenta regalia* (London: s. n., 1641).

Nichols, John, *The Progresses and Public Processions of Queen Elizabeth*, 3 vols (London, 1823).

Norden, John, *A Prayer for the Prosperous Proceedings and Good Successe of the Earle of Essex and His Companies* (London: E. Alde, 1599).

Osborne, Francis, *A Miscellany of Sundry Essayes, Paradoxes, and Problematicall Discourses, letters and characters; together with politicall deductions from the history of the Earl of Essex, executed under Queen Elizabeth* (London: J. Grismond for S. Royston, 1659).

Peele, George, *An Eglogue Gratulatorie. Entituled: to the right honorable, and renowmed Shepheard of Albions Arcadia: Robert Earle of Essex and Ewe, for his welcome into England from Portugall* (London: J. Windet for Richard Jones, 1589).

——, *The Life and Minor Works of George Peele*, 3 vols, ed. David H. Horne (New Haven, CT: Yale University Press, 1952).

Pérez, Antonio, *A Spaniard in Elizabethan England: The Correspondence of Antonio Pérez's Exile*, 2 vols, ed. Gustav Ungerer (London: Thamesis Books, 1974–76).

Phillip, John, *The Life and Death of Sir Phillip Sidney, late Lord gouernour of Flushing: His funerals Solemnized in Paules Churche where he lyeth interred; with the whole order of the mournfull shewe, as they marched thorowe the citie of London, on Thursday the 16 of February, 1587* (London: Robert Waldegrave, 1587).

Pollard, A. F., *Tudor Tracts* (Westminster: A. Constable, 1903).

Pricket, Robert, *Honors Fame in Triumph Riding* (London: R. Blower for Roger Jackson, 1604).

PRO, *List and Analysis of State Papers, Foreign Series, Elizabeth I*, vol. 6, ed. Richard Bruce Wernham (London: HMSO, 1989).

Purchas, Samuel, *Purchas his pilgrimes* (London: Henry Fetherstone, 1625).

Rainolds, John, *De Romanae Ecclesiae Idololatria* (Oxford: Joseph Barnes, 1596).

The Records of Early English Drama, ed. Sally Beth Maclean *et al.* (Toronto, University of Toronto, 1979–2010).

The Records of Early English Drama, 'The Patrons and Performances Web Site', http://link.library.utoronto.ca/reed/.

R. T., *Orlando Inamorato* (London: Valentine Sims, 1598).

Savile, Henry, *The Ende of Nero and the Beginning of Galba*, in Tacitus, *Fower bookes of the Histories ... The Life of Agricola* (Oxford: Joseph Barnes, 1591).

Saviolo, Vincentio, *His Practise in two Bookes. The first intreating of the vse of the Rapier and Dagger. The second, of Honor and honorable Quarrels* (London: Thomas Scarlet for John Wolfe, 1595).

Shakespeare, William, *As You Like It*, ed. Alan Brissenden (Oxford: Oxford University Press, 1993).
——, *As You Like It*, ed. Juliet Dusinberre (London: Thomson Learning, 2006).
——, *The Tragicall Historie of Hamlet* (London: N. L. and Iohn Trundell, 1603).
——, *The Tragicall Historie of Hamlet* (London: I. R. for N. L., 1604).
——, *Hamlet*, in *The Riverside Shakespeare*, ed. G. Blakemore Evans (Boston, MA: Houghton Mifflin, 1974), pp. 1135–97.
——, *Henry V*, ed. Gary Taylor (Oxford: Clarendon Press, 1982).
——, *The Merchant of Venice*, ed. John Russell Brown (Surrey: Arden, 1955).
——, *A Midsummer Night's Dream*, ed. Harold E. Brooks [1979] (London: Routledge, 1988).
——, *Mr William Shakespeares Comedies, Histories, & Tragedies* (London: Isaac Jaggard and Ed. Blount, 1623).
——, *King Richard II*, ed. Andrew Gurr (Cambridge: Cambridge University Press, 1984).
——, *King Richard II*, ed. Charles R. Forker (London: Thomson Learning, 2002).
——, *Troilus and Cressida*, ed. David Bevington (London: Arden/Cengage, 1998).
——, *Troilus and Cressida*, ed. Jonathan V. Crewe (Harmondsworth: Penguin/Pelican Shakespeare, 2000).
Sidney, Philip, *An Apology for Poetry or The Defence of Poesy*, ed. Geoffrey Shepherd (London and Edinburgh: Thomas Nelson & Sons, 1965; reprint, Manchester: Manchester University Press, 1973).
——, *The Countess of Pembroke's Arcadia*, ed. Maurice Evans (Harmondsworth: Penguin, 1977).
——, *The Countess of Pembroke's Arcadia (The New Arcadia)*, ed. Victor Skretkowicz (Oxford: Clarendon Press, 1987).
——, *The Countess of Pembroke's Arcadia (The Old Arcadia)*, ed. Jean Robertson. (Oxford: Clarendon Press, 1973).
——, *Defence of Poesie, Astrophil and Stella, and Other Writings*, ed. Elizabeth Porges Watson (London: Everyman, 1997).
——, *Sir Philip Sidney*, ed. Katherine Duncan-Jones (Oxford: Oxford University Press, 1989).
Smith, A. J. (ed.), *John Donne: The Complete English Poems* (London. Penguin, 1996).
Smith, Sir Thomas, *Sir Thomas Smithes voiage and entertainment in Rushia* (1605).
Spedding, James (ed.), *The Letters and the Life of Francis Bacon, Including all his Occasional Works*, 8 vols (London: Longman, Green, Longman and Roberts, 1861–74).
Speed, John, *The Theatre of the Empire of Great Britaine* (London: William Hall for John Sudbury and George Humble, 1612).
Spenser, Edmund, *Edmund Spenser, A View of the State of Ireland (1633): from the first printed edition*, eds Andrew Hadfield and Willy Maley (Oxford: Blackwell, 1997).
——, *The Faerie Queene* (London: William Ponsonby, 1590).
——, *The Faerie Queene*, eds A. C. Hamilton, Hiroshi Yamashita and Toshiyuki Suzuki, 2nd edition (London: Pearson, 2001).
——, *Prothalamion or A Spousall Verse … In honour of the double mariage of the two honorable & vertuous ladies, the Ladie Elizabeth and the Ladie Katherine Somerset, daughters to the Right Honourable the Earle of Worcester and espoused to the two worthie gentlemen M. Henry Gilford, and M. William Peter Esquyers* (1596).
Stow, John, *The Annales of England*, Folger Shakespeare Library cs309(London, 1601).
Sully, Maximilien de Béthune, duc de, *Memoirs of the Duke of Sully … a new edition, revised and corrected; with additional notes, and an historical introduction, attributed to Sir Walter Scott*, trans. Charlotte Lennox (London: H.G. Bohn, 1856).

Tacitus, P. Cornelius, *Fower bookes of the Histories of Cornelius Tacitus. The Life of Agricola*, ed. and trans. Henry Savile (Oxford: Joseph Barnes, 1591).
——, *The Annales of Cornelius Tacitus*, trans. Richard Greenway (London: Arnold Hatfield for Bonham and John Norton, 1598),
Tanner, J. R. (ed.), *The annales. The description of Germanie*, trans. Richard Greneway (1598)
——, *Tudor Constitutional Documents, A.D. 1485–1603* (Cambridge: Cambridge University Press, 1951).
The Tatler: or, Lucubrations of Isaac Bickerstaff, Esq. 4 vols (Dublin, 1777).
Vaughan, William, *The Golden Grove* (London: Simon Stafford, 1600).
Vere, Francis, *The commentaries of Sr. Francis Vere being diverse pieces of service, wherein he had command* (Cambridge: John Field, 1657).
Virgil, *Aeneid VII–XII*, trans. H. Rushton Fairclough (Cambridge, MA./London: Harvard University Press – Loeb Classical Library, 2000)
——, *Eclogues, Georgics, Aeneid I–VI*, trans. H. Rushton Fairclough, rev. G. P. Goold (Cambridge, Mass./London: Harvard University Press – Loeb Classical Library, 1999).
Voltaire, *The Works of M. de Voltaire. Translated from the French. With notes, historical and critical. By T. Smollett, M.D. T. Francklin, M.A. and others*, 34 vols (London: J. Newbery, 1762).
Warner, William, *Albions England. Or a historicall map of the same island* (London: the Widow Orwin for Joan Broome, 1586).
Wentworth, Peter, *A Pithie Exhortation to her Maiestie for establishing her successor to the crowne. Whereunto is added a discourse containing the authors opinion of the true and lawfull successor to her Maiestie* (Edinburgh: Robert Waldegrave, 1598).
White, J. Lincoln, *The Abdication of Edward VIII: A Record with all the Published Documents* (London: George Routledge & Sons, 1937).
Wilbraham, Rogert. 'The Journal of Sir Roger Wilbraham ... 1593–1616', ed. Harold Spencer, *The Camden Miscellany*, 10, Camden Society, 3rd series, 4 (London: The Camden Society, 1902), pp. 27–30.
Wotton, Sir Henry, *A Parallel betweene Robert Late Earle of Essex, and George Late Duke of Buckingham* (London: s.n., 1641).
——, *Reliquiae Wottonianae*, 3rd edition (London: T. Roycroft for R. Marriott, F. Tyton, T. Collins and J. Ford, 1672).

Secondary sources

Adams, Simon, 'Faction, Clientage and Party: English Politics, 1550–1603', *History Today* 32 (December 1982), pp. 33–39.
——, 'Eliza Enthroned? The Court and its Politics', in *The Reign of Elizabeth I*, ed. Christopher Haigh (Basingstoke: Macmillan, 1984; reprint 1994), pp. 55–77.
——, 'Dudley, Lettice, countess of Essex and countess of Leicester (1543–1634)', in *Oxford Dictionary of National Biography*, eds H. C. G. Matthew and Brian Harrison (Oxford: Oxford University Press, 2004). Online edition, ed. Lawrence Goldman, January 2008.
——, 'Sidney, Mary, Lady Sidney (1530x35–1586)', in *Oxford Dictionary of National Biography*, eds H. C. G. Matthew and Brian Harrison (Oxford: Oxford University Press, 2004). Online edition, ed. Lawrence Goldman, January 2008.

Akrigg, G. P. V., *Shakespeare and the Earl of Southampton* (London: H. Hamilton, 1968).

Albright, E. M., 'Shakespeare's *Richard II* and the Essex Conspiracy', *PMLA* 42:3 (1927), pp. 686–720.

——, 'The Folio Version of *Henry V* in Relation to Shakespeare's Times', *PMLA* 43:3 (1928), pp. 722–756.

——, 'Shakespeare's *Richard II*, Hayward's History of Henry IV, and the Essex Conspiracy', *PMLA* 46 (1931), pp. 695–719.

——, 'Reply to Ray Heffner's "Shakespeare, Hayward and Essex again"', *PMLA* 47 (1932), pp. 899–901.

Alexander, Gavin, *Writing After Sidney: The Literary Response to Sir Philip Sidney, 1586–1640* (Oxford: Oxford University Press, 2006).

Armstrong, William A., 'The Audience of the Elizabethan Private Theatres', *The Review of English Studies*, new series 10: 39 (August 1959), pp. 234–249.

Barroll, Leeds, 'A New History for Shakespeare and His Time', *Shakespeare Quarterly* 39 (1988), pp. 441–464.

Batchelor, Anne, 'Daniel Bacheler: The Right Perfect Musician', *The Lute* 28 (1988), pp. 3–12.

Bate, Jonathan, *Soul of the Age: The Life, Mind and World of William Shakespeare* (London: Viking, 2008).

——, 'Was Shakespeare an Essex Man?' *Proceedings of the British Academy*, 162 (London: The British Academy, 2009), pp. 1–28.

Beal, Peter, *In Praise of Scribes: Manuscripts and their Makers in Seventeenth-Century England* (Oxford: Clarendon Press, 1998).

Bellamy, John, *The Tudor Law of Treason: an Introduction* (London: Routledge, 1979).

Benjamin, Edwin B., 'Sir John Hayward and Tacitus', *Review of English Studies* 8: 31 August 1957), pp. 275–276.

——, 'Bacon and Tacitus', *Classical Philology* 60: 2 (April 1965), pp. 102–110.

Berry, Philippa, *Of Chastity and Power: Elizabethan Literature and the Unmarried Queen* (London: Routledge, 1994).

Bevington, David, *Tudor Drama and Politics: A Critical Approach to Topical Meaning* (Cambridge, MA: Harvard University Press, 1968).

Blackburn, Thomas H., 'The Date and Evolution of Edmund Bolton's *Hypercritica*', *Studies in Philology* 63 (1966), pp. 196–202.

Bossy, John, *Christianity in the West, 1400–1700* (Oxford: Oxford University Press, 1985).

Bowers, Fredson, 'Essex's Rebellion and Dekker's *Old Fortunatus*', *Review of English Studies*, 3 (1952), pp. 365–366.

Bradbrook, M. C., 'Authority, Truth, and Justice in *Measure for Measure*', *The Review of English Studies*, 17: 68 (October 1941), pp. 385–399.

Brady, Ciaran, 'The Road to the *View*: On the Decline of Reform Thought in Tudor Ireland', in *Spenser and Ireland: An Interdisciplinary Perspective*, ed. Patricia Coughlan (Cork: Cork University Press, 1989), pp. 25–45.

Briggs, John Channing, 'Chapman's *Seaven Bookes of the Iliades*: Mirror for Essex', *SEL* 21 (1981), pp. 59–73.

Brooke, C. F. Tucker, *The Tudor Drama: A History of English National Drama to the Retirement of Shakespeare* (Boston, MA: Houghton Mifflin, 1911).

Bruster, Douglas, *Shakespeare and the Question of Culture: Early Modern Literature and the Cultural Turn* (Basingstoke: Palgrave, 2003).

Burgess, Glenn, Wymer, Rowland and Lawrence, Jason (eds), *The Accession of James I. Historical and Cultural Consequences* (Basingstoke: Macmillan, 2006).

Campbell, Lily B., *Shakespeare's* 'Histories'*: Mirrors of Elizabethan Policy* (San Marino, CA: The Huntington Library, 1947).

Canny, Nicholas P., *Making Ireland British 1580–1650* (Oxford: Oxford University Press, 2001).

——, 'O'Neill, Hugh, 2nd earl of Tyrone (c. 1550–1616), magnate and rebel', *Oxford Dictionary of National Biography*, eds H. C. G. Matthew and Brian Harrison (Oxford: Oxford University Press, 2004). Online edition, ed. Lawrence Goldman, 2008.

Caraman, Philip (ed.), *The Other Face: Catholic Life under Elizabeth I* (London: Longmans, 1960).

Carroll, Clare, 'The Text, its Sources, and Traditions', in Richard Beacon, *Solon his Follie, or a Politique Discourse Touching the Reformation of Common-weales Conquered, Declined or Corrupted*, eds Clare Carroll and Vincent Carey (Binghampton, NY: Medieval and Renaissance Texts and Studies, 1996), pp. xxvi–xliii.

Carron, Helen. 'William Sancroft (1617–93): a Seventeenth-Century Collector and his Library', *The Library* 7th series, 1: 3 (2000), pp. 290–307.

Cerasano, S. P., 'Must the Devil Appear?: Audiences, Actors, Stage Business', in *A Companion to Renaissance Drama*, ed. Arthur F. Kinney (Oxford: Blackwell, 2002), pp. 193–211.

Chambers, E. K., *William Shakespeare: A Study of Facts and Problems*, 2 vols (Oxford: Clarendon Press, 1930).

——, *The Elizabethan Stage*, 4 vols (Oxford: Clarendon Press, 1923; reprint 1951).

Chew, Samuel S., 'Time and Fortune', *English Literary History* 6: 2 (June 1939), pp. 83–113.

Clare, Janet, *'Art Made Tongue-Tied By Authority': Elizabethan and Jacobean Dramatic Censorship* (Manchester: Manchester University Press, 1990).

Clark, Peter, 'Thomas Scott and the Growth of Urban Opposition to the Early Stuart Regime', *The Historical Journal* 21 (1978), pp. 1–26.

Clegg, Cyndia Susan, *Press Censorship in Elizabethan England* (Cambridge: Cambridge University Press, 1997).

——, 'Archival Poetics and the Politics of Literature: Essex and Hayward Revisited', *Studies in the Literary Imagination* 32: 1 (Spring 1999), pp. 115–466.

Cogswell, Thomas, 'The People's Love: The Duke of Buckingham and Popularity', in *Politics, Religion and Popularity in Early Stuart Britain*, eds Thomas Cogswell, Peter Lake and Richard Cust (Cambridge: Cambridge University Press, 2002), pp. 210–234.

Colclough, David, *Freedom of Speech in Early Stuart England* (Cambridge: Cambridge University Press, 2005).

Collinson, Patrick, 'One of Us? William Camden and the Making of History', *Transactions of the Royal Historical Society*, sixth series, 8 (1998), pp. 139–163.

Considine, John, 'Davison, Francis (1573/4–1613x19)', *Oxford Dictionary of National Biography*, eds H. C. G. Matthew and Brian Harrison (Oxford: Oxford University Press, 2004). Online edition, ed. Lawrence Goldman, 2008.

Cox, Angela, *Sir Henry Unton, Elizabethan Gentleman* (Cambridge: Cambridge University Press, 1982).

Craig-McFeely, Julia, 'English Lute Manuscripts and Scribes 1530–1630', University of Oxford DPhil thesis, 1993, http://www.ramesescats.co.uk/thesis, accessed 29 April 2013.

Croft, Pauline, 'The Reputation of Robert Cecil: Libels, Political Opinion and Popular Awareness in the Early Seventeenth Century', *Transactions of the Royal Historical Society*, sixth series, 1 (1991), pp. 43–69.

——, 'Rex Pacificus, Robert Cecil, and the 1604 Peace with Spain', in *The Accession of James I. Historical and Cultural Consequences*, eds Glenn Burgess, Rowland Wymer and Jason Lawrence (Basingstoke: Macmillan, 2006), pp. 140–154.

Crowley, Lara M., 'Donne, not Davison: Reconsidering the Authorship of "Psalme 137"', *Modern Philology* 105: 4 (2008), pp. 603–636.

Davis, Joel, 'Multiple *Arcadias* and the Literary Quarrel between Fulke Greville and the Countess of Pembroke', *Studies in Philology* 101: 4 (Fall 2004), pp. 401–430.

——, *The Countesse of Pembrokes Arcadia and the Invention of English Literature* (Basingstoke: Palgrave Macmillan, 2011).

Dawson, Lesel, 'The Earl of Essex and the Trials of History: Gervase Markham's *The Dumbe Knight*', *The Review of English Studies* 53 (August 2002), pp. 344–364.

——, 'Dangerous Misogyny: John Ford's *The Queen* and the Earl of Essex's 1601 Uprising', *Explorations in Renaissance Culture* 33: 1 (2007), pp. 64–82.

Daybell, James, 'Women, Politics and Domesticity: The Scribal Publication of Lady Rich's Letter to Elizabeth I', in *Women and Writing c. 1340-c.1650: The Domestication of Print Culture*, eds Anne Lawrence-Mathers and Phillipa Hardman (York: York Medieval Press, 2010).

Dobson, Michael and Nicola J. Watson, *England's Elizabeth: An Afterlife in Fame and Fantasy* (Oxford: Oxford University Press, 2002).

Dodd, A. H. 'Wales and the Scottish Succession', *Transactions of the Honourable Society of Cymmrodorion*, Session 1937 (1938), pp. 201–225.

——, 'North Wales in the Essex Revolt', *The English Historical Review* 59: 235 (1944), pp. 348–370.

Doebler, John, 'Beaumont's *The Knight of the Burning Pestle* and the Prodigal Son Plays', *Studies in English Literature, 1500–1900* 5: 2 (Spring 1965), pp. 333–344.

Dollimore, Jonathan, 'Introduction: Shakespeare, cultural materialism and new historicism', in *Political Shakespeare: Essays in Cultural Materialism*, eds Jonathan Dollimore and Alan Sinfield (Manchester: Manchester University Press, 1985), pp. 18–47.

——, and Sinfield, Alan, 'History and Ideology: The Instance of *Henry V*', in *Alternative Shakespeares*, ed. John Drakakis (London: Methuen, 1985), pp. 206–227.

Doran, Susan, *Monarchy and Matrimony: The Courtships of Elizabeth I* (London: Routledge, 1996).

Doughtie, Edward, 'Sidney, Tessier, Batchelar and *A Musicall Banquet*: Two Notes', *Renaissance News* 18: 2 (1965), pp. 123–126.

Du Maurier, Daphne, *Golden Lads: A Study of Anthony Bacon, Francis and Their Friends* (London: Virago, 2007 [1975]).

Duncan-Jones, Katherine, 'Ford and the Earl of Devonshire', *Review of English Studies* 29: 116 (November 1978), pp. 447–452.

Dusinberre, Juliet, 'Pancakes and a Date for *As You Like It*', *Shakespeare Quarterly* 54: 4 (2003), pp. 371–405.

Dutton, Richard, *Mastering the Revels: The Regulation and Censorship of English Renaissance Drama* (Basingstoke: Macmillan, 1991).

——, 'Buggeswords: Samuel Harsnett and the Licensing, Suppression and Afterlife of Dr. John Hayward's *The First Part of the Life and Reign of King Henry IV*', *Criticism* 35:3 (1993), pp. 305–339.

——, '"Methinks the truth should live from age to age": The Dating and Contexts of *Henry V*', in *The Uses of History in Early Modern England*, ed. Paulina Kewes (The Huntington Library: San Marino, CA, 2006), pp. 169–199.

——, '*The Famous Victories* and the 1600 Quarto of *Henry V*', in *Locating the Queen's Men, 1583–1603: Material Practices and Conditions of Playing*, eds Helen Ostovich, Holger Schott Syme and Andrew Griffin (Surrey: Ashgate, 2009), pp. 135–144.

Falls, Cyril, *Mountjoy: Elizabethan General* (London: Odhams Press, 1955).

Fitter, Chris, 'Historicising Shakespeare's *Richard II*: Current Events, Dating, and the Sabotage of Essex', *Early Modern Literary Studies* 11: 2 (September 2005), http://extra.shu.ac.uk/emls/11–2/fittric2.htm, accessed 22 August 2012.

Fleay, F. G., 'On the History of Theatres in London, from their First Opening in 1576 to their Closing in 1642', *Transactions of the Royal Historical Society* 10 (1882), pp. 114–133.

Fletcher, Anthony and Roberts, Peter (eds), *Religion, Culture and Society in Early Modern Britain: Essays in Honour of Patrick Collinson* (Cambridge: Cambridge University Press, 1994).

Fox, Alastair,'The Complaint of Poetry for the Death of Liberality; the Decline of Literary Patronage in the 1590s', in *The Reign of Elizabeth: Court and culture in the 1590s*, ed. John Guy (Cambridge: Cambridge University Press 1995), pp. 229–257.

Freedman, Sylvia, *Poor Penelope: Lady Penelope Rich, An Elizabethan Woman* (London: Kensal Press, 1983).

Gair, W. Reavley, *The Children of Paul's: The Story of a Theatre Company, 1553–1608* (Cambridge: Cambridge University Press, 1982).

Gajda, Alexandra, '*The State of Christendom*: History, Political Thought and the Essex Circle', *Historical Research,* 81:213 (2008), pp. 423–446.

——, 'Debating War and Peace in late Elizabethan England', *The Historical Journal* 52 (2009), pp. 851–878.

——, *The Earl of Essex and Late Elizabethan Political Culture* (Oxford: Oxford University Press, 2012).

Gazzard, Hugh, 'The Patronage of Robert Devereux, Second Earl of Essex, *c.* 1577–1596', DPhil thesis, University of Oxford, 2000.

——, '"Those Graue Presentments of Antiquitie": Samuel Daniel's *Philotas* and the Earl of Essex', *The Review of English Studies,* new series 51: 203 (2000), pp. 423–50.

——, '"Many a Herdsman More Disposde to Mourn": Peele, Campion and the Portugal Expedition of 1589', *The Review of English Studies* 57 (2006), pp. 16–42.

Gibson, Kirsten, '"So to the wood went I": Politicizing the Greenwood in Two Songs by John Dowland', *Journal of the Royal Musical Association,* 132: 2 (2007), pp. 221–251.

Gittings, Robert, *Shakespeare's Rival: a Study in Three Parts* (London: Heinemann, 1960).

Goldberg, Jonathan, *Writing Matter: From the Hands of the English Renaissance* (Stanford, CA: Stanford University Press, 1990).

Gordon, Andrew, '"A Fortune of Paper walls": the Letters of Francis Bacon and the Earl of Essex', *English Literary Renaissance* 37:3 (2007), pp. 319–336.

——, '*Copycopia,* or the Place of Copied Correspondence in Manuscript Culture: A Case Study', in *Material Readings of Early Modern Culture: Texts and Social Practices, 1580–1700,* eds James Daybell and Peter Hinds (Basingstoke: Palgrave, 2010), pp. 65–81.

Gottfried, R. B. 'Spenser's *View* and Essex', *PMLA* 52: 3 (1937), pp. 645–651.

Gouws, John, 'Greville, Fulke, first Baron Brooke of Beauchamps Court (1554–1628)', in *Oxford Dictionary of National Biography,* eds H. C. G. Matthew and Brian Harrison (Oxford: Oxford University Press, 2004). Online edition, ed. Lawrence Goldman, May 2007.

Greenblatt, Stephen, 'Introduction' to 'The Forms of Power and The Power of Forms In the Renaissance', *Genre,* 15 (1982), pp. 3–6.

Gurr, Andrew, *The Shakespearean Stage, 1594–1642* (Cambridge: Cambridge University Press, 1980).

——, *Playgoing in Shakespeare's London,* 3rd edition (Cambridge: Cambridge University Press, 2004).

Guy, John, *Tudor England* (Oxford: Oxford University Press, 1988).

——, (ed.), *The Reign of Elizabeth I: Court and Culture in the Last Decade* (Cambridge: Cambridge University Press, 1995).

Hackel, Heidi Brayman, *Reading Material in Early Modern England: Print, Gender, and Literacy* (Cambridge: Cambridge University Press, 2005).

Hackett, Helen, *Virgin Mother, Maiden Queen: Elizabeth I and the Cult of the Virgin Mary* (Houndmills: Macmillan, 1995).

——, *Shakespeare and Elizabeth: The Meeting of Two Myths* (Princeton, NJ: Princeton University Press, 2009).

Hadfield, Andrew, *Spenser's Irish Experience: Wilde Fruit and Salvage Soyl* (Oxford: Clarendon Press, 1997).

——, 'The Political Significance of the First Tetralogy', in *The Monarchical Republic of Early Modern England*, ed. John McDiarmid (Aldershot: Ashgate, 2007), pp. 149–164.

Hammer, Paul E. J., 'The Earl of Essex, Fulke Greville, and the Employment of Scholars', *Studies in Philology* 91 (1994), pp. 167–180.

——, 'The Uses of Scholarship: the Secretariat of Robert Devereux, Second Earl of Essex, c. 1585–1601', *The English Historical Review* 109 (1994), pp. 26–51.

——, 'Letters of Travel Advice from the Earl of Essex to the Earl of Rutland: Some Comments', *Philological Quarterly* 74: 3 (1995), pp. 317–325.

——, 'A Reckoning Reframed: the "Murder" of Christopher Marlowe Reconsidered', *English Literary Renaissance* 26 (1996), pp. 225–242.

——, 'Essex and Europe: Evidence from Confidential Instructions by the Earl of Essex, 1595–6', *English Historical Review* 111 (April 1996), pp. 357–381.

——, 'Myth-Making: Politics, Propaganda and the Capture of Cadiz in 1596', *The Historical Journal* 40: 3 (1997), pp. 621–642.

——, 'Upstaging the Queen: The Earl of Essex, Francis Bacon, and the Accession Day Celebrations of 1595', in *The Politics of the Stuart Court Masque*, eds David Bevington and Peter Holbrook (Cambridge: Cambridge University Press, 1998), pp. 41–66.

——, *The Polarisation of Elizabethan Politics: The Political Career of Robert Devereux, Second Earl of Essex, 1585–1597* (Cambridge: Cambridge University Press, 1999).

——, *Elizabeth's Wars: War, Government and Society in Tudor England 1544–1604* (Basingstoke: Palgrave 2003).

——, 'The Crucible of War: English Foreign Policy, 1589–1603', in *Tudor England and its Neighbours*, eds Susan Doran and Glenn Richardson (New York: Palgrave Macmillan, 2005), pp. 235–266.

——, 'Devereux, Robert, second earl of Essex (1565–1601)', in *Oxford Dictionary of National Biography*, eds H. C. G. Matthew and Brian Harrison (Oxford: Oxford University Press, 2004). Online edition, ed. Lawrence Goldman, October 2008.

——, 'Shakespeare's *Richard II*, the Play of 7 February 1601, and the Essex Rising', *Shakespeare Quarterly* 59: 1 (2008), pp. 1–35.

——, 'The Smiling Crocodile: the Earl of Essex and Later Elizabethan "Popularity"', in *The Politics of the Public Sphere in Early Modern England*, eds Peter Lake and Steven Pincus (Manchester: Manchester University Press 2008), pp. 95–115.

——, '*The Private Lives of Elizabeth and Essex* and the Romanticization of Elizabethan Politics', in *Tudors and Stuarts on Film: Historical Perspectives*, eds Susan Doran and Thomas S. Freeman (Basingstoke: Palgrave Macmillan, 2009), pp. 190–203.

Hammons, Pamela S., *Gender, Sexuality, and Material Objects in English Renaissance Verse* (Aldershot: Ashgate, 2010).

Hannay, Margaret P., *Philip's Phoenix: Mary Sidney, Countess of Pembroke* (Oxford: Oxford University Press, 1990).

Harrison, G. B., *The Life and Death of Robert Devereux, Earl of Essex* (Bath: Cedric Chivers, 1970 [1937]).

Harwood, Ian, 'Holborne, Antony (d. 1602?)', in *Oxford Dictionary of National Biography*, eds H. C. G. Matthew and Brian Harrison (Oxford: Oxford University Press, 2004). Online edition, ed. Lawrence Goldman, January 2007.

Headlam Wells, Robin, *Shakespeare on Masculinity* (Cambridge: Cambridge University Press, 2005).

Heffner, R., 'Shakespeare, Hayward and Essex', *PMLA* 43 (1930), pp. 754–780.

——, 'Shakespeare, Hayward and Essex again', *PMLA* 47 (1932), pp. 898–899.

——, 'Essex, the Ideal Courtier', *English Literary History* 1:1 (1934), pp. 7–36.

——, 'Essex and Book Five of *The Faerie Queene*' *English Literary History*, 3: 1 (1936), pp. 67–82.

Heinemann, Margot, 'Rebel Lords, Popular Playwrights, and Political Culture: Notes on the Jacobean Patronage of the Earl of Southampton', *Yearbook of English Studies* 21 (1991), pp. 63–86.

Henry, L. W., 'The Earl of Essex as Strategist and Military Organizer (1596–7)', *English Historical Review* 68 (1953), pp. 363–393.

——, 'The Earl of Essex and Ireland, 1599', *Bulletin of the Institute of Historical Research* 32: 85 (1959), pp. 1–23.

Hicks, Leo, S. I., 'Sir Robert Cecil, Father Persons and the Succession, 1600–1601', *Archivum Historicum Societatis Iesu* 24 (1955) pp. 95–139.

Highley, Christopher, 'Wales, Ireland, and *1 Henry IV*', *Renaissance Drama* 21 (1990), pp. 91–114.

——, *Shakespeare, Spenser, and the Crisis in Ireland* (Cambridge: Cambridge University Press, 1997).

Hillebrand, Harold Newcomb, 'The Child Actors', *University of Illinois Studies in Language and Literature* 11: 1–2 (February 1926), pp. 128–131.

Hinton, E. M. (ed.). 'Rych's "Anothomy of Ireland" [1615], with an account of the author', *PMLA* 55: 1 (1940), pp. 73–101.

Hodgdon, Barbara, *The Shakespeare Trade: Performances and Appropriations* (Philadelphia, PA: University of Pennsylvania Press, 1998).

Holmes, Peter, 'The Authorship and Early Reception of *A Conference about the Next Succession to the Crown of England*', *Historical Journal* 23 (1980), pp. 415–429.

Hopkins, Lisa, *Writing Renaissance Queens: Texts by and about Elizabeth I and Mary, Queen of Scots* (Newark, DE: University of Delaware Press, 2002).

——, 'Harington, *Troilus and Cressida*, and the Poets' War', in *Italian Culture in the Drama of Shakespeare and his Contemporaries: Rewriting, Remaking, Refashioning*, ed. Michele Marrapodi (Aldershot: Ashgate, 2007), pp. 127–140.

Houliston, Victor, *Catholic Resistance in Elizabethan England. Robert Persons's Jesuit Polemic, 1580–1610* (Aldershot: Ashgate, 2007).

Hudson, Hoyt. H., 'Penelope Devereux as Sidney's Stella', *Huntington Library Bulletin* 7 (April 1935), pp. 89–129.

Hunt, William, 'Colfe, Abraham (1580–1657)', rev. Vivienne Larminie, *ODNB online*, www.oxforddnb.com/view/article/5900, accessed 3 September 2010.

Husken, Wim, 'Queen Elizabeth and Essex: A Dutch Rhetorician's Play', *Leeds Studies in English* 32 (2001), pp. 151–170.

Hutchins, John, *The History and Antiquities of the County of Dorset*, vol. IV [1870] (Dorchester: Dorset County Library, 1973).

Hutson, Lorna, *The Usurer's Daughter: Male Friendship and Fictions of Women in Sixteenth-Century England* (London: Routledge, 1994).

Ioppolo, Grace, *Dramatists and their Manuscripts in the Age of Shakespeare, Jonson, Middleton and Heywood: Authorship, Authority and the Playhouse* (London: Routledge, 2006).

——, '"Your Majesties most humble faythrullest and most affectionate seruant": The Earl of Essex constructs himself and his Queen in the Hulton Letters', in *Elizabeth I and the Culture of Writing*, eds Peter Beal and Grace Ioppolo (London: British Library, 2007), pp. 43–69.

Ivic, C., '"Our inland": Shakespeare's *Henry V* and the Celtic Fringe', *Ariel: A Review of International Literature* 30: 1 (1999), pp. 85–103.

James, Henry and Walker, Greg, 'The Politics of *Gorboduc*', *The English Historical Review* 110: 435 (1995), pp. 109–121.

James, Mervyn. *Society, Politics and Culture: Studies in Early Modern England* (Cambridge: Cambridge University Press, 1986).

Jardine, David (ed.), *Criminal Trials*, 2 vols (London: Charles Knight, 1832).

Jardine, Lisa and Grafton, Anthony, '"Studied for Action": How Gabriel Harvey read his Livy,' *Past and Present* 129 (1990), pp. 30–78.

Jardine, Lisa and Sherman, William, 'Pragmatic Readers: Knowledge Transactions and Scholarly Services in Late Elizabethan England', in *Religion, Culture and Society in Early Modern Britain: Essays in Honour of Patrick Collinson*, eds Anthony Fletcher and Peter Roberts (Cambridge: Cambridge University Press, 1994), pp. 102–124.

John, Lisle C, 'The Date of the Marriage of Penelope Devereux', *PMLA* 49: 3 (1934), pp. 961–962.

Jones, Frederick M., *Mountjoy, 1563–1606: The Last Elizabethan Deputy* (Dublin: Clonmore and Reynolds, 1958).

Kearney, H., *Strafford in Ireland, 1633–41: A Study in Absolutism* (Manchester: University of Manchester Press, 1959, reprint 1989).

Kewes, Paulina (ed.), *The Uses of History in Early Modern England* (The Huntington Library: San Marino, CA, 2006).

——, 'Henry Savile's Tacitus and the Politics of Roman History in Late Elizabethan England', *Huntington Library Quarterly*, 74:4 (2011), pp. 515–551.

King, Maureen Claire, '"Essex, that could vary himself into all shapes for a time": The Second Earl of Essex in Jacobean England', PhD thesis, University of Alberta, 2000.

Kinney, Arthur F., 'Shakespeare versus Hayward', *Shakespeare Quarterly*, 44 (1993), pp. 464–466.

Knutson, Roslyn L., 'Influence of the Repertory System on the Revival and Revision of *The Spanish Tragedy and Dr Faustus*', *English Literary Renaissance* 18: 2 (Spring 1988), pp. 257–274.

——, *The Repertory of Shakespeare's Company, 1594–1613* (Fayetteville, AR: The University of Arkansas Press, 1991).

——, 'The Repertory', in *A New History of Early English Drama*, eds John D. Cox and David Scott Kastan (New York: Columbia University Press, 1997), pp. 461–480.

——, *Playing Companies and Commerce in Shakespeare's Time* (Cambridge: Cambridge University Press, 2001).

Kökeritz, Helge, 'Elizabethan che vore ye "I warrant you"', *Modern Language Notes* 57: 2 (February 1942), pp. 98–103.

Lacey, Robert, *Robert, Earl of Essex: an Elizabethan Icarus* (London: Weidenfeld and Nicolson, 1971; reprint London: Phoenix Press, 2001).

Lake, Peter. 'From *Leicester his Commonwealth* to *Sejanus his Fall*: Ben Jonson and the politics of Roman (Catholic) Virtue', in *Catholics and the 'Protestant Nation': Religious Politics and Identity in Early Modern Britain*, ed. Ethan H. Shagen (Manchester: Manchester University Press, 2005), pp. 128–161.

——, 'The politics of "Popularity" and the Public Sphere: the "Monarchical Republic" of Elizabeth I Defends Itself', in *The Politics of the Public Sphere in Early Modern England*, eds Peter Lake and Steven Pincus (Manchester: Manchester University Press 2008), pp. 59–94.

Lamb, Mary Ellen, *Gender and Authorship in the Sidney Circle* (Madison, WI: University of Wisconsin Press, 1990).

Laoutaris, Chris, 'Translation / Historical Writing', in *The History of British Women's Writing: 1500–1610*, eds Caroline Bicks and Jennifer Summit (Basingstoke: Palgrave, 2010), pp. 296–327.

——, 'The Radical Pedagogies of Lady Elizabeth Russell', in *Performing Pedagogy in Early Modern England: Gender, Instruction, and Performance*, eds Kathryn M. Moncrief and Kathryn R. McPherson (Aldershot: Ashgate, 2011), pp. 65–86.

Lea, Kathleen M., 'Sir Anthony Standen and Some Anglo-Italian Letters', *English Historical Review* 47: 187 (July 1932), pp. 461–477.

Lee, Sidney. 'Devereux, Robert, second Earl of Essex (1566–1601)', in *Dictionary of National Biography* XIV (1888), eds Leslie Stephen and Sidney Lee, 22 vols (London, Smith, Elder & Co., 1885–1900). Online edition, Oxford *Dictionary of National Biography* Archive.

Lemon, Rebecca, 'The Faulty Verdict in "The Crown v. John Hayward"', *Studies in English Literature 1500–1900* 41 (2001), pp. 109–132.

Levy, F. J., *Tudor Historical Thought* (The Huntington Library: San Marino, California, 1967).

——, 'Hayward, Daniel, and the Beginnings of Politic History in England', *Huntington Library Quarterly* 50 (1987), pp. 1–34.

——, 'The Theatre and the Court in the 1590s', in *The Reign of Elizabeth I*, ed. John Guy (Cambridge: Cambridge University Press 1995), pp. 274–300.

Lindberg, Kevin, 'Thomas Heywood's *The Royal King, and the Loyal Subject* and the Fall of Robert Devereux, Second Earl of Essex', *Comparative Drama* 39 (2005), pp. 31–53.

Lindheim, Nancy, *The Structures of Sidney's Arcadia* (Toronto: University of Toronto Press, 1982).

Lisak, C., '"Succession" versus "Usurpation": Politics and Rhetoric in Shakespeare's *Richard II*', in *The Struggle for the Succession in Late Elizabethan England: Politics, Polemics and Cultural Representations*, ed. Jean-Christophe Mayer (Montpellier: Institute de Recherche sur la Renaissance, l'Âge Classique et les Lumières, 2004), pp. 352–369.

Lloyd, Howell A, *The Rouen Campaign 1590–1592: Politics, Warfare and the Early-Modern State* (Oxford: Clarendon Press, 1973).

Love, Harold, *Scribal Publication in Seventeenth-Century England* (Amherst, MA: University of Massachusetts Press, 1993).

McCabe, R. A., 'Making History: Holinshed's Irish *Chronicles*, 1577 and 1587', in *British Identities and English Renaissance Literature*, eds David J. Baker and Willy Maley (Cambridge: Cambridge University Press, 2002), pp. 51–67.

MacCaffrey, Wallace T., *Elizabeth I: War and Politics, 1588–1603* (Princeton, NJ: Princeton University Press, 1992).

McCarthy, Jeanne H., 'Elizabeth I's "picture in little": Boy Company Representations of a Queen's Authority', *Studies in Philology* 100: 4 (Autumn 2003), pp. 425–462.

McConica, James (ed.), *The History of the University of Oxford. Volume 3. The Collegiate University* (Oxford: Clarendon Press, 1986).

McCoy, R., '"*A Dangerous Image*": The Earl of Essex and Elizabethan Chivalry', *Journal of Medieval and Renaissance Studies* 13 (1983), pp. 316–323.

——, *The Rites of Knighthood: The Literature and Politics of Elizabethan Chivalry* (Berkeley, CA: University of California Press, 1989).

——, 'Lord of Liberty: Francis Davison and the Cult of Elizabeth', in *The Reign of Elizabeth I: Court And Culture in the Last Decade*, ed. J. Guy (Cambridge: Cambridge University Press, 1995), pp. 212–228.

McDiarmid, John (ed.), *The Monarchical Republic of Early Modern England* (Aldershot: Ashgate, 2007).

McIntyre, Jean, *Costumes and Scripts in the Elizabethan Theatres* (Edmonton: University of Alberta Press, 1992).

McKerrow, R. B. (gen. ed.), *A Dictionary of Printers and Booksellers in England, Scotland and Ireland, and of Foreign Printers of English books 1557–1640* (London: The Bibliographical Society, 1910).

McMillin, Scott and Sally-Beth MacLean, *The Queen's Men and their Plays* (Cambridge: Cambridge University Press, 1998).

Maley, Willy, 'The Irish Text and Subtext of Shakespeare's English Histories', in *A Companion to Shakespeare's Works Vol. II: The Histories*, eds Richard Dutton and Jean Howard (Oxford and Malden: Blackwell, 2003).

Marcus, Leah S., 'Jonson and the Court', in *The Cambridge Companion to Ben Jonson*, eds Richard Harp and Stanley Stewart (Cambridge: Cambridge University Press, 2000), pp. 30–42.

Margetts, Michele, 'Lady Penelope Rich: Hilliard's Lost Miniatures and a Surviving Portrait', *Burlington Magazine* 130, no. 1027 (October, 1988), pp. 758–761.

Markham, Clements R., ed., *Markham Memorials* (London: Spottiswoode and Co., 1913).

Marotti, Arthur, *Manuscript, Print, and the English Renaissance Lyric* (Ithaca, NY: Cornell University Press, 1995).

Martin, W. C., 'The Date and Purpose of Spenser's *Veue*', *PMLA* 47: 1 (1932), pp. 137–143.

Mathew, David, *The Celtic Peoples and Renaissance Europe: A Study of the Celtic and Spanish Influences on Elizabethan History* (London: Sheed and Ward, 1933).

Mears, Natalie, '*Regnum Cecilianum*? A Perspective of the Court', in *The Reign of Elizabeth*, ed. John Guy (Cambridge: Cambridge University Press 1995), pp. 46–63.

——, 'Counsel, Public Debate, and Queenship: John Stubbs's *The Discoverie of a Gaping Gulf*, 1579', *The Historical Journal* 44: 3 (September 2001), pp. 629–650.

——, *Queenship and Political Discourse in the Elizabethan Realms* (Cambridge: Cambridge University Press, 2005).

Ménager, Daniel, *Diplomatie et Théologie à la Renaissance* (Paris: Presses Universitaires de France, 2001).

Michel, Laurence, 'Introduction', in Samuel Daniel, *The Tragedy of Philotas*, ed. Laurence Michel, pp. 1–94 (New Haven, CT: Yale University Press, 1949).

Molhuysen, P. C., and P.J. Blok (eds), *Nieuw Nederlandsch biografisch Woordenboek*, 10 vols (Leiden 1911–37).

Morash, Christopher, *A History of Irish Theatre, 1601–2000* (Cambridge: Cambridge University Press, 2002).

Morgan, H., *Tyrone's Rebellion: The Outbreak of the Nine Years War in Tudor Ireland* (Woodbridge: Boydell, 1993).

Mullett, Charles F., 'Gervase Markham, Scientific Amateur', *Isis* 35 (1944), pp. 106–118.

Munro, Lucy, 'The Humour of Children: Performance, Gender and the Early Modern Children's Companies', *Literature Compass* 2: 1 (January 2005), pp. 1–26.

Murphy, Andrew, 'Gold Lace and a Frozen Snake: Donne, Wotton and the Nine Years War', *Irish Studies Review* 2: 8 (1994), pp. 9–11.

——, '"'Tish ill done": *Henry the Fift* and the Politics of Editing', in *Shakespeare and Ireland: History, Politics, Culture*, eds Mark Thornton-Burnett and Ramona Wray (Basingstoke: Macmillan, 1997), pp. 213–234.

Myers, Micki, 'The Earl of Essex Unsuccessfully Defends his Return from Ireland Before the Privy Council, 29 September 1599', *Critical Quarterly*, 49: 4 (2007), p. 123.

Neale, J. E., *Queen Elizabeth* (New York: Harcourt, Brace and Company, 1934).

——, 'The Elizabethan political scene', in *The Age of Catherine de Medici and Essays in Elizabethan History*, pp. 145–70 (London: Jonathan Cape, 1963; reprint 1965).

Neill, Michael, '"What Strange Riddle's This?": Deciphering *'Tis Pity She's a Whore*', in *John Ford: Critical Revisions*, ed. Michael Neill (Cambridge: Cambridge University Press, 1988).

——, 'Broken English and Broken Irish: Nation, Language, and the Optic of Power in Shakespeare's Histories', *Shakespeare Quarterly*, 45: 1 (1994), pp. 1–32.

Nicholl, Charles, *The Reckoning: The Murder of Christopher Marlowe* (London: Vintage, 1992).

Norbrook, David, *Poetry and Politics in the English Renaissance* (London: Routledge and Kegan Paul, 1984).

Oakely, Francis, 'Almain and Major: Conciliar Theory on the Eve of the Reformation', *American Historical Review* 70: 3 (1965), pp. 673–690.

Orr, Alan, *Treason and the State: Law, Politics and Ideology in the English Civil War* (Cambridge: Cambridge University Press, 2002).

Parker, Patricia, *Shakespeare from the Margins: Language, Culture, Context* (Chicago: University of Chicago Press, 1996).

Peck, D. C. (ed.), *Leicester's Commonwealth: The Copy of a Letter Written by a Master of Art at Cambridge (1584) and Related Documents* (Athens, OH: Ohio University Press, 1985).

Perry, Curtis, *Literature and Favoritism in Early Modern England* (Cambridge; Cambridge University Press, 2006).

Pigeon, Renée, 'Gloriana Goes Hollywood: Elizabeth I on Film, 1937-1940', in *Reinventing the Middle Ages and the Renaissance: Constructions of the Medieval and Early Modern Periods*, ed. William F. Gentrup (Turnhout: Brepols, 1998).

Piper, David, 'The Lumley Inventory: Hilliard, Segar and the Earl of Essex-II', *The Burlington Magazine* 99: 654 (September 1957), pp. 299–302.

Pitcher, John, 'Essex, Robert Devereux, Second Earl of', in *The Spenser Encyclopedia*, ed. A. C. Hamilton (Toronto: University of Toronto Press, 1990), p. 535.

Poulton, Diana, *John Dowland* (London: Faber and Faber 1982).

Poynter, F. N. L., 'Gervase Markham and Genevieve Petau', *Times Literary Supplement* (16 October 1959), p. 600.

——, *A Bibliography of Gervase Markham, 1568?–1637* (Oxford: Oxford Bibliographical Society, 1962).

Preston, Claire. 'Arcadia'. In *The Literary Encyclopedia*, www.litencyc.com/php/sworks.php?rec=true&UID=6542, accessed 11 July 2012.

Randall, David, 'Epistolary Rhetoric, the Newspaper, and the Public Sphere', *Past and Present* 198 (2008), pp. 3–32.

Read, Conyers, *Lord Burghley and Queen Elizabeth* (London: Jonathan Cape, 1960).

Reiss, Timothy J., '"Seated Between the Old World and the New": Geopolitics, Natural Philosophy, and Proficient Method', in *Francis Bacon and the Refiguring of Early Modern Thought*, eds Julie Robin Solomon and Catherine Gimelli Martin (Aldershot: Ashgate, 2005), pp. 223–246.

Richardson, L. J., Sir John Hayward and early Stuart historiography', 2 vols, PhD thesis, Cambridge University, 1999.

Rickman, Johanna, *Love, Lust, and License in Early Modern England: Illicit Sex and the Nobility* (Aldershot: Ashgate, 2008).

Robertson, James C., *The Casablanca Man: The Cinema of Michael Curtiz* (London: Routledge, 1993).

Rodger, Ian, 'Sweet England's Pride', in *Plays of the Year Special: Elizabeth R*, ed. J.C. Trewin (London: Paul Elek, 1972).

Rogge, H. C. *Caspar Janszoon Coolhaes, de Voorlooper van Arminius en der Remonstraten*, 2 vols (Amsterdam, 1856–58).

Rouse, Charles A., 'Was Heywood a Servant of the Earl of Southampton?' *PMLA* 45 (1930), pp. 787–790.

Rowley, Anthony, 'A Portrait of Sir Henry Unton', in *Companion to Medieval and Renaissance Music*, eds Tess Knighton and David Fallows (New York: Schirmer Books, 1992), pp. 85–92.

Rowse, A. L., *The Expansion of Elizabethan England* (London: Cardinal, 1955).

Ruff, Lillian M. and D. Arnold Wilson, 'The Madrigal, the Lute Song and Elizabethan Politics', *Past & Present* 44 (1969), pp. 3–51.

Saint-Foix, Monsieur de (Germain-François Poullain), *Essais historiques sur Paris*, fifth edition (Paris: Veuve Duchesne, 1776–77).

Salmon, J. H. M., 'Stoicism and Roman Example: Seneca and Tacitus in Jacobean England', *Journal of the History of Ideas* 50: 2 (1989), pp. 199–225.

Schrickx, Willem, *Foreign Envoys and Travelling Players in the Age of Shakespeare and Jonson* (Ghent: State University of Ghent, 1986).

Schurink, Fred, '"Like a hand in the margine of a booke": William Blount's Marginalia and the Politics of Sidney's *Arcadia*', *The Review of English Studies* 59 (2008), pp. 1–24.

Scott-Warren, Jason, 'Reconstructing Manuscript Networks: the Textual Transactions of Sir Stephen Powle', in *Communities in Early Modern England: Networks, Place, Rhetoric*, eds Alexandra Shepard and Phil Withington (Manchester: Manchester University Press 2000), pp. 18–37.

——, *Sir John Harington and the Book as Gift* (Oxford: Oxford University Press, 2001).

Serjeantson, Richard and Thomas Wollford, 'The Scribal Publication of a Printed Book: Francis Bacon's *Certaine Considerations Touching … the Church of England* (1604)', *The Library*, 7th series: 10 (2009), pp. 119–156.

Shapiro, James, *1599: A Year in the Life of William Shakespeare* (London: Faber & Faber, 2005).

Shapiro, Michael, *The Children of the Revels: The Boy Companies of Shakespeare's Time and their Plays* (New York: Columbia University Press, 1977).

Sharp, Buchanan, 'Shakespeare's *Coriolanus* and the crisis of the 1590s', in *Law and Authority in Early Modern England: Essays Presented to Thomas Garden Barnes*, eds Buchanan Sharp and Mark Charles Fissel, pp. 27–63 (Newark, DE: University of Delaware Press, 2007).

Sharpe, Kevin and Peter Lake, eds, *Culture and Politics in Early Stuart England* (Basingstoke: Macmillan, 1994).

Shenk, Linda S., '"To Love and Be Wise": the Earl of Essex, Humanist Court Culture, and England's Learned Queen', *Early Modern Literary Studies* Special Issue 16 (2007), http://extra.shu.ac.uk/emls/si–16/shenwise.htm, accessed 29 April 2013.

——, *Learned Queen: The Image of Elizabeth I in Politics and Poetry* (New York: Palgrave Macmillan, 2010).

Shephard, Robert, 'Sidney, Robert, first Earl of Leicester (1563–1626)', in *Oxford Dictionary of National Biography*, eds H. C. G. Matthew and Brian Harrison (Oxford: Oxford University Press, 2004). Online edition, ed. Lawrence Goldman, January 2008, http://www.oxforddnb.com/view/article/25524, accessed 31 May 2010.

Shuger, Debora Kuller, *The Renaissance Bible: Scholarship, Sacrifice, and Subjectivity* (Berkeley, CA: University of California Press, 1994).

——, '"In a Christian Climate": Religion and Honor in *Richard II*', in *Shakespeare and Religious Change*, eds K. J. E. Graham and P. D. Collington (Basingstoke: Palgrave Macmillan, 2009), pp. 37–62.

Simoni, Anna E. C., *Catalogue of Books from the Low Countries 1601–1621 in the British Library* (London, 1990).

Sinfield, Alan, 'Sidney and Astrophil', *Studies in English Literature 1500–1900* 20: 1 (Winter 1980), pp. 25–41.

Skinner, Quentin, *The Foundations of Modern Political Thought*, 2 vols (Cambridge: Cambridge University Press, 1978).

Smith, Lacey Baldwin, *Treason in Tudor England: Politics and Paranoia* (London: Jonathan Cape, 1986; reprint Pimlico, 2006).

Smith, Warrren D., 'The *Henry V* Choruses in the First Folio', *Journal of English and Germanic Philology* 53 (1954), pp. 38–57.

Smith, Winifred, 'The Earl of Essex on the Stage', *PMLA* 39:1 (March 1924), pp. 147–73.

Smuts, R. Malcolm, 'Court-Centred Politics and the Uses of Roman Historians', in *Culture and Politics in Early Stuart England*, eds Kevin Sharpe and Peter Lake (Basingstoke: Macmillan, 1994), pp. 21–43.

Spencer, Robert, *The Mynshall lute book* (Leeds: Boethius Press 1975).

——, 'Three English Lute Manuscripts', *Early Music* 3:2 (1975), pp. 119–24.

Stafford, Helen Georgia, *James VI and the Throne of England* (New York and London: D. Appleton-Century Company, 1940).

Steggle, Matthew. 'Markham, Gervase (1568?–1637)', in *Oxford Dictionary of National Biography*, eds H. C. G. Matthew and Brian Harrison (Oxford: Oxford University Press, 2004). Online edition, ed. Lawrence Goldman, October 2006, http://www.oxforddnb.com/view/article/18065, accessed 25 February 2010.

Stern, Virginia F., *Gabriel Harvey. His Life, Marginalia and Library* (Oxford: Clarendon Press, 1979).

Stewart, Alan, 'Francis Bacon's Bi-lateral Cipher and the Materiality of Early Modern Diplomatic Writing', in *Diplomacy and Early Modern Culture*, eds Robyn Adams and Rosanna Cox (Basingstoke: Palgrave, 2011), pp. 120–37.

Stillman, Robert E., *Sidney's Poetic Justice: The Old Arcadia, Its Eclogues, and Renaissance Pastoral Traditions* (Lewisburg, PA: Bucknell University Press, 1986).

——, *Philip Sidney and the Poetics of Renaissance Cosmopolitanism* (Aldershot: Ashgate, 2008).

——, Stone, Lawrence, *The Crisis of the Aristocracy, 1558–1641* (Oxford: Clarendon Press, 1965).

Stonex, Arthur Bivins, 'The Sources of Jonson's *The Staple of News*', *PMLA* 30: 4 (1915), pp. 821–830.

Stopes, Charlotte Carmichael, *The Life of Henry, Third Earl of Southampton, Shakespeare's Patron* (Cambridge: Cambridge University Press, 1922).

Strachey, Lytton, *Elizabeth and Essex* (London: Chatto and Windus, 1928).

Strong, Roy, 'Queen Elizabeth, The Earl of Essex and Nicholas Hilliard', *Burlington Magazine* 101: 673 (April 1959), pp. 145–149.

——, *The Cult of Elizabeth: Elizabethan Portraiture and Pageantry* (London: Thames and Hudson, 1977).

——, *The English Renaissance Miniature* (London: Thames and Hudson, 1983).

Stump, Donald and Susan M. Felch (eds), *Elizabeth I and Her Age* (New York: W. W. Norton, 2009).

Sturgess, Keith, *Jacobean Private Theatre* (London: Routledge & Kegan Paul, 1987).

Tenison, E. M., *Elizabethan England: Being the history of this Country 'In Relation to all foreign Princes' … From Original Manuscripts, many hitherto unpublished*, 13 vols (Leamington Spa, 1933–61).

Tennenhouse, Leonard, *Power on Display: The Politics of Shakespeare's Genres* (London: Methuen, 1986).

Thomas, Sidney, 'Richard Smith: "Foreign to the Company"', *Library* 5 (1948), pp. 186–192.

Tipton, Alazada J., '"Lively Patterns … For Affayres of State": Sir John Hayward's *The Life and Reigne of King Henrie IIII* and the Earl of Essex', *Sixteenth Century Journal* 33: 3 (2002), pp. 769–794.

Tuck, Richard, *Philosophy and Government, 1572–1651* (Cambridge: Cambridge University Press, 1993).

Van Doorninck, J. I., *Vermomde en naamlooze schrijvers opgespoord op het gebied der Nederlandsche en Vlaamsche letteren*, 2 vols (Leiden, 1883–85).

Varlow, Sally, *The Lady Penelope: The Lost Tale of Love and Politics in the Court of Elizabeth I* (London: André Deutsch, 2007).

Venn, John and J. A., *Alumni cantabrigienses* (Cambridge: Cambridge University Press 1922).

Vickers, Brian, 'The Authenticity of Bacon's Earliest Writings', *Studies in Philology*, 94:2 (1997), pp. 248–296.

Walker, D. P., 'Ways of Dealing with Atheists: A Background to Pamela's Refutation of Cecropia', *Bibliothèque d'Humanisme et Renaissance* 17: 2 (1955), pp. 252–277.

Walker, Greg, *The Private Life of Henry VIII* (London: I. B. Tauris & Co., 2003).

Wall, Wendy, 'Renaissance National Husbandry: Gervase Markham and the Publication of England', *Sixteenth Century Journal* 27 (1996), pp. 767–785.

Wallace, Malcolm William, *The Life of Sir Philip Sidney* (Cambridge: Cambridge University Press, 1915).

Ward, John M., 'Tessier and the Essex Circle', *Renaissance Quarterly* 29: 3 (Autumn 1976), pp. 378–384.

Watson, Andrew G., *The Library of Sir Simonds D'Ewes* (London: British Museum, 1966).

Weir, Alison, *Elizabeth the Queen* (London: Jonathan Cape, 1998).

Wernham, R. B., *The Return of the Armadas: The Last Years of the Elizabethan War against Spain, 1595–1603* (Oxford: Oxford University Press, 1994).

Wickham, Glynne, Herbert Berry and William Ingram (eds), *English Professional Theatre, 1530–1660* (Cambridge: Cambridge University Press, 2001).

Williams, Franklin B, Jr., *An Index of Dedications and Commendatory Verses in English Books before 1641* (London: The Bibliographical Society, 1962).

Williams, Penry, 'Elizabethan Oxford: State, Church and University', in James McConica, *History of the University of Oxford* (Oxford: The Clarenon Press, 1986), pp. 397–440.

Williams, Susan, *The People's Kin: The True Story of the Abdication* (London: Penguin, 2004 [2003]).

Wilson, J. Dover, 'Richard Schilders and the English Puritans', *Transactions of the Bibliographical Society*, 1st series: 11 (1909–11), pp. 65–134.

Womersley, David, 'Sir Henry Savile's Translation of Tacitus and the Political Interpretation of Elizabethan Texts', *The Review of English Studies* 42: 167 (1991), pp. 313–342.
——, 'Sir John Hayward's Tacitism', *Renaissance Studies*, 6:1 (1992), pp. 46–59.
Wood, Richard, '"The representing of so strange a power in love": Philip Sidney's Legacy of Anti-factionalism', *Early Modern Literary Studies* Special Issue 16 (October, 2007), http://purl.oclc.org/emls/si–16/woodsidn.htm, accessed 29 April 2013.
Woolf, D. R., 'Genre into Artifact: the Decline of the English Chronicle in the Sixteenth Century', *Sixteenth Century Journal* 19.3 (1988), pp. 321–354.
——, *The Idea of History in Early Stuart England* (Toronto: University of Toronto Press, 1990).
Worden, Blair, *The Sound of Virtue: Philip Sidney's* Arcadia *and Elizabethan Politics* (New Haven, CT: Yale University Press, 1996).
——, 'Favourites on the English Stage', in *The World of the Favourite*, eds Laurence W. B. Brockliss and John H. Elliot (New Haven, CT and London: Yale University Press, 1999), pp. 159–183.
——,'Which Play was Performed at the Globe Theatre on 7 February 1601?', *London Review of Books* 25: 13 (2003), pp. 22–24.
Woudhuysen, H. R., *Sir Philip Sidney and the Circulation of Manuscripts, 1558–1640* (Oxford: Clarendon Press, 1996).
——, 'Sidney, Sir Philip (1554–1586)', in *Oxford Dictionary of National Biography*, eds H. C. G. Matthew and Brian Harrison (Oxford: Oxford University Press, 2004). Online edition, ed. Lawrence Goldman, May 2005.
Wright, Gillian, 'Samuel Daniel's Use of Sources in *The Civil Wars*', *Studies in Philology* 101: 1 (2004), pp. 59–87.
——, 'The Politics of Revision in Samuel Daniel's *The Civil Wars*', *English Literary Renaissance* 38:3 (2008), pp. 461–482.
Wright, Louis B., 'Propaganda against James I's "Appeasement" of Spain', *Huntington Library Quarterly* 6 (1943), pp. 149–172.
Yates, Frances A., *John Florio: The Life of an Italian in Shakespeare's England* (Cambridge: Cambridge University Press, 1934).
Young, Alan, *Tudor and Jacobean Tournaments* (London: George Philip, 1987).
Ziegler, Philip, *King Edward VIII* (London: Fontana, 1991 [1990]).
Zitner, Sheldon P., 'Introduction', in Francis Beaumont, *The Knight of the Burning Pestle*, ed. Sheldon P. Zitner (Manchester: Manchester University Press, 1984; revised edition 2004), pp. 1–49.

Index

Accession Day Tilts 19–30, 38, 74, 81, 103, 155, 189
Adams, Simon 33
Albright, Evelyn May 13, 144
Alexander, Gavin 41, 50
Anderson, Maxwell 279–281, 283, 285
Anjou, François, Duke of 33
Azores expedition 5–6, 8, 49, 51–52, 58, 153, 183, 191–192

Bacheler, Daniel 160–1
Bacon, Anthony 40, 105, 115, 156, 183, 186, 189, 210–212, 214–215, 218, 224, 240, 244
Bacon, Francis 8–9, 12, 18, 40, 74, 82, 107–108, 110–111, 114, 183, 185, 191–192, 212, 214, 218, 220, 238–240, 242, 246, 250, 265–267, 272–273
Banks, John
  The Unhappy Favourite 8, 119–20
Barnes, Barnabe 104, 109, 111, 115–116, 118
Barroll, Leeds 13–14
Beal, Peter 188
Betteridge, Thomas 281, 285–286
Burghley, William Cecil, Lord 4–5, 8, 29, 33, 36, 70, 82, 86, 89, 107, 111, 133, 137–140, 145, 154, 185, 202–203, 206, 208–209, 212, 239, 243, 270, 273
Butler, Chris 6, 16, 108

Cadiz expedition 5, 29, 106–107, 112, 114, 145, 153, 155, 189, 241, 270
Camden, William 109, 111, 116, 120, 153, 185, 210, 266, 269, 271, 274
Carleton, George 104, 107, 111, 114, 121
Carney, Jo Eldridge 285
Cecil, Sir Robert 5, 7–8, 29, 32, 72, 75, 82, 106–107, 110, 112, 115, 133, 135, 139–142, 144, 155, 180–182, 184–185, 187, 209, 212, 216–217, 219, 223–227, 238–239, 242–244, 247–248, 250
Chapman, George 73–4, 107, 155
  Byron plays 73, 274
Churchyard, Thomas 111, 116, 134–135, 144
Clegg, Cyndia 239–240
Colclough, David 158
Connolly, Annaliese 105
Constable, Henry 202, 204–205, 207
Cuffe, Henry 48, 106, 108, 146, 161, 181, 189, 210, 218, 220–221, 271–274
Cornwallis, William 180
Curtiz, Michael
  The Private Lives of Elizabeth and Essex 10, 18, 279–291

Daniel, Samuel 48–49, 74, 239, 242–243, 250
  Delia 41
  Philotas 8, 18, 73, 106, 118, 193, 274
Davis, Joel 28, 33, 50
Davison, Francis 2–3, 8, 105, 112, 159
Dawson, Lesel 55
Devereux, Dorothy 3–4, 52, 73, 153–154, 204, 209, 214, 217, 224

Devereux, Penelope *see* Rich, Penelope
Devereux, Walter (Essex's brother) 3, 5, 52, 192–193
Dobson, Michael 6, 9, 281, 284, 290
Dollimore, Jonathan 13
Doran, Susan 290
Drake, Francis 5, 29, 84–85
Duplessis-Mornay, Philippe 34–35, 40, 113, 141
Dusinberre, Juliet 16, 141–143

Earl of Essex's Men, The 15, 65–67, 69–72
Edward VIII 18, 286–290
Egerton, Thomas 17, 65, 156, 159, 163, 215, 273
Elizabeth I 1, 3–6, 8–13, 15–18, 25, 29–30, 32–36, 38, 40, 48–53, 55, 64–67, 69, 71, 74, 81–95, 101–104, 109, 111, 113, 115–117, 134, 137–140, 142–143, 153–154, 156–157, 159, 161, 180–181, 189, 201, 206–209, 211–212, 215–217, 220, 222–227, 241–244, 246–252, 263, 266–270, 272–274
Elizabeth I (television series) 10–11, 291
Elizabeth R (television series) 11–12
Essex, Frances Walsingham, countess of 4, 29, 41, 110, 161, 214, 217, 226
Essex, Lettice Knollys, countess of 3–4, 15, 66–67, 69–71, 77, 253, 209, 224
Essex, Robert Devereux, 2nd earl of
  and chivalry 15, 30–31, 49, 51–53, 57–58, 103, 110, 141
  and espionage 5, 202–203
  and illness 7, 16, 153–154, 216
  and Ireland 2, 6, 11–12, 16, 32, 38, 49, 52, 65, 87, 115–116, 133–148, 153–155, 159, 161, 215–226, 242, 244–247, 253, 266–267
  and Protestantism 5, 28–29, 32, 34–35, 49–52, 58, 89, 134, 193
  as Achilles 3, 16, 107–108, 112, 155, 239
  Apology 16–17, 115, 136–137, 156–58, 179–194, 224, 243
  as author 38, 74, 81–82, 90, 155–164, 179–194
  as Chancellor of Cambridge University 5, 104
  as dedicatee 3, 12, 18, 104, 133, 155, 239, 246
  as earl marshal 5, 104
  patronage of 15, 17, 26, 33, 49, 63–64, 69, 77, 83, 104, 111, 114, 133, 155
  portraiture of 10, 15, 141, 207
  as Privy Councillor 5, 38, 103–104
  Rebellion 6–7, 11–14, 17, 26, 32, 40, 63, 145, 163, 227, 237, 247–248, 250, 267
Essex, Robert Devereux, 3rd earl of 8, 49, 111, 192
Essex, Walter Devereux, 1st earl of 3–6, 15, 65–66, 69–71, 77, 108, 115–116, 133, 136–139, 142, 145, 147–148

Ford, John 7, 74, 283
  The Queen 73–74

Gajda, Alexandra 17, 31, 184, 219
Gazzard, Hugh 17, 48, 203, 263
Goldberg, Jonathan 163
Gordon, Andrew 16–17, 239
Gorges, Ferdinando 244
Greenblatt, Stephen 13, 163–164
Greville, Fulke 15, 26–28, 30–35, 41, 116, 186, 189, 238–239, 242

Hackett, Helen 206
Hammer, Paul 14, 25–26, 33–34, 40–1, 48, 108, 136–137, 147, 226, 238, 248, 270, 282, 284
Hannay, Margaret P. 35, 41
Harington, John 116, 141, 207
Hayward, John 12–14, 17–18, 75–76, 104, 114, 155, 220, 237, 239–243, 245–247, 250
Heffner, Ray 13–14, 38
Heinemann, Margot 48, 71
Henri IV 5, 30, 33–35, 51, 82, 86–89, 91–92, 112–114, 136, 184, 204, 210, 244
Heywood, Thomas 71–73, 107, 119, 239
Highley, Christopher 143–144
Hilliard, Nicholas 202, 204–207
  Young Man among the Roses 10, 206–207
Hiscock, Andrew 5, 16
Hodgdon, Barbara 280, 286
Hopkins, Lisa 18, 36, 39, 105
Howard, Lord Henry 40, 108, 116
Hutton, Lorna 40

Ioppolo, Grace 6, 15, 188, 263
Isabella, Infanta 7, 184, 241–243, 248

James VI and I 8, 17, 31, 58, 103, 110–112, 135, 140, 145–146, 201–204, 206–209, 239, 241–244, 247, 249, 251
James, Mervyn 26, 30–32
Jones, William 240
Jonson, Ben 49, 75, 109–110, 218, 220
Catiline 110
Cynthia's Revels 18, 274
Sejanus 8, 18, 110

Kermode, Frank 14, 75
Knollys, Francis (Essex's grandfather) 4, 137, 270
Knollys, Lettice *see* Essex, Lettice Knollys, countess of
Knollys, William (Essex's uncle) 7, 139, 154

Lacey, Robert 8–9
Lake, Peter 156
Lambarde, William 12–13
Languet, Hubert 34–35, 39–40
Laoutaris, Chris 5, 10, 17, 36, 240
Lee, Sidney 25
Leicester, Robert Dudley, earl of 4–5, 10–11, 15, 28–29, 32–33, 36, 49, 66–71, 77, 83, 137–138, 202–203, 208–209
Leicester, countess of *see* Essex, Lettice Knollys, countess of
Levin, Carole 285
Levin, Harry 9
Levy, Fritz 263
Liberality and Prodigality 18, 263–274
Lindheim, Nancy 37
Love, Harold 158, 187–188

McCoy, Richard 141
Maley, Willy 5, 16, 108
Markham, Gervase 15, 27, 47–59, 74, 104, 117
Marlowe, Christopher 9, 11, 133, 145, 287–288
Doctor Faustus 280
Edward II 124–125, 145, 243
Tamburlaine 11
May, Steven W. 81–82
Mears, Natalie 33, 35–36
Meyrick, Gelly 7, 145, 271–272, 274
Monopoly of sweet wines 5–6, 12, 157, 266, 284, 291
Mountjoy, Charles Blount, Lord 41, 52, 73, 101, 106, 108, 139–140, 145–146, 203, 205, 225–226, 242, 271, 284
Mynshall, Richard 17, 141, 159–163

Neill, Michael 140–141, 283
Norris, John 5, 29, 52, 107
Northumberland, Dorothy Devereux, countess of, *see* Devereux, Dorothy
Northumberland, Henry Percy, earl of 4, 73, 117, 154
Nottingham, Charles Howard, earl of 7, 82, 139, 225, 227

Of Love and Self-Love 74, 81–83, 93–94
Oxford, Edward de Vere, earl of 36

Parker, Patricia 144
Parsons, Robert
A Conference about the Next Succession to the Crown of England 17, 145, 242–243, 246, 248, 251
Partridge, Mary 18
Peele, George 28, 110
Pérez, Antonio 17, 86, 91–92, 107, 112, 139, 209–210, 212–215, 218–220, 239–241, 245
Philip II 5, 7, 86, 185–186, 210, 219, 239, 244
Philips, Augustine 11–12
Pigeon, Renée 282
Pleasant Comodie, Shewing the Contention Betweene Liberalitie and Prodigalitie see *Liberality and Prodigality*
Popham, John 7, 226, 240
Portugal 5, 29, 50, 110, 113, 115, 183
Private Life of Henry VIII, The 282, 285, 289

Ralegh, Walter 4, 121, 147, 155, 192, 238–239, 244, 247, 265
Reynolds, Edward 64–65, 154, 161, 180, 187, 189, 210
Rich, Barnaby 133, 142
Rich, Penelope 3–4, 6–8, 10, 17, 36–37, 41, 52, 73, 103, 112, 179–182, 187, 204–227
Rich, Robert 4, 72, 179–180, 183, 202–203
Robertson, James C. 282
Rodger, Ian 12

Savile, Henry 3, 108–109, 218–221, 238, 240, 244–246
Scott-Warren, Jason 158, 161
Seeing Love 15, 81–85, 87–90, 92–95
Shakespeare, William 1, 7, 10–16, 49, 63, 68, 71–76, 133, 140, 279
Antony and Cleopatra 10, 282
As You Like It 16, 141–143, 207
Coriolanus 10, 108, 274
Hamlet 69, 76–77, 140
Henry IV, Part One 73, 280
Henry V 1, 10, 15–16, 63, 73, 108, 143–146, 280
Henry VIII 146–147
Julius Caesar 73
King Lear 193
Love's Labour's Lost 72, 75
Macbeth 10
Midsummer Night's Dream, A 83, 94–95, 279–280
Much Ado About Nothing 280
Othello 10
Richard II 1, 7, 11–14, 63, 73–76, 108, 134, 140–142, 237–239, 243, 248, 51, 279
Richard III 75, 288
Troilus and Cressida 107–108
Shapiro, Michael 269
Shenk, Linda 15–16
Sidney, Mary, countess of Pembroke 14–15, 26–8, 34–6, 41
Sidney, Philip 3–4, 14–15, 25–41, 49, 51–52, 54, 68, 73, 83, 106, 110, 161, 206
Arcadia 14–15, 26–41, 49–50, 54, 205, 213
Astrophel and Stella 3–5, 36, 54, 201
Defence of Poesy 31–32
Lady of May, The 85
Letter to Queen Elizabeth Touching her Marriage with Monsieur 33, 35–36, 39
Sidney, Robert 35, 73, 88–89, 92, 116, 181, 185, 210–211, 216–217, 221, 266, 270
Skretkowicz, Victor 26, 35
Southampton, Henry Wriothesley, earl of 6, 8, 11, 48–49, 51–52, 71–72, 117, 145–146, 203, 216, 221
Spenser, Edmund 49–51, 58, 111, 133, 136, 140
A View of the Present State of Ireland 16, 133–136, 138
The Faerie Queene 16, 49–54, 56, 104, 113–114, 133–134, 136
The Shepheardes calender 33, 35
State of Christendom, The 17, 40, 219, 240, 243–4, 248–51
Steggle, Matthew 14–15, 27, 104
Stillman, Robert E. 39
Strachey, Lytton 8–9, 18, 280–283, 285, 290
Strong, Roy 10, 206
Stubbs, John 33, 35–36

Tacitus, influence of 3, 6, 8, 15, 17–18, 28, 31, 33–34, 105, 109–110, 185, 202, 218–223, 225, 237–238, 240–241, 243–246
Taylor, Gary 144
Tennenhouse, Leonard 13
Tyrone, Hugh O'Neill, earl of 6, 32, 111, 114–115, 117, 134, 137–141, 143–145, 215, 247

Ungerer, Gustav 218
Unton, Henry 15–16, 82, 89–92, 107, 112

Vere, Francis 51–52
Virgin Queen, The (television series) 11

Walker, D. P. 38–39
Walker, Greg 282, 289
Wall, Wendy 58
Walsingham, Frances, *see* Essex, Frances, countess of
Walsingham, Francis 4–5, 33, 40, 49, 210
Watson, Nicola J. 6, 9, 281, 284, 290
Wilson, J. Dover 13
Wingfield, Edward 52
Womersley, David 31, 220
Wood, Richard 14–15, 50, 54, 110
Woolf, D. R. 17–18
Worden, Blair 14, 37–38, 75, 243
Wotton, Sir Henry 40, 48, 106, 115, 135, 146, 187, 191, 210, 218–219, 270
Woudhuysen, Henry 188

CPSIA information can be obtained at www.ICGtesting.com
Printed in the USA
BVOW08s2114130616

451907BV00002B/2/P

9 781784 993542